The Cambridge Handbook of Linguistic Code-switching

Code-switching – the alternating use of two languages in the same stretch of discourse by a bilingual speaker – is a dominant topic in the study of bilingualism and a phenomenon that generates a great deal of pointed discussion in the public domain. This handbook provides the most comprehensive guide to this bilingual phenomenon to date. Drawing on empirical data from a wide range of language pairings, the leading researchers in the study of bilingualism examine the linguistic, social, and cognitive implications of code-switching in up-to-date and accessible survey chapters. *The Cambridge Handbook of Linguistic Code-switching* will serve as a vital resource for advanced undergraduate and graduate students, as a wide-ranging overview for linguists, psychologists and speech scientists, and as an informative guide for educators interested in bilingual speech practices.

BARBARA E. BULLOCK is Professor of Linguistics and French in the Department of French and Francophone Studies at The Pennsylvania State University.

ALMEIDA JACQUELINE TORIBIO is Professor of Linguistics and Spanish Linguistics in the Department of Spanish, Italian, and Portuguese at The Pennsylvania State University.

CAMBRIDGE HANDBOOKS IN LINGUISTICS

Genuinely broad in scope, each handbook in this series provides a complete state-of-the-field overview of a major sub-discipline within language study and research. Grouped into broad thematic areas, the chapters in each volume encompass the most important issues and topics within each subject, offering a coherent picture of the latest theories and findings. Together, the volumes will build into an integrated overview of the discipline in its entirety.

Published titles

The Cambridge Handbook of Phonology, edited by Paul de Lacy
The Cambridge Handbook of Linguistic Code-switching, edited by Barbara E. Bullock and Almeida Jacqueline Toribio
The Cambridge Handbook of Child Language, edited by Edith L. Bavin

Further titles planned for the series

The Cambridge Handbook of Sociolinguistics, edited by Rajend Mesthrie and Walt Wolfram
The Cambridge Handbook of Endangered Languages, edited by Peter Austin

The Cambridge Handbook of Linguistic Code-switching

Edited by
Barbara E. Bullock
and
Almeida Jacqueline Toribio

CAMBRIDGE UNIVERSITY PRESS
Cambridge, New York, Melbourne, Madrid, Cape Town, Singapore, São Paulo, Delhi

Cambridge University Press
The Edinburgh Building, Cambridge CB2 8RU, UK

Published in the United States of America by Cambridge University Press, New York

www.cambridge.org
Information on this title: www.cambridge.org/9780521875912

First published 2009

Printed in the United Kingdom at the University Press, Cambridge

A catalogue record for this publication is available from the British Library

Library of Congress Cataloguing in Publication data
Cambridge handbook of linguistic code-switching / edited by Barbara E. Bullock
and Almeida Jacqueline Toribio.
    p.   cm.
Includes bibliographical references and index.
ISBN 978-0-521-87591-2
1. Code switching (Linguistics)   I. Bullock, Barbara E.   II. Toribio, Almeida
Jacqueline, 1963–
P115.3.C36 2008
306.44–dc22
                                                                2008026924

ISBN 978-0-521-87591-2 hardback

Contents

List of figures		*page* vii
List of tables		viii
List of contributors		ix
Acknowledgements		xi
Aims and content		xii
List of abbreviations		xiv

1 Themes in the study of code-switching *Barbara E. Bullock and Almeida Jacqueline Toribio* — 1

Part I Conceptual and methodological considerations in code-switching research — 19

2 Research techniques for the study of code-switching *Marianne Gullberg, Peter Indefrey, and Pieter Muysken* — 21

3 On the notions of congruence and convergence in code-switching *Mark Sebba* — 40

4 Code-switching and transfer: an exploration of similarities and differences *Jeanine Treffers-Daller* — 58

5 Loan translations versus code-switching *Ad Backus and Margreet Dorleijn* — 75

Part II Social aspects of code-switching — 95

6 Sociolinguistic factors in code-switching *Penelope Gardner-Chloros* — 97

7 The Conversation Analytic model of code-switching *Joseph Gafaranga* — 114

8 Code-switching and the internet *Margreet Dorleijn and Jacomine Nortier* — 127

9 Phonetic accommodation in children's code-switching *Ghada Khattab* — 142

Part III   The structural implications of code-switching   161

10   Phonetic reflexes of code-switching   *Barbara E. Bullock*   163

11   Code-switching between typologically distinct
languages   *Brian Hok-Shing Chan*   182

12   Language mixing in bilingual children: code-
switching?   *Natascha Müller and Katja Francesca Cantone*   199

13   Code-switching between sign languages   *David Quinto-Pozos*   221

Part IV   Psycholinguistics and code-switching   239

14   Code-switching and language disorders in bilingual
children   *Adele W. Miccio, Carol Scheffner Hammer,
and Bárbara Rodríguez*   241

15   Code-switching, imperfect acquisition,
and attrition   *Agnes Bolonyai*   253

16   Code-switching and the bilingual mental
lexicon   *Longxing Wei*   270

17   Code-switching and the brain   *Marta Kutas, Eva Moreno,
and Nicole Wicha*   289

Part V   Formal models of code-switching   307

18   Generative approaches to code-switching   *Jeff MacSwan*   309

19   A universal model of code-switching and bilingual
language processing and production   *Carol Myers-Scotton
and Janice Jake*   336

References   358
Index of subjects   416
Index of languages   421

Figures

Figure 7.1 Approaches to language alternation in bilingual
conversation   *page* 119

Figure 9.1 Phonetic patterns of English code-switches
produced by each of the bilinguals during a
45-minute Arabic session with their mothers
(N = 337)   150

Figure 10.1 Waveform of English *cat* showing long voicing lag
and accompanying aspiration for initial /k/
between the vertical lines   168

Figure 12.1 The Three-Stage-Model   210

Figure 12.2 The architecture of the bilingual (Italian–German)
language faculty, following MacSwan (2000)   214

Figure 16.1 Lemma activation in speech production (adapted
from Levelt 1989)   271

Figure 16.2 Lemma activation in the bilingual mental lexicon
(adapted from Myers-Scotton and Jake 2000)   273

Figure 16.3 A bilingual lemma activation model (adapted
from Levelt 1989)   279

Figure 18.1 Model of the minimalist framework   322

Tables

Table 2.1   Schematic overview of the studies on
            Finnish–English code-switching   *page* 24
Table 2.2   Experimental tasks and example studies   27
Table 2.3   Task and output modes   38
Table 5.1   Synchronic and diachronic instantiations
            of contact phenomena, classified by the nature
            of the source material   79
Table 8.1   Advantages of three types of internet data
            for code-switching research   133
Table 11.1 Code-switching between a VO and an OV language:
            options of the processor   193
Table 11.2 Code-switching between languages with different
            types of DP: options of the processor   197
Table 13.1 Differences between LSM FUEGO and ASL FIRE   234

Contributors

Ad Backus, Assistant Professor, Faculty of Arts, Tilburg University.

Agnes Bolonyai, Assistant Professor, Department of English, North Carolina State University.

Barbara E. Bullock, Professor, Department of French and Francophone Studies, The Pennsylvania State University.

Katja Cantone, Research Assistant, Languages and Literature, Universität Bremen.

Brian Hok-Shing Chan, Assistant Professor, Department of English, University of Macau.

Margreet Dorleijn, Associate Professor, Institute of Linguistics, Universiteit van Amsterdam.

Joseph Gafaranga, Lecturer, Department of Linguistics and English Language, University of Edinburgh.

Penelope Gardner-Chloros, Lecturer, School of Languages, Linguistics and Culture, Birkbeck College, University of London.

Marianne Gullberg, Principle Investigator, Max Planck Institute for Psycholinguistics, Nijmegen.

Carol Scheffner Hammer, Associate Professor, Department of Communication Sciences, The Pennsylvania State University.

Peter Indefrey, Principal Investigator, Max Planck Institute for Psycholinguistics, Nijmegen.

Janice Jake, Lecturer, English Department, Midlands Technical College.

Ghada Khattab, Lecturer, Speech and Language Sciences Section, University of Newcastle.

Marta Kutas, Professor, Department of Cognitive Science, University of California, San Diego.

Jeff MacSwan, Associate Professor, Department of Language and Literacy, Arizona State University.

Adele Miccio, Associate Professor, Department of Communication Sciences, The Pennsylvania State University.

Eva Moreno, Researcher, Brain Mapping Unit, Universidad Complutense de Madrid.

Natascha Müller, Professor, Department of Romance Languages, Bergische Universität Wuppertal.

Pieter Muysken, Professor, Linguistics, Universiteit Radboud.

Carol Myers-Scotton, Professor Emerita, Linguistics Program and English Department, University of South Carolina.

Jacomine Nortier, Associate Professor, Utrecht Institute of Linguistics, Universiteit Utrecht.

David Quinto-Pozos, Assistant Professor, Department of Speech and Hearing Sciences, University of Illinois at Urbana-Champaign.

Bárbara Rodríguez, Assistant Professor, Department of Speech and Hearing Sciences, University of New Mexico.

Mark Sebba, Reader, Department of Linguistics, Lancaster University.

Almeida Jacqueline Toribio, Professor, Department of Spanish, Italian and Portuguese, The Pennsylvania State University.

Jeanine Treffers-Daller, Principal Reader, Faculty of Humanities, Languages and Social Sciences, University of West England, Bristol.

Longxing Wei, Associate Professor, Linguistics Department, Montclair State University.

Nicole Y. Y. Wicha, Assistant Professor, Department of Biology, University of Texas, San Antonio.

Acknowledgements

We would like to express our gratitude to a number of people who have helped to bring this Handbook to completion.

First and foremost, we thank our contributing authors who responded to our many requests and suggestions with understanding and grace. Without their knowledge and passion for this subject and their willingness to commit it to paper, this work would not have been possible.

We thank Paul de Lacy, editor of *The Cambridge Handbook of Phonology*, for his support and advice. We are grateful that he went through this process first and was then so helpful in ushering us through it.

Our many thanks to Andrew Winnard at Cambridge University Press for helping us to develop this Handbook and for his patience and good humor throughout this process, and to Sarah Green for her editorial help and her rapid responses.

To Aaron Roggia, who compiled and hand-checked every single reference in this Handbook for consistency and accuracy, we owe an inestimable debt. If any errors remain, they are entirely ours.

Finally, we express our heartfelt thanks to the students of our Contact Linguistics seminar, whose continued interest in issues of bilingualism and language contact inspired us to produce this volume: Hilary Barnes, Joshua Brown, Amanda Dalola, Verónica González, Ana de Prada Pérez, Aaron Roggia, and Eva María Suárez Budenbender.

Aims and content

This handbook overviews the major issues in the linguistic study of code-switching (hereafter CS), the alternating use of two languages in the same stretch of discourse by a bilingual speaker. Comprised of chapters written by experts in a concise, accessible, and comprehensive format, the volume is intended to serve multiple audiences as a guide to the main theoretical and empirical contributions to the study of CS.

The handbook is targeted to a readership ranging from advanced undergraduate students to researchers with specializations in syntax, phonetics/phonology, morphology, bilingualism, language contact, discourse pragmatics, language acquisition, language attrition, psycholinguistics, neurolinguistics, speech science, and sociolinguistics. Most of the chapters are comprehensible to students and scholars of general linguistics who need not be experts in the study of bilingualism or in any of the specific theories pertaining to the subfields of linguistics.

Since the phenomenon of CS falls firmly within the fields of bilingualism and language contact, we expect that the chapters of this volume will serve as relevant companion readings to more general works such as Romaine's (1995) *Bilingualism*, second edition, Winford's (2003) *An introduction to contact linguistics,* and Myers-Scotton's (2006a) *Multiple Voices: An introduction to bilingualism*. A major goal of this volume is to provide its readers with the background necessary to move from introductory texts on bilingualism, sociolinguistics, or general linguistics to research articles devoted to the analysis and implications of CS. Our broader objective is to help dispel the myths and misperceptions that surround the bilingual practice of CS.

Bilingual speech practices such as CS have engaged the interests of scholars from diverse disciplines, among them Communication Sciences, Education, and Cultural Studies, to name but a few; this volume focuses on the analysis of CS within the discipline of Linguistics. In the introductory chapter, Bullock and Toribio present the broad themes in the linguistic study of CS. Part I, "Conceptual and methodological considerations in code-switching," consists of three chapters: Gullberg, Indefrey and Muysken (Chapter 2) survey and critique pertinent research techniques, and Sebba (Chapter 3), Treffers-Daller (Chapter 4), and Backus and Dorleijn (Chapter 5) seek to clarify the conceptual assumptions that underlie much CS research. Four chapters make up Part II, "Social aspects of code-switching." Gardner-Chloros (Chapter 6) addresses the social motivations implicated in CS practices and Gafaranga (Chapter 7) examines CS as a communicative resource. CS on the internet as a new community of practice is considered by Dorleijn and Nortier (Chapter 8), and CS as accommodation is the focus of Chapter 9 by Khattab. The coverage in this section, though by no means exhaustive, is intended to be representative of the various types of approaches to sociolinguistic research on CS. Part III, "The structural implications of code-switching," considers CS at all levels of linguistic analysis. Bullock (Chapter 10) addresses the phonetic/phonological patterns of CS, Chan (Chapter 11) considers the grammatical patterns attested in CS between typologically dissimilar languages, Müller and Cantone (Chapter 12) investigate CS patterns in bilingual first language acquisition, and Quinto-Pozos (Chapter 13) discusses CS in signed modality. Part IV, "Psycholinguistics and code-switching," contemplates developmental and psycholinguistic aspects of CS. Miccio, Hammer, and Rodríguez (Chapter 14) distinguish CS from disordered speech in children, Bolonyai (Chapter 15) distinguishes CS from language attrition, Wei describes and theorizes the bilingual mental lexicon (Chapter 16), and Kutas, Moreno, and Wicha (Chapter 17) overview the psycholinguistic and neurolinguistic facets of CS. Finally, Part V, "Formal models of code-switching," presents and further advances two influential theoretical models of bilingual morpho-syntactic patterns: MacSwan's generativist framework (Chapter 18) and Myers-Scotton and Jake's psycholinguistic processing and production model (Chapter 19).

The structure of this handbook follows a defined scheme, progressing from general methodological and definitional issues in the study of CS (Part I) through the three major linguistic approaches to CS – sociolinguistic (Part II), structural (Part III), and psycholinguistic (Part IV) – to formal models of CS (Part V). However, many issues recur throughout the volume. For instance, readers with interests in child language will benefit not only from the chapters in Part IV, but also from Chapter 9 and Chapter 12, both of which address first language acquisition; and language processing is invoked in Chapter 2, Chapter 4, Chapter 10, Chapter 16, and Chapter 19, as well as in Chapter 17, which is devoted to CS and the brain. Indeed, readers will discover a good deal of overlap among the themes discussed throughout this volume; this is to be expected, as linguists are converging on the view that CS must be examined from structural, social, and psycholinguistic perspectives concurrently.

Abbreviations

ABIL	Ability marker	FEM	Feminine
ABL	Ablative Case	FUT	Future
ACC	Accusative Case	GEN	Genitive
AD	Adessive Case	GER	Gerund
AFFIRM	Affirmative	HAB	Habitual
AOR	Aorist	IL	Illative Case
ART	Article	IMP	Imperfect
ASP	Aspect	IN	Inessive Case
ASSOC	Associative	INDEF	Indefinite
AUX	Auxiliary	INF	Infinitive
BEN	Benefactive Case	INFL	Inflection
C	Class	INT	Intransitive
CIS	Cislocative (near or	INTERJ	Interjection
	toward the speaker)	INTERROG	Interrogative
CL/CLIT	Clitic	IP	Inflectional Phrase
CLAS	Classifier	LOC	Locative Case
COND	Conditional	MASC	Masculine
CONSEC	Consecutive	ML	Matrix Language
CONT	Continuative	N	Noun
COP	Copula	NOM	Nominative Case
CS	Code-switching	NEG	Negation
DAT	Dative Case	NP	Noun Phrase
DEM	Demonstrative	NSF	Noun suffix
DET	Determiner	O	Object marker
DP	Determiner Phrase	OBJ	Object
DUR	Durative	P	Preposition or
EL	Embedded Language		Postposition
EMPH	Emphasis marker	PART	Participle
EVID	Evidential	PAST	Past

PERF	Perfective	REL	Relativizer
PP	Prepositional	S	Subject marker
	Phrase	SFP	Sentence Final
PL	Plural		Particle
POSS	Possessive Case	SG	Singular
PREP	Preposition	SUBJ	Subject
PRES	Present	SUBJUNC	Subjunctive
PRET	Preterite	SUBL	Sublative Case
PRT	Partitive Case	TAM	Tense or aspect
PROG	Progressive		marker
PRT	Participle	TNS	Tense
PST	Past	TOP	Topic marker
Q	Question marker	TP	Tense Phrase
QUE	Question particle	V	Verb
REDUP	Reduplication	VP	Verb Phrase

1

Themes in the study of code-switching

Barbara E. Bullock
and
Almeida Jacqueline Toribio

1.1   Introduction

Of all of the contact phenomena of interest to researchers and students of bilingualism, code-switching (hereafter CS) has arguably dominated the field. Broadly defined, CS is the ability on the part of bilinguals to alternate effortlessly between their two languages. This capacity is truly remarkable and invites scientific and scholarly analysis from professionals, but, at the same time, generates a great deal of pointed discussion that reflects popular misperceptions of the nature of CS in particular and bilinguals more generally. While CS is viewed as an index of bilingual proficiency among linguists, it is more commonly perceived by the general public as indicative of language degeneration. This disparity can be best understood by reference to notions of grammar. Most laypeople define grammar as a set of statements about how we should correctly use our language. Such an understanding of grammar is properly called *prescriptive*, because it attempts to mandate or prescribe the way language should be used. Linguists, who study language objectively, are more interested in *descriptive* grammars, which represent speakers' unconscious knowledge of their languages as manifested in their actual linguistic behavior. Bilinguals in language contact situations commonly use forms that integrate their two languages to some degree, a behavior that is disparaged by language purists, who insist that each language maintain its integrity according to prescribed norms. For the linguist, on the other hand, CS provides a unique window on the structural outcomes of language contact, which can be shown to be systematic rather than aberrant. Further, the act of CS can be studied as a reflection of social constructs and of the cognitive mechanisms that control language switching. From the perspective of linguistics, then, CS is worthy of study for a variety of reasons.

The significance of this phenomenon in illuminating bilingual cognition and behavior cannot be underestimated, first and foremost because CS is exclusive to bilinguals. Nevertheless, many controversies exist in the study of CS, in large part because the phenomenon has been approached from different disciplinary perspectives, and as a consequence has evaded a uniform definition and explanation. The purpose of this chapter is to present an overview of CS from the perspective of linguistics, with a view towards defining CS, identifying who engages in CS and for what purposes, and delineating the various approaches to the study of CS. The overarching goal of the chapter is to set out why the study of CS is important, and by so doing to dispel misconceptions regarding language alternation among bilinguals.

1.2   What is code-switching?

All speakers selectively draw on the language varieties in their linguistic repertoire, as dictated by their intentions and by the needs of the speech participants and the conversational setting. Even monolinguals are capable of shifting between the linguistic registers and the dialects they command and, as such, there are parallels that can be drawn between monolingual and bilingual language use. For convenience, we can refer to such monolingual behavior as *style shifting*. In turn, bilinguals have available not only different registers and dialects of one language, but of two. As is true of monolingual style shifting, it is not uncommon for bilinguals to segregate their languages, speaking exclusively in one language in certain domains (e.g. at home, with friends) while shifting to another in other contexts (e.g. school, work), a bilingual behavior commonly referred to as *language shifting*. Given the appropriate circumstances, many bilinguals will exploit this ability and alternate between languages in an unchanged setting, often within the same utterance; this is the phenomenon understood as CS.

CS comprises a broad range of contact phenomena and is difficult to characterize definitively. First, its linguistic manifestation may extend from the insertion of single words to the alternation of languages for larger segments of discourse. Second, it is produced by bilinguals of differing degrees of proficiency who reside in various types of language contact settings, and as a consequence their CS patterns may not be uniform. Finally, it may be deployed for a number of reasons: filling linguistic gaps, expressing ethnic identity, and achieving particular discursive aims, among others. Given these factors, it is not surprising that there exists debate in the literature concerning the precise characterization of CS and how various kinds of language contact varieties are to be classified.

An incontrovertible example of CS is to be found in the English–Spanish bilingual title of Poplack's (1980) seminal article:

(1)   *Spanish–English*
      Sometimes I'll start a sentence in Spanish [*sic*] ***y termino en español***
      " . . . and I finish in Spanish."

Note that there are readily identifiable constituents from English and Spanish and that their combination here does not violate the grammar of either language. This type of language alternation has been termed *Classic* CS (Myers-Scotton 1993a) or *alternational* CS (Muysken 2000), but is most widely known as *intra-sentential* CS (Poplack 1980). This contrasts with *inter-sentential* CS, as in (2), where alternation occurs at clause boundaries.

(2) *Swahili–English*
     That's too much. **Sina pesa**.
     " ... I don't have [much] money."
     (Myers-Scotton 1993a:41)

Like intra-sentential CS, inter-sentential switching requires an advanced level of bilingual proficiency as it often entails the production of full clauses in each language. However, the former, but not the latter, can offer insights into the ways in which the two grammars of the bilingual interact at the sentence level.

Muysken (2000) advances a typology of CS patterns, suggesting that bilinguals employ three distinct strategies: *alternation*, where the two languages remain relatively separated in an A–B configuration, as exemplified in (1) and (2) above; *congruent lexicalization*, in which the two languages share a common grammatical structure that can be filled with lexical elements from either language, as in (3); and *insertion*, which involves the embedding of a constituent – usually a word or a phrase – in a nested A–B–A structure, as in (4).

(3) *Dutch–Sranan*
     wan heri **gedeelte** de ondro **beheer** fu **gewapende machten**
     one *wholepart* COP under *control* of *armed force*
     "One whole part is under control of the armed forces."
     (Bolle 1994:75, cited in Muysken 2000:139)

(4) *Persian–Swedish*
     xob pas **falsk-an** pesa-â
     well then false-COP3PL boy-PL
     "Well then boys are false."
     (Naseh Lotfabbadi 2002:101)

Congruent lexicalization is most prevalent between languages that are closely related typologically (Sranan in (3) is a Dutch-based creole). Alternations such as in (3) have been analyzed as constituting a *composite matrix language* (Myers-Scotton 2003), which arises "when speakers produce structures for which the source of structure is split between two or more varieties (2003:99)." Myers-Scotton further maintains that composite structures arise in contexts of language shift. For this reason alone, congruent lexicalization differs from Classic CS, i.e. intra-sentential CS, for which it is assumed bilinguals fully maintain both language systems. Insertion, as in (4), can also arguably be viewed as distinct from intra-sentential CS, as it has much in common with lexical borrowing, which does not necessitate bilingual proficiency. Similarly, *tag-switching* may also occur among bilinguals with limited abilities in one language, as it is defined by the insertion of a formulaic expression from language B (e.g. *so, well, d'accord?*) into an utterance in language A, primarily for pragmatic effect, as in (5).

(5) *Frenchville French–English*
     Les autres pourraient [*sic*] **parler français comme lui**, ya know
     "The others could speak French like him, . . . "

(Bullock fieldnotes)

In brief, although all of the above forms can be classified as CS, it is Classic or intra-sentential CS that may reveal the most about language structure. Consider, again, the example in (1). Because Spanish and English have similar surface structures for this expression, the lexemes can be aligned more or less in a one-to-one fashion. Thus, numerous other CS patterns should be possible. However, consider the hypothetical examples in (6):

(6) a. *Sometimes **yo** will **empezar** a **oración** in **inglés** and **termino** in **español**.
     b. *Sometimes I'll **empezar una oración en inglés y** I finish in Spanish.
     c. *****A veces yo** will start a sentence in English and I **termino en español**.

In (6a), the alternation between English and Spanish occurs at every other word. In (6b, 6c), the switching is less frequent, allowing for longer stretches of English and Spanish. Significantly, though, none of these sentences would be attested nor accepted among Spanish–English bilinguals because each is in violation of core principles of CS.

Clearly, CS is not the random mixing of two languages, as is popularly assumed. Nevertheless, this misperception endures, as evidenced by the various metaphors and terms ascribed to bilingual speech varieties. For instance, metaphors whereby contact varieties are likened to a mix of grains are common (e.g. *trasjanka* for mixed Russian–Byelorussian speech, literally "hay and straw," and *surzhyk* for mixed Ukranian–Russian, literally "wheat and rye"). Also common are portmanteau creations such as *finnglish, ingleñol, franglais, portinglês,* and so on. While these terms are playful they often carry pejorative connotations that the speech varieties they reference are nothing but a linguistic hodgepodge and that the speakers who use them are uneducated and incapable of expressing themselves in one or the other language. However, a significant body of research has amply demonstrated that CS does not represent a breakdown in communication, but reflects the skillful manipulation of two language systems for various communicative functions. This is articulated through a different – and to our mind, more apt – metaphor offered by Valdés: "[I]t is helpful to imagine that when bilinguals code-switch, they are in fact using a twelve-string guitar, rather than limiting themselves to two six-string instruments (1988:126)."

1.3 Distinguishing CS from other contact phenomena

CS is to be distinguished from other types of contact phenomena, although it is not always the case that clear-cut distinctions can be drawn. For instance, as noted above, insertional CS can be equated with borrowing. However, the term *borrowing* has been used to describe many different forms, from the transfer of structural features (e.g. phonemes, suffixes) to that of whole clauses. Lexical borrowing normally involves the morphological and phonological integration of a single lexeme, as in the Japanese word *basubaru*, from English "baseball," which is fully established in the monolingual Japanese lexicon. But unassimilated loan words, also called *nonce* borrowings (Poplack et al. 1988), can occur spontaneously in the speech of bilinguals, blurring any boundary that can be drawn between these contact forms on structural criteria alone. It is evident that nonce borrowing is akin to CS because both are attested in the speech of bilinguals and unlikely to be found in that of monolinguals; hence some researchers (e.g. Treffers-Daller 1991; Myers-Scotton 1993a) view borrowing and CS as falling along a continuum (see Bullock, Treffers-Daller, this volume).

Other contact forms are more easily differentiated from CS, although they too implicate the transfer of material from one language into the other (see Treffers-Daller, this volume, on the relation between transfer and CS). *Loan translations* or *calques*, as in (7), involve the importation of foreign patterns or meanings with the retention of native-language morphemes (see Backus and Dorleijn, this volume). Also attested in bilingual speech are cross-linguistic *semantic extensions*, where a word from language A takes on additional meanings that are modeled by language B, as in (8).

(7) a. *US Chicano Spanish*
        escuela alta "high school"
        literally "school high"
        (cf. Spanish *secundaria*)
     b. *US French*
        étudiant gradué "graduate student"
        literally "student graduated"
        (cf. French *étudiant de troisième cycle*)

(8) a. *US Spanish*
        mayor [madʒor] "mayor"

literally "older"
(cf. Spanish *alcalde*)
b. *US French*
enregistrer "register (for a course)"
literally "check a bag"
(cf. French *s'inscrire*)

CS is also distinct from *mixed languages*, which are contact varieties that derive components of their grammatical systems from diverse genetic sources. For example, Media Lengua, spoken as a native language in the highlands of Central Ecuador, has been described as a prototypical mixed language (Muysken 1988, 1996). The general properties of Media Lengua include Quechua morpho-syntax combined with Spanish lexical stems, as shown in (9).

(9) *Media Lengua*
Unu fabur-ta pidi-nga-bu bini-xu-ni
one favor-ACC ask-NOM-BEN come-PROG-1SG
"I come to ask a favor"
cf. Quechua: Shuk fabur-ta maña-nga-bu shamu-xu-ni
one favor-ACC ask-NOM-BEN come-PROG-1SG
cf. Spanish: Vengo para pedir un favor
I-come for ask-INF a favor

(Muysken 1981:68–69)

Media Lengua is structurally distinct from Quechua and Spanish and is not intelligible to monolingual speakers of those languages. Unlike mixed languages, CS does not constitute a composite or hybrid system. However, it is conceivable that mixed languages may have arisen within communities where bilingual CS was prevalent; indeed, this is explicitly argued to be the case for at least one mixed language, Gurindji Kriol, spoken in the Northern Territory of Australia (McConvell and Meakins 2005). However, the origins of most mixed languages are not well understood and whether CS lies at their source remains an issue of debate within contact linguistics.

Finally, CS should not be confused with *diglossia*. Diglossia describes a community where languages or language varieties are functionally compartmentalized. Within such a situation, each language form is associated with a particular social function. A well-cited example is the functional distribution of languages in Paraguay, where Spanish is used in official and institutional contexts, and Guaraní is relegated to informal domains. In diglossic settings, the selection of which language to use is not free, but determined by community norms; that is, diglossia is socially imposed. In contrast, CS is understood as an individual phenomenon wherein a speaker chooses when, why, and how to alternate between languages.

1.4　Who engages in CS?

Any healthy individual who speaks more than one language has the capacity to select the appropriate language in a given situation. Only in certain instances of brain damage is language selection impaired with *pathological switching* as a result (see Kutas et al., this volume). CS, in the normal case, is under the conscious control of the speaker and, significantly, not all bilinguals are observed to engage in CS. Thus, a relevant domain of inquiry is to examine the individual, discursive, and social conditions under which a bilingual deploys both languages simultaneously. Since CS is manifested only in the speech of the bilingual it is also necessary first to ask, who is a bilingual?

1.4.1　CS and bilingual proficiency

"Bilingual" is a cover term that encompasses speakers who fall along a "bilingual range," a continuum of linguistic abilities and communicative strategies (Valdés 2001). As a consequence, there may be a relationship between a speaker's place in the bilingual continuum and the quality and quantity of CS attested. Therefore, a careful consideration of how a bilingual is defined is in order. The layperson's definition holds that a bilingual is an individual who has native-like control of two (or more) languages (a definition also offered by the linguist Bloomfield in 1933). Specialists, too, have employed terms such as *balanced bilingual*, *true bilingual*, and *symmetrical bilingual* to describe such a person. But consider what this would involve: no accent, no non-target word selection, and the ability to converse on any subject with any interlocutor at any time in either language. Such a bilingual would be like the putative "two monolinguals in one," a metaphor made current by Grosjean (1998). However, monolingual-like control of two languages over all aspects of linguistic knowledge and use within all domains is rare, if possible at all. Most bilinguals show disparate abilities in their component languages, for a myriad of reasons, including age of second language acquisition, the quality of linguistic input received, the language most used, and the status of the language in the community.

Speakers who have been exposed to two languages from birth or early childhood – *simultaneous* or *early* bilinguals – and who have maintained the use of their languages throughout their lifespan most closely approximate what is meant by true bilingual. These speakers possess advanced linguistic and communicative abilities in both languages, and are able to deploy each as required. The examples in 10, taken from Köppe and Meisel (1995:285), show the language alternations of Ivar (age 2;05), as he interacts with a French-speaking interviewer (F) and a German-speaking interlocutor (G).

(10) Iv (to G):   oh der kann nich fahr(en) der auto
                   "Oh this one can't move the car."
       F: qu'est-ce qu'elle a fait l'auto la voiture?
                   "What has it done the auto the car?"
       Iv: peut peut pas rouler
                   "can can not move"

As demonstrated in (10), Ivar is clearly able to separate his languages yet, at the same time, he is also reported to code-switch. Veh (1990) and Meisel (1994) report a high rate of language mixing for Ivar until around the age of 2;05, mostly between deictic elements and nouns (11a) and between verbs and nouns (11b). In (11c), Ivar uses translation equivalents, a common strategy for emphasis among bilinguals.

(11)   a. *das* bateau (2;00,02)
          "this boat"

                                        (Köppe and Meisel 1995:291)

       b. sent *füße* (2;04,09)
          "smell feet"

                                        (Köppe and Meisel 1995:291)

       c. j'ai trouvé – *i gefunden diese*! (2;08,15)
          "I have found – I (have) found these."

                                        (Schlyter 1990:114)

CS, then, is not indicative either of the bilingual's inability to separate his languages or of a lack of proficiency. Rather it is an additional communication resource available to bilinguals. CS also speaks to a bilingual's competence in each of the two languages. Various researchers have demonstrated that the ability to switch at the intra-sentential level correlates with increased mastery of linguistic structures. In particular, Genesee and his colleagues in Canada and Meisel and his colleagues in Germany have charted the language patterns of bilingual children and demonstrated that development in each language proceeds independently and that as the acquisition of the syntax of their component languages progresses, their language mixing patterns become more adult-like (see Müller and Cantone, Miccio et al., this volume).

Simultaneous bilingualism is frequently encountered in immigrant and guest-worker communities. Such communities also give rise to second generation, or *heritage*, bilinguals who, unlike their parents, may be dominant in the majority language. As their contact with the majority language increases, their use of and exposure to the home language may become more restricted. Thus, in addition to CS, their productions may also demonstrate features that are typical of language attrition including loan translations or calquing, semantic extensions and convergence (see Sebba, Bolonyai, this volume). It is usually the case that by the third generation the descendants of immigrants will have shifted to the dominant language, retaining only residual, formulaic traces of the heritage language in their speech. Oftentimes, this may be reflected in their CS patterns, which have been reduced to lexical insertion and/or tag-switching. In this respect, heritage speakers' linguistic forms come to resemble those attested among second language learners.

Second language acquirers or *late bilinguals* are those who have a linguistic system fully in place when their exposure to the second begins. Clearly, under this definition, we find a vast range of patterns of acquisition and outcomes. *Naturalistic* or *folk* bilinguals who learn a second language without formal instruction (e.g. immigrants and guest-workers) will differ greatly from so-called *elite* bilinguals whose language learning is primarily classroom based. Not only do these two types of bilinguals differ according to the context of second language learning, but they may also differ in terms of motivation. For many naturalistic bilinguals, second language learning is a necessity, as they cannot function easily in the dominant society without such knowledge. Elite bilinguals, on the other hand, often choose to learn a second language for personal or professional gain. Among speakers of both groups, particularly in the early stages of acquisition, CS results from an inability to produce a target form. Due to temporary or permanent lapses in knowledge, learners may switch to the native language, a process referred to as *crutching*. But as their proficiency develops, CS among second language learners and folk bilinguals, if attested, will resemble that of more fluent bilinguals. Thus, even among incipient bilinguals, CS patterns may be used as a measure of bilingual *ability*, rather than deficit. In fact, the degree of language proficiency that a speaker possesses in two languages has been shown to correlate with the type of CS engaged in. Poplack (1980) observes that adult bilinguals who reported to be dominant in one language tended to switch by means of tag-like phrases; in contrast, those who reported and demonstrated the greatest degree of bilingual ability favored intra-sentential switches. Similar patterns were attested among the school-age children studied by McClure (1981), who concludes that

... just as the monolingual improves his control over his verbal resources with age, so too does the bilingual. Further, just as there is a developmental pattern in the monolingual's syntactic control of his language, so too may such a pattern be found in the bilingual's control of the syntax of code-switching, which begins with the mixing of single items from one code into discourse in the other and culminates in the code changing of even more complex constituents (1981:92).

1.4.2 Why bilinguals code-switch
Despite the fact that CS has been shown to index bilingual linguistic and communicative skills rather than shortcomings, CS remains largely

stigmatized. Nevertheless bilinguals *do* choose to code-switch, a decision that is influenced by a number of social and discursive factors (see Gafaranga, Gardner-Chloros, Khattab, this volume). At the community level, the persistence of CS may reflect the covert prestige ascribed to this linguistic behavior. In particular, CS may serve as a marker of group membership and solidarity. Importantly, bilinguals only code-switch with other bilinguals with whom they share a dual language identity. For many, CS is a speech form that allows for the expression of their membership in two cultures: the dominant and the minority. Within some strata of bilingual communities, CS carries *overt* prestige. For example, Sankoff (1980) reports that in some areas of lowlands New Guinea, villagers are trilingual in Buang, Tok Pisin, and Yabem, and switching among them is the most prestigious form of public-speaking and is expected of persons in possession of power. In other instances, switching into a particular language may confer status on a speaker. For example, in Bulgaria, trilingual Muslim Roms who speak Romani, Bulgarian, and Turkish will code-switch into Turkish, as it has higher prestige than the other languages they command (Kyuchukov 2006).

There are also discursive functions that motivate the presence of CS in bilingual conversation. These pertain to the speaker's communicative intentions. Gumperz, in his seminal work on bilingual discursive strategies (1976, 1982a), describes many important functions served by CS. The premise underlying his and subsequent studies is that CS is a conscious choice on the part of the speaker, used to mark quotations, emphasis, realignment of speech roles, reiteration, and elaboration, among others. In (13), from Romaine (1995:162), a girl from Papua New Guinea inserts an English quotation from a cartoon into a Tok Pisin utterance. In (14), from Frenchville, PA (USA), the speaker uses English for translation/repair of an ill-formed French sentence that he is quoting. In (15), from Zentella (1997:94), the speaker switches from Spanish to English to mark a role shift. Finally, in (16), a Japanese–English bilingual uses Japanese to introduce the discourse topic (Nishimura 1985a, cited in Romaine 1995:163).

(12) *Tok Pisin–English*
   Lapun man ia kam na tok, "oh you poor pusiket," **na em go insait**.
   "The old man came and said, ..., and then he went inside."

(13) *Frenchville, PA, French–English*
   Elle m'a dit, "il pleuve [sic] **maintenant**." It's raining now. That's not good French, is it?
   "She said to me 'it's raining now [cf. *il pleut*]' ..."

(14) *Spanish–English*
   Mi nombre es Lourdes. Now we turn to my sister.
   "My name is Lourdes..."

(15) *Japanese–English*
   Yano-san-wa he was speaking all in English.
   "As for Mr. Yano, he was speaking all in English."

A great deal of research has been devoted to analyzing bilingual speech and ascribing particular functions to specific language alternations (see Gafaranga, this volume). However, it merits pointing out that not all language alternations in bilingual speech do signal a particular communicative intent or purpose; for many bilinguals, CS merely represents another way of speaking; that is, some bilinguals code-switch simply because they can and oftentimes may not be aware that they have done so.

Although bilinguals may possess the linguistic resources that allow for CS, this is not to suggest that all bilinguals *do* code-switch. As noted, it is commonly the case that social norms will confer prestige on monolingual forms but stigma on bilingual varieties such as CS. This is especially true in immigrant communities, where bilingualism is expected to be transitional. In educational settings in particular, CS may be perceived as a form of *semilingualism* among bilingual students and efforts have been taken to eradicate CS from the classroom. And in other professional contexts (e.g. the workplace), CS may be interpreted as reflecting negatively on speakers' cognitive abilities, social manners, etc. Not surprisingly, many bilinguals internalize the stigma attached to CS and disavow its use altogether. Even in communities where languages are in sustained contact, stable bilingualism is not necessarily accompanied by CS. Aikhenvald (2003) reports that among the Tariana in northwest Amazonia (Brazil), CS is considered taboo and those who engage in it, even accidentally, are ridiculed. One young man inadvertently produced a Tucano word in Tariana, illustrated in (16), and "this mistake of his was long remembered as a shameful thing, constantly mentioned in conversations about this young man (otherwise respected as a good hunter) and in discussing what is and what is not correct Tariana (Aikhenvald 2003:8)."

(16) Rafael matʃa **basa-mi**.
   Rafael good SING-PRES.3SGN
   "Rafael sings well."

In Tariana society, CS is permitted only in two specific contexts: in direct quotations and in the expression of the speech of animals and evil spirits in narratives. The Tariana situation is insightful because, even though the society holds strict taboos regarding CS, speakers in this contact situation are nonetheless observed to inadvertently code-switch. This is consistent with the well-known sociolinguistic fact that speakers' attitudes do not coincide with their behaviors. That is, many bilinguals will voice negative attitudes towards CS all the while deploying it in their own speech.

There are increasingly more contexts in which CS is accepted, if not admired, as a display of linguistic virtuosity. For example, CS is common on the web (see Dorleijn and Nortier, this volume), and also frequently found in prose, poetry, and music that depict culturally and linguistically diverse experiences. For example, Gustavo Pérez Firmat, a Cuban–American poet, employs CS in "Bilingual blues," excerpted in (17), whose title anticipates the purposeful musicality of the poem that is achieved through CS.

(17) ... psycho soy, cantando voy: ... Soy un ajiaco de
                                                    contradicciones,
      You say tomato,   un potaje de paradojas:
      I say tu madre;   a little square from Rubik's Cuba
      You say potato,   que nadie nunca acoplará.
      I say Pototo.   (Cha-cha-chá.)
      Let's call the hole
      un hueco, the thing
      a cosa, and if the cosa goes into
      the hueco,
      consider yourself en casa,
      consider yourself part of the family

In (18), the "multilingual wordsmithing" of Quebec Hip-Hop artists Muzion manifests a combination of French, English, Haitian Creole, Jamaican Creole, and Spanish (see Sarkar and Winer 2006:185).

(18) Hey, yo, uno. Teste moi pas, puto. Flow, c'est mon boulot. Phat comme
      un sumo, mes mots tranchent comme un couteau. Nouveau standard,
      j'emmène avec D et J. Ko. Pas d'égo que des échos: Les mc's bite mon
      steelo.
      "Hey, yo, first. Don't test me, whore [m]. To flow, it's my job. Phat like
      a sumo, my words cut like a knife. New standard, I'm bringing it with
      D and J. Ko. No ego except echoes: the mc's steal my style."

And in (19), the Arabic–French alternations of Cheb Hasni introduces additional authenticity into the Algerian rai genre.

(19) gelbek lli kan *vicieux*
      enti lxasra zzerga dxalti l *milieu*
      lukan kunti Sabra w kan 'sqek *sérieux*
      kun rak bdarek w gulti ll'du *adieu*
      lakin kunti makra lhubbi w xallSek *mon dieu*
      kunit 'duja *contre* w qsemti gelbi *en deux*

Indeed, Bentahila and Davies (2002) report that CS in rai lyrics generally conforms to the norms of conversational CS in the community in which they originate; for North African listeners, such lyrics are "instantly familiar examples of a form of discourse they know well" (Davies and Bentahila in press).

The above extracts are to be contrasted with those of others who at once laud CS as a creative process but at the same time demonstrate a misunderstanding of the phenomenon, especially with regard to its linguistic structure. Consider the text produced by Ilan Stavans and his university students, in (20), where Spanish and English are randomly mixed, purportedly to represent authentic *Spanglish* (Stavans 2003:15).

(20)   The United States Constitution
       Nosotros joldamos que estas truths son self-evidentes, que todos los hombres son creados equally, que están endawdeados por su Creador con certain derechos unalienables, que entre these están la vida, la libertad, y la persura de la felicidad.

As Lipski states, such a "grotesque creation not only contains numerous syntactic violations of code-switching, but also phonetically unlikely combinations in either language" (Lipski 2004:12). Unfortunately, this type of text contributes to the popular misperceptions of CS as an uncontrolled speech form and reinforces the stigma associated with it.

1.4.3   Social contexts for CS

Diverse social contexts give rise to language contact, which, in turn, provides the environment in which CS can take place. Societal bilingualism arises from various social forces and historical events, including colonization, invasion and annexation, migration and deportation. Political boundaries, which are often mutable, may place divisions within or between linguistic groups. These factors may lead to short-term or sustained language contact, which can have different outcomes in terms of language dominance and linguistic practices. For example, following the British colonial expansion into Asia, sustained contact between English and other languages is prevalent in India, Pakistan, Malaysia, Singapore, Hong Kong, etc. Thus it is not uncommon to find that speakers command a repertoire of languages available for various uses and that, for instance, a Malaysian may switch between a Chinese dialect, a colloquial form of English, formal English, and Malay in everyday conversation. Early textual evidence from ancient bilingual societies provides concrete evidence that when there is language contact, CS is likely to follow (see Adams 2003).

Because social conditions for language contact are malleable, different patterns of bilingual language use are to be expected. For instance, Bentahila and Davies (1995) demonstrate that the patterns of code-switching they observe among Moroccan Arabic–French bilinguals differ according to the role that each language may have played among different generations. The older, more balanced bilinguals displayed the ability to use sustained sequences of French in their discourse, whereas younger speakers primarily speak Arabic with French lexical insertions. These linguistic patterns reflect not only the bilinguals' proficiency in each language but also the changing status of French within Moroccan society, where it can be seen to be in regression following a movement toward Arabization. The opposite situation, where French is in ascension, is witnessed in Quebec, following the recognition of French as the official language of the province in 1977. This has led to increased parity between English and French, which is reflected in the patterns of language choice in contemporary Quebec, where switches into French from English are no longer viewed negatively (Heller 1995).

In sum, the individual and social factors that are implicated in CS are complex and difficult to isolate. For this reason, a uniform account of the phenomenon of CS is beyond the scope of any single research paradigm. Consequently, CS is addressed from a variety of different disciplinary perspectives, each focusing on a particular aspect of this behavior, and with different explanatory goals. The major approaches to the study of CS are overviewed below.

1.5   Approaches to the study of CS

There are three major strands in the study of CS. The *structural* approach is concerned with what CS can reveal about language structure at all levels (lexicon, phonology, morphology, syntax, semantics); the *psycholinguistic* approach investigates CS to better understand the cognitive mechanisms that underlie bilingual production, perception, and acquisition; and the *sociolinguistic* approach attends to the social factors that promote or inhibit CS and views CS as affording insights into social constructs such as power and prestige. Although, in principle, a full account of CS cannot be achieved without the integration of findings from each of these strands, in practice, such an all-encompassing task would be unwieldy. The methodologies employed within these various approaches are often incompatible, and the frameworks into which findings are couched can be diametrically opposed. For example, psycholinguistic studies are most often conducted within laboratory settings, using controlled stimuli, a methodology foreign to ethnographic studies, where language behavior must be observed in its natural context. Likewise, while some researchers would argue that there are no structural restrictions on CS, others build full-scale models based on structural considerations. In brief, because there is a lot of latitude in what comprises the study of CS, it is not surprising to find disagreements in the literature.

The theoretical linguistic or structural approach to CS research is primarily concerned with addressing the question that defines the field of linguistics: what constitutes knowledge of language? Most of this literature has been dedicated to the study of the morphological and syntactic patterns in CS. While syntactic theories are intended to be universal, they have been largely constructed to represent the knowledge of the mono-lingual. In this respect, the knowledge of the bilingual, as manifested through CS, provides the linguist with a challenging and unique source of data. Specifically, any universal theory of linguistic knowledge should be able to take account of bilingual as well as monolingual structures. Thus, bilingual researchers have sought to interpret data from CS within extant linguistic models.

From the structural perspective, CS is not aberrant but rule-governed and systematic (see Part III, this volume). Just as monolingual speakers possess intuitions about what constitutes well-formed utterances in their native language, bilinguals have the capacity to differentiate ill-formed from grammatical patterns of CS. Moreover, it has been demonstrated that CS does not constitute a distinct or third grammar, instead CS forms emerge from and conform to the constraints of both language systems. Early attempts at characterizing CS grammars examined notions of linear equivalence between the contributing languages. While it is expected that CS be facilitated between structurally similar languages (e.g. French and Italian), such an approach failed to account for CS between languages with distinct surface renderings (e.g. French and Arabic). Thus in accounting for how bilinguals reconcile the contradictory constraints of particular language pairings, researchers have sought to elaborate models that draw on more general principles (see Müller and Cantone, Chan, and Part V, this volume).

While there is a vast literature on the morpho-syntactic properties of CS, much less is known of its phonological implications (but see Bullock, Khattab, this volume). An overarching concern in this domain is whether there is an immediate and complete changeover from the phonetic system of one language to that of the other during CS. Note that this line of inquiry differs conceptually from that adopted by syntacticians – that is, syntacticians seek to examine the effect of morpho-syntax on CS, while here the issue is the impact of CS on phonological structure. Extant research on CS and sound structure has focused on the discrete phonetic properties of individual segments in CS production and perception. Thus, little is known about the effect of CS on the pronunciation or perception of larger units of analysis (e.g. syllables, words, intonational phrases). In sum, the interaction between phonology and CS invites further scrutiny.

Within the discipline of psycholinguistics, researchers have examined the cognitive mechanisms and neuro-anatomical structures that are implicated in the control of two languages (see Part IV, this volume). The simultaneous activation of two languages is commonly examined through language switching tasks, which can be used to assess lexical access, working memory, bilingual control, and attention, among others. Language switching tasks typically involve single lexical items, so it is not clear whether the bilingual process being examined is representative of CS. Psycholinguistic experimental methods rely on on-line techniques, where language processing, as reflected by reaction times, eye-movements, etc., can be directly assessed. Such tasks often reveal a cost associated with language switching, but it remains to be further examined whether this is necessarily the case for CS. As discussed by Kutas et al. (this volume), there may be circumstances in which CS, if it occurs in a sufficiently rich semantic context, is beneficial to bilingual language processing. To be sure, psycholinguistic studies of CS, rather than language switching, would be welcome (see Gullberg et al., this volume, for further discussion).

It is widely recognized that structural and cognitive dimensions are inadequate in accounting for the attested patterns of CS behavior; the social motivations and contexts for CS must also be considered (see Part II, this volume). Of all of the approaches to the study of CS, the sociolinguistic is the most diverse, as it attends to a multiplicity of linguistic-external factors: age, class, gender, social networks, community norms, identity, and attitudes, among others. As was noted above for the structural approach to CS, sociolinguists analyze CS in terms of existing frameworks that apply equally to the analysis of monolingual behavior at the micro- and macro-levels. The micro-level, which is the most well-studied, is focused on an individual's motivations for CS. In particular, it examines CS in the service of discursive functions (see Gumperz 1982a; Auer 1984), identity construction (see Le Page and Tabouret-Keller 1985), and accommodation (see Giles 1977), as well as CS as a reflection of the social networks in which an individual bilingual participates (see Milroy 1980). Scholars pursuing the micro-level sociolinguistic analysis of CS have contributed much to our current understanding of bilingual behavior and, as a consequence, have greatly helped to dispel the myths and misperceptions surrounding it. Complementing these analyses, researchers investigating CS as a community behavior (i.e. at the macro-level) have helped to situate individual bilingual behavior within diverse social contexts and by reference to societal norms (see Bentahila and Davies 1992; Li Wei 1994).

CS presents the sociolinguist with the complex task of correctly isolating the external variables that are relevant for analyzing bilingual behavior. These variables are often inter-related and their relative importance may change according to the social context. In this respect, a combined micro- and macro-level analysis may be warranted since it is difficult to appreciate an individual's performance independently from the social context in which it unfolds. In other words, the sociolinguist must know a great deal about the community in which she or he works, ideally including knowledge about the socio-historical situation of language contact. The case of the development of Gurindji Kriol into a mixed language may provide an illustration of this point. From studying Gurindji speech over several decades, McConvell and his students have been able to persuasively argue that the Gurindji Kriol spoken among the younger generations is no longer the manifestation of CS between Gurindji and Kriol (an English-based pidgin), although it resembles it. This is illustrated in (21) where Gurindji forms are italicized (McConvell and Meakins 2005:11).

(21)   *Gurindji–Kriol*
       nyawa-ma wan **karu** bin plei-bat pak-**ta nyanuny warlaku–yawung-ma**.
       this-TOP one child PAST play-CONT park-LOC.3SG. DAT dog-having-TOP
       "This one kid was playing at the park with his dog."

Here, Kriol provides most of the syntax and verbal morphology and Gurindji the case markers on nouns and pronouns, as well as much of the vocabulary for nouns. In his work on aboriginal CS in the 1980s, McConvell (1988) noted that Kriol predominated in the verbal domain, which appears to be the pattern that has become replicated in the mixed language utterances of the younger generations. Strong support for the notion that Gurindji Kriol constitutes a mixed language is provided by the different sociolinguistic profiles across generations. Significantly, while older Gurindji were proficient bilinguals capable of engaging in alternational, as well as insertional CS, the younger generation is restricted to the insertional types as in (21) because they are no longer proficient in Gurindji. By concurrently studying Gurindji from sociolinguistic and structural perspectives over a period of many years, McConvell and his colleagues have been able to shed new light on the CS versus mixed language controversy. In doing so, they have demonstrated that language contact within the same ethnic group can lead to different, but related, structural outcomes as changes in sociolinguistic conditions give rise to different language varieties.

1.6   Conclusion

As this chapter has demonstrated, there are many facets to the study of CS. Those with interests in CS behavior range from poets to neurologists, and from parents to politicians. As should be clear, much is misunderstood about CS and those who engage in it. Thus it falls to linguists and to students of linguistics to unveil the nature of CS – its structural properties, its biological underpinnings, and its social meanings – and to communicate their findings to a broader audience.

Part I

Conceptual and methodological considerations in code-switching research

2

Research techniques for the study of code-switching

Marianne Gullberg
Peter Indefrey
and
Pieter Muysken

2.1 Introduction

The selection of techniques to include in a review of methods for studying code-switching (henceforth CS) inevitably raises the question of what constitutes CS. In addition to the distinctions made between CS and code-mixing (see Muysken 2000), a further distinction can usefully be made between CS and so called language switching.

The term CS can be reserved for studies where the focus is on internally generated switches, i.e. switches produced spontaneously by a multilingual speaker. Studies of CS are mainly concerned with the nature of the constraints governing CS and its processing. The focus is typically on phrases or sentences, on the semantic or structural relationships, and on the linguistic constraints governing switching. The methods used to study CS defined this way are almost exclusively found in the domain of free production.

In contrast, language switching studies generally concern the mechanism of switching itself, including language selection, control, attention, and switching costs, the structure of and access to the bilingual lexicon, and bilingual memory (see Costa 2005; Costa and Santesteban 2006; Dijkstra 2005; La Heij 2005; Meuter 2005). The general domain is the lexicon at the single word level. Typical of language switching paradigms is the use of externally induced switching whereby participants change language on an external cue or respond to an externally generated switch. Frequent techniques are word recognition and lexical decision tasks.

The overarching methodological problem regarding experimental techniques is how to study CS without compromising the phenomenon, i.e. how to induce, manipulate, and replicate natural CS. Arguably, CS as defined above is a production phenomenon whereas the comprehension of CS can only be studied using language switching techniques, i.e. methods relying on external cues or materials with pre-existing switches to which bilinguals must respond. This raises methodological issues. Although some experimental methods use internally generated switches to study CS, externally generated switches (i.e. language switching techniques) are often used to study both language switching and CS. Language switching techniques can naturally be used to gain insights into CS, but it is important to validate such techniques to ensure that data from language switching methods are actually comparable to CS in the sense of internally generated switching.

The importance of this point can be underscored by considering attempts to study CS using intuition data. Some of the earlier studies on syntactic properties of CS used this technique (Di Sciullo et al. 1986; Mahootian 1993; Woolford 1983). While there may be some degree of correspondence between intuition data and naturalistic data, there is no guarantee that the results coincide. Sobin (1984) systematically studied judgements of adjective/noun orders in Spanish–English CS, where the orders in both languages often differ (*the* **white** *house* versus *la casa* **blanca**). In addition to considerable disagreement between speakers, the overall tendencies reported only partially correspond to what is actually found in naturalistic data. Reliability may vary between different speech communities and different constructions, but is certainly not a given.

It is further crucial to stress that different methods and techniques allow different questions to be answered. Depending on whether the focus of interest is on language switching or on CS, on sociolinguistic aspects, grammatical constraints, phonetic properties, development, on-line processing, bilingual memory, the cost of switching, or the neurocognitive underpinnings of CS, different techniques must be employed. The tension between naturalistic, ecologically valid approaches and more artificial, controlled, experimental techniques should be recognized but also be embraced as a source of complementary information rather than as a (false) dichotomy between "good" and "bad" approaches to the study of CS. A more important consideration in the study of CS is that techniques are validated, and that the behavior they elicit in some measure corresponds to the phenomenon "in the wild" (see Myers-Scotton 2006b). Converging evidence from a range of techniques is perhaps the best way to ensure such validity.

2.2 Naturalistic data and corpus methods: the limits of the observational paradigm

Before the development of good recording techniques made it possible to gather naturalistic data, CS could be studied either through written observations of naturalistic speech (a technique used by Schuchardt 1890; Weinreich 1953), or through the study of texts containing CS. Incidental observations of naturalistic speech have the advantage of at least reflecting actual language use, but may be inaccurate in various ways. No representative sample can be gathered this way. The study of written texts containing CS can take various forms:

(1.)   Studying literary authors who represent the CS of their characters. The best known of these is Tolstoy, who represents Russian–French CS in *War and Peace* (Timm 1978). A number of studies have examined literary texts, but the same reservations apply as for written observations.

(2.)   Studying poetic genres where bilingual language use and CS are central to the genre itself. In modernist "high" literature, examples would be some of the *Cantos* of Ezra Pound or portions of *Finnegans Wake* by James Joyce. More amenable to systematic analysis of CS are various types of bilingual poetry, ranging from the Hebrew–Arabic–Spanish *kjarkas* of medieval Spain (Zwartjes 1997) to Yiddish–Hebrew–Russian mixed songs (Weinreich 1950, alas only available in Yiddish), to the *calypso* of Trinidad and the bilingual Quechua–Spanish *wayno* of the Andes (Muysken 2005). The trouble with these bilingual genres is (i) that some switches may be due to requirements of meter or rhyme, and hence do not represent naturalistic speech; (ii) there may be more outrageous mixing than is ever encountered in naturalistic speech, for poetic effect (see Muysken 1995).

(3.)   Studying archival material (e.g. trade registers) in which two languages are systematically used (e.g. Middle English and Latin). The drawback of these materials is that they are often quite formulaic, and only represent a limited range of constructions.

To overcome these disadvantages, many researchers, starting at least with Poplack (1980), record naturalistic data in a variety of settings: the public domain, peer group interactions, family gatherings, sociolinguistic interviews, classroom interactions, etc. The work of the last thirty years has produced an impressive corpus of bilingual speech illustrating CS and a host of other language interaction phenomena. Clearly the field owes whatever achievements have been attained to this technique.

Why, then, not simply continue using this method as the main data gathering technique? The naturalistic data method has a number of drawbacks:

(1.)   **Costs**. Gathering and transcribing a large corpus of bilingual speech is complicated and costly.

(2.)   **Accountability**. For various reasons (competition between researchers, the privacy of the bilingual speakers recorded, incomplete or fragmented transcription, negligence), virtually none of the bilingual corpora on which the CS studies are based are publicly available. It is therefore not possible to study the same materials in order to test the conclusions reached or explore other interpretations.

(3.) **Inherent limitations**. A corpus of naturalistic data has inherent limitations. Some questions are very difficult to answer on the basis of a corpus. These are not only questions that generative syntacticians might ask (e.g. Is it possible to switch in a clause with a parasitic gap?), but fairly standard research questions as well.

We will illustrate the final point with the example of Finnish–English, perhaps surprisingly the most systematically studied language pair with respect to CS. A number of excellent studies exist, listed in Table 2.1.

Table 2.1 Schematic overview of the studies on Finnish–English code-switching

Author	Date	Location
Lehtinen	(1966)	Northern US
Poplack et al.	(1987)	Canada
Lauttamus	(1990)	US
Halmari	(1997)	Southern US
Kovács	(2001)	Australia

We will focus here on determiner phrases with their attendant case marking. The following observations are made by the various researchers, with different interpretations given to the material. In the Finnish examples the following abbreviations are used: PRT = partitive case; IL = illative case; ACC = accusative case; PL = plural; SG = singular; PAST = past; IN = inessive case; AD = adessive case; IMP = imperfect tense; FS = Finnish stem marker.

(1.) In many switched clauses the English noun is marked with the appropriate Finnish case:

(1)   Kerran sä olit pannu si-tä mun ***lunchbox***-iin
       once you had put it+PRT my lunchbox-IL
       "You had once put it in my lunchbox."

(Halmari 1997: 59)

Halmari (1997) interprets this pattern as consistent with a syntactic-theoretical account (the Government Constraint of Di Sciullo et al. 1986): the Finnish verb *pannu* 'put' carries a Finnish language marker, requiring its direct object to be Finnish, as signaled by the case marking on *lunchbox*. In the view of Poplack et al. (1987) the inserted noun *lunchbox-iin* is instead a borrowing, not a code-switch. Finally, Kovács (2001) claims that the phenomenon is a case of "smooth" switching.

(2.) In many cases there is also a deictic element preceding the switched element, both of which are marked for the same case:

(2) Sit se jätti sen sinne **library**-in
then it left it-ACC there-IL library-IL
"Then she left it in the library."

(Halmari 1997:59)

(3) Molemmat niinku teki ton **language**-in koulussa
both-PL as/like do-PAST3SG that-ACC language-ACC school-IN
"Both liked the language at school."

(Kovács 2001:152)

Halmari (1997) suggests that the deictic element is a language carrier, requiring that *library* also be marked with a Finnish case, while in the view of Poplack et al. (1987) the phenomenon is a sign of flagging. Kovács (2001) explains it as a characteristic of new information in dialectal spoken Finnish.

(3.) In almost one third of the data, the case marking is missing on the inserted element. Sometimes a case-marked pre-nominal deictic is present:

(4) Siell-o-n iso intiaanimuseo siell-ä **Prescott**-Ø
there-AD-is big Indian.museum there-AD
"There is a big Indian museum in Prescott."

(Halmari 1997:64)

(5) Se sai semmose-n **stroke**-Ø
s/he get-IMP3SG like-ACC stroke
"She had like a stroke."

(Kovács 2001:153)

Again, Halmari (1997) explains the phenomenon by saying that the language marking is carried by the deictic element. Poplack et al. (1987) again evoke flagging. Kovács (2001) explains this as fully marked, flagged switching.

(4.) In some cases, there is considerable pausing:

(6) Nekin pelaa sitä ... pel- jotain **softball**-i-a
They-also play-3SG that-PRT play-some-PRT softball- FEM.SG.PRT
"They also play softball."

(Kovács 2001:191)

All researchers interpret this as an indication of flagged CS.

(5.) Sometimes, however, the flagging element is not present:

(7) Partitive case missing
Teeksää vai **Irish-Irish coffee**-Ø?
Make- Q-you ... or
"Are you making Irish coffee or what?"

(Halmari 1997:64)

(8) Mä ostan yleensä **spruce**-Ø taikka **Douglas pine**-Ø
I buy-1SG usually spruce or Douglas pine
"I usually buy spruce or Douglas Pine."

(Kovács 2001:153)

According to Halmari (1997) this lack of marking is characteristic of attrition among second generation speakers. Poplack et al. (1987) view it as an example of a non-smooth noun switch, whereas Kovács (2001) explains it as L2-oriented switching.

Even in a case like this, where extensive research has been carried out, observational techniques will not help us answer all the questions, and more specific controlled experiments are called for to determine the contributions of the various factors involved.

2.3   Experimental data and methods

Controlled or experimental methods for studying CS beyond the single-word level are still relatively rare, especially if the distinction between language switching and CS is maintained. Semi-experimental techniques range from controlled elicited production tasks to grammaticality or acceptability judgement tasks. Experimental techniques, usually conducted in the laboratory, involve strict designs with a balanced set of experimental and control conditions and test and filler items. Statistical treatment of the results can be found in corpus-based and experimental paradigms alike.

Experimental methods can be divided into *off-line* techniques, where no time constraint is involved and participants can reflect on their responses as long as they like, and *on-line* techniques, where the time course of language processing itself is at stake. These different methods rely on different measures or dependent variables. Off-line methods often draw on metalinguistic judgements or written production. On-line methods typically involve measuring response/reaction times, and accuracy or error scores. Response times are assumed to reflect processing difficulty such that the longer the reaction time, the more difficult something is to process compared to a control item. By inference, the more difficult it is to process an item, the less grammatical, acceptable, or accessible it is assumed to be. Other indicators of difficulty, especially in production, are hesitations, disfluencies, and repetitions. In both types of techniques, features whose influence is examined and manipulated include the nature of the switched element (e.g. a content vs. a function word), the location of a switch, language choice, proficiency and dominance, word frequency, ambiguity, the preceding sentence context, and the nature of the immediately preceding response. Bilingual and CS experimentation calls for very careful design to control for all relevant factors.

In the following, methods will be briefly presented with a short description of the task, its underlying logic, and the measures it yields. For more detailed descriptions, references are given to example studies in Table 2.2. A final remark must be made about the distinction between

Table 2.2 Experimental tasks and example studies

Task	Example studies
Phonetic/phonological level	
Phonetic categorization/ categorical perception	Bürki-Cohen et al. (1989)
Gating	Grosjean (1980, 1988), Li (1996)
Lexical level	
Cued shadowing	Li (1996), Bates and Liu (1996)
Lexical decision	
Visual	Beauvillain and Grainger (1987)
Auditory	Soares and Grosjean (1984)
Naming	
Simple naming	Macnamara (1967a), Meuter and Allport (1999)
Translation	Altarriba and Mathis (1997), Kroll and Stewart (1994)
Stroop	Altarriba and Mathis (1997), Hamers and Lambert (1972)
Picture naming	Costa and Santesteban (2004)
Word association	Taylor (1971)
Sentence level	
Grammaticality/acceptability judgements	
Written	Sobin (1984)
Auditory	Aguirre (1985), Sobin (1984)
Contrastive pairs	Toribio (2001b)
Content judgements	Kolers (1966), Macnamara and Kushnir (1971)
Sentence matching	Dussias (2001)
Reading times	Altarriba et al. (1996), Dussias (2003)
Auditory moving window	Ferreira et al. (1996)
Reading aloud	Grosjean and Miller (1994), Kolers (1966), Toribio (2001a)
Free speech in switch mode	Azuma (1996), Grosjean and Miller (1994), Toribio (2001a)
Sentence repetition, elicited imitation	Azuma and Meier (1997), Clyne (1972), Meijer and Fox Tree (2003)
Sentence completion	Dussias (2002)
Sentence recall (priming)	Meijer and Fox Tree (2003)
Confederate scripting	Kootstra et al. (in prep.)
fMRI, PET	Hernández et al. (2001)
ERP	Moreno et al. (2002)

comprehension and production tasks. Experimental tasks are generally speaking more numerous for the study of comprehension than production (see Bock 1996). While intuitively convenient, the distinction between comprehension and production is not always easy to uphold since much language activity involves both modalities. Wherever possible, a note will be made regarding whether a task focuses mainly on comprehension or production.

2.3.1 The phonetic–phonological level

To probe the role of phonetic–phonological knowledge in bilinguals' comprehension and production of CS, language switching paradigms have mainly been used, i.e. tasks measuring responses to externally generated switches (but see Bullock, this volume).

2.3.1.1   Phonetic categorization and categorical perception

Phonetic categorization tasks are used to examine whether bilinguals categorize CS words as belonging to language A or B and what factors influence such categorization. Listeners hear a range of speech sounds forming a continuum between two unambiguous endpoints with ambiguous sounds in between. In CS research an endpoint is a sound or a word clearly belonging to language A or B. The ambiguous sounds are often synthesized or digitally manipulated versions of the endpoint sounds. Listeners are required to identify all sounds as being either language A or B. The task measurements are proportions of responses categorized as A or B, reaction times, and accuracy scores on a companion discrimination task of the endpoints. This task has been used to investigate whether bilinguals mainly use phonetic information or also preceding context to decide what language a CS word is (Bürki-Cohen et al. 1989).

2.3.1.2   Gating

Gating is used to examine how much and which information is necessary for listeners to identify words in speech (Grosjean 1980). For CS, the role of phonetic and phonotactic properties of words, the preceding context, word frequency, etc., can be examined. Typically, participants hear sentences with a spoken target word presented in segments of increasing duration (increments of between 30 and 50 milliseconds) until the entire word has been presented. For each presentation, participants must identify or guess the word (and/or the language) and give a confidence rating of their guess. The task yields measures of the number of segments, or gates, required for participants to reach the isolation point (i.e. the amount of exposure needed for identification), confidence ratings, and the word guesses, which can be characterized for language.

2.3.2   The lexical level

Methods that target individual words are almost exclusively language switching techniques and can be argued to tap general bilingual processing rather than CS.

2.3.2.1   Cued shadowing

Cued shadowing (or single-word shadowing, auditory naming, word repetition) (Bates and Liu 1996) is also used to study the recognition of code-switched items in bilingual speech. The task allows the influence of phonological, structural, and contextual information on the recognition of CS words to be examined. Listeners are presented with a spoken phrase or sentence, which contains a target word that they must repeat as quickly and accurately as possible once they detect it. The task yields reaction times and accuracy scores. In monolingual contexts, the target word can be recorded in another voice. Li (1996) adapted the task for CS research by presenting the target word in the other of the bilingual's languages (Chinese or English). Participants were told beforehand where in the sentence structure the target word would occur. A variation on this task is to indicate that the target word will start with a particular sound (a phoneme-triggered task, suggested by Heredia and Stewart 2002).

2.3.2.2 Lexical decision

Lexical decision tasks are used extensively in studies on language switching to examine issues of lexical access, the structure of the bilingual mental lexicon, and control issues. Lexical decision tasks examine what determines how long it takes listeners to decide whether a written or a spoken string is a word or not. Participants hear or read words, presented in isolation or in sequence. For a given target word, they must decide whether the string is a real word or not by pressing a button for Yes or No. The response measures are reaction times and accuracy or error scores. The logic of the task is that, if bilinguals consider words in both languages for every decision, it should take them longer than monolinguals to decide whether a string is a word or not. If, in contrast, only one language is active, then response times should be the same as for monolinguals.

The basic task can be modified in many ways. Written versions manipulate orthographic properties of words. For instance, issues of lexical access are studied by measuring the influence of words that are orthographically similar but mean different things in two languages (interlexical or interlingual homographs, "false friends," Beauvillain and Grainger 1987). Orthographic systems with both overlap and differences, as in Greek and Latin scripts, are also manipulated (see Dijkstra 2005 for an overview of studies of visual word recognition). In auditory versions participants are asked to listen for a string starting with a particular sound in a sentence and then to indicate whether that string is a word or not (phoneme-triggered lexical decision, e.g. Soares and Grosjean 1984).

In cross-modal versions, e.g. cross-modal priming, participants listen to speech (the "prime," e.g. *dog*) while watching a fixation mark on a screen. A written test word then appears on the screen, which can be semantically (e.g. *cat*) or phonologically (e.g. *doll*) related or unrelated (e.g. *apple*) to the prime. Participants must then make a lexical decision or name the word. Reaction times are measured to determine whether priming occurs, i.e. whether the prime word led to facilitation (shorter reaction times) or to interference (longer reaction times).

2.3.2.3 Naming tasks

Naming tasks are often used in the study of language switching to examine the structure of the lexicon, the strengths and nature of associations between words of the same versus different languages, and the cost of switching language. Naming tasks are used to study both comprehension and production. The simplest version requires participants to name as many words as possible in a given time window using a particular language or a particular mode, for instance, to name only in one language, to switch language for every word, or to give a translation equivalent for every word offered (Macnamara 1967b). The dependent variable is generally the number of words produced and response times. Monolingual naming is compared to switched naming. The logic is that the strength of association between words, levels of activation, and facilitation/inhibition of lexical access will be reflected in the number of words produced.

Other versions constrain the task by asking participants to name particular stimuli and by providing an external cue for switching. For example, participants may be asked to name digits with the language to be used indicated by a geometrical shape (Macnamara et al. 1968), background color (Meuter and Allport 1999), or a particular digit system (Campbell 2005). A translation version requires participants to provide the translation equivalent of a keyword, varying the directionality of the translation from language A to B or vice versa (e.g. Chan et al. 1983; Kroll and Stewart 1994). In these tasks, naming latencies and accuracy or error scores are measured. Participants may also be required to read monolingual or mixed word lists out loud in which the switching frequency is manipulated (Dalrymple-Alford 1985). Naming latencies in such studies are measured to examine whether switching language takes longer than not switching. A further variation is a translation recognition task in which participants are presented with two words, one in each language. They are required to decide whether the second word is an accurate translation of the first by pressing a button for Yes or No (e.g. Altarriba and Mathis 1997). Again, reaction times and accuracy/error scores are measured.

A particular type of naming task is the bilingual Stroop task (MacLeod 1991). Participants must name a color patch (e.g. in red) on which are printed either incongruently colored words (*blue*), congruently colored words (*red*), or neutral words (*car*). The task is to name the color of the patch, and to ignore the words. The difference in response times between naming patches with incongruent words and neutral words is known as the interference effect. In bilingual versions color words appear in both languages, and participants are asked to respond in language A on some trials and in B on other trials. The question is whether it is easier to ignore the printed word when it is in another language than the response language, e.g. to ignore the printed word *"red"* printed on a blue patch, when you must respond "azul" in Spanish. Although interference is typically greater within a language, there is also a robust interference effect between languages. Interference is also likelier from a dominant into a weaker language than the opposite (see Altarriba and Mathis 1997;

MacLeod 1991). The Stroop task can also be auditory. Listeners may be asked to decide whether the pitch of a speaker's voice is high or low as the speaker pronounces the words "high" or "low" in either a high or low pitch and in alternating languages (see Hamers and Lambert 1972).

Another type of naming is picture naming. The simplest kind presents pictures to be named on different colored backgrounds to cue the use of a particular language (e.g. Costa and Santesteban 2004). The picture names are manipulated to examine the effect of cognates, for instance. The measures are reaction times and error/accuracy scores. In picture-word interference tasks a picture is presented on a computer screen and participants are asked to name the picture (e.g. a dog) as quickly and accurately as possible. They are also asked to ignore an auditory or visual interfering stimulus that can be semantically (e.g. *cat*) or phonologically (e.g. *doll*) related to the picture, or not related at all (e.g. *apple*). In bilingual versions the distractors can come from both languages, and the naming can take place in either or both of the bilinguals' languages (see La Heij 2005 for an overview). Again, the rationale is that if naming in language A is affected by the names of distractors in language B, this is an indication that access to the bilingual lexicon is not language-specific.

2.3.2.4   Word associations

Word association tasks in spoken and written form are used to study the relationship and associations between words in the bilingual lexicon and bilingual memory. Participants are asked to provide word associations to keywords in their two languages. They can be requested to respond monolingually, in either language, or to switch at particular rates, such as once every two words or at every other word (e.g. Ervin-Tripp 1964; Taylor 1971). The dependent variable is the number of words provided. The task can also be used to probe whether bilinguals will make semantically or conceptually different associations in either of their languages.

2.3.3   The sentence level

Only at the sentence level are techniques found that draw on internally generated switches to study CS, as opposed to language switching paradigms where the switch is externally imposed. Both written and auditory stimuli are used to elicit written and spoken output.

2.3.3.1   Grammaticality or acceptability judgement tasks

Traditionally, grammaticality and acceptability judgement tasks are written off-line tests probing participants' grammatical knowledge. In bilingual studies, participants must respond by indicating whether a sentence with a particular type of switch is grammatical or not, or indicate its degree of acceptability on Likert scales (e.g. Bhatia and Ritchie 1996; Sobin 1984). To reduce the risk of prescriptive attitudes towards switching, auditory versions have been developed in which participants instead hear the sentences to be judged (e.g. Aguirre 1985; Sobin 1984), and instructions can be phrased in familiarity terms, for instance, "Does this sentence sound like something you might have heard?" (Aguirre 1985). In addition to the judgement, participants are occasionally asked to correct or improve unacceptable sentences (e.g. Lederberg and Morales 1985). Another variation presents sentences in contrastive pairs, drawing attention to switching sites (Toribio 2001b). This procedure can fruitfully be combined with scalar responses or be turned into a preference response rather than an absolute one to avoid some of the artifacts and validity problems connected with the task (e.g. Sorace 1996). The technique can be used to examine the acceptability of particular switch locations (e.g. Toribio 2001b).

2.3.3.2   Content judgements

A more indirect measure of acceptability are content judgements such as comprehension questions or sentence verification tasks calling for true–false judgements. The assumption here is that if a switch of a particular type (e.g. manipulation of switching site or element switched) incurs a processing difficulty, then response times should be longer and error rates higher. Such tasks are typically language switching tasks since the materials are pre-switched and artificially created. Comprehension questions are often off-line tasks where participants respond after silently reading or listening to monolingual and code-switched passages of text or speech (e.g. Kolers 1966). True–false judgements can be on-line tasks in which participants read or hear a monolingual or code-switched passage. They are then asked to judge whether the sentence is true or false by pressing a button for Yes or No. The task yields reaction times as well as accuracy/error scores (Macnamara and Kushnir 1971; Rakowsky 1989; Wakefield et al. 1975).

2.3.3.3   Sentence matching

Sentence matching is an on-line task that also taps acceptability indirectly without asking explicit metalinguistic questions (Freedman and Forster 1985; Gass 2001). Participants see two written sentences on a computer screen, one presented slightly after the other. They must indicate whether the two sentences are identical or not by pushing a button for Yes or No. The time needed for this same–different decision is measured, as are accuracy/error scores. The pacing of presentation time can be fixed or self-paced, in which case participants themselves bring up the second sentence by a button push when they have read the first one, the so-called response-contingent sentence matching technique. The first technique provides only one response time, the second provides one response time for reading the first sentence, and another for the matching decision. Generally, the first reading time is given most weight, as it is assumed that reading time reflects complexity of processing. In general, grammatical sentences are responded to faster than ungrammatical sentences. A promising modification for CS research would be an auditory version of the task (see Roberts and Verhagen forthcoming). In CS research, Dussias (2001) has used the written task to investigate the effects of switch locations in Spanish–English, comparing switches before function words like determiners (***la maestra compró*** the books "the teacher bought …") to switches between function and content elements (***la maestra compró los*** books "the teacher bought the …"). Switches at dispreferred locations or in dispreferred directions (from English to Spanish or from Spanish to English) are assumed to affect response times.

2.3.3.4   Silent reading

Reading is used to tap processing in language switching. Reading times are assumed to reflect processing difficulty such that the longer the reading time, the more difficult the processing. The unit for which reading time is measured ranges from whole text passages to sentences, phrases or individual words. Eye-tracking techniques allow one to measure the time the eye fixates on an individual word during reading. The number of times an element is fixated on can also be counted, again assuming that more fixations indicate greater processing difficulty (see Dussias 2003; Altarriba et al. 1996). The technique can be used to examine reading times of switched words in mixed sentences.

2.3.3.5   Auditory moving window

In this task participants listen to sentences one or two words at a time and must press a button to receive successive segments (see Ferreira et al. 1996). The time needed to process each segment is recorded. The technique has been employed to study the effect of context, word frequency, and phonetic realization in the processing of switched sentences (Heredia et al. 2002).

2.3.3.6   Reading aloud

A simple sentence-level language switching technique is to ask bilinguals to read texts aloud that are either monolingual or that contain switches (e.g. Chan et al. 1983; Grosjean and Miller 1994; Kolers 1966; Toribio 2001a). The measure is always reading (plus speaking) speed and the aim is to investigate the influence, if any, of switching itself. Switching can be "blocked" with switching occurring at alternating sentences, or before a particular word class (e.g. each noun). Switching can also be random but conform to the word order of one of the languages, or it can be entirely random. The contrasts between acceptable versus unacceptable switches have also been examined. The task has also been used to assess whether bilinguals change to language-appropriate phonetics at the critical word or not by measuring voice onset times (see Bullock et al. 2006).

2.3.3.7   Free speech in "code-switch mode"

A straightforward CS task is to ask bilinguals to speak freely over a given topic, either monolingually in language A or B, or to deliberately code-switch. Although speakers are required to code-switch, they are free to decide when and how to do so. Switches are therefore internally generated and constitute true CS. The assumption is that the procedure will yield "natural" switches compatible with the bilinguals' grammars. The measure is the number or proportion of switches produced per some speech unit (per clause, per 100 words, etc.), as well as more qualitative measures like types of switches, switch locations, phonetic–phonological properties of switches, etc. The degree of fluency can also be measured. Speech can be entirely free (Blot et al. 2003), consist of story retellings in speech or in writing (Grosjean and Miller 1994; Toribio 2001a), or be spoken summaries of texts that are either monolingual or switched (Kolers 1966). This method generates ecologically valid data, but does not allow much control over factors that constrain CS. A language switching version of the task asks bilinguals to speak freely over a given topic and then to switch language when they hear a tone randomly generated at irregular intervals. With this method Azuma (1996) examined the planning units of switched speech. He noted the type of word uttered at the time of the tone (noun, preposition, etc.), measured the time it took the bilingual to stop speaking and switch language, and noted the type of element where language was switched (word, phrasal boundary, etc.).

2.3.3.8   Sentence repetition

In sentence repetition or elicited imitation participants hear a sentence and must then repeat it back as accurately as possible. The rationale of the technique is that when listeners hear a sentence that exceeds the capacity of their short-term memory, they will pass it through their own grammar before repeating it. If a particular grammatical element in the input sentence is not part of the individual's grammar, that element will be changed during the repetition (Vinther 2002). The dependent measures are therefore number or proportion of accurately repeated sentences, alternatively, number or proportion of changes, the time elapsed between the offset of the prompt and the onset of the repetition, and qualitative aspects of types and locations of changes. Because the nature of switches and their locations is predefined, it is typically a language switching task. However, the repetitions produced may be considered to be CS. The delay between hearing the sentence and the required repetition can vary from immediate repetition (Azuma and Meier 1997), to a ten-second delay with intervening music (Clyne 1972), to delays involving distractor tasks (Meijer and Fox Tree 2003). The longer the delay, the more likely the response is to reflect the individual's own grammar.

2.3.3.9   Sentence completion

In sentence completion tasks, participants are presented with sentences with missing elements. Participants must read and complete the sentence by filling in the blank as quickly and accurately as possible. The time between the last read element and the naming of the blank or of a corresponding picture can be measured as a response time and accuracy/ error scores can be recorded. Properties of the filled-in element can also be recorded, like language chosen, word order, grammatical category, etc. The task relies on internally generated switches, i.e. on CS proper, since no force is applied to make the bilingual switch. If a switch occurs, it is self-generated. The task can be used to examine, for instance, preferred switch locations such as between functional and content elements.

2.3.3.10   Sentence recall (priming)

Sentence recall tasks combine comprehension and production aspects. Participants are asked to read and memorize a sentence. They then read a prime sentence with a different syntactic construction, and/or in a different language. After reading the prime, participants are asked a distractor question, for example, whether a certain word was part of the prime sentence. Finally, they are asked to recall the original sentence aloud. The key question is whether the structure of the prime will influence recall of the original sentence. The task has been used to examine syntactic priming effects, i.e. whether listeners are more likely to repeat syntactic constructions they have just heard than to use another construction (Hartsuiker et al. 2004; Loebell and Bock 2003). For example, Meijer and Fox Tree (2003) used the opposition between double-object and prepositional object constructions in English and Spanish to examine whether a construction in one language would prime the corresponding construction in the other. These studies are not CS studies *per se*, but could be modified for the study of CS.

2.3.3.11   Confederate scripting

A related technique is confederate scripting (Branigan et al. 2000; Hartsuiker et al. 2004) where two participants take turns describing a picture. The confederate participant is instructed (scripted) to use a particular lexical or syntactic construction. The extent to which the real participant then uses the same construction in his/her own description is measured. Kootstra et al. (in preparation) use the task to elicit Dutch–English CS. Participants are given a lead-in sentence fragment like "on this picture" and are asked to describe a picture, switching language somewhere in the sentence. The confederate produces code-switched sentences that conform either to Dutch or English word order given the lead-in fragment. The confederate's contribution constitutes a language switch but the real participant's output is CS. The dependent measure is the number of times the real participants use a primed word order, which word order is used, and where in the structure the switch occurs.

2.3.4   Neurocognitive methods

Recently neurocognitive methods have been used to investigate the neuro-cognitive underpinnings of bilingual processing (see papers in Gullberg and Indefrey 2006). Both hemodynamic (PET, fMRI) and electrophysiolog-ical (ERP, MEG) techniques are promising research tools for the study of language switching and CS. Normally, participants need to perform no additional experimental task other than reading or listening for compre-hension. With some limitations due to possible movement artifacts, the techniques can also be used to investigate language production. A number of studies have examined the neural correlates of language switching using explicit cues to switch language (see Rodriguez-Fornells et al. 2006 for an overview). Electrophysiological methods are very sensitive to the time course of neural events in relation to a particular word. The tech-nique therefore provides precise measurements of the effects of a code-switch on processing and is also suited to examine neural events preceding a code-switch in production.

The ERP technique provides a means for distinguishing semantic from syntactic difficulties, and for assessing task control and attention. The monolingual literature has already established signatures for semantic integration difficulties. When a participant has difficulties integrating the semantics of a word with the preceding context, this is typically reflected in an increased negativity peaking approximately 400 ms after the onset of the unexpected word in comparison to a condition where there is no integration difficulty. This is the so-called N400 effect (Kutas and Hillyard 1984). Similarly, difficulties integrating syntactic information are reflected in an increased positivity peaking approximately 600 ms after the onset of the critical element, the so-called P600 effect (Osterhout and Holcomb 1992; Hagoort et al. 1993). These signatures can be exploited to study the effects of CS on bilingual lexical and sentence processing. A recent study investigated the electrophysiological responses of English–Spanish bilinguals to sentences and idioms that ended either in the expected English word, in an English synonym of the expected word (a lexical switch) or in a Spanish translation equivalent (a code-switch) (Moreno et al. 2002). See Kutas et al. (this volume) for an expanded dis-cussion of ERP research in CS.

2.4   A multi-task approach to studying CS production

The above review of experimental techniques highlights the challenges involved in choosing tasks that ensure ecological validity of experimental data, that take the sociolinguistic and contextual sensitivity of CS into account, and that acknowledge the tension between tasks operating with externally and internally generated switches, here labeled language switching versus CS (see Grosjean 1998). One possibility is to use multiple tasks to probe the same phenomenon and to generate converging evidence. This is not a new idea. For instance, in an early study, Ervin-Tripp (1964) used word association tests, sentence completion tasks, semantic differentials, and so-called problem stories in the assessment of Japanese–English bilingual speech. Recently, Toribio (2001a) has combined the reading aloud of manipulated texts with spoken and written story retellings in a forced output mode to assess code-switching competence. Similarly, Dussias (2002) has examined the processing of a particular structure in both comprehension and production using eye tracking in reading and a sentence completion task.

In a research project targeting the study of code-switched sentence production, researchers can fruitfully combine multiple methods and collect data from the same participants performing a variety of tasks. The procedure allows for several types of baseline and within-subject comparisons. Baseline data are necessary to establish what constitutes natural CS in a particular population and language pair (see Muysken 2000 for a typology of different switching types in different bilingual communities). The experimental tasks and the data they yield can further be validated against this baseline. This approach allows researchers to examine whether the patterns of sentence-level CS observed "in the wild" are replicable experimentally, which is a worthy research goal in itself.

An example of this approach is a project that targets Papiamentu–Dutch bilinguals living in the Netherlands (Gullberg et al. in preparation). Papiamentu is a creole language of mixed Spanish–Portuguese origin spoken in the Dutch Antilles, where it co-exists with Dutch, which has a colonial past as an official language (e.g. Gordon 2005; Kouwenberg and Muysken 1995). The Papiamentu–Dutch bilinguals in the Netherlands code-switch as a normal part of everyday interactions (see Muysken et al. 1996; Vedder et al. 1996).

In a study of CS, the effect of language mode must be controlled for (Grosjean 1998). Bilingual experimenters therefore recruit and instruct participants in code-switched mode, except when the tasks call for monolingual performance, in which case different, monolingual experimenters are called upon. The tasks move gradually from interactive, multiparty settings where CS is more likely to occur, to individual settings and tasks; from spontaneous and naturalistic to controlled and experimental tasks; and from tasks where no constraints are applied to make participants code-switch, to more constrained tasks. A list of sample tasks is presented in Table 2.3.

The conversations and the Director–Matcher task are entirely unconstrained. The Director–Matcher task is a referential communication task

Table 2.3 Tasks and output modes

Task	Language output mode
Conversations	Free (incl. CS)
Director–Matcher (CS)	Free (incl. CS)
Sentence completion task with picture naming	Free but stimulated CS
Shadowing	Constrained CS
Auditory acceptability judgement task	Constrained CS
Director–Matcher (Dutch)	Constrained mono Dutch
Standardized Dutch proficiency test	Constrained mono Dutch

(Yule 1997) in which two participants have to solve a problem together. One of them has the information necessary to solve the task and must convey it so that the other participants can "match" the information and thereby solve the task. Although the task can be designed to encourage speakers to use particular constructions, they are not coerced to use a particular language. The sentence completion task is also free but stimulates switching. The shadowing and acceptability judgement tasks are fully constrained.

The output from the various tasks can be compared qualitatively and quantitatively to examine the validity of the more constrained tasks. For example, lexical noun phrases (NPs) with a modifying color adjective of the type *the white flag* could be targeted. Within-NP switches are of particular interest because they represent potential conflict sites given the word order properties of the two languages: Dutch adjectives are prenominal, *de witte flag*, and Papiamentu color adjectives are typically postnominal, *e bandera blanco*. The Director-Matcher data – e.g. elicited items such as "arrange *the green bottle* first" – may be compared to the conversation data to determine whether the switches from the former task are "natural." In this way, the data from the Director-Matcher task constitute a baseline for complex NPs and possible within-NP switches against which to validate the experimental items in the sentence completion task.

The sentence completion task is designed to examine whether the language of the first sentence element, the subject-NP, or the finite verb will influence the naming of the direct object. In this task speakers are not forced but implicitly encouraged to switch. The experimental items are transitive sentence frames consisting of a subject-NP and a finite transitive verb. These are presented as text and the direct object is a colored picture to be named as quickly and as accurately as possible. The lead-in sentences can be either monolingual Dutch or Papiamentu (9–10), or have the subject NP in one language and the finite verb in another (11–12). The participants read the sentences and name the picture in whatever language they choose. The task is designed to examine whether the language of the first sentence element, the subject-NP, or the finite verb will influence the naming of the direct object.

(9)   *Papiamentu*
      e homber den e bar ta kibra [picture of green bottle]

(10) *Dutch*
      de man in de bar breekt [picture of green bottle]

(11) *Papiamentu–Dutch CS*
      e homber den e bar ***breekt*** [picture of green bottle]

(12) *Papiamentu–Dutch CS*
      de man in de bar ***ta kibra*** [picture of green bottle]
      "The man in the bar breaks [picture of green bottle]."

If constructions similar to those from the Director–Matcher task are attested, the sentence completion task may be said to yield qualitatively ecologically valid output. In addition, these tasks can be complemented with a battery of more controlled tasks, such as shadowing (Marslen-Wilson 1973) and auditory acceptability judgement. Output from these tasks allows for a comparison of bilinguals' explicit metalinguistic judgements with their on-line processing of a particular structure.

2.5   Conclusions

Research techniques employed in the study of CS have clearly progressed in their methods of data collection, mirroring the progress made with other phenomena of psycholinguistic inquiry. The earliest studies focused on individual and incidental observations. Later studies involved increased attention to the importance of relative frequencies in the observed data. Most recently, CS studies involve the careful variation of experimental conditions in controlled, laboratory settings. Despite the recent trend toward more experimental techniques, it should be clear from this chapter that, even though naturalistic data have their limits, experiments can never fully replicate or replace observations of naturalistic CS. There are benefits to be gained from integrated studies that seek to validate experimental methods and data against naturally occurring CS.

3

On the notions of congruence and convergence in code-switching

Mark Sebba

3.1   Introduction

Intra-sentential code-switching (hereafter CS) can be viewed as a remarkable achievement on the part of bilingual speakers. In spite of all the differences in lexis, morphology, and syntax that exist between most pairs of languages, code-switchers successfully communicate in mixed-language utterances which are fluent (at least, no less fluent than monolingual utterances) and which on the whole do not violate the grammar of either language (or at least, violate it no more than monolingual utterances). This chapter will be devoted to examining exactly what this means and how it comes about.

What do code-switchers actually achieve? An analogy from the world of sports is useful here. Consider two team games, for example, football (soccer) and basketball. It is relatively easy to identify certain components of each game that have an equivalent in the other (though we should not be too complacent about assuming this equivalence): for example, in each game there are two teams that compete, there are players, there is a ball, there is a net that acts as a goal. Equally easily we could identify certain things that are different between the two games, for example, the number of players, the parts of the body that are allowed to be used for moving the ball, the areas used or not used for certain purposes, the specific roles or functions of players, and many other things. The achievement of code-switchers is to play both games at once in a way that is satisfactory to the participants, while keeping (sufficiently if not absolutely) to the rules of both.

In our games analogy, it is clear that the fact that certain key components are "the same" across the two games is helpful in allowing them to be combined. Yet somehow the combined game is being played in spite of the differences as well. Looking at CS, we can say that part of explaining how it is possible must involve looking at what is similar in the two languages, while another part of the explanation must involve looking at the differences and how code-switching bilinguals might resolve (or avoid) these differences when they speak. In the CS literature, various terms have been given to this quality of "sameness" of grammatical categories across languages, in particular, *correspondence*, *equivalence*, and *congruence*.

3.2 Cross-linguistic identity in the CS literature: "equivalence," "correspondence," and "congruence"

Much of the work on formal (as opposed to sociolinguistic) aspects of CS starts from an assumption that it involves the interaction of two autonomous language systems, each with its own grammatical system, but with some shared elements. The notion that structural elements of one language may have equivalents in another language seems to be so taken for granted that it has rarely been discussed as problematic (but see below); rather, researchers tend to begin with an assumption that some categories or structures are "the same" across languages. An early mention of this in the literature comes from Weinreich (1964:33, footnote omitted), who remarks in connection with the transference from one language to another of bound morphemes:

It stands very much to reason that the transfer of morphemes is facilitated between highly congruent structures; for a highly bound morpheme is so dependent on its grammatical function (as opposed to its designative value) that it is useless in an alien system unless there is a ready function for it.

In fact, some notion of "congruence" or "equivalence" of categories of the grammar is implicit in many accounts of the syntax of CS even where it is not mentioned. The cross-linguistic equivalence of categories is in keeping with Chomskyan ideas of language acquisition, which require that all children be capable in principle of acquiring the same categories. Surprisingly, however, few writers on the subject of CS have produced any direct evidence that grammatical categories (in particular, phrase structure categories) *are* equivalent across language pairs. Rather, the existence of CS is itself taken as *evidence* for such equivalence. For example, Woolford (1983:535) concludes that "the ability of grammars to cooperate in this fashion to produce structurally and lexically mixed sentences strongly indicates that the category labels of different grammars have a cross-linguistic identity."

While Woolford asserts this "cross-linguistic identity" of category labels explicitly, most other CS researchers seem to assume it. For example, Poplack's formulation (1980) of the Equivalence Constraint[1] appears to imply an assumption that the phrase structure categories of the languages involved are equivalent, at least at the surface level, i.e. X_e (the category X in English) is treated by the phrase structure rules as the same thing as X_f (the category X in French). Bentahila and Davies (1983) make similar assumptions (see below). Joshi (1985a) describes a formal system to account for Marathi–English CS that requires "correspondence" between categories of G_m (grammar of Marathi) and G_e (grammar of English).

Myers-Scotton (1993a, 1995), Myers-Scotton and Jake (1995, this volume), and Jake and Myers-Scotton (1997) make use of a notion of "congruence" within their Matrix Language Frame (MLF) Model. Within this model, the Matrix Language provides the grammatical frame of the bilingual clause, but the Embedded Language may supply content morphemes that are inserted within it. "However, in order for these Embedded Language morphemes to appear, they must be checked for 'sufficient congruence' with their Matrix Language counterparts (Myers-Scotton 2002a:20)." This checking occurs at three levels in the mental lexicon: lexical–conceptual structure, predicate–argument structure, and morphological realization patterns. What exactly this means in practice is uncertain, however; as Myers-Scotton says (2002a:20):

However, the fly in the ointment is the issue of what sufficient congruence means. This notion has not yet been adequately refined. Very definitely, *sufficient* does not mean *complete* congruence – because, of course, content morphemes across languages are rarely completely congruent [...] what constitutes congruence in contact phenomena is still largely unstudied.

3.3 Cross-language equivalence of phrase structure categories

In spite of the lack of clarity mentioned by Myers-Scotton, some notion of cross-linguistic identity of categories in language pairs seems to be present in all attempts to account for the syntax of CS. Usually, this takes the form of an implicit assumption that phrase structure categories (X-bar categories in the sense of Jackendoff 1977) – N, N', N", V, V', V", etc. – are identical across languages when they exist in both. To what extent is this assumption justified? As Deuchar points out (2005:257), "one might argue that the use of universal labels for categories such as NP, VP, IP has helped to perpetuate the view that these are equivalent categories across languages." But clearly, if switching between languages at an intra-sentential level is known empirically to be a fact, there must be some kind of "sameness" between the categories of the two languages.

An example of an argument in the literature that relies on the cross-linguistic identity of categories is a discussion of switching among Moroccan Arabic–French bilinguals by Bentahila and Davies (1983:321). They show that while expressions like (1a) and (1b) are acceptable and common, expressions like (2a) and (2b) do not occur and are judged odd by informants. The reason, they say, is that the French demonstrative *cette* and the Arabic demonstrative *had* subcategorize different complements: *cette* requires N', while *had* requires N" (which includes the article). In (2a) *cette* has a N" complement, and in (2b), *had* has a N' complement; this accounts for the unacceptability of these examples.

(1) (a.) cette **xubza**
            this-FEM bread
            "this bread"
     (b.) **had** le pain
            this the-MASC bread
            "this bread"

(2) (a.) *cette **l xubza**
     (b.) *had* pain

Bentahila and Davies' (1983:329) conclusion that "switching is freely permitted at all boundaries above that of the word, subject only to the condition that it entails no violation of the subcategorisation restrictions on particular lexical items of either language" is clearly dependent on the categories of French having a direct correspondence with those of Moroccan Arabic which have the same labels; $X_a = X_f$ for the purposes of the subcategorization rules.

3.4 Cross-language equivalence of other grammatical categories

In the tradition begun by Poplack's (1980) now classic proposal to account for the syntax of CS by means of constraints on surface phrase stucture and morphology, research has tended to emphasise the cross-linguistic equivalence of phrase structures. However, grammars of languages are not simply sets of X-bar type structures, and while identity of phrase category labels across languages may be a *necessary* condition for CS it is not a *sufficient* condition. In concentrating on identity of phrase category labels, researchers have tended to overlook other types of identity between systems that manifest themselves in CS behavior. There are numerous other categories such as number, gender, tense, aspect, definiteness, and indefiniteness, which in many languages are fully grammaticalized in spite of having some semantic basis. For CS to take place, there must be some kind of identity (or "compatibility") between these categories in the different languages concerned as well. One of the relatively few researchers who recognizes this explicitly is Deuchar (2005:256), who defines "congruence" as "a notion of equivalence between the grammatical categories or word classes of different languages" and separates this into two types: "Paradigmatic congruence is defined as similarity or equivalence between the grammatical categories of two languages, whereas syntagmatic congruence is defined in terms of similarity of word order (2005:256)." Let us look now at some examples where congruence between non-phrasal categories seems to be an essential requirement for CS.

3.4.1   Gender in French and Arabic

In their 1983 article, Bentahila and Davies have many examples of agreement between determiners, nouns, and adjectives in Moroccan Arabic. French demonstratives can combine with Arabic nouns, as in (3) (repetition of (1a) above). Both French and Arabic have grammatical gender and require gender agreement between nouns and certain modifiers (e.g. determiners and adjectives). In this example, the French demonstrative has the form *cette*, which is used with feminine nouns. The Arabic noun *xubza* is indeed feminine, although the French word that is its translation equivalent, *pain*, is masculine.

(3)   ***cette*** xubza
     this-FEM bread
     "this bread"

On the face of it, this may seem unremarkable. The determiner and noun show agreement in gender. However, note that while gender in French and Arabic works in rather similar ways, it is in both languages a grammatical category. While certain animate nouns (*man, mother, daughter, cow* …) have their natural or "expected" gender, all inanimate things are also assigned to masculine or feminine gender, to a large extent arbitrarily. Thus "bread" is masculine in French but feminine in Arabic, while "moon" is masculine in Arabic, but feminine in French, and "sun" is exactly the other way around. Therefore, the fact that linguists have given the same labels, "masculine" and "feminine," to the two genders in Arabic and French obscures the fact that here we actually have two largely arbitrary sets that divide the whole of the nominal vocabulary of the language into two. We could equally well say that in French all words belong either to one of two disjoint sets, Set A and Set B, while in Arabic each word is assigned either to one of two other disjoint sets, C and D. Now what the bilingual speakers of Moroccan Arabic and French have done seems more noteworthy. They have treated the French Set A as equivalent to the Arabic Set C, and the French B as equivalent to the Arabic D. Just as the use of the same labels across languages for phrasal categories has led to a default view that these are equivalent (as Deuchar has pointed out), we could say that calling these sets "masculine" and "feminine" in both French and Arabic has somewhat obscured the work that code-switchers must do to treat them as "the same."

3.4.2 Noun class agreement in Swahili

Swahili, in common with other Bantu languages, has a rather large number of noun classes (about ten), each of which induces a distinctive set of
agreement markers on verbs, adjectives, possessive markers, and various
other morphemes. All native Swahili nouns belong to one of these classes
and the class of each noun in a sentence will be displayed by other words
in the sentence that show agreement with it. Where a non-Swahili noun is
present, as in (4) and (5) below, normally one of three markers occurs
on items in grammatical agreement with it: **wa-** = Class 2 nominal prefix:
agreement prefix for "living things" (singular or plural); **i-** / **y-** = Class 9
nominal prefix: agreement prefix for "inanimate things" (singular); **z-** =
Class 10 nominal prefix: agreement prefix for "inanimate things" (plural).

(4) *Swahili–English*
 mwaka wa tatu i-le long paper **i-li-kuwa ya nini**
 year CL3-of three CL9-that long paper CL9-PAST-INF-COP CL9-of what
 "In the third year what was that long paper for?"
              (Kibogoya 1995)

(5) *Swahili–English*
 Tour Operators **wa-na-wa-chukua** across the border to Tanzania
 tour operators *cl2subj-pres-cl2obj*-carry across the border to Tanzania
 "Tour Operators take them across the border to Tanzania."
              (Kibogoya 1995)

Thus the Swahili/English bilingual who produces sentences like (4) and (5)
has treated at least 4 categories as equivalent across the two languages:
(i) English "inanimate" = Swahili "inanimate"; (ii) English "animate" =
Swahili "animate"; (iii) English "singular" = Swahili "singular"; (iv) English
"plural" = Swahili "plural." Although it could be argued that the Swahili
agreement prefixes are assigned partly on a semantic basis even with
native Swahili nouns (animate nouns take the **wa-** agreement prefix even
if they belong morphologically to another class), the categories mentioned
above are nevertheless also *grammatical* categories in Swahili, and it is still
the case that Swahili–English speakers are recognizing the categories of
English and treating them as if they were Swahili categories. This case is
quite analogous to that of (3), except that the Swahili noun classes are
much more numerous. It is clearer that there is no *a priori* one-to-one
mapping from the English to the Swahili categories, and that some kind
of conceptual work is going on to make the systems compatible.

3.4.3 Auxiliary + participle constructions: examples from Alsatian–French, Spanish–English, and Swahili–English

Many languages have tense/aspect systems that make use of structures
of the form auxiliary + participle. Where this similarity of form exists,

we might expect it to be exploited in CS. In this section we will look at three examples.

The verb systems of French and the Germanic languages are structurally similar in many ways, but also have differences both in form and in semantics. There is no general one-to-one mapping between the two, though certainly the similarities of form lead to some "false friends" and difficulties for French and German speakers learning each other's languages. A particular construction that French and German have in common (and which English has too) is the auxiliary + past participle construction. In example (6) we have a code-switch within such a construction between French and Alsatian (a Germanic dialect spoken in Strasbourg in France).

(6) *Alsatian–French*
     Noch schlimmer, wenn de **client recalé** wurd am permis
     still worse when the candidate failed is in licence
     "Even worse, when the candidate fails in the driving test . . . "
                                                    (Gardner-Chloros 1991:152)

In (6), the French *recalé* ("failed") is treated "as if" it were an Alsatian past participle.[2] The bilingual speaker who produced (6) has clearly chosen the most likely candidate of the available French structures to replace the Alsatian past participle required by *wurd*; or looking at it from a different angle, the speaker has chosen the most appropriate Alsatian auxiliary, *wurd*, to do the work of the French *est* (for which a more "literal" substitute would be Alsatian/German *ist*). Clearly some explanation is required for the ability of bilingual speakers to do this.

Spanish and English also have similar auxiliary + participle constructions, using both past and present participles. In (7), the English present participle form *promising* is treated as equivalent to the Spanish *prometiendo*, which could appear in this context following *está* "he is."

(7) *Spanish–English*
     Siempre está **promising** cosas.
     always be-PRES3SG promising things
     "He's always promising things."
                                                    (Poplack 1980:596)

While in (6) and (7) the structural similarities may make the substitution of one participle for the other an "obvious" strategy for bilingual speakers, example (8) shows a more complex case from Swahili and English, where it is far from clear that there is structural compatibility.

(8) *Swahili–English*
     ilikuwa discussed **kwenye** approximants

CL9-PAST-INF-BE discussed in approximants
"It was discussed under approximants."

(Kibogoya 1995)

In (8) the English past participle *discussed* forms a passive construction with the Swahili verb *ilikuwa*, which generally would be translated as "it was." The verb *kuwa* is used as an auxiliary with certain verb forms in monolingual Swahili, for example, *ilikuwa imelala* "it was sleeping." In this example, *imelala* is identical to a finite form, composed of the class 9 nominal prefix *i-*, the perfect tense affix *-me-*, and the verb stem. However, as Kibogoya (1995) points out, there is nothing corresponding to the English BE + Past participle passive construction in monolingual Swahili.[3] Rather, Swahili passives are formed by using verbal affixes on the main verb stem. Compare the Swahili–English phrase (9) with its monolingual equivalent (10). Thus according to Kibogoya, (8) and (9) are not consistent with Kiswahili forms; rather, they are calqued on the English passive construction.

(9) wa-li-ku-wa **beaten**
     3PL-PAST-INF-COP beaten
     "They were beaten."

(10) wa-li-pig-wa
      3PL-PAST-beat-PASSIVE
      "They were beaten."

In this case again, bilingual speakers are treating a category of the grammar of language L1 as equivalent to a category of language L2. This is more complex than in the Alsatian–French and the English–Spanish examples. There, each language has a very similar construction consisting of an auxiliary verb that subcategorizes for a past or present participle. In the Swahili–English case, these obvious similarities are absent. If we treat the Swahili–English mixed passive as a basically Swahili construction that incorporates an English element, we have to see the English past participle *beaten* as filling the Swahili slot that normally is occupied by a dependent, but nonetheless finite, verb form. The alternative is to view the mixed passive as a basically English construction, but with the English *it was*, in (8), or *they were*, in (10), being substituted by the Swahili verb *kuwa* "to be" with the appropriate affixes. In this case also, the equivalence is not "given"; although *kuwa* is a possible literal translation of *to be*, it is not true in general that English *it was* should be translated as *ilikuwa*.

The above examples show that code-switching bilinguals must recognize, in specific language pairs, the cross-language identity of various grammatical categories. While all of these are potentially semantic categories, what is important is that they are also *grammatical* categories in at least one of the languages concerned.

3.5   Playing two games at once: the achievement of grammaticality in intra-sentential CS

In the previous sections we have seen how both phrase structure categories and other categories of grammar can be treated as equivalent or congruent across languages. In this section we will look at some of the strategies that code-switchers use to integrate two linguistic systems.

3.5.1   Strategies of harmonization

When congruent categories exist across the languages involved, CS can proceed straightforwardly with the grammatical categories of one language being treated as though they were the identical category in the other language. We have seen several examples of this already. Another example comes from Joshi (1985a) in his discussion of CS between Marathi and English. In Marathi the verb *pataw* ("persuade") takes the complementizers *la* (which Joshi glosses as "to") and *ca* (which he glosses as "ing"). The corresponding English verb *persuade*, however, only takes the complementizer *to*. Hence, when the English verb *persuade* takes a Marathi complement, only the complement *la* (corresponding to *to*) is allowed. Hence (11a) is acceptable in the code-switching mode, but (11b), Joshi says, is not:

(11)   (a.) Mi tyala ghar ghyayla **persuade** kela la
             I he-DAT house to buy persuade did "to"
       (b.) *Mi tyala ghar ghyayca **persuade** kela ca
             I he-DAT house to buy persuade did "ing"
             "I persuaded him to buy a house."

(Joshi 1985a:197)

Joshi's judgment here is based on his native intuitions as a Marathi–English code-switcher, and his assertion that *la* = "to" and *ca* = "ing" may be an oversimplification, but it appears that speakers do indeed treat *la* but not *ca* as congruent with *to*. Thus the requirement that English *persuade* should be followed by a verb with a *to* complementizer is met only by the Marathi verb with *la*.

3.5.2   Strategies of neutralization

Where the grammars of the languages concerned are too divergent to allow harmonization strategies to operate in a particular construction, speakers may nevertheless effect code-switches by means of a *neutralization* strategy (also called *nativization*, e.g. by Appel and Muysken 1987). This refers to a case where an existing structure in L1 is used to incorporate an element from L2 that belongs to an easily "switchable" category such as N or V. By doing this, the bilingual speaker avoids the necessity to inflect or otherwise adapt the L2 item. A common strategy found across language pairings is one in which a morpheme meaning something like "do" or "make" in L1 is used with a content word from L2 as a way of enabling the L2 content word to appear without affixations that are required by the monolingual L1 grammar. Example (12), taken from Dutch–Turkish data discussed by Backus (1996:278), is typical:

(12)   bir sürü **taal**-ları **beheersen** yapıyorken
       many language-PL master-INF make/do-while
       "while s/he spoke many languages"

Here the Dutch *beheersen* "to master" is combined with an inflected Turkish verb, a form of the verb *yapmak* "do, make." Very similar strategies are common in CS modes involving languages of the Indian subcontinent, where the verb *karnaa* "do" or its cognates function as the inflected operator, creating a "slot" for a more syntactically neutral element from L2. Typically this is a lexical category (such as a noun or verb) either in a bare form or in a grammatically "neutral" form such as an infinitive. However, a little caution is necessary here in identifying these forms; for example, the Dutch *beheersen* in example (12) is indeed the infinitive form of "to master" but it is also homophonous with the inflected present tense forms (except the third person singular).

3.5.3   Compromise strategies

In spite of the opportunities for using harmonization and neutralization strategies, in some cases where switching takes place we find structures that appear to violate the grammar of *both* languages. Nortier (1990) studied CS between Moroccan Arabic and Dutch and found that it followed different rules from the CS between Moroccan Arabic and French reported by Bentahila and Davies (1983). One of her findings was that about a quarter of all the Dutch nouns inserted within Moroccan Arabic stretches in her corpus were lacking obligatory definite articles (Nortier 1990:197, 208). The resulting stretches containing "bare nouns" were therefore ungrammatical from the point of view of *both* Dutch and Arabic grammar.

   This apparent anomaly affects the Demonstrative + Noun construction as well. In Nortier's corpus, the CS in (13b) is common, but that in (13a) is absent (note the form of the demonstrative is different from that in the data from Bentahila and Davies).

(13)   (a.) *__dik__ het gesprek
             this the conversation
       (b.) dik gesprek
             "this conversation"
             see Dutch *dit gesprek*, "this conversation"

Unlike the French–Moroccan Arabic examples (e.g. (3) above) in the data of Bentahila and Davies, it seems that in Dutch–Moroccan Arabic switching the Dutch *Det+N* combination may not occur following the Arabic demonstrative. Nortier suggests a possible explanation that relates to the difference between Arabic and French articles on the one hand, and Dutch articles on the other (1990:208–9): "… if French articles are assumed to be more proclitic than articles in Dutch it follows that Dutch nouns can more easily be separated from their articles than French nouns, so when a Dutch NP is inserted the article can more often be lacking than when a French NP is inserted."

Whatever the explanation, the Dutch–Moroccan Arabic structure appears to be a compromise. It resembles the monolingual grammar of Dutch in having the form *Demonstrative + (bare) Noun* but it does not conform to the Moroccan Arabic structure, which is *Demonstrative + Determiner + Noun*. It is interesting, but at this stage not fully explained, that the grammars of French and Moroccan Arabic can be harmonized in respect of this construction, but the grammars of Dutch and Moroccan Arabic cannot. This kind of grammatical compromise is, of course, not the only way of dealing with incompatibilities that make harmonization or neutralization impossible or unlikely. Gardner-Chloros and Edwards (2004:108) observe that

> … code-switchers take advantage of various "let-outs" to avoid the straightjacket of grammatical rules. [...] Speakers use pauses, interruptions, "left/right-dislocation" and other devices to neutralize any grammatical awkwardness resulting from switching at a particular point in the sentence [...] allow[ing] the full resources of both varieties to be exploited while sidestepping any grammatical difficulties. They can "legitimize" combinations from languages which are typologically different, for example as regards word-order.

Some of these strategies – in particular, pauses and interruptions – are equally available in monolingual speech. While they provide convenient opportunities for code-switchers to avoid the complexities of harmonizing divergent grammatical systems, they may be frustrating for linguists looking for evidence of how grammatical harmony is achieved.

Returning to the question of how code-switchers succeed in playing two games at the same time, let us look again at one of our early examples, that of the harmonization of gender in French–Moroccan Arabic CS. From different viewpoints we could suggest at least three possible explanations for how this comes about:

(1.)   The gender systems of French and Moroccan Arabic are "naturally" congruent and map on to each other in such a way that bilinguals will always automatically treat the French category "masculine" as equivalent to the Arabic category "masculine" and the French category "feminine" as equivalent to the Arabic category "feminine." If this is the case, we should expect few or no exceptions (as long as the bilingual code-switchers have native-like competence in both languages), and little or no variation between different CS communities where the same language pairs are involved.

(2.) The gender systems of French and Moroccan Arabic are similar in function, but the equation of the French and Arabic categories of masculine and feminine is the result of *educated* speakers, who have some explicit knowledge of the grammar of both languages, treating them as equivalent. The strategy of using the French feminine form of a demonstrative with a noun that is feminine in Arabic is then more of a conscious attempt to make the systems behave harmoniously in keeping with learned rules of grammar. We would expect some level of variation between speakers as a result of different levels of (prescriptive) grammatical knowledge, and we would expect those who have no explicit grammatical knowledge in one or both of the languages to use different strategies from this one or to exhibit high degrees of variability.

(3.) The harmonized gender system is conventional, in the same way and to the same extent as the norms of monolingual language systems are conventional. In this view, CS could be seen as a "mixed system" which is the product of norms and conventions, just like any "monolingual" system, and as in the case of any language they must be acquired through a social process, whether in early childhood, youth, or adulthood. In this case, inter-speaker and intra-speaker variability should be fairly limited within a single code-switching community, but there could be substantial differences between communities with different histories of bilingualism even where the same language pairs are involved.

The first of these views is implicit in much of the literature and is in keeping with widely accepted notions of universal grammar. The second allows for the possibility that congruence between categories is partly constructed by individual speakers, while the third sees it as a product of both linguistic and social processes that may lead to different outcomes in spite of the same languages being involved. This is a view less widely held, but taken, for example, by Sebba (1998) (see also Hamers and Blanc 2000:269).

3.6   From congruence to convergence

As pointed out above, many researchers of CS start from the assumption that two independent grammars are involved. These grammars interact with each other through a CS mechanism of some kind, but in other respects retain their integrity and separateness.

These assumptions can be and have been challenged. Alvarez-Caccamo (1998:36), for example, believes that neither the assumption that "speakers who code-switch possess two (or more) identifiable linguistic systems or languages" nor the assumption that "'code-switched' speech results from the predictable interaction between lexical elements and grammatical rules from these languages [...] is proven yet." Gardner-Chloros and Edwards (2004:106–108) agree, and give four reasons why CS data are "likely to pose problems for grammatical descriptions." In brief, these are: variability; uncertainty over the applicability of abstract categories such as noun, verb, noun phrase, clause, and, particularly, sentence; the use by code-switchers of strategies to neutralize what would otherwise be "grammatical awkwardness"; the fact that CS "frequently involves creative, innovative elements, often based on exploiting similarities between the two varieties."

The assumption that CS is the product of two monolingual grammars can be seen as a consequence of studying CS from the viewpoint of a monolingual norm, and a reluctance to deal with linguistic variation. For the sake of objectivity, it would be desirable to study CS systems *without* reference to the monolingual norm, and also to bear in mind that a "mixed system," like any other language system, is subject to development over time. In particular, prolonged interaction between languages, given the right social conditions, may lead to a greater or lesser degree of language convergence. Furthermore, if circumstances are conducive to it, the grammatical norms of the "switched" code may converge on a *new*, mixed, or "hybrid" set of norms (see Auer 1999).

Examples of emerging hybrid systems were observed in the Swahili–English data (8) and (9), the latter repeated here as (14):

(14)   wa-li-ku-wa **beaten**
       3PL-PAST-INF-COP beaten
       "They were beaten."

According to Kibogoya (1995), utterances like this are modeled on English and do not correspond exactly to Swahili. Here again, there appears a construction that is possible only in the mixed code, as the Swahili verb, with its array of Swahili tense and nominal affixes (many of them without counterparts in monolingual English), functions as an auxiliary to the English past participle (which has no counterpart in monolingual Swahili).

The development of a mixed system may not involve only new, hybrid syntactic structures, but also new semantic structures. Let us look again at Poplack's example (7), repeated here as (15):

(15)   Siempre está **promising** cosas.
       always be-PRES3SG promising things
       "He's always promising things."

Here the Spanish and English present participles are treated by speakers as being "the same category," i.e. English V+*ing* is congruent with Spanish V+*ndo*. But in spite of their formal similarity and a good deal of overlap in meaning, the Spanish be + present participle construction does *not* map semantically on to the English one, i.e. there are pragmatic contexts where one is appropriate but not the other. However, longstanding varieties of contact Spanish in the United States have been shown to remap *estar* + present participle as the simple present progressive (e.g. Klein 1980; Silva-Corvalán 1994). Romaine comments (1995:178–179):

If bilingual speakers of typologically different languages can realign their usage in areas of the grammar where choice exists and where one or more of the possible variants overlaps with choices in the contact language, they can maximise the structural equivalence between the two languages to create more potential loci for switching. Intensive bilingualism with frequent code-switching [. . .] can in this way lay the groundwork for massive convergence.

As in the Swahili–English example above, the Spanish–English example (15) shows a structural integration of the Spanish and English systems. In the Spanish–English case, unlike the Swahili–English one, there is a clear *structural* similarity to begin with; but there are *semantic/pragmatic* differences in how the tenses are used according to the monolingual norms of English and Spanish. Whether the CS utterance in (15) conforms pragmatically to the norms of monolingual English or monolingual Spanish, or neither, we have a form that is different (by virtue of being structurally mixed) from both.

   If CS is subject to norms and conventions like other language behavior, we should expect to find variability. For example, we should expect to find that where there are potential alternative strategies that will allow switching to take place, both (or all) alternatives will be realized. Thus in addition to the examples like (3), which show harmonization of the Arabic and French gender systems, Bentahila and Davies's data also contain others like (16) and (17):

(16)   **les moustaches** l xaburi
         the-PL moustaches-PL the yellow-SG
         "the yellow moustache"

(17)   dak **le trajet** kulha
         that the-MASC journey whole-FEM
         "that whole journey"

As Bentahila and Davies (1983:327) point out, the lack of agreement (in number in (16), and gender in (17)) "is not due to ignorance, for the correct use of the French determiners in each case shows that the speakers are aware of the gender of the French nouns." However, they point out that in each case, the Arabic adjective has the inflection that would be required to agree with the equivalent *Arabic* noun, though not the French one. The Arabic for *moustache* is singular (though plural in French) and the Arabic for *journey* is feminine (though masculine in French). Thus we find a hybrid kind of agreement in both these examples, the determiner agreeing with the gender of the noun that is actually present, while the postposed adjective agrees with the gender of the translation equivalent.

Following Poplack (1980), it is accepted that the ability to code-switch, especially within sentences, correlates with a high degree of fluency in both languages. It is maximally fluent bilinguals, then, who should show the greatest propensity for CS and the most skill and success in using those strategies that allow it to happen. This will be true especially when the languages involved have roughly equal social as well as linguistic status, so that speakers have no motive to minimize the use of one of the languages, and where CS behavior itself is not seen as illegitimate due to purism or other prescriptive notions. This type of situation might be taken to typify the "healthiest" environment for CS, where switches are not limited by lack of competence on the part of speakers and take place in response to a positive motivation rather than as a strategy for avoidance.

The particular Spanish–English, Swahili–English, and Moroccan–French contexts that have provided a number of examples already are probably good examples of such "healthy" CS environments. Others might be "Taglish," mixed Tagalog and English discourse in the Philippines, which Bautista (2004:226) describes as "the language of informality among middle-class, college-educated, urbanized Filipinos," and the mixing of English and Malay in Brunei Darussalam, as described by McLellan (2005). In the latter case, typological similarities between English and Malay seem to permit a large number of categories to be treated as congruent, as shown by examples from McLellan's corpus of (written) postings to a message board. For example, one finds English prepositions governing Malay nominal phrases (18), English complementizers or conjunctions introducing Malay verbs (19), and verbal groups containing mixed Malay–English passive constructions as in (20) and (21):

(18)   the Task Force **yang**-REL discover the big black secret behind **projek rumah** expo **atu**-DEM
       "the Task Force which discovered the big black secret behind that expo housing project"

(McLellan 2005:120)

(19)   **tapi** its time to **lapaskan** daddy/**bapa**/ mummy/**ibu**
       but AV-leave father mother (AV = Active Verb)
       "but it's time to leave daddy and mummy"

(McLellan 2005:122)

(20) So far are we really-really **tertindas** by the concept
      so far are we really-really REDUP AV-oppressed
      "So far are we really oppressed by the concept?"

                                                    (McLellan 2005:117)

(21) How sure are you all **yang**-REL the ex minister **atu**-DEM, **kana**-PAST
      remove from office
      "How sure are you all that that ex-Minister was removed from
      office?"

                                                    (McLellan 2005:115)

In the above examples we can see how CS and convergence may go hand
in hand. A number of researchers have noted a connection between the
two, for example, Clyne (1987:750), who writes: "Our studies of German
and Dutch in Australia suggest that (a) the syntactic system of L1 in many
individuals converges toward L2, and (b) syntactic convergence in specific
sentences often accompanies code switching." Clyne uses a notion of local
syntactic convergence (perhaps similar to *harmonization* as discussed
above) that favors switching within an utterance: "syntactic convergence
will take place around the switch, apparently IN ORDER to ease code
switching (Clyne 1987:753)." However, if identifying congruences is a
strategy for enabling CS, as has been argued above, then these local "con-
vergences" are the product of a more global process of convergence that is
driven by the CS itself. This seems to coincide with the view of Thomason
and Kaufman (1988:96), who say it is likely that convergence in a multi-
lateral Sprachbund situation involves "bi- and multilingual speakers favor-
ing structures [...] that are common to some or all of the languages." If we
accept that CS is one of the mechanisms by which language convergence
comes about, then we must also accept that the monolingual grammatical
norms for the languages involved are subject to alteration as a result of
switching (or of language contact phenomena more generally). According
to this view, part of the work that bilingual code-switchers do is to "create
congruence" between the two existing languages, if necessary by making
adjustments to the monolingual norms.

3.7 Conclusions

What might we reasonably expect of a theory about the grammar of CS,
given the central place that it has assumed in linguists' attempts to understand both bilingual and monolingual language behavior? Here are some
suggestions of desiderata for such a theory (Sebba 1998:2):

(1.) It should set the syntactic and phonological limits within which
      CS *may* occur, while allowing a role for pragmatic and social
      factors that may determine what switching actually *does* occur.

In other words, it should take into account both competence and performance.

(2.) It should be inclusive enough to account for different observed phenomena across different language pairs and situations. Identifying a new CS outcome in a previously studied language pair should not automatically falsify the hypothesis; non-structural factors should be allowed to account for differing outcomes.

(3.) It should be able to account for different observed phenomena from different code-switching individuals, even those who may reasonably be considered to belong to the same "speech community."

(4.) It should allow for a separation of the phonological, syntactic, and pragmatic levels so that a switch at one level need not necessarily be taken to be accompanied by a corresponding switch at another level.

(5.) It should be sensitive to sociolinguistic features of individual speakers as well as of the situation, such as the individual's bilingual competence, the norms of language use within the community (for example, the extent to which CS is approved of or frowned upon), the length and closeness of language contact, and the power relations between the languages.

(6.) It should take into account the acquisition of CS behavior, including such factors as the age at which CS practices emerge in speakers and how code-switchers become socialized into these practices.

To this we might add:

(7.) It will be part of an account of other phenomena of bilingualism and language contact such as relexification, language convergence, interlanguage, and language death; perhaps also of pidginization, creolization, and language mixing/intertwining.

Clearly, the grammar of CS involves something more than just the individual grammars of two languages put together. In explaining the syntax of CS, the notion of equivalent or congruent categories across languages seems to be essential and is implicit or explicit in much of the literature. In this chapter we have looked at some of the issues involved in identifying categories as "the same" across languages and have described some strategies – harmonization, neutralization, and compromise – which speakers may use when they engage in CS. There are many researchable issues here, for example, examining the extent of compatibility ("congruence" or "equivalence") between the languages of different CS pairs, as measured by the extent to which the different strategies are used. Another important question is the extent to which the grammar of CS is dependent on what we might broadly call "sociolinguistic factors" such as the history of bilingualism in the individual speaker and the bilingual community. Is it reasonable to expect different structural outcomes depending on, for example, the extent to which speakers have explicit, school-based knowledge of the grammars of the languages concerned? Will the grammar of CS be different in two communities where the language pairs involved are the same, but the contact is old and pervasive in one case, but recent and superficial in another? In the last section of this chapter it was suggested that not only is this likely, but also that continued close contact between languages in a CS community may lead to the emergence of new norms and the gradual convergence of the languages into a new hybrid system. Thus *congruence* of categories may lead over time to *convergence* of languages.

Notes

1. "Switches will tend to occur at points in discourse where juxtaposition of L1 and L2 elements does not violate a syntactic rule of either language, i.e. at points around which the surface structures of the two languages map onto each other (Poplack 1980:586)."
2. Myers-Scotton (1993a:89) observes rightly of this example that *recalé* "precedes the Alsatian auxiliary *wurd* in accordance with Alsatian syntactic specifications." The equivalent French order would be *est recalé*. However, she does not comment on the fact that speakers are at the same time treating the French *category* of past participle as equivalent to an Alsatian one.
3. Myers-Scotton and Jake (1995:1007) point out that the English past participle "does not fit into the morpho-syntactic frame normally projected in the Swahili passive construction. It does, however, fit into a frame of *copula 'be' + predicate adjective* in Swahili."

4

Code-switching and transfer: an exploration of similarities and differences

Jeanine Treffers-Daller

4.1 Introduction

Over the past thirty years, and in particular since the publication of the groundbreaking work of Pfaff (1979) and Poplack (1980), a wealth of information about code-switching (hereafter CS) between a wide range of language pairs has become available. While the popularity of the topic is perhaps unrivalled in the field of language contact, there are important controversies over the nature of the phenomenon and how to delimit it from other contact phenomena, in particular borrowing. Sometimes the problem is that researchers use different terminology for data that are in essence the same, but in other cases researchers appear to be investigating different phenomena altogether, which means that drawing conclusions from a range of studies is difficult (see Jarvis 2000 for similar comments regarding research about transfer). As Meuter (2005:350) puts it, the focus of most psycholinguistic studies is on "the controlled and willed selection of single responses in a bilingual setting and not on language switching as it occurs spontaneously and (un)intentionally in code switching." Psycholinguists often use the term *language switching* for the controlled and willed switching to another language, while this term is hardly ever used by linguists working on naturalistic CS (see Gullberg et al., this volume).

The confusion around terminology and definitions is compounded when one tries to incorporate findings from neighboring disciplines, such as second language acquisition (SLA) or psycholinguistics, into research on CS, because each discipline favors its own terminology. Linguists use a wide variety of terms to indicate different bilingual behaviors, including CS (see §4.2). There is also an abundance of terms used to refer to the influence of one language on another. Since the demise of contrastive analysis (Lado 1957), researchers in SLA avoid the term *interference* and use *transfer* or *cross-linguistic influence* instead, while psycho-linguists continue to use the term *interference*, and researchers in contact-induced language change talk about *convergence, intersystemic influence,* or *substrate/superstrate/adstrate influence.*

The focus of this chapter is to present a review of the definitions of CS and transfer employed in the extant literature on bilingualism and language contact. Although many researchers think of CS and interference or transfer as different phenomena, instances of CS and transfer can be seen as similar in that they involve the occurrence of elements of language A in stretches of speech of language B. The term "elements" is used for want of something better, as there is no other term to cover the wide variety of phonological, morphological, syntactic, semantic, and conceptual features, lexical items, phrases, clauses, multiword chunks, and graphemic symbols that can be transferred from one language to another.

One of the important developments in the past few years is that scholars are increasingly seeking to show how CS research can be made relevant for different fields, such as psycholinguistic models of speech processing or theories of language change. Thus, CS is studied not only as a subject in its own right, however justified the aim of formulating (universal) constraints on this phenomenon or proving its significance in a particular sociolinguistic context may be. Instead, it is becoming increasingly evident that CS research needs to inform and be informed by models of speech processing, theories of language variation and change, and SLA, and that studying CS in isolation from other disciplines may not be fruitful (see Boeschoten 1998). Using a unified conceptual framework will also considerably enhance the potential impact of insights from CS studies on other fields.

For the purposes of this chapter, the evidence accumulated by researchers in SLA on L1 transfer (Kellerman and Sharwood Smith 1986; Gass 1996; Jarvis 2000; Pienemann 1999) is particularly relevant. As will be shown, a fuller understanding of the similarities and differences between CS and transfer can no doubt be obtained if we cross the boundaries of various disciplines and integrate the findings from SLA into our models.

4.2   Pertinent distinctions across the disciplines

Poplack (1990) and de Bot (1992) point to the difficulty of distinguishing different contact phenomena from each other. According to de Bot (1992:19), "Many instances of cross-linguistic influences [*sic*] are related to code-switching and cannot be simply separated from this on theoretical or empirical grounds." For Poplack (1990:39), "each of the mechanisms for combining material from two grammars within a single utterance results from different processes and is governed by different constraints," and Grosjean (1995:263) expresses a similar point of view, but Paradis (1998, in de Bot 2002:291) argues that in terms of processing, cross-linguistic influence cannot be distinguished clearly from CS phenomena.

Poulisse and Bongaerts (1994) draw parallels between CS and speech errors, and argue that accidental switches to the L1 are very similar to substitutions and slips in monolingual speech, but Winford (2003:109) sees clear linguistic and sociolinguistic differences between CS and interference. Whether or not CS and transfer correspond to the same or different psycholinguistic processes, and whether or not contact phenomena are intrinsically different from substitutions and slips in monolingual speech is a key issue for research in bilingualism, but it is far from being settled, as the different positions of researchers indicate.

Considering CS and transfer as similar phenomena is helpful if one wants to create a theory that is as parsimonious as possible, and therefore it is worth attempting to aim for such a unified approach, unless there is compelling evidence that this is not possible. A key issue that needs further investigation in this context is how speakers can control CS and transfer. While it is clear that speakers can decide when to switch and when not to, it is less obvious that they can control transfer in the same ways. As Grosjean (2001:7) puts it, speakers may produce interference "even in the most monolingual of situations." This inability of speakers to control (certain forms of) transfer may be an indication that there are at least some differences in the psycholinguistic processes behind CS and transfer. The issue of control also seems important to distinguish *smooth* from *flagged* CS (Poplack 1987). Smooth CS is effortless and fluent, whereas flagged switching draws attention to itself, marked by repetitions, hesitations, metalinguistic comments, and the like.

De Bot (2002) uses the term *motivated switching* for those instances of CS where speakers switch deliberately to the other language, whereas unintentional CS is labeled *performance switching*. While this terminology is not frequently used, the difference between the flagged CS patterns of French–English bilinguals in Ottawa-Hull and the smooth CS practiced by Puerto Rican Spanish–English bilinguals in New York City described by Poplack (1987) can illustrate these two types of CS.

Researchers working on CS from a discourse analytical perspective (Myers-Scotton and Ury 1977; Myers-Scotton 1993b; Auer 1984, 1998; Li Wei 1998; Heller 1988a; Moyer 1998) have shown that CS can indeed be intentional and that individual reasons for choosing particular items can be spelled out in detail. However, most researchers would probably agree that it would be hard to come up with reasons for every individual switch in examples such as (1), from Valdés (1976:70–71), in which there is a continuous back and forth switching between Spanish and English.

(1)   ***Oyes*** [sic], when I was a freshman I had a term paper to do … ***Y este***
      I waited till the last minute two days before to take notes, to do the
      typing, to do everything … And all of a sudden, I started acting real

curiosa, you know. I started going like this. **Y luego decía**, look at the smoke coming out of my fingers, like that. And then **me dijo**, stop acting silly. **Y luego decía yo, mira** can't you see. **Y luego este**, I started seeing like little stars all over the place. **Y volteaba yo asina y le decía** look at the … the … **no sé era como brillosito así like stars. Y luego** he started acting silly and he was getting mad at me.

"Hey, when I was a freshman I had a term paper to do … And uh I waited until the last minute two days before to take notes, to do the typing, to do everything … And all of a sudden, I started acting real strange, you know. I started going like this. And then I said, look at the smoke coming out of my fingers, like that. And he said, stop acting silly. And then I said, look can't you see. And then uh, I started seeing like little stars all over the place. And I turned like this and I said, look at the … the … I don't know, it was sort of shiny like this, like stars. And then he thought I was acting silly and he was getting mad at me."

Transfer of linguistic features can also happen spontaneously and unintentionally, but this is clearly not the case whenever transfer is used as a strategy (see below) or when the elements that have been transferred have permanently entered the borrowing language.

The distinction made by Paradis (1993) and Grosjean (2001) between *dynamic interference* and *static interference* is very useful in this context. Paradis sees dynamic interferences as performance errors in speech production, when an element of one language appears inadvertently in a sequence of another language. For Grosjean (2001:7) dynamic interferences are "ephemeral deviations due to the influence of the […] deactivated language." Static interferences are those that have become part of the implicit grammar of an individual. An example of the latter is the use of *une fois* (literally, "once") in Brussels French, which can be traced back to the influence of Dutch in some uses, and has become established in Brussels Dutch (Treffers-Daller 2005b).

One might equally want to explore to what extent CS can be seen as dynamic or static. While most researchers emphasize the creativity involved in CS behavior, and thus appear to see CS as a dynamic process in which grammars interact in speech production, not all forms of CS are necessarily entirely creative or dynamic. An example could be the use of the slogan *Let's make things better*, as used in Dutch advertisements by Philips. Other examples are switches of chunks (Backus 2003) or multi-word units (Treffers-Daller 2005a) which illustrate the occurrence of fixed patterns in CS. Finally, there are situations where CS has become more or less institutionalized, for example when a mixed code has become the norm of an elite, as Swigart (1992a, 1992b, 1992c) shows to be the case for Wolof–French CS in Dakar. A new perspective on the controversy around the distinction between borrowing and CS may also be possible if the former was redefined as static CS. Thus CS, transfer, and borrowing may have more in common than has been previously thought (see §4.3), especially if these phenomena are considered from a psycholinguistic perspective.

The distinction between static and dynamic interference appears not to have been picked up by researchers working on transfer in either SLA or language contact studies (see Treffers-Daller 2005a, 2005b), possibly because the term interference is suspect for many researchers outside the field of psycholinguistics. As evidence from speech processing becomes more and more important in a range of disciplines, it may well be timely to exploit the distinction more fully in theories of CS and transfer. One of the questions that would need to be answered in research in the future is, of course, to what extent dynamic and static forms of CS are processed differently.

4.3   Psycholinguistic approaches to language selection, switching, and interference

Normally functioning bilingual speakers are able to separate their languages in speech production; they can produce monolingual utterances whenever the situation or the interlocutor require it. This rather obvious fact is a problem for models of speech processing, which need to account for bilinguals' ability to control their output so that they do not code-switch continuously or experience continued interference (Costa et al. 2006). Like bilinguals, monolinguals also need to exercise control in choosing the right words from a number of competing alternatives. In contrast to monolinguals, bilinguals have translation equivalents for at least a proportion of their vocabularies. As a consequence, accounting for the "hard problem" (Finkbeiner et al. 2006:153) of how to avoid inappropriate choices is particularly difficult in models of bilingual speech production. Recent psycholinguistic research is focused on identifying the locus and manner in which bilinguals control their language choices. Kroll et al. (2006:124) opt for a language-nonselective model of speech production because there is "a great deal of evidence that suggests that candidates in the unintended language are active, that they compete with one another for selection." La Heij (2005), on the contrary, assumes a language-selective model, in which only those lexical items are activated that correspond to the information contained in the pre-verbal message. La Heij assumes that in bilingual speakers the intention to speak is part of the preverbal message, so that translation equivalents from the non-response language become less activated than words from the intended language. While the debate is far from being settled, it is clear that all models of bilingual speech production need to account for different kinds of interference from the non-response language (speech errors, blends, etc.), and all models also need to be able to account for different kinds of CS, as will be illustrated below.

Before reviewing the implications of these models and findings for CS research, it is important to note a number of relevant facts of bilingual processing. First of all, there is a consensus in psycholinguistics that bilinguals can perhaps "turn down" one of their languages, but that they cannot completely "turn off" that language (Grosjean 2001). Second, bilingual word recognition is basically language non-selective (Dijkstra 2005), that is, words from *both* languages are activated in the process of understanding the incoming speech signal. Third, languages are probably not stored separately, but, according to the "subset hypothesis" (Paradis 1981, 2004; de Bot 1992), they form subsets within a larger unit in the brain. Fourth, evidence from neuro-imaging suggests that no major differences in brain activity are found in processing of stories in L1 and L2 among highly proficient bilinguals, but that different patterns of cortical activity are found for less proficient bilinguals performing the same task (Abutalebi et al. 2001). Thus, one cannot easily locate the two languages of a bilingual in separate areas of the brain (see Kutas et al., this volume), at least not in highly proficient bilinguals, although each language is "susceptible to selective pathological inhibition" (Paradis 2004:111), a fact that is compatible with the subset hypothesis.

Most authors adopt Levelt's (1989) speech production model (see Wei, this volume), but assume it needs adaptation to account for bilingual speech production. The best-known adapted models are Grosjean's (1988) Bilingual Model of Lexical Access, Green's (1998) Inhibitory Control model, and Dijkstra and Van Heuven's (1998, 2002) Bilingual Interactive Activation model (BIA). De Bot (1992, 2002), Green (1998), and La Heij (2005) propose, with most other authors in the field, that the decision to speak one language or the other must be taken at the level of the preverbal message, i.e. this is the task of the conceptualizer in Levelt's model. Poulisse and Bongaerts (1994) and Green (1998) propose that lemmas, which contain the lexical entry's meaning and syntax, are tagged with a language label.[1] In Green's Inhibitory Control model, it is the activation of this tag together with the conceptual information that leads to the selection of a given lemma, with any highly active competing lemma inhibited. According to Paradis (2004), however, there is no need for a language tag, and language processing in monolinguals and bilinguals is very similar. He assumes that it is lexical meaning that drives the selection of the appropriate lexical item. As the meaning of a word is language-specific, and the meanings of translation equivalents overlap only partly, the formulator should be able to select the right lemma on the basis of its semantic information, by selecting the lemma that maps best onto the information in the preverbal message.

According to Paradis (2004:212), the implicit grammar of code-mixing (see §4.4 for this notion) does not require anything beyond the requirements of the individual languages; "the only constraint seems to be that each speech segment of a mixed utterance should not violate the grammar of the language of that segment," a proposal that MacSwan formulated earlier in syntactic-theoretical terms (see MacSwan 1999a, 1999b, this volume). Paradis recognises that not every single switch can be the result of a decision at the initial planning stage (i.e. at the stage of the pre-verbal message). It would be counter-intuitive, given the frequency of switching within a stretch of speech such as (1), that speakers plan in detail at which points to switch at this early stage, when the focus is on conceptual organization rather than form. He assumes that deliberate CS occurs by virtue of the same principles that make "inadvertent" CS possible.

Most researchers agree that the decision to choose one language as the basic language of the conversation enhances the likelihood that lemmas from that language are being activated. Paradis's (1987, 2004) Activation Threshold Hypothesis accounts for this in such a way that the activation levels of the selected language are raised so as to avoid interference. When speakers are in a bilingual mode (Grosjean 1995), the activation thresholds for both languages are lowered, to allow for CS. As we will see below, the Activation Threshold Hypothesis is however not sufficient to account for the different types of naturalistic CS that Muysken (2000) distinguishes, and it makes a number of predictions that are not borne out by the facts.

Paradis's hypothesis that lexical selection in monolinguals is similar to lexical selection in bilinguals is attractive in that it is a parsimonious theory, in fact a null hypothesis, and researchers from different fields can look for evidence in support for or against it. It is not difficult to see that the tools provided in Paradis's model are necessary but not sufficient to account for naturalistic CS. According to Paradis's (2004:224) Activation Threshold Hypothesis, "in the case of extremely frequently used items, such as closed-class grammatical morphemes, the threshold may be so low as to show no fluctuation because of the strong frequency effect." This is problematic for theories of CS, because it predicts that, in the absence of additional constraints on CS, interference in the use of closed class items should be frequent. It also predicts that switching of adpositions (pre- and postpositions), which are frequent in most languages that possess this category, should be common. These two predictions are not borne out by the data. The reason for the lack of CS in these categories is probably the lack of *categorial equivalence* (Muysken 1995, 2000) or *congruence* (Sridhar and Sridhar 1980; Sebba 1998, this volume; Myers-Scotton 2002a; Deuchar 2005) between adpositions from different languages or between functional categories across languages. As is well known, the spatial systems covered by adpositions differ from language to language, and determiner systems differ widely from language to language as well, which may inhibit CS (see the discussion about Arabic versus Dutch determiners in Nortier 1990). Paradis does not clarify the role of congruence in his framework, but it is clear that it needs to have a role, for example as a metalinguistic tool which can be used by speakers to identify where languages have parallel categories or structures. This issue is important for theories of transfer in SLA as well, because the extent to which speakers perceive their L1 and their L2 to be similar or different has an impact on their use of transfer as a strategy for language learning (Odlin 2003). The discussions around perceptions of interlingual identification in SLA are unfortunately currently completely separate from the discussions around congruence in CS, but researchers would benefit from knowledge exchange in this area too.

Paradis's model cannot explain either why there are systematic differences in CS patterns (*alternation, insertion* and *congruent lexicalization*), as distinguished by Muysken (2000), or how this typology interacts with issues of control, language typological factors, and societal factors. While Paradis's model is able to account for inter-individual differences in lexical choice and/or switch habits in terms of differences in activation of rules or words from both languages, it cannot explain the systematic differences in types of CS which go beyond the idiosyncratic choices of an individual and which linguists explain on the basis of principles of linguistic theory in interaction with societal factors.

Some models of processing of bilingual speech are based on the idea that languages are either "on" or "off." However, this is not plausible given the psycholinguistic evidence sketched above (see Muysken 2000). Rather, we probably need to assume with Sridhar and Sridhar (1980:413) that both systems are "on" at the same time, although we now know that they can be "on" to different degrees. Furthermore, while some researchers define CS as a "complete" switch from one language to the other (Poplack and Meechan 1995; Grosjean 2001), it is not clear what switching "completely" to the other language means, given the psycholinguistic evidence about continued activation of both languages in production and perception.

4.4   Definitions and types of code-switching

Weinreich (1953:1), a pioneer of contact linguistics, uses the notion *interference* as the overarching concept for a range of language contact phenomena, "those instances of deviation from the norms of either language, which occur in the speech of bilinguals as a result of their familiarity with more than one language, i.e. as a result of language contact." In Weinreich's definition, interference can be observed at different levels of analysis, including the lexical level. Under this view, borrowing and CS can be seen as instantiations of interference, although he does not explicitly formulate it in this way. As is well known, Weinreich (1953:73) adopts a negative attitude towards CS:

[T]he ideal bilingual switches from one language to the other according to appropriate changes in the speech situation (interlocutors, topics, etc.), but not in an unchanged situation, and certainly not within a sentence.

Some researchers continue to use one umbrella term for CS, borrowing and transfer. Clyne (2003:72), for example, uses the notion *transference* to cover the phenomena that Weinreich describes as interference, as the term CS has become so polysemous and unclear. For Clyne, transference can take place at a range of levels of analysis, and certain types of CS (in particular insertional code-mixing – see below) are seen as instantiations of transference, whereas he considers other types of CS (alternation and congruent lexicalization) as examples of *transversion* (see below). Furthermore, he distinguishes between the process (transference) and the product (transfer) of language contact.

Other authors see transfer and CS as different phenomena that cannot be subsumed under a single term. Poplack and Meechan (1995:200) emphasize the fact that in CS the languages are clearly separate from each other, and they define CS as "the juxtaposition of sentences or sentence fragments from two languages, each of which is internally consistent with the morphological and syntactic (and optionally, phonological) rules of its lexifier language." This definition is reminiscent of McClure's (1977) use of the terminology. McClure (1977:97) uses the term code-switching to cover code-changing and code-mixing. In McClure's definition, *code-changing* is the alternation of languages at the level of the major constituents (e.g. NP, VP, S). Importantly, she sees code-changing as involving a complete shift to another language system, in that all function words, morphology and syntax are abruptly changed, whereas code-mixing takes place within constituents. Grosjean (1995:263) defines CS along similar lines as shifting completely to the other language for a word, a phrase, a sentence, etc. Finally, Clyne (2003:76) uses the term transversion "to express 'crossing over' *to* the other language rather than alternating *between* the languages (original emphasis)." The emphasis on separation probably results from the need felt by many researchers in the 1990s to distinguish between borrowing and CS. Borrowing is seen by many researchers as the integration of features from one language into another. In Thomason and Kaufman's (1988) definition of borrowing (see below) the source language and the recipient language play very different roles, but in some CS models the contact languages are also assumed to be unequal partners, so that CS and borrowing are not necessarily different on this point.

For Myers-Scotton (1993a) CS does not necessarily involve a complete switch to the other language. In her Matrix Language Frame (MLF) model, one of the two languages generally takes a more predominant role in CS in that it determines the grammatical frame of the utterance. This language is considered to be the matrix language (or "base" language) of the interaction, and the other is the embedded or "guest" language. In what

Myers-Scotton (2006a:241) calls *classic* CS, "elements from two or more language varieties are found in the same clause, but only one of these varieties is the source of the morpho-syntactic frame for the clause." Arguably then, in classic CS, there is no complete switch to the other language, because the syntactic frame of the entire utterance comes from one language. The interaction between the grammars of both languages is more pronounced in another type of CS, which is called *composite* CS, in which the guest language contributes some of the abstract structure underlying surface forms in the clause (Myers-Scotton 2006a:242).

Muysken (2000:1) uses the term *code-mixing* instead of intra-sentential CS to refer to "all cases where lexical items and grammatical features from two languages appear in one sentence." Muysken's typology of code-mixing (insertion, alternation, and congruent lexicalization) is very helpful in that it shows that there is CS in which the languages are clearly kept separate (alternation), as in (2), where the main clause is in French and the subordinate clause is in Dutch, but also that the two are separated by an interjection.

(2) ***Je téléphone à Chantal*** he, meestal voor commieskes te doen en eten
     I call to Chantal INT, mostly for shopping to do and food
     "I call Chantal to go shopping and get food."
                                                   (Treffers-Daller 1994:213)

There are forms of CS in which the contact languages are not kept separate at all (congruent lexicalization). When the two languages in contact are closely related through either the lexicon or the grammar or both, or perceived by speakers to be related, it is often not possible to attribute the syntactic structure of the language to one or the other of the two languages. Thus, while Haugen (1972b:80) felt that "except in abnormal cases speakers have not been observed to draw freely from two languages at once," in congruent lexicalization there is a syntactic frame which is shared by both languages, and this is also filled with lexical items that can come from both languages. This kind of CS is often found in those contact situations where convergence of the contact languages is taking place, and it is somewhat similar to *style-shifting* in monolingual discourse (see Hymes 1972). The following example is from Sranan–Dutch CS.

(3) wan heri **gedeelte** de ondro **beheer** fu gewapende **machten**
     one wholepart COP under control of armed forces
     "One whole part is under control of the armed forces."
                                          (Bolle 1994:75; in Muysken 2000:139)

In Muysken's third type of code-mixing, insertional code-mixing (which corresponds to Myers-Scotton's classic CS), lexical items or entire constituents from one language are inserted into a structure from the other language, as in (4), where the Spanish phrase *las dos de la noche* "two at night" is surrounded by matrix language elements (from Quechua) in which the Spanish words are nested (A-B-A structure), and *noche* is integrated into Quechua with the help of the accusative suffix *–ta*.

(4) Chay-ta **las dos de la noche**-ta chaya-mu-yk
     That-ACC the *two of the night*-ACC arrive-CIS-1PL
     "There at two in the morning we arrive."

(Muysken 2000:63)

If we were to rank the three types of code-mixing distinguished by Muysken on a scale of separation of the languages, then alternation would be a type of code-mixing with maximum separation, and congruent lexicalization would be at the opposite end (minimum separation), with insertional code-mixing occupying the middle ground.

Separation continuum

We do need to keep in mind, though, that researchers' understanding of separation between languages may not correspond to speakers' perceptions, as Auer (1984:26) points out. Auer (1984, 1995) uses a terminology that differs from that used by others by adopting the overarching concept of *language alternation*, which covers CS and transfer. CS is defined by Auer as "language alternation at a certain point in conversation without a structurally determined (and therefore predictable) return into the first language," whereas "transfer is defined as language alternation for a certain unit with a structurally provided point of return into the first language (Auer 1984:26)."[2] These distinctions correspond – roughly – to Muysken's alternational code-mixing and insertional code-mixing. As the term transfer is used in a very different way in research on language contact and SLA, Auer's terminology has not been widely adopted.

It is also possible to hypothesize that these three types of code-mixing differ from each other with respect to speakers' ability to control their switching. Alternational code-mixing seems to be on the side of maximum control, whereas congruent lexicalization is on the opposite side of the continuum, with insertion occupying the middle ground. Of course this hypothesis needs to be corroborated with experimental evidence.

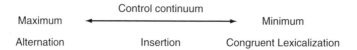

Control continuum

Separation between contact languages, and the fact that languages can become more or less similar to each other through contact is key in any discussions of convergence and transfer, to be addressed next.

4.5   Convergence and transfer in language change and in Second Language Acquisition (SLA)

As the terms convergence and transfer are often used alongside each other by many researchers working on contact-induced language change, these concepts are discussed together in this section, with an attempt to clarify how researchers see the relationship between CS on the one hand and transfer/convergence on the other. The discussion first addresses the work of researchers who focus on the role of transfer/convergence in language contact and language change, and then the work of researchers in SLA, who prefer to use the term "transfer" or "crosslinguistic influence" (Kellerman and Sharwood Smith 1986). Researchers working on transfer or convergence from the perspective of theories of language change have most often focused on the outcome of language contact, or what Paradis (1993) and Grosjean (2001) have termed static interference, referring to features that have become part of the implicit grammar (see §4.1). Researchers working on SLA tend to focus on dynamic interference. The discussion below will reflect those tendencies in the literature.

4.5.1   Convergence and transfer in contact-induced variation and change

According to Salmons (1990:476) the notion of convergence goes back to Schmidt's (1872) *Wellentheorie* (wave theory), and it is also used by Trubetzkoy (1939) and later by Weinreich (1953:395), who defines convergence as "partial similarities increasing at the expense of differences." Hock (1991:492) adds an important dimension by proposing that "convergence between different languages may be mutual (between adstratal languages) or unidirectional (in an unequal prestige relationship)," and the same point is made by Bullock and Toribio (2004).

Pfaff (1979:315) is probably the first to raise the issue of the relationship between CS and convergence. According to Pfaff, CS may lead to convergence, whereas Clyne (1987:753) appears to imply that convergence may lead to CS, when stating that "syntactic convergence will take place around the switch, apparently *in order* to ease code switching" [original emphasis]. Clyne (2003:79) uses the term convergence in general to denote "making languages more similar to each other," and specifically distinguishes between syntactic transference and convergence. Syntactic transference leads to a morpheme-to-morpheme correspondence between the contact languages, as in (5a). Syntactic convergence results in an approximation of the two languages, but not in completely parallel structures, as in (5b), where there is convergence to English in the choice of the auxiliary (*haben* "to have" instead of *sein* "to be"), in the extraposition of *in Tarrington* to the right-hand side of the verb, and in the omission of case marking on the preposition *zu* "to."

(5) (a.) *syntactic transference*
         Wir haben gegangen zu Schule **in Tarrington**
         we have gone to school in Tarrington
     (b.) *syntactic convergence*
         Wir haben zu Schule gegangen **in Tarrington**
         we have to school gone in Tarrington
     (c.) *Standard German*
         Wir sind **in Tarrington** zur Schule gegangen
         We are in Tarrington to school gone
         "We went to school in Tarrington."

(Clyne 2003:79–80)

While Thomason and Kaufman (1988) do not discuss CS in any detail, their framework for contact-induced language change is one of the most influential works on transfer, which they term interference. They distinguish two basic mechanisms of contact-induced change: *borrowing* and *interference through shift*. Borrowing is defined as "the incorporation of foreign features into a group's native language by speakers of that language: the native language is maintained but is changed by the addition of the incorporated features (Thomason and Kaufman 1988:37)." Interference through shift is "a type of interference that results from imperfect group learning during a process of language shift." That is, in this kind of interference, a group of speakers shifting to a target language fails to learn the target language perfectly (Thomason and Kaufman 1988:39). In an application of these mechanisms to Brussels, Treffers-Daller (1999) showed that the contact phenomena found in Brussels French are the result of interference through shift, because large groups of speakers of Brussels Dutch learned French, and often abandoned Dutch in the process, whereas the contact phenomena found in Brussels Dutch are the result of a process of borrowing from French. The concepts of borrowing and interference through shift roughly correspond to Van Coetsem's (1988) notions *recipient language agentivity* (e.g. when speakers of Brussels Dutch borrow features from French) and *source language agentivity* (e.g. when Dutch learners of French import features of Dutch into their interlanguages).

Bullock and Toribio (2004:91), like Silva-Corvalán (1994), argue that convergence is not necessarily externally induced, and in their view this distinguishes convergence from interference or transfer, as the latter concepts refer to externally motivated innovations. They also make an important point regarding the areas of the grammatical system that are particularly prone to external influence and point out that "the convergence of grammatical properties is either of a lexical nature or it occurs primarily at the interface of syntax and pragmatics/semantics" (Bullock and Toribio 2004:92). In addition, they claim that syntax proper (the purely formal system) is immune to convergence (see Treffers-Daller and Mougeon 2005 and Backus 2004 for counter-arguments).

Silva-Corvalán (1994:4) points to the fact that "transfer leads to, but is not the single cause of convergence, defined as the achievement of greater structural similarity in a given aspect of the grammar of two or more languages." She also mentions the importance of the fact that the languages are assumed to be different at the onset of contact, a point which is crucial, but not always easy to establish if historical data are not available. She discusses different types of transfer, described as *direct transfer* and *indirect transfer*. The former refers to the importation of a new form from another language, such as *lonche* "lunch" in Los Angeles Spanish. When *registrarse* incorporates the meaning "to register in school" from English, this is also considered an example of direct transfer. Indirect transfer refers to a higher frequency of usage of a form that corresponds to a structure of the contact language (e.g. the more frequent use of progressives in Spanish by Puerto Rican Spanish-English bilinguals in comparison with monolinguals). These terms are similar to the ones used by Mougeon et al. (2005) who apply the terms *overt transfer* and *covert transfer* for these phenomena. For Silva-Corvalán, the loss of a category that does not have a parallel in the contact language is also a form of indirect transfer. An example is the loss of adjective gender marking in some Spanish varieties of Los Angeles, or in (5a) and (5b) the loss of case marking on the German preposition *zu* "to."

Importantly, Silva-Corvalán (1994:5) points to the fact that "convergence may result as well from pre-existing internally motivated changes in one of the languages, most likely *accelerated* [original emphasis] by contact, rather than as a consequence of direct interlingual influence." Researchers have often failed to disentangle internal and external causes in their study of the emergence of particular innovations, and have jumped to conclusions about transfer in cases where the result is most likely due to *multiple causation* (Thomason and Kaufman 1988). There are however many researchers – in particular historical linguists – who dismiss explanations based on external factors. As Farrar and Jones (2002:4) explain, "Examining whether contact plays a role in change is [...] seen as a last resort, and 'if in doubt' we should 'do without' and simply not take this final step." Rather than resorting to a multiple causation explanation, perhaps the true challenge for researchers in contact linguistics is to find better methodologies for teasing apart the effects of transfer from those of internal change.

Despite the terminological confusion, the key differences between convergence and transfer appear to be as follows. First, convergence is not necessarily externally motivated, whereas transfer by definition must be. Second, transfer implies directionality (for instance, from language A to language B), while convergence does not. Third, convergence used in the sense of Mougeon and Beniak (1991) often involves simplification of structures or features, whereas transfer can lead to *complexification* (i.e. an unmarked feature is replaced by a marked feature).

An issue that will need to be investigated in future is to what extent internal and external change draw on the same mechanisms. According to Croft (2000:148) "essentially the same mechanism that causes interference also causes the innovation of certain types of internal language changes." Croft reserves the term *intraference* for processes of internal change such as morphological leveling whereby one form in a morphological paradigm spreads to other forms of that paradigm. A key aspect of this process is *intralingual identification*, i.e. "the recognition of the semantic relatedness of words, inflections and constructions" (Croft 2000:148). Interference works in the same way, in his view, except that a form spreads from one language to another, rather than from one subsystem of a language to another subsystem of the same language, through a process of interlingual identification. This issue is important, as it raises the question to what extent contact-induced change is fundamentally different from internal mechanisms of language change.

4.5.2   Transfer in Second Language Acquisition (SLA)

It is clear from all introductions to SLA that transfer is a key concept that needs to form part of any theory of SLA, despite the efforts of Dulay and Burt (1974) to minimize its role. Dechert and Raupach (1989:xii) consider language transfer to be a metaphorical concept, "because nothing is really 'transferred' from one domain to the other when we speak or listen to a new language." They distinguish no less than seventeen "shades of meaning" attributed to the term language transfer, and even this list is not intended to be complete. Depending on the aims of the study and the theoretical framework in which researchers work, transfer is seen, for example, as a research paradigm (Osgood 1953), a central process underlying language performance (Selinker 1972), a production strategy or a communication strategy (Gass and Selinker 1983), or a constraint on the hypotheses that learners will formulate about the target language (Schachter 1993). It is also clear that transfer can take place from L1 to L2 or from L2 to L1 (Pavlenko 2000; Cook 2003).

While researchers working from the perspective of Universal Grammar (UG) do not always think of transfer as key, White (2000) identifies five different approaches to this issue. The most extreme position taken in relation to transfer in SLA is expressed in what has become known as the Full Transfer/Full Access model (Schwartz and Sprouse 1996). Adherents of this model believe that learners initially transfer all the parameter settings from their first language into the L2. Subsequently they revise their hypotheses on the basis of positive evidence from the input (Mitchell and Myles 2004). If such evidence is not available or is obscure, learners do not become fully competent in the L2, which explains fossilization.

Other researchers believe that learners have access to UG via their L1, or that only lexical categories are transferred, but not functional categories (Vainikka and Young-Scholten 1996a, 1996b).

Jarvis (2000) points out that there are so many conflicting findings about the importance of transfer in SLA because researchers do not agree about the "nature" of transfer and they adopt different definitions of the concept. He proposes a working definition of L1 transfer: "L1 influence refers to any instance of learner data where a statistically significant correlation (or probability-based relation) is shown to exist between some features of learners' IL [interlanguage] performance and their L1 background (Jarvis 2000:252)." This definition focuses on the empirical evidence that supports an explanation that transfer is the likely cause for a particular phenomenon.

4.6   Conclusion: towards a unified account of code-switching and transfer

In this chapter we have seen that the wide variety of concepts used for contact phenomena makes it difficult for researchers to incorporate findings from neighboring fields into their research. The key question is, of course, whether researchers are only using different labels for essentially the same phenomena, or whether the phenomena under investigation are fundamentally different either in their surface manifestations, or in the processes and mechanisms that lead to those surface forms. The problem is often that surface forms as found in corpora of spontaneous bilingual speech can be the result of different processes that cannot be directly observed, whereas in strictly controlled experiments only a small proportion of the phenomena that can be observed "in the wild" can be tested (see Gullberg et al., this volume, who call for a multi-task approach).

A number of general points can however be made to advance the discussion. While many researchers have argued that CS and transfer are different phenomena altogether, new insights from psycholinguistics may well point to a different direction. As we have seen in §4.1, Paradis (1998) argues that in terms of processing, cross-linguistic influence cannot be distinguished clearly from CS phenomena. The position that CS and transfer are manifestations of the same phenomenon, i.e. the influence of one language on another, is an attractive null hypothesis that can be tested in experimental settings. A key question to be investigated in this context is the issue of control. A further investigation of the locus and manner in which speakers control CS and transfer will no doubt shed new light on this matter.

Another key point that needs further investigation is to what extent the language selection processes that are involved in CS are the same or different from those that are used in lexical access in monolinguals. If Paradis (2004) is right, language processing in bilinguals and monolinguals works in the same way, so that no additional mechanisms are needed to account for CS. As we have seen above, Poulisse and Bongaerts (1994) provide evidence to support a unified approach to processing in monolinguals and bilinguals. While Paradis's position is an interesting null hypothesis, this chapter has argued that we do need additional mechanisms, such as a mechanism for establishing congruence between languages (see Sebba, this volume). Independent support for the existence of such a mechanism comes from Croft (2000), who sees interlingual identification as a key mechanism behind contact-induced change.

It may be possible to go further and see intralingual processes such as analogy in language change or overgeneralization in L1 development as manifestations of transfer. If speakers regularize irregular verbs (e.g. *goed* for *went*) this can also be seen as transfer of a pattern to a new domain. Similarly, it is possible to see accommodation (Giles and Powesland 1975) as a form of transfer of features between interlocutors. Transfer may thus well be a powerful mechanism that can be seen to work in monolingual and bilingual contexts. Whether or not the same processes are at work in these different contexts, and whether or not the notion language transfer is merely a metaphor or more than that, are empirical questions, surely worth investigating in the future.

Notes

1. Long ago, Haugen (1972a:314) also assumed the existence of language tags to ensure speakers are able to keep their languages apart.
2. Auer (1984:103) points out that the terms *Umschaltung* (switching) and *Einschaltung* (transfer) coined by Stolt (1964) are at the basis of his use of the terminology.

5

Loan translations versus code-switching

Ad Backus
and
Margreet Dorleijn

5.1 Introduction

Loan translations or *calques* are defined as words or phrases that are reproduced as literal translations from one language into another. These terms figure prominently in lists of contact phenomena, and sit comfortably besides relatively well-described linguistic consequences of language contact such as code-switching (hereafter CS), *interference*, and *attrition*. However, actual theoretical treatments of loan translation are surprisingly rare. This contribution aims to summarize extant theoretical treatments, and to provide the basis for furthering a theoretical account that integrates loan translation with these other language contact phenomena, specifically with CS. The two are closely related because they are both arguably lexical contact phenomena.

While theoretical treatments may be rare, individual examples of loan translations, or calques, are easy to find in the literature on contact linguistics, especially in work on CS. Somewhat surprisingly though, textbooks on language contact and historical linguistics generally just mention one or more of a handful of standard examples. A classic example is the literally translated compound noun, such as the words for "skyscraper" in various European languages, which all use morphemes for "sky" and "scrape": French *gratteciel*, Spanish *rascacielos*, German *wolkenkratzer*. However, the phenomenon is found across a wide range of linguistic constructions, including complex verbs, prepositional phrases, and idiomatic expressions. An example culled from the CS literature is given in (1), in which the English phrasal verb *work out* is calqued with the equivalent German morphemes *schaff* and *aus*.

(1) *Pennsylvania German*
     Es hat juscht net **aus**-ge-**schaff**-t far Amisch Leite, so ham mer vehicle
     grieg-t

it have.3SG just not out-PRT-work-PRT for Amish people so have we
vehicle get-PRT

"It just didn't work out for Amish people, so we got vehicles."

(Fuller 1999:49)

Loan translation has received limited attention because it has been
assumed to be relatively rare. However, its frequency in actual data
depends on how you define it. Traditionally, it has been limited to clear
cases of translated lexical combinations only, as in *skyscraper*. However,
there are at least two good reasons for expanding this definition. The first
one is empirical: many other cases are a lot like *skyscraper* in the sense that
some degree of literal translation seems to have taken place, but the
translation process involved is rarely one of total translation. As will be
demonstrated below, most cases involve what is best termed partial translation. However, since the mechanism that produces these cases is the
same as that which produced *skyscraper*, it would be sound academic
practice to group together all cases that involve some form of concrete
translation. The second reason is more theoretical: having a wider definition of loan translation allows us to better explore its relationship to CS,
lexical borrowing, semantic extension, and what is often called structural
or grammatical borrowing. Having a narrow definition isolates loan translation as a relatively minor phenomenon; having a wide definition allows
us to explore the boundaries it shares with these other phenomena.

5.2 Definitions

We will begin illustrating the basic division between loan translation and
CS on the one hand, and loan translation and structural borrowing on the
other, by defining the phenomena as explicitly as possible. For each phenomenon, we tease apart whether it is synchronic (i.e. linked to specific
utterances, and, therefore, directly observable in speech data) or diachronic (i.e. related to historical development, and thus not directly
observable in the transcript of a conversation), and discuss its structural
implications.

(1.) ***Code-switching***: the use of overt material (from single morphemes to
entire sentences) from Language B in Language A discourse. CS
roughly comes in two types (see Muysken 2000):

(a.) *Alternational CS*: the alternation of material in two languages in
bilingual discourse, as in the Turkish–Dutch example in (2).

(2) sen de kalkma-n lazım onlar-la ***en hoe moet je dan op de rest
letten***?

you too get.up-POSS.2SG necessary them-with and how can
you then on the rest keep.an.eye?

"You must get up with them as well, and then how can you keep an eye on the rest?"

(b.) *Insertional CS*: the use of material from one language, the Embedded Language (EL), in bilingual discourse. In this type, the foreign material is embedded in clauses that are clearly recognizable as in the Matrix Language (ML), as exemplified in the Turkish–Dutch example in (3). Note that in this contact phenomenon both form and meaning are from the EL (see Myers-Scotton and Jake, this volume).

(3) mesela okul-da iki tane kız da bana **verkering** sor-du
for.instance school-LOC two CLAS girl too me.DAT engagement ask-PAST-3SG
"For instance, two girls at school have asked me out on a date."

(2.) **Lexical Borrowing**: the process whereby words from a lending language become entrenched as conventional words in the receiving lexicon. It is often difficult to distinguish "new" code-switches from "established" loan words in synchronic data. For example, because of their frequency, the words *uitgaan* "to go out," *opleiding* "school," *afstuderen* "to graduate," and *Hemelvaart* "Ascension Day" may very well have become established Dutch-origin loan words in Dutch Turkish, rather than code-switches.

(3.) **Loan translation**: any usage of morphemes in Language A that is the result of the literal translation of one or more elements in a semantically equivalent expression in Language B. In this type of contact phenomenon, only the meaning, and not the overt morphemes, is from Language B, as for example, the use of the word for "to play" (*oynamak*) in (4).

(4) piano oynamak
piano play; "to play piano"
cf. Standard Turkish: piano çalmak (literally "piano to.sound")
cf. Standard Dutch: piano spelen (literally "piano to.play")

(4.) **Lexical change**: the process whereby the use of words or morphemes, or morpheme combinations, from the lending language, becomes entrenched as conventional usage and/or combinations in the receiving language lexicon. Again, it is not always possible to determine whether a particular foreign-inspired combination or usage is used for the first time (i.e. as a result of on-line translation) or has been already conventionalized. For example, the collocation *piano oynamak* mentioned above has been attested various times by different researchers, so it is possible that it has become a borrowing in Dutch–Turkish.

(5.) ***Interference/Transference***: any structure used in discourse in Language A that is the result of influence from Language B but where there is no evidence that this usage was produced by the translation of a concrete expression in Language B. As in loan translation, only the formal structure comes from Language B. Consider example (5):

(5)   hiç Türkçe kitap-***lar*** oku-ya-m-ıyor-um
      no Turkish book-PL read-ABIL-NEG-PROG-1SG
      "I can't read Turkish books."
      cf. Standard Turkish: *hiç Türkçe kitap okuyamıyorum*, with singular noun *kitap*
      cf. Standard Dutch: *ik kan geen Turkse boeken lezen*, with plural noun *boek-en* (book-pl; "books")

(6.) ***Structural borrowing***: the process whereby the use of a structure originally from the donor language becomes entrenched as a conventional part of the grammatical structure of the receiving language. It can sometimes be shown that a foreign-inspired structure has become conventionalized if it is used exclusively, or with much more frequency, than the native structure it is replacing or has replaced.

Three important distinctions are made in the above definitions. The first is the difference between the use of overt words and morphemes from Language A and Language B versus the use of Language A forms with Language B semantic and/or structural characteristics. The use of overt material from two languages unites CS and lexical borrowing, against the four other phenomena. The second difference allows us to distinguish loan translation and lexical change, on the one hand, from interference/transference and structural change, on the other. The crucial point here is whether there is a concrete lexical model that acts as the source or not. Note that the definitions of loan translation and interference/transference are almost identical. They only differ in the specificity of the element that is copied from the other language: a specific expression in the case of loan translation (e.g. a word, a collocation, or an idiom), and general grammatical structure in the case of interference/transference. As we shall see below, the line between the two is often hard to draw.

Finally, it is important to distinguish between synchronic and diachronic facts. Note that the definitions of CS, loan translation and interference/transference make reference to synchronic discourse. That is, they are seen as characteristics of "speech" or of the actual utterances people produce while talking. "Speech" is a synchronic entity, while "language" is a diachronic one. Every synchronic utterance has diachronic effects, i.e. it contributes to the development of the language involved. The result of insertional CS, especially if the same foreign word is repeatedly used in discourse by many different people, may be that the foreign word in question becomes a normal word in the recipient language discourse: it becomes a loan word. We refer to this diachronic process as "lexical

Table 5.1 Synchronic and diachronic instantiations of contact phenomena, classified by the nature of the source material

Linguistic Source	Synchronic	Diachronic
Foreign words	Insertional code-switching	Lexical borrowing
Foreign meaning/combinations	Loan translation	Lexical change
Foreign structure	Interference/Transference	Structural change/borrowing

borrowing." Loan translation, likewise, may have the diachronic effect that the new expression catches on in the speech community. The language has then undergone "lexical change": the new collocation has become a fixed unit in the language, alongside the numerous other conventional collocations, but with the distinguishing feature that its ultimate etymological origin lies in another language. Note that we cannot call this development "lexical borrowing" because that term is traditionally used for loan words only. A similar relationship holds for "interference/transference" and "structural change." These dimensions are summarized in Table 5.1.

5.3 Theoretical interest: why study loan translation?

How exactly CS and loan translation relate to each other has not been the focus of much study, and this chapter aims to elucidate this relationship. Descriptively, the issue is fairly clear: we are either dealing with words from the other language (CS) or with native words that are used in a new way, one inspired by the other language (loan translation). But accounting for the two phenomena is much harder. What governs a speaker's choice? Can we predict when CS rather than loan translation will take place? While most of this chapter will consist of a presentation of types of loan translation, we will come back to this question in the conclusion.

Apart from its link with CS, there are at least three independent reasons for studying loan translation. The first has to do with scientific accountability. Loan translation simply figures in contact data, so it needs to be explained. In fact, since CS and loan translation tend to co-occur in corpora, the question arises whether they are in free distribution, or whether there are patterns to uncover about when a speaker will opt for CS versus loan translation. The second motivation is that studying loan translations in contact settings provides us with an opportunity to identify conventional combinations in a language, something that is not so easy in speech from monolinguals. Loan translations stand out, certainly for speakers of non-contact varieties of the same language, precisely because they break the conventions those speakers are used to. Such conventional combinations are central to the perspective of cognitive linguistics, in which there is intense interest in the division between structures that are fixed in language and those that are innovated in speech. Given enough of these new structures, a language may come across as significantly different from other, non-contact, varieties of the same language, despite using the same words and the same syntax. Third, the study of loan translations provides insights that monolingual data cannot through the dissociation of semantic from phonological structure. Contact phenomena, particularly loan translation, show that this can be done relatively easily, at least for some elements. Loan translation provides unique data in this respect.

5.3.1   Previous treatments of loan translation

Owens (1996) presents one of the few systematic synchronic corpus studies of loan translation. He demonstrates that Nigerian Arabic sounds distinctly "un-Arabic" to Arabic speakers from the Middle East, because of the many unfamiliar collocations and idioms. Nigerian Arabic shares these lexical collocations and idioms with most languages of the Lake Chad Basin area, even though these stem from different families. A typical example is that all languages of the area render the meaning <roof> as *head of house*, i.e. as a possessive combination. As Owens maintains, "loan translation" is actually not a very accurate term since speakers are using established collocations, rather than innovating on the spot through translation from another language. Such expressions often arise in Sprachbund-type situations, such as the Lake Chad Basin, and it is often impossible to identify the source language that originally provided the model for the loan translation. Speakers using these forms are not necessarily bilingual.

Treatments of loan translation in general accounts of language contact that abstract away from particular bilingual settings are very rare, with the exception of taxonomies of contact effects (e.g. Haugen 1972a). These, however, contain little theorizing about what brings loan translations about, and especially about what constraints may be placed on its application. There are at least two exceptions, however. First, Johanson (1998) provides a descriptive model of contact effects in which loan translation finds a place among the other phenomena. His model, the Code Copying model, makes a distinction between Global Code Copying (taking over forms from another language, i.e. insertional CS and lexical borrowing) and Selective Code Copying. The latter type of copying comes in four different kinds, which all have in common that only part of a foreign model is copied: phonological characteristics, semantic features, the way in which words and morphemes are combined, and/or its relative frequency of usage. Loan translation can be considered a type of selective code copying, and can be of the semantic or combinational type, or both.

In Myers-Scotton's (2002a) Matrix Language Frame model, loan translation and structural borrowing are discussed together under the rubric of the "Composite Matrix Language." If words or morphemes are combined in unexpected ways due to contact, a new variety of the Matrix Language, the Composite ML, has come into being. Incorporated into this new variety are some lexical and structural changes. Specifically, in the case of lexical change, one or more aspects of a morpheme or a word, such as a shade of meaning, or the words or morphemes it can combine with, are replaced by those of its equivalent in the other language. Interestingly, for Myers-Scotton and associates it seems to make no difference whether the pivotal element is a content word or a functional morpheme (e.g. a conjunction or a case marker). For most others in the field, the former would be a loan translation or lexical change, and the latter a case of interference or structural borrowing. We will discuss examples of each further on; in fact, the distinction between content and function elements will be used as a dimension on which to classify types of loan translation.

Discussing loan translation and structural borrowing together is reasonable, since there are quite a lot of similarities between the synchronic phenomena, loan translation and interference/transference, and between the diachronic processes, lexical change and structural borrowing (recall that we cannot talk of "lexical borrowing" here, because that term is reserved for loan words) (see Winford 2005:385). Though we classified loan translation as a lexical phenomenon, it is more accurate to say that it is lexical as well as structural in nature. As will be seen from examples presented below, the term "lexical" leaves room for a broad interpretation. We want to emphasize that the crucial property of a loan translation is that the model is a specific expression in the other language. If the result of this translation produces not just an unconventional combination of morphemes, but also an unconventional structure, interference/transference has occurred as well, but only as an accidental by-product of the loan translation. Normally, however, loan translations do not violate the grammar of the language in which they are coined, as will be shown below. Otheguy (1993) goes so far as to reject the term loan translation because of this. According to him, since loan translations have no systemic impact on the receiving language, they reflect cultural rather than linguistic influence. It is the foreign concept that is imported. The point is exemplified with the often-cited construction [Verb + *para atrás*] in American varieties of Spanish, assumed to be a calque of English [Verb + *back*], in (6). Otheguy's position is that the combination of lexemes *para atrás* "exploits inherent Spanish possibilities" (Otheguy 1993:23), and does not violate Spanish syntax. However, it should be noted that although no grammatical structure is introduced, it is nevertheless a new expression in Spanish, brought about through language contact.

(6) *US Spanish*
     Papi, tú me prestas esa pluma y yo te la doy ***para atrás***; please, please, préstamela y yo te la doy ***para atrás***.
     "Daddy, you lend me that pen and I'll give it back to you, please, please, lend it to me and I'll give it back to you."

(Otheguy 1993:22)

We will now review the various kinds of loan translation, and see how they vary systematically along the dimension "lexical to grammatical"; this will be illustrated with examples from our data on contact varieties of Turkish.[1] Similarities and differences with CS will be highlighted throughout the discussion and summarized in the conclusion.

5.4   Identifying loan translations

The definition of loan translation formulated above is vague with respect to what counts as a literal translation. Foreign influence can take a variety of forms, ranging from exact translation to mere resemblance. Identifying a loan translation is not always easy, since it often requires subtle knowledge of the norms of the pre-contact variety. In many contexts, of course, we know very little of certain linguistic varieties, particularly in situations in which the entire speech community is bilingual. However, among bilingual immigrants, identification of loan translation is a bit more straightforward. If a putative calque is produced only by bilinguals, while monolinguals use a different form, this provides evidence for loan translation. By way of example, the combination *piano oynamak* ("piano play"; "to play the piano"), is only produced by Turkish speakers in Holland, as a loan translation, see example (4) above.

Loan translations can be categorized according to the type of morpheme involved in the calque, allowing a continuum in which the specificity of the semantics of the calqued morphemes decreases gradually:

(1.)   loan translations involving content morphemes
(2.)   loan translations involving function morphemes
(3.)   loan translations involving grammatical morphemes
(4.)   loan translations involving discourse patterns

In the first three types, some element of meaning is the source of the translation, but it must be emphasized that if the meaning is relatively abstract, the translated element tends to be a functional element, and thus the translation may have structural consequences. Therefore, the continuum shades into the realm of interference and structural borrowing. The fourth category, the copying of discourse patterns, has, to our knowledge, not received much attention in the literature on contact linguistics. We discuss each category in turn.

5.4.1   Loan translations involving content morphemes

As stated above, the most familiar type of calque is a compound noun such as English *sky-scraper*, French *gratte-ciel*, Spanish *rasca-cielos*. This type may be subdivided according to the number of words involved. Classic loan translations are mostly two-word combinations, while one-word translations are often discussed as *semantic extension*. An example is *registrarse* "to register (for class)" in contact Spanish (cf. non-contact Spanish *matricularse*).

5.4.1.1   One-word loan translations: semantic extension
Semantic extensions are not commonly understood by speakers of non-contact varieties of the language involved. An example is the use of Turkish *kalabalık* ("crowded"), in which it is semantically extended on the model of Dutch *druk* ("noisy," "crowded," "busy"), as in examples (7) and (8). Such translations do not normally have implications for the structure of the receiving language.

(7) çocuk-lar bugün çok kalabalık
     child-PL today very crowded
     "The children are very crowded (> noisy) today."

(8) bugün çok kalabalığım
     today very crowded.COP.1SG
     "I am very crowded (> busy) today."

5.4.1.2   Two-word loan translations
Two-word loan translations, like one-word loan translations, can be semantic extensions, but more importantly it is the combination of the two particular morphemes that is unconventional. There may be structural consequences, too, in that, for instance, the relative ordering may be "ungrammatical" (see the un-English ordering of adjective and noun in translated expressions such as *Surgeon-General*, modelled on French with the word order intact), but this does not seem to be common.

Two-word loan translations are found in all the morpho-syntactic domains in which content words are combined to form a new, more complex "word," notably compound nouns, adjective–noun units, and verb–object collocations. A particularly frequent type seems to be the translated Object + Verb construction. Interestingly, in the case of Turkish–Dutch contact, whenever such loan translations appear, the object is often generic, or non-specific, as in (9).

(9) iyi olan hasta-nın hal-in-den anlamaz ama doktor mecbur anlama-sı
     lazım bi de ***para soruyo*** yani o doktora doktor de-mi-yce-n ki
     healthy bePART ill.person-GEN condition-POSS-ABL understand.AOR.
     NEG.3SG. but doctor necessary understand-POSS.NOM necessary and
     too money ask.PRES.3SG so.that doctor.DAT doctor say-NEG-FUT-2SG
     EMPH
     "A healthy person does not understand how an ill person feels, but a
     doctor should [understand], and then on top of that he asks [for]
     money, I mean, you can't very well call such a doctor a doctor."

Here Turkish *para soruyo* "money ask," is modelled after the Dutch collocation *om geld vragen* "for money ask" ("to ask for money"). The expected

Turkish counterpart would be: *para istemek*, "money want" ("to want/ demand money"). Generic objects are not case-marked in Turkish (only specific direct objects are marked with the accusative case in Turkish), and this stimulates an incorporation reading, in which verb and noun form a single semantic unit. Such verb–object combinations are as much cases of word formation (of compound verbs) as of synchronic syntactic composition.

Empirically, most examples concern unique fixed combinations of two words or morphemes, directly translated from the source language. These are usually inserted into regular syntactic constructions, and therefore have no structural consequences beyond the distribution of the words involved. However, structural implications do arise if functional elements within a combination get translated as well. This can be seen in (10), another Object + Verb loan translation:

(10)   suç-u bana ver-di
       guilt-ACC to.me give-PAST.3SG
       "He accused me."

The monolingual Turkish equivalent is the single verb *suçlamak* "to accuse"; the Dutch expression *de schuld geven*, "to give the blame" is the model. Note that the translation involves more than the simple juxtaposition of the content morphemes for "guilt" and "give." The presence of the accusative marker and the indirect object are also the result of the translation process because they are required in the Dutch model. The use of the definite article *de* "the" in the Dutch model is idiomatic (*guilt* is construed as inherently definite), and the speaker has copied this through the use of the accusative marker *-u*, the relatively transparent equivalent of the definite article. The replacement of the single transitive verb by the Object + Verb construction has the further consequence that the Dutch subcategorization frame is also copied – a third argument is needed to encode the person or thing being blamed. As in Dutch, this must surface as an indirect object. Though the loan translation is more complex than in the case of *para soruyo* above, the translation is still lexical in nature, because the borrowing is the entire Dutch lexical unit *give blame to someone*. That is, speakers do not borrow the abstract double object construction or the partially schematic construction [Direct Object + Indirect Object + give], but rather the specific collocation.

Evidence of slightly more abstract structural change as the consequence of loan translation can be seen in the next example. In monolingual Turkish, the dative-marked directional adverbs *öne* ("to the front") and *arkaya* ("to the back") can only be combined with motion verbs, but in Dutch Turkish they co-occur with the stative verb *durmak* "stand." This combination is normal in Dutch, presumably the model for this usage: *naar voren staan* "stand towards the front" and *naar achteren staan* "stand towards the back."

(11) erken gel-ir-se-n ön-e doğru dur-ur-sun, geç gelirsen, arka-ya doğru
      dur-ur-sun.
      early come-AOR-COND-2SG front-DAT towards stand-AOR-2SG late if.you.
      come, back-DAT towards stand-AOR-2SG
      "If you come early, you stand towards the front; if you are late, you
      stand towards the back."

It is unclear whether this effect should be interpreted as lexical or as
structural. Under a lexical interpretation, a specific Dutch collocation
has been copied using Turkish morphemes. From a grammatical point of
view, the Dutch rule permitting the combination of directional adverbs
and stative verbs may have been copied. It is in principle impossible to
decide on the correct option on the basis of isolated examples, but at this
point the available data are simply lacking. Data demonstrating the use of
directional adverbs with different stative verbs would indicate a grammatical interpretation rather than a lexical one.

5.4.1.3 Multi-word loan translations

The source of a multi-word loan translation is generally a conventional
phrase or expression that is translated along with some or all of its structural features. Since loan translations of this kind tend to occur at sentence
boundaries, as can be seen in example (12), they are not unlike alternational
CS, only, of course, they have the phonological shape of the receiving
language. They differ from the one-word and two-word loan translations
in that they are not separate lexical items. Instead, they often constitute a
clause on their own.

(12) bazı-ki-ler işde anne baba-m oku /oku di-yo işde oku-mu-yo-lar işde
      istek ol-ma-dıkça o / *o* aile oku / oku diy-ince/ **bi şey yardım et-mez**
      some-N-PL well mother father-POSS.1SG read/read say-PRES.3SG well
      read-NEG-PRES-3PL well motivation be-NEG-as.long.as that/ that family
      read / read say-when a thing help do-AOR.NEG.3SG
      "Some people, well, their parents say 'come on, study, do your home-
      work,' but they don't, if you have no motivation [for it] that family can
      say 'come on, study,' as often as they want, but it doesn't help one bit."

The phrase *bir şey yardim etmez* is modeled after the Dutch phrase *dat helpt
niks*, literally "it helps nothing." Though this phrase instantiates the syntax
of a normal Dutch intransitive clause, the expression itself is so common
and has such idiomatic meaning that it can be safely assumed to be a fixed
unit (see Wray 2002). Further evidence of its status as a unit is the fact that
helpen would otherwise require a direct object: *hij helpt hem*, "he helps him."
Its impersonal use is also a conventional part of the idiom. The Turkish
verb *yardım etmek* normally has a different subcategorization frame: the
person who is helped is encoded as an indirect object (by the dative): *birine
yardım etmek* "to help someone." None of these characteristics of the verb
surface in the Dutch idiom nor in the loan translation in (12). Most features

of the Dutch unit, i.e. the idiomatic impersonal use of the verb *helpen* and the adverbial reinforcer "nothing," are copied and translated (through the use of the Turkish verb for "to help" and the discontinuous unit consisting of "something" (*bi şey*) and the negation on the verb).

The final example in this section, another translated idiom, takes us to the limits of what can be identified as a loan translation. While all cases discussed so far were easily detected on the basis of relatively clear unconventional semantics and/or structure, some loan translations are less noticeable, and this causes a serious methodological problem. In Example (13), the highlighted segments are unconventional, but the phrases in question are semantically transparent.

(13) (a.) ama işde bazen insan-lar unut-uyo-lar doktor ve hemşire-ler de *insan-lar, yanlış yap-abil-ir-ler.*
            but well sometimes people-PL forget-PRES-3PL doctor and nurse-PL too *people-PL, mistake make-can-AOR-3PL*
            "But sometimes people forget that doctors and nurses are human and can make mistakes."
       (b.) *Monolingual Turkish*
            hata yap-ar-lar
            mistake make-AOR-3PL
            "They may make mistakes."

The plural noun *insanlar* "people" is the translation of Dutch *mensen*, also a plural noun, while conventional Turkish would use singular *insan* in this context. The reason why the plural is used is probably the fact that the whole Dutch phrase *x en x zijn ook mensen* ("X and X are people too") is used as the idiomatic basis for the Turkish expression. While the unconventional plural provides us with at least one reason to assume that this is what has happened, the clause that follows **yanlış yap-abil-ir-ler** is virtually impossible to establish as a loan translation, yet it may very well be one. Again, the phrase is semantically transparent, and in this case it also follows default Turkish structure. Possibility is expressed through an explicit modal marker, the derivational suffix *–abil-*, possibly translating the Dutch use of the modal auxiliary verb "can" in the expression *die kunnen fouten maken* "they can make mistakes." At least according to some of our informants, conventional Turkish would prefer to use the expression in (13b), with a different word for "mistake" and the aorist tense. This example illustrates the methodological problem one runs into: sometimes there are no objective features that can incontrovertibly demonstrate that something is a loan translation. Because of this, loan translations may well be considerably under-identified.

5.4.2 Loan translations involving function morphemes

In this section, we will discuss cases of loan translation that clearly revolve around grammatical elements, such as case markers, but we will begin with an example that could just as well have been differently classified. Because function morphemes have largely grammatical meaning, cross-linguistic influence involving such morphemes as the crucial element is close to what is traditionally called structural borrowing or contact-induced grammaticalization (Heine and Kuteva 2003). If, for instance, an indefinite article is used like its counterpart in another language, and this usage deviates from what is conventional in its own language, one could argue that indefiniteness marking has changed. The examples to be discussed operate on this line between lexical and grammatical change, and we will discuss to what extent they should be considered loan translations. We will make one subdivision in presenting the examples: either the entire loan translation consists of a function morpheme, or a function morpheme is the most crucial part of it.

One-word loan translations of functional morphemes have much in common with semantic extensions of content words, see (7) and (8) above. Adpositions especially, because of their concrete semantic content, are often analysed as somewhere in between a function word and a content word, so one may argue that in (14), just as in (7) and (8), the loan translation is purely lexical. There is no real structural effect, because only one lexical element is involved, and in addition it replaces a word from the same part of speech, which is structurally used in an identical way. In monolingual Turkish, the postpositional phrase *önünde* ("in front of") would be the expected choice, but a Turkish translation of the Dutch convention, which uses the preposition *achter* ("behind"), is used instead.

(14) bütün gün kompüter ***arka-sın-da*** otur-du-m
      whole day computer back-POSS.3SG-LOC sit-PAST-1SG
      "I have been sitting behind the computer all day (i.e. I have been at the computer all day)."

Other elements that are in between content and function morpheme status include adverbs, particles, and conjunctions. In (15), the use of the sentential adverb *belki* "maybe" betrays direct copying of how its Dutch equivalent *misschien* is used, as a sentential modifier in a question with the effect of making the question more polite.

(15) ***belki*** sen de farket-ti-n mi?
      maybe you too notice-PAST-2SG Q
      "Did you happen to notice that, too?"

In example (16) the particle *te* "also" is used like its Dutch counterpart. In Turkish, normally the somewhat more specific forms *bir de* or *aynı zamanda* ("at the same time") would be expected, but bilinguals may feel that these have too strong an additive meaning ("and then on top of that, you also …"), probably because Dutch *ook* is used in both strong and weak additive contexts. The usage of simple *te*, therefore, has its semantic motivations in the usage of its translation equivalent, and thus it qualifies as a loan translation (for another example, see the conjunction *ve*, "and," in example 21 below).

(16)   çok iyi, öğretmenlik *te* yap-ıyo-sun, değil mi?
       very well, teaching also do-PRES-2SG, not Q?
       "Very well, and then you teach, right?"

The comitative suffix in (17) is the result of translating the Dutch way of saying "burden someone with responsibility." Dutch, like English, uses "with" and marks the person saddled with the responsibility as a direct object. Turkish, on the other hand, normally construes the responsibility as the direct object and the person involved as an indirect object (through the dative). Dutch Turkish has copied the subcategorization pattern for this expression from its Dutch equivalent.

(17)   (a.) birin-*i* sorumluluk-*la* yükledi
            somebody-ACC responsibility-with burden.PAST.3SG
       (b.) *Monolingual Turkish*
            sorumluluğ-*u* birin-*e* yükledi
            responsibility-ACC somebody-DAT.burden.PAST.3SG
            "He burdened somebody with the responsibility."

As long as we are dealing with morphemes that have a clear semantic core, loan translation seems to be an apt term, since bilingual speakers have operated on the basis of a transparent link between Form A in Turkish and Form B in Dutch, both with Meaning X. The effect of the various examples we have seen is more lexical than structural. In the examples that follow, however, bound morphemes are involved, and their meaning is more grammatical than lexical, and hence their effect is more like structural borrowing than like loan translation. The question is: where does loan translation end and structural interference begin?

5.4.3   Loan translations involving grammatical morphemes

In (18), accusative marking is used instead of dative, but this should not be seen as an example of a generalized morpho-syntactic change. Rather, the change in case marking is the result of the translation of the Dutch expression: *iemand (iets) vragen* ("to ask somebody (something)"). Dutch construes the person who is being asked as a direct object, while Turkish marks it as an indirect object. In monolingual Turkish the meaning of (18) would be: "My mother asked for information about (the well-being of) her friends." Although no content morphemes are involved in this loan translation (in neither of the languages), some concrete translation of semantic content has nevertheless taken place, namely the construal of the Recipient (the person being asked) as a Direct Object.

(18) anne-m sor-du arkadaşları-**nı**
      mother-POSS-1SG ask-PAST.3SG friends-ACC
      "My mother asked her friends [something]."

In the following example, the use of the plural ending on the noun seems to be modeled on Dutch syntax, rather than on a particular Dutch plural noun. In fact, we come across this pattern quite often, especially when generic or categorial reference is intended. Dutch tends to use the plural ending in such cases (combined with the absence of an article), while Turkish normally uses a singular noun. In (19), it is unlikely that the whole noun phrase is a translation from Dutch; most likely it really is just the plural marking that is copied, in which case we have passed into the realm of foreign-modeled morpho-syntax. This, therefore, is not loan translation according to our definition. On the other hand, it illustrates that there is a scale from one realm to the other, since we might say that the plural meaning is translated from Dutch.

(19) hiç Türkçe kitap-**lar** oku-ya-mı-yor-um
      no Turkish book-**PL** read-ABIL-NEG-PRES-1SG
      "I can't read Turkish books."

If grammatical morphemes are used like their Dutch counterparts, the effect is often the extended use of a syntactic construction, since functional elements are not selected on their own. A case in point in our data is the distal, non-anaphoric use of the demonstrative pronoun, to encode some sort of "mental distance" from the referent of the noun that follows the pronoun, as in (20), in which the English translation indicates the connotation that is implied by the use of the deictic marker. This usage is copied from Dutch, in which demonstratives are often used in this way.

(20) yani kendi-m-i ifade etmek ist-er-se-m bile ed-e-mem çünkü *o* sözcük-
      ler-i bul-a-mam
      so self-POSS-ACC expression to.do want-AOR-COND-1SG even do-ABIL-AOR.
      NEG.1SG because those word-PL-ACC find-ABIL-AOR.NEG.1SG
      "So even if I want to express myself I can't because I can't find those damn words."

5.4.4 Loan translations involving discourse patterns

Finally, discourse patterns from the other language may be incorporated. These are generally better seen as cases of structural borrowing, but sometimes there is a clear lexical model. So, there are good arguments to group these under either loan translation or interference/transference. In the following question–answer sequence, the follow-up question (A2) follows an unconventional pattern that is similar to what is done in Dutch.

(21)   A1:   Ilke, sen daha çok yani Hollandaca konuş-uyo-sun değil mi gün-
lük hayat-ın-da sadece aile içerisinde Türkçe konuş-uyo-sun?
Ilke, you more so Dutch speak-PRES-2SGnot Q daily life-POSS.2SG.
LOC only family in Turkish speak-PRES-2SG
"Ilke, you speak more Dutch, isn't it, in daily life, only in the
family you speak Turkish?"

       B1:   evet sadece aile içerisinde.
yes only family in
"Yes, only in the family."

       A2:   ***ve arkadaş-lar-ın-la Türkçe*** [*sic*]
and friend-PL-POSS.2SG -with Turkish
"And with your friends Turkish?" [*sic*: "Dutch" is meant]

       B2:   ***ja***, arkadaş-lar-ım-la Türkçe [*sic*].
yes, friend-PL-POSS.1SG -with Turkish
"Yes, with my friends Turkish."

According to monolingual conventions the follow-up question (A2) would
require repetition of the finite verb of the main question (A1). It is probably
no coincidence, however, that this pattern co-occurs with the use of the
clause-initial conjunction *ve* "and," inspired by the Dutch convention of
starting such questions with *en* "and." In monolingual Turkish, this conjunction is not used much at all, especially not for the resumption of a
topic.

5.4.5   The translation process

What do all these examples have in common? The basis of any loan translation is an urge that a bilingual feels, consciously or not, to say something
in a base language in the way that it is said in the other language. This
much may be similar to the motivation for CS. Yet, for some reason, in loan
translation incorporating the full form from the other language is not
judged to be the right thing to do. Instead, the form is translated. This
can only be done if there is a transparent link between Form A in Language
X and Form B in Language Y, in the sense that they mean the same thing in
some way (see Sebba, this volume). This is, of course, not equivalence as
established by linguists, but is based on what speakers perceive to be
equivalent across the languages (Bolonyai 2000). The forms A and B are
translation equivalents, but this is not to be understood as "identical" in
meaning. In fact, by definition, loan translations alter the meaning of the
involved morpheme, since it is used in a novel way. For this reason, what
Weinreich (1953:51) calls "loan rendition" seems to be much more common than "real" loan translation (see Grzega 2003). In loan rendition, the
translation is not exact, but there is still a clear similarity in meaning
between the source form in the other language and the target form in
the native language.

5.5   Pervasiveness of loan translation

Loan translations may play a large role in creating the impression that immigrant varieties are different from their non-contact counterparts. It is not clear, though, how pervasive loan translations actually are. Do immigrant varieties seem different because there are so many of them, or are loan translations, when they occur, simply very salient and noticeable? Owens (1996) gives some indication of how widespread loan translation is in Nigerian Arabic. He mentions having collected some 200 idioms that deviate from other varieties of Arabic, in a corpus of about 500,000 words. However, Owens limited his investigations to clearly idiomatic combinations, and left the more modest forms of semantic extension out of his analysis. Therefore, it is possible that the pervasiveness of the phenomenon in his corpus is underestimated. Moreover, we should take into account that many loan translations may be under-identified since their deviation from the conventional norm in the non-contact variety is so minimal that they cannot be detected, but that nevertheless they contribute to the perception of a variety that deviates considerably from monolingual norms. In any case, quantitative analyses are needed.

   Another unknown is the degree to which individual loan translations have spread to all or most idiolects in a given bilingual community. As far as we know, there is no information on this for situations of on-going language contact, but studies of past contact situations certainly show that, given time, a language can undergo serious semantic restructuring as the end result of calquing numerous expressions from another language (Ross 2001).

5.6   Final remarks

In this chapter, we have presented a classification of loan translations along a cline of abstractness, going from translations of specific meanings, as embedded in lexical items and fixed expressions, to translations of abstract, partially grammatical meanings, as embedded in functional elements that are themselves part of larger constructions. Imposing a strict boundary between loan translation and structural borrowing seems elusive. It is an empirical point whether the same cline can be filled in with data from other language pairs, with less or more typological distance, and in different sociolinguistic settings.

   At least two intriguing questions remain to be answered by further research:

(1.)   Since bilinguals have the possibility to choose between CS and loan translation (and the two co-occur frequently in our bilingual speech data), is it in any way predictable which form they will choose?

Our tentative answer is that most lexemes involved in loan translation are from the stock of the basic vocabulary. Relatively specific meanings, on the other hand, tend to be imported along with the morpheme expressing it, through CS (see Backus 2000; Dorleijn 2002). It remains to be seen, however, whether this suggestion can be upheld once a larger and more diverse set of data has been examined. It stands to reason, however, that faced with the task of planning an utterance containing a concept that is best expressed by a complex lexical item from the other language, speakers have a choice between overtly code-switching for that item or calquing it. For instance, if Turkish speakers in Holland wish to express a concept easily produced through a particular verb-object collocation in Dutch, e.g. *schuld geven* "blame give" ("to accuse"), then they have various possibilities for doing this. First, they can take both the noun and the verb from Dutch. Or they may take just one of these forms from Dutch and translate the other. Or they may produce the loan translation exemplified in (10) above. Bilingual data seem to indicate that all options occur, but that there are preferential patterns. Specifically, CS is most often used for nouns and verbs that do not belong to the basic vocabulary. Those that do belong to the basic vocabulary are subject to calquing. This suggests that basic vocabulary patterns with functional elements are being produced without much conscious attention, while specific vocabulary is consciously selected. Though it remains a problem how exactly we should distinguish between basic and specific vocabulary, we may eventually be able to establish a complementary distribution of CS and loan translation. This would considerably clarify the empirical basis of a theory of contact linguistics (see Weinreich 1953).

(2.)   Why are some elements translated and others not?

One possibility is that there exist, apart from semantic criteria, structural criteria also that would favor loan translation. Counting the loan translations in a limited set of bilingual Turkish–Dutch data has revealed a numerical preponderance of translated Object–Verb and Prepositional Phrase–Verb combinations (Dorleijn and van der Heijden 2000). Whether this is a coincidence, whether this applies only to Turkish–Dutch data or also to other language pairs, and what exactly the theoretical implications would be if indeed Object–Verb combinations were relatively "translation-prone," remains open for further investigation.

To conclude, we are aware of the fact that in this chapter we have raised more questions than we have answered, but we hope to have convinced the reader that the study of loan translations needs to be considered as an integral part of the study of CS behavior.

Note

1. The data used to illustrate language contact outcomes in this chapter are all taken from recordings of spontaneous conversations involving men and women who were born in Holland and were between 18 and 25 years old. Interviews were conducted by Ad Backus, Seza Doğruöz, and Margreet Dorleijn.

Part II

Social aspects of code-switching

6

Sociolinguistic factors in code-switching

Penelope Gardner-Chloros[1]

6.1 Introduction

Sociolinguistics is an extremely broad field within linguistics. It incorporates topics as different in scope as the study of policy in multilingual states, the role of "linguistic markets," the different linguistic behavior of women vs. men, middle-class vs. working-class and other social groups, and the analysis of individual conversations. Sociolinguistic factors are relevant to our understanding of code-switching (hereafter CS) at a variety of different levels, but obviously their impact at all these levels cannot be treated in one chapter. For the purposes of this chapter, a selective approach will be adopted to the study of relations between social factors and the speech of individuals, groups, or communities. The selection will draw on some of the macro-level factors as well as the micro-level ones, the purpose being to show how sociolinguistics can help us understand CS, as opposed to, say, factors deriving from linguistic similarities/dissimilarities between the varieties involved or psycholinguistic factors.

It is argued here that CS should be considered first and foremost from a sociolinguistic perspective, that is to say from a perspective where language behavior and use are related to speakers' (social) identity and characteristics, or to aspects of their social life in the broad sense. There are several reasons for this. First, the study of CS developed in tandem with the study of sociolinguistics and has therefore evolved in response to similar developments. Sociolinguistics took off in the 1970s and 1980s, when, particularly following the work of Labov, the study of "natural" vernacular speech, bearing in mind the Observer's Paradox, became a focus for linguistic study. This is not to say that nobody had studied language, or even CS, in a naturalistic context before that (see Benson 2001, on the neglected early history of CS), but such studies as existed were "one-offs" rather than part of a trend. This changed with studies of CS carried out by Blom and Gumperz (1972) and Gumperz (1982a), from an ethnographic perspective on the one hand, and of Poplack (1980) from a grammatical perspective on the other. Both used data collected in natural conversational settings in order to analyze different aspects of CS.

Secondly, CS is in fact a construct derived from the behavior of bilinguals. In observing the daily interactions of people in plurilingual communities, linguists noticed that such speakers often appeared to be drawing on two or more different varieties and combining them in socially meaningful ways. Although, as this volume shows, CS is now studied from a number of different perspectives and with different methodologies, the primary source of data remains in the sociolinguistic arena.

Thirdly, as will be argued here, sociolinguistic factors are the prime source of variation in CS behavior. This can be seen most clearly in relation to the grammatical patterning of CS in different communities. Although there is evidence that different typological combinations favor different ways of combining varieties within the sentence (Muysken 2000), the same languages can be combined in radically different ways grammatically speaking when, for example, speakers of different generations are involved, or when the languages are combined in an immigrant, as opposed to a native multilingual, setting.

At a time when sociolinguistic approaches are sometimes under attack for positing correlations between language and society which are too simplistic and positivistic (Williams 1992; Cameron 1990), it is worth bearing in mind that such approaches retain some considerable explanatory power, which can provide a first step towards understanding the significance of CS in social life. In this chapter, various ways in which CS can be elucidated with reference to sociolinguistic factors will be reviewed. For example, studies that consider CS in relation to gender will be discussed, so as to clarify whether, and in what ways, the two can be related. The conclusion, however, warns against using sociolinguistic parameters in too direct a way as an explanation of CS.

6.2   Types of factor

A wide range of factors determine whether or not CS occurs at all in a given language contact situation. From a sociolinguistic point of view, three types of factor contribute to the form taken by CS in a particular instance:

1. Factors independent of particular speakers and particular circumstances in which the varieties are used, which affect all the speakers of the relevant varieties in a particular community, e.g. economic "market" forces such as those described by Bourdieu (1991), overt prestige and covert prestige (Labov 1972; Trudgill 1974), power relations, and the associations of each variety with a particular context or way of life (Gal 1979).

2. Factors directly related to the speakers, both as individuals and as members of a variety of subgroups: their competence in each variety, their social networks and relationships, their attitudes and ideologies, their self-perception and perception of others (Milroy and Gordon 2003).
3. Factors within the conversations where CS takes place: CS is a major conversational resource for speakers, providing further tools to structure their discourse beyond those available to monolinguals (Auer 1998).

There are many overlaps and inter-relations between the three sets of factors, and some understanding of all three is necessary in order to understand why particular CS patterns arise. The classification above provides a semblance of order within the huge range of factors that attach neither to the varieties themselves as linguistic entities, nor to cognitive/psycholinguistic factors that affect the individual. For example, the individual's competence in the relevant varieties is a product of their (reasonably permanent) psycholinguistic make-up; at the same time, it has sociolinguistic implications, as it is closely connected with factors such as age, network and identity. Thus, whether or not a second or third generation member of the Chinese community on Tyneside can converse fluently in Chinese determines the extent to which they can take part in conversations with the oldest members of the community, who may be to all intents and purposes monolingual Chinese speakers. At the same time, their social networking with people their own age is also partly determined by their linguistic abilities, and their association with English or Chinese speakers is likely to reinforce their preferences and abilities in those languages (Milroy and Li Wei 1995; Li Wei 1998).

6.3   Macrolinguistic approaches

As sociolinguistics covers a wide range of issues, CS can be studied at the level of multilingual societies (e.g. India), right down to the inter-individual and idiolectal level. Gumperz and Hernández (1971) wrote that, "CS occurs whenever minority language groups come into close contact with majority language groups under conditions of rapid social change." In the next section a few of the broader-based studies are described.

Heller (1988a) was perhaps the first volume in which CS was treated principally as a broad societal phenomenon. Heller's own paper (1988b) shows how CS can be used to manage and avoid conflict when different varieties are associated with different roles in a society. She gives examples from a Montreal company and a school in Toronto to show how CS allows people to gain access to different roles or "voices" by switching from French to English or vice versa, and thereby exploit various ambiguities inherent in the situation. In the same volume, Woolard (1988) describes the use by a comedian, Eugenio, of Catalan–Castilian CS in Barcelona, not as a test of ingroup membership but rather as a way of addressing two audiences at once and thereby *leveling*, rather than maintaining, the boundary between them; and McConvell (1988) describes switching between dialects of an aboriginal language, Gurindji, and English in terms of the inter-related social "arenas" where these are used.

Gal's (1988) chapter points out that CS often involves one state-supported and one stigmatized minority language. Vernacular linguistic forms continue to be used because they represent a form of resistance to domination, so such patterns of use do not simply *reflect* the socio-political situation, they help to shape it. The latter point is an important one. Several others have also pointed out that traditional sociolinguistics tends to present the stratification which it portrays in society (e.g. class or gender based) as if it were the result of a consensus, and thereby to gloss over the fact that the observable differences may in fact embody conflict or dissatisfaction (Williams 1992; Cameron 1990; Pujolar 2001). As Cameron (1990:57) puts it, "The language reflects society account implies that social structures somehow exist before language, which simply 'reflects' or 'expresses' the more fundamental categories of the social."

6.3.1 Diglossia, markedness theory, and networks

Ferguson's description of certain linguistic situations as "diglossic" (1959, reprinted in Li Wei 2000), continues to form a useful basis for discussing bilingual situations. This is not because the diglossic communities described by Ferguson are unchanged – the description was not totally accurate even when first written – but because these proposals focused attention on the functional differences between different varieties of the same language and provided a set of structural parameters which allowed one situation to be compared with another. Language use in bidialectal situations – the model was subsequently extended by others to bilingual ones – is described in terms of complementary domains[2] of usage, of the varieties' relative prestige, their role in official life, religion, education, and literature. The schema was the subject of significant amendments by Fishman (1965, 1967, also reprinted in Li Wei 2000). Breitborde (1983) subsequently pointed to some difficulties with connecting the abstract notion of domain with its impact in actual interactions: the features which make up a domain are rarely a perfect fit, so in each case some aspects are likely to be more significant than others. The concept of diglossia was specifically related to CS by Myers-Scotton (1986). Myers-Scotton also developed the concept of markedness in order to explain the socio-psychological motivations for CS, using data collected in various settings in Africa, Kenya in particular (1983, 2002b). It was suggested that in any given situation, a language choice could be either unmarked (i.e. the expected choice for this speech act) or marked (i.e. a choice which contributes in some way to the message because it is unexpected, and therefore carries particular implications or associations).

Li Wei et al. (2000) proposed social networks as an alternative means of relating CS and the language choices of individuals to the broader social, economic, and political context. They claim that a social (as opposed to sociolinguistic) theory that associates network patterns with the sub-groups that emerge from political, social, and economic processes remains to be developed. Højrup's (1983) division of the population into sub-groups described in terms of different "life-modes" provides one possibility. Li Wei et al. found that these life-modes corresponded well with the linguistic behavior of members of different types of network in their study of the Tyneside Chinese.

6.3.2 Comparisons between and within communities

One of the challenges posed by CS is to explain the variation within it, or, viewed another way, to decide how broadly it should be defined. It has been defined here as inclusively as possible, because, in the present state of knowledge, it has not been demonstrated that the differences between CS and other language contact phenomena are categorical differences as opposed to differences of degree. CS merges with lexical borrowing at one end of the scale, one of the most "minimal" manifestations of contact, and with convergence/interference/code-mixing at the other end, which can be seen as the last step before total fusion. If the process of language contact always started and ended in the same way and always proceeded along a similar path, it would be easier to divide it into distinct phases. Instead, our task is a messier one, namely, to try and apprehend the variations involved and to tie them in with the factors that may help explain this variety. Variation in CS can be divided for practical purposes into variation between communities and variation within communities or groups.

6.3.2.1 Variation between communities

Making systematic comparisons between CS in different language combinations and different contexts is the best way to elucidate the contribution of typological factors on the one hand, and sociolinguistic ones on the other, to the patterns of CS in different communities. So far, only a few such comparisons are available. On the whole, researchers base their discussions of CS on their own data, collected in a single community, and do not have access to comparable data sets from other communities. The LIPPS Project has set up a database of CS texts coded according to a common protocol and thus facilitating such comparisons (Barnett et al. 2000). Meanwhile, some existing comparisons between communities or sub-groups are discussed below. Treffers-Daller (1994, 1999), Cheshire and Gardner-Chloros (1998), and Muysken (2000), also employ a comparative approach.

6.3.2.2   Comparisons between communities

6.3.2.2.1   McClure and McClure (1988)

McClure and McClure (1988) took a broader perspective than in much CS research when they described a multilingual Saxon community in Romania in terms of the macrolinguistic relationships between the groups. The Saxon and Romanian communities are quite separate, but unlike other minority groups, the Saxons do not occupy a subordinate position vis à vis the majority. Consequently, their CS is more limited in type than that described elsewhere. Situational switching, mainly dictated by changes in participant, is dominant over the conversational variety. Where the latter does occur, its main function is to highlight quotations.

McClure (1998) compared written CS – a more common phenomenon than might be supposed[3] – between English and the national languages in Mexico, Spain, and Bulgaria. The characteristic type of CS encountered in each of these countries reflects the functions of and attitudes toward English. In Mexico and Spain, English is widely known, and is used in the press in various expressions denoting concepts expressed more economically in English or using "English" concepts (e.g. "Latin lover"). But in Mexico, which shares a border with an English-speaking country and resents the latter's economic and cultural domination, CS is functionally richer than in the other two settings. It is used in ironic contexts to reflect a certain rejection of the US culture, as for example in the use of "by the way" in this quotation from the Mexican press:

(1)   La hipocresia norteamericana no estriba tanto en los lamentos exagerados por la muerte de un agente de la DEA, y en la indiferencia o incluso el desprecio ante la muerte de decenas de agentes mexicanos (o, **by the way**, de miles de civiles panameños).
"The North- American hypocrisy does not rest so much on the exaggerated laments over the death of an agent of the DEA, and on the indifference or even the scorn with respect to the death of tens of Mexican agents (or, by the way, thousands of Panamanian civilians)."
(*Proceso*, January 15, 1990; cited in McClure 1998:141).

By contrast, in Bulgaria English has increasingly been used, since the fall of the Communist regime, as a symbol of the West, a cultural and economic world to which many Bulgarians aspire. English is not yet sufficiently well known for more subtle uses of CS, but is widely present in advertising and in other documents, such as the "yellow pages" for Sofia.

6.3.2.2.2   Poplack (1988)

Poplack (1988) made a three-way comparison between data collected in the Puerto Rican community in New York (Poplack 1980) and a later data-set from five neighborhoods within the Ottawa–Hull community in Canada, which is divided by a river that constitutes both a geographic and a linguistic border (not in the dialectologist's sense of "isogloss," but in a sociolinguistic sense). On the Quebec side (Hull), French is the official and majority language, and on the Ontario side (Ottawa), it is a minority language. The comparison is of particular interest as the differences between the communities cannot be attributed to linguistic factors but only to the different status of French in the two communities. The method of data collection and the definition of what constituted CS was the same in both cases. For the purposes of this study, Poplack considered as CS the use of English material in the context of French conversations (i.e. in practice she operated with the notion of French being the *base language*). In keeping with her view as to the demarcation line between CS and borrowing (Poplack and Sankoff 1984), she did not count as CS single English words that were morphologically or phonologically integrated with French.

The most striking finding was that in the Ottawa communities, where French is a minority language, CS was "three to four times as frequent" as in Hull, i.e. the stronger influence of English in the environment was directly reflected in the amount of CS (Poplack 1988:226). The same switch-types were found in both communities, but the distribution of the four main types was radically different. In both communities the most common switches were *mot juste* switches, switches for metalinguistic comments, switches where the English intervention is flagged, as in (2a), and switches in the context of explaining/translating. This points to a fairly self-conscious use of English in both cases, with switches in Quebec being largely restricted to metalinguistic commentary, which, as Poplack points out, show the speaker's full awareness of using English, as in (2b).

(2)   (a.) Excuse mon anglais, mais les **odds** sont là
           "Excuse my English, but the odds are there."
     (b.) Je m'adresse en français, pis s'il dit "***I'm sorry***", ben là je recommence en anglais
           "I begin in French and if he says, 'I'm sorry,' well then I start over in English."

Poplack comments that this reflects the fact that in Hull people believe that good French must of necessity exclude Anglicisms.

6.3.2.2.3   Reasons underlying the differences

The comparison with Puerto Ricans in New York is less direct. There is a wide range of differences between the two situations, such as the fact that the Puerto Ricans are of immigrant origin, and these differences could account for the differences in the prevalent types of CS. We are also dealing with another language combination, but as Poplack points out the linguistic distance between English and Spanish is not much more remarkable than that between English and French. It is probably more significant that different data collection techniques were used, the Puerto Ricans being studied through participant observation, whereas the Canadian studies were conducted by means of interviews with out-group inter-viewers. The latter technique might mask the extent of CS and give rise to heightened purism on the speakers' behalf. Regardless of this, Poplack describes switching found in New York as fluent and varied, with many unflagged switches, as opposed to the limited, and more stilted, CS found in the two Canadian contexts. She ascribes this mainly to the fact that for the Puerto Ricans both languages are an intrinsic part of their identity and of their communicative practices. The cohabitation of the two varieties within CS is a natural consequence of this integrated duality.

CS therefore arises, in different forms, in a wide variety of sociolinguis-tic circumstances. There are also, more unusually, communities that appear to shun it, as in the case described by Sella-Mazi (2001). This is the Muslim, Turkish-speaking community in Thrace (Greece), who were afforded a special status and elaborate protection of their linguistic rights under the Treaty of Lausanne (1923). Although the younger members of this community are perfectly fluent in Greek, they are described as avoid-ing CS, owing to a high level of awareness of the need to protect their language and culture from Greek influence. A second reason given is that the two languages are of widely differing importance in terms of speaker attitudes. A similar avoidance of CS between two of the languages spoken in Nigeria, Igbo and Yoruba, has been described in the literature (see Goglia 2006).

6.3.3 The Gumperz tradition

John Gumperz, whose early work on CS put the latter on the sociolinguistic map, investigated it in contexts ranging from Delhi to Norway, from the point of view of its historical genesis, its linguistic consequences, its signifi-cance for speakers, and its conversational functions (see Gafaranga, this volume). Here, the discussion concentrates on two aspects of his analysis which continue to be influential: the notions of *we-code* vs. *they-code*, and the distinction between *situational* and *conversational CS*. Much of Gumperz's earlier work on CS, originally published in less accessible sources, was recapitulated in *Discourse Strategies* (1982a), so for the sake of convenience most of the references here are to that volume.

6.3.3.1 *We-codes* and *they-codes*

Gumperz (1982b) suggested that as a direct consequence of diglossia the ethnically specific, minority language comes to be regarded as a *"we-code"* and to be associated with in-group and informal activities, whereas the majority language serves as the *"they-code,"* and is associated with more formal, out-group relations. However, he emphasized that the relationship between the occurrence of a particular set of linguistic forms and the non-linguistic context is indirect, and that there are only very few situations where one code exclusively is appropriate: "Elsewhere a variety of options occur, and as with conversations in general, interpretation of messages is in large part a matter of discourse context, social presuppositions and speakers' background knowledge (1982b:66)." In CS, the *we-code* and the *they-code* are often used within the same conversation, as in (3), in which a Punjabi–English bilingual talks to a friend about the likely loss of Punjabi culture in Britain.

(3)   culture tha aapna ... rena tha hayni **we know it, we know it, we know it's coming**
      culture [tha = stress marker] our ... stay [stress marker] is-not ...
      "Our culture is not going to last, we know it, we know it, we know it's coming."

                                        (Gardner-Chloros et al. 2000:1322)

The threat to Punjabi culture is poignantly embodied in the switch from the *we-code* to the *they-code* half way through the sentence, and by the use of the English word "culture."

From an early stage, variations on the *we-code/they-code* dichotomy were reported. Singh (1983) wrote that, although the minority language is usually the *we-code*, this is not always the case. In India, for example, speakers with social aspirations may use English as their *we-code* and Hindi with ironic intent, to show themselves to be a different kind of minority, whose apartness is based on privilege. Sebba and Wootton (1998) also state that even where there are two or three distinct codes available, a multiplicity of social identities may be evoked and manipulated through them, and the relationship between code and identity is far from being one to one. They illustrate the point by showing unexpected configurations of *we-* and *they-codes* in various contexts. Cantonese is the *we-code* in Hong Kong classrooms, where English is learned as an L2, but cannot be equated with an insider-code as Cantonese is the majority language. For British-born Caribbeans, London English and London Jamaican are both *we-codes*, since it is the ability to use *both* that characterizes the "Black British" speaker.

The *we-code/they-code* distinction also breaks down in situations such as that described in Meeuwis and Blommaert (1998). In the Congolese community in Belgium, CS can be a variety in its own right, with the same functions and effects as those usually attributed to "languages." In communities where this is the case, speakers vary in the extent to which they are able to speak the two varieties monolingually. All the national languages of Congo (Kinshasa) are spoken as CS varieties peppered with French (French being the official language in Congo). Lingala–French and Swahili–French CS varieties (Lingala and Swahili being the two most widespread national languages) have their own range of social, stylistic, and register-related variation. A similar situation is reported by Swigart (1992c) with respect to the CS variety known as Urban Wolof in Dakar. Such cases point to the dangers of viewing CS from a monolingual reference point in which meaning is seen as being negotiated through the interplay of two differentially marked "languages." Beyond this, there are cases where the *we-code/they-code* distinction completely fails to account for the variation and CS that are observed. Instead, the contrast between the two varieties is used to bring about "local" meanings in a variety of ways, only some of which make use of the associations of the two languages. Similar criticisms can be levelled at the markedness model (see above), which also assumes that each variety indexes fairly clear values in a given society, although Myers-Scotton does allow that CS itself may be the "unmarked choice."

The adoption of CS may in itself be an "act of identity," a fact which is clearly illustrated in the phenomenon known as "crossing" (Rampton 1995). Rampton describes adolescents in Britain using features of Punjabi and Creole in order to create a trans-racial "common ground." By contrast with other types of CS, crossing, according to Rampton (1995:280), "focuses on code-alternation by people who are not accepted members of the group associated with the second language they employ. It is concerned with switching into languages that are not generally thought to belong to you" (see also Hewitt 1986). Franceschini (1998:56–57) gives a bilingual example:

In a fashion house in Zurich, I am served by a ca. eighteen-year-old shop assistant in Swiss-German. After about ten minutes, a group of young men, obviously friends of the shop assistant, enter the shop. All of them use the common Swiss-German/Italian CS style, which is certainly not surprising. There is nothing unusual about the scene. The group seems to me to be one of many second-generation immigrant peer-groups. ... In order to exchange my purchase, I go to the same fashion house the following day. I am now served by the owner of the shop, a ca. forty-year-old Italian. In the course of our conversation, I am told that the shop assistant I overheard the previous day is not a second-generation Italian immigrant at all but a Swiss-German. She grew up in a linguistically strongly mixed area of the town and has had Italian friends since her school years.

The young shop assistant code-switches, not out of linguistic necessity, but in order to identify herself with a particular peer-group. However, CS due to necessity and CS as the product of choice, are not always easy to separate. Many instances of CS are combinations of the two, or somewhere on the border *between* the two. Auer (2005) shows that it is not always easy in practice to disentangle *discourse*-related CS from such displays of identity.

6.3.3.2 Situational and conversational CS

Equally influential with the *we-code/they-code* distinction was Gumperz's subdivision of CS into *situational* and *conversational* types. Situational CS occurs when distinct varieties are associated with changes in interlocutor, context, or topic, and is therefore a direct consequence of a diglossic distribution of the varieties. Conversational CS occurs when there are changes in variety without any such external prompting. Such switching is also termed *metaphorical* when the purpose of introducing a particular variety into the conversation is to evoke the connotations, the metaphorical "world" of that variety. Blom and Gumperz (1972) give the example of two villagers in a Social Security office in a Norwegian village, switching from Standard Norwegian to discuss business, to the local dialect to discuss family and village matters.

Although this type of switch and the compelling motivation for it are familiar to anyone who has observed CS in this type of minority situation, it was asserted by Mæhlum that the dialect and standard varieties taken as a prototype by Gumperz were in fact "Idealized entities" which in practice are subject to interference at different linguistic levels: "Most probably, the switching strategies which Blom and Gumperz recorded in Hemnes actually represent some form of *variant switching* whereby, in certain contexts, single words, (idiomatic) expressions and grammatical forms from the standard are introduced into otherwise dialectal utterances (1990:758)." Mæhlum claims that the misapprehension is due to the researchers' insufficient knowledge of the ins and outs of the dialectal situation in that area. Gumperz himself (1982a:62) remarked that recordings of informal conversations in the same town, which *speakers* claimed were conducted entirely in the local dialect, "revealed frequent conversational switching into standard Norwegian." Along with classic diglossia, situational CS appears to be a somewhat idealised notion, rarely found in practice.

6.4 Gender

Gender is considered one of the most important sociolinguistic categories. Studies of the interaction of gender with linguistic performance have become increasingly subtle, avoiding the broad generalizations of some earlier studies of the 1970s. Gender has assumed more prominence within the discipline rather than less, as the ways in which it is studied have become more diversified. Various studies show that CS cannot be correlated in any direct way with gender, but intersects with a large number of intervening variables which are themselves connected with gender issues. Following a brief survey, one study (Gardner-Chloros and Finnis 2004) is presented slightly more extensively to show how CS is woven in with female discourse strategies and discourse needs, via the notion of politeness.

6.4.1 CS and gender in various communities
The long-established finding that women use more standard forms than men (Labov 1972; Trudgill 1974; Chambers 2003) arose in monolingual

settings. In its simplest form, it can usefully be tested in bilingual contexts. First we need to know whether, in a given case, the choice of one or the other variety corresponds with a choice between the vernacular and the prestige code. In some cases, as we have seen, it is the CS mode itself that carries the "in-group" connotations and may be considered the "local" type of speech (Swigart 1992c).

Given the generally negative judgements of CS, a study was carried out to find out whether the widespread finding that women use more standard and less non-standard language than men was reflected by a clear gender difference in the amount of CS they used. The finding would gain support if women were found to code-switch substantially less than men (Cheshire and Gardner-Chloros 1998). Transcribed recordings from two immigrant communities in the UK, the Greek Cypriots and the Punjabis, were used to test the hypothesis. The results were negative – there were no significant differences between men and women in either community regarding the use of any kind of CS, though there were substantial differences *between* the two communities, both as regards quantity and type of CS. Other studies, however, *have* found differences in either the amount or the type of CS used by women and men within the same community (Poplack 1980; Treffers-Daller 1992). In a study in the Gambia, Haust (1995) found that men used CS twice as much as women, especially using discourse marker insertions, whereas women tended to change varieties outside the turn unit.

Such differing findings in different communities may be accounted for given the shift which has taken place within language and gender studies from essentialist to constructionist views (Winter and Pauwels 2000). As Swigart (1992c) argued, women, even *within* a given society, do not all behave as a monolithic group. Gender is no longer viewed as a fixed, stable, and universal category whose meaning is shared within or across cultures. It cannot be separated from other aspects of social identity and its meaning varies in different domains: "A non-essentialist view sees gender as a dynamic construct, which is historically, culturally, situationally, and inter-actionally constituted and negotiated (Winter and Pauwels 2000:509)." Conversely though, the variation within these findings should lead us to relativize the usual pattern of sex differentiation, which Chambers (2003) referred to as a "sociolinguistic verity." This can come about if we look not only at statistical information about how many instances of variable X are produced by women or men, but at the discourse context and the reasons why particular choices are made.

Furthermore, use of particular linguistic forms does not always signal the same underlying motivations. Traditionally polite or indirect forms do not necessarily indicate underlying compliance. Brown (1993) found that in Tenejapan society, even when women are not being polite in essence, characteristic female strategies of indirectness and politeness are nevertheless manifested in their speech. Brown suggests that this might help us make sense of the finding that women appear more cooperative than men in interaction. While cooperative strategies are being used, what is being achieved may be opposition and disagreement. But the way in which this is done in particular instances, the strategies which are typical of women or of men in specific communities, and the particular types of discourse where CS is brought to bear, are often associated with different genders in a given community.

6.4.2   CS, gender, and politeness

In Gardner-Chloros and Finnis (2004), the link between language and gender is explored by considering whether *certain specific functions* of CS are more common among women or men in the Greek Cypriot community. Findings from Cheshire and Gardner-Chloros (1998), mentioned above, provided a starting point. The earlier study did not eliminate the possibility that, although the overall switching rate between the sexes did not differ significantly, women and men were code-switching for very different purposes. Two sets of data were used: thirty interviews carried out in the London Greek Cypriot community (Gardner-Chloros 1992) and transcriptions of recordings carried out at meetings of a Greek Cypriot youth organization (Finnis 2008). These meetings were informal, and took place at a range of venues, including a community centre, a coffee shop, and the home of one of the participants. The participants were five males and five females between the ages of twenty-three and twenty-nine who had all completed higher education.

Sifianou's (1992) comparative study of politeness in England and Greece also proved a useful starting point. It was pointed out there that different cultures place emphasis on different values, values which are moreover interpreted differently. Basing her work on Brown and Levinson's (1999) theory of positive and negative politeness, Sifianou argued that, "Politeness is conceptualised differently and thus, manifested differently in the two societies; more specifically that Greeks tend to use more positive politeness devices than the English, who prefer more negative politeness devices (1992:2)." It is not the case that some cultures or societies are *more* polite than others. The difference is the quality, rather than the quantity of politeness strategies, in that speakers are polite in different, culturally specific, ways.

In particular, Greek speakers are more direct when it comes to making requests, when giving advice or making suggestions. The cultural norm in England requires a more distant code of behavior, and requests, among other speech acts, are expressed more elaborately and indirectly. Sifianou argues that, in England, requests are perceived to a greater extent as impositions, and as such, need to be accompanied by more elaborate politeness strategies. Therefore a variety of options are available to the interlocutor when making a request, allowing the imposition created by the request to be minimized, e.g. *You don't have a pen, do you?* (1992:140). In contrast, Greeks define politeness in very broad terms. Sifianou found that their definition included attributes that might be better described in English in terms of "altruism, generosity, morality, and self-abnegation" (1992:88). Greeks reported that "a warm look, a friendly smile, and in general a good-humoured disposition and pleasant facial expression are integral parts of polite behaviour (1992:91)." Her overall message is that English culture values distance, and Greek culture values intimacy.

This is supported by several examples in Gardner-Chloros and Finnis (2004), which indicate that, when being direct, Greek Cypriot speakers prefer to switch to Greek, as directness is more acceptable in Greek culture. This seems especially to be the case for women, of whom, as in many western societies, there is an expectation that they will be more polite and consequently more indirect than men. At the same time, because Greek is a more positively polite language, when being intimate, speakers may also prefer to use Greek. Similarly, Zentella (1997) notes that in the Puerto Rican community in New York, commands are often repeated in Spanish, after being delivered in English, in order to soften their impact or harshness.

Three of the functions that are noticeably associated with CS, which are labeled *humor*, *bonding*, and *dampening directness*, are illustrated below. There are significant overlaps between the three, which reinforces the idea that there is a general politeness function associated with CS. For different reasons that are discussed in each case, it was considered that these uses of CS were particularly typical of women in the community, though by no means exclusive to them:

(4)   CS used for *humor*
      1. M1[4] ... Happen to know anyone that has like a colour laser jet?
      2. F1   I know a place where they do.
      3. M1   Yeah.
      4. F1   ???
      5. M1   What make are they?
      6. F1   En ixero, en leptomeries.
             "I don't know, these are details."
         (general laughter)
                                    (Gardner-Chloros and Finnis 2004:524)

The speaker is relying on her interlocutors' familiarity with Greek culture, in that she adopts the "voice" of a particular Greek stereotype, that of a laid-back type who won't bother with too much detail. The fact that she is playing a part is indicated by a change in voice quality for the remark in Greek. In this way, she justifies her ignorance of the technical details of the photocopier by adopting a "voice" that represents this particular Greek attitude.

(5)   CS used for *bonding*
      CS was often used to indicate identification or intimacy. In the follow-
      ing example, the speakers are talking about a conference they are
      organizing. Speaker F1 suggests the topic of arranged marriages, a
      traditional aspect of Greek Cypriot culture. She refers to her own
      mother's concern about her finding a husband and getting married:
      1.   F1   Am I the only person that gets??? by their parents already?
      2.   M1   What, about getting married?
      3.   F1   Yeah, she started today.
      4.   F2   ???mana sou?
               "Your mother?"

                              (Gardner-Chloros and Finnis 2004:525)

In line 4, Speaker F2's intervention in Greek can be viewed as an act of
positive politeness, or identification with F1, as another female Greek
Cypriot. She uses the language of the culture in which such traditional
maternal attitudes towards the marital status of daughters prevail. Gender
therefore plays an important role in this switch. While the topic of marriage within the community is relevant to all its members, it has much
greater consequences for women, and, as such, requires more positive
politeness strategies in order to indicate solidarity.

(6)   CS used for *dampening directness*
      In this example, speaker F1, after asking the same question in English
      twice and failing to get a response from speaker M1, switches to Greek
      to elicit a response. Having succeeded in doing so, she then switches
      back to English.
      1.   M1   All right.
      2.   F1   Stop, how many days is the conference?
      3.   M1   Guys, I wanna finish at seven o'clock.
      4.   F1   I'm asking! How many days is the conference?
      5.   M1   ??? It's half past six.
      6.   F1   Kirie Meniko, poses imeres ine?
                         'Mr Meniko, how many days is it?'
      7.   M1   It will be around four days, I imagine.
      8.   F1   OK, four days, good … and what time?
                              (Gardner-Chloros and Finnis 2004: 527)

The potentially face-threatening act – an escalation of repeated questions
that had been phrased pretty directly from the beginning – is carried off
thanks to the switch to Greek, which not only allows greater directness but
is also the *we-code* and the language of humor. CS is shown to offer a
powerful toolkit for women in the community, who can get away with
jokes and strong repartee without appearing aggressive or unfeminine.
   Among the London Greek Cypriots, women seemed to make use of these
strategies to get around some of the traditional constraints on female

discourse, such as the expectation that it will be less forceful, pressing, or direct than that of men, or that making jokes is unfeminine. Women also use CS for solidarity in certain contexts that are directly relevant to them, e.g. in talking about mothers and their attitudes towards their daughters' marital status. It would not be surprising to find that, being more directly concerned, women talked about these issues more than men, and so had occasion to use these strategies to a greater extent.

To the extent that one can show that gender differences are contingent upon culturally determined norms, the role of gender as such is relativized. It is shown to be mediated by other factors, such as the power relationship between the speakers and the conventions governing behavior – which of course include gendered behavior – in the community. "We must criticize explanations of difference that treat gender as something obvious, static and monolithic, ignoring the forces that shape it and the varied forms they take in different times and places ... Feminism begins when we approach sex differences as constructs, show how they are constructed and in whose interests (Cameron 1992:40)."

6.5 Conclusion

Broadly, "sociolinguistic" approaches to CS are extremely varied and cover multiple levels of engagement with plurilingual data, from the societal to the intra-individual. Dividing these approaches up is a partly arbitrary exercise, since the societal level and the individual are in constant dynamic interaction. The issue of gender is a case in point: whereas one might think of it as a broad sociolinguistic differentiator, it turns out in practice to have some potential explanatory power only through its inter-action with finely tuned conversational factors which require a close knowledge of the community.

We should also bear in mind that CS is the plurilingual embodiment of techniques that have equivalents in the monolingual sphere (Gardner-Chloros et al. 2000). Theories linking the social phenomenon of register and style variation to individual performance are highly relevant to CS (see the papers in Eckert and Rickford 2001). Barrett (1998), for example, has illustrated style alternation, largely in phonological terms, amongst African-American drag queens, identifying three basic styles (African-American vernacular English, gay male style, and a style based on stereotypes of white women's speech) and showing how the subjects' performances are "tuned" to highlight the audience's assumptions about sex, class, and ethnicity.

The concept of "audience design" developed by Bell (1984, 1997) and Coupland (1985) can help explain many cases of why bilinguals code-switch. Speakers may for example explicitly account for their own CS with reference to similar CS on behalf of their interlocutor. A speaker recorded in a Strasbourg insurance office during the course of a working day switched between several different styles of CS and monolingual speech depending on her audience (Gardner-Chloros 1991:92–94). The effect of audience design/accommodation on CS is also well illustrated in Zhang (2005), where callers to a radio phone-in program in a bi-dialectal area of China are addressed in Cantonese by the host unless they themselves reply in Putonghua, in which case the host switches to match. It is to be hoped that in the future there will be more studies systematically comparing CS and dialect- as well as style/register-shifting.

More recently, the linguistic *styles* adopted by individuals have become an important focus of interest in sociolinguistics. Broad, quantitative approaches that obscure the differences between individuals are being put into perspective by approaches such as that of Eckert (2000) based on the notion of "community of practice." This notion too could prove extremely useful in relation to CS: research has shown that CS is only in exceptional cases to be understood as alternation between externally defined "languages," and more often represents an amalgam determined by the individual as rooted in their community practices.

To sum up, we have seen that CS embodies, or corresponds with, a wide range of sociolinguistic factors that interact or operate simultaneously. We should therefore be wary of ascribing particular "reasons" to particular instances of CS, as these are likely to present only a partial picture. Methodologically speaking, this dictates a pluralistic, interdisciplinary approach, in which, ideally, both quantitative and qualitative methods are combined, and the research is "triangulated." CS is indeed a major sociolinguistic indicator, but we should not underestimate the complexity of its interaction with the numerous factors that allow individuals to produce discourse "in their own image."

Notes

1. Sections of this Chapter will appear as Chapters 3 and 4 of *Code-switching*, by the same author, Cambridge: Cambridge University Press, forthcoming. CUP's permission to reprint these sections is acknowledged with thanks.
2. Fishman defines domains in terms of "institutional contexts and their congruent behavioral co-occurrences," e.g. family, employment (1972:441).
3. CS in written texts occurs copiously nowadays in advertising all over the world, and in email and text messaging. Before the spread of nationhood and compulsory education in the nineteenth century, it was found in texts of all kinds, from sermons to poetry to personal letters.
4. In this study M1 indicates the first male speaker, M2 the second male speaker, F1 the first female speaker, etc. "???" indicates inaudible speech.

7

The Conversation Analytic model of code-switching

Joseph Gafaranga

7.1 Introduction

The term Conversation Analysis (CA), as Have (1999) notes, can be used in two different ways. Used in a broad sense, it can "denote any study of people talking together, 'oral communication' or 'language use'." And, used in a more restricted sense, "it points to one particular tradition of analytic work" on talk-in-interaction (Have 1999:5). This chapter is concerned with the latter sense of CA. However, it is important to note from the outset that the availability of these two understandings of the same term leads to a situation where some researchers might claim to be working within the CA paradigm while others may not recognize their work as CA at all. The situation becomes even more confusing in the case of Applied CA (see Have 1999; Richards 2005) where researchers claim not to be conducting CA as such, but rather only to be using it.

The aim of this chapter is twofold. First, it will discuss the key aspects of the CA "mentality" (Schenkein 1978), including its intellectual background, its aims, and its procedures. Second, it will show how those general aspects of the CA mentality have been retained in current CA work on bilingual conversation. Previous accounts of the CA perspective on code-switching (hereafter CS) have been proposed by Li Wei (1998, 2002, 2005) among others. Particularly interesting in Li Wei's work is the comparison and contrast he draws between the CA perspective and other approaches to CS. But in this chapter, no comparison of the models will be attempted so as to focus solely on the CA perspective.

7.2 The CA mentality

CA has been described as a "mentality" (Schenkein 1978), as an "attitude" (Psathas 1995), and as a "style of work" (Wooffitt 2005). By characterizing

CA in this way, these authors emphasize the fact that CA practitioners do not follow any fully established theory. Indeed one of the most striking features of CA is that it has consistently resisted theorizing its object. The fact that there is no fixed CA theory has attracted criticisms of all sorts, out of a lack of proper understanding of its goals. For the present purpose of presenting an overview of the CA mentality, the fact that it has no fully developed theory presents a descriptive difficulty. That is, CA resists summarizing. Because the body of CA knowledge consists of a variety of research findings that have not been put together into one coherent whole, any summary will necessarily give preference to certain aspects over others. This chapter is no exception. Only those aspects that are considered most important for a CA model of CS will be discussed.

To begin to understand the CA mentality, it is important to place it in its intellectual and historical context. CA's original disciplinary home is sociology. This sociology background is obvious in the often-cited passage below from Sacks (1984):

So the question was, *could there be some way that* **sociology** *could hope to deal with the details of actual events, formally and informatively* (...) It was not from any large interest in language or from some formulation of what should be studied that I started with tape-recorded conversations, but simply because I could get my hands on it.   (Sacks 1984:26, my emphasis)

That is to say, in analyzing conversations, Sacks and colleagues were hoping to contribute to sociology. Nowadays, CA methods have been adopted in other disciplines, including linguistics, anthropology, and psychology.

A major consequence of its origin in sociology on current CA work is that, despite its expansion to other disciplines, its main concern remains unchanged. The aim of CA is to study "the order/organization/orderliness of social action, particularly those social actions that are located in everyday interaction, in discursive practices, in the sayings/tellings/doings of members of society" (Psathas 1995:2). The two main assumptions of this formulation of the object of CA must be made explicit. First, CA starts from the assumption that *talk is social action*, i.e. that people do things while talking. In assuming that talk is action, conversation analysts are not alone; Speech Act theorists such as Austin (1965) and Searle (1969) have long held the same position. According to Speech Act Theory, while talking, people accomplish acts such as promising, agreeing, and threatening. Consider line 1 below.

(1)   1.   D: Didju hear the terrible news?
      2.   R: No. What?
      3.   D: Y'know your Grandpa Bill's brother Dan?
      4.   R: He died.
      5.   D: Yeah.
                   (Terasaki 1976; cited in Levinson 1983:350)

From a grammatical point of view, line 1 is a question, which receives an answer in line 2. From a pragmatic and CA perspective on the other hand, line 1 is a *pre-announcement*. Also consider the grammatical question in turn 3 in example (2) below:

(2) 1. C: Right. hh .hh (.) Erm: (0.5) You've come just for an HIV te:[st
     2. P: [uh-hum
     3. C: .hh (.4) **Can I just ask you briefly:: (.2) erm: one or two questions before we start**..hh Have you ever had a test before,
     4. P: N:o
     5. C: No. .hhh Have you ever injected drugs?
     6. P: No
     (2.0)
     7. C: Have you ever had a homosexual relationship?
     (.5)
     8. P: No

(Silverman 1997:49–50)

If we took the highlighted item merely as a question, we would be faced with the problem of why it does not receive any answer. On the other hand, if we view talk as action, then we must ask what act is accomplished by the highlighted element. If we do so, the problem of the absence of an answer disappears. Following Schegloff (1980), Silverman analyzes the above instance as a *preliminary*, an act through which "a speaker projects some type of action by mentioning something they will do (. . .) or something they would like the recipient to do" (Silverman 1998:157). In other words, in the example, C is not asking a question as such (despite the grammatical form), but rather telling P what she is going to do. Therefore, no answer is necessary.

However, although both Speech Act Theory and CA are interested in what people do, they are interested in them in ways that are significantly different. While Speech Act Theory focuses on showing the various ways in which the same action can be accomplished, CA considers actions vis-à-vis other actions in the same conversation, hence the notion of *organization*. Consider the following opening of a Doctor–Patient consultation.

(3) 1. D: **So what can I do for you then?**
     2. P: Oh.
     3. D: **What's the problem?**
     4.   (0.2)
     5. P: I've got rashes.

(Gafaranga and Britten 2005:83)

The highlighted two items are both attempts by D to get P to display his presenting problem. They are, according to Gafaranga and Britten (2003, 2005), *first concern elicitors*. In other words, both questions are doing the same work. Speech Act Theory would be interested in the fact that turns 1 and 3 are two ways of accomplishing the same action. In contrast, from a CA perspective, what is important is not that 1 and 3 are two ways of doing the same action (requesting), but rather why both are used. A CA analysis of the situation is that the question in turn 3 is produced because no answer has been obtained following the question in turn 1. To use Goffman's words, CA is interested in the "syntactical [*sic*] relations among the acts of different persons mutually present to one another" (1967:2). Its interest is in inter-action.

The second assumption that underlies CA work is that *talk is an orderly activity*. In this context, the job of the analyst is to describe that order. Consider example (4):

(4) 1. D; right. okay. And what can I do for you today?
     2. P: you- my blood test er from er my gout ((laughs))
     3. D: right. yes yes yes. th:e uric acid is- is high
     4. P: it is. yeah

(Gafaranga and Britten 2005:83)

In turn 1, through the use of the first concern elicitor "What can I do for you?", D proposes to see the interaction as a new consultation. However, the patient, presenting with a concern for which he has already seen the doctor, sees it as a follow-up consultation, hence the use of the "retrospective tying reference" (Firth 1995) "my" in "my blood" and "my gout." This clash of interpretation leads to a delicate situation, hence the laughter. In turn, in 3, D acknowledges being reminded through the repetition of "Yes." In other words, D's actions in turn 3 are intelligible only with reference to P's action in turn 2, and P's action itself is intelligible with reference to D's action in turn 1. Conversation analysts refer to this connectedness of conversational participants' actions as *sequentiality*. Talk-in-interaction, they maintain, is organized sequentially, step-by-step, turn-by-turn and their analysis itself is often referred to as *sequential analysis*.

CA proposes emic accounts of order in talk-in-interaction. Pike (1967) makes a distinction between *etic* and *emic* perspectives on human behavior. In an etic perspective, one approaches human behavior from outside, while in an emic perspective, one approaches it from inside. An emic perspective on talk is the participants' own viewpoint. In an emic approach it is necessary to ask: what does this observable mean for participants themselves? Take the phenomenon of openings in general practice consultation. Gafaranga and Britten (2005) argue that there is order here, for it is possible to distinguish consultations which open with "How are you?" (follow-up consultation) and those which open with "What can I do for you?" (new consultation). As seen in example 4, when the doctor used "What can I do for you?", the patient noticed its inappropriateness and went on to propose a redefinition of the consultation.

The possibility of an emic perspective and the strength of a sequential analysis are both built on the assumption that conversational orders are *resources* that participants draw on in organizing their interaction. That is to say, conversational orders are not mere products of the analyst's imagination. Rather they are tools that are available for participants themselves to use. As the last two examples show, the order of the opening sequence is something participants themselves use in achieving an orderly entry into the consultation. This assumption is so important for the CA mentality that it deserves further discussion. Garfinkel and Sacks (1970) discuss a conversational phenomenon they refer to as *formulation*, which consists of summarizing the gist of the immediately preceding talk (Heritage and Watson 1979). As research shows, formulation is one of the resources that participants in a conversation use to negotiate orderly exit from a topic. Therefore, while talking, participants constantly monitor each other for closing implicative activities and react accordingly. Alternatively, they display them in their own talk for the benefit of their interlocutors. Consider example (5) below from a general practice consultation.

(5) 1. D: What can I do for you?
     2. P: The pain in my chest and belly. (0.2) E:r I;t's not going away. No matter what I'm doing even I can't eat properly now.
     3. D: [Right
     4. P: [I just er- I can't eat because every time I eat the pain starts. I mean last night I couldn't even stand up straight (0.2) So I'm sorry but I don't- can't see it being just muscular pain.
     5. D: Right. Right
     6. P: F- I'm sick all the time. Feeling sick all the time now and I've got a belly ache (0.2) so-
     7. D: **So you're ha- having a lot of problem**
     8. P: Yeah
     9.   (0.4)
     10. D: Where about's- is the- this pain then?

(Gafaranga and Britten 2005:156)

Through the formulation in turn 7, D shows understanding of P's presenting concern and, by implication, opens the possibility for talk on this topic to be closed. In 8, P ratifies that understanding and abstains from any further talk. And after a short silence, D takes the turn (10) and initiates another topic. In other words, this is a successful and concerted exit by means of a formulation.

Where do conversational resources derive their value from? In other words, how can participants be confident that, in using conversational resources such as formulation, interlocutors will understand their meanings as intended? The answer to these questions resides in another CA assumption, namely the *normative* nature of conversational orders. Each conversational structure works as "a scheme of interpretation" (Garfinkel 1967), or as "a grid" with reference to which actions are interpreted (Heritage 1984) either as normative or as deviant.

To summarize, some, although by no means all, assumptions of the CA mentality include the following:

- The aim is to describe talk organization.
- Talk is viewed as action.
- Talk activities are organized sequentially.
- Talk organization is described from an emic perspective.
- Aspects of talk organization are viewed as resources for conversational participants.
- A normative framework gives value to conversational resources, thus allowing their meaningful use.

The section below examines how these different aspects of the CA mentality have been used in the study of CS.

7.3   CA model of code-switching

Torras and Gafaranga (2002) use the representation in Figure 7.1 to capture different approaches to CS. The CA model corresponds to the node *Organizational explanation.*

As stated above, the first assumption of CA is that talk is action, that, while talking, people accomplish a variety of activities. Therefore, a CA approach to language alternation views language choice itself as an activity. In this respect, Auer (1988:167) writes:

I propose then to examine bilingualism primarily as a set of complex linguistic activities … We need a model of bilingual conversation which provides a coherent and functionally motivated picture of *bilingualism as a set of linguistic activities.*

One aim of CA, as we have seen, is to account for the orderliness of talk organization. In the case of CS, the main research agenda is to investigate

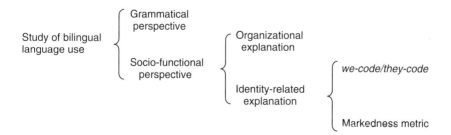

Figure 7.1 Approaches to language alternation in bilingual conversation

the role of CS in the organization of bilingual conversation. Auer, for example, sees CS as fulfilling a "discourse-related" function, which he defines as "the use of code-switching to organize the conversation" (1998:4). Likewise, Gafaranga (1999) states that language choice is "a significant aspect of talk organization," while Alfonzetti (1998:186) maintains that CS "can be exploited to cope with the several tasks related to the organization of conversation itself." Many studies conducted from a CA perspective support these general statements. Studies have shown that, in bilingual conversation, CS contributes to many of the aspects of talk organization that CA studies of monolingual conversation have described. These include turn-taking, preference organization, repair, and side-sequences. Consider the following extract from a Chinese–English dinner-table interaction between a mother (A) and her daughter (B).

(6) 1. A: Oy-m-oy a? A Ying a?
              "Want rice or not rice?"
     2. B: (No response)
     3. A: Chaaufaan a. Oy-m-oy?
              "Fried rice. Want or not?"
     4. B: (2.0) I'll have some shrimps.
     5. A: Mut-ye? (.) Chaaufaan a.
              "What? Fried rice."
     6. B: Hai a.
              "OK."

(Li Wei 1994:86)

In turn 1, A makes an offer, and in turn 2, B fails to accept or reject the offer. Such noticeable absences of a response after an offer are often interpreted as potential rejections. After such anticipated rejections, as Davidson (1984, 1990) shows, speakers often formulate *second versions*, presenting the offer in a more attractive way. This is precisely what happens in 3. After this upgraded offer, B has no option but to reply, either explicitly accepting the offer or rejecting it. Studies in CA show that, after an offer, the preferred response is acceptance, while rejection is dispreferred. They also show that dispreferred second parts are flagged by *dispreference markers* (Pomerantz 1984), including prefaces, delays, and accounts. In the example above, at least one of these dispreference markers is used, namely delay in the form of a two-second pause. In addition to the pause, language alternation occurs as a further signal of dispreference. In this case, switching from Chinese to English contributes to preference organization.

Recall that another important assumption of CA is sequentiality. As a turn may consist of different units, known as *turn constructional units* (Sacks et al. 1978), sequential analysis also requires viewing each unit relative to immediately preceding and immediately following units. Auer (2000:137) remarks:

I want to argue that … we should look at language choice on a turn-by-turn level in order to do justice to bilingual participants' conversational practices. This means describing and explaining patterns of conversational code choice on a local basis, i.e. by analysing speakers' language choices for one particular turn, or turn constructional unit, with reference to language choices directly or indirectly preceding it, as well as in their consequences for language choices in the turns to follow.

By way of an illustration of the sequentiality of language alternation, consider the choice of Catalan and Spanish in (7) below. Conversation takes place between a receptionist (REC) and an enquirer (EN) at a town hall reception area in Barcelona.

(7) 1. REC: *Bon dia senyora.*
         "Good morning madam."
     2. EN: Mire quería hacer una pregunta # a ver # ¿para inscribir al
         niño al instituto de aquí?
         "I would like to ask you a question # let's see # how do I
         register my son for secondary school here?"
     3. REC: Directamente al instituto # ¿está empadronado aquí el
         chico? "Just at the secondary school # was the boy
         registered here?"

                                          (Gafaranga and Torras 2001:201)

This is a case of what researchers refer to as *implicit language negotiation* (Auer 1995; Codó 1998; Torras 1998). In turn 1, REC greets the customer in Catalan. In 2, the customer moves to a service request without returning the greeting and she uses Spanish. Against the background of Catalan in 1, the choice of Spanish in 2 must be seen as divergent, a necessary condition for language negotiation (Auer 1984, 1998). In turn 3, REC answers EN's question in Spanish, shifting from her own choice of Catalan in 1. That is to say, REC takes EN's action in 2 to be a request to use Spanish as the medium of the encounter and grants it in 3. Thus, participants' actions are organized sequentially because the value of EN's action in 2 is understood against the background of REC's action in 1 and is confirmed by REC's action in 3.

   Further, CA takes an emic perspective on the orderliness of talk as social action. The short analysis of extract (7) above begins to give a flavor of what an emic perspective on language alternation looks like. The analysis has revealed, not simply what the analyst thinks about language choice in the instance, but what participants themselves have taken it to mean. To further illustrate the emic perspective on language alternation, consider the following instance of *medium repair* (Gafaranga 2000):

(8) Kinyarwanda (normal font)–French (***bold italics***)–English (**bold
     underlined**)
     1. A: Nonelıo rero nka bariya b' impunzi ukuntu bigenda (.) babagira
        ba (.) a a amashuri hano ni ***privé*** *quoi* (.) ni ***privé*** mbega (.)

kuburyo rero kugirango aze muri iyi **université** agomba kwishyura.

"Refugees like him are (.) schools here are private (.) they are private so that he must pay to study at this university."

2. B: umh

3. A: **Mais comme** nta mafaranga afite ay yatse **bourse le** (.) babyita **local government.**

"But as he doesn't have money he has had to apply for a grant from the (.) they call it local government."

4. B umh

5. A: **Local authority** *donc* ni nkaaa.

"Local authority well it's like ..."

6. B: Ni nka **municipalité.**

"It's like a municipality."

7. A: Ni nka **municipalité c'est ça** (.) **municipalité** yahano niyo yamuhaye **bourse.**

"That's right it's like a municipality (.) he got a grant from the local municipality."

(Gafaranga 2000:338)

An external (etic) perspective on this example reveals only that three languages are used. An emic perspective on the other hand demonstrates that participants themselves do not treat the languages as having equal status. Indeed, as the transcript shows, the English elements have been repaired while neither Kinyarwanda nor French elements have.

An emic perspective on CS is possible because it is arguably viewed as a resource by speakers themselves. Consider example (9) below.

(9) 1. STU: *I'm sorry it's not your fault right.*

2. SEC: *No // uh no that's you you you.*

3. STU: *//I'm erm I offended you.*

4. SEC: mmm (.) **Le le droit** [to RES] el dret.

"mmm (.) The the right [to RES] the right."

5. RES: *The right.*

6. SEC: *The right (.) you have the right to protest eh OK.*

(Gafaranga 2000:338)

Three participants are involved in this exchange: a foreign student (STU), a secretary (SEC) and a researcher (RES). Both SEC and RES are Catalan and understand French in addition to Catalan and English. While speaking English (*italics*), SEC runs into difficulties (line 4). Changing from English to French (**bold**), she signals exactly what her problem is, namely the lack of the correct word in English. She then moves into Catalan (underlined). In 5, RES provides the needed English word. Thus, language alternation is used as a resource to signal the nature of the problem without stating it and to select the next speaker.

Language alternation, like other conversational resources, can be meaningfully used because it works within a normative framework. One way of explaining this normativity of language choice among bilingual speakers is in terms of the principle of *preference for same language talk* as proposed by Auer (1984, 1988, 1995). According to this principle, once a turn, or turn constructional unit, has occurred in a particular language, participants have to decide whether to continue in the same language or whether to use a different one. It is against the background of this preference for the same language that language alternation can be identified and interpreted. Consider example (9) above again. In the example, alternation to French works as a signalling device because the preceding talk has been in English. Likewise, the shift to Catalan deviates from language choice in the preceding turn constructional unit and is likely to be perceived as intentional. A similar local explanation applies to example (7). After SEC chose Catalan (turn 1), the norm was for EN to keep talking in the same language. Thus, against this expectation, EN's choice of Spanish in turn 2 is noticeable and is interpreted, by REC, as a request to use this language as the medium.

7.3.1   Some findings on code-switching

Research on CS using the CA approach as sketched above has been concerned with two main issues. On the one hand, research has aimed to refine the very notion of CS as a theoretical concept and, on the other, it has aimed to describe the functions of CS vis-à-vis specific aspects of talk organization. When Gumperz initiated the study of CS, he defined CS as "the juxtaposition within the same speech exchange of passages belonging to two different grammatical systems or subsystems" (1982a:59). That is to say, CS was defined from a grammatical perspective. Such a grammar-based definition was obviously felt to be problematic since, as we have seen, CA takes an emic perspective.

In the literature, two attempts at refining the notion of CS from a CA perspective have been proposed. As we have seen, starting from the CA view that talk is organized turn-by-turn, Auer proposes that CS be "conceptualised as a divergence from the language of the prior turn or turn constructional unit" (Auer 1988:137). We have seen how this definition can be operationalized by looking at language choice in a particular instance against the backdrop of immediately preceding choices (sequentiality). In Auer's definition, it is important not to lose sight of the key concept of "turn constructional unit." A turn constructional unit is any stretch of talk that potentially can form a full turn (Sacks et al. 1978). Consider the following piece of an interview conducted in Nairobi (Swahili in plain, English in **bold italics**).

(10) 1. Int: Unapenda kufanya kazi yako lani? Mchana au usiku?
                  "When do you like to work? Days or nights?"

2. Nurse: *As I told you, I like my job*.
3.   Sina ubaguzi wo wote kuhusu wakati ninapofanya kazi.
          "I have no difficulty at all regarding when I do work."
4.   *I enjoy working either during the day*
5.   au usiku yote ni sawa kwangu.
          "or at night, all is OK as far as I'm concerned."
6.   Hata *family members* wangu wamezoea mtindo huu.
          "Even my family members have gotten used to this plan."
7.   *There is no quarrel at all*.

(Myers-Scotton 1991; cited in Auer 1995:131)

In the example, language alternation between 1 and 2 corresponds to the shift from Int's and Nurse's turn. It is inter-turn. On the other hand, language alternation between 2 and 3 takes place within the same turn by Nurse. However, it occurs at a point where turn transition could have taken place. The fragment "I like my job" is a complete turn constructional unit. Therefore, in both cases, one can speak of CS in Auer's sense. However, the same cannot be said of language alternation in line 6. Here, alternation from Swahili to English takes place within the same turn and at a point where turn transition was not possible. On its own, the element "hata" (even) is not a complete turn constructional unit. In this case, Auer (1999) speaks, not of CS, but rather of *language mixing*.

However, it is easy to demonstrate that, from an emic perspective, the definition of CS with reference to turn constructional units is problematic. Consider example (9) again. In this example, most switches occur within the same constructional units. Yet, as we have seen, participants themselves have not treated them as equivalent. To overcome difficulties such as this, more recent research, especially work by Gafaranga and Torras (2001, 2002) and Torras and Gafaranga (2002), has proposed to refine the notion of CS, starting with the overall level of talk organization. According to these authors, each conversation (or conversational episode) has a base code. This code may or may not be monolingual. Referring to this code as a *medium*, they argue that, in bilingual talk-in-interaction, there is a *preference for same medium talk*. When language alternation occurs, participants notice the deviance and either repair it or hold it to be motivated, i.e. functional. According to this view, the term CS is to be reserved for this latter category. CS is "any instance of deviance from current medium which is not oriented to by participants themselves as requiring any repair" (Gafaranga and Torras 2002:18). In example (8), two types of language alternation have occurred, but none of them can be seen as CS. Alternation between French and Kinyarwanda constitutes the bilingual medium, while alternation to English is a case of medium repair. For a case of CS, consider the conversation among Rwandan refugees in Belgium, in example (11) below. The conversation adopts a bilingual medium (Kinyarwanda–French language alternation). In 1, A departs from this medium and uses Swahili (bold and underlined) to do direct speech reporting. As the transcript shows, this deviance from the medium is not repaired. Therefore, it must be seen as CS.

(11) *Kinyarwanda–French*

    1. A: Ubu rero ab- buretse (.) **abazayiruwa bagiye gutan-gira ngo (.) fukuza munyarwanda.**
               "Now Zai- wait a minute (.) Zairians are going to start saying kick out Rwandese."

    2. B: *Avec raison puisque* turi imbwa.
               "Rightly so as we do not deserve any respect."

    3. A: [xxx [laughter] ariko
               "[xxx [laughter] but . . . "

    4. C: *Avec raison* (.) none se wanzanira ibibazo iwanjye.
               "Rightly so (.) if you brought problems to my door . . . "

    5. A, B, C: [laughter]

                              (Gafaranga 2005:286)

While some researchers are focused on refining the concept of CS from a CA perspective, others address the issue of what CS can contribute to talk organization. In this respect, the strategy has mostly been to focus on conversational structures that CA studies of monolingual conversation have found to be significant, and to ask the question whether and to what extent CS contributes to them in bilingual conversation. Thus, CS has been found to contribute to the following aspects of talk organization, many of which have been illustrated in this chapter: turn-taking (participant selection), opening sequences (see language negotiation), repair organization, preference organization, and inserted and aside sequences. As indicated, this organizing function of CS is also known as its "Discourse-relatedness" (Auer, 1984).

7.4   Conclusion

The focus of CA is primarily talk organization. In its workings, CA draws on a number of interconnected assumptions. The first aim of this chapter has been to explore some of those assumptions that are most relevant for the CA model of bilingual conversation. As indicated, the starting assumption in CA is that talk is social action and that the acts that participants accomplish are orderly. CA work on language alternation starts from this very same assumption. The prerequisite for any meaningful CA account of CS is the view that language choice is a significant aspect of talk organization (Gafaranga 1999) and its object must be to describe the various ways in which language choice contributes to the organization of talk in two or more languages. In examining the organization of social interaction, in monolingual as well as in bilingual conversation, CA adopts an emic perspective, which in turn is possible only through sequential analysis. An emic perspective on bilingual conversation assumes the view that language choice, like any other aspect of talk organization, is a resource that participants can draw on and do so because of the normative nature of conversational resources. The second aim of this chapter has been to illustrate the findings of research that has been conducted under the CA model of CS. Two main lines of research were identified, namely research that focuses on refining the definition of CS from a CA perspective and research that investigates the role of CS vis-à-vis specific conversational structures.

8

Code-switching and the internet

Margreet Dorleijn
and
Jacomine Nortier

8.1 Introduction

Along with the general trend in sociolinguistics, there has always been consensus among researchers of code-switching (hereafter CS) that only in spontaneous speech, produced as unconsciously as possible, would the real patterns and regularities (be they of a structural or a pragmatic nature) of CS emerge. Therefore sociolinguistic studies of CS are generally based on the analysis of more or less spontaneous speech. However, during the last few years, the focus of interest of much CS research has, again, along with general trends in sociolinguistics, shifted to issues like stylistic uses of CS and the role of CS in identity construction, processes in which conscious use of CS is involved (Rampton 1999). Written data from the internet seem to be extremely suitable for this latter type of CS research, judging from the increasing number of studies of this kind that draw on it. This has, obviously, to do with the nature of these data. Internet data are not written language in the traditional sense. Language on the internet, referred to in the literature as Computer Mediated Communication (CMC), is felt by most users to be much more informal, and much less reflected upon by its authors than written texts. Consequently, the kind of language used in CMC contains a lot of colloquial forms and other features that are usually associated with spoken language. The fact that CS occurs in CMC at all is an indication of its informal character, CS being in general a highly informal mode of speech. But still, since CMC is a written medium, a certain level of consciousness on the part of its authors is presupposed. The conscious use of colloquial forms is valuable for research that focuses on stylistic uses of CS, and/or the use of CS in identity construction and presentation. In fact, this conscious use of CS on the internet is an explicit object of study (see Hinrichs 2006).

CS research is traditionally split up into two branches: the pragmatic/interactional and the structural/psycholinguistic. CMC data, then, appear to be valuable for the first branch of research. But does this type of data have something to offer to those who study structural or psycholinguistic aspects of CS as well? Is CS in CMC comparable with spontaneous data, at least when certain relevant aspects are concerned? The answer is, tentatively, yes. One important argument is that in some speech communities the mixed code is the preferred variety for in-group communication: the members of those communities automatically switch to this mixed code when they meet (or when they write to each other on the internet), because it is the easiest, the most "relaxed" and therefore most "spontaneous," least monitored, and most unconsciously produced way of speaking for them. In that case, when it is used for in-group communication, CS does not particularly serve the aim of identity construction or style. In other words, one may argue that CS in CMC is in some cases produced consciously, and in other cases less consciously, not unlike spoken language. The fact that the production of these data, because they are written, presupposes a higher level of consciousness may even be advantageous for certain aspects of the study of structural CS.

This chapter discusses whether CMC may have something to offer to those who study structural aspects of CS as well as to those who study style and identity construction. First, §8.2 overviews studies concerning characteristics of spoken vs. written texts and introduces the notion of *written speech*. The question to what degree these data can be put on a par with spontaneous data is then addressed. In §8.3, an overview of studies on CS in CMC is presented. Finally, in §8.4, we report on ongoing research into CS on Moroccan–Dutch and Turkish–Dutch internet forums. Data from these different language pairings will be compared and used to illustrate the advantages and disadvantages of CMC for both structurally and socially or interactionally oriented research. It will be shown that CMC data of different language combinations may differ in terms of suitability for the study of either of these two research questions.

8.2   The usefulness of CMC as data in code-switching research

8.2.1   Written speech?

In studies on the nature of (monolingual) internet communication, it is often noted that CMC is a hybrid between speaking and writing, which is indeed what internet users intuitively feel to be the case. Hence the term written speech is often used to refer to CMC. To make this broadly shared intuition explicit, studies on internet language frequently refer to earlier studies on the differences between oral and written texts. One often-cited study is Biber (1988). In this quantitative analysis of corpora of spoken and written English, Biber defined and investigated six dimensions that are relevant for the description of the difference between the two genres. Each of these dimensions is associated with specific bundles of linguistic features. Although not one single linguistic feature was exclusively present in only one of the genres, Biber found in his corpus that spoken and written language would take almost opposite positions on three of the six dimensions he had defined. These are *involved vs. informational production, explicit vs. situation dependent reference*, and *abstract vs. non-abstract information*. The other dimensions where the contrast found was less extreme are *narrative vs. non-narrative, overt expression of persuasion, on-line informational elaboration*. For instance, examples of linguistic features that Biber found to correlate with abstract information are passive constructions and adverbial conjunctions, which occur more often in written than spoken texts.

Collot and Belmore (1996) applied Biber's model to a corpus of CMC data and found no extreme scores on most dimensions, which would indeed suggest that CMC is positioned between speech and writing. However, on two of the six dimensions, their CMS data scored almost the same as written texts (i.e. the dimensions *overt expression of persuasion* and *abstract vs. non-abstract information*). Yates (1996) analyzed corpora of spoken, written, and CMC language and found that CMC data are similar to written data in terms of lexical density, i.e. the relatively high rate of tokens of content words in a text. At the same time, CMC data are similar to spoken data in the use of first and second person pronouns, which occurred even more frequently than in the spoken data. He found modal verbs to be used significantly more frequently in CMC data than in both written and spoken texts.

In an accessible treatise on language on the internet, Crystal (2001) lists seven criteria that are typical for written versus oral texts. Most of Crystal's criteria relate to extra-linguistic circumstances and, unlike Biber, he does not attribute specific linguistic features to them.[1] In his analysis of different text types on the internet, Crystal concludes that some CMC texts have more in common with writing and others with speaking. These and other studies suggest that, indeed, CMC data show characteristics of both spoken and written genres. In some instances (as for example can be seen from Yates's study) some linguistic features occur more frequently in CMC data than in either written or spoken language. Add to this the peculiarities that are typical of CMC (e.g. the extensive use of abbreviations and emoticons – see Crystal for ample examples) and one is justified in speaking of CMC as a "third medium."

Studies on the specific character of language on the internet in its own right abound. But the question raised (and partly answered) in this chapter is whether this third medium is suitable for CS research in the traditional sense and, further, whether it affords new perspectives for CS research.

8.2.2 Types of informal CMC texts

Not all texts on the internet are suitable for CS research. Although texts from the internet are generally felt to be more informal and therefore closer to the colloquial than the average written text, this is certainly not true for scientific articles, lectures etc. that can also be found on the internet. CS research texts must be informal. This is an absolute pre-requisite, because CS is typically used in informal situations and reflects colloquial language. Interaction may be important, especially for those who study CS from the Conversation Analytic perspective (see Gafaranga, this volume), but is not an absolute prerequisite for those who study other aspects of CS, e.g. structural aspects or identity construction strategies.

Crystal distinguishes four types of internet texts: the Web, e-mail, real-time chatgroups ("synchronous chatgroups" in his terms), forums ("asyn-chronous chatgroups" in his terms), and virtual worlds. The weblog (or blog) should perhaps be added to these four types because it has become increasingly popular since Crystal's book was published, but because of its similarity with what Crystal labels as asynchronous chatgroups, it will not be discussed separately. Which of these four types meet the conditions of informality and colloquial language use? Crystal concludes that the Web is closest to written language, e-mail is the most variable, and a chatgroup, a virtual world, and a multi-user dungeon/domain/dimension (MUD) show a high degree of similarity to oral language. In MUDs a certain number of participants play a game together. As a consequence, MUDs are centered around the game and this often entails a highly specific jargon. For this reason, MUDs will not be considered further here.

E-mail cannot be considered one single type of text. Hinrichs (2006:19), who based his study of Jamaican Creole–English CS on a corpus of e-mail, observes that:

... its language is becoming more varied as the range of its application broadens. If the predominant style among the first generation of e-mail users was mostly informal, this is likely so because e-mail, due to the newness as a medium, was trusted mostly with communicative purposes of a less important and by themselves informal nature. Recently, users have trusted e-mail with much more critical communicative applications, including business consultations, the negotiation of legal contracts, etc.

Obviously, then, for CS research, a sample of e-mails from the informal end of the continuum will prove more fruitful than those of a more serious nature.

Users in real-time chatgroups interact directly on-line with each other, a means of communicating that seems to be the closest to speaking and may therefore be of great value for CS research. To date, however, no studies have been based entirely on this type of data. The nature of texts in forums, where moderators start a certain topic to which participants react through "threads," may vary from long stretches of text like news reports or narratives, to shorter reactions, and quite often also synchronous inter-action. The diverse, but at the same time intrinsically informal nature of this type of data seems promising. In the next section, the advantages and disadvantages of each of the three text types will be examined: e-mail, real-time chat, and asynchronous chat.

8.2.3 Advantages and disadvantages of CMC data for code-switching research

This section examines some advantages, disadvantages, and ambiguous aspects of e-mail, synchronous chat, and forums, the three interactional text types that offer the most promising data for CS research. One important point to bear in mind is that the data may differ enormously in nature, not only according to text type, but also depending on the language pair involved. The nature of the data is probably determined by sociolinguistic factors in particular, centering around questions like: Are the languages involved standard written or oral languages? Is CS the unmarked choice for in-group communication? As will be shown in §8.4, factors like these have enormous consequences for the suitability of certain datasets in certain types of research. Be that as it may, at least one obvious methodological advantage that applies to research on all three types of texts is the amount of time that is saved, since the data need not be transcribed. In addition, since the data are written, utterances cannot be misunderstood or misinterpreted.

While written data are not suitable for the investigation of phonological aspects of CS, there may be interesting clues revealed through orthography. Other aspects are neither clearly advantageous nor disadvantageous. For example, the fact that written data contain no false starts and hesitations is an advantage for some types of research, but obviously not for those areas concerned with such speech properties. The assumed higher level of consciousness that seems inevitable in producing written CS may be seen as a disadvantage for the "traditional" macro- or micro-level sociolinguistic CS research in the vein of Gumperz (1982a), Myers-Scotton (1993b), and Auer (1998). But for the type of study that investigates CS as a tool in the construction of identity and expression of style, the conscious use of CS is the explicit object of study (e.g. Hinrichs 2006; Rampton 1995). For the study of structural aspects, a consciously stylized text is not useful, since atypical and deliberately "incorrect" use of language is often involved. But in contexts where CS is simply the unmarked mode of expression, the slightly higher conscious production of a written text is not a disadvantage. For those researchers who are interested in the emergence of conventions in mixed lects, written CS may have added value, because it captures existent norms in writing. This is a line of research that may in the future benefit greatly from this kind of data.

Apart from these general characteristics, some features are specific for each of the three text types:

(1.) *e-mail*
   Advantages
   (a.) The background of the authors can be retrieved. This information may be important when interpreting the data. It is

indispensable in types of research where network analyses play a role.

(b.) The authors often know each other in real life, therefore their communication is embedded in a larger context.

(c.) The texts may be of a very diverse nature, from informative texts to merely phatic exchanges.

Disadvantages

(a.) Data collection requires an effort from the authors to submit their (often) private e-mail to the researcher.

(b.) There is no control over possible censorship or self-censorship that may be done on the material before it is submitted.

(2.) *Real-time chatgroups*

Advantages

(a.) Probably closest to spoken language.

(b.) Highest similarity to natural conversation.

(c.) Manipulation is possible by introducing topics, language, linguistic forms etc.

(d.) Easily accessible.

Disadvantages

(a.) Ephemeral. In most instances, data cannot be stored.

(b.) The authors are not known to the researcher. In the case of instant messaging, researchers depend on the authors' willingness to cooperate.

(c.) The phatic function is often dominant, including long sequences of greetings and curses. Overall, the sentences are often very short, one-word or two-word.

(3.) *Forums*

Advantages

(a.) Easily accessible.

(b.) Texts are very diverse in nature, ranging from informative to phatic. However, in all instances they are intrinsically informal.

(c.) Just as with real-time chat, manipulation is possible.

(d.) Discussions are often archived and, in some cases, texts from years ago are available, allowing for the possibility of longitudinal study.

(e.) Each is catered to a different demographic group, in terms of age, educational level, linguistic background, and gender. This may reveal something about macro-linguistic patterning in CS.

Disadvantages

(a.) The individual authors' backgrounds are usually unknown to the researcher.

(b.) Access is open to everyone, which makes it difficult to capture interactions between the same individuals. However, in practice, it is often the case that only a few persons dominate the discussions.

The above characteristics of each of the three types of data can be summarized as in Table 8.1.

Table 8.1 Advantages of three types of internet data for code-switching research

Characteristics	e-mail	chat	forum
Easily obtainable	−	+	+
Background of authors is known	+	−	−
Easy to store	+	−	+
Longitudinal data	?	−	+
Manipulable	−	+	+
Diversity in text type	+	−	+
Informal/colloquial	?	+	+
Interactional	?	+	?
Embedding in real-life relationships	+	−	−

8.3   The literature on internet CS

8.3.1   Definitions

Before we discuss the literature on CS on the internet, we feel it necessary to dedicate some discussion to definitions of CS. In order to avoid confusion, all uses of two languages within one conversational or situational setting will be referred to as CS. Following Muysken (2000) the term insertion will be used when there is one clearly distinguishable matrix or base language, into which elements from the other language are inserted. Code alternation is the complete transition from one language system to the other. Both insertion and alternation are instances of CS. The term intra-sentential CS will be used for switching within sentence boundaries.

8.3.2   Studies on bilingualism on the internet

The study of digital CS is a very young field. However, there are recurrent topics in the extant literature: the relation between conscious vs. unconscious CS in oral and digital speech, the function of oral vs. digital CS, the base language in oral vs. digital CS, and the question of markedness and the standardization of non-standard varieties by its use in written form. Compared to the general literature on CS, grammatical issues seem to be less prominent in the literature on digital CS.

Rather than being focused on bilingualism, extant studies are generally exponents of the broader field of research into language on the internet. However, the study of CS on the internet may potentially inform us about linguistic aspects of contemporary societies. For instance, from the moment that large groups of migrants have settled in their countries of destination, they have used the available media to represent their social status, to stay informed about their country of origin, and to contact each other within the country of migration. Since the 1990s the predominantly used medium is the internet, particularly among young people. In Germany, for example, ethnic groups have developed their own websites, where German usually is the basic language. Androutsopoulos (2006) discusses language choice and CS in so-called "Ethno Portalen," websites with a mix of information and interaction. In his analysis of language choice and CS on a Persian–German website, he concludes, among other things, that there is not always a clear relation between language choice and topic of discussion. Inter-sentential CS ("Sprachwechsel") is the main form of language contact in internet forums; intra-sentential CS ("Sprachmischung") occurs only sporadically and is caused by local changes in the discussions. The logical consequence, therefore, is that CS on the German Ethno Portalen is of the insertional type, where material from the migrant language (Persian) is inserted into German. Goodbyes, addresses, congratulations, proverbs, and slogans are typically elements that are expressed in the migrant language.

Thus, there is a clear distinction between what Gumperz (1982a) calls the "*we-code*," used among insiders and group members, and the "*they-code*," used in inter-group exchange. However, this may not always be the case. Hinrichs's (2006) findings on English–Jamaican Creole exchanges diverge from Gumperz's observations: in his study he found that there is no one-to-one relation between language and group identity. Siebenhaar (2005) carried out a study on CS between formal Standard German ("Schriftdeutsch") and informal Schwitzerdütsch ("Mundart"). One of the hypotheses he tested was that the function of CS in internet chat is comparable to its function in oral speech. This hypothesis was not confirmed. There are similarities with spoken language, but in chat the languages have a more equal status than in the spoken form, therefore there is more frequent CS and it is less marked than in spoken or written forms.

Digital CS and oral CS appear to have different characteristics. Hinrichs (2006), for example, found that the unmarked language in daily digital use is English. This is in accordance with recent developments in the Jamaican diaspora, where English has become the unmarked language of communication, but it is contrary to the oral situation in Jamaica, where Jamaican Creole (or Patois, the basilect) is unmarked. The use of English is a consequence of the fact that English has a standard spelling, while there is no such thing for Patois. On the internet, the long established and functional distinction between the two languages has thus shifted. In Jamaica, CS is unmarked, but on the internet, English is unmarked and a shift to Patois is the marked choice. This is possibly medium-related because of the difficulty of writing Creole as compared to English.

Analyses of digital CS can reveal the emergence of a written form of a non-standardized variety. This is discussed by Hinrichs (2006) and by Palfreyman and al Khalil (2003), the latter who report on the use of spoken

Gulf Arabic in Roman transcription, which is not standardized. They focus on the use of ASCII code for Arab-language texts. They also studied the relation between language choice (English or Arabic) and topic. They found a correlation with (change of) topic, Arabic for formulaic phrases, English for topics such as university courses.

The difference between the two contexts is that the Jamaican Creole studied by Hinrichs has a low status while the status of Arabic is very high. What Patois and Arabic on the internet have in common, though, is the unconventional way in which the varieties are written. An even more complex situation arises for Moroccans in The Netherlands, who use both a high and a low variety of Arabic in the Latin script. Their home language is either Moroccan Arabic or Berber, both with very low prestige. The language they use on the internet is mainly Dutch, with some Arabic or Berber inserted into it. Standard Arabic, of high prestige, is used in formulaic expressions, and despite the existence of a digital Arabic script, it is written in Roman script. Boumans (2002) analyzed the use of Moroccan Arabic and Dutch on www.maroc.nl, used by both Dutch Moroccans and native Dutch visitors. He concludes that Arabic is mainly used in formulaic expressions of a religious nature.

Axelsson et al. (2003) examine a specific virtual environment, Active Worlds (AWs), which allow interaction with a 3D computer-generated virtual environment. They focus on situations in which a new language is introduced in a conversation held in another language. They find that factors such as type of language, interactional setting, and speaker intentions influence language choice in AWs.

Given that so little work has been carried out on CS on the internet and, in particular, on its structural properties, the following section presents a case study highlighting identity construction, the functions of contributing languages, and the structural properties of CS on the internet.

8.4   An illustration of code-switching on the internet in two minority communities in the Netherlands

8.4.1   Immigrant groups in The Netherlands

The Moroccan and Turkish communities in The Netherlands are comparable in terms of size. By 2006, there were approximately 323,000 persons of Moroccan background, and 364,000 of Turkish background living in the Netherlands. Their migration history is quite similar: the majority are descendants and family members of former guest workers who arrived in the 1960s and 1970s. These groups share a low socio-economic status and a Muslim background. The sociolinguistic situation of the two communities, however, differs considerably, and this is reflected in the way each community employs CS on the internet. Each group will be considered separately.

8.4.1.1 The linguistic situation of Moroccans in Morocco and in The Netherlands

Moroccans speak one of two languages: Berber and Moroccan Arabic. Although Moroccan Arabic (a Semitic language) and Berber (a Hamito-Kushitic language) have been spoken alongside one another for centuries, and therefore have influenced each other, the languages differ to a high degree and are not mutually intelligible. Moroccan Arabic and Berber do not have standardized written forms. This absence has consequences for their use on the internet.

An estimated 70–80% of the Moroccans living in The Netherlands are Berber-speaking. And although most Berber-speaking Moroccans are more or less familiar with Moroccan Arabic, this does not imply that every Berber speaks Moroccan Arabic fluently (El Aissati 1996). In Morocco, Moroccan Arabic functions as the lingua franca, but in The Netherlands, Dutch seems to have taken over this function (El Aissati 2002). There are several reasons why Moroccans would choose Dutch: in the first place, one can never be sure whether the interlocutor speaks Arabic or Berber; second, among the second and third generations, proficiency in Dutch is higher than in the ethnic languages; and third, Berber is stigmatized. Although there is a strong emancipatory movement, the relation between Berber and Arabic is far from equal, and an Arabic speaker may be insulted to be addressed in Berber. Thus, Dutch is the most neutral choice.

8.4.1.2 The linguistic situation of Turks in Turkey and in The Netherlands

The linguistic situation in Turkey differs substantially from the situation in Morocco. The overwhelming majority of Turkey's inhabitants are familiar with standard Turkish, the result of a strict language policy during the history of the modern Turkish Republic (founded in 1923). A standardized, nearly phonemic spelling in Roman script has existed since 1928. Standard Turkish is the only official language and functions as the language of education and the media.

Relative to other migrant groups in The Netherlands, the immigrant language is vital in the Turkish community (Broeder and Extra 1999; Extra et al. 2001). The Turkish language is highly valued and considered to be an essential part of one's Turkish identity. Members of the community have easy access to standard Turkish through all kinds of media, and it is common practice to send children to Turkey in order to learn proper Turkish and complete their education there. Turkish–Dutch CS is frequent (Eversteijn 2002) and this is reflected in language use on Dutch–Turkish websites, as will be discussed below.

8.4.2 Analysis of code-switching on Dutch/Turkish and Dutch/ Moroccan websites

8.4.2.1 Description of some popular websites visited by Moroccans and Turks

Dutch is the main language used on Moroccan/Dutch websites. The use of Moroccan Arabic and Berber occurs predominantly at the insertional level. Just as in everyday Dutch, English is inserted frequently, as in the contributions in (1). Note that in all examples, **bold italics** are used for languages other than Dutch.

(1) **Ok, I admit**, maar h0e wil je dan 00it **mr Right** vinden als je t0ch geen relaties mag aangaan … behalve het huwelijk?
  "OK, I admit, but how will you ever find Mr Right if you're not allowed to have any relations … except marriage?"

  (posted on www.maroc.nl)

Authors use the Roman alphabet for Berber and Arabic. There is no orthographic standard and authors can be very creative, for example when they want to communicate phatically, as in (2):

(2) *amazigh* roos: En **Aythwayagh**ers praten met een vraagteken.
  "amazigh rose: And people from A. speak with a question mark."
  Ahraifi: Soms ook met een uitroepteken! (…)
  "Professor: Sometimes also with an exclamation mark! (…)"
  IkHaatWerken: **maghaaaaaaaaa**?
  "IHatetoWork: whyyyyy?"
  amazigh roos: **hahaha nishan ayomahhhhhh**??
  "amazigh rose: hahaha right my brotheeeeeer?"

  (posted on www.amazigh.nl, July 2004)

CS itself is used as a source of play and wit, as illustrated in the following example, where rhyme is achieved via inserted Moroccan Arabic nouns. (The symbol "7" in (3) is the convention used on the internet to represent a pharyngealized "h.")

(3) Je bent nog mooier dan mijn **remra7**, gezien vanaf de **sta7**, bij het krieken van de **sba7**.
  "You are even prettier than my court-yard, seen from the roof, at the dawn of the morning."

  (posted on www.maroc.nl, September 2006)

In sum, the language used on Dutch/Moroccan websites is almost always Dutch. Berber and Arabic have partly different, partly overlapping functions. What Berber and Arabic primarily share is their function as a mode to express bilingual identity. Examples are given in (4) and (5) where the authors seem proficient enough to use Dutch, but choose Moroccan Arabic for proper nouns.

(4) Ik vertelde hem dat het hier brrrrrrrrrrr-koud was. Dat het zelfs een beetje gesneeuwd had. Hij had het gehoord en gezien op het nieuws.

Beelden van ondergesneeuwde plekken in **Fransa, L'allemagne, Taljan** en **Turkja**. Voor de rest ging het goed met iedereen.
"I told him that it was brrrr-cold here. That it even had snowed a bit. He had heard it and seen it on the news. Images of snowed-under places in France, Germany, Italy, and Turkey. Furthermore everyone was doing fine."

(posted on www.maroc.nl)

(5)   zolang we 1 gemeenschappelijke vijand hebben (**sjarron wa boesj**) zijn we allemaal moslimbroeders en zusters
"As long as we have 1 common enemy (Sharon and Bush) we are all muslim brothers and sisters."

(posted on www.maroc.nl)

8.4.2.2   Languages and their functions

On the Dutch/Turkish websites, both Turkish and Dutch are used. In the general format of CS in informative exchanges (e.g. educational matters or job opportunities), the base language is mostly Dutch, with Turkish insertions. The function of the Turkish insertions in these text types is often to mark Turkish identity, and sometimes also to try and find out whether the interlocutor is Turkish as well. For example, a job offer was posted on the site www.lokum.nl in July of 2006, in Dutch; reactions to this offer were partly in Turkish, as in (6). The answer to this question was posted entirely in Dutch and the exchange continued in Dutch as well.

(6)   Dat klinkt goed, **ama ne kadar para aliyorsun**?
"This sounds great, but how much money do you get for it?"

Narratives and jokes are usually monolingual (either Dutch or Turkish, depending on topic and protagonists), with side-comments and other conversational cues in the other language, as illustrated in (7):

(7)   Maar wat wil het lot … (**büyük konusmusuz**)[2] ik ben verliefd en zwaar ook.
"But fate strikes … (that was easy to say at the time) I am in love and heavily too."

(posted on www.lokum.nl, September 2006)

The selection of Dutch or Turkish in the types of texts above can, in most instances, be analyzed in terms of either conversational cues, negotiation of identity, topic-relatedness, or other communicative functions.

CS in texts that resemble oral conversation (e.g. in a chat context) is of a slightly different nature. Both intra- and inter-sentential CS are used, as in (8) and (9) below, found on www.Turksestudent.nl in October 2006:

(8)   bende havo 4 en 5 in 1 jaar **yapdim**
      me too havo 4 and 5 in 1 year I-finished

"Me too I finished havo 4 and 5 in 1 year." [Havo 4 and 5 are school type and grades.]

(9) ***daha yasin neki***? Als je met zo'n instelling over school/studie denkt, dan ...

"How old are you anyway? If that is how you think about school/study, then ..."

Frequently, the Dutch and Turkish elements are completely intertwined, as in (10), posted on www.TurkishTexas.nl in October of 2006:

(10) Is er geen moppen topic of zo, ***fikralar topigi falan var, mop guzel ama, her mopa bir topic acilirsa***, is een beetje onnodig.

is there no jokes topic or so, joke-PL topic-POSS or-so there-is joke nice-ls, but each joke-DAT one topic open-PASS-COND-3SG, is a little unnecessary.

"Isn't there a topic for jokes, there is a special topic for jokes, joke(s) (are) nice but, if a topic is opened for every joke, it is a bit too much."

In these text types, the choice of either Turkish or Dutch seems to be random and difficult to analyze in terms of communicative functions. In fact, closer inspection of these data reveals a certain intertwining of the two linguistic systems, where Dutch structural features may appear in Turkish phonological guise and vice versa (see also Backus and Dorleijn, this volume).[3]

8.4.3 Future directions

While attention in the analysis of digital CS in general focuses on its communicative function, this does not necessarily have to be the case. For instance, Nortier (1995) has shown that in oral Moroccan Arabic–Dutch CS, definite articles are deleted frequently, but they are almost never deleted in the monolingual speech of the same speakers. An example from Nortier (1995) in which a definite article is required but not realized is given in (11):

(11) ***waHed*** gesprek[4]
"one conversation"

In (11), the noun should have been preceded by a definite article, either in Moroccan Arabic or in Dutch, thus obeying the grammatical rules of the two langues (Bentahila and Davies 1983). Intriguingly, in Dutch–Moroccan Arabic CS, this constraint is frequently violated while French–Moroccan Arabic CS doesn't show any violations of the constraint at all:

(12) ***had*** le truc
"that the thing"

(13) ***waHed l-*** paysage
"one the landscape"

In both (12) and (13) the definite article is realized; in (12) in French and in (13) in Moroccan Arabic, according to grammatical requirements.

While the deletion of definite articles has not been systematically studied in Dutch–Moroccan Arabic CS on the internet, it may bring novel insights to research on grammatical constraints on CS across different media. An examination of data from CS on the internet may reveal similar patterns with respect to the omission of these and other functional elements. If this should prove to be the case, then internet CS data may indeed serve as an easily accessible source of data that replicates many of the aspects of spontaneous, oral CS corpora. That the Turkish definite marker -*i* is often omitted with intrinsically definite objects in the Turkish–Dutch bilingual mode both in oral as well as in written speech is a case in point. Furthermore, comparing spontaneous data with internet data may reveal interesting resemblances in patterns of use, which may tell us something about conventionalization patterns. On the other hand, if the patterns in either type of data differ, this in its turn may prove to be revealing of the role of spontaneous vs. planned language production. Written speech where CS is not too consciously deployed seems fit for these types of research.

8.5 Concluding remarks

Because of its informal nature, CS abounds on many internet forums. Internet CS may be unique in that it demonstrates characteristics of both oral and written speech. While research on digital CS has hitherto focused on communicative and stylistic aspects, CMC data seem to offer promising possibilities for other types and aspects of CS research as well, be it from a structural, a psycholinguistic, or even a diachronic perspective. The Dutch–Moroccan and Dutch–Turkish internet sites we have examined have revealed, however, that different language pairings may manifest different CS patterns of usage. Whereas Moroccan–Dutch data appear to be extremely suitable for research in the field of style and identity construction, Turkish–Dutch data prove valuable for, among others, research into structural aspects. This difference between these two language pairings has nothing to do with typological considerations, but rather with the respective sociolinguistic situations of the two immigrant communities that speak the languages.

As should be clear, there remains much to be investigated concerning CS on the internet. For example, the degree to which the structures attested conform to or deviate from spontaneous oral CS speech is an area open to study. In addition, investigations of digital CS between the same language pairs in different social contexts may provide insights into macro-level issues such as the relative power and prestige of a particular language variety and about the acceptability of CS across diverse communities of practice.

Notes

1. The criteria Crystal lists are the following: 1. time-bound vs. space-bound; 2. spontaneous vs. contrived; 3. face-to-face vs. visually decontextualized; 4. loosely structured vs. elaborately structured; 5. socially interactive vs. factually communicative; 6. immediately revisable vs. repeatedly revisable; 7. prosodically rich vs. graphically rich.
2. The texts are presented as they were found on the internet. For Turkish in the Dutch context a slightly "Dutchified" orthography is used, and often Turkish diacritics (e.g. ö, ü, ç, ş) are omitted.
3. In contrast to the Moroccan/Dutch forums, in Turkish/Dutch forums we have not found that bilingualism in itself is employed as a source for wit or wordplay.
4. Capital H is used for pharyngealized [h] for which the Latin alphabet does not have a separate letter.

9

Phonetic accommodation in children's code-switching

Ghada Khattab

9.1 Introduction

It is well known that bilingual children develop sociolinguistic competence, i.e. they learn which language(s) to use with whom and in which situational and physical context, topic, register, activity, etc. (e.g. Ervin-Tripp and Reyes 2005; Fantini 1985; Fishman 2000a; Genesee et al. 1996; Goodz 1994). However, discussion of sociolinguistic competence in bilingual environments often concentrates on the child's ability to switch between languages rather than language varieties, e.g. between different dialects, standard and non-standard varieties, or native and non-native varieties of the same language. This might be due to the tendency in bilingual phonological research to concentrate on cross-language rather than within-language differences and to deal with each of the bilingual's target languages as a stable system made up of easily identifiable and/or invariable target sounds and structures.

The influence of the sociolinguistic environment on bilingual development is paramount, since many bilinguals acquire their two languages in different physical and social contexts, only one of them corresponding to monolinguals' experience (the home language, if there is only one). Even then, depending on the status of that language, the bilinguals might quickly attach more significance to the community language and might experience first language (L1) attrition as they develop their second language (L2). In cases where both parents are L2 speakers of the community language, their children might be exposed to native and non-native varieties of the L2 in monolingual and bilingual conversations. While it is generally assumed that second-generation immigrants learn the L2 in a native-like manner regardless of their parents' accent (Chambers 2002), this chapter explores the bilingual child's ability to code-switch not only between languages, but also between native and non-native varieties of one of their languages for communicative purposes. In order to understand how children may develop that ability, the chapter examines the development of sociolinguistic competence and accommodation in monolingual settings (§9.2). A parallel is then drawn with bilingual settings, with a review of a small body of literature which shows that children can harness their phonetic repertoire for sociolinguistic purposes (§9.3). This is followed by data from English–Arabic bilinguals in the UK that adds to the scarce literature on the phonetics of code-switching (hereafter CS) (§9.4). A discussion follows on the role of input and on how to label and fit these data within existing models of CS (§9.5 and §9.6).

9.2 Sociolinguistic competence in monolingual settings

As Andersen (1990), Ervin-Tripp (1973), Hymes (1974), and Schieffelin and Ochs (1986) point out, children develop sociolinguistic competence along with grammatical competence. That is, they learn "when to speak, when not, and … what to talk about with whom, when, where, in what manner" (Hymes 1974:277). The ability to achieve sociolinguistic competence might stem from one of the most common characteristics of interpersonal communication, the adaptation of two speakers to each other's speech, also known as *accommodation* (Hamers and Blanc 2000:242). Accommodation is defined by constant movement toward and away from others by changing one's communicative behavior (Sachdev and Giles 2006). This can take place at the linguistic (e.g. voice quality, accent), paralinguistic (e.g. pauses, floor-time), and non-verbal (e.g. smiling, gazing) levels. One strategy for doing so is *convergence* (Giles 1973), whereby speakers may adapt their communicative behavior to match that of their interlocutor. Phonetic convergence has been demonstrated by looking at interlocutors' adaptation of speaking rate, fundamental frequency, amplitude contour, and other segmental and suprasegmental aspects of speech (see Coupland and Giles 1988; Giles et al. 1991; Giles 1973; Gregory 1990; Pardo 2006). An important motivation for convergence is the desire to gain approval from the addressee and/or improve the effectiveness of the communication. On the other hand, *divergence* involves emphasizing linguistic (and cultural) differences. Divergence accentuates individual identity and helps the speaker signal distinctiveness from their interlocutor, normally in relation to their ethnic or social identity.

The ability to adapt to others' speech patterns starts very early, as infants have been shown to be predisposed to imitate what they perceive (see Boysson-Bardies and Vihman 1991; Vihman and Boysson-Bardies 1994; Kuhl and Meltzoff 1996). The socialization process also begins at birth. Verbal interactions between infants and mothers are culturally organized and exhibit patterns that are specific to the particular social group into which the developing child is being socialized (Schieffelin and Ochs 1986). Children learn the meaning of speech events and the socially acceptable or unacceptable contexts for those events. Early phonetic accommodation is exhibited in the way children learn how to use intonation, rhythm, and stress to convey or alter the meaning of semantic choices, e.g. to agree or disagree with what is said, plead, ignore, or persuade (Cook-Gumperz and Gumperz 1976). Therefore, learning to use language and learning to use language in context become inseparable.

Throughout their development, children participate in a variety of speech situations with people who differ in age, gender, status, and familiarity, and whose speech will therefore vary in a number of systematic ways. These experiences trigger the acquisition of a dialect or set of dialects that will mark children as belonging to a particular social class, ethnic group, age, and gender. For instance, children as young as 3;6 exhibit the acquisition of gender-correlated phonological variation (Docherty et al. 2006). Comparable results have been found for older children with regard to the use of standard and non-standard pronunciation and grammar, suggesting that girls are more likely to produce standard variants than boys (see Cheshire 1982; Ladegaard and Bleses 2003; Gleason 1987). Young girls and boys may also exhibit gender-specific behavior in pitch and voice quality well before they undergo physical changes that will lead to this behavior (Lee et al. 1995; Sachs et al. 1973). Young children also show social class stratification in the use of phonological variables such as final /t/ and /d/ deletion, postvocalic /r/, and -ing in English (see Romaine 1984; Macaulay 1977; Reid 1978; Trudgill 1975; Wolfram 1969), and local versus non-local features (Docherty et al. 2006; Mees 1990; Roberts and Labov 1995).

Children acquire a repertoire of registers and pragmatic rules that will allow them to style-shift in order to express a wide range of social meanings relevant to particular contexts (Andersen 1990:32). For instance, children as young as two develop the ability to perceive dialectal variation in their input and to adopt appropriate variants according to the relevant social and linguistic constraints (Smith et al. 2007). Four-year-olds have been shown to vary loudness, rate, pitch variation, voice quality, and accent when playing different social roles such as parents, doctors, and teachers (Andersen 1990). Children as young as three also adapt non-linguistic aspects of speech relative to interlocutors, e.g. reciprocating conversational floor-time, response latency, and speech rate (Street and Capella 1989). Eight-year-old children speaking to younger children have been shown to use less complex structure and their speech was slower, higher in pitch, and had exaggerated pitch contours compared with their speech to adults (Andersen and Johnson 1973). Eleven-year-olds have been found to use variants of -ing differently depending on whether they were reading, in interview, in peer conversation, or on the playground (Reid 1978).

In the early years of sociolinguistic development, children's production is heavily influenced by parental input, especially with regard to the acquisition of the phonological features of their local variety (Kerswill

1996:190). It is at this stage that the initial transmission of dialect features and sociolinguistic competence might take place. At the pre-adolescent age, however, children begin to assert themselves outside the home and their friends and classmates become linguistically and socially more influential than teachers and parents (Chambers 2003; Kerswill 1996; Ervin-Tripp and Reyes 2005). For children whose parents belong to a different speech community from the one in which the children are being raised, the influence of peers over parents becomes most obvious. The children may become bi-dialectal (Dyer 2004) but they will almost always prefer their peers' dialect over their parents' (Chambers 2002). The same applies in bilingual situations with respect to languages and varieties spoken by children and their parents, but bilinguals may have more opportunities and motivations to choose one variety as their most preferred one and switch to others for communicative purposes. This will be discussed in more detail in the next section.

9.3   Sociolinguistic competence in bilingual settings

Bilingual children demonstrate sociolinguistic competence by adopting one code or the other according to the needs of the situation (see Ervin-Tripp and Reyes 2005; Fishman 2000b; Genesee et al. 1996; Goodz 1994) and grammatical competence by using language alternation at specific intervals that generally do not interfere with the syntactic and morphological constraints of the languages involved (see Myers-Scotton 1993a, 2002b; Meisel 1994; Poplack 1980; Poplack and Meechan 1995, 1998). The first of these abilities is also known as bilingual accommodation (Sachdev and Giles 2006) and has been known to develop from a very early age as part of children's developing sociolinguistic competence. Bilingual children as young as two have been shown to modify their language or language mixing patterns in response to particular language characteristics of their interlocutor (Genesee et al. 1995) even when the interlocutor speaks their less dominant language (Genesee et al. 1996). Bilinguals take into consideration their interlocutor's proficiency in each of the languages and become aware of the relative status of certain languages and ethnolinguistic groups. For instance, Aboud (1976) observed a six-year-old Spanish–English bilingual converging more frequently to Anglophone than Hispanophone interlocutors. Moreover, bilingual children learn how to associate non-verbal characteristics of the interlocutor with ethnolinguistic backgrounds and accommodate their speech accordingly. For instance, Beebe (1981) found that Thai–Chinese bilingual children used Chinese phonological variants in their Thai speech when interviewed by a speaker of Standard Thai who looked ethnically Chinese.

Bilingual speech accommodation is influenced by social factors similar to those found in monolingual situations, except that bilinguals have a choice of language as well as varieties within each language. Therefore, bilinguals possess a much wider repertoire of adaptive strategies than monolinguals, since they have a whole range of intermediate strategies which include the adaptation of either code and the relative use of both (Hamers and Blanc 2000:255). Few studies, however, have considered the phonological repertoire of bilingual children with the particular local accent(s)/dialect(s) in mind in order to examine the motivating factors that trigger the production of one realization over competing alternatives. These alternatives might include standard, local, and L1 influenced realizations, especially if the second language is acquired outside the home (see Agnihotri 1979; Heselwood and McChrystal 2000; Verma et al. 1992). In such cases, the parents are usually immigrants who speak a second language variety that includes features from their first language. As in monolingual situations, speakers of the same age will presumably have more influence in shaping the accent/dialect that the bilinguals will develop than their parents. However, the initial parental model that should provide the child with the basic phonological and sociolinguistic patterns of the dialect may be impoverished or missing. Sociolinguistic factors such as speech style, gender, social background, and area of residence of the families will play an important role in the adoption of particular accent features and their use for communicative purposes. Some of the studies that have looked at linguistic choice within each language as a way to signal social affiliation by the bilingual are reviewed below.

For some researchers, CS is seen as the alternation between not only languages but also dialects, styles, prosodic registers and paralinguistic cues. In the very first issue of *Language and Society* in 1974, Gumperz emphasized linguistic diversity (rather than uniformity) both in bilingual and monolingual urbanized societies where multi-dialectalism must be the norm. Zentella's (1997) work is particularly interesting here because it shows that in the case of communities where different ethnic groups live, children learn different varieties of each of their languages. Her study of Puerto Rican children growing up in East Harlem showed how Spanish was being lost in the younger generation but how children were still able to establish their identity by speaking Puerto Rican English. The children were being exposed to standard and non-standard varieties of Spanish and English. One of these varieties in each case became the one they spoke best, but the others became part of their repertoire, and were influenced by their social networks. For instance the Puerto Ricans who stayed in *el bloque* neighborhood in El Barrio mainly spoke Puerto Rican English and considered their identity as distinct from "American." Those who moved away from the neighborhood to areas populated by Anglos found themselves speaking more Standard English as a way to facilitate their entry into new educational and employment networks and were described as "acting/sounding white." On the other hand, those who mixed with

African-Americans spoke African-American varieties of English (AAVE) the most and identified with "talking and acting Black."

Al-Khatib (2003) looked at CS patterns in Lebanese–English bilinguals growing up in London and found that a particular choice of language and variety can be used by the bilingual in defiance in cases of social conflict. She gives an example of morphemically marked language alternation where one speaker apparently opts for the adolescent London dialect during an interaction at home despite the fact that this variety is normally reserved for interactions outside the home (the youngsters associate it with power display and credibility among young Londoners):

(1) W (addressing his mother):   inti bta'mli aTyab akil
                                  "You make the tastiest food!"
     L (his brother):   baddu yjeeb SaHbu hal**suck up**!
                                  "He wants to invite his friend, this suck up!"

Al-Khatib does not provide phonetic transcription nor does she explain what the home English variety sounds like, if not like London English, but her study is one of the very few investigations into the different language varieties that bilingual children might develop as part of what Al-Khatib calls *socio-pragmatic competence*. This level of competence is more evident with increasing age, as the older bilinguals in her study used more marked (salient) alternations to make a point, while the younger ones use both marked and unmarked alternations.

The use of different varieties of a language for different communicative purposes was also demonstrated by Di Luzio (1984) when he described German–Italian bilingual children's switches from German and Standard Italian to the native Italian dialect that they had learned at home. The native dialect was used to perform particular speech activities that had emotional and expressive functions that were connected with the children's home socialization process. For instance the children normally used German for their everyday interactions and learned Standard Italian at school, but they switched to their native Italian dialect to tell personal stories, make funny comments, plead, or protest.

Purcell (1984) refers to the alternation between different dialects or prosodic registers as *code-shifting*. She describes the case of young Hawaiian residents who learn General American English and Hawaiian English together with the associated sociolinguistic rules for their occurrence. Microanalyses of young children's interactions with various members of their speech community showed evidence of code-shifting at the lexical, grammatical, phonological, and prosodic levels between General American English and Hawaiian English that correlated with the children's convergence and divergence strategies, i.e. depending on shifts in topic, the ethnosocial background of their interlocutor, and their desire to maintain or minimize distance with that interlocutor.

Cases of dialect- or accent-shifting in children are comparable to what is normally observed in bilingual CS, especially where the purpose of the shift or switch is to express a change in addressee or audience, topic, emphasis, emotion, or stance (Giles 1973; Gumperz 1982a; Hymes 1974). However, the apparently fluid boundaries in terms of constraints governing the occurrence of certain features in dialects have led some researchers to discount cases of accent-shifting as CS behavior due to the suggestion that only the latter is rule-governed (e.g. Alvarez-Caccamo 1998). But research on phonological variation in adult- and child-directed speech shows that variation is rule-governed and is part of the overall linguistic competence that a child must acquire in order to be a speaker of his/her language (Docherty et al. 2006; Roberts 1997). Some researchers have gone as far as suggesting that social factors in speech events restrict the selection of linguistic variables in the same way as syntactic environments determine grammatical variables (Blom and Gumperz 1972:421). But while this view might suggest that selection rules are not simply a matter of conscious choice, studies like Al-Khatib's, Zentella's, and Purcell's present an intermediate position by showing that choice does play a role and is intricately related to communicative intent.

9.4 Children's sociophonetic competence in bilingual settings

Very little research to date has examined the fine-grained phonetic detail of bilingual children's verbal interactions. This may, perhaps, be due to the view that bilinguals' component languages constitute discrete systems. However, it is the aim of this chapter to demonstrate that bilingual children manifest subtle forms of phonetic accommodation both within and across their languages and language varieties. The following sections are devoted to illustrating and elaborating this claim.

9.4.1 English–Arabic bilingual data

The CS data discussed here are taken from a detailed sociophonetic study of three English–Arabic bilinguals growing up in the United Kingdom (Khattab 2003). The children were a five-year-old female (Maguy) and two brothers aged seven (Mazen) and ten (Mohamed). All three had Lebanese parents who had immigrated to the UK and had been living there for over ten years. The children were born and raised in Yorkshire and were exposed to Arabic from birth and to English from around 6 months when they started attending nursery school. The parents used mainly Arabic at home and were keen on their children learning spoken and written Arabic for religious and cultural reasons. The children, however, had all become English-dominant and were in danger of experiencing L1 attrition due to the lack of other Arabic speakers in their environment, the lack of support for their language at school, and the higher status of the society language.

The children were audio-recorded in various settings including free play sessions with monolingual English friends, picture-naming and story-telling in English with the investigator, and similar tasks in Arabic with their mothers. Each session lasted for 30–45 minutes. The children used only English in all but the sessions with their mothers. This limited the code-switched data that will be discussed here to 337 utterances, which should be interpreted with care since the original aim of the study was not to look at CS; rather, the main interest was in looking at whether the bilinguals' production in English and Arabic showed any interaction between their languages. Results reported elsewhere (see Khattab 2002a, 2002b, 2002c, 2003, 2006, 2007) showed that they produced native-like English (with Yorkshire features) and Arabic in each of the sessions, but that their Arabic production occasionally exhibited English phonetic patterns. There were no Arabic code-switches during the English-only sessions by any of the children. However, during the Arabic sessions with the mothers, the three children frequently code-switched to English for various reasons that will be discussed below.

It must be noted that the term CS is here used as an umbrella term for discourse phenomena which also included borrowing, mixing, loan words, alternation, code-shifting, and sometimes cases where the children reverted to an English monolingual base for a short while before they were encouraged to speak Arabic by the mothers. Moreover, single-word switches were analyzed as they occurred frequently in the picture-naming data. Single-word switches have been traditionally discarded from analyses in the CS literature since there may be no morphological or syntactic criteria for determining whether the item is following L1 or L2 rules, which makes it difficult to determine whether they constitute cases of CS or borrowing (Poplack et al. 1988; Romaine 1995). In this study, however, these utterances proved interesting to look at since their phonetic behavior varied depending on external as well as internal factors. A micro-analysis approach was adopted (Auer 1995) by looking at the context of the interactions, including what was said by the children and their mothers before, during, and/or after the switches.

All three children produced English utterances with both English- and Arabic-like phonetics and in both single- and mixed-language utterances (Fig. 9.1). However, there was no straightforward correlation between phonetic patterns (English-like or Arabic-like) and utterance length (single or multiple words) or utterance type (one language or mixed utterances). For instance, Maguy produced most switches with English-like phonetics (67%) and had very few mixed-language utterances. Mazen code-switched more than the other children and his switches included a more balanced mix of English- and Arabic-like phonetics and of single- and mixed-language

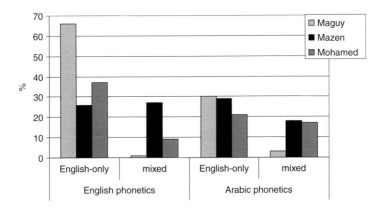

Figure 9.1 Phonetic patterns of English code-switches produced by each of the bilinguals during a 45-minute Arabic session with their mothers (N=337)

utterances. Mohamed had the fewest code-switches. His switches included a mix of English- and Arabic-like phonetics comparable to Mazen's but more single- than mixed-language utterances. All types of switches by all children comprised English- and Arabic-like phonetics, including single words and English-only utterances. These complex and sometimes un-expected patterns according to the linguistic context can be explained by relating them to sociolinguistic factors such as the communicative role they played in the interactions and the language mixing abilities of each child.

9.4.2   Switching patterns
The three children were English-dominant and frequently inserted single words and short phrases from English during the Arabic sessions, which is very common in child bilingualism. A small number of switches could be considered cases of code-mixing, since they occurred without the partici-pants (the children or their mothers) noticing and/or meaning to mix for a social purpose (Auer 1998:16). However, there were many more cases of what Auer refers to as *functional code-switches*, i.e. switching for a particular communicative purpose.

9.4.2.1   Role of English-like phonetics
Some of these switches were only produced with English-like phonetics and mainly occurred when the children did not know the Arabic target. These could be considered cases of nonce borrowing, i.e. of lexical items borrowed from English due to the inevitability of lexical gaps in the child-ren's Arabic vocabulary (Ervin-Tripp and Reyes 2005:89). Myers-Scotton (2006a:205) argues for these to be called "code-switches" and to be distin-guished from established borrowings that have "tags" for both languages.

If "tags" refers to phonetic as well as morphological detail as originally used in Myers-Scotton's model, then this could explain the number of English utterances that were produced with English- or Arabic-like phonetics depending on the context. Unlike Myers-Scotton's model, though, the context here is taken to be social as well as grammatical (see §9.4.2.2). The children also used English code-switches with English-like phonetics in order to make metalinguistic comments or to negotiate meaning, as in (2). Here, while telling a picture story in Arabic, Mazen disputed particular translations with his mother when she tried to help:

(2) Mazen: ʔɪ-sːɑbe keːn **ʃɒkt**
                                   "The boy was shocked."

     Mother (trying to help):   koːn ɹɪʕleːn
                                   "He was sad."

     Mazen (protesting):   laʔ **hi wəʃ ʃɒkt**
                                   "No he was shocked."

     Mother: ʔe, jaʕne zɪʕleːn
                                   "Yes, it means he was sad."

9.4.2.2   Role of Arabic-like or mixed phonetics

All three children showed awareness of the communicative role that English and Arabic phonetic patterns can convey if applied to their English switches. They all resisted speaking Arabic and one way this was achieved was by sometimes producing English utterances with Arabic phonetics for targets that they knew in Arabic, as evidenced by the mothers' request for the Arabic word. Their interactions with their mothers varied between convergence and divergence depending on the needs of the situation and on their co-operative mood. Examples of convergence included reverting back to Arabic when the mothers encouraged them to do so or persevering with the English switches but applying Arabic phonetics to them. In the following example, Maguy's [k] in "castle" is unaspirated, her raised [ä] is typical of Arabic /a/, and her final /l/ is clear. Maguy had produced 'castle' as [kʰasɫ] or [kʰasʊ] during the English sessions, with aspirated /k/s, a more open /a/, and a syllabic or a vocalized /l/, the latter due to the dark /l/ quality in English.

(3) *Maguy and Mother, looking at a picture book*
     Mother: ʃu haɪda?
                                   "What's this?"

     Maguy: *k*äsəl
                                   "Castle"

     Mother (in a cheeky tone):   w bɪl ʕarabe?
                                   "And in Arabic?"

     Maguy: ʔasˤɪr
                                   "Castle"

The resulting accented pronunciations were very similar to those found in the parents' English accent as evidenced in the example that follows (see Khattab 2002a, 2002b, 2002c, 2003, 2006, 2007) and suggest that the children might be applying phonetic accommodation as a way of converging to the speech of their interlocutor.

(4) *Maguy and Mother*
     Mother: l-*weɪl* ʔɪsmo ħuːt, ʃu ʔɪsmo l-*weɪl*?
                "The whale is called whale, what's the whale called?"
     Maguy: ħuːt
                "Whale"
     Mother: w haɪda?
                "And this?"
     Maguy: ʃaːɾk
                "Shark"
     Mother: ʃɑːɾk, braːvo maːːgi
                "Shark, bravo Maguy!"

Here, the mother's production of "whale" is noticeably non-native due to the final clear /l/. Maguy produces the word "shark" with a fronted vowel and a post-vocalic /r/ despite the fact that her English accent is generally non-rhotic and that she had produced this word during the English sessions as [ʃɑːk]. The mother does not notice that the answer was in English and simply moves on to the next picture. Sometimes, the accented patterns were exaggerated versions of the parents' foreign accent and may suggest that the children are aware of particular phonetic features that convey "Arabic-ness" and can exaggerate them for particular effects. For instance, while some of the Arabic realizations that Mazen applied to those English words were reminiscent of his parents' production of those words in English, he also applied these to words that his parents would not have produced with that degree of foreign accent:

(5) *Mazen, referring to one of the cartoon characters*
     Mazen: lamːa *fəlik* bjɪʒe
               "When Flick comes."

Here even Mazen's parents, who are advanced speakers of English, would have produced "Flick" as [flɪk], but Mazen overcompensated by breaking the initial cluster and producing a high tense vowel in the second syllable.

Some other times, the children's behavior seemed less conscious but rather driven by the mothers' use of accented English in the same interaction (6) or the child's treatment of an accented English word as Arabic (7).

(6) *Mazen and Mother*
     Mazen: *tʰɔːtəs*
                                                     "Tortoise"
     Mother (construing *tortoise* as *turtle*):   *tɜɾtəl*
                                                     "Turtle"

Mazen (looking confused):	*tɜrtəl*, laʔ *tʰɔːtəs*
	"Turtle, no, tortoise"
Mother (realizing mistake):	ʔe, z ɪ lɪħfe
	"Yes, tortoise"
Mazen (a bit later on):	*tɜrtəs . . . tɜrtəl . . . tɔrtəs*
	"Tortoise … turtle … tortoise"

(7) *Mazen and Mother, looking at a picture of a nose*

Mazen:	*noːz*
	"Nose"
Mother:	ʃu ʔɪsmo bɪl ʕarabe
	"What is it called in Arabic?"
Mazen (annoyed):	*noːz*, ʔolet *noːz*
	"Nose, I said nose!"

In (6), Mazen had produced the right target in English ("tortoise") but his mother confused him by calling it a "turtle" (there is only one word for both "tortoise" and "turtle" in Arabic). Mazen initially repeats his mother's non-native production (with an unaspirated /t/, a post-vocalic /r/, and clear final /l/) but then objects to it and calls it "tortoise" with English-like pronunciation. As the story goes on Mazen starts shifting back and forth between the two lexical options as well as exploring the various possible pronunciations for these words, with "tortoise" being produced at one point as [tɜrtəs]. In (7) Mazen was surprised that his mother was asking for the Arabic target because he was convinced that he had just produced it. His realization of this word in English is [nəʊz].

Examples of divergence include switching back to native English as a reaction to a conflict in the conversation:

(8) *Mazen and Mother, in the middle of a story*

Mother:	ʃu eːxdɪ-t-l-a?
	"What is she taking for her?"
Mazen:	*grosəriːz*
	"Groceries"
Mother:	ʃuʔˈ
	"What?"
Mazen (annoyed):	*gɹəʊsəɹiz*
	"Groceries!"

Here Mazen first replies in English but produces the word "groceries" with a tap and a monophthongal realization of /əʊ/. When the mother asks for clarification, Mazen decides to switch to a native-like realization, which is more typical of how he realizes these sounds in English.

Other factors that influenced the children's production included the type of activity and the progress of the interaction. For instance, one activity that triggered English production the most for all the children was looking at pictures of children's films that they had watched in

English and being asked to tell the stories in Arabic. Since these were English films, Maguy attempted to tell the stories entirely in English and refused to use Arabic, while Mazen and Mohamed used a combination of English-only and mixed utterances. The mixed utterances had more English-like phonetic patterns than Arabic-like ones, until the mothers pleaded for Arabic. On the other hand, after a long stretch of Arabic production by the children and their mothers, an English switch was more likely to have Arabic-like phonetic features than English ones. This points to the important role of lexical as well as phonetic access in the production process and suggests that phonetic implementation can be influenced by the highly activated language at a particular period in the interaction. However, as can be seen in (9), the levels of activation leading to a more English or Arabic mode can quickly change depending on communicative needs for divergence or convergence.

(9) *Mohamed and Mother*
    Mother: ʔaj:a fi:lm ʕaʒabak
                    "Which film did you like?"
    Mohamed: ***dʒɔːrdʒ əv ðə dʒʌŋgəl***
                    "George of the Jungle"
    Mother: ʃu sˤaːr fi?
                    "What happened in it?"
    Mohamed: marːa keːn fi hal ***hʌntɚ*** keːn ʕindo ***lɪtəl vɪlədʒ*** baʕdeːn. . .
                    "Once there was this hunter who had a little village
                    then . . ."
    Mohamed (after a while with no input from mother):
                    ðə hʌntə lɒst-ɪz waɪf ðɛn hi smaʃt ɪntu-ə tʃɹiː
                    "The hunter lost his wife and then he smashed into a tree."
    Mother (catching up and interrupting):
                    ʔeː w ʃu sˤaːr
                    "Yes, and what happened?"
    Mohamed: baʕdeːn ***dʒɔːrdʒ əv ðə dʒʌŋgəl seɪvd hɚ***
                    "Then George of the Jungle saved her."

Here Mohamed starts by inserting English utterances with Arabic phonetics when the mother leads the interaction in Arabic, moves to English phonetics when she accepts his switches, and then moves back to Arabic phonetics when she decides to interrupt again to remind him of the language of the interaction.

9.4.3 The role of the caregiver in raising the child's linguistic awareness

The mothers played a major role in facilitating interaction. When the children struggled to remember the Arabic word for the target in question, the mothers were very accommodating and asked the children to say them in English. Only when the mothers knew that the children were capable of producing the Arabic version did they insist on eliciting these. Their elicitation methods were varied, skillful, and effective. One technique was to request a translation ("What is X in Arabic?"), which was common after the child's production of the target in English, but sometimes occurred without an English prompt. Another technique was to relate the word to an Arabic context by mentioning a previous experience in which the child produced it in Arabic due to the needs of the situation or interlocutor, e.g. "What do you ask Grandma to make you?" (Grandma is a monolingual Arabic speaker); "What did we watch at our neighbor's house in Beirut?" etc. A third technique was to produce the first sound or syllable of the target word as a reminder, and in all these cases the children immediately remembered the target and produced it in full. A final technique was to produce the full target and ask the children to imitate. Repeated performances are common in both monolingual and bilingual child-caregiver interactions in many cultures as a way of reminding children of the target or familiarizing them with linguistic and sociocultural information (Döpke 1992:147; Schieffelin and Ochs 1986:172). Regardless of the technique used, a correct response was often followed by the mother's repetition of that response as a way to positively reinforce it and increase the teaching opportunity. This happened more often with the younger child's interactions with her mother, which might suggest an age-graded use of this technique.

When the parents were interviewed about language use at home they all reported that the recording sessions were representative of the daily struggles that they experience while encouraging the children to speak Arabic. However, informal observations showed that the family's daily interactions included more CS, and the parents did not insist on their children speaking Arabic as much as they did in the recorded sessions. Still, the parents were very aware of the fact that they are the main source of Arabic input to the children and they were very keen to resist L1 attrition for their children. The parents' relentless efforts may have played a major role in raising linguistic awareness in the children and in their harnessing of fine phonetic detail for communicative purposes. The children have learned to associate various people and activities not only with particular languages, but also with accents. Bilinguals also generalize their skill of knowing which language to use with whom to strangers who are similar in appearance (Fantini 1985; McClure 1981).

9.4.4 Modeling the bilingual children's code-switching behavior

The dominant perspectives on CS have been psycholinguistic (looking at the processes underlying single and mixed-language production and perception), grammatical (looking at intra-sentential code-switching in order to find rule-governed patterns), or sociolinguistic (looking at the relation between linguistic structure and social factors). While psycholinguistic and grammatical approaches have mainly outlined language-specific and online processing constraints on the bilingual and their output, social approaches have looked more closely at external constraints. These range from topic, interlocutor, and setting to more detailed examinations of bilingual interactions in order to understand processes that might lead to language alternation. More and more studies are following a micro-analytical approach in order to take into account the changing needs of the individuals in terms of their relations to others within an interactional setting. But the emphasis has often been on language (rather than linguistic) choice as a way to reflect issues of identity, empowerment, conflict development and resolution, and negotiation of meaning. In trying to explain the bilinguals' speech production, insights from all three approaches to CS are helpful, but the one that best explains the above data is the sociolinguistic approach.

From a psycholinguistic perspective, Roelofs and Verhoef (2006) suggest that the bilingual may have shared representations for phonologically "similar" material, e.g. similar phonemes, and that this similarity triggers phonetic activation from both languages, leading to the "wrong" one being used at times. Evidence for bilinguals treating phonological material from their languages as "similar" could be taken from their use of phonetic realizations that are typical of one language in the production of the other language. Examples from this study included the production of taps and trills in English switches instead of approximant /r/, clear final /l/, and raised /a/. However, the bilinguals were not simply choosing the wrong variant, since they largely restricted the production of these accented variants to the Arabic sessions and, within these sessions, often showed evidence of producing them for particular communicative effect. When pictures were being named in the L1, the L2 was still active because it behaved like the L1 and was required for lexical gaps and other functions. Therefore the L2 lexical representations were still available and the mapping from concepts to words likely to be stronger, resulting in more answers in the L2 in this case than the L1 (Kroll et al. 2006). The bilinguals still, however, produced some of these English words with English phonetics and others with Arabic phonetics. They must therefore be exerting some choice at a later level in the processing stage in order to produce one or the other. Instead of just having links between the morphemes of translation equivalents which activate English and Arabic sounds at the morpheme level (Roelofs and Verhoef 2006:168), the bilinguals in this study might also have established links between English- and Arabic-accented versions of the same lexical item, with one realization making it to the articulation stage.

From a grammatical point of view, grammatical structure and base language did not play a major role in explaining the phonetic patterning of the children's CS, since comparable mixed and single-language utterances were produced with both English-like and Arabic-like phonetics. This is not to suggest that structure has no role to play in the patterning of CS, but the data discussed here contained many more inter- than intra-sentential switches, and only the latter could constitute a real test for grammatical models. Moreover, a flexible view of the matrix language could explain some of the patterns observed. While the matrix language is often assumed to be the language of the interlocutor, this can change if the child's dominant language is the guest language (Lanza 1997). The mothers here were mainly using Arabic but the children were sometimes operating from an English matrix language.

The CS behavior presented here is better evaluated from a sociolinguistic perspective as a manifestation of the macro- and micro-social influences of the situation determining not only language choice, but also detailed phonetic choices within each language (Fishman 1972; Auer 1998). In terms of macro-influences, the home setting did certainly influence the bilinguals' linguistic behavior since CS was common during family interactions, and Arabic-accented English was commonly produced by the parents. Since the bilinguals were aware that their mothers spoke English and Arabic, they did not have to limit themselves to one language as they would if they were addressing monolinguals. They did, however, accommodate to the mothers in a different way, by using foreign-accented English regardless of whether or not the utterances were mixed or English-only.

As for micro-influences, specific interactions led to the particular phonetic patterns observed. For instance, the phonetic patterns of English responses varied depending on whether the Arabic target was known or unknown. They also varied according to whether the bilinguals were being cooperative or challenging the situation. Myers-Scotton (1993a) notes that bilinguals can switch between the unmarked and marked code during interactions with other bilinguals to signal harmony or conflict. Since the unmarked code during the interactions described here (Arabic) is not the bilinguals' dominant language, one way to maintain harmony within the constraints of their English dominance could be by producing English utterances with Arabic-like phonetics. The bilinguals might be showing what Al-Khatib (2003:412) calls their individual social, interpersonal, and pragmatic behavior, which might stem from their attempt to create their own identity and convey their own agenda within the larger social context. This takes the form of convergence in some cases and divergence in other cases in order to challenge the situation. Looking at the social and situational context of the interactions as well as the responsiveness and orientation of both child and mother during, before, and after the utterance of interest helped explain the English and Arabic phonetic patterns, especially in single-word utterances.

9.4.5　Labeling the switches

Some of the English switches encountered in the data share similarities with bilingual behavior that have been labelled as *code-switching style*

(Gumperz 1982a), *code-switching mode* (Poplack 1980), "unmarked choice" (Myers-Scotton 1993a), or *crossing* (Rampton 2005). While Alvarez-Caccamo (1998) has argued that these types of interactions should not count as CS since it is not obvious whether the speakers are actively combining items from two separate systems, what is certain is that the speakers are aware of switching and are using these switches for communicative purposes. Woolard (1998) uses the term *bivalency* to refer to the bilingual's use of words or segments that could "belong" equally to both codes and are therefore ambiguous. Her examples are from related languages like Catalan and Spanish where the lexical items in both languages are similar or the same, but the phonetic realization is different (e.g. the verb *saben* "(they) know," which is differentiated in the two languages by the quality of the second vowel, [e] in Castilian and [ɛ] in Catalan). Bilinguals can in this case strategically use one pronunciation or another for social, ideological, and communicative purposes. In the case of unrelated languages like English and Arabic, there are fewer shared words and the bilinguals engaged in the type of bivalency described by Woolard might have to be a little bit more creative. One way the bilinguals achieve this is by producing words with varying patterns. In this case, the different realizations could be seen as belonging to separate codes since the English-like one is produced by the bilinguals' native English community and friends and the Arabic-like one is produced by their parents and other non-native speakers in their environment. The productions with Arabic-like phonetics by the bilinguals should not be described as cases of interference because they seemed able to control their realization depending on the linguistic and social context.

9.5   Conclusion

A shift in children's dominant language is common in immigrant situations and often results in L1 attrition unless the parents and the children make an extra effort to preserve it. As a result of L2 dominance, the L2 of the children in this study was often activated while they were in L1 interactions with their mothers. While bilinguals are encouraged to speak the L1, much of their behavior often shows partial accommodation, which is normally used to refer to CS as a means to converge to an interlocutor's language while at the same time producing elements from the other language (Sachdev and Giles 2006). In the case of bilingual children, however, they may be using their L2 with an L1 foreign accent.

Bilingual children use whichever linguistic means is available to them to establish themselves as bilingual speakers. If dominance in one language stands in the way of conversing in the other, children compensate by producing accented speech and making sure that they restrict this to home conversations with their parents. This creates a different identity for them from the one they convey to their monolingual English friends, whom they address with the local features that they have acquired from the immediate monolingual community. This identity may also be used at home when the bilinguals are challenging their parents and establishing their linguistic credentials.

There are many reports of caregivers accommodating to their children to help them convey their message and to understand other people's utterances, but fewer reports concentrate on the child's accommodation to the caregiver. The bilinguals described here sometimes used "foreign" rather than "foreigner talk" with their mothers. Previous analyses of the mothers' speech and a micro-analytical approach to mother–child interactions suggest that the children were sometimes accommodating to the mothers' non-native English accent. This evidence contrasts with Chambers' (2002) claim that the children of immigrants have an innate accent-filter which allows them to filter-out their parents' non-native accent as part of their developing sociolinguistic competence. While Chambers is correct in observing that many children of immigrant families end up speaking more like their peers than with the second language accent of their parents, children can store information about native and non-native patterns in the input around them and can draw upon that information for communicative purposes. Single word productions are particularly interesting to examine because they show native- and non-native-like features despite the fact that the base language effect in this case would be minimal.

Bilingual studies that have paid attention to phonetics in CS have normally involved carefully controlled experimental designs where stimuli are created to elicit a monolingual or a bilingual mode and the resulting production and perception behavior of the bilingual is taken as evidence for or against their ability to switch at the phonetic level or whether they might be influenced by factors such as the base language (see Bullock, this volume). This chapter suggests that bilinguals may constantly move between bilingual and monolingual modes during the course of the interaction depending on the needs of the situation. Microanalyses of interactions between bilinguals and their mothers showed that the base language does not always determine the phonetic patterns of the bilingual's utterance. Bilinguals constantly negotiate meaning and identity with their interlocutors and the phonetic detail of their utterances can reveal a lot about their convergence and divergence strategies.

Part III

The structural implications of code-switching

10

Phonetic reflexes of code-switching

Barbara E. Bullock

10.1 Introduction

While there is abundant descriptive and theoretical literature on the morpho-syntactic aspects of code-switching (hereafter CS) in a variety of language pairings, the phonetic and phonological reflexes of CS remain relatively unexplored. The paucity of research on these latter properties of CS may reflect the widespread assumption that, in contrast to borrowing, CS utterances manifest an abrupt transition between the sound systems of each language. When this view is challenged, it is generally done so on the basis that it inaccurately describes the degree of phonological integration that lexical borrowings, but not code-switches, may undergo. The adaptation of loan words has received considerable attention from phonologists, but the relationship between CS and the sound system of a language has not. If borrowing and CS fall along a single continuum, as many linguists have argued, then it is possible that CS utterances, as well as borrowings, may manifest some degree of integration or convergence.

This chapter presents an overview of the extant research on the phonetics of CS and attempts to address the types of questions that a full linguistic inquiry into the phonetics/phonology of CS should explore. Much of the current literature on phonetics and CS arises from the field of psycholinguistics, where the focus is on the mechanisms underlying CS in bilinguals (see Kutas et al., Gullberg et al., this volume) rather than on understanding the role of phonetics/phonology in relation to the structural aspects of bilingual CS. By examining both the psycholinguistic and the structural aspects of the phonetics of CS, this chapter demonstrates that many of the controversies that arise in explorations of the morpho-syntax of CS exist as well for the phonetic domain. In this respect, three broad questions regarding the role of the sound system in CS can be raised:

(1.) Does CS have an effect on phonological/phonetic production and perception?

(2.) Can phonological/phonetic properties be observed to constrain CS production?

(3.) Is there a phonetic base or matrix language in CS?

Each of these questions has been addressed in the small body of research on the phonetics and phonology of CS, but the findings of these studies are often contradictory. Nevertheless, this chapter will advance tentative answers to these questions and address the many challenges that await future researchers in this field.

As has often been noted, there is a good bit of terminological confusion surrounding the term "code-switching." This may be particularly true of some of the literature on CS and phonetics, where "code-switching" may refer not to the alternation of languages within a single utterance but instead to a bilingual's performance in one language rather than the other (see Bahr and Frisch 2002 on "code-switching" and voice identification in forensic phonetics; Hazan and Boulakia 1993 on phonetic production). The focus of this chapter will be limited to a consideration of the perception and production of bilingual speakers when they are performing simultaneously in both languages either via alternational or insertional CS (see Muysken 2000). The organization of this chapter is as follows: § 10.2 examines the use of phonological integration as a metric for distinguishing borrowing from CS. In § 10.3 we turn to a review and analysis of psycholinguistic "switching studies" that are largely devoted to examining bilingual perception and that rely on the notion of a phonetic base language. § 10.4 reviews the findings of a handful of recent linguistic studies on the phonetics and phonology of CS productions that, in part, advance answers and introduce new complexities into the question of whether bilinguals truly switch completely from the phonetic structure of one language to the next. The possibility that prosody constrains CS is considered in § 10.5. Finally, § 10.6 concludes with areas to be investigated and challenges for future research on CS and sound structure.

10.2   The phonology and phonetics of contact phenomena

There has been a great deal of debate within the field of contact linguistics on whether or not borrowing can be distinguished from CS on the basis of phonological structure. It is important to clarify what is intended by phonological, as opposed to phonetic, structure. Phonology is commonly held to be distinct from phonetics. Where phonological differences are envisioned as categorical, phonetic ones are seen as gradient. For instance, /b/ defines the phonemic category of a voiced stop which, depending on the language and the context, may in actuality be only partially or gradiently voiced. Similarly, L(ow)H(igh) defines the distinctive phonological category of a rising tone but the slope of the LH tone may be more or less steep depending on the distance of the interval between the pitch alignment positions of the valley and the peak. Phonological distinctions, such as /b/ or LH, are generally salient to native speakers, whereas the gradient phonetic properties of an utterance, such as more or less voicing or steeper pitch rises, are not.

In a general way, the division between phonology and phonetics is analogous to the segregation of research strands in borrowing and CS, respectively. Much of the work on borrowing is undertaken at the phonological level, analyzing broadly transcribed data to advance the notion that a borrowing conforms to the sound pattern of its recipient language. Conversely, research on the interaction between CS and sound structure invariably involves examining (or manipulating) the discrete phonetic properties of an utterance since it is assumed that code-switches should manifest only marginal cross-linguistic assimilation or, ideally, none at all. The following sections discuss, in turn, the phonology of borrowing and the phonetics of CS.

10.2.1   Phonology as a metric of lexical borrowing

It is popularly accepted that established borrowings tend to show a high degree of phonological integration to the recipient language. This observation has inspired a subdiscipline of theoretical linguistics, the study of *loan phonology*, which attempts to account for the perceptual, articulatory, and prosodic constraints that map donor language inputs onto well-formed recipient language outputs (see Coetsem 1988 for a theory of loan phonology, Jacobs and Gussenhoven 2000 for a review of loan phonology analyses within Optimality Theory). Established loan words typically manifest the application of an array of common strategies – deletion, epenthesis, sound substitutions – that reveal the systematic properties of the phonology of the recipient language. For instance, throughout the Caribbean, Vick's® VapoRub®, widely used as a cure-all salve, has been adapted into Spanish as *vivaporú* [biβaporú], manifesting the appropriate distribution of the Spanish labial allophones [b] and [β] as substitutes for /v/, which is absent from the Spanish inventory. Its syllabic structure, as well, conforms to Spanish via the deletion of the coda consonants from the English input form.

That *vivaporú* is a borrowing is hardly in doubt; it is fully integrated into the grammatical system of the recipient language and Spanish monolinguals and bilinguals alike use it ubiquitously. Yet identifying the status of a donor language lexeme as a borrowing versus a CS is not always so straightforward even when such criteria as structural integration and high frequency of use are taken as indexes of borrowing. In fact, many researchers agree that CS and borrowing cannot be fully differentiated but, instead, form a continuum of non-assimilated to assimilated forms (Myers-Scotton

1993a; Treffers-Daller 1991). Still others find it necessary to distinguish these phenomena (Poplack and Meechan 1995), reflecting the intuition that the processes underlying them are different; CS arises from the ability of bilinguals to alternate between two linguistic systems on-line, whereas borrowing derives from lexical storage. Of the two, only CS is held to be a uniquely bilingual behavior.

In early theoretical works that attempted to distinguish single lexeme borrowings from CS, phonological integration was held to be an important factor in identifying loan word status. However, many researchers soon objected that borrowings of any vintage (new or established) do not always manifest phonological integration. For instance, even monolingual speakers of English may manifest a reasonable phonological approximation of the French culinary term *jus* [ʒy] despite the fact that established French loan words in English, such as *jury, justice, Julian,* show fortition of the post-alveolar word initial fricative [ʒ] to the affricate [dʒ] to conform to English phonotatic patterns.

The failure of all borrowings to be consistently adapted to the phonology of the source language led to the abandonment of phonological integration as a necessary property of loan words. Unassimilated loans are now either classified as "nonce borrowings" (Poplack et al. 1988) or are considered to belong within a continuum that spans from fully integrated borrowings to unassimilated code-switches (Myers-Scotton 1993a). Whether the degree to which a lexeme has assimilated *phonetically*, as opposed to phonologically, can be used as a diagnostic for situating it along such a purported continuum remains an open question.

Rarely considered in the debate over whether one can distinguish borrowing from CS is the potential objection that switches, as well as borrowings, may manifest phonological adaptation. In a study of Finnish–American English CS, Lehtinen (1966:191) remarked early on that, "The phonological switching point cannot always be established with precision." In particular, Lehtinen notes that English stem-final consonants preceding Finnish suffixes appear to undergo Finnish consonant gradation while in all other respects the speakers are faithful to the English phonological form of the stem. Such forms, then, are only partially integrated so that the phonetic transition between English and Finnish is obscured. Under one view, these forms would likely be classified as "nonce borrowings" rather than code-switches, but regardless, Lehtinen's observation about a potential interplay between phonology and CS passed largely unnoticed.

Intuitively, it would seem apparent that bilinguals may show signs of phonological adaptation in CS since many bilinguals speak with a detectable accent in one, or perhaps both, of their languages. Accents may be attributed to various individual factors such as language dominance, age of acquisition, or to external factors such as the quality of the ambient input that they receive which, particularly in immigrant settings, may differ substantially from the norms of the monolingual community. In fact, it has been demonstrated that many bilinguals in such situations acquire the ability to calibrate their speech to phonetically accommodate to the non-native pronunciations of their interlocutors, even when they may pass as native speakers in monolingual contexts (see Khattab, this volume). Given that very few bilinguals are equally proficient in both their languages and that they likely command a variety of socio-phonetic registers that they may be able to consciously control, it is reasonable to expect some degree of cross-linguistic convergence in their speech. Of particular relevance to the study of CS, then, is the question of whether bilinguals alter the sound structure of one of both languages *particularly* when switching between them. In order to investigate this question, the level of linguistic analysis must shift from the phonological, where sound alternations are generally salient, to the acoustic phonetic, where degrees of difference, rather than wholesale sound substitutions, may be revealed.

10.3   The processing of acoustic information in bilingual switching studies

Psycholinguists interested in the mechanisms that underlie bilingualism, such as lexical access, inhibitory control, and selective attention, have conducted a series of studies investigating the acoustic and phonetic properties of language switching. These works largely aim to test proposals similar to those put forth by Macnamara (1967a, b) and Macnamara and Kushnir (1971) that bilinguals' control of the input (perception) operates independently from their control of the output (production). Under such a view, the input switch is said to be automatic and biased toward the language of the incoming signal. That is, speakers expect the input signal to continue in the same language, and hence their processing strategies are tuned to that language. Thus, language switching has a processing cost. On the other hand, the output switch would operate under the conscious or voluntary control of the speaker. The normal design of a switching study involves the insertion of a "guest" word into what is termed a "base" or "precursor" language that provides the language set for the input. The aim is to determine whether the base language affects the recognition, perception, or production of the guest word.

Gullberg et al. (this volume) define language switching studies as those that induce participants to switch at a predestined point in an utterance. This is distinct from CS, which is assumed be voluntary. For the purposes of this chapter, though, switching studies are additionally characterized as experiments that examine the insertion of only a single guest word into a base language utterance. Thus, from a linguistic point of view, this kind of switching may fall more toward the borrowing than the CS end of the continuum of contact phenomena. However, at least one switching study (Li 1996, discussed below) endeavors to control for these different contact phenomena by manipulating the phonological structure of the guest word.

In the phonetic realm, switching studies normally target bilingual perception and are nearly exclusively dedicated to examining one phonological parameter, the categorical perception of the voiced /b,d,g/ versus voiceless /p,t,k/ series of stop consonants. One acoustic cue for the voiced–voiceless distinction is voice onset time (VOT), which defines the interval between the burst release of the consonant and the onset of voicing of the vowel. VOT spans a continuum with different languages situating the transition between a voiced and voiceless stop at different points. In Spanish and French, voiceless stops are produced with very short VOT values and are said to be short lag stops. In English, by contrast, VOT values for voiceless stops are relatively long and such stops are produced with a period of aspiration following the consonant burst, as indicated in the waveform diagram in Figure 10.1. The gradient nature of the voicing lag makes it an ideal testing ground for perceptual switching studies since the VOT value can be manipulated either through the creation of synthetic stimuli or through edited natural speech tokens. This allows for the establishment of clear end-points; for instance, VOT values of − 60 ms would be perceived as voiced by all listeners and, at the other extreme, values of 60 ms, as voiceless. Between the two endpoints lie ambiguous stimuli that could be perceived as either voiced or voiceless. In general, phonetic switching studies have been designed to test whether the language of presentation, the base language, has an effect on the perceptual categorization of ambiguous inputs. The results have been contradictory, so it is worth considering the relevant experiments in turn.

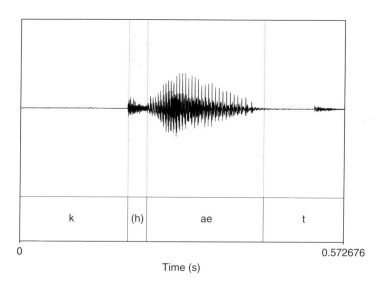

Figure 10.1 Waveform of English *cat* showing long voicing lag and accompanying aspiration for initial /k/ between the vertical lines

Using synthetically generated nonce syllables, Caramazza et. al (1973), testing French–English bilinguals, and Williams (1977), testing Spanish–English bilinguals, found that listeners were unaffected by the language of the experimental instructions, taken as the precursor language, and that bilinguals appeared to have fixed (i.e. merged) perceptual boundaries for the voicing distinction across their two languages. Elman et al. (1977) directly assessed the effect of the precursor language on bilingual perceptual switching, using natural stimuli embedded in either English (1a) or Spanish (1b) base language contexts, as shown by the translations equivalents in (1).

(1)　Elman et al. (1977:972) switching stimuli
　　(a.) "Write the word /pa/"
　　(b.) "Escriba la palabra /pa/"

In contrast to the previous findings in VOT switching studies, Elman et al. found that bilinguals did shift their perceptual boundary in response to the precursor language. Further, the effect remained when their listeners were divided into groups reflecting different levels of bilingual proficiency. Even the highest proficiency bilinguals performed differently from the corresponding monolingual groups. The researchers hypothesized that their results differed from those of the previous studies primarily due to the use of natural versus synthetic speech tokens.

A number of subsequent studies confirm the dominance of the base language on the perception of the guest language in CS but acknowledge that there might be numerous factors – structural, contextual, and psychological – that impinge on a listener's access of a CS word (Soares and Grosjean 1984; Grosjean and Soares 1986; Grosjean 1988). With respect to structural factors, Bürki-Cohen et al. (1989) hypothesize that the phonetic structure of the stimuli itself may have a bearing on bilingual perception during CS. They constructed two different sets of stimuli, one in which the switched tokens could be homophonous across languages (French *dé* "dice" and English *day*), and one in which the phonology provides a distinctive cue to the guest language (French *ré* [ʁe] and English *ray* [ɹe]). They edited the tokens by splicing French and English productions together to create ambiguous or hybrid stimuli for the perception tasks. As in the Elman et al. study, the stimuli were embedded into base language carrier phrases as in (2).

(2)　Bürki-Cohen et al. (1989:365) switching stimuli
　　(a.) "We have to categorize (ray/day)"
　　(b.) "Il faut qu'on catégorise (ré/dé)"

They found that the base language had no effect on the listener's categorization of the language-neutral series of stimuli. The ambiguous stimuli of this series were identified as the same regardless of the precursor. However, they found a polarizing effect of the base language on the perception of the language-selective tokens. Here, the hybrid tokens were categorized more toward the guest language, in contrast to the base language. This implies that any effect of the base language is not necessarily assimilatory.

The use of the distinctive phonetic and phonotactic structure of a guest word as a perceptual cue to a language switch is also investigated by Li (1996). Li uses phonological criteria to distinguish English borrowings from code-switches in a Chinese–English context. For instance, the English word *flight* is pronounced [faɪ] as a borrowing but as a CS, it retains the English phonetic and phonotatic structure [flaɪt]. Li shows that the structurally distinctive properties of a CS allow listeners to recognize an English word in a Chinese base language as quickly as monolingual English listeners do. The recognition of borrowings that are phonologically integrated into Chinese was found to take much more time. Li uses this evidence as an argument against an automatic language input switch since the precursor language does not affect the perception of a CS. His results can be seen to affirm those of Bürki-Cohen et al. (1989) in that a significant phonological *dissimilarity* between languages can apparently facilitate the recognition or perception of CS.

The studies by Bürki-Cohen et al. (1989) and Li (1996) show that the effect of the precursor language on the perception of the guest language is probably not independent of the phonological properties under examination. This may be true of the acoustic level as well. Hazan and Boulakia (1993) examine an additional phonetic cue to the voicing distinction in stops, the frequency of the first formant (F_1) at the onset of the voicing of the vowel. F_1 onset frequency can present a strong perceptual cue for the voicing distinction in English but not in French. In contrast to the VOT continuum that serves as a distinctive voicing cue in both English and French, the cue weighting of F_1 onset frequency, then, is categorically different across these languages. In their study, edited tokens of /bɛn/ and /pɛn/, real words in both English and French, were edited to have an identical VOT range but to vary in F_1 frequency at the onset of the syllable rhyme. As in previous studies, the test materials were constructed in a base language + guest word series to test the effect of switching, as in (3), and presented to French–English bilinguals who differed in language dominance.

(3)   *Hazan and Boulakia (1993:22) switching stimuli*
      (a.) repeat /pɛn/
      (b.) répète /pɛn/

Their results showed only a small effect of the precursor language on phoneme categorization and, for a majority of the bilinguals, the precursor language failed to affect cue-weighting at all. They tentatively conclude that language dominance, defined as the language learned first, determines cue-weighting in bilinguals.

Taken together, the results of the perceptual studies offer only tentative evidence that the base or precursor language affects the perception or recognition of the guest word. Soares and Grosjean (1984) enumerate various linguistic and psycho-social factors of CS that might impinge upon bilingual listeners' performance in these tasks, few of which are ever taken into account in psycholinguistic studies of CS. Nevertheless, given the available evidence, it is unlikely that the base language functions as the phonetic equivalent of the morpho-syntactic matrix language (see Myers-Scotton and Jake, this volume), providing an acoustic frame for the perception of a mixed language utterance.

10.3.1 Production in bilingual switching studies

In the few available switching studies of production, the base language has been found to have no effect on the production of categorically distinct sets of stop phonemes. For instance, Hazan and Boulakia (1993) complemented their perception analysis with a production task administered to their French–English bilinguals. They found that all groups (monolingual French, monolingual English, French dominant bilinguals, and English dominant bilinguals) showed categorical differences between /p/ and /b/ in both English and French (an effect that they refer to confusingly as evidence of code-switching). Caramazza et al. (1973:427) reported similar results from their production study and conclude that, "It seems that language switching is easier for production than for perception. In perception, the stimulus itself seems to determine the type of analysis to be performed." This statement is in line with Macnamara's (1967a, b) proposal of independent input and output switches.

Grosjean and Miller (1994:201), who declare, perhaps precipitously given the available evidence, that there is a "momentary dominance of base-language units" in the perceptual domain, find that the precursor language has no such effect in production and that the French–English bilinguals in their study switched immediately and completely from the phonetics of one language to that of another. It merits noting that this study attempts to test whether bilinguals anticipate a switch in production and assimilate earlier than the switch point to the phonetics of the guest language. One task requires bilinguals to code-switch for the proper names *Paul, Tom, Carl* into the phonetics of the guest language, as shown in (4).

(4) *Grosjean and Miller (1994:203) stimuli for production study*
    (a.) "During the first few days, we'll tell him to copy **Carl** constantly."
    (b.) "Pendant les premiers jours, il faudra qu'il **c**opie **Carl c**onstamment."

The construction of these test stimuli in this way allowed Grosjean and Miller to measure the VOT values of the initial consonants of the French base language words, underlined in (4b), in contexts immediately preceding and following the switch (*Carl*, pronounced with English phonetics in (4b)). These values could then be compared with the values for the French phoneme /k/ when it occurs at a switch juncture (*Carl*, pronounced with French phonetics in (4a)). Again, their results showed a categorical shift between English and French language phonetics, irrespective of the context.

10.3.2   Reconsidering the switching paradigm for production

There is an apparent disparity between the findings of the perceptual studies, where the acoustics of the base language arguably affects the processing of the guest language, and those of the production tasks, where the separation between the phonetics of the base and guest language is claimed to be complete. This would seem to provide support for the notion that bilinguals have voluntary control over the output but that the processing of the input shows an influence from the precursor (unless the phonetics of the guest language provides a salient cue to the language switch). In other words, it would appear from these studies that bilinguals are able to completely suppress or inhibit their non-target language in production, a result that would be entirely at odds with more current thinking that both languages of a bilingual are simultaneously "on," although to different degrees of activation. A deeper consideration of the switching paradigm may help to resolve this paradox.

Note that the materials for the various switching studies, as illustrated in examples (1) through (4), show a similar design in that they consist of a base language carrier phrase into which is inserted a single guest language word. The vast majority of these guest words (with the exception of some of the tokens in (2)) are intentionally selected, or synthesized, to be bilingual homophones. This choice may be appropriate for the perception studies, but may have unintended effects on production. While bilingual speakers have been repeatedly shown to produce merged or compromised VOT values relative to monolinguals, they have also demonstrated the opposite tendency; that is, they may be observed to exaggerate these same values to maximize the phonetic contrast between their component languages (Flege and Eefting 1987). When faced with a production task that requires them to pronounce isolated homophones in the alternate language from the carrier phrase, some speakers may indeed maximize the cross-linguistic contrast while others may assimilate the homophones to the phonetics of the base. Group averages would effectively efface the effect of different strategies, making it appear as if bilinguals are impervious to the influence of the base language in production.

10.4   Laboratory research on the phonetics of CS

There are a number of conceptual issues underlying switching studies that limit their possible extension to understanding the phonetics of naturalistic CS. First, the guest language is represented only by a single syllable or word, a structure that is representative of a lexical insertion rather than an intra-sentential CS. As noted above (§ 10.2.1), the status of such items, even when they are real words rather than synthesized ones, is questionable and they may be interpreted by bilinguals as borrowings (therefore easily assimilated to the base language) rather than switches. Second, switching studies are predicated on the idea that the language you start in affects the language you switch to. Yet if we admit that bilinguals can activate both languages simultaneously, a state surely to be achieved during CS or when accessing interlingual homophones, then we would expect that cross-linguistic interaction may operate bi-directionally (from base to guest or vice-versa). Third, switching studies, by their current design, cannot be informative regarding how long before or after a CS any cross-linguistic effect can be detected. In theory, it is possible that bilinguals adopt a bilingual production (or perceptual) mode, in which they may behave quite differently from when they expect to produce (or hear) in only one language. Given that bilinguals should not be assumed to perform to the phonetic norms of monolinguals, it is crucial to investigate the effects of CS relative to their own non-switching norms.

Linguistic studies devoted to describing the phonetic effects of CS, rather than the cognitive mechanisms underlying language switching, are few (Toribio et al. 2005; Bullock et al. 2006; Khattab 2006, this volume). Like switching studies, these have often induced CS in bilinguals in order to insure that the specific phonetic features under examination appear in the appropriate contexts with the difference that the materials used are intra-sentential CS constructions with grammatically constrained junctures, occurring either at the Subject–Predicate or Verb–Object boundaries. In this respect, the stimuli resemble natural bilingual CS. In laboratory studies of linguistic CS, researchers have attempted to redress the limitations imposed by the switching paradigm with respect to bilingual language production by posing additional questions, such as those cited in (5).

(5)   *Research questions adapted from Bullock et al. (2006:11)*
   (a.) Are there within-language differences between bilingual production in monolingual versus code-switched natural speech?
   (b.) Is one language affected more than the other?
   (c.) Is the speaker's L1 less permeable to convergence than the L2?
   (d.) Does the direction of the switch matter (from L1→L2 or from L2→L1)?
   (e.) If an effect of CS occurs, how long does it persist into an utterance?

These research questions are cited here because they pose fundamental issues that any inquiry into bilingual CS should take into consideration. Item (5a) considers the general effect of CS on bilingual production because it is possible, in theory, that bilinguals manifest no difference between modes, or that they adopt compromised or merged phonetic values across a CS utterance relative to a monolingual one. Notice that questions (5b–c) raise the possibility that the effects of CS on phonetic production may be asymmetrical. That is, perhaps due to inherent linguistic differences or to speaker proficiency, to mention but a few factors, only one language of the pair may be affected (5b). Additionally, given that L1 phonetic values are assumed to be set early, it is possible that the language first acquired may be more stable during CS than the L2 (5c). Item (5d) aims to test the directionality assumption implicit in language switching studies and (5e) is designed to tease apart the effects of CS from that of language mode by examining whether perturbations to the phonetic system in CS are temporary or global.

Interestingly, the results of phonetic CS studies to date do not converge with those of the production switching studies reviewed above in § 10.3.1. In particular, the study by Bullock et al. (2006) showed a robust effect of CS on phonetic production that would not be predicted by a switching study. They tested the production of Spanish–English bilinguals in both monolingual and bilingual modes, separating their participants into two groups who were mismatched in proficiency. The Spanish (L1) bilinguals were strongly Spanish dominant and most had detectable foreign accents in their English. The English (L1) speakers, however, were Spanish instructors and, thus, more balanced across their languages. Each group was tested on their productions of /p,t,k/ in separate Spanish and English monolingual sessions. They were then tested in a bilingual session where they read CS sentences in both directions, randomly ordered. Embedded in each sentence were counterbalanced tokens of /p,t,k/ at strategic sites: pre-switch, at the switch juncture, and post-switch, as illustrated in (6).

(6)   *CS stimuli from Bullock et al. (2006:11)*
    (a.) Spanish to English

       Todos mis amigos   talked Spanish as   kids.

       Pre-switch   Switch   Post-Switch
       "All my friends talked Spanish as kids."

    (b.) English to Spanish

       The typhoon damaged   **techos y**   **paredes**.

         Pre-switch   Switch   Post-Switch
       "The typhoon damaged roofs and walls."

The results showed that both groups, regardless of mode or switch site, maintain significantly distinct categories for Spanish versus English, a result that confirms the findings from the production switching studies. However, despite the participant group differences in L1 and in L2 proficiency, both groups showed an identical *asymmetric* pattern of phonetic shift in CS; that is, the effect of CS on production was manifested only in their English language productions. Specifically, their English language VOT values merged toward (but did not converge with) Spanish language values only when CS, but their Spanish language VOT productions remained constant across modes. The influence of Spanish on English occurred regardless of the direction of the switch. Intriguingly, the phonetic merger was most pronounced *before* switching from English to Spanish, rather than in the reverse direction. That is, bilinguals showed the highest degree of phonetic merger *in anticipation of* CS. When switching from Spanish to English, their English VOT productions at the switch site also merged significantly toward the Spanish language values while, at the post-switch position, they recovered their own monolingual values.

These findings suggest that there is a cross-linguistic effect in CS but one that is more complex than anticipated by switching studies. This effect appears to be local, rather than global, as it is concentrated before and directly after the switch. It is also independent of the base language (i.e. the language that you start in) because it occurred regardless of the direction of the switch. In fact, the English language productions of both groups were most Spanish-like when speakers began an utterance in English. Finally, the effect can be asymmetric, affecting only one language of the pair whether it is the base or the guest language. Importantly, the convergence between languages is not complete; these bilinguals, regardless of proficiency level, maintained separate voicing categories across their two languages, although not necessarily in the identical range to those of monolinguals of the respective languages.

The authors of the study speculate that the observed asymmetry may be due to inherent linguistic differences. That is, the VOT range for voiceless stops in English is expansive compared to the relatively compressed range of the short lag stops of Spanish. This could potentially allow more flexibility in the production of voiceless stops in English, permitting convergence toward (but not confusion with) Spanish during CS.[1] By contrast, expanding the VOT continuum of voiceless stops for Spanish past a certain interval (>30ms) may push them noticeably out of the Spanish range. This would suggest that inherent phonetic differences may condition CS behavior and, as within the morpho-syntactic domain, the output of CS must respect the phonological constraints of both languages, albeit allowing for phonetic variability in their expression.

Only one study to date examines directly whether CS can confound phonological distribution. Bullock et al. (2005) investigated whether CS could impact the production of syllable final lateral allophones among Puerto Rican Spanish (PRS)–American English (AE) bilinguals. Both languages possess phonological processes that impact syllable final liquids. In AE, a final lateral is produced with a retracted tongue dorsum and realized as a velarized, or dark l: [ɫ]. A salient (and sociolinguistically stigmatized) property of PRS is the variable application of lamdacization where an underlying rhotic surfaces as a lateral (e.g. *vivir* "to live" → [biβil]). In PRS, syllable final laterals are apico-alveolar but they may surface as the reflex of either an underlying /l/ or of an underlying /r/. This means that the distributional as well as the phonetic properties of laterals differ between these two languages. The study was designed to test whether bilinguals could be observed to confuse the phonologies of their two languages by producing the alternate language allophone while engaged in reading CS sentences such as as in (7):

(7)   The perfume smells **suti/l/ pero fuerte**.
      "The perfume smells subtle but strong."

Extracting each lateral produced in both monolingual and CS contexts, the researchers measured the degree of velarization of all lateral productions by reference to the position of the second formant (F_2) – a velarized lateral will show a significantly lower F_2 than an apico-alveolar lateral (i.e. "clear l"). There was a small effect of CS within the Spanish language productions among individual speakers in that one speaker only produced lambdacization of underlying /r/ and another produced significantly velarized variants for underlying /l/ only while CS. The researchers suggest that, "it may be more difficult to ... self-monitor pronunciation" while CS (Bullock et al. 2005:110). However, overall, the results showed that these bilinguals, even in CS, maintain separate, correctly distributed allophones across their two languages. That is, they did not confuse their phonologies while engaged in CS.

In sum, laboratory studies investigating the effect of CS on production demonstrate that cross-linguistic influence is present at the phonetic level even though bilinguals are successful in maintaining separate phonological categories across languages. However, it also shows that the interplay between CS and phonetics is complex and may, in part, be determined by the specific phonetic properties under investigation.

10.4.1   The phonetics of naturalistic CS

An objection that can be raised with respect to the studies of CS reviewed so far is that the participants are induced to code-switch and that this fails to reflect the natural behavior of bilinguals. This is a valid concern because the motivations underlying a speaker's choice to code-switch are complicated and we cannot simply assume that a speaker's CS productions are invariable across the different conversational contexts in which they use both languages simultaneously. Laboratory findings into the consequences of CS on phonetic structure, then, need to be weighed against findings from bilinguals engaged in natural CS.

Khattab (2002a, 2002b, in press, this volume) provides insight into the phonetic properties of naturalistic CS through her investigations of the phonetic productions of Arabic–English bilingual children. She demonstrates that the children under study often engage in CS with their bilingual (Arabic dominant) parents and that when they do so, their English productions display Arabic phonetic features that are absent when they are speaking English in monolingual settings. Khattab reasons that the children are accommodating in their CS speech to the non-native productions of their parents. Importantly, she argues that the apparent "interference" of Arabic on their English language productions may not be accidental at all, but rather that the children are capable of fine phonetic control, displaying evidence of an expanded and sophisticated phonetic repertoire relative to monolinguals.

Notice that the findings from naturalistic studies indeed confirm the findings of the laboratory studies that CS has an effect on the phonetic production of bilinguals. However, the observed phonetic convergence revealed by these two study paradigms may arise for entirely different reasons. The naturalistic data, unlike the laboratory data, suggest that bilinguals can intentionally *enhance* linguistic crossover between their two linguistic systems while CS. This implies that the laboratory studies may actually present a conservative picture of the potential effects of CS on phonetic production. We can hypothesize that in spontaneous bilingual interactions, we might expect even more dramatic evidence of phonetic overlap during CS. Whether this prediction is borne out awaits future study.

10.5   Can phonology constrain CS?

Up to this point we have considered only whether CS affects phonological/phonetic structure. The issue can be viewed the other way around: can phonological/phonetic structure affect CS? This question is the natural corollary to the syntactic theoretic literature devoted to CS, yet only rarely has a role for phonology been acknowledged in the search for linguistic constraints on CS. The few proposals that exist view the role of phonology as *facilitating*, not constraining, CS and at a lexical rather than a phrasal level (Clyne 2003). The idea behind facilitation, as envisioned by Clyne (2003), is that certain lexical items can act as triggers for CS in bilingual speech. Because there generally needs to be some similarity in the surface form of a trigger word across the component languages, facilitation is more likely to arise in closely related languages, but it is not unattested in typologically distinct languages.

According to Clyne, certain types of words – bilingual homophones, unassimilated lexical transfers (i.e. nonce borrowings), and proper names – may facilitate a shift in language, as illustrated in (8).

(8)   *Dutch–English CS triggered by a bilingual homophone*
      En we reckoned Holland was too **smal vor uns. Het was te benauwd allemaal**.
      "And we reckoned Holland was too narrow/small for us. It was too oppressive altogether."

(Clyne 2003:146)

The bilingual homophone **smal** (Dutch "narrow") has converged phonetically for the speaker cited in (8) and he pronounces it identically across
Dutch and English: [smɑl]. The coincidence of the phonetic surface form
across languages triggers a CS in an unlikely syntactic context (between a
modifier and adjective). This implies that facilitation (triggering) can con-
travene syntactic constraints.

Facilitation has also been reported at the prosodic level in Vietnamese–
English CS (Tuc 2003). Standard Vietnamese has a repertoire of six distinctive tones, each designated by a name and represented orthographically
by a diacritic (or by the absence of a diacritic for the "neutral" tone *ngang*),
as given in (9).

(9) *Vietnamese tones*
     sắc: high (or mid) rising
     ngang: mid level (neutral)
     huyền: mid falling
     ngã: rising contour, constricted
     hỏi: dipping-rising contour
     nặng: low, constricted

Tuc (2003) shows that of these six tones, the last three, characterized
by contours, by glottalization, or a combination of both, are virtually
excluded from occurring immediately before CS into English.[2] The
remaining tones have a relatively high or mid pitch, which Tuc argues
facilitates switching into English because Vietnamese speakers establish
a perceptual equivalence between the high and mid Vietnamese tones
with the stressed and unstressed syllables of English, respectively. Thus,
CS into English overwhelmingly occurs at the tonal range that is most
appropriate for both languages. Zheng (1997, cited in Clyne 2003) finds
that switching between Mandarin and English is similarly restricted
to a particular tonal range that is perceived to be compatible to both
languages.

On another interpretation of these data, one could argue that the
tonal properties of Vietnamese (and perhaps Mandarin) do more than
facilitate a CS; they appear to constrain it. It is not simply the case that
lexemes bearing particular tones trigger CS but CS is virtually blocked
unless certain tones appear at a switch juncture. This can be seen when a
particle with no syntactic function in an utterance is inserted before a
CS, as in the example in (10), where the determiner *đó* "that" has been
inserted.

(10) *Vietnamese–English*
      Những gì nó nói mày phi đó **recall** lại hết
      PL what he say you must DET recall again FINAL PARTICLE
      "You have to recall whatever he said."

                                                         (Tuc 2003:107)

As Tuc shows, the CS sentence would be fully grammatical without *đó*. In fact, the corresponding monolingual phrase would be ungrammatical if the determiner were to precede the equivalent Vietnamese verb for "recall." But the presence of the dummy determiner, which Tuc endows with the pragmatic function of signaling CS, can be understood to be prosodically motivated. Without it, the sentence may be grammatical but the CS would likely be ill-formed as it would be directly preceded by a contour tone, rather than a mid or high tone. This implies that the particle is inserted not simply to facilitate CS but, instead, to allow it.

In sum, the data summarized in this section provide empirical support to the notion that CS can be conditioned by phonological structure. The Vietnamese data, in particular, strongly suggest that CS may be subject to prosodic constraints. This implies that although the search for structural constraints on CS has largely been confined to the morpho-syntactic component of grammar, it may be time to expand the quest to consider the role of prosody in CS. This is but one of a number of topics that awaits future study.

10.6   Conclusion: challenges for future research

This chapter began by laying out three general questions concerning the role of phonology and phonetics in CS. Here, we consider them in turn in an attempt to advance some conclusions.

(1.) *Does CS have an effect on phonological/phonetic production and perception?*
      This question probes whether two languages may overlap or influence one another in CS. As we have seen, there is clear evidence of crossover between languages in the production domain but only at the phonetic level; phonological categories do not appear to overlap in CS. In the perceptual domain, there is also reported evidence of cross-linguistic influence on the processing of acoustic stimuli. In particular, phonological dissimilarity between languages has been shown to have a facilitative effect on both perception and word recognition. The answer to question (1.), then, depends upon the degree and type of overlap concerned but, by and large, we do find effects of CS on both production and perception. Indeed, this is the expected result under models that assume that bilinguals maintain both languages simultaneously activated.

(2.) *Can phonological/phonetic properties be observed to constrain CS production?*
      Although constraints on CS have been the main preoccupation of syntacticians interested in bilingualism, this issue has been only cursorily addressed in the phonological literature. Results from studies of CS between languages with typologically distinct prosodic systems suggest that the answer to this question is affirmative. But, clearly, this is an area that merits much more consideration.

(3.) *Is there a phonetic base or matrix language in CS?*

If the base language is construed to be the language that initiates a CS utterance then the answer to this question is <u>negative.</u> Phonetic overlap can occur irrespective of the direction of CS. However, there remains the possibility that some bilinguals may show a greater influence of one language over the other only in their CS pronunciations.

The answers to the questions posed in this chapter are only tentative and an exploration of the phonetic reflexes of CS remains very much an open field of inquiry. Clearly, the factors underlying phonetic production and perception in CS are complicated and present significant challenges to future researchers. Data collection, alone, is an obstacle because future work must undertake rigorous acoustic phonetic analyses of CS speech as impressionistic transcriptions are not detailed enough to detect the myriad cues that may be present. The addition of data from spontaneous CS corpora is an absolute necessity but, here, researchers will be hampered by the difficulty of collecting a sufficient amount of target tokens in the appropriate contexts.

A significant challenge to understanding the phonetics of CS arises from the fact that bilingual phonology, in general, is much understudied. Not all bilinguals are "accent free" in both languages and it is quite likely that even those who pass as monolinguals differ substantially from true monolinguals at the phonetic level. Thus, it is imperative that researchers examine bilinguals' CS behavior in relation to the participants' own monolingual performance. In addition, researchers repeatedly underscore the highly variable nature of bilingual phonetic performance; even bilinguals of virtually identical sociolinguistic profiles can behave quite differently at the phonetic level. Thus, group results must be treated with caution as they tend to efface the often dramatic differences that individuals may manifest in their speech production.

Finally, although there are many avenues of bilingual phonology to investigate in relation to CS, this chapter will conclude with one in particular. Neglected in much of the discussion regarding CS is the fact that phonology and syntax *interface* in bilingual performance. In this respect, a fruitful area for research in CS will likely be found at the prosodic level where pitch contours range across an utterance and, in many languages, are used for various discourse-pragmatic purposes. Prosodic or accentual boundaries are not necessarily isomorphic to syntactic or lexical ones. For instance, pitch peaks in many languages, like Spanish, are not bound to the stressed syllable of a lexical item but may, at times, be aligned to a syllable in the following word. Does this affect CS? How do bilinguals jointly reconcile the syntactic constraints of their component languages with the prosodic ones? These are unanswered questions but it seems quite likely that the interface between prosody and syntax, and not merely syntax alone, may play a role in circumscribing the domain of CS.

Notes

1. This observation, if sustained, could explain why Grosjean and Miller (1994) failed to find any phonetic effect of preplanning during CS on VOT values in their production study, since they only examined these values for French, which patterns like Spanish with respect to VOT.
2. It is worth noting that the contour tones are absent, as well, from French borrowings in Vietnamese where only the mid tones occur by default. In these borrowings, the high tone, *sắc*, and the constricted low tone, *nặng*, replace the mid level tones when a voiceless stop appears in the coda of the syllable (Hoi Doan, p.c.).

11

Code-switching between typologically distinct languages

Brian Hok-Shing Chan

11.1 The search for universal constraints on code-switching

In the last few decades there has been a burgeoning growth in the literature of code-switching (hereafter CS), the use of two (or more) languages between sentences (i.e. inter-sentential) or within a sentence (i.e. intra-sentential). Whereas the pioneering works focused on bilingual communities in the United States (e.g. Poplack 1980), by now there are also studies on bilingual CS in different parts of the world, including Europe (e.g. Backus 1996), Asia (e.g. Chan 1998a, 1998b), Africa (e.g. Myers-Scotton 1993a, 1993b) and the Middle East (e.g. Berk-Seligson 1986). In terms of language typology, while Indo-European language pairs tend to attract attention, there have been additional studies on languages that come from families other than Indo-European. These efforts have been spurred by a growing interest in CS around the world and an increasing recognition of bilingualism as a proper sub-discipline of linguistics – the broader field to which CS belongs (Li Wei 2000, Myers-Scotton 2006a, Romaine 1995). In addition, researchers have recognized that CS is not an indicator of deficiency in either or both language(s). Instead, it is most often viewed as a resource that bilinguals tactfully utilize to achieve various communicative effects (see Gardner-Chloros, this volume), to index social roles and identities (Myers-Scotton 1993b), and/or to manage ongoing talk (see Gafaranga, this volume). Furthermore, researchers have come to realize that (intra-sentential) CS – far from being random – is patterned and structurally governed, although there is still debate about the nature of grammatical constraints on CS and whether these constraints are universal (but see Myers-Scotton and Jake, MacSwan, this volume).

The search for universal constraints on CS has been instrumental in spawning much research on new data involving various language pairs. Based on Spanish–English data collected from Puerto Ricans in New York

City, the classic paper by Poplack (1980) proposed The Free Morpheme Constraint and The Equivalence Constraint, the two constraints that have probably been most frequently discussed in the literature. The Free Morpheme Constraint holds that CS does not take place within a word between a free morpheme and a bound morpheme (e.g. CS between "eat," an English verb stem, and "*-iendo,*" the Spanish present progressive, is impossible (Poplack 1980:586) unless the former is phonologically integrated into Spanish (Sankoff and Poplack 1981). The Equivalence Constraint stipulates that CS only takes place where the surface order of constituents surrounding the switch point is the same in the participating languages (e.g. CS is possible between an adjective and a noun if the participating languages both have the same pre-nominal (or post-nominal) positioning of adjectives (Pfaff 1979)).

Poplack (1980) concluded that the two constraints apply to her Spanish–English data irrespective of L2 proficiency and sociolinguistic variation; Sankoff and Poplack (1981:7) further suggested that the constraints might well be universal. This claim was the impetus for testing the validity of these constraints on other language pairs, which often resulted in revised or new constraints. Nartey (1982) was quick to point out that data of Adaŋme–English (spoken by educated Ghanaians in Ghana) present counter-examples to both constraints, and she was probably the first one to suggest that different linguistic constraints may apply in different sociocultural environments – a precursor of more recent works such as Bhatt (1997) and Muysken (2000). Much as data from Spanish–Hebrew collected in Jerusalem (Berk-Seligson 1986) and Arabic–French collected in Morocco (Bentahila and Davies 1983) supported The Free Morpheme Constraint, counter-examples were found against The Equivalence Constraint. Bentahila and Davies (1983) suggested that subcategorization restrictions (or *selection*) – rather than word order equivalence – are always respected in CS. Di Sciullo et al. (1986) refuted The Equivalence Constraint for reasons which are empirical (i.e. many possible switching sites allowed by The Equivalence Constraint show little CS in Poplack's dataset) and theoretical (i.e. The Equivalence Constraint does not refer to deeper structural relations). They examined data from Italian–French–English CS and Hindi–English CS, and put forth The Government Constraint, which bars CS between a lexical head (e.g. a verb) and the "highest" element in the constituent this head governs (e.g. the determiner in the verb's object noun phrase). The Government Constraint was found to be empirically inadequate by Belazi et al. (1994), among others. These authors propose The Functional Head Constraint, which precludes CS between a functional head (i.e. Determiner, Inflection, Complementizer, Quantifier and Negation) and its complement (e.g. Noun Phrase, Verb Phrase, Inflection Phrase), which the functional head *f-selects* (see Abney 1987). Again, counter-examples were soon brought to light by Bhatt (1995), Halmari (1997) and Mahootian and Santorini (1996) from various language pairs documented in previous literature.

Poplack and her associates also examined CS in more exotic language pairs, including Finnish–English (Poplack et al. 1989), Tamil–English (Sankoff et al. 1990), Wolof–French and Fongbe–French (Poplack and Meechan 1995). Facing apparent counter-examples to The Free Morpheme Constraint and The Equivalence Constraint, they concluded that these instances are in fact "nonce borrowings" rather than CS. The suggestion generated a series of debates as to the definition and delineation between CS with respect to (nonce-)borrowing (Myers-Scotton 1993b, 2002a; Muysken 2000). In any case, Poplack's original constraints have not faded away in current literature. The empirical predictions of The Free Morpheme Constraint have been preserved in the PF (Phonetic Form) Adjunction Theorem of MacSwan (1999a, 1999b, 2000), based on Nahuatl-Spanish data, whereas The Equivalence Constraint is still seen as facilitating CS (Muysken 2000) if not strictly constraining it (Deuchar 2005, based on Welsh–English data).

In many datasets there is an obvious asymmetry between the participating languages in terms of the morpho-syntax of CS sentences. Most of these data involve an Indo-European language and an Asian or African language (e.g. Kamwangamalu 1989 on Bantu–English/French; Sridhar and Sridhar 1980 on Kannada–English; Nishimura 1985a, 1985b on Japanese–English; Park 1990 on Korean–English; Joshi 1985a, 1985b on Marathi–English in which both languages are Indo-European). All these works eventually paved the way to the Matrix Language Frame Model (henceforth the MLF Model) of Myers-Scotton (1993a, 1997, 2002a), which drew support primarily from Swahili–English CS data. This remains a dominant paradigm in the grammatical approach to CS. The basic premise of the MLF Model is that in a code-switched "sentence," defined as a Complementizer Phrase (CP) by Myers-Scotton, the Matrix Language (ML) generates the sentence structure. This implies two things. First, the ML determines word order, a constraint formalized as *The Morpheme Order Principle*, and, second, the ML supplies system morphemes (largely bound morphemes and function words), a constraint formalized as *The System Morpheme Principle* (see Myers-Scotton and Jake, this volume). The Embedded Language (EL), on the other hand, can only contribute content morphemes, i.e. content words that take part in theta-marking such as nouns, verbs, adjectives, and most prepositions. In addition to these two core principles, there are a number of subsidiary principles that deal with alleged counter-examples, mostly cases involving system morphemes from the EL. For instance, the Embedded Language Island Principle allows EL system morphemes to appear in EL phrases consisting of all words from the EL. The Double Morphology Principle licenses an EL system morpheme (e.g. a plural morpheme) if it is "doubled" with its counter-part from the ML. Apart from positing subsidiary principles, the content/system morpheme distinction has also been fine-tuned to account for apparent counter-examples to the two overarching principles and now there are four types of morphemes rather than the original two. In any case, skeptics may still be dissatisfied with the subsidiary principles and the new morpheme models that water down the original force of The System Morpheme Principle. Also, the additions have made the MLF model perhaps too sophisticated and uneconomical to be desirable as a model of bilingual *competence* (Chomsky 1965), in marked contrast with a more recent view that there are actually *no* constraints or principles specific to CS in the language faculty of bilinguals. This alternative is known as The Null Theory (see MacSwan 1999a, 1999b, this volume; Mahootian 1993; Chan 2003).

Indeed, many constraints and models in the CS literature have been challenged and modified by the discovery of new empirical data. Unlike linguistic research with monolingual participants, it is unclear whether a bilingual's intuitions of CS sentences are consistent and trustworthy. For one thing, grammaticality judgments on hypothetical CS sentences may be affected by the social stigma that has always been attached to CS (Pfaff 1979). A more deep-rooted problem lies in the fact that many bilinguals are non-balanced, i.e. they have not attained a proficiency level in their weaker language that is akin to that of a native speaker of that language. In this respect, some researchers have been able to solicit consistent grammatical judgments (Bentahila and Davies 1983), while others have found varied intuitions among different proficiency groups (Toribio 2001b). Still others have been most careful to elicit judgments only from balanced bilinguals (MacSwan 1999a, 1999b), only to leave aside the copious data produced by non-balanced bilinguals, whereas others avoided grammaticality judgments altogether (Mahootian 1993).

Given that consistent and trustworthy judgments are not always obtainable and that CS data display considerable variation, it is understandable that some researchers have become disgruntled with the constraint approach to CS. Nonetheless, one must be careful in differentiating three different responses:

(1.) The constraint approach to CS is misguided and futile; it does not provide any insights into CS (see Bokamba 1989; Gardner-Chloros and Edwards 2004).
(2.) There are no *universal* constraints on CS, but there are *specific* constraints which are followed in different bilingual communities (see Bhatt 1997; Muysken 2000).
(3.) There are no constraints that operate *specifically* on CS. It is governed by abstract constraints or principles underlying universal grammar on a par with "pure" languages (see Mahootian 1993; MacSwan 1999a, 1999b, 2000; Chan 2003).

Position (1.) downplays the fact that, although universal constraints are not yet in sight, CS does exhibit certain structural regularities, patterns that led researchers to arrive at various constraints or models. CS is often produced fluently and understood instantly by bilinguals in the manner of spontaneous monolingual conversations, and the CS sentences do show structure; they are not a loose array of words glued together randomly, nor do they look similar to those sentences produced by severe agrammatic aphasics. Even linguists who have dismissed the constraint approach have never denied that there is syntactic structure underlying CS; rather, they prefer accounts of CS patterns based on social–pragmatic factors instead of syntactic theory.

Position (2.) is exemplified by Bhatt (1997), who adheres to grammatical constraints, but not those that are absolutely inviolable. Rather, he explains variation in CS patterns by different rankings of constraints, as envisioned in Optimality Theory. As a particular language pair is assigned a certain constraint ranking, there remains a problem of how to capture variation *within* a language pair. Muysken (2000) does not employ Optimality Theory, but he attempts to accommodate various CS patterns by devising a typology of language mixing. In particular, a bilingual may exploit one of these three strategies, namely, *alternation, insertion* or *congruent lexicalization* when engaging in CS. Alternation refers to a "total" switch to another language, including lexicon and grammar. In insertion, bilinguals do not switch totally; they insert words and phrases from one language (i.e. the EL) into a sentence frame generated by the grammar of another language (i.e. the Matrix Language). Congruent lexicalization applies to a language pair with languages that are typologically related (e.g. Dutch and German); the structure of a CS sentence is very similar to that found in both participating languages, to the extent that CS apparently can take place at any point of the sentence with words drawn from either lexicon. The ingenuity of Muysken's (2000) model lies in its attempt to connect the syntax of CS with sociolinguistics and psycholinguistics. He suggests that alternation is typical in stable bilingual communities with balanced bilinguals, whereas insertion is commonly found in former colonial settings where bilinguals are more fluent and at home with their first language. Congruent lexicalization is found where bilinguals, often second-generation immigrants, are fluent in two typologically similar languages, and these languages have equal prestige in society. Yet, syntax still plays a crucial role in this model. The three strategies represent the limits within which CS may vary on an individual or community level, although the three strategies are themselves defined by diagnostic criteria which are syntactic.

Position (3.) is associated with The Null Theory (Mahootian 1993; MacSwan 1999a, 1999b; Chan 2003). This theory considers that CS is possible as long as no principle or constraint in universal grammar is violated, and therefore it departs from most previous models or constraints that are supposed to operate on CS specifically. The idea is motivated by Occam's Razor – in an attempt to devise the most economical model of CS (Mahootian 1993; MacSwan 1999a, 1999b, 2000), as well as by a consideration of cognitive economy (Chan 2003). It would be more parsimonious for a bilingual mind not to have a separate grammar for CS. That is, considering that only some speakers in the world are bilinguals who may engage in CS, it is uneconomical to propose a code-switching grammar within the language faculty or universal grammar, which is supposed to be innate, inborn, and biologically endowed in *all* human beings, bilingual or monolingual. And even though there may be a CS grammar, it still begs an explanation as to why the putative constraints (e.g. The Free Morpheme Constraint, The Equivalence Constraint, the MLF Model, etc.) look so radically different from principles or constraints in other languages (e.g. structural dependence, locality, binding principles).

The major drawback of The Null Theory is that constraints are necessarily expressed in theory-specific terms, and therefore the empirical predictions may vary when researchers are committed to different linguistic theories or assumptions.[1] One may say that The Null Theory is more of a spirit rather than a coherent framework, treating CS on a par with other "pure" languages rather than as a "peripheral" phenomenon, and applying to CS various syntactic theories which are independently grounded in monolingual grammatical phenomena. Despite the thrust of The Null Theory, it is in this connection that it meets with another problem – there are a number of CS constructions which do seem to arise specifically through language contact and which are absent in either participating language, including the mixed compound verbs (i.e. a code-switched verb and a helping verb from the host or matrix language – see below), the portmanteau construction (e.g. a "mirror" sentence in which a verb from a VO language co-occurs with another one from an OV language – see below), and the omission or double marking of function words or bound morphemes (e.g. the omission of determiner(s) – see below). To explain these phenomena, general syntactic rules or principles (e.g. word order parameters, agreement, etc.), which The Null Theory appeals to, seem insufficient, but *additional, construction-specific* rules or principles, apart from those of the two participating languages, appear necessary.

The above survey hardly solves the intricate empirical and theoretical problems involved in the grammatical study of CS, but merely highlights the main dilemmas that researchers have been facing. On the one hand, CS data often turn out to be more diverse and varied than the proposed models or constraints would have predicted. On the other hand, there is structural regularity underlying most CS sentences, which requires an explanation. The tension between constraining CS by grammatical theories and describing the diversity of real data is indeed daunting. A related issue is whether to account for the various CS patterns in sociolinguistic or pragmatic terms (which are more concerned with variation) or by syntactic theories (which are more concerned with underlying regularity). A third dilemma concerns adopting a uniform, universalist theory (e.g. the MLF Model), which is supposed to apply in all language pairs, or a typological approach (e.g. the Bilingual Speech Model of Muysken 2000), which posits different constraints in different bilingual communities. Yet a fourth one is whether to devise constraints that operate on CS specifically, or to resort to syntactic theories independently grounded in monolingual grammatical phenomena.

One way of resolving the above dilemmas and synthesizing the insights of various approaches is to envision a greater role for processing strategies, conceived as part of linguistic *performance* in the generative literature (Chomsky 1965). Performance is also the site where pragmatic, discourse-functional and other sociolinguistic factors may come into play and interact with grammar. This is consistent with the typologists' view that processing strategies and other language-external factors may shape grammars and grammatical constructions (Comrie 1989; Croft 2003). In the context of CS, a bilingual gets to know not only words but also syntactic rules from both languages. Should the two languages have different rules for a construction (e.g. a noun phrase or a verb phrase), the bilingual has access to more than one syntactically viable *option* in forming a CS construction. Various options are taken in different bilingual communities, hence the diversity of patterns. The following sections illustrate how such an approach can be applied to two cases where CS involves typologically different languages.

11.2   Code-switching between VO and OV languages

One area where languages vary from each other syntactically is word order. Typologists have long treated subject–verb–object order as a major parameter by which to classify languages. In those cases where a bilingual code-switches between a VO language and an OV language, what patterns are produced? There are four logical possibilities:

CS between a VO language and an OV language: possible patterns
(1.) VO order: verb from VO language
(2.) OV order: verb from OV language
(3.) VO order: verb from OV language
(4.) OV order: verb from VO language

Most researchers have believed that word order follows the language of the verb; in other words, VO order is attested if the verb comes from the VO language (i.e. pattern (1.)), whereas OV order is realized if the verb comes from the OV language (i.e. pattern (2.)). The following are some examples found in the literature.

(1)   *VO order: verb from VO language (pattern (1.))*
      (a.) *English–Farsi*
           you'll **buy** *xune-ye jaedid*

you'll buy house-POSS new
"You'll buy a new house."

(Mahootian 1993:152)

(b.) *Japanese–English*
nisei no jidai ni wa *we never* **knew anna koto nanka**
Nisei POSS days P TOP we never knew such thing sarcasm
"In the days of Nisei, we never knew such a thing as sarcasm."

(Nishimura 1985a:76)

(c.) *English–Hindi*
He **keeps *daarimuunch***
he keeps beard moustache
"He has a full beard."

(Pandit 1986:92)

(d.) *English–Korean*
I **like *koki***. *Koki's* good.
I like meat meat's good
"I like meat. Meat's good."

(Choi 1991:886)

(2)   *OV order: verb from OV language (pattern (2.))*
(a.) *English–Japanese*
Only small prizes *moratta* *ne*
only small prizes get-PAST
"We got only small prizes."

(Nishimura 1985a:128)

(b.) *Hindi–English*
ki *Syria* uske sath ***diplomatic relations* kayam** kare
that Syria it with diplomatic relations establish do
" . . . that Syria establishes diplomatic relations with it."

(Bhatt 1997:228)

Patterns (3.) and (4.) appear to be ruled out. Various grammatical theories have been invoked to explain this apparent restriction. Mahootian (1993) appeals to Tree Adjoining Grammar in which the lexical content of a verb is specified for its arguments (i.e. subject and object of the verb) as well as the position of these arguments. MacSwan (1999a, 1999b) proposes that a verb carries a case feature that derives VO or OV order in a Minimalist fashion. Nishimura and Yoon (1998) suggest that the directionality of the head (verb in this case) has to be followed. In spite of different explanatory tools, all of these approaches assume a *lexicalist* account of VO/OV order – that the latter is in some way specified by the head verb.

One may wonder whether this restriction is universal. For one thing, The MLF Model would have allowed that a bilingual inserts a verb, a canonical *content morpheme*, from a VO language into an OV order, or insert a verb from an OV language into a VO order, provided that the Matrix Language is OV or VO respectively. A deeper probe into the literature indeed yields data where verb–object order does not follow the language of the verb (Chan 2003, 2008), as shown here:

(3) *VO order: verb from OV language (pattern (3.))*
   (a.) *Tamil–English*
      naan pooyi **paaDuvein** *Hindi song***-ei**
      I go-INF sing.1-SG.FUT Hindi song-ACC
      "I will go and sing a Hindi song."

(Sankoff et al. 1990:79)

   (b.) *English–Korean*
      I have to ***ttakē* my hand**
      I have to wash my hand
      "I have to wash my hand."

(Choi 1991:889)

(4) *OV order: verb from VO language (pattern (4.))*
   (a.) *Mandinka–English*
      n buka **wo *understand*** – noo
      1-SG TAM that understand – AUX
      "I'm not able to understand that."

(Haust and Dittmar 1998:87)

   (b.) *Tsotsitaal–English*
      want ou Tex laat ons **daai *group join***
      because old Tex make 1PL DEM group join
      "Because old Tex made us join that group."

(Slabbert and Myers-Scotton 1997:332)

The mixed compound verbs further attest pattern (4.) in which apparently a verb from a VO language assumes OV order, for instance, in the Matathi–English example in (5).

(5) *OV order: verb from VO language: mixed compound verb*
      mula **khurcyā** *paint* kartāt
      boys chairs paint do+TNS
      "Boys paint chairs."

(Joshi 1985a:193)

There has been quite some dispute as to the proper status of the code-switched verb, though. As the name "mixed compound verb" suggests, some researchers consider that the code-switched verb (from the VO language) is actually adjoined to the helping verb from the OV language (e.g. *kartāt* in (5)); in other words, the code-switched element and the helping verb together form a V node. The helping verb somehow "nativizes" the code-switched element (Kachru 1978), and so the "mixed compound verb" functions as any other verb in the OV language, hence the OV order. The code-switched element may be a verb or a nominalization. There is, however, evidence that, at least in some cases, the code-switched element is a verb on its own. For instance, in (6) below, the English verb ("*force*") takes a Panjabi object ("*baceã*") inflected by an accusative marker ("*nũ*"). The helping verb in Hindi ("*kər*") most probably rests in a higher syntactic position, since it is separated from the English verb ("*force*") by a negation marker ("*nəi*") (see Muysken 2000 for more discussion on these "bilingual verbs").

(6)　*OV order: verb from VO language: mixed compound verb*
　　　baceã nũ tusī ***force*** nəi kər sakde
　　　children ACC you force NEG do
　　　"You can't force children."

(Romaine 1995:140)

　　The existence of examples in (3), (4), and (6) (i.e. patterns (3.) and (4.) above) resist a *lexicalist* account of verb–object order in CS, where verb–object order is specified in the head verb. Alternatively, VO or OV order could be stipulated by a *syntactic* rule as more traditionally envisioned, for instance, a verb-initial and a verb-final parameter (Neeleman and Weerman 1999, Saito and Fukui 1998). Now, suppose the bilingual has access to both rules. Either VO or OV would comply with the input and thus both orders can be found in the production data. On the other hand, if the bilingual's languages both have VO order (e.g. Spanish–English, Cantonese–English), the bilingual does not have the OV option and OV order would never be yielded, unless the objects are moved or pre-posed for pragmatic effects. By the same token, it is hypothesized that CS between two OV languages does not yield VO order unless it is for "pragmatic" effects.

　　Consider again the bilingual who code-switches between a VO and an OV language. The idea that either VO or OV is an "optimal" strategy may sound like a mere description of the above data, but it is not: Both VO and OV rules may be co-activated, leading to "portmanteau" constructions such as those in (7).

(7)　*Portmanteau constructions*
　　　(a.)　*English–Japanese*
　　　　　We **bought** about two pounds *gurai* ***kattekita*** *no*
　　　　　we bought about two pounds about bought
　　　　　"We bought about two pounds."

(Nishimura 1985a:139)

　　　(b.)　*English–Tamil*
　　　　　They **gave** me a research grant ***koDutaa***
　　　　　They gave me a research grant give (3PL.PAST)
　　　　　"They gave me a research grant."

(Sankoff et al. 1990:93)

　　　(c.)　*Dutch–Turkish*
　　　　　Dus in Nederland **zijn** zoveel *devlet hastanesi* **var**
　　　　　so in Holland are-3PL so-many state hospital there-are
　　　　　"So in Holland there are so many state hospitals."

(Backus 1996:348)

The markedness of "portmanteau" constructions in comparison with VO or OV order (Backus 1996; Nishimura 1985a; Sankoff et al. 1990) may well be due to the relative *economy* of the latter option. In portmanteau constructions semantic information is duplicated in two verbs: one from the VO language and another from the OV language, while the selection of VO or OV order is non-redundant.

There is also a third possible option: neither VO nor OV order. It is difficult to conceive how this option can be realized if both verb and object are coded, in consideration of the fact that all sentences need to be linearized, a requirement which is imposed by the PF (Phonetic Form) Interface in the Minimalist Program (Chomsky 1995). Another possibility is that the whole VP is not realized at all (hence neither VO nor OV), thus best respecting economy. Nonetheless, this would violate *syntagmatic isomorphism* – the principle that a meaning is expressed by a linguistic form (Croft 2003; Haiman 1980). Since the verb also licenses the subject argument, the non-coding of VP implies the non-coding of the whole proposition. Yet another possibility is that the object is not expressed, which again respects economy but violates isomorphism. Empirically, there are indeed some instances where the object of a CS verb is dropped, such as the English–Japanese example in (8) below. However, Nishimura (1985a:138) attributed the object drop in (8) to the grammar of Japanese in which an object may be null where it is salient in the context. In this light, it is unlikely that object drop is induced by CS between a VO and an OV language, which is not attested elsewhere in the literature (see examples in (1), (2), (3) and (4) above).

(8)   *Object drop*
      She **karita**
      she borrow-PAST
      "She borrowed [it]."

(Nishimura 1985a:137)

Table 11.1 below summarizes the options of the processor for a bilingual who code-switches between a VO language and an OV language.

Portmanteau constructions are not ruled out strictly as ungrammatical. The sociolinguistic or pragmatic contexts where portmanteau constructions appear have not been adequately studied. However, the available data are often documented from immigrants, mostly of the second or intermediate generation (Nishimura 1985a; Backus 1996). They tend to engage in extensive conversational CS within their peer groups, and they stand midway between two different identities (i.e. those of their origin and of the new settlement). It may be the case that the portmanteau constructions, in juxtaposing the lexicons and observing the grammars of both languages, are a convenient strategy to signal these bilinguals' dual identity or to involve mixed audiences of different groups (Nishimura 1995). If this is on the right track, the portmanteau constructions would have been justified by sociolinguistic reasons even though they are not optimal.

Table 11.1 Code-switching between a VO and an OV language: options of the processor

Strategy taken	Linguistic consequences	Functional principles respected or violated
Activate either VO or OV order (most optimal)	VO or OV order	Economy respected Isomorphism respected Linearization respected
Activate both VO and OV order (less optimal)	Portmanteau constructions	Isomorphism respected Linearization respected Economy violated
Activate neither VO or OV order (least optimal)	Object drop, VP not coded, or syntactically impossible	Economy respected Isomorphism violated or Linearization violated

The least optimal strategy – i.e. neither VO nor OV – is *theoretically possible* but it may be syntactically impossible (where both verb and object are coded without a recognizable order, hence violating *linearization*) or impossible to prove (where both verb and object are not coded, hence violating *isomorphism*). Object drop appears to be permissible only where one of the participating languages (e.g. Japanese in (8)) licenses null objects in discourse contexts where the objects are readily recoverable, hence not clearly induced by CS. The apparent impossibility of CS inducing object drop may be due to other grammatical principles.

How does the bilingual select VO or OV order out of the two alternatives? There are two main approaches: the syntactic approach and the processing approach. In the former, some built-in syntactic mechanism derives the preferred OV/VO order. Under one view, consistent with Kayne's (1994) Linear Correspondence Axiom, VO is the unmarked, base-generated order, whereas OV is derived through movement of the object to a higher position. As for the processing approach (Chan 2003, 2008), both VO and OV can be considered to be base-generated word orders, selected by the processor under the influence of various "usage" factors. For instance, a particular order (OV or VO) has been in use and much more accessible, possibly because the speakers have been primed by using that language. The choice of one particular construction (e.g. VO or OV) is conventionally seen as governed by sociolinguistic norms (e.g. speakers, formality of occasion).

11.3 Code-switching between languages with different types of DP

Apart from word order, languages systematically vary from each other in terms of morpho-syntactic marking, functional words, and bound morphemes that encode grammatical information such as definiteness, tense, aspect, number, case, gender. In generative grammar, it has widely been assumed since Abney (1987) that noun phrases are actually determiner phrases (DP) headed by the determiner, although by "determiner" Abney had in mind various function words attached to nouns (e.g. articles, quantifiers, demonstratives). More recently, it has been recognized that the "functional domain" of nouns is more articulated than a Determiner (D) head (Cheng and Sybesma 1999; Giusti 1997; Ritter 1995). There are other functional heads hosting function words and even noun affixes, such as Quantifier (Q), Number (Num), Classifier (CL) and Case (K), and the functional domain may vary greatly from one language to another. For instance, whereas a referential argument (i.e. a DP that receives a theta-role in subject or object position) in English is mostly marked by an article, in Chinese languages, it is normally marked by a classifier which primarily expresses its attribute (e.g. shape), unit (e.g. similar to "cup" as in "*a cup of tea*"), or quantity (e.g. similar to "dozen" as in "a *dozen* cakes"). In other languages with morphological case (e.g. Hindi, Japanese, Korean, Turkish), an argument is always framed by a case marker that signals its role in an event (e.g. a nominative marked subject, an accusative marked object), although the case marker may be covert. For the sake of exposition, this difference can be captured by proposing that English DPs are Article Phrases (ArtP), whereas Chinese languages project Classifier Phrases (CLP) and languages with morphological case markers project Case Phrases (KP).

When there is CS between languages in which nouns are expanded into different functional projections, it seems that one functional template of the participating languages is chosen (i.e. ArtP, CLP or KP), as shown in (9) through (11).

(9)   *English noun in CLP (Cantonese–English)*
      nei5 zou6 saai3   [di1 **assignment**]$_{CLP}$ mei6[2]
      you do ASP CL assignment SFP
      "Have you done all the assignments?"

                                                    (Chan 1998a:193)

(10) *English noun phrase in KP (Tamil–English)*
      naan pooyi paaDuvein [**Hindi song**-ei]$_{KP}$
      I go-INF sing Hindi song-ACC
      "I will go and sing a Hindi song."

                                                    (Sankoff et al. 1990:79)

(11) *Korean noun in ArtP (English–Korean)*
      I command you to do [the **nokum**]$_{ArtP}$
      I command you to do the recording
      "I command you to do the recording."

                                                    (Choi 1991:889)

The scenario is similar to that of the bilingual's selecting either the VO or OV rule as elaborated in § 11.2 above. That is, CLP is projected instead of

ArtP in (9), although the bilingual speaker is supposed to have access to the latter template as well. In a similar fashion, KP is projected instead of ArtP in (10), and ArtP is projected rather than KP in (11).

The plural morpheme in English (e.g. the English "-*s*") is more likely to be expressed on a CS noun, when plurality is also expressed with determiners from another language (e.g. (12)) or is "double-marked" with another plural morpheme (e.g. *ma-game-s* (13) below). Myers-Scotton (2002a, also Myers-Scotton and Jake, this volume) has explained these phenomena by stating that the plural morpheme is an "early system morpheme," easily activated with the code-switched noun even though it may be from the EL.

(12)   *Cantonese–English*
      ngo5 duk6 zo2 [gei2 go3 **chapters**]_{CLP}
      I read ASP several CL chapters
      "I've read several chapters."

(Chan 1998b:269)

(13)   *Shona–English*
      … dzimwe dzenguva tinenge tichiita ma-**game**-s panze
      " … sometimes we will be doing games outside."

(Myers-Scotton 1993b:132)

Notice, however, that the DP in (12) is essentially a Classifier Phrase (CLP), the functional template from Cantonese. The plural morpheme arguably does not expand into a functional projection; that is, the plural noun "*chapters*" remains a noun (N) and hence it can be selected by the Cantonese classifier (Chan 1998b, 2003). All in all, the Cantonese CLP template, as indicated by the numeral and classifier "*gei2 go3/several*," is chosen even though English plural morphology is activated due to the context.

Sometimes, determiners from both languages are used to frame a noun, but the pattern appears to be specific to certain language pairs, for example, Moroccan-Arabic and French, as in (14) below.

(14)   *Moroccan Arabic–French*
      haduk **les gens**
      these the people
      "these people"

(Bentahila and Davies 1983:317)

Despite the co-occurrence of determiners in Arabic and French, apparently it is the Arabic functional domain rather than the French one that is selected in (14). Bentahila and Davies (1983) explained that in Arabic demonstratives and numerals select a DP – a noun with the definite article – and so in CS they also select a French DP with an article. A complementary point is that the French articles, unlike those in English and other languages, are always present with French nouns. The French article may easily be activated together with the French noun, which is similar to what the English plural morpheme is to an English noun in CS (see (12) and (13) above). Elsewhere, the use of determiners from both languages appears to be rare. The projection of functional templates from both languages is also rare and motivated by meaning. For instance, in (15) below the Korean case marker is required by Korean grammar, and the English definite article is motivated by the "superlative" meaning.

(15)   *English–Korean*
       [[**The** most difficult structure]$_{\text{ArtP}}$-***lul***]$_{\text{KP}}$ *sseya hako*
       the most difficult structure-ACC use must
       "They must use the most difficult structure."

(Park 1990:120)

Sometimes, code-switched nouns may be bare, without determiners or affixes. Nonetheless, a number of these cases are explained by the grammar of the Matrix Language which licenses null determiners, especially in indefinite, generic, or predicative contexts, such as in (16), (17), and (18) below. In other words, the English nouns may well project to a CLP with a null classifier in (16) and (17), whereas in (18) the English noun projects to a KP with a null case particle.

(16)   *Cantonese–English*
       ngo5 dei6 haa6 go3 lai2-baai3 hoei3 teng1 [***concert***]$_{\text{CLP}}$ (indefinite)
       1 PL next CL week go hear concert
       "We are going to hear a concert next week."

(Chan 2003:199)

(17)   *Cantonese–English*
       keoi5 go3 zai2 zing3-jat1 hai6 [***naughty boy***]$_{\text{CLP}}$ (predicative)
       3 CL son really COP naughty boy
       "Her son is really a naughty boy."

(Chan 1998a:196)

(18)   *Tamil–English*
       pooTuruvaan [***letter***]$_{\text{KP}}$ (indefinite)
       put-3SG.MASC.FUT. letter
       "He will write a letter."

(Sankoff et al. 1990:79)

It is hard, if not impossible, to find bare nouns in syntactic environments where the grammar of either language would have required determiners and noun affixes – Berk-Seligson (1986) calls them code-switching "errors" – see (19). The functional template of neither of the participating languages is coded. This does not seem to be the normal case in and across language pairs.

(19)   *Spanish–Hebrew*
       Izítis [***taút***]$_{\text{NP?}}$
       "You made [a] mistake."

(Berk-Seligson 1986:328)

Table 11.2 Code-switching between languages with different types of DP: options of the processor

Strategy taken	Linguistic consequences	Functional principles respected or violated
Activate the functional template of either language (most optimal)	Different types of DP (e.g. Article Phrase (ArtP), Classifier Phrase (CLP), Case Phrase (KP))	Economy respected Isomorphism respected
Activate the functional templates of both languages (less optimal)	Double-marking, determiners from both languages within a DP	Isomorphism respected Economy violated
Activate the functional template of neither language (less optimal)	Bare nouns without determiners	Economy respected Isomorphism violated

Overall, the case of morpho-syntactic marking of nouns in CS described in this section is parallel to that of VO/OV order expounded in § 11.2 above, and hence the two may receive a unified account. When a bilingual code-switches between two languages with different types of DP, he or she has access to two morpho-syntactic rules with which to project the DP. The strategy is to activate one of the rules, probably as a "balance" of economy and isomorphism, but in some cases both may be activated, resulting in double marking, or neither may be activated, resulting in bare nouns without determiners. Double marking or bare nouns are more marked in terms of their occurrences in and across different language pairs.

11.4   Summary and areas for further research

This chapter has surveyed the major constraints and models that have been proposed to account for the structure of CS, highlighting the main controversies within the grammatical approach. The long-standing problem of these attempts has been the diversity and variation of CS patterns, which appear to defy any economical, unified, and universal syntactic account. It has been suggested that this diversity be construed as the interaction of the grammars of the two languages, which gives rise to more than one syntactically viable option. The selection of one of these options is the result of the influence of processing strategies and various sociolinguistic factors.

Despite the diversity of CS patterns, there seems a universal *tendency* to select one morpho-syntactic rule, probably a result of the balance between "economy" and "isomorphism" (Haiman 1980, 1983; Croft 2003), which are functional principles rather than formal syntactic constraints. Less optimal patterns may appear when there is a functional motivation (socio-linguistic, pragmatic or processing), a hypothesis that opens avenues for further research. It might well be most efficient to select the morpho-syntactic rules consistently from one language, and that language would become what is conceived as the Matrix Language in the MLF Model. If this were correct, the Matrix Language would be an *epiphenomenon*, arising from language use or performance rather than competence. Then, theoretically, the series of principles that stipulate the role of the Matrix Language and the Embedded Language would be unnecessary. In other words, data that comply with the MLF Model represent "optimal" strategies under certain settings, but there may well be other strategies activating grammatical rules from both languages, when these choices are functionally motivated by sociolinguistic, pragmatic, or processing factors.

Notes

1. Works that claim to follow The Null Theory – Mahootian 1993; MacSwan 1999a, 1999b, 2000; Chan 2003 – have adopted slightly different theoretical frameworks, and indeed they make different empirical predictions (see § 11.2 above).
2. The transcription of Cantonese follows the scheme "Jyut6 Ping3 (Cantonese Romanization)" as devised by the Linguistic Society of Hong Kong. The number at the end of each word refers to one of the six tones in Cantonese.

12

Language mixing in bilingual children: code-switching?

Natascha Müller
and
Katja Francesca Cantone

12.1 Introduction

Code-switching (hereafter CS) is a very common feature in the speech of bilinguals and has attracted the attention of sociolinguists and psycholinguists for many years. In the last forty years, syntacticians have become interested in the study of the structural aspects of CS. A wide range of (typologically different or similar) language pairs has been studied in order to find out whether constraints, both pragmatic and syntactic in nature, govern this speech style. A distinction has been made between inter-sentential and intra-sentential CS. The examples in (1) demonstrate inter-sentential CS in children, taken from Cantone and Müller (2005:210). In these examples, the bilingual German–Italian child Aurelio (age 2;5,21 in years;months,days) switches into Italian while speaking to a German interlocutor.

(1) Aurelio: ***ieio battone*** (= bottone)
            ieio (= Aurelio) button
     Adult: was möchtest du habn?
            what want you have?
            "What do you want?"
     Aurelio: ***battone ieio (o) voio***
            button ieio it want
     Adult: was möchtest du?
            what want you?
            "What do you want?"
     Aurelio: ***il battone***
            "The button."

In the study of structural constraints in CS, researchers have mainly focused on intra-sentential mixes. Intra-sentential CS is the juxtaposition of elements from two (or more) languages within one sentence. In (2), each child switches into the respective other language within the same utterance, like Céline, a French–German bilingual child at age 2;11,15 in the French recording, and Leo, a Spanish–English bilingual child, at age 2;7 (see Liceras et al. 2005:239).

(2) (a.) *French–German*
       ça c'est pas **warm**
       this it is not warm
       "This one is not warm."
     (b.) *Spanish–English*
       un **sheep**
       "a sheep"

As for the alternation of both languages in child speech, researchers often use the term "code-mixing," referring to the very early stages of bilingual first language development. The use of the term code-mixing reflects the idea that the alternation of the languages is not yet constrained (see Meisel 1994; Köppe and Meisel 1995).

   In the following sections, this chapter summarizes the most important constraints proposed for adult CS (§12.2) and the main studies on child language mixing (§12.3). §12.4 presents a radically monolingual view of adult CS, which implies that nothing, apart from the two grammatical systems involved, constrains adult CS (see MacSwan, this volume). This view applies to child code-mixing which, as a result, can be analyzed in the same way as adult CS.

12.2   Code-switching as a rule-governed behavior of bilingual speakers

12.2.1   The grammar of code-switching: a third grammar

The literature on CS has been marked by a lively debate about the syntactic constraints specific to CS. Two famous constraints are The Free Morpheme Constraint and The Equivalence Constraint, presented and discussed in Poplack (1980, 1981). Both constraints are tested and confirmed on a large database of Spanish–English Puerto Ricans living in New York City. The Free Morpheme Constraint states that "codes may be switched after any constituent in discourse provided that constituent is not a bound morpheme" (Poplack 1980:585f.). Switching is therefore impossible between a bound morpheme and its host. However, there has been criticism that undermines the empirical power of The Free Morpheme Constraint since it cannot account for the observation made by Belazi et al. (1994: 224f.) who claim that CS is at times impossible even between free morphemes. For instance, in the case of Spanish–English bilinguals, switching is ungrammatical between an auxiliary verb (a free morpheme) and the past participle (a free morpheme), as shown in (3a) and (3b). Examples (4a) and (4b) show that the complementizer of a complement clause must be in the same language as the complement clause, rather than the selecting verb. In sum, The Free Morpheme Constraint is not restrictive enough.

(3)   (a.)   *The students had ***visto la película italiana***.
              the students had seen the movie Italian
      (b.)   ****Los estudiantes habían*** seen the Italian movie.

(4)   (a.)   ****El profesor dijo que*** the student had received an A.
              the professor said that the student had received an A
      (b.)   ****El profesor dijo*** that the student had received an A.

Apart from some counter-examples cited in the literature which show that a bound morpheme can occasionally be the target of CS, there are language pairs (Finnish–English, for example; see Halmari 1997) for which the switching between a bound morpheme (a Finnish case marker) and its host (an English noun) represents a recurrent pattern of that speech style. Of course, one could argue that such examples are not counter-examples to The Free Morpheme Constraint but reflections of a different phenomenon than CS, namely borrowing or nonce borrowing. However, it is unclear whether borrowing and CS are distinct phenomena or related with slightly different characteristics. Muysken (1995) advances convincing arguments for the latter view. Borrowing is a sub-lexical (i.e. below or at the word level) phenomenon, whereas CS is supra-lexical (above the word level). If further research can show that borrowing and CS are related phenomena, the reservations about The Free Morpheme Constraint are well grounded.

The Equivalence Constraint restricts CS to points in the clause where the surface structures of the languages map onto each other. It prohibits switching at points where the surface strings differ in the two languages involved: "Code-switches will tend to occur at points in discourse where juxtaposition of L1 and L2 elements does not violate a syntactic rule of either language, i.e. at points around which the surface structures of the two languages map onto each other (Poplack 1980:586)." As The Free Morpheme Constraint, The Equivalence Constraint is insufficiently restrictive since it would incorrectly allow (3a,b) and (4a). In Spanish and in English, the word order is identical for complementizers in relation to their selecting main verbs and to the embedded IP-clause. Word order is also identical for auxiliary verbs and past participles in both languages. Notwithstanding, CS is prohibited in (3a,b) and (4a). Furthermore, counter-examples have been presented in the literature which stem from natural data on CS. Di Sciullo et al. (1986:155) report CS within noun phrases for the language pair Italian–English although the two languages have different orders for adjectives and nouns, as exemplified in (5).

(5) Ma ci stanno dei **smart** italiani.
     but there are of-the smàrt Italians
     "But there are smart Italians."

Finally, Joshi's (1985a, 1985b) attempt to restrict CS to open-class elements
like nouns, lexical verbs, and adjectives and to disallow it with closed-class
items like determiners, auxiliary verbs, and prepositions suffered from the
same problems, namely insufficient restrictiveness. Belazi et al. (1994:227)
present an example of a switch between a preposition, a closed-class element, and its complement, a DP. Example (6) from a Tunisian Arabic–French
corpus should be ungrammatical under the Constraint on Closed-Class
Items, unfortunately a wrong prediction.

(6) *Tunisian Arabic–French*
     J'ai joué avec il-ku:ra
     "I played with the ball."

The advantages of the above-mentioned constraints clearly are that they
were not intended to apply to particular language pairs and that they were
not construction-specific. However, two kinds of criticism have been
advanced which undermine the view of a grammar particular to CS: The
constraints are both too powerful and not powerful enough. In other
words, switches that do occur are incorrectly excluded and switches that
are not attested in natural data are incorrectly allowed. Researchers have
attempted to remedy this situation and have formulated restrictions on CS
in terms of structural constraints.

12.2.2 Restrictions on code-switching formulated in terms of structural constraints

Some researchers assume that CS is constrained structurally. However, they
reject the idea that there are constraints specific to CS. This line of research
considers mixed utterances to be like monolingual utterances, both being
regulated by the same formal syntactic relations. One of the early influential
proposals comes from Bentahila and Davies (1983). The Subcategorization
Constraint is formulated as follows: "All items must be used in such a way as
to satisfy the (language-particular) subcategorization restrictions imposed
on them (Bentahila and Davies 1983:329)." An example from Moroccan
Arabic–French is that the complementizer *baš* is always followed by a finite
clause. This should be the case in monolingual Arabic as well as in mixed
utterances; *baš* combined with a French infinitival clause is excluded by the
constraint since the selectional restriction of the complementizer on finite
complements is violated. Unfortunately, counter-examples against The
Subcategorization Constraint are reported in the literature.

One of the first attempts to analyze CS within Chomsky's Government
and Binding Theory is The Government Constraint by Di Sciullo et al.
(1986). This constraint disallows switching when a government relation

exists between elements. It has been evaluated as being too restrictive since it makes the incorrect prediction that CS will not occur between a verb and its complement or that the complementizer of a complement clause must be in the same language as the selecting verb, rather than that of the complement clause. Thus, (4a) should occur, while (4b) should be ungrammatical. However, (4b) is part of the Spanish–English bilingual corpus discussed by Belazi et al. (1994:224f.), not (4a).

Belazi et al. (1994) argue on the basis of CS by Tunisian Arabic–French and Spanish–English bilinguals in favor of a refinement of f(=functional)-selection, a constraint of Universal Grammar which holds between functional heads and their complements. The authors introduce *The Functional Head Constraint*, which presupposes that "The language feature of the complement f-selected by a functional head, like all other relevant features, must match the corresponding feature of that functional head (Belazi et al. 1994:228)." They identify five functional heads and their complements: C and IP, INFL and VP, D and NP, Q (Quantifier) and NP, and NEG and VP. The Functional Head Constraint predicts that there is no switching between a functional head and its complement. Mahootian and Santorini (1996) cite numerous counter-examples to the constraint, two of which are listed below:

(7)   (a.) *Italian–French*
        No parce que hanno ***donné des cours***.
        no because have given of-the lectures
        "No because they gave lectures."

      (b.) *English–Spanish*
        I seen everything 'cause ***no cogí na*'.
        I saw everything because not took nothing
        "I saw everything because I didn't take anything."

In sum, the validity of the structural constraints reported in the literature is in doubt due to the existence of numerous counter-examples. Although intended as universal constraints that restrict CS without extra machinery, the structural approaches view CS as a phenomenon that has to be restricted. The result is a CS grammar, governed by formal grammatical relations that are important for monolingual grammars as well. Chan (2003:59) deduces that

The counter-examples to these constraints show that code-switching is possible even between constituents which are held by formal syntactic relations such as government. [...] within a code-switched sentence, phrases and sentences project in ways similar to pure languages – code-switching is not bound by formal syntactic relations (e.g. government); rather, as long as the relations between constituents are respected [...], code-switching may occur. In other words, constituents drawn from different lexicons can combine and form syntactic relations which are found in pure languages.

Researchers have taken the existence of counter-examples to CS constraints as a motivation to revise the constraints. What other factors than non-validity could account for the constant revision of the CS constraints? Perhaps one of the main reasons why constraints on CS have been revised and rejected is the diversity of speakers' proficiency in both languages: many were adult learners rather than bilinguals who acquired both languages from birth. It is quite plausible to assume that grammaticality judgments on CS differ depending on whether the two languages are acquired simultaneously, as first languages, or successively. Another reason for the continual rejection and revision of constraints lies in the methodologies used (see Gullberg et al., this volume). Early analyses of CS were mostly based on speech samples collected in spontaneous interaction. But later studies asked speakers to give acceptability judgments on CS examples constructed by linguists.

The question of whether only spontaneous speech should be admitted for the analysis of CS, as proposed by Mahootian and Santorini (1996), or whether it is problematic to analyze only data coming from spontaneous speech, as argued in Toribio (2001a), remains a disputed topic among CS researchers. Toribio (2001a) assumes that CS data should always be double-checked, that is, it should consist of both natural conversation and acceptability judgments. As a matter of fact, acceptability judgments are subject to debate as they can be substantially influenced by external factors like attitude toward bilingualism or the status of the contributing languages.

Given these problematic aspects of CS research in adult speakers, researchers have been using child data for the purpose of checking the grammaticality of CS in bilinguals. Child speech is less influenced by the external factors mentioned above than adult speech. Hence, what children utter reflects what is possible in CS in the most unfiltered way. This situation clearly contrasts with adult speech, where learning and attitudes may intervene. Additionally, given that age of onset of language acquisition may influence language proficiency, and since the more fluent bilinguals are said to be more accurate code-switchers, future research should study the different acquisition types (simultaneous vs. successive) separately.

12.3   Code-switching in bilingual children

12.3.1   Is child code-mixing constrained?

Researchers have tested bilingual children's knowledge of the CS constraints presented in §12.2.1 and that of other constraints. The main results of these studies are compatible with the criticism about the constraints in adult language. That is, language acquisition researchers found that the constraints were violated by the children and that not all cases of observed switch points were correctly predicted by the constraints. Thus, these constraints when applied to child language corpora are, as with adult corpora, both too restrictive and not restrictive enough.

Lindholm and Padilla (1978) analyze the speech of five Spanish–English bilingual children between the age of 2;10 and 6;2. They observe that only 2% (110 utterances) of the children's utterances are mixed in the sense that they contain material from both languages. The category most affected in mixed utterances is the noun (75%). Verbs and adjectives, although open-class categories, are rarely mixed. Conjunctions, clearly closed-class items, are not expected to be mixed, following Joshi's Constraint on Closed-Class Items; however, mixing is not completely excluded within this category. Lindholm and Padilla's observations cannot be captured by Joshi's Constraint on Closed-Class Items for two reasons. First, the children mix closed-class items, and second, the prevalence of nouns – versus verbs and adjectives – in mixing is unpredicted.

In another important study, Redlinger and Park (1980) investigate four children who have become bilingual in Germany with a French (two), an English (one), or a Spanish (one) mother. The children were observed for a period of five to nine months, between the ages of two to three. In three children, they observe that the category involved most in mixed utterances is again the noun (34%). However, closed-class items are mixed to a considerable extent: 23% adverbs, 13% articles, and 13% pronouns, a result that is unexpected on the basis of Joshi's Constraint on Closed-Class Items. Adverbs and pronouns also figure among the mixed categories of the two German–Italian bilingual children studied by Taeschner (1983) between the ages 3;9 and 4;5 (see also Vihman 1985; Jisa 2000). Although the authors have different definitions for what they call "function words" in child language, it is nevertheless clear that Joshi's Constraint on Closed-Class Items does not hold.

Lanza (1992), Lindholm and Padilla (1978), Taeschner (1983), Fantini (1985), Petersen (1988), and Vihman (1985) report mixing at the word-level, an observation that contradicts The Free Morpheme Constraint. Examples from these studies appear in (8).

(8) (a.) **Shoté** ese.
      shot this-one
      "I shot this one."

                        (Spanish–English, child between 1;5 and 2;2,
                                Lindholm and Padilla 1978:334)

   (b.) Io **trinko**, io **esso**.
      "I drink, I eat."

                (Italian–German, Giulia, 3;0, Taeschner 1983:175)

   (c.) Giulia hat aus**bevuto**.
      Giulia has everything-drunk
      "Giulia has drunk everything."

           (Italian–German, Lisa, 2;4–3;0, Taeschner 1983:131)

(d.) Io ho **ge***vinto.*
I have won
"I won."

(Italian–German, Lisa, 2;8, Taeschner 1983:131)

In (8a) and (8b) an English/German verbal root is combined with Spanish/Italian inflection. (8c) is an example of the combination of a German verb particle with an Italian past participle. (8d) shows the combination of the German past participle prefix with an Italian past participle form.

With respect to the validity of The Equivalence Constraint, the same doubts are in order. McClure (1981) reports the same problematic data for Spanish-English bilingual children between the ages of three and fifteen as Di Sciullo et al. (1986) report for adults – switching is allowed within noun phrases although the two languages have different orders for adjectives and nouns, as illustrated in the examples in (9) (see also Taeschner 1983:95; Redlinger and Park 1980:346; Paradis et al. 2000:255, English–French).

(9)   (a.) Yo tengo un **brown** perro
"I have a brown dog."

(Spanish–English, age unclear, McClure 1981:88)

(b.) Ich hat **trovato un** schwarze **capello**
"I have found a black hat."

(Italian–German, Giulia, 2;9, Taeschner 1983:170)

(c.) pour l'auto **rot**
for the car red
"for the red car"

(French–German, Marc, period 3, 2;10,23–3;0,4,
Redlinger and Park 1980:346)

(d.) L'auto est pas cassé, l'auto **grün**
the car is not broken, the car green
"The car is not broken, the green car."

(French–German, Marc, 3, 2;10,23–3;0,4,
Redlinger and Park 1980:346)

(e.) my **rose** bat
"my pink bat"

(English–French, Olivier, 2;10, Paradis et al. 2000:255)

Another switch point that is not predicted by The Equivalence Constraint but attested in child data is between the object and the verb in OV and VO language pairs. Switching should be prohibited between the verb and the object within language pairs like German-Italian. However, as illustrated in (10), where German would require a verb-final structure, the Italian verb is preposed to the German object (see also Redlinger and Park 1980:350 and Saunders 1982:62, both for German-English).

(10)   Mami Giulia will ***lavare*** die hände.
       Mummy Giulia wants to-wash the hands
       "Mummy Giulia wants to wash her hands."
                         (Italian–German, Giulia, 2;8, Taeschner 1983:95)

   In sum, data from research on child language mixing, as with adult CS, have provided counter-examples to the structural constraints proposed to account for restrictions on CS. However, there is another way to deal especially with the problem that children violate CS constraints, namely to allow that "The structure of code-switched utterances undergoes developmental change from the immature to the mature bilingual speaker (Paradis et al. 2000:246)." In essence, the idea is that the constraints hold in adult language but they are not activated from the beginning of language acquisition; the bilingual child has to acquire them. Within this approach, the term code-mixing has been introduced in order to cover the use of utterances with elements from language A and language B before the developmental shift in structural properties of mixed utterances from a non-adult to an adult-like system of CS. One example is Vihman's study (1985) of the mixed utterances of an Estonian–English bilingual child. She finds that the most prevalent category in mixed utterances during early ages (before 2;0) are function words, not nouns and verbs. Later in development, from age 2;8 onwards, mixed categories are lexical, i.e. nouns and verbs (Vihman 1998). The same result is reported in Meisel (1994) for German–French bilingual children. However, Lanza (1997) observes the trend that function words figure more frequently in mixed utterances than content words only in some children, and the opposite pattern is apparent in others. Nicoladis and Genesee (1997) also underline the individual aspect of prevalence of mixed categories among bilingual children. A further problem, discussed in Meisel (1994), is the definition of the category function word. Some authors, like Vihman, subsume under this category elements like *yes* and *no*. Although it is clear that these elements are not nouns or verbs, they do not figure in grammatical relations and therefore are peripheral to syntax in a strict sense.

   The importance of individual differences with respect to the violation of The Free Morpheme Constraint and The Equivalence Constraint is pointed out by Vihman. The comparison of two Estonian–English bilingual children shows that these CS constraints are still being violated at the age of seven years in one of the children, whereas the other child behaves in an adult-like way by the age of three. Although control of language choice may increase with age (but see Cantone and Müller 2005 for the view that language choice is related to readiness to speak the language, not to age), these findings are in line with the study by Nicoladis and Genesee (1997), who convincingly unravel individual differences in code-mixing. Together with the criticism of the CS constraints applied to adult switching, the discussion of language acquisition data indicates that it is not completely implausible to question the existence of constraints particular to CS altogether.

12.3.2 Structural constraints on language mixing in bilingual children

Language acquisition researchers have also tested the structural CS constraints outlined in §12.2.2 against child language corpora. The general result is that children violate such constraints. The examples in (11) are violations of The Government Constraint (11a-d) and The Functional Head Constraint (11e-h), taken from Veh's (1990) study of German–French bilingual children and from Cantone's (2007) investigation of German–Italian bilingual children.

(11) (a.) CS between verb and complement
            weck nounours un peu
            wakes-up teddy a bit
            "[The puppet] wakes up the Teddy a little bit."
                                    (Ivar, 2;4,9, Veh 1990:Appendix p. 18)

      (b.) CS between verb and complement;
            je cherche mein hammer
            "I look for my hammer."
                                    (Ivar, 3;2,14, Veh 1990:Appendix p. 25)

      (c.) CS between verb and complement
            ho fatto zimtsterne
            have made cinnamon-stars
            "I made cinnamon-stars (= cookies)."
                                    (Carlotta, 4;6,8, Cantone 2007:175)

      (d.) CS between verb and complement
            io ti dò fünfzig mark
            I you give fifty marks
            "I give you fifty marks."
                                    (Lukas, 2;11,27, Cantone 2007:175)

      (e.) CS between INFL and VP
            et puis Patti a sein arm gebrochen
            " . . . and then Patti has his arm broken."
                                    (Annika, 3;7,13, Veh 1990:109)

      (f.) CS between NEG and VP
            ich kann nicht attraper baguette
            I can not catch stick
            "I can't catch it with the stick."
                                    (Ivar, 2;4,9, Veh 1990:Appendix p. 17)

      (g.) CS between INFL and VP
            noi abbiamo gewonnen
            "We have won."
                                    (Aurelio, 3;8,13, Cantone 2007:178)

(h.) CS between C and IP
   hai visto che geht leicht
   have seen that goes easy
   "Have you seen that it goes easy?"

   (Lukas, 3;4,25, Cantone 2007:191)

The existence of such examples casts doubt on the validity of the structural CS constraints. As pointed out earlier, not all language acquisition researchers interpret the data in (11) as counter-examples to the constraints, at least when they appear early in development (which is, however, not the case for all the examples in 11).

Meisel (1994) investigates CS in two bilingual German–French children in order to examine the validity of The Government Constraint during the age of 1;6 to 3;0. He concludes that the children adhere to The Government Constraint in a modified version, but that its application (and that of other structural constraints) is irrelevant at the early stages of grammatical development since the necessary ingredients of the constraints (functional categories for example) have not evolved yet. Trivially, constraints can only hold if the syntactic configuration in which the constraint applies is activated in child grammar. In particular, Meisel (1994) formulates The Grammatical Deficiency Hypothesis, which assumes that there is a stage in language development in which the child's word combinations are not constrained by principles of grammar, and thus language mixing at this stage is not constrained by structural principles either. The proto-syntactic stage correlates with the stage in language acquisition characterized by the absence of functional categories. The plausibility of this approach relies heavily on two assumptions: (1) absence of principles of grammar during the early stages and (2) consistent use of grammatical morphemes signals the presence of functional categories, hence the activation of principles of grammar.

Paradis et al. (2000) test French–English bilingual children's adherence to the structural constraints on intra-sentential code-mixing and come to the conclusion that children violate structural constraints rarely during the early stage of language development, ranging from 0% to 9.7%. Furthermore, there are no discernible changes over time. "Thus, taken together, these patterns are not consistent with an across-the-board qualitative shift from no sensitivity to structural constraints to a stage where code-mixing adheres to structural constraints (Paradis et al. 2000:259)." Specifically, the children in the Paradis et al. study show evidence of the structural CS constraints before sufficient use of INFL-related morphology occurs in both languages, which is indicative of a view shared by many acquisitionists, namely that syntactic knowledge associated with INFL can be apparent before use of morphemes marking tense and agreement. We may thus conclude that the language acquisition studies can be interpreted as supporting evidence for the view in adult CS that the validity of the structural constraints is seriously in doubt.

12.3.3   The relation between language mixing and cross-linguistic influence

In 1978, Volterra and Taeschner published a longitudinal study on the simultaneous development of two languages (German and Italian) in two girls raised in Italy. Their view on simultaneous bilingualism is known as *the three-stage-model*. In this model, bilingual children necessarily pass through each of three stages until they reach the point of being truly bilingual, as illustrated in Figure 12.1.

The first stage in development is characterized by the existence of one lexicon and one syntactic system (or grammar). This does not necessarily mean that the children use the grammar of one language in understanding and producing two languages; instead the syntactic system used by the children is best seen as a fused system, with properties from both languages. The view of a fused syntactic system will be illustrated further below. In general, the existence of one lexicon means that a bilingual child will not refer to a book as, for example, both *buch* (German) and *libro* (Italian) but will use only one of these words when producing in either language. From Volterra and Taeschner's perspective, the results are mixed utterances of the type *buch rotto* "book_{German} broken_{Italian}" – *buch voglio* "book_{German} (I) want_{Italian}," if *buch* is the word stored in the child's lexicon.

The second stage is characterized by the development of two language-specific lexicons while there is still one syntactic system shared by both languages. As a result, the children use one grammar while drawing on two language-specific lexicons. In other words, the mixing between the two languages observed during the first stage (*buch rotto* and *buch voglio*) ceases to occur. Volterra and Taeschner present several examples of a fused grammatical system. For example, both children place attributive adjectives post-nominally, which gives target-like results for Italian, e.g. *scarpe marrone scuro*, "shoes brown dark" and *il riso buono* "the rice good," but target-deviant placements in the German equivalents – *schuhe dunkel-braun* and *reis gut*.

During the third stage, the bilingual children, in addition to two separate lexicons, possess two separate syntactic systems. The view of Volterra and Taeschner that language mixing is due to a fused lexicon has been criticized, particularly since the seminal work of Genesee (1989). Genesee demonstrates that there are other reasons for language mixing at the

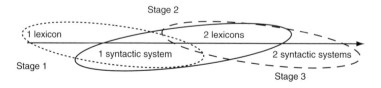

Figure 12.1 The Three-Stage-Model

lexical level than the absence of an equivalent word in the lexicon of the respective other language. That his criticism is indeed plausible is indicated, among other things, by the observation that there are bilingual children who mix a lot in both languages, others only in one language, and still other children who do not mix at all or very rarely. One may thus conclude that code-mixing cannot be considered as evidence in favor of one, fused lexicon (see also Cantone and Müller 2005).

Is language mixing in young bilingual children an instance of cross-linguistic influence? Cross-linguistic influence can be defined very generally by the influence of one language on the other (see Müller et al. 2006). Hulk and Müller (2000) and Müller and Hulk (2001) describe particular grammatical domains that are vulnerable for cross-linguistic influence in bilingual children. They propose conditions under which cross-linguistic influence affects bilingual first language acquisition. The interesting conclusion is that cross-linguistic influence seems to be determined only by linguistic properties of the grammatical phenomenon in question. The outcomes of cross-linguistic influence are acceleration (speed of acquisition is accelerated in language A due to the influence of language B), delay (speed of acquisition is reduced in language A due to the influence of language B), and transfer (the syntactic analysis of language A is used while speaking language B). With respect to language mixing in children, it seems that nothing, except the fact that lexical material from both languages has been used, will indicate that the two languages are influencing each other in the bilingual child. The mixed utterances produced by the children are well-formed from a syntactic point of view. Language mixing therefore has to be viewed and analyzed as a bilingual phenomenon that can occur independently of cross-linguistic influence, as evidenced in monolingual utterances.

In a study on gender marking in mixed DPs, i.e. in DPs that contain a determiner from language A and a noun from language B, Cantone and Müller (2008) find that German–Italian bilingual children respect the lexical gender of the noun when gender is marked on the determiner. This result is particularly revealing when the equivalents of these nouns have a different gender in the other language. For example, in (12a) Carlotta uses the Italian feminine noun *pentola* with a German indefinite article that carries the feminine suffix *–e* in the German context. The German equivalent of *pentola* is *topf*, which, however, is a masculine noun.

GC = German context, IC = Italian context.

(12) (a.) eine$_{\text{FEM}}$ ***pentola*$_{\text{FEM}}$** (Carlotta, GC, 2;9,25)
      a pot
      cf. German ein$_{\text{MAS}}$ topf$_{\text{MAS}}$
   (b.) il$_{\text{MAS}}$ ***schwanz*$_{\text{MAS}}$** (Jan, IC, 3;7,1)
      the tail
      cf. Italian la$_{\text{FEM}}$ coda$_{\text{FEM}}$

(c.) il_{MAS} mio_{MAS} **stuhl_{MAS}** (Carlotta, IC, 2;7,13)
   the my chair
   cf. Italian la_{FEM} mia_{FEM} sedia_{FEM}

(d.) una_{FEM} **blume_{FEM}** (Aurelio, IC, 3;8,13)
   a flower
   cf. Italian un_{MAS} fiore_{MAS}

(e.) für die_{FEM} **cintura_{FEM}** (Carlotta, GC, 3;6,3)
   for the belt
   cf. German für_{MAS} den_{MAS} gurt_{MAS}

(f.) un_{MAS} **stern_{MAS}** (Lukas, IC, 3;5,8)
   a star
   cf. Italian la_{FEM} stella_{FEM}

If the alternation of languages were construed as cross-linguistic influence, one would expect bilingual children to use the gender of the translation equivalent noun when marking the determiner, but they do not.

In another recent study on mixed DPs, Liceras et al. (2005) assume that the language of the functional category D will be the dominant one, in accordance with the *grammatical features spell-out hypothesis* formulated in Liceras (2002) and Spradlin et al. (2003). The idea is that when bilingual children code-switch, the language with the richest array of uninterpretable (i.e. purely formal) features (Chomsky 1995, 2001a,b) is the dominant one and therefore provides the surface realization of the functional category. Liceras et al. analyze data from Spanish–English bilingual children. Given that in Spanish the determiner carries two uninterpretable features, namely gender and number, and that the English determiner only carries the feature for number, in the mixed DP the determiner will come from Spanish, whereas the noun will be provided by English. This prediction is corroborated by the data: the sequence Spanish DET – English NOUN occurs in 98% of the cases. The authors also predict that if both languages have rich arrays, then no sequence will be preferred.

12.3.4 The relation between language mixing and language dominance

The next important factor to be considered in language mixing among bilingual children is language dominance. Studies on bilingual first language acquisition often observe that the two languages develop differently with respect to time; that is, one language develops faster than the other one (see e.g. Petersen 1988; Lanza 1992; Schlyter 1993). In these cases, researchers assume that one language is *dominant* with respect to the other one. Several studies relate mixing to language dominance (see Petersen 1988; Genesee et al. 1995; Deuchar and Quay 1998, 2000). These approaches can be summarized as follows: the bilingual child uses language mixing as a strategy to cope with situations in which one language is less advanced than the other. This strategy has been defined as *Bilingual Bootstrapping* by Gawlitzek-Maiwald and Tracy (1996) or as the *Ivy Hypothesis* by Bernardini and Schlyter (2004). Gawlitzek-Maiwald and Tracy (1996) observe that some grammatical domains develop separately, but the bilingual child may use language A to bootstrap aspects of the syntactic system of language B for others. On the basis of the monolingual utterances produced by a German–English bilingual child, they find that German is much more advanced than English with respect to lexical and syntactic aspects of temporal and modal auxiliary verbs. In order to "help herself out" when speaking English, the child produces mixed utterances of the type in (13), with a German left periphery and an English lexical verb and an adverb.

(13) ***Kannst du*** move a bit
      "Can you move a bit?"

Until the English system of modal and temporal auxiliaries has been fully acquired by the child, she will fill in such material from German. This is a strategy that may also help the child to instantiate the English system. Language dominance in this study is not seen as a concept that applies for a whole language during a developmental stage, but in relation to particular grammatical phenomena. For other grammatical phenomena, English might be more advanced than German, and the child may benefit from the knowledge already acquired in English when she speaks German.

Bernardini and Schlyter (2004) study the simultaneous acquisition of Swedish and Italian and propose that unbalanced bilingual children use the more developed language in order to build sentences in the weaker language. The authors assume that children benefit from language dominance by filling gaps with material from the dominant language while speaking the weaker language. In contrast to *bilingual bootstrapping*, language dominance in Bernardini and Schlyter's study refers to the whole language system and not to single grammatical phenomena in the respective languages. The authors' approach makes the prediction that mixing is uni-directional during a particular stage of language development and that non-balanced bilingual children mix more in their weak language. However, Cantone (2007) fails to find corroborating evidence for this prediction. As mentioned, there are bilingual children who mix a lot in both languages, others only in one language, and still other children who do not mix at all. Moreover, uni-directional mixing does not necessarily affect the weaker of the two languages. In sum, language mixing seems to be an individual choice rather than a developmental stage (Cantone 2007).

12.4   A radically monolingual approach to code-switching

12.4.1   Recent syntactic-theoretical approaches

A recent syntactic-theoretical approach to adult CS is offered by MacSwan (2000, this volume), in the Minimalist framework to syntactic theory (Chomsky 1995). He argues that CS can be explained by the same grammatical machinery that also underlies monolingual speech. MacSwan claims that the computational system and its operations are shared by both languages in the bilingual, whereas the lexicon is language-specific and thus has to be duplicated. The architecture of the bilingual speaker's language faculty is represented in Figure 12.2.

MacSwan suggests that there is a general ban on CS within a morphological word, which is captured by the PF Disjunction Theorem ("code switching within a PF component is not possible"; MacSwan 2000:45). Morphology is located in the PF component of the grammar and the PF component is not a possible locus for CS since phonological rules have different orderings across languages. All cases of mixing within words are violations of the PF Disjunction Theorem and are therefore analyzed as cases of borrowing.

Puzzling for the PF Disjunction Theorem is the data presented by Cantone (2007) who reports word-internal "switches" in child bilingual speech. Cantone observes that Italian nouns that are used in German utterances are adapted to German syllable structure. That is, the children elide the Italian vocal nominal ending: *león* is the noun used for adult Italian *leone* ("lion"), *pappagall* for *pappagallo* ("parrot"), *scimm* for *scimmia* ("monkey"), *conchil* for *conchiglia* ("shell-fish"), *volp* for *volpe* ("fox"), *cavall* for *cavallo* ("horse"), *farfall* for *farfalla* ("butterfly"), *ranocc* for *ranocchio* ("frog"). In the Italian context, the children sometimes add the vocal nominal ending to German nouns: *Krona* for adult German *Krone* (corona, "crown"). The age of the children ranges from three to four years, demonstrating that even older children exhibit this kind of word-internal creativity. Of course, one may interpret these instances as borrowing. Notice, however, that the lexical stem of the nouns is not phonologically integrated into German or Italian.

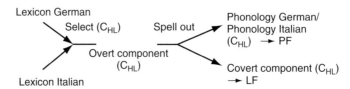

Figure 12.2 The architecture of the bilingual (Italian–German) language faculty, following MacSwan (2000)

Also problematic for the PF Disjunction Theorem are the following instances of switches between the two languages, where genuine morphological
processes are involved, like derivation and inflection and compounding.
The German–Italian examples in (14) are taken from Cantone (2007), the
German–French examples from Veh (1990), the English–Spanish examples
from Liceras et al. (2005).

(14) (a.) switch between French derivational prefix and German
        inflected verb
        deddy **re**sucht
        Teddy again-look-for

                                               (Ivar, 2;4,9, Veh 1990:98)

    (b.) switch between German derivational prefix and French
        inflected verb
        dies on peut **an**mis- mise
        This one can on-put$_{[masc]}$-put$_{[fem]}$

                                               (Ivar 2;5,7, Veh 1990:98)

    (c.) switch between German noun and Italian diminutive suffix
        topfino
        little pot

                                       (Carlotta, 3;7,13, Cantone 2007:181)

    (d.) switch between English adjectival stem and Spanish diminutive
        suffix
        sill**ito**
        little silly

                                       (Simon, 3;10, Liceras et al. 2005:248)

    (e.) switch between Italian nominal stem and German plural affix
        gelaten
        ice-creams

                                       (Aurelio, 3;0,19, Cantone 2007:181)

    (f.) switch between a French noun and a German genitive suffix
        ça c'est Daniel**s** et puis moi
        This it is Daniel's and then me

                                               (Annika, 3,7,2, Veh 1990:99)

    (g.) switch between Italian verbal stem and German inflectional
        suffix
        e poi è fin**iert**
        and then is finished

                                       (Aurelio, 4;0,28, Cantone 2007:181)

    (h.) switch between German verbal stem and French inflectional
        suffix
        il a **reit**é ne?
        he has ridden right?

                                               (Ivar, 2;0,29, Veh 1990:98)

(i.) switch between Spanish verbal stem and English suffix

I am **lav**ing myself

I am washing myself

(Leo, 3;3, Liceras et al. 2005:248)

There are other cases of word-internal mixes that are problematic. For example, compounding differs between Germanic languages and Romance languages. Whereas German exhibits morphological heads on the right edge of the complex word, French/Italian compounds are left-headed. Examples in (15) show compound-internal switches:

(15)   (a.) fruchtgust

fruit-flavor

cf. Italian *gusto di frutta*, German *fruchtgeschmack*

(Carlotta, 4;3,23, Cantone 2007:181)

(b.) himbeerodore

raspberry-scent

cf. Italian *odore di lampone*, German *himbeergeruch*

(Carlotta, 4;9,1, Cantone 2007:181)

(c.) kartoffelsoupe

potato-soup

cf. French *soupe de pommes de terre*, German *kartoffelsuppe*

(Ivar, 3;5,28, Veh 1990:99)

(d.) ein monsieurhut

a man-hat

cf. German *herrenhut*, French *chapeau de monsieur*

(Ivar, 4;8,17, Veh 1990:99)

(e.) ein omamasque

a grandma-mask

cf. French *masque de grand-mère*, German *omamaske*

(Ivar, 4;11,14, Veh 1990:99)

According to MacSwan's model, the head of the compound should determine the position of the other elements. This is neither the case for *kartoffel*soupe, nor for *himbeer*odore. Hence, these cases of CS seem to violate the language-specific requirements of the two languages involved. Nevertheless, they cannot be considered borrowings, because the children do not integrate the mixed words phonologically into the recipient language.

12.4.2 Word order in code-switching

Word order has been a crucial and strongly debated topic in structural analyses of CS. It has been established from cross-linguistic studies on word order that functional categories play an essential role in determining the order of their complements. It has been argued that the properties of functional categories differ from language to language (Ouhalla 1993; Chomsky 1995). Given that functional elements are responsible for determining word order, word order differences among languages are due to the language-specific properties of functional heads. In order to check whether a functional category can also have an influence on the word order of mixed utterances, researchers have studied word order sequences in languages with contrasting word orders for functional heads.

Chan (2003, this volume) claims that in CS, as well as in monolingual speech, functional categories always determine the position of their complements. In contrast, the language of lexical categories like nouns and verbs does not always determine the position of their complements. If this theoretical assumption is correct, then CS between languages that differ with respect to word order should be allowed as long as the language-specific properties of the functional element are respected. On the basis of this difference, it would be possible to explain the compounding data in (15) which show that the language of the lexical head does not determine the position of the other elements in the compound.

12.4.3 Code-switching in child speech: nothing additional to acquire apart from the two grammars involved

As the discussion of word order in CS shows, there are approaches that try to account for the importance of functional and lexical heads in determining the position of their complements when studying CS. Following are results that underline (i) that switching between functional elements and their complements is grammatical, and (ii) that predictions regarding word order in CS can be made by looking at the language of the functional head.

Cantone (2007) studies CS in simultaneous bilingual Italian–German children from age 2;6 to 5. Her results show that children do mix between functional heads and their complements, as shown in the following examples (from Cantone 2007:191):

(16) (a.) perché ***ihr seid böse***
            because you are bad

                                                                    (Lu, 3;11,2, IC)

      (b.) pecché ***ich war kleiner***
            because I was younger

                                                                    (Lu, 4;0,5, IC)

      (c.) wir sind aus- ***perché*** wir sind aus-aus-aus- auf deutsch- auf
            Deutschland
            we are from- because we are from-from-from- in German- in
            Germany

                                                                    (Ja, 3;1,1, GC)

(d.) hai visto che **geht leicht**
      have [you] seen that [it] goes easy?

(Lu, 3;4,25, IC)

(e.) guarda che **war hier**
      look that [it] was here

(Lu, 3;10,3, IC)

Cantone hypothesizes that the language of the complementizer determines the word order of its complement. Subordinate clauses are a good
testing ground for this hypothesis since German subordinate clauses are
verb-final, whereas Italian subordinates follow SVO order. Since German
weil ("because") clauses can be non-verb-final in spoken language, (16a-c)
do not constitute clear examples. However, (16d) and (16e) prove that an
Italian complementizer determines Italian word order in the subordinate
clause, although the clause is made up of German lexical items. With
German word order, the child should have said *hai visto che leicht geht* and
guarda che hier war. Furthermore, in these examples, the German finite
verb in the subordinate clause is not accompanied by an overt subject, a
possibility characteristic of Italian but not of German. Cantone specifies
that if the complementizer is Italian, then the structure below the functional head C is Italian, too, independent of whether its syntactic positions are filled with Italian or with German elements. In the examples,
Italian C can be combined with an underlying structure that contains a
null-subject.

   CS also occurs within the TP. For example, there are mixes between a
temporal/modal auxiliary and a past participle/infinitive with the object
realized as a clitic pronoun (note that syntactic clitics exist in Italian, but
not in German). Again, CS between the functional head T and its complements is constrained by the language of T, the language of the latter being
responsible for word order in the structure below (examples from Cantone
2007:205):

(17) (a.) il papà lo ha **gekauft**
            the dad it CLIT has bought

(Lu, 3;6,13, IC)

      (b.) non lo devi **verraten**
            not it CLIT must [you] tell

(Au,3;6,14, IC)

Further interesting cases are switches between the lexical verb and its non-
pronominalized complement. (18a) and (18b) show that the language of
the head T does not always determine word order in the structure below
(examples from Cantone 2007:207).

(18) (a.) devi **finden** un seil
            [you] must find a rope

(Lu, 2;11,27, IC)

(b.) adesso deve il cameliele **wandern**
     now must the waiter walk around

(Lu, 3;6,30, IC)

German is an OV language, whereas Italian is VO. In (18a) and (18b) we have an Italian modal auxiliary, hence the head of T is filled with an Italian element, whereas the infinitive is German. The direct object is a mixed DP in (18a) and an Italian DP in (18b). Having an Italian T (modal auxiliary), one should expect VO word order, which is corroborated by the example in (18a) but not in (18b).

CS also occurs within the DP. The following examples are again taken from Cantone (2007:217–218).

(19) (a.) **ein** treno
         a train

(Ma, 2;5,26, GC)

   (b.) **la** überraschung
        the surprise

(Ca, 5;0,15, IC)

   (c.) **un** hund
        a dog

(Au, 3,5,30, IC)

   (d.) **sulle** wolken
        on the clouds

(Ja, 2;7,7, IC)

   (e.) **le** erdbeeren
        the strawberries

(Lu, 2;8,26, IC)

Since the position of determiners is similar in the language pair German–Italian, CS at this point is not particularly revealing for a word order analysis. Consider, however, mixes involving an adjective. Attributive adjectives are always pre-nominal in German. In Italian, both orders, pre-nominal and post-nominal, exist, depending on the adjective. As in the case of ordering between lexical verbs and non-pronominalized objects, the language of the determiner does not establish adjective–noun order, as shown in (20). Together with Chan (2003), Cantone claims that the language of the noun is responsible for the position of the adjective. Whenever a German noun occurs, the adjective will be pre-nominal. By contrast, if we have an Italian noun, the adjective will occur pre- or post-nominally. The data in (20a-d) are predicted, but (20e) presents a counter-example (all from Cantone 2007:223–224).

(20) (a.) io sono un **grüne** monstere sono un mosto [mosto = monster/ mostro]
         I am a green monster am a monster

(Au, 3;5,2, IC)

(b.) ci mettiamo una cosa **schwer**
there put [we] a thing heavy

(Au, 4;0,9, IC)

(c.) però ho visto un-un grosso **nest**
but have [I] seen a-a big nest

(Ja, 4;4,27, IC)

(d.) un **lustiges gesicht**
a funny face

(Lu, 3;6,13, IC)

(e.) la **schaufel** magica
the shovel magic

(Lu, 3;1,30, IC)

Analyzing monolingual data from bilingual English–French children, Nicoladis (2006) shows that bilingual children also have problems with adjective placement in monolingual utterances. If this turns out to be true also for the children mentioned under (20), what looks like a counter-example may be interpreted in the same vein as mixing between lexical verbs and their non-pronominalized objects. In sum, bilingual children's monolingual utterances have to be analyzed in addition to the mixed ones, since they may reflect differences from the respective target-systems.

12.5 Conclusions

The present chapter has demonstrated that what researchers have criticized when analyzing adult CS is mirrored in the study of bilingual children's language mixing. The investigation of children's language mixing has taken a radically monolingual perspective, which implies that mixed utterances may be analyzed with the same linguistic machinery as monolingual utterances. The view of adult CS as a speech style which is constrained by nothing apart from the two grammatical systems involved has paved the way for monolingual analyses of children's language mixing. Future research will have to take into account the difference between functional and lexical categories in child CS with the goal of distinguishing competence-driven from performance-driven explanations of the mixing datas.

13

Code-switching between sign languages

David Quinto-Pozos

13.1   Introduction

Code-switching (hereafter CS) can occur when signers of two sign languages interact. This is not surprising since CS is presumably a phenomenon that occurs regardless of the modality in which language is produced and perceived. Even so, the signed language researcher of CS is faced with challenges that may be unique to that modality. In particular, the question of how to attribute various signs or meaningful elements within an utterance (e.g. from Language A, Language B, both languages, or neither language) is among the main concerns. Admittedly, this phenomenon is not unique to signed language CS research, as evidenced by the discussion of congruence in spoken language literature and its role in CS (see Sebba, this volume). However, the potential for similarities between sign languages perhaps makes this issue much more pronounced in CS between sign languages.

Some signed languages are related historically, and this can be noted, in some cases, by examining lexical and grammatical similarities between the languages. However, regardless of the history of any combination of sign languages, there seem to be similar ways that signers use their bodies – not simply their hands – to create meaning across such languages, and this results in the production – within a signed stream – of elements whose meanings are relatively transparent to an interlocutor. Essentially, such characteristically transparent communicative devices exist across sign languages, and in some cases they take on linguistic roles. For example, an extended index finger directed at the signer herself, often at the chest but possibly at the face, usually acts as the first person singular pronoun, and points in the signing space often indicate locative references such as *here* or *there*. So-called "classifier" constructions and bodily actions that appear mimetic in nature are also found in the utterances of signers of different sign languages, and those constructions and actions are often difficult to attribute to one particular sign language as opposed to another. If one also considers the articulation, within the sign stream, of common gestures that are used throughout various cultures (e.g. the thumbs-up gesture to indicate that something is good), the degree to which meaning creation is transparent across sign languages – even those that are unrelated – is significant. CS researchers who work on signed language data must carefully consider a broad spectrum of meaningful devices that signers produce because they influence the ways in which CS analyses are performed. Since users of spoken languages can also accompany their speech with points and gestures, it would appear that such productions could also present a challenge for researchers of CS in speech – not only for sign linguists. In essence, the signed modality forces us to consider ways in which linguistic and gestural devices interact, and this could be extremely valuable to CS analyses of spoken or signed languages.

In addition to communicative devices that are somewhat similar across sign languages, it appears that various linguistic structures of signed languages are more similar to each other than is the case for spoken languages, and this holds true even when one considers unrelated sign languages. One could suggest that this is the case at the level of phonology, morphology, and even syntax. As a result, whether or not a particular form can be described as a code-switch could be questionable. This situation may be akin to types of CS that occur between two historically related spoken languages like Spanish and Portuguese, but it is perhaps very different for examples of CS between structurally diverse languages.

There is at least one other major challenge that is faced by the researcher of signed language CS, and it also relates to the primary question of how to determine what language is operating at any one time during the articulation of various elements within the sign stream. This challenge stems from the fact that the articulators that a signer uses – body parts that allow sign languages to express meaning in certain ways – differ from those used in spoken languages. In essence, a signer can use more than one body part (e.g. hands, arms, head, torso) simultaneously to create meaning, and this fact influences how CS is examined in signed language research.

13.2   Notions to consider: differences between sign and speech

Despite similarities in various facets of linguistic structure between signed and spoken languages (e.g. the existence of phonological primitives, various word-formation processes, and syntactic structures), there are some noteworthy differences between languages across the two modalities. Several of these likely stem from having the hands, arms, and other upper body parts as articulators as well as from the use of the immediate area in front of the signer as an important space in which signs are articulated.

The simultaneous nature of signed language has been recognized since the beginning of linguistic research on American Sign Language (ASL) and other sign languages (Fischer 1974; Klima and Bellugi 1979). For example, morphemes that communicate person, number, and aspectual information can occur concomitantly with some verbs, and a signer's two hands can be used to simultaneously articulate two different classifier constructions, referred to hereafter as *polycomponential* signs, following Schembri (2003) and Slobin et al. (2003). A signer can also produce non-manual signals (e.g. mouth and head movements, torso shifts, and patterns of eyegaze) simultaneously with a lexical sign in order to modify that sign (or phrase). As an example, a non-manual signal such as an adverbial mouth movement can co-occur with verb signs. The mouth and lips can also serve to articulate, without voice, a spoken language word while the signer produces a semantically equivalent sign, and this is commonly referred to as "mouthing." Even if one considers tonal contrasts in some of the world's languages and prosodic features that provide meaningful information, spoken languages do not tend toward exhibiting simultaneity to the degree that signed languages do.

One reason for differences between signed and spoken languages may lie in the purported speed of sign production versus spoken word production. Klima and Bellugi (1979) claim that, on average, a spoken word can be uttered in half the time required to articulate a sign.[1] Meier (2002) hypothesizes that the rate of signing versus speaking plays a prominent role in the simultaneous nature of signed languages because it discourages sequential affixation.[2] Essentially, an "articulatory constraint may push natural sign languages, such as ASL, in a particular typological direction, that is, toward nonconcatenative morphology" (Meier 2002:8).

Another factor that may play an important role in leading to the simultaneous nature of signed languages has been described in terms of the amount of information that can be communicated simultaneously in one modality versus the other. Meier (2002:10) suggests that, "at any instant in time more information is available to the eye than the ear, although in both modalities only a fraction of that information is linguistically relevant." Emmorey (2002) is consistent with Meier's argument in her claim that it is easier to visually perceive spatially disparate information in parallel than to perceive and decipher different types of auditory information simultaneously. In other words, it is easier to perceive complex visual displays at once than auditory signals that may contain disparate types of information.

The use of three-dimensional space in the articulation of sign seems to also lead to some interesting differences between sign and speech. Sign languages allow for the simultaneous communication of various types of information about one or more objects. As mentioned earlier, a signer can articulate a polycomponential sign with one hand and a different one with the other hand, and the two hands interact in specific ways (Supalla 1986).[3]

Such articulations, referred to here as *entity* polycomponential signs, can provide information about motion and/or location of the objects, including to what type or class each item belongs. The kinds of productions that have been labeled polycomponential signs are also used to describe how objects are handled (*handle* polycomponential signs) as well as how objects can be described in visual–geometric ways (*size* and *shape* specifiers) (Emmorey 2002; Schembri 2003).

In addition to the use of 3-D space by signers when they articulate polycomponential signs, users of all sign languages also have access to the gestural medium for meaning generation. As a result, signers can alternate linguistic signs with non-linguistic gestures, and the signs and gestural material can also co-occur in some cases – such as with deictic pointing and verbs that indicate person and number, referred to commonly as "agreement" verbs or "indicating" verbs. The gestures themselves are sometimes culturally specific emblems that are also produced by members of the hearing community (McNeill 1992). However, the gestures can also be deictic and pantomimic in nature. The latter are particularly intriguing because they tend to be used regularly in sign languages. Signers across different sign languages produce similar mimetic gestures that alternate with linguistic material, which are referred to by some researchers as *constructed action*. Constructed action has been described for sign as the way in which a signer uses her body to depict aspects of an animate entity (Metzger 1995; Aarons and Morgan 2003). For example, a signer might "act" like another person or an animal when describing something about that being or something that occurred. Clark and Gerrig (1990) describe a similar phenomenon as an accompaniment to spoken language use, and they develop an argument for why demonstrations, as they call these mimetic actions, function as quotations. The alternation of gestural material such as emblems and constructed action with linguistic/grammatical material might be rule-governed, although such systematic relationships have been addressed only minimally in the literature (e.g. Aarons and Morgan 2003). The fact that signers have access to gestural resources within the same channel of communication poses a challenge for the researcher who is analyzing CS data, as will be demonstrated later in this chapter.

With regard to linguistic structure, some authors have suggested that sign language phonologies are more similar to each other than spoken language phonologies when compared cross-linguistically. Lucas and Valli (1992) note that signs referencing names of foreign countries have become incorporated into ASL from other signed languages, but the phonologies of the source languages are so similar to the phonology of ASL that it is difficult to determine if the incorporation should be considered a lexical borrowing or an example of CS. Borrowings in spoken language have often been characterized by the phonological integration of the borrowed word into the phonology of the other language, but this integration may not be so evident in signed language. For instance, the sign ITALY as signed in Italian Sign Language (LIS) has now been incorporated into ASL, in some cases replacing the older sign for Italy. Lucas and Valli suggest that LIS and ASL have similar phonological inventories of handshape, palm orientation, and location, and this is true even though they are not related or mutually intelligible as languages. They also note that the languages may have similar segmental structure. One part of the authors' rationale for claiming that sign languages have similar phonologies lies in the assertion that such languages have many more basic components (i.e. basic handshapes, movements, places of articulation, etc.) than the sets of inventories that spoken languages contain. They cite as evidence the suggestion of a colleague (Robert Johnson) that:

> ... pure minimal pairs of the kind used to demonstrate contrast in spoken languages are hard to find in ASL and that this may be so because there are so many more basic components from which to build contrastive units – so many handshapes, locations, palm orientations, and facial expressions – as opposed to the relatively limited number of components available in spoken languages.   (Lucas and Valli 1992:30–31)

The paradox is that while there may be more basic components in signed language, various signed languages in their present forms seem to share a significant percentage of those large sets. Visual iconicity in signed languages – such as the use of deictic forms, polycomponential signs, and construction action – perhaps contributes to this situation.

In terms of grammatical items, there are cross-linguistic differences in some aspects of sign language morphology and syntax, such as word order (Newport and Supalla 2000), the existence of auxiliary verbs that use locations in the signing space to indicate subjects and objects (Rathmann 2000; Quadros 1999), and even the grammar of negation (Pfau 2002). By some accounts, syntax is the level of structure in which sign languages may most closely resemble spoken languages. Yet, sign languages seem to demonstrate similar morpho-syntactic structures. They all appear to have different categories of verbs, e.g. verbs that indicate the subject and object of the verb by movement through space and verbs that rely on word order for the assignment of case. Other examples of cross-linguistic similarities concern aspectual modifications to verbs, the use of pronouns, and the use of polycomponential signs.

Additionally, sign languages appear to possess a base level of lexical similarity that is greater than that found for spoken languages, a fact that is likely influenced by a significant degree of iconicity in sign languages. Iconicity is a complex phenomenon, but for the purposes of this chapter it can be defined as the ways in which a signer creates visual correspondences between her own body (hands, arms, torso, head, etc.) and the referent. The modest degree of lexical similarity between sign languages is even true for sign languages with no known historical or genetic relationship. The potential for visual iconicity in the signed modality influences signed languages in this regard. However, there are many lexical items in sign languages that are not considered iconic and others that have become less iconic over time. A higher degree of iconicity can make it difficult for the CS analyst to determine if a particular sign – especially if it is very iconic – is really a sign of one language and not the other or just a visually meaningful way of representing a concept that may not be a lexical item in either language. While common methods for determining lexical similarity across sign languages are useful, they are also somewhat arbitrary and may not reflect the ways in which signers recognize and process signs. For instance, similarity has been determined by comparing articulations across the parameters of sign formation, and a similarly articulated sign is one that is determined to share at least two of the three values of the major phonological parameters (handshape, movement, and place of articulation) (Guerra Currie et al. 2002). As will be noted later, this method, while useful for various analyses, may allow for important information to be overlooked.

In summary, when one considers the various ways in which sign and spoken languages differ from each other, it becomes clear that analyses of CS in signed language are challenging. There are times when it is not clear how to differentiate the languages used in a particular utterance. However, there are also instances when signs that are unique to one or the other language can be identified, and sometimes a switch occurs at a location where such signs occur in sequence. This is, perhaps, the best place to begin a discussion of CS in sign. This chapter provides some illustrations of what seem to be clear cases of CS between two sign languages, although the presentation will also include various examples of issues in the labeling of meaningful elements.

13.3   Code-switching in sign

13.3.1   Code-switching between sign and speech
Most of the work on CS in signed language focuses on the interaction between a signed and a spoken language. Some researchers have looked at the manner in which the interlocutor's language background and language use influence the form that CS takes as it is performed by Deaf adults (Hoffmeister and Moores 1987; Kuntze 2000; Lee 1983), while others have focused on the language of Deaf children (Kachman 1991).

A common theme of the sign–speech work on CS involves the various ways in which a signer can produce elements from the spoken and the signed language simultaneously. As noted earlier, the use of multiple articulators (the hands, face, etc.) at once is common in signed languages. For instance, Davis (1989, 1990) refers to the simultaneous mouthing of English words with the production of ASL signs in his data of English–ASL interpreters and their voice-to-sign productions as *code-mixing*. As noted earlier, the challenge for analyzing this type of language contact phenomenon is that two meaningful elements can co-occur, so determining the source (e.g. English or ASL) of the two elements in sequence is problematic. An example of a signed language interpreter producing code-mixing, as adapted from Davis (1989:93), is found in (1). Following conventions for the transcription of ASL, signs are represented by English words in capital letters, dashes that separate the letters within a word represent fingerspelling, and non-manual signals are indicated immediately above the English glosses of the ASL signs with which they co-occur.

(1) mouthing: most households   mouth: mm
     MOST U-S HOME ...   IN-GENERAL
     "Most households in the United States ... "

In (1), the interpreter signs MOST U-S HOME while mouthing the English words "most households." This simultaneous phenomenon is what Davis refers to as code-mixing. Then, the interpreter signs IN-GENERAL while producing an ASL mouth movement ("mm"), also considered a non-manual signal, that is a common non-manual modifier of various signs. Note that there is a switch from the ASL mouthing to the ASL non-manual signal in this segment as well. It seems apparent that a CS analysis of ASL and English needs to take into account the simultaneous code-mixing of the two languages along with sequential CS.

Lucas and Valli (1992) note that CS following spoken language criteria would mean that the language user would need to completely change from one type of language production (e.g. signing) to "switch" to the other type of production (e.g. speaking). That type of CS is mostly not the focus of the works mentioned previously, but this phenomenon has been reported to occur, albeit minimally, in the language use of people who are fluent in both languages. Petitto et al. (2001) and Emmorey et al. (2005) suggest that this type of CS is relatively rare – comprising approximately 5–6% of switches in their corpora. Petitto et al. reported this result based on the development of three hearing children – all less than five years old at the commencement of one year of data collection – acquiring Quebec Sign Language (*Langue des Signes Québécoise*, LSQ) and French simultaneously, whereas the Emmorey et al. study focused on the language use of eleven ASL–English adults who acquired both languages natively. Petitto et al. report that one child performed the sequential switch found in (2):

(2) Ça ressemble   MOUCHOIR
     this resembles   [facial] tissue
     "This looks like facial tissue."

One example of ASL–English consecutive CS as reported by Emmorey et al. is the following:

> For example, after saying "pipe," participant 2 then produced an ASL classifier construction indicating a vertically-oriented thin cylinder without any accompanying speech.   (Emmorey et al. 2005:665)

Interestingly, both studies reported very similar percentages of sequential CS in two different spoken–signed language pairs and in both adults and children.

As expected, since these hearing bilinguals produced sequential CS approximately 5% of the time, the majority of the language mixing can be categorized as *code-blends* – the simultaneous production of a spoken word with a semantically equivalent sign. Code-blending has been described as being different from Simultaneous-Communication (Emmorey et al. 2005). The difference between code-blends and code-mixes (as defined here) is that the former involve the use of speech – along with sign – while the latter involve the voiceless mouthing of words.

Contact between ASL and English has also been described in terms of CS that occurs for some Deaf users of ASL and Cued Speech – a way to make spoken language visible through the use of manual "cues" articulated by a hand of the cue-er. Consonant and vowel sounds are represented by the hand in this system and, in theory, any spoken language can be "cued." Hauser (2000) describes the signing of a ten-year-old girl who is fluent in both ASL and cued English and how she code-switches between the two forms of manual communication. An example from Hauser (2000:65) is found in (3); the Cued English is represented in non-capital letters and ASL in capital letters.

(3)   ... brothers are WAKE-UP so woke up so TIRED so I said ...

In this example, the person is switching sequentially between a manual form of English, which represents the sounds of the language, and ASL.

13.3.2   CS between signed languages

Thus far, all the examples of CS that have been described concern the mixing of a signed language and some form of a spoken language. It seems that little work has been done on the mixing of two signed languages, and examples of sign–sign CS are mostly lacking in the literature. One work that does provide some examples of such phenomena is Quinto-Pozos (2002), and it focuses on contact between ASL and Mexican Sign Language (LSM) along two areas of the Mexico–US border in Texas. There are other areas of the world where one would expect contact between two signed languages, although it appears that no published works exist that document such contact. One such area might be along the border of two provinces of Canada, Quebec and Ontario, where different signed languages, Quebec Sign Language (LSQ) and American Sign Language (ASL), are used. Contact between signed languages may also occur in parts of Spain, where Spanish Sign Language (LSE) and Catalan Sign Language (LSC) are used by populations of Deaf signers.

For the study of LSM and ASL contact, Quinto-Pozos (2002) videotaped interactions between users of Mexican Sign Language (LSM) and American Sign Language (ASL) who live on the United States side of the US–Mexico border. Both LSM and ASL have been reported to be historically related to the Old French Sign Language (OLSF) of the 1800s (Guerra Currie 1999; Adams 2003), although the two languages are distinct and not mutually intelligible (Faurot et al. 1999). Yet, there do exist lexical and grammatical similarities between the two languages.

The CS data reported in Quinto-Pozos (2002) come from deaf signers who were fluent bilinguals in the two languages and others who were mostly proficient in one of the two languages. The data collection involved group discussions (four participants per group in each of two locations) and one-on-one interviews, and those sessions were examined for various contact phenomena in the signed modality.

13.3.2.1 Reiterative CS

One type of CS described in Quinto-Pozos (2002) is the switching of synonymous signs. In these cases, each of these code-switched elements was produced after a participant would articulate a semantically equivalent sign from the other language that differed in form. Of the 40 switches of this type from 64 minutes of conversation, more than half (n= 23) were nouns, one-fifth (n= 8) were verbs, one-eighth (5) were adjectives, and there were also a couple of possessive pronouns and adverbs. A seemingly similar type of CS in spoken language contact situations has been termed *reiteration* (Auer 1995; Eldridge 1996; Pakir 1989; Tay 1989). This is the phenomenon of a message in one code being repeated in another code. Various social functions have been attributed to the phenomenon of reiterative CS and among them are: negotiation of a collective social identity, accommodation, amplification of a message, emphasis, reinforcement or clarification of a message, and attention-getting, as in the regulation of turn-taking (Pakir 1989; Tay 1989; Auer 1995; Eldridge 1996). In the LSM–ASL data that were analyzed by Quinto-Pozos (2002), the CS seems to have served several of the social functions just mentioned such as emphasis, clarification, accommodation, and reinforcement. However, there are also cases where the functions of switching are not clear.

In many cases, CS (not only reiterative switching) can serve what Appel and Muysken (1987:119) call a directive function – the desire to "include a person more by using her or his language." This directive function that Appel and Muysken describe is not unlike the concept of accommodation that Pakir (1989) described as a function of reiterative CS. The first example from Quinto-Pozos (2002) can be seen in (4), where the code-switched sign is bolded. In these examples, LSM signs are represented by Spanish words in capital letters and those from ASL are indicated via English. Points are indicated by their form (e.g. "point to finger") or by their function in the case of pronouns (e.g. ME/YO).

(4)   point: middle finger (for listing) TOMATO   **TOMATE**
      ADD-INGREDIENTS   MIX   gesture: "thumbs-up"
      "(. . . and then you take) tomatoes and you add them to the other ingredients and mix everything together. It's great."

Example (4) contains a few items that do not allow for easy classification as elements from LSM, ASL, both languages, or neither language. One example is the point that begins the segment; it seems to be a common listing strategy that is not attributable to only one of the sign languages. Also noteworthy is that the ASL signs indicated as ADD-INGREDIENTS and MIX are quite transparent (or iconic), although they have been labeled as ASL simply because they were not confirmed by the author to also be LSM signs. It is likely that both of those purported ASL signs would be understood by signers of both languages. Example (4) does contain CS, however, and that is the focus of the following discussion.

In (4), the bilingual interviewer was mostly looking in the direction of two users of LSM who were raised in Mexico as they recapped cooking instructions that were presented earlier by another participant. The interlocutors who engaged the signer frequently produced LSM signs in other segments of the discussion, which is why the signer may have made a conscious decision to add the LSM nominal sign TOMATE after the ASL sign TOMATO. There was a very brief pause between the sign TOMATO and TOMATE, which gives the code-switched item a certain degree of emphasis. In some respects, the code-switched sign could also be viewed as a clarification – a sign used to clarify an ASL sign that might not be entirely familiar to at least one of the other participants. Also, note that the final meaningful element in (4) is the emblematic gesture "thumbs-up," which provides a positive comment about what had just been described. Whether or not such an element should be considered an LSM or ASL sign – having become lexicalized into either or both of those languages – is another question that should be addressed, and this would also apply to other emblems that are used within the sign stream.

In another example of CS from the group discussions, the interviewer code-switched a verb while asking a question about what one of the participants regularly does for her birthday. The sequence of signs that contains that verb appears to be a serial verb construction, a type of syntactic construction that is common in ASL and perhaps other sign languages (see Supalla 1990). The example can be found in (5), and the code-switched item is in bold. Like (4), the example given in (5) shows the use of deictic points to a second-person singular interlocutor. Such points would be produced in either language, although they are also common outside of the two languages within the gestural communication of hearing people. They have been labeled in (5) as pronouns from both languages.

(5) TÚ/YOU CUMPLEAÑOS TÚ/YOU   HACER FORM-GROUP INVITE
    2SG   birthday   2SG   do
    INVITAR SELF   TÚ/YOU   INVITAR
    invite   yourself   2SG   invite
    "For your birthday, do you usually invite people to get together?
    Do you do that (yourself)?"

In (5), there are several clear switches from unique signs in one language to unique signs in the other. For instance, HACER ("do") to FORM-GROUP is the first clear switch, and INVITAR to SELF is the second. It very well could be the case that the second-person singular switches were influenced by only one of the sign languages, although the surface forms do not allow for such a determination.

In (5) the signer did not pause, even briefly, before the code-switched item. Thus, this example does not exhibit the emphasis that characterized the CS in (4). Yet, this example might still function as accommodation or even identification with the other signer. The interlocutor who held the signer's gaze during this sequence was one of the participants who produced the most LSM in the border data collection sessions. Further, the interview session with that interlocutor was characterized by relatively large amounts of LSM production. As in that interview session, the interviewer, during this example from the group discussion, may have presumed that this particular interlocutor preferred LSM and thus made an effort to produce LSM signs. This type of CS can also be described as serving a reinforcing function, which is one of the roles that reiterative CS has been claimed to perform.

In example (5) it is not clear what function the code-switched element served. This is also true of other examples of reiterative CS that occurred in the group discussions and interviews as reported in Quinto-Pozos (2002). During a discussion of whether or not participants' families are Deaf or hearing and how the participants communicate with their families, a Deaf female participant who was raised in Mexico commented on the fact that most of her family are hearing. The example is given in (6), and the code-switched item, the LSM noun FAMILIA, is in bold. Similarly articulated signs (those that differ by the value of one phonological parameter at most but that are similar in meaning) in LSM and ASL are represented in capital letters in Spanish and English separated by a slash.

(6) NO/NO   ME/YO   NO/NO++   ME/YO
    gesture: shake-finger   DEAF/ SORDO
    __ head shake for negation __
    gesture: "wave hand to negate" ME/YO FAMILY   **FAMILIA** MY/MI
    gesture/emblem: "well"
    "As for me, my family is not Deaf. Oh well."

In (6), there was no pause between FAMILY and FAMILIA. The sign FAMILIA was not stressed and no other means were used to draw attention to this sign. This does not seem to be a clear case of emphasis. Further, while the female participant signed FAMILIA she was looking at another participant who signed mostly ASL during the group discussion and interviews. Thus, this code-switch does not seem to be a case of accommodation either. Perhaps this instance of CS was intended to display an identification with the interlocutor, but there are no explicit features (emphasis of the sign, a pause, change of eyegaze, etc.) that would suggest what the signer's intent was when she produced this code-switch. As can be seen, the reason(s) for using CS are not always clear. Sometimes there are no explicit features that would suggest that the code-switch was deliberately produced for a specific reason(s). Thus, lists of CS functions do not seem to account for all instances of CS.

Another point that is noteworthy about (6), in consideration of the challenge for determining how to attribute various elements in the sign stream, is that the only signs that are unique to the two languages are the signs FAMILY and FAMILIA – the actual location of the CS. So, while it is possible to note that the signer code-switched here, it is not possible to determine how to label the other meaningful elements (points, similarly articulated signs, and common gestures) within the sequence. This is a problem for CS analyses that rely on clearly identifying the source language for each lexical item.

13.3.2.2   Non-reiterative code-switching

The corpus of US–Mexico border data collected by Quinto-Pozos also contains examples of CS that are not of the reiterative variety. These are presented here to further illustrate why it is often difficult to clearly attribute a meaningful element from the sign stream for purposes of CS analyses. In the examples presented in this section, the code-switched item does not follow a semantically-equivalent sign from the other language, as was done in examples (4) through (6). In some cases the switches are of single signs, but the switch might also contain a sequence of signs and/or other meaningful productions (e.g. polycomponential signs, gestural productions, and/or constructed action).

In the first example of non-reiterative CS, the participant describes how candy from Mexico is quite different from that of the United States. The signer is left handed, and that is her default dominant hand for signed language production. But, as will be noted in (7), she switches hand dominance for a short sequence of signs for comparison purposes, which is a common non-manual strategy for providing comparisons in ASL and perhaps in other sign languages as well. In (7) through (9), the bolded item represents a clear switch from a previous sign or sequence in the other language. Any sign unique to either LSM or ASL that immediately follows a similarly articulated sign is not represented in bold in (7) because it is not clear if the similarly articulated sign should be labeled an LSM or ASL production using the current methods of sign analysis. Other transcription conventions pertinent to this example include: [lh] or [rh] to indicate an articulation with the signer's left or right hand, and the use of "+" to indicate a single repetition of the sign, "PS2" (or Polycomponential Sign 2) to indicate a possible item from the set of so-called handle classifier forms, and "CA:" with a brief description of the signer's enactment to indicate the use of constructed action.

(7)   BUT   [lh]: point: upward and leftward FOOD/COMIDA   DULCE
       there   sweet/candy
      DIFFERENT/DIFERENTE   HOT+   **PICANTE-CHILE**   DELICIOSO
                                           spicy   delicious
      [rh]: point: downward   CA: signer tasting candy/PS2: holding a small item here
      LOUSY   BUT [lh]: CHOCOLATE [ASL] DELICIOUS
      point: upward and leftward   CHOCOLATE [ASL]   LITE   HIGH
      DULCE   RIGHT point-TV3   HIGH
      sweet/candy
      "However, the candies in Mexico are different; they are spicy and delicious. Here, they are lousy. But, the chocolate here is also sweet. There the chocolate is lighter and not so full of sugar as it is here."

As can be noted, (7) contains two examples of LSM-ASL similarly articulated signs (FOOD/COMIDA and DIFFERENT/DIFERENTE), and it also contains several examples of pointing, but there are also several unique signs from each of the languages. LSM signs include DULCE, PICANTE-CHILE, and DELICIOSA. ASL signs include BUT, HOT, LOUSY, CHOCOLATE, LITE, RIGHT, and HIGH. The passage begins with an ASL sign as a conjunction, and ASL signs outnumber LSM signs. One could claim that the passage seems to contain more ASL than LSM (lexically and in terms of grammatical function words), although the similarly articulated signs, points, and brief use of constructed action present challenges for CS analyses.

The next two examples include instances of polycomponential signs. The sequence in (8) is about the preparation of a food dish in Mexico that does not need to be cooked before serving; [bh] indicates the signer's articulation with both hands; PS3 is a size and shape specifier.

(8)   THAT (response to the interviewer)
      [bh]: PS3: meat exiting a grinder
      [bh]: PS3: motion of gears that are grinding something
      TOMATO   ONION[4]   **PICANTE/CHILE**   MIX
                                 spicy
      [rh]: PS3-shape of bowl, [lh]: PS2: stirring as if with spoon
      NOT   NEED   FUEGO/FIRE   NOT   NEED FUEGO/FIRE
      COLD/FRÍO   EAT/COMER   DELICIOSO
                                delicious

Table 13.1 Differences between LSM FUEGO and ASL FIRE

	LSM FUEGO	ASL FIRE
handshape	LSM bent-5 (i.e. fingers bent at two joints beyond the knuckle)	ASL 5
hand internal movement	none	wiggling of four digits (not the thumb)
path movement	up and down and circular (toward and away from the signer)	up and down
place of articulation	the signing space in front of the signer	the signing space in front of the signer

> "That's it. It's the tomato, onion, chile that is mixed together and you stir it up in a bowl. You don't need to cook it; you just eat it cold. It is delicious."

Note that the sequence in (8) begins with an ASL sign (THAT), which is an affirmation of what the interviewer had just signed. The signer goes on to describe a grinding action with polycomponential signs and follows that with two ASL nouns and an LSM noun. It is not clear if the polycomponential signs should be analyzed as LSM structures, ASL structures, or both. Three other elements surface that are difficult to label as either ASL or LSM, and they are the highly iconic sign MIX, a polycomponential sign depicting the side of a large bowl, and the signer showing the mixing of something in the bowl. The final sign of the entire sequence is the LSM sign DELICIOSO, an adjective that describes the food that is prepared in that manner. In some respects, this sequence appears to have more of an ASL character because of the several ASL noun signs (TOMATO, ONION), and the negation and modal signs (NOT NEED) that were signed twice. However, it should be noted that even though FUEGO/FIRE is coded as being a similarly-articulated sign, there are nonetheless some differences between FUEGO and FIRE, specifically, articulations for hand internal movement, path movement, and whether or not the fingers are fully extended or bent. See Table 13.1 for a comparison of the two signs. Even though FUEGO/FIRE seem to differ in several ways, an analysis that would consider only the three major parameters of sign formation for the determination of similarly articulated signs might lose the distinctions between the signs (either because the two handshapes would be considered variants of a 5-handshape or because the up-and-down path movements would be considered similar, even though one occurs with a circular movement and one does not). However, if one were to consider more fine-grained phonetic analyses of the two signs, the results would likely suggest that the sequence with the purported similarly articulated sign should probably be shown as in (9):

(9)   NOT NEED **FUEGO** NOT NEED **FUEGO**

Then, the code-switching analysis could focus on the switch between a verb (NEED) and its object (FUEGO).

The final example, given in (10), also includes polycomponential signs. This sequence describes a participant explaining to the interviewer and the others in the group that it is easier to understand a written Spanish recipe than a written English recipe. In this example, the item denoted as "PS1" should be considered within the entity category of polycomponential signs.

(10)   EASY (10+)
       BUT [lh]: ME/YO MÉXICO THINK MÉXICO FÁCIL
       [rh]: point-downward TOUGH INGLÉS PS1:flat object CA:signer looks
       at paper
       [lh]: UNDERSTAND EXPLAIN LONG/LARGO PS1: paper CA: signer
       looks at paper
       WRONG TIME TWO/DOS WRONG THREE TIME BIEN/GOOD
       "That's easy [referring to reading Spanish]. I think it's easy in Mexico.
       Here [United States] English is tough. In order to understand some-
       thing written in English, it takes a long time. Sometimes I get some-
       thing wrong two times, then the third time is fine."

In (10), the signer begins with ASL signs, interjects LSM signs for the country Mexico, but then also uses a mixture of LSM and ASL signs in the next few signs. The adjective FÁCIL ("easy") is in a clause (assumedly beginning with the conjunction BUT and ending with the adjective) that has only two signs that are clearly from LSM: MÉXICO and FÁCIL. Although, as mentioned ear-lier, the country signs used in foreign sign languages (e.g. JAPAN in Japanese Sign Language, MÉXICO in LSM, etc.) are more common in ASL than they used to be; perhaps they could currently be considered borrowings. This complicates matters because now it is not clear if the clause is mostly LSM or ASL, and there are no function word signs in this sequence to provide information about which grammar is being utilized at various points in the sign stream. Further, it is not clear how to label the source language of the polycomponential sign (to represent a paper or other written document) and the constructed action of the signer gazing at the paper.

Based on the data presentation and the brief discussion of examples (7), (8), and (9), it is clear that some examples of CS are quite challenging to analyze because of the issues raised earlier. Note that there is little discussion of non-manual signals (mouth gestures, eyebrow movements, torso shift, etc.) in these passages, which would present yet another example of simultaneous articulations that would need to be examined. Additionally, possible switches could be lost because of the current system of classification for similarly articulated versus non-similarly articulated signs. Also, the segments that contain polycomponential signs and constructed action are particularly difficult to attribute to one language or the other. All of these issues create challenges for CS analyses in sign.

13.4   Conclusion

As was suggested throughout the data presentation section, CS analysts of sign data are faced with the challenge of determining how to label some of the meaningful elements from a signed conversation. And, such labeling should occur before the data can be examined within any particular model or theory. Current frameworks for CS analyses are primarily based on sequential analyses of meaningful elements (i.e. words, bound morphemes, etc.) without taking into account the alternations with gestural material or influences from visual iconicity that occur in the signed modality. There are also challenges in sign analyses that have to do with simultaneity in that modality. These issues pose challenges and difficulties for analyses of sign data.

Yet, in some cases, sequential CS can be identified and analyzed for sign. This is true for the LSM–ASL reiterative switches presented in examples (4), (5), and (6), and these examples do not seem to contain simultaneous articulations that would leave the researcher wondering how to label each of the code-switched signs. They also contain sign pairs – the reiterative switch and the sign that precedes it – that are clearly articulated differently in the two languages. Even though ASL and LSM are related historically and have similar phonologies, the lexical items in those examples differ from each other, which allows the analyst to determine when the signer is producing one language versus the other. However, those examples also contain the use of gesture (both in the form of widely used emblems and also in the form of constructed action) that alternates with signs, and some of the signs are highly iconic. This can be problematic for language labeling.

Signed languages have some structures that pose challenges for the CS researcher. In particular, the simultaneous nature of sign (e.g. polycomponential signs, code-mixes, and code-blends), the apparent similarity of some sign language structures, and the interaction of signs with non-linguistic gestures need to be considered carefully. One way to address those challenges is to produce more fine-grained descriptions of the phonetic, phonological, morphological, and syntactic structures of signed languages. Knowing, in specific ways, how sign languages differ from each other will allow for the examination of possible examples of CS between such languages. Further, lexical comparisons between sign languages need to concern themselves with more than the major parameters of sign formation; specific details of orientation, finger positions, contact locations, and the like are also necessary. More cross-linguistic work in sign could perhaps help to understand how polycomponential signs differ from each other (if they do), and offer suggestions about how researchers can identify differences between such signs in different sign languages. Research on how specific languages constrain or govern the use of constructed action as it interacts with the linguistic system is sorely needed. Work of this nature can inform CS analyses in sign, and will allow for the inclusion of sign data in theories and models of CS. Assumedly, theories of CS should be equally applicable to sign and speech data, but that remains to be confirmed with more empirical data.

Finally, it seems that all CS researchers should be faced with the challenge of accounting for multi-modal data. Two possible questions for such a line of inquiry could be: how does the use of gesture and demonstration influence the way people code-switch in their communication? And, how does the use of spoken words and phrases interact with emblematic gestures in spoken language conversations? Signed language data can provide exciting opportunities to consider how non-verbal ways of communicating interact with linguistic systems.

Notes

1. Despite the purported differences in speed of sign versus spoken word production, a proposition is articulated, on average, in ASL within the same time frame that a similar proposition is uttered in English (Klima and Bellugi 1979).
2. The simultaneous character of natural signed languages has also been advanced as evidence for the purported ineffectiveness of invented sign systems, which happen to primarily employ sequentially affixed morphemes, to aid in the acquisition of English for Deaf children (Supalla and McKee 2002).
3. These constructions are also known by various other terms such as *classifiers, classifier predicates,* and *verbs of location and motion.*
4. The ASL lexical item ONION was articulated by the participant without the normal wrist-twist of that sign. Rather, contact was made between the index finger and the temple area of the signer's head. This articulation might reflect an LSM accent in ASL, although one would need to investigate what part of the phonology of LSM influenced the signer to fail to provide the common wrist-twist of the ASL sign.

Part IV

Psycholinguistics and code-switching

14

Code-switching and language disorders in bilingual children

Adele W. Miccio
Carol Scheffner Hammer
and
Bárbara Rodríguez[1]

14.1   Introduction

Speech-language pathologists are required to proficiently serve children from diverse backgrounds. To be clinically competent, knowledge of bilingual language development and code-switching (hereafter CS) as a part of normal bilingual language acquisition is crucial. The purpose of this chapter is twofold: to provide insight into the act of CS for professionals who have begun to see an increase in the number of bilingual children on their caseloads, and to address the controversy of viewing CS as evidence of a speech–language disorder in bilingual children. Through a better understanding of what CS is and what it reflects about a child's linguistic competence, it is less likely that bilingual children will be misdiagnosed as having a language disorder and more likely that CS will be encouraged in certain social and academic settings as an added resource available to the bilingual child for effective communication.

14.1.1   Definitions

The term "code-switching" has been used in the field of speech–language pathology to refer to the pragmatic shifts that occur in monolingual conversational discourse. A child would be said to have a CS deficit if he or she was not adept at altering the formality of his or her language when switching between speech with friends and speech with the school principal, for example. (In the linguistic literature, this is known as *style shifting*.) CS has also been used to describe the alternate use of two or more dialects, for example African-American Vernacular English versus "Standard" American English in different social settings. For the purposes of this chapter, the term CS is more narrowly defined as the alternation between two languages. We follow Meisel (1994:114), who defines CS as

... a specific skill of the bilingual's pragmatic competence, that is, the ability to select the language according to the interlocutor, the situational context, the topic of conversation, and so forth, and to change languages within an interactional sequence in accordance with sociolinguistic rules and without violating specific grammatical constraints.

CS between languages can occur between whole stretches of speech, between sentences, or within sentences, clauses, or phrases. Those switches that occur between sentences or utterances are referred to as inter-sentential or inter-utterance CS, whereas those that occur within a single sentence or utterance are called intra-sentential or intra-utterance CS. Pragmatically motivated switches at early ages are typically not of the intra-sentential type. Because intra-sentential switches require a mastery of more complex syntactic structures, they typically are not observed in children at a young age or in those who are just acquiring a second language (Köppe and Meisel 1995). Examples of inter-sentential and intra-sentential CS by a Spanish–English bilingual child follow:

(1) *Intra-sentential CS*
Estaba snowing
"It was snowing."

(2) *Inter-sentential CS*
Cinco dólares. Sorry.
"Five dollars. Sorry."

One misconception about CS that is commonly held by parents and professionals is that it indicates linguistic confusion or lack of proficiency; but as is evident from the above definition, CS, especially of the intra-sentential type, requires a high degree of both pragmatic and grammatical competence in both languages. It reflects the ability of the speaker to appropriately select a language while obeying socially and culturally imposed constraints. In addition, the CS utterances generally adhere to grammatical constraints imposed by the syntactic structures of both languages such that they conform to the surface structure of each language.

Early in development, children's CS may not adhere to the constraints imposed on adult CS (see Müller and Cantone, this volume). To distinguish language alternations that appear to adhere to the constraints of adult CS and those that do not, some researchers refer to the latter type as *code-mixing* (Köppe and Meisel 1995). Code-mixing can occur in the phonological, lexical, morpho-syntactic, or pragmatic domains of language production (Genesee et al. 2004). It can also occur at any linguistic level: from syllable to words, phrases, clauses or pragmatic patterns and is more likely to occur in less-proficient speakers, such as children who are just learning language. While the act of CS also involves the alternation of languages at the word, phrase, clause, or sentence level, it is done so with intent or as a matter of choice on the part of the speaker, whereas code-mixing may occur more often because of a lack of proficiency in one of the languages and does not adhere to the principles of CS with regard to pragmatic and morpho-syntactic rules. Two examples include lexical mixing within a word, as in (3), and morpheme mixing as in (4):

(3) **La som**brella (mix of *sombrilla* and *umbrella*)
"the umbrella"

(Miccio and Hammer 2006)

(4) **Es de papá's**
"It's papa's."

(Bergman 1976)

As a child matures and acquires competence in both languages, the language alternations that occur begin to conform to the grammatical principles of the languages in question. When this occurs, particularly in the domain of syntax, the use of both languages together is clearly CS. Code-switches tend to occur at points where the concurrence of elements from the two languages does not violate a morpho-syntactic rule of either language, as for example, in (5):

(5) I'm going with her **a la esquina**
"I'm going with her to the corner."

(Zentella 1997)

CS should not be confused with *word borrowing*. For instance, English words, such as *fax*, appear regularly in the monolingual Spanish of some speakers in US Latino communities. These words have been adapted phonologically and morpho-syntactically over time and appear to new learners to be part of the Spanish language. The same can be true of borrowed Spanish words found in English (e.g. *patio*). These single-word borrowings are not considered code-switches, and sometimes, as in the case of a single-word CS, make it difficult to determine if CS has indeed occurred.

14.2 The pragmatics of code-switching

Bilingual speakers code-switch in a variety of ways and for different reasons. Zentella (1997) noted that adults tend to code-switch more in familiar informal settings where the conversation partners share the same languages. In more formal settings, however, adults tend to code-switch less, particularly where one language or the other is being used by the majority of participants. Timm (1975) suggested that extralinguistic factors such as group identity, age, and gender play a role in determining whether or not speakers will code-switch. She found that Mexican-American Spanish–English bilingual speakers switched to Spanish to convey personal feelings or to converse about aspects of their culture, but switched to English to convey more objective information.

Proficient bilinguals may also code-switch to signal to a conversation partner that they are bilingual or that they identify with a particular cultural group. Poplack (1980) and Zentella (1997) observed that the Puerto Rican community in New York City engages in fluent mixing of Spanish and English. In smaller communities where minority language users are greatly outnumbered, the community norm may be different and result in less CS. Genesee et al. (2004), for example, noted that CS among French–English bilinguals in Canada varies greatly depending on whether or not the individual identifies as French-Canadian versus Anglo-Canadian.

14.3   CS as a measure of proficiency

There is a general consensus in the CS literature that CS of the intra-sentential type is produced by the most proficient bilinguals. Research with adults indicates that intra-sentential switches do not include randomly inserted elements in either language, but rather CS occurs fluently at predictable syntactic points in the sentence and that the most proficient bilinguals are able to easily switch between languages within a sentence without violating the grammatical rules of either language. Despite these findings with regard to adult CS, child CS is often viewed negatively.

There is a widespread misperception that the bilingual child does not truly engage in CS as a proficient bilingual adult would, but is instead using a "mixed-up" language that signals lack of linguistic and sociocultural knowledge or the cognitive inability to separate the two languages. This "mixed-up" language is likely due to the fact that children who are just acquiring their languages may not have developed the competence necessary for production of a complete, syntactically correct utterance in either language. Therefore, code-switched utterances may not adhere to the constraints evident in the adult switches due to production errors. As a result, bilingual CS or code-mixing in children may result in a referral to a speech-language pathologist. In such cases, it is often assumed that the mixing of linguistic elements is indicative of atypical language development. But, in fact, as is the case with adult bilinguals, children who are able to switch between their two languages effectively demonstrate a high degree of language proficiency.

14.4   CS as language choice in children

The ability to choose which language to use in a particular situation develops early in a bilingual child. As with adults, language choice by children is determined by a number of variables including characteristics of the interlocutor, e.g. the degree of intimacy of the relationship to the child, the interlocutor's role (i.e. babysitter, teacher, etc.), languages known and used by the interlocutor, and other listeners in the environment. In addition, the setting (e.g. home, classroom), the function (e.g. to emphasize a previous statement), and the form (e.g. storytelling, role-playing, quoting others) all play a role in the child's language choice.

Even at very young ages, children use their languages in a context-sensitive manner. Comeau et al. (2003) studied six French–English bilingual children (average age 2;4 years) as they played with an assistant who deliberately used a relatively low or a relatively high rate of mixing on three separate occasions. Their results showed that the children adjusted their rates of mixing according to the rate used by the assistant. They also matched their language choice with that of the interlocutor. These examples indicate a sophisticated ability to use two languages and to accommodate to the language of the interlocutor at very young ages (see also Khattab, this volume).

In their longitudinal study of eighty-one Spanish–English bilingual children, Miccio and Hammer (2006) observed that three-year-old children are sensitive to the preference for English in their preschool setting. When tested at school with a Spanish-speaking examiner, some children who spoke Spanish fluently at home offered few responses in Spanish in a Spanish testing situation. An implication of this study is that a teacher may misidentify a bilingual child as having minimal abilities in both languages. Consequently, the child is referred for speech-language services based on the lack of demonstrated language ability at school. A proficient bilingual or a second language learner may appear, in a particular setting, to have a speech or language delay, whereas their language use is a reflection of choice with respect to whether or not mixing is an accepted behavior at home, at school, or in the greater community. Thus, school programming has a great deal of influence on whether or not two languages may be used (Hammer 2000).

In addition to inappropriately referring typically developing bilingual children to a speech-language pathologist for suspected language delay, professionals who are unfamiliar with CS as a linguistic skill may advise families and children to stop switching between languages (McCardle et al. 1995) or may suggest that the parents not speak in their native language to their children. In so doing, a message is conveyed that CS is harmful and will delay language acquisition or even be the source of a language disorder. This advice presents a difficult, if not impossible, challenge to a family. If parents are second language learners themselves, they will not be able to provide a rich linguistic environment for their children and the entire family dynamic will be affected. If a family is bilingual, CS may be a common characteristic of language use at home. To ask families not to code-switch jeopardizes the quality of the linguistic input the child receives and may endanger the socio-emotional stability of the home environment.

Thus, it is counter-productive to discourage CS in bilingual families. Even if the adults in a family are proficient bilingual speakers, stopping the natural CS that occurs within a family or community is extremely difficult to accomplish. For adults to exert the conscious control necessary to inhibit what is an automatic and naturally occurring phenomenon will alter the spontaneity of language use within the family. There is no scientific evidence, to date, that learning language in a mixed language environment is detrimental to language acquisition in children (Kohnert and Bates 2002). In fact, the likelihood of language impairment would possibly increase if parents and children no longer engage in the quantity of communicative interactions that occur naturally in the bilingual environment.

14.5   The grammaticality of children's CS

A number of investigators have studied the grammaticality of children's CS to determine if it is constrained in the same way that adult code-switches are (see Müller and Cantone, this volume). Intra-utterance CS in children who use multiword utterances has been shown to be systematic in a variety of language pairs, e.g. French and English (Genesee and Sauve 2000; Paradis et al. 2000), French and German (Meisel 1994), English and Inuktitut (Allen et al. 2001), English and Norwegian (Lanza 1997), and English and Estonian (Vihman 1998).

Genesee et al. (1995), in a study of French–English bilingual children in Montreal, found more occurrences of inter-utterance code-mixing than intra-utterance mixing, noting that development played a role in this distribution. Younger children with one- or two-word utterances tended to switch between utterances, whereas children at the multi-word level produced more intra-sentential switches. Compared to adult CS, that of young children involves single words, likely due to the fact that young children are not yet using complex sentences with multiple constituents (Genesee et al. 2004). Nonetheless, the single word switch generally follows the grammatical construction of the language in which it is inserted. This was evident in a study by Paradis et al. (2000) who found that a French–English bilingual child prior to age four was able to code-switch single pronouns based on the rules of pronoun use of each language. The insertion of a single code-switched word may, however, be the result of a gap in the lexicon, where the child has not yet acquired the lexical item in one language and so substitutes the word from the second language (Genesee et al. 1995). This is not usually the case in fluent adult bilinguals.

Another difference between CS among young children as compared to adults is manifested in the grammatical categories of switched words. Lanza (1992) found that in the utterances of a two-year-old bilingual

English–Norwegian child, 43% involved prepositions, 22% adjectives, and only 15% were nouns. Vihman (1985) found that, at age two, her bilingual English–Estonian son code-switched from Estonian into English in 42% of his utterances. Of the words switched, 67% were function words as opposed to content words. Vihman did not include the categories of inter-jections, auxiliaries, or articles in her definition of function words. In a study of a bilingual Spanish–English child, Deuchar (1999) found that 85% of the child's utterances that included a function word were switched. Deuchar's definition of function words more closely resembled that of closed-class words and included articles, pronouns, prepositions, and conjunctions. Taking into account this difference in inclusion criteria, the results of Deuchar (1999) and Vihman (1985) are strikingly similar. According to Deuchar (1999) the reason function words are so often switched is that they do not play as important a role in conveying meaning.

Hulk and van der Linden (2005) also found that function words were switched more often than content words in the language samples of three Dutch–French bilingual subjects; however, once the children progressed beyond the two-word stage, the switching of function words declined. This decline in the switching of function words coincided with the children's acquisition of more complex grammar, which included a greater variety of structures in each of the monolingual languages. Similar results were found by Köppe and Meisel (1995), who report that the two children in their study did not appear to violate The Free Morpheme Constraint beyond age 2;5. After that, CS occurred most frequently with nouns and between determiners and nouns in object noun phrases. Similarly, Vihman (1985) found that switched categories changed from mostly function words early in production to nouns and verbs after 2 years of age. The finding that CS on function words gradually declines, but increases with content words indicates that the CS of the child is becoming more adult-like.

It can be concluded, therefore, that the earliest CS observed to occur in children does not follow the same pattern of switching observed in highly proficient bilingual adults. It is likely that the earliest CS reflects a lack of development in either language of the bilingual and single word switches are used to fill gaps in a child's developing systems. Syntactic elements may be mixed for the same reason. Because children are in the process of acquiring two languages, it can be expected that their CS will neither be as fluent nor as grammatically correct as that of an adult. Therefore, errors in grammar are likely to occur in each language as well as in CS. Most of the code-switched utterances of bilingual children are grammatically correct according to both languages involved in the switch once the children are able to produce utterances greater than three words in length (Meisel 1994; Lanza 1997; Paradis et al. 2000; Köppe and Meisel 1995). It is evident that the ability to code-switch using grammatical sentences develops in tandem with the acquisition of grammar in each language. Additionally, as children become more proficient with each of their languages, the code-switched word categories appear to be more similar to those of the switches involved in adult CS, indicating that the later switches occur out of choice and not out of necessity.

14.6   Is CS a language disorder?

Is code-switching in children ever indicative of a language disorder? First it is necessary to define the term *language disorder* or *impairment*. Leonard (2001:116) defines a child with specific language impairment (SLI) as one "who exhibits a significant deficit in language ability yet displays normal hearing, age-appropriate scores on tests of nonverbal intelligence, and no obvious signs of neurological damage." Children with SLI usually express first words and two word combinations later than typically developing peers. Difficulties with grammar and, in particular, overgeneralizations of grammatical morphemes are also characteristic of SLI; however, individuals with SLI differ widely in their language abilities. A broader definition of language disorder can be found in Paul (2001:3), who defines a language disorder as "a significant deficit in learning to talk, understand, or use any aspect of language appropriately, relative to both environmental and norm-referenced expectations for children of similar developmental level." According to this definition, CS would not, in and of itself be considered a disorder due to the fact that CS is likely very common in bilingual communities. In order to be considered a disorder, the child's CS behavior would have to be significantly different from the CS patterns of other bilingual children in the same environment.

One might be tempted to assess a bilingual child in his or her dominant language to determine if a disorder is present. However, many bilingual children do not have a dominant language and their skills in each language may be lower than that of their monolingual peers (Gutiérrez-Clellen 1996). The use of tests developed for monolinguals is inappropriate because the acquisition rate of linguistic elements has been found to vary between bilingual and monolingual speakers of a language. For example, Merino (1992) found that the rate and order of acquisition of Spanish morphemes was different for bilingual (Spanish–English) children residing in the US as compared to monolingual Spanish speaking children living in Mexico. The use of a test normed on monolingual speakers for bilingual children is therefore inadequate and may result in the misdiagnosis of a disorder in a typically developing bilingual child.

The extant literature provides little insight with regard to what is considered typical and atypical CS in bilingual children for those who must assess a bilingual child's competence. This is because few studies have looked at CS in bilingual children identified as having a language disorder. In a report of grammatical impairments in Spanish–English speaking children, Restrepo and Gutiérrez-Clellen noted that bilingual children with specific language impairment do not exhibit code-switching behaviors that violate grammatical constraints. Restrepo (2003) did find that second language learners may, for example, use English "the" with Spanish nouns, an error commonly found in learning English as a second language. In general, however, no significant differences have been found in the amount or type of CS in bilingual children with and without SLI (Patterson and Pearson 2004; Restrepo and Gutiérrez-Clellen 2004).

14.6.1   Is intervention necessary?

It is likely that, during the course of language acquisition, bilingual children will overextend their speech and language patterns to settings where they will not be able to effectively communicate. Given adequate time, most children will adjust and learn without intervention by a speech–language pathologist. This does not mean, however, that professionals should assume that all CS among bilingual children is simply a feature of bilingualism and not worthy of attention. As with monolinguals, bilingual children may persist in using inappropriate patterns even after considerable experience in a new setting. If a child continues to use CS inappropriately or without pragmatic or linguistic purpose, this may be an indication that the communicative demands on the child are too great given his or her level of language competence. In this case, Genesee et al. (2004) suggest that the context in which the inappropriate CS is occurring should be evaluated and opportunities for language enhancement should be provided. Rather than assume that a bilingual child has a language delay or disorder due to observed instances of CS, Genesee et al. further suggest that professionals screen for CS that serves to fill lexical gaps, shows a pragmatic purpose, or is used to assert identity with a particular cultural group. Language behaviors that can be explained in one of these ways should be ruled out before considering whether or not a disorder is present.

Keeping in mind that bilingualism is shaped by the sociocultural environment, behaviors that differ from those of mainstream monolingual children should not be singled out for attention or referred for remediation. Like adults, bilingual children will acquire the social norms of their environment if given sufficient time and encouragement. To determine if a child's CS pattern is what would be expected for a particular child, it is imperative that the speech–language pathologist becomes knowledgeable about the communication norms for the child's community and family. It is therefore essential for a professional to obtain a detailed language history for the child to assure that an assessment of the child's current linguistic abilities takes into account the family context and the culture of the community in which the child has learned language (Tabors 1997; van Tuijl et al. 2001). Knowing which language or languages are encouraged in the home and community and how those languages are used in various social situations will help professionals determine how to provide the best language enhancement opportunities in the school setting.

Home visits and observations with conversation partners are likely to be an important part of the diagnostic evaluation. In addition to understanding the linguistic patterns of a child's family, professionals must make an effort to understand the linguistic patterns of the child's peer group. If a child's language ability differs significantly from the peer group with which they identify, then an evaluation is recommended so that any linguistic deficit can be addressed and the child can be provided with appropriate strategies to overcome the problem. It is important always to provide positive recognition of the minority culture, but also give assistance to becoming socialized into the majority culture so that children communicate effectively and function well in various environments.

Although over-identification of disorders has received attention, there is also a problem of under-identification of disorders in bilingual children. Professionals may incorrectly assume that any language characteristics they observe are due to bilingualism and consequently ignore a serious language learning problem. Specifically, the professional should gather information about: (a) when the child was exposed to and expected to communicate in each language; (b) who serves as the child's communicative partners; (c) the languages and topics of conversation between the child and the respective partners; and (d) how frequently the child sees and interacts with the partners (Crago and Cole 1991; Gutiérrez-Clellen and Kreiter 2003; Hammer 1998). Knowledge about language usage at school will also be valuable, as the language of instruction and the language used between peers can vary from school to school and even classroom to classroom. In addition, observations of the child interacting with key conversational partners at home and school can provide valuable insights about the nature of these interactions and how the two languages are used. Information from interviews and observations will enable the speech–language pathologist to ascertain how much exposure a child has had to each language as well as changes that have occurred in the language environment. This information may explain much of the variation among children and why children will speak in a certain way. Most importantly, the speech–language pathologist will be able to determine if the child's CS is typical of his environment and/or if the child's CS may be due, in part, to limited knowledge of the second language. Furthermore, difficulties in communicating may reflect the child's inability to conform to particular social norms because those norms are in conflict with what the child has learned at home (Crago 1992). CS may have resulted from the language learning environment rather than a language delay or disorder. Thus, detailed attention to the language and cultural history of a bilingual child is a crucial part of assessment.

The bilingual child presents even more of a challenge to speech–language pathologists who are expected to decide whether or not a disorder exists, and, if one does exist, what to do about it. This problem is further exacerbated by the shortage of bilingual speech–language pathologists in many parts of the world. Consequently, professionals who are not bilingual and who do not belong to the children's cultural group are faced with the responsibility of making very difficult decisions. Individuals from a child's community can be called upon to assist in these cases. Thus, a speech–language pathologist working with children from different cultural and linguistic backgrounds must not only be willing to do the research necessary to understand the linguistic background of the children in question, but also be very careful in the selection and training of allied professionals when seeking to determine the most appropriate educational program and level of special services for a bilingual child.

A model of assessment and treatment that has gained attention, particularly for bilingual children, is *dynamic assessment* (Gutiérrez-Clellen and Peña 2001). Dynamic assessment implies that assessment is ongoing and is interspersed with opportunities for the child to learn new behaviors. A speech–language pathologist may observe a child on more than one occasion both prior to and after the teaching of a new behavior to determine if a child is able to learn a new skill without significant intervention. If the use of language by the child in question changes positively, the child is most likely able to acquire language typically. Utilizing these strategies either instead of or in addition to traditional methods of assessment will minimize the likelihood of misdiagnosis. Even if a disorder is present, it does not mean that the child's language acquisition is random or grammatically unpredictable. The language abilities of children with disorders will usually be more static and learning new rules, those for CS for example, will be more challenging for the child.

Finally, it must be remembered that young children are in the process of acquiring language. Children under the age of five who are in educational programs that do not provide systematic support for the first language are extremely vulnerable to backsliding in their knowledge and use of the their first language (Kan and Kohnert 2005; Kohnert et al. 2005; Leseman 2000; Montrul 2002; Schaerlaekens et al. 1995; Wong-Fillmore 1991; Bolonyai, this volume). Positive interaction in bilingual children's two languages is important, not only for maintaining what has been learned, but also for acquisition of more complex forms in each language (see Cummins 1979). In addition, findings of intervention studies involving bilingual children with language impairments suggest that increasing skills in a child's first language does not impede learning of the second (Paradis et al. 2003; Perozzi and Sánchez 1992; Thordardottir et al. 1997) and may, in fact, contribute to learning of the second (Miccio and Hammer 2006; Tabors et al. 2003). Thus, if a bilingual child is to become a successful communicator in all of her or his language environments, direct support needs to be provided for both languages.

14.7 Conclusion

CS is a linguistic behavior frequently used among bilinguals for a variety of reasons and should not generally be considered a cause for referral to a speech–language pathologist. CS does not occur in random fashion, but rather is constrained by grammatical rules as well as social and cultural norms, and reflects the child's developing linguistic competence in two languages. To alternate between languages appropriately, a child must be acquiring both grammars and be able to access them on-line and integrate them into a single utterance. A bilingual child must also develop functional communication that is context-sensitive so that he or she can distinguish between familiar and unfamiliar interlocutors and situations. Because CS is a sign of proficiency in two languages, it should not be considered deviant or be discouraged as a form of self-expression.

In addition, professionals should not recommend that children use only one language with the assumption that this will stop CS. CS should be viewed as a resource for children who have not yet achieved proficiency in their two languages, much in the same way that CS is a resource for adults who can express themselves best in a particular way in a particular setting. Like monolinguals, bilingual children adapt to their communicative environment with appropriate encouragement. Insight into the development of both the pragmatic and grammatical aspects of CS will allow for a more complete evaluation of a bilingual child's overall language competence and perhaps can be useful in determining whether a bilingual child's language development is disordered or delayed. Since CS is often used as a means for a child to identify with a social group, preventing him or her from doing so could lead to isolation and could be more detrimental than beneficial with regard to the child's communication development.

Note

1. The authors would like to thank Shelley Scarpino for her valuable comments and indispensable assistance in the preparation of earlier versions of this chapter.

15

Code-switching, imperfect acquisition, and attrition

Agnes Bolonyai

15.1 Introduction

Many, if not most, immigrant parents wonder how raising a child with two languages might impact the child's linguistic development. Perhaps not surprisingly, parental concern is extremely widespread regarding the causes and consequences of code-switching (hereafter CS) in the child's speech. Is using words from two languages in the same sentence a sign of language confusion or delay? Could extensive switching back and forth from one language to another have a negative effect, resulting in a "broken" mixture? And moreover, can language mixing cause the child to lose the mother tongue, the language of the home and ethnic heritage? These questions merit attention not only because they reveal sentiments that run wide and deep in the public discourse of bilingual mixing, but also because they resonate with pervasive issues in the study of CS in relation to child bilingual first (L1) language attrition and/or imperfect acquisition. The goal of this chapter is to provide an overview of the research that explores what role, if any, CS might play in minority language attrition and incomplete acquisition in children who grow up in a majority language setting.

It is important to point out that there has been no scientific evidence to date that would suggest that switching or mixing between languages is *inherently* damaging or that it *automatically* leads to erosion of either of the child's languages. In fact, several studies have demonstrated that, just as adult bilinguals use CS as a communicative resource, children, too, can skillfully alternate between languages for a variety of sociolinguistic and conversational–pragmatic purposes (Auer 1988; Bolonyai 2005; Cromdal and Aronsson 2000; Halmari 2005; Jørgensen 1998; Zentella 1997). Nonetheless, recent work in contact linguistics has suggested that a possible link might exist between CS and various forms of language decline such as L1 attrition and imperfect acquisition, particularly in bilingual contact situations where a second language (L2) is socially dominant (Bolonyai 1998, 2000; Halmari 1992; Kaufman 2001; Kaufman and Aronoff 1991; Schmitt 2000; Seliger 1996; Viberg 1993). While research findings concerning the precise nature of the interaction between language mixing and L1 attrition/incomplete acquisition are far from conclusive, investigations in this area have offered insights that inform our current understanding of some key issues and perennial questions. These include the following:

(1.)   A fundamental issue concerns whether CS can be taken as an indicator of the child's bilingual proficiency. What can CS tell us about the nature or degree of erosion of language skills or competence? Is "normal" CS that occurs in the absence of language deterioration different from the type of CS that occurs in the context of attrition? If so, what are the linguistic characteristics of CS with attrition and what mechanisms can account for them? Can the pattern of CS in the child's speech tell us whether vulnerable L1 structures have been acquired and forgotten, or whether they have never been fully acquired in the first place? Does CS correlate with dynamic changes of bilingual competence and contact? Can CS prohibit attrition and promote language maintenance? What are the characteristics of CS at different stages of language decline?

(2.)   Another set of issues focuses on the nature of the connection between CS and language deterioration. Is there a cause-and-effect relation between the two phenomena? If there is, does CS bring about attrition or does attrition lead to the switching and mixing of languages? In the absence of causal links, what other explanation could account for observed co-occurrences between CS and language erosion? Can CS be shown to facilitate other language contact phenomena (e.g. cross-linguistic influence, structural borrowing, restructuring, innovation) in the eroding or incompletely acquired language? If there is interaction between CS and L1 vulnerability, what linguistic domains and aspects are the most affected?

   For the purposes of this chapter, the review of the literature will focus largely on research pertaining to the two sets of issues mentioned above. The resurgence of interest in how a uniquely bilingual behavior such as CS – a phenomenon that, folk wisdom notwithstanding, some researchers view as "language at its best" (Broersma and de Bot 2006:1) – may figure in the complex processes of minority L1 loss and/or restricted acquisition in immigrant children should not be surprising. In addition to its broader societal and educational implications, research in this area is important for theoretical reasons. The study of bilingual L1 attrition and imperfect acquisition in children can teach us about the nature of bilingual competence from a perspective that can complement, and possibly sharpen, some of what we know from research into bilingual contact and change in adult populations. Pre-pubescent school-age children in particular tend to exhibit a degree of bilingual plasticity, or fluidity, along with rapid developmental changes – both in terms of language acquisition and loss – that are largely unobserved in adults (Kaufman and Aronoff 1991; Kuhberg 1992; Bolonyai 1998; Isurin 2000; Jisa 2000; Halmari 2005). Investigations of the dynamic moves "in and out of bilingualism" (Grosjean 1985:473) can help address questions about the flexibility and fragility of the unique, "compound state of mind" (Cook 2003) that is thought to characterize bilingual speakers.

From a sociolinguistic perspective, linguistic practices of pre-adolescent immigrant children may have a profound impact on the success or failure of intergenerational mother-tongue transmission at the level of the family, the most important social unit in language maintenance (Fishman 2000a). Compared to younger bilingual children, whose language use is largely determined by the structuring influence of parental language practices and attitudes, school-age children are more likely to make linguistic choices for themselves. In particular, after children enter grade school, "the natural attraction of the majority language" (Pearson 2007:402) becomes very powerful and their language use preference may diverge from that of the L1-dominant parents. Newly experienced social pressure and/or desire to assimilate and succeed outside the home environment can give rise to sociolinguistic tensions that children will seek to solve through increasing allegiance to the societal language vis à vis the home language. Late bilingual children who immigrate during or after puberty – i.e. whose primary language socialization took place in the homeland – are generally better equipped for, and often more self-invested in, maintaining their linguistic, cultural, and ethnic heritage in the L2 environment. In this sense, pre-pubescent bilingual children of first-generation immigrants often seem to be situated on the frontline of vulnerability to primary language attrition and shift. Their distinct position makes the study of this age group particularly interesting, with implications for a better understanding of how social, cognitive, and linguistic factors interact to shape processes of bilingual contact, language progression, and language regression in the individual and at societal levels.

15.1.1   What is attrition?

Broadly defined, and as used here, language attrition refers to the temporary or permanent decline of language skills, knowledge, and/or use in individuals. It is both a process and a potential outcome of the dynamic sociolinguistic conditions of language contact in which individuals may find themselves. De Bot and Weltens (1985) and Van Els (1986) distinguish four bilingual situations in which language attrition occurs, each one marking a different combination of the language that is lost (L1 or L2) and the environment in which language loss takes place (L1 or L2 environment). This chapter is mainly concerned with L1 attrition that occurs in L2 environments, such as the deterioration of the native language of immigrants. L1 attrition is a non-pathological, commonly occurring phenomenon in individuals, but in situations of unstable contact it may create conditions for language shift at the community level (Myers-Scotton 2002b). From a linguistic point of view, erosion in the immigrant L1 is a result of intensive language contact; that is, changes that occur in the L1 "would have been less likely to happen if it were not for the contact situation" (Thomason 2001:62). Nevertheless, contact-induced erosion of L1 knowledge is rarely a "total phenomenon" (Clyne 1986); rather, it is a gradual and selective process in which distinct aspects of the waning language can be affected differently (Seliger 1991). Some of the changes appear as loss, reduction, or replacement of certain L1 features, while others seem to enrich the L1 system through innovation, addition, and borrowing from the L2 (Gal 1989; Sharwood Smith 1989). Indeed, L2 influence on L1 as a major mechanism in the attrition process has been the focus of much recent work on adult bilinguals (Pavlenko 2000; Gürel 2004).

More narrowly defined, attrition is the forgetting or "loss of aspects of a previously *fully* acquired primary language resulting from the acquisition of another language" (Seliger 1996:606, emphasis added). Assuming that attrition proper presupposes complete L1 knowledge before the onset of bilingualism and subsequent L1 loss, the use of the term seems more felicitous in reference to adult bilinguals than young children. There is ample evidence that most healthy, monolingual children attain mature and stable competence in the basic structures of their native language by the age of five; mastering the most complex constructions may take a few additional years, while vocabulary acquisition continues for another decade or so (Aitchison 1996). Strictly speaking, then, attrition may not take place before the age of linguistic maturation – after all, what has never been acquired cannot be forgotten. Such a narrow definition of L1 attrition may be difficult to apply to simultaneous and early bilingual children growing up with a minority L1 and majority L2, since the L1 may begin to erode before it has been fully mastered due to persistent dominance of the societal L2.

15.1.2   Incomplete L1 acquisition in children

In an attempt to mitigate the problem of terminological ambiguity, recent studies refer to bilingual L1 erosion in children as developmental attrition and/or as imperfect or incomplete acquisition (Kaufman and Aronoff 1991; Polinsky 1995; Halmari 2005; Bolonyai 2007). Clearly, the distinction between forgetting and incomplete acquisition is an essential one; however, it is also important to recognize that the two processes can co-occur and reinforce each other, resulting in linguistic outcomes that may not be clearly assigned to one or the other process.

Incomplete L1 acquisition is fairly common in first- and second-generation minority children who acquire their L1 mainly as the home language while being immersed in a socially and functionally L2-dominant environment. The language dynamism associated with these children is regarded as a "special case of language acquisition and use" (Andersen 1982: 86). What makes this acquisition–attrition process unique is that it involves "divergent change" (Sharwood Smith 1989) in performance and/or competence and concomitant linguistic behavior that appears to violate "normal" – i.e. native, monolingual – linguistic and sociolinguistic norms. In most cases, changes and deviations in an L1 system that has not fully developed or stabilized can be attributed to the child's restricted contact with the native language (i.e. when the quantity and/or quality of L1 exposure and functional use is limited) alongside intensive contact with L2 (i.e. when the predominant source of linguistic input and active use is L2). The onset of the process of contact-induced divergence is important because "the earlier a child's L1 input becomes restricted and the more restricted the continued input is, the more likely the child is to show signs of incomplete acquisition in the areas of morphology, syntax, semantics, and lexicon, as well as phonology" (Halmari 2005:340).

This claim is in line with the view that children must be exposed to a "critical mass" of input, both in quantity and quality, during a certain period for language maintenance to be successful (Neisser 1984; de Bot and Clyne 1989). If exposure to the minority language continues to be curtailed through puberty and adulthood, the individual may ultimately remain an *incomplete learner* (Polinsky 1995) or *imperfect speaker* (Dorian 1981) of his/her native tongue. Indeed, several studies of second-generation adult speakers of heritage languages report a positive correlation between reduced access to the full, native L1 variety over time and the emergence of a qualitatively divergent, imperfect adult language system (Silva-Corvalán 1991; Polinsky 1995; Montrul 2002). Undoubtedly, when an imperfectly learned variety of the heritage language is transmitted to subsequent generations, it is even more likely to undergo additional structural changes.

15.2 Sociolinguistic and psycholinguistic aspects of bilingual L1 attrition and incomplete acquisition

Intensive language contact in most bilingual scenarios takes on a distinct characteristic: asymmetry. Asymmetry can be a feature of both the sociolinguistic and psycholinguistic dynamics of contact situations, including those that operate in minority L1 attrition and imperfect acquisition.

15.2.1 Language status
On the sociolinguistic level, asymmetry is most commonly implicated in the political and symbolic economy of the languages in contact. Linguistic inequality between a majority and a minority language is constructed on the dominant "linguistic market" that endows languages with different

values and helps to (re-)produce asymmetrical power relations (Bourdieu 1991). Thus, in the context of minority language attrition among immigrants, the societal language is presumably more highly valued than the minority L1. Supported by legitimating language ideologies, the socially dominant language is typically recognized as the language of power, status, authority, prestige, and the beacon of socio-economic mobility. As linguistic capital, the immigrant language is rarely positioned to carry equal clout as the societal language. Of course, that is not to say that the immigrant language is always lacking currency or that possessing any two (or more) languages in one's repertoire is not a valuable asset. In fact, the more linguistic capital that speakers accumulate, the more they should be able to profit from the hierarchy between languages (Bourdieu 1991). Yet, it is not an exceptional case when the symbolic value of ethnicity, cultural heritage, in-group solidarity, and emotional intimacy associated with a minority L1 fails to provide the incentive necessary for successful trans-generational language maintenance.

15.2.2   Language attitudes and use

It is also not uncommon for an asymmetrical sociolinguistic order to promote psycholinguistic imbalance between the L1 and L2, for example, in terms of speakers' attitudes towards their languages. Parents' language attitudes are generally considered crucial in children's L1 retention. When parents view the native language as an integral part of ethnicity, regard it as a valuable economic asset, and/or a highly prestigious source of cultural capital, and its trans-generational retention important, they are more likely to use the ethnic L1 at home as the primary means of communication. Yet, numerous studies indicate that parental encouragement and prevalent L1 use notwithstanding, immigrant children who leave their native country at a very young age or are born in the host society may develop more positive attitudes toward the majority L2 than the minority L1 over a period of time (Hakuta and D'Andrea 1992; Kouritzin 1999; Young and Tran 1999; Luo and Wiseman 2000). For example, Hakuta and D'Andrea (1992) investigated the relationship between language attitudes and use in Mexican-American adolescents of first- and second-generation immigrants in California. They found that teenagers who held positive attitudes toward L2 (English) reported using English more often. Self-reports of estimated proficiency in both L1 and L2 were predicted by their attitudes toward each language. Another study by Kaufman (2001) explored the role of attitudes in L1 attrition among children of Israeli immigrants residing in the United States. This study too argues for a powerful link between language attitudes and outcomes of bilingual contact by reporting that children's low affective attachment to the L1 (Hebrew) and high integrative orientation toward the L2 (English) make the L1 particularly vulnerable to attrition.

15.2.3   Language and identity

While negative attitudes toward the immigrant language can play a significant role in its deterioration, L1 attrition, incomplete acquisition, or shift
to L2 may occur even when speakers maintain strong and positive identification with the heritage language and culture (Bankston and Henry
1998). Due to sociolinguistic conditions brought about by migration and
language contact, immigrant minorities' conception of what it means to
be, for example, Puerto Rican, or who counts as a legitimate speaker of
Spanish, might change. Assumptions, taken for granted before migration,
about a "natural" and intimate connection between ethnic language, identity, and culture may be revised such that the notion of retaining one's
ethnic identity while not speaking the ethnic language is perceived as
normal. As a case in point, Zentella's (1997) study of Puerto Rican children
growing up in New York demonstrates that a Puerto Rican identity for the
youth born and/or raised in *El Barrio* does not depend on speaking Spanish.
The study reports that given the "concrete reality" of immigrant life, this
community "drew the boundaries of Puerto Rican identity wide enough to
encompass the monolingual children of Puerto Rican descent" (Zentella
1997:54). Parents aim for their children to achieve a minimal level of
Spanish comprehension; in fact, community norms define those with
passive comprehension in one language and fluent speaking and understanding in the other language as bilinguals. Predictably, language choice
patterns are often non-reciprocal in that parents may speak Spanish and
children respond in English. Similar asymmetrical language choice patterns in inter-generational communication are well documented in the
literature (Gal 1979; Bentahila and Davies 1992; Extra and Verhoeven
1998; Li Wei 1994; Hlavac 2000; Clyne 2003). Zentella further notes that
children who lack minimal Spanish skills are accommodated through
code-switches to English or translation both in peer and adult-child interactions. The function of switching between languages, however, goes
beyond accommodation. It is "the most obvious expression" (Zentella
1997:271) of the multiple and complementary identities immigrant bilinguals forge for themselves as they (re-)define what it means to belong to an
ethnolinguistic minority community within the political economy of a
broader social context. Questions of how CS may be implicated in the
linguistic processes and outcomes of children acquiring a minority L1 in
a majority L2 setting is discussed next.

15.3   Distinguishing "normal" CS from CS in language erosion

CS is an integral part of being bilingual. It is motivated by three basic
factors – sociolinguistic, psycholinguistic, and structural – and it is used
by fluent or stable bilinguals as well as by those who are becoming or

"un-becoming" bilingual and therefore their languages are undergoing change and restructuring. In general, normal bilingual CS can be distinguished from CS in language erosion in terms of all three motivating factors, although the fact that some forms of CS could be used by full bilinguals and incomplete bilinguals, albeit for different reasons, may blur the distinction.

15.3.1   Sociolinguistic evidence

CS in language erosion can be distinguished from normal CS on a sociolinguistic basis. Unlike fluent bilinguals, whose linguistic competence enables them to use their languages in accordance with relevant sociolinguistic norms and situational characteristics, those undergoing L1 attrition may be forced to code-switch when it is not appropriate. Seliger (1996:613) claims that, "[c]ode-mixing can be considered a precursor condition for primary language attrition when mixing begins to occur in contexts that are not motivated by external factors such as interlocutor, topic, or cultural environment." Empirical evidence for this claim comes from a study of a Russian–English-speaking child's speech prior to and after attrition (Turian and Altenberg 1991). Prior to attrition (3;0 to 3;7 years;months), the child appropriately used CS to address each family member in his or her respective L1, or for emphasis. By contrast, post-attrition data (at 4;3 and 4;4 years of age) show continuous CS to English, unrelated to interlocutor, topic, or context of conversation. In example (1), J's mixing English words into Russian when speaking to a monolingual Russian speaker, A, is prompted by his lack of proficiency.

(1)   A: Eto shto takoye? Eto imeniny?
              "What is it? Is it a birthday party?"
         J: Eto **was** kogda moy **birthday**.
              "It was when my birthday."

                                                      (Turian and Altenberg 1991:223)

15.3.2   Psycholinguistic evidence

Psycholinguistic factors triggering CS include on-line lexical retrieval difficulties, fluency problems, and gaps in "an incomplete knowledge base" (Poulisse 1999). Lack of availability or accessibility of certain words and structures can be reflected in the use of CS and borrowings "flagged" with pauses, hesitations, false starts, repetitions, fillers, inaccuracy, avoidance, and reformulations (Olshtain and Barzilay 1991). While any bilingual may produce flagged CS, it is much less likely to be used by fluent bilinguals than those who are in the process of language attrition. Bilingual speakers, who use their languages with sufficient frequency, are generally able to control, access, and activate each language according to their communicative goals with great facility, accuracy, and fluency (Green 1998;

Paradis 2001). Nevertheless, occasional CS due to lexical retrieval problems is considered normal, since even fluent bilinguals rarely develop equal, perfectly balanced proficiency or pattern of use in their two languages (Grosjean 1998). CS may also be prompted by a momentary, tip-of-the-tongue memory lapse, which, of course, occurs in bilinguals and monolinguals alike.

In L1 attrition and incomplete acquisition, reduced use and accessibility of L1 may result in frequent or involuntary CS to the stronger L2 (Turian and Altenberg 1991). Speakers use CS as a "crutch" in coping with permanent or temporary inaccessibility of specific words and complex or unstable structures (Zentella 1997). When CS is motivated by L1 erosion, it often co-occurs with pauses and other disfluency phenomena, appeals for help, and metalinguistic comments (e.g. "*I forgot*," "*I don't know how to say it*") that explicitly signal a breakdown in communication. In (2), two English-dominant Hungarian-American children, ages eight and nine, talk about their favorite movies in their weaker L1. The child's (CH1) difficulty finding the appropriate Hungarian word manifests itself in the use of repeated pauses, a filler, and finally CS to English, her stronger language.

(2) CH1: Amikor én megláttam a … ahm … a … **movie**-t.
   "When I saw the uhm th movie."
   CH2: Filmet.
   "Movie."
   CH1: A filmet.
   "The movie."

(Bolonyai 1998)

Although it is often assumed that the main reason bilingual children use CS is to compensate for their linguistic deficiency, empirical research does not uniformly support this assumption. Zentella (1997) examined the CS strategies used by five Puerto Rican children (aged six to eleven) in New York and found that CS for "crutching" (i.e. when the child did not know or remember a word) accounted for only about 14% of all instances of CS in the corpus. The majority of CS served conversational functions such as change in footing and clarification and/or emphasis, as shown in examples (3) and (4). Crutching occurred most frequently in CS to English, suggesting children's dominance in English. Overall, however, the findings show that "even non-fluent children do less 'crutching' than most people assume" (99).

(3) *Topic shift*
   Vamo/h/ a preguntarle. It's raining!
   "Let's go ask her. It's raining!"

(Zentella 1997:94)

(4) *Quotations, direct and indirect*
   El me dijo, "Call the police!" **pero yo dije, "No voy a llamar la policía na(-da)**."

"He told me, 'Call the police!' but I said, 'I'm not going to call the police nothin'.'"

(Zentella 1997:94)

15.3.3   Linguistic evidence

From a grammatical perspective, CS has been characterized in the literature as a sophisticated, structurally coherent, rule-governed behavior that requires a great deal of bilingual competence. While there is little consensus with respect to the nature of linguistic rules or constraints involved in CS, most researchers agree that the degree of bilingual competence constitutes a source of variability in the type of CS that is produced (Weinreich 1953; Clyne 1967; Myers-Scotton 1993a; 1997; 2002a; Muysken 2000). For example, studies based on both adult and child populations have found that unbalanced bilinguals tend to favor single-word and tag-like switches intra-sententially. The direction of these switches is typically from speakers' stronger language to the weaker language. This pattern has been used to support claims that the less morpho-syntactic anchoring an alien element requires in the base language, the easier it is to use in CS.

Another CS pattern that is likely to occur in unbalanced bilinguals is alternational CS between sentences or speech turns (Poplack 1980). When speakers are constrained in their grammatical abilities in one of the languages, this CS style may help to avoid the production of longer and morpho-syntactically more complex stretches of speech. By the same token, intra-sentential CS involving larger segments and constituents (phrases, clauses) requires a high level of proficiency in both grammars, and therefore is, arguably, more likely to occur in the most fluent and balanced bilingual speakers. The following examples from Hungarian–English data may illustrate the distinction between intra-sentential word-level switching (5), phrasal-level switching (6), and inter-sentential turn-level switching (7).

(5)   Mi történik az utolsó **part**-ban?
       "What happens in the last part?"

(Bolonyai 2000:85)

(6)   Hogy tudsz rákapaszkodni … **to the branch**.
       "That you can cling onto … to the branch."

(Bolonyai 2000:99)

(7)   Mother: Mind a ketten nagyon-nagyon jókat mondtatok, nagyon
                  okosakat.
                  "Both of you said very-very good things, very smart things."
       Emma: No! Who was the best? Mommy?

(Bolonyai 2005:21)

It is important to realize, however, that the aforementioned correlations are probabilistic rather than absolute. For example, Bentahila and Davies's

(1992) study of two generations of Arabic–French bilinguals in Morocco reported a different patterning of CS. The older generation of bilinguals, who had an equally high command of both languages, used the socio-linguistically more acceptable inter-sentential CS more frequently, whereas the younger bilinguals, who were Arabic-dominant, used intra-sentential CS with more frequency. Additionally, there is some evidence that intra-sentential CS may be a more frequent pattern in CS involving an agglutina-tive language than CS involving a fusional language (Myers-Scotton 1993a; Halmari 1997; Clyne 2003). Indeed, it is incumbent on future research to systematically account for the exact ways in which sociolinguistic and typological factors may interact with psycholinguistic and cognitive (competence related) factors to produce the actual type of CS.

Unlike "normal" bilingual CS, where the grammatical autonomy of each language is maintained and shows largely predictable structures, CS in L1 erosion is lacking in structural coherence, predictability, and well-formedness, as measured by community norms (Myers-Scotton 1997). Motivated primarily by the speaker's linguistic needs rather than socio-pragmatic goals and linguistic constraints, CS showing attrition has been characterized as linguistic "intermixing" where the autonomy and integrity of the L1 system is no longer observed (Sridhar and Sridhar 1980; Seliger and Vago 1991). According to Seliger (1996:611), language mixing in attrition "leads to the nonobservance of language-specific constraints" on L1, and, eventually, the fusion or merging of the two grammatical systems in contact into a single system. Due to reduced accessibility of the L1 grammar and intensive contact with L2, the L2 linguistic system becomes a source of "indirect positive evidence" (Seliger 1991), a model for imitation, or "copying" (Johanson 1993). While this process is selective, perceived cross-linguistic congruence – on the basis of the speaker's subjective assessment of equivalence between any given structure in L1 and L2 – has been claimed to have an important effect on determining how and what linguistic features of the L1 will undergo change (Johanson 1993; Bolonyai 2000; Muysken 2000; Backus 2005). As numerous studies have shown, L2 influence on the unstable L1 may manifest itself in various forms of language mixing, such as transfer, interference, transference, structural borrowing, selective copying, calquing, convergence, restruc-turing, creative innovation, incorporation of L1 into L2, covert CS, com-posite CS, or "third-system" innovation, among others. The following examples from the speech of young immigrant children in the United States illustrate the type of language mixing that could be considered as a sign of L1 attrition and/or imperfect acquisition (Bolonyai 1998, 2002, 2005, 2007).

(8) mert [én] vol-t-am meleg akkor
     because NOM1SG be-PAST.1SG hot then
     "because I was hot then"

Cf. Standard Hungarian
mert [nek-ém] meleg-em vol-t akkor
because DAT1SG hot-POSS.1SG be-PAST.1SG then

(Bolonyai 1998:36)

Example (8) comes from a Hungarian–English-speaking, four-year-old child residing in the US. The utterance illustrates what has been referred to as *covert CS*, or *convergence*: "bilingual speech appearing in the disguise of monolingual speech" (Bolonyai 1998:23). In covert CS, all lexical material comes from one language, but abstract structural features from both languages converge in a composite grammatical structure, or "composite Matrix Language" (Myers-Scotton 1998, 2002a; Bolonyai 1998; Schmitt 2000). Composite grammatical structures are likely to be found in situations of L1 attrition/imperfect acquisition, when unbalanced, non-fluent bilinguals attempt to communicate in their linguistically unstable, weaker language. In (8), all the words are in Hungarian, although some of the structural properties of the utterance are copied from English. The word order is directed in part by Hungarian, in part by English. In line with Standard Hungarian rules, subject pro-drop is observed. Following English, however, the verb *voltam* "I was" precedes the complement *meleg* "hot," which is in violation of the Hungarian rule for marking pragmatic emphasis. Also, the argument structure (Dative Experiencer Subject) of the Hungarian construction "to have hot" is replaced by the argument structure (Nominative Experiencer Subject) of its English equivalent "to be hot." Thus, the monolingual surface form of the utterance is supported by a composite structure, with parts of abstract lexical structure from two linguistic systems combined in a way that, arguably, reflects the child's subjective perspective on "interlingual equivalence" (Johanson 1993) and structural compatibility between Hungarian and English.

Example (9) is taken from a study that examines the vulnerability of the Hungarian case system in the speech of six Hungarian-American children, ages seven to nine (Bolonyai 2002).

(9)   Hogy megy-ünk **P.E.**-be, **music**-ba, **art**-ba
      that go-PRES.1PL P.E.-IL/into music-IL/into art-IL/into
      "that we are going to P.E., music, art"
      Cf. Standard Hungarian
      Hogy megy-ünk **P.E.**-re, **music**-ra, **art**-ra
      that go-PRES.1PL P.E.-SUBL/onto music-SUBL/onto art-SUBL/onto

(Bolonyai 2002:22)

The example illustrates composite CS, where code-switched L2 lexemes are incorporated into the L1 system along with some L2-specific abstract structural properties. Specifically, English influence on Hungarian is noticeable in the use of semantic case morphology, which, in turn, indicates signs of restructuring at the conceptual–semantic level – in the mental representation of topological space, such as "container" ("in"), "surface" ("on"), and "proximity" ("to"). Unlike in English, in Standard Hungarian a classroom as an "imagined" place, associated with particular disciplinary knowledge, discourse, and identities (as opposed to a concrete place of a classroom), is conceptualized as a surface and therefore takes *on* case endings (e.g. sublative *-ra* "onto"). In (7), however, the English code-switched nouns for classes (*P.E.*, *music*, *art*) receive an *in* case (illative *-ba* "into"), which marks them as a container – just as they are in English, where the distinction between the two senses of "class" is not grammaticalized but shows a partial overlap with Hungarian. According to the findings of the study, morphological case replacements were most frequent in the L1-specific structuring of topological space due to cross linguistic influence from the children's dominant L2/English on spatial "thinking for speaking" (Slobin 1996).

Examples such as these are commensurate with the suggestion that "interface" structures, such as topological spatial expression – which require the integration of conceptual–semantic and morpho-syntactic knowledge – might constitute a vulnerable area in bilingual L1 attrition and imperfect acquisition. The hypothesis that cross-linguistic influence is most likely to occur in grammatical phenomena that involve the semantics–syntax or pragmatics–syntax interface has been in the forefront of more recent work within generative approaches to bilingualism and language contact (Hulk and Müller 2000; Sorace 2000; Montrul 2002, 2004; Bullock and Toribio 2004; Gürel 2004; Sorace 2004; Toribio 2004; Tsimpli et al. 2004; Bolonyai 2007). Studies of different types of bilingual development, such as bilingual L1 acquisition, adult L2 acquisition, and L1 attrition, have indicated that grammatical interfaces are particularly unstable and open to cross-linguistic influence, leading to optionality and variability in the production/interpretation of affected features (Sorace 2004). According to Sorace, interface instability in attrition/imperfect acquisition can be attributed to two main factors. First, interfaces are more complex than narrow syntax and therefore may be acquired late, partially, or never – that is, certain grammatical properties remain underspecified or "permanently indeterminate" (2004:143) at the level of competence. Second, speakers may lack processing resources that are required to integrate both (morpho-)syntactic and conceptual (pragmatic, semantic) constraints governing a particular linguistic structure. Although cross-linguistic influence and CS often co-occur in bilingual L1 attrition/imperfect acquisition, the question of whether CS may be connected to the vulnerability of interface structures has received very little attention (see Bolonyai 2007).

Finally, an important, although sometimes neglected, aspect of L1 attrition/incomplete acquisition in the context of bilingualism is its potential for linguistic creativity and innovation (Gal 1989; Seliger 1989; Thomason 2001; Skaaden 2005). Driven by linguistic need, sociolinguistic incentives, or perhaps ludic motivations for expressiveness, bilingual speakers (their limited L1 resources notwithstanding) may produce unconventional innovations that evidence lexical and structural creativity. While some of the innovations are intra-lingual, i.e. based on monolingual L1 resources, many others exploit L2 resources and/or involve CS. Examples (10) and (11) show innovative bilingual verb formation patterns found in the spontaneous speech of pre-pubescent Hungarian–English bilingual children.

(10)   Akkor három **yard**-ot **donate**-el-ek.
       then three yard-ACC donate-PRES.1SG.INDEF
       "Then I am going to donate three yards [of fabric]."

(Bolonyai 2007)

(11)   Szeret-n-ém meg-**hear**-ni.
       like-COND-1SG PERF-hear-INF
       "I'd like to hear it."

(Bolonyai 2002)

Previous research has demonstrated that fluent Hungarian speakers use a verbalizer suffix (-ol) to integrate borrowed and code-switched words into Hungarian. According to Moravcsik (1975), foreign verbs are borrowed into Hungarian as nominal forms; therefore, they must be verbalized. In the children's data, however, the verbalizer may attach to unambiguous verb stems from English such as *donate* in (10). Since this construction (verb + denominal verbalizer + inflection) does not exist in either Hungarian or English but does occur in bilingual contact, it can be seen as an innovative structure. It suggests change in the semantic features of the verbalizer, which enables creative productivity in bilingual verb formation. In other cases, code-switched English verbs are inserted into Hungarian without a verbalizer, as in (11). This strategy may indicate that the English verb ("hear") is treated as fully equivalent with a Hungarian verb – rather than a "foreign non-verb" needing to be nativized. Linguistic creativity in intensive language contact thus can be linked to the speaker's assessment of perceived equivalence between L1 and L2, whereby linguistic asymmetries and boundaries that mandate the presence of the verbalizer in "normal" CS are being reconfigured. Of course, ultimately, as Gal points out, both innovation and loss are the consequences of an ongoing conflict and competition between cognitive, interactional, and social/symbolic forces: "in the midst of diminishing use and input from Hungarian, young speakers must nevertheless use that language to communicate effectively" in their family or community networks (1989:330). That is, linguistic creativity can be seen as a response to the interactional demand of family and ethnic community networks.

15.4   Can CS lead to language erosion?

Finally, an intriguing question raised in the literature concerns whether CS itself can lead to L1 attrition and/or imperfect acquisition. The answer to this question is far from straightforward. On the one hand, it has been argued that occasional CS to the stronger L2 may be used as an "achievement" strategy to bolster up the weaker L1 when necessary, keeping the communication fluent and efficient. This, in turn, may lead to more use, better maintenance, and less deterioration of L1 (Rindler-Schjerve 1998; Jisa 2000; Field 2005; Pearson 2007). Similarly, in advanced stages of native language attrition, even the use of simple word insertions, tag-switches, set expressions, and lexical borrowings from the L1 in the L2 may keep the eroding L1 alive and temporarily forestall its attrition (Field 2005:351). On the other hand, claims have been made that switching to the L2 "deprives the children of the opportunity to use L1 productively" (Kaufman 2001:187). In other cases, as Halmari has argued, CS "may provide a camouflage under which … L1 attriters may, indeed, be able to (unconsciously) hide their incompetence in L1 by successfully avoiding many or most L1 structures" (1992:201). This, in turn, may halt language development and contribute to further decline of proficiency in the already waning L1. In the same vein, an influential hypothesis in contact linguistics predicts that frequent CS can induce language change, lexical and structural interference, and ultimately language shift, or even language death in some bilingual communities (Myers-Scotton 1993a; Thomason 2001; Backus 2005). This proposal was formalized most prominently in Myers-Scotton's "Matrix Language (ML) turnover" hypothesis (Myers-Scotton 1993a; 1998).

Empirical support for a pattern of changing asymmetry in the L1–L2 relationship comes from studies of bilingual immigrant children (Kaufman and Aronoff 1991; Halmari 1992; Kuhberg 1992; Bolonyai 1998). Halmari (1992) examined the CS patterns of two Finnish-American children and found that highly frequent "language assignment shifts" in CS were indicative of incipient language loss. Two years after the children immigrated to the United States, the eight-year-old child demonstrated a strong tendency to switch from Finnish to English "both inter- and especially intra-sententially by resorting to language assignment shifts" (Halmari 1992:207). Halmari argues that by switching completely to English, the child was able to avoid violating Finnish morpho-syntactic constraints on the use of complex inflectional L1 morphology. By contrast, the nine-year-old child, whose Finnish was stronger than her younger sister's, preferred the opposite strategy: she would start with an English discourse marker, and then switch to monolingual Finnish. Examples (12) and (13) illustrate the two types of CS.

(12) ***Tota noin tota me*** we-er when we go to the fieldtrip we're gonna go see something and it's gonna be e:r Secret Garden
"Well so well we-er when we go to the fieldtrip we're gonna go see something and it's gonna be e:r Secret Garden."
(Halmari 1992:210)

(13)   Oh yeah, *miks sen nimi eli VeePee*?
       "*Oh yea*h, why was its name VP?"

(Halmari 1992:209)

Another study followed a winding path of change in the CS patterns of a young Hungarian-American immigrant child over the course of one and a half years, between ages 3;7 and 4;10 (Bolonyai 1998). At age 3;7, the child produced mostly inter-sentential CS. In the few intra-sentential switches that occurred, the ML was Hungarian or a composite showing convergence to English. By age 4;2, the child's language use showed a significant (40%) increase in intra-sentential CS. The pattern of these intra-sentential switches, however, indicated a turnover in the ML; English functioned as the Matrix Language almost 40% of the time. There also appeared a slight increase in the occurrence of composite CS. The most significant changes were apparent at age 4;10, after the child returned from a month-long visit to Hungary. The findings showed further increase in CS, but this time with a strong preference for Hungarian as the ML. It was also evident that the increase in CS co-occurred with a significant increase in composite grammatical structures. Indeed, the fact that across all stages of observation, composite structures were much more common in clauses with a composite ML with CS (i.e. in composite CS) than in clauses with a composite structure but without CS (i.e. in convergence, or covert CS), appeared to suggest a possible correlation between CS and L1 change and erosion. The study argued for a lexically based explanation as to how CS may serve as a catalyst and bring about structural change in the L1. Assuming that L2 lexical structure is always present in CS as a potential source for restructuring bilingual speech, the study suggested that "L2 lexemes can 'drag along' their grammar into L1 with them" and replace aspects of the waning L1 (Bolonyai 1998:39).

Further evidence indicating Hungarian L1 erosion in the presence of CS was found in school-aged immigrant children's divergent use of the accusative case marker (Bolonyai 2000, 2002) and the possessive agreement suffix (Bolonyai 2007). Both studies showed that lack of morphological marking was particularly high on code-switched nouns from English, suggesting again that, given certain social and structural conditions, CS may mediate L2 lexically induced change in an unstable L1 linguistic system. This is in line with the claim that CS can exert "indirect effects" on the structure of another language (Backus 2005). Frequency of CS counts because the cumulative effect of a great many lexical switches and borrowings is "that a foreign pattern may slowly but surely gain a foothold" (Backus 2005:321). Hence, Backus postulates that CS may facilitate and serve as a mechanism for structural change when "internally complex insertional as well as alternational codeswitching ... function to model syntactic patterns which are then subsequently imitated in the base language" (2005:334).

15.5   Conclusion

A complete understanding of the nature and role of CS in bilingual L1 attrition and/or incomplete acquisition can only be achieved by examining the interactions between the social, cognitive, and linguistic aspects of children's bilingual language use. This chapter has identified some of the key issues in recent work on L1 attrition and imperfect acquisition in immigrant contexts. In particular, it has examined the sociolinguistic and psycholinguistic factors that interact with and potentially alter the linguistic processes and outcomes of these language contact phenomena. It has additionally compared patterns of "normal" CS produced by fluent bilinguals, distinguishing it from CS in attrition in terms of its sociolinguistic, psycholinguistic, and structural characteristics, and summarized research investigating the relationship between CS and contact-induced language change and erosion.

16

Code-switching and the bilingual mental lexicon

Longxing Wei

16.1 Introduction

This chapter explores bilingual speech production processes and constraints by studying the nature of the bilingual mental lexicon and its activity in intra-sentential code-switching (hereafter CS). More specifically, it confronts and expands on Levelt's model of speech production and Myers-Scotton's Matrix Language Framework (MLF) model with data drawn from Chinese–English and Japanese–English CS in natural conversations. The research findings provide empirical evidence that CS itself is a linguistic system, and, like any linguistic system, it is governed and constrained by a set of morpho-syntactic principles and rules, and CS cannot be accounted for without exploring the nature and the activity of the bilingual mental lexicon. Based on this evidence, this chapter presents a bilingual activation model of CS. It concludes that any CS phenomenon depends on bilingual cognitively based operations of an abstract nature.

16.2 The bilingual mental lexicon

Levelt defines a lemma as the "nonphonological part of an item's lexical information," including semantic, syntactic, and some aspects of morphological information, and argues that "it is in the lemmas of the mental lexicon that conceptual information is linked to grammatical function" (1989:162). In other words, lemmas are abstract entries in the mental lexicon and underlie surface configurations of speech production. Each item in the mental lexicon contains its own lemma specification, comprising declarative knowledge about the word's meaning as well as information about its syntax and morphology. Thus, lemmas contain directions regarding three subsystems of lexical structure: lexical–conceptual structure, predicate–argument structure, and morphological realization patterns.

Each subsystem plays a specific role. Lexical–conceptual structure draws on universally available semantic/pragmatic information. Predicate–argument structure specifies the properties of verbs in different subcategorization frames and how the expressed arguments are encoded grammatically. Morphological realization patterns spell out surface devices for word order, case, agreement, tense/aspect marking, and so on (de Bot and Schreuder 1993; Wei 2001). For example, the lemma for the verb "like" requires a subject that expresses the role of Experiencer and an object that expresses the role of Theme; the lemma for "she" specifies that the word must refer to a female and that any following present-tense main verb must have the suffix "-s" attached to it for subject-verb agreement.

It seems obvious that the mental lexicon, or, to be specific, the activation of lemmas in the mental lexicon, plays a central role in speech production. According to Levelt, the whole set of formulation processes is lexically driven:

This means that grammatical and phonological encodings are mediated by lexical entries. The preverbal message triggers lexical items into activity. The syntactic, morphological, and phonological properties of an activated lexical item trigger, in turn, the grammatical, morphological, and phonological encoding procedures underlying the generation of an utterance.   (Levelt 1989:181)

Thus, lemma activation of particular lexical items in the mental lexicon mediates between conceptualization and speech formulation as a necessary level of speech production. The role of lemma activation in speech production can be schematized as in Figure 16.1.

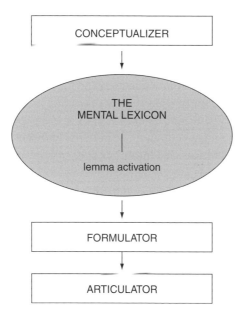

Figure 16.1 Lemma activation in speech production (adapted from Levelt 1989)

Although there is some disagreement about the exact nature of lemma representation in the mental lexicon, it is generally assumed that lemmas are language-specific for lexicalization patterns of a particular language. One often cited example is from Talmy (1985:69) for the notion of language-specific lemmas: (English) *The bottle floated into the cave* versus (Spanish) *La botella entró a la cueva flotando* (The bottle moved-into the cave floating). The lexicalization pattern differs across the two languages. English can conflate motion with manner into a lemma, i.e. FLOAT, while Spanish must express the notion of FLOATING periphrastically using the gerund.

Lemmas in the mental lexicon are argued to form a connection between the lexical features and conceptual features, which map to and from syntax (see Kroll and de Groot 1997). In addition, lemmas in the bilingual mental lexicon are argued to be language-specific and each lemma is tagged for a specific language and supports the realization of an actual lexeme at the surface or positional level. In CS, language-specific lemmas in the bilingual mental lexicon activate language-specific sets of morpho-syntactic procedures in the speech production Formulator. However, speech production is so rapid and fluent that these procedures must involve parallel, rather than separate, processing, but with one procedure in one language blind to the workings of another in a different language. Lemmas from one language may receive more activation at a certain point than the corresponding lemmas from another language if the speaker's preverbal message contains the specification of a particular language (i.e. the Matrix Language). Representative CS instances to be discussed provide evidence for such parallel processing. This means that the two languages involved in CS do not equally control the selection of morpho-syntactic procedures, instead the Matrix Language (ML) has greater input in the resulting string of CS (Myers-Scotton and Jake 1995; Wei 2000a, 2000b).

In Levelt's model of speech production (1989) semantic and syntactic information constitute the lemma of the lexical item while morphological and phonological information constitute the form of the lexical item. The conceptual information in the preverbal message activates the appropriate lexical items during the formulation of a message. This model was designed for describing the major components and processes of monolingual language production, and it must be adapted to account for bilingual speech behavior such as CS. Consequently, it is proposed here that it is the preverbal message/intention that activates language-specific lemmas in the bilingual mental lexicon. In other words, it is the semantic/pragmatic feature bundles selected by the Conceptualizer at the conceptual level (see Figure 16.1) that trigger the appropriate lemmas into activity before the Formulator has access to the relevant lexical items in the mental lexicon.

Figure 16.2 illustrates that the speaker's preverbal message/intention at the conceptual level activates language-specific feature bundles, which are then mapped onto lemmas in the mental lexicon. Lemmas activated at

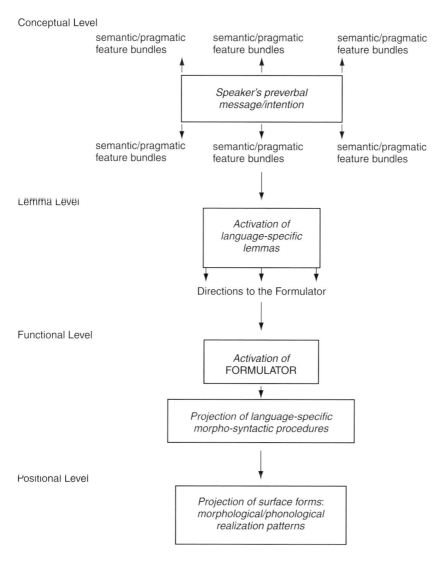

Conceptual Level

semantic/pragmatic feature bundles   semantic/pragmatic feature bundles   semantic/pragmatic feature bundles

Speaker's preverbal message/intention

semantic/pragmatic feature bundles   semantic/pragmatic feature bundles   semantic/pragmatic feature bundles

Lemma Level

Activation of language-specific lemmas

Directions to the Formulator

Functional Level

Activation of FORMULATOR

Projection of language-specific morpho-syntactic procedures

Positional Level

Projection of surface forms: morphological/phonological realization patterns

Figure 16.2 Lemma activation in the bilingual mental lexicon (adapted from Myers-Scotton and Jake 2000)

the lemma level send directions to the Formulator at the functional level for projecting language-specific morpho-syntactic procedures. Finally, at the positional level, morphological/phonological surface patterns are realized. As shown, lemmas in the mental lexicon mediate between the conceptual level and the functional level.

16.3   Essential principles governing CS

Proposed in the MLF model of Myers-Scotton (1993a [1997]) are two fundamental distinctions in CS: the content vs. system morpheme distinction and the Matrix vs. Embedded Language distinction (ML vs. EL). The first distinction is assumed to determine what type of morphemes can be switched, and the second is assumed to determine which language builds the sentential frame into which items are inserted. These two distinctions constrain CS configurations and are briefly reviewed in turn.

16.3.1   Content vs. system morphemes

Content morphemes assign or receive thematic roles. Prototypical content morphemes are nouns, most verbs, descriptive adjectives, most prepositions, and free-standing pronouns. Prototypical system morphemes are quantifiers, specifiers, and inflectional affixes. However, there exists cross-linguistic variation in assigning morphemes to either content or system morpheme status. That is, cross-linguistically, not all members of a particular lexical category pattern alike. Morphemes of different languages may be conceptually congruent but may differ in their status as content or system morphemes. (For cross-linguistic variation and categorization of morphemes, see Jake 1994, 1998 and Myers-Scotton and Jake 2000, this volume.)

The content vs. system morpheme distinction can be slightly recast in light of sources of morphemes, i.e. when they are activated. Lemmas contain all aspects of lexical information necessary to project a morphosyntactic frame. Morphemes activated at the lemma level are referred to as "directly-elected" (Bock and Levelt 1994). Along with these directly-elected elements are "indirectly-elected" morphemes that are required by certain lexical items for the realization of their predicate–argument structure, but they themselves do not represent lexical concepts independent of the directly-elected elements with which they are accessed. Indirectly-elected morphemes include prepositions such as *to* in *listen to the radio* and *at* in *look at the photo*, and verbal particles such as *up* in *pick up the wallet* and *on* in *turn on the light*. In contrast to directly-elected and indirectly-elected morphemes are "structurally-assigned" morphemes required for the spelling out of aspects of morphological realization. Such structurally-assigned morphemes include morphemes for case assignment which reflect predicate-argument structure and phi-features.

Myers-Scotton's 4-M Model classifies directly-elected morphemes as content morphemes, and indirectly-elected morphemes as "early" system morphemes. They are called "early" in the sense that, like content morphemes, they are activated at the conceptual level when they realize the conceptual content of the semantic/pragmatic feature bundles of certain content morphemes. Structurally-assigned morphemes are late system morphemes and include two types: "bridges" and "outsiders." They are called "late" in the sense that they are activated later at the functional level to build larger linguistic units in the speech production process (see Myers-Scotton and Jake, this volume, for elaboration). CS data indicate that content and system morphemes are accessed differently. That is, these two types of morphemes have different types of lemma entries in the mental lexicon.

16.3.2   Matrix vs. embedded languages

The ML vs. EL distinction is much more than a heuristic device for labeling CS constituents but underlies the differential participation of the ML and the EL in shaping CS utterances. The ML vs. EL distinction is crucial in analyzing and explaining CS configurations. The ML and the EL play unequal roles in CS in that the ML has the dominant role in sentential frame building. It is the ML that projects the sentential frame, i.e. the morpheme order, inflectional morphology, and other functional items. The ML is more activated than the EL in CS discourse and the occurrence of its morphemes is more frequent and freer than that of the EL. The ML is the language that the speakers engaged in CS will identify as the "main language" being used. At the conceptual level the speaker's preverbal message/intention determines which language is to be used as the ML for CS. It is the ML chosen at the conceptual level, together with the semantic/pragmatic feature bundles as desired, which activates language-specific lemmas and sends directions to the Formulator.

16.3.3   Structural principles

Three structural principles are essential in explaining grammatical constraints on CS and predicting possible occurrences of ML + EL constituents. In the MLF model, two principles are proposed under the Matrix Language Hypothesis: the Morpheme Order Principle, which specifies that in CS, surface morpheme order must not violate that of the ML, and the System Morpheme Principle, which specifies that in ML + EL constituents, all syntactically relevant system morphemes must come from the ML.

In Figure 16.3, the distinctions of the MLF model are integrated into a model of lemma activation in the bilingual production process. The implications of this model are discussed in the following sections with reference to Chinese–English and Japanese–English CS.

16.4   Evidence for the ML vs. EL distinction

16.4.1   Lemma activation for content morphemes in CS

In the Chinese–English CS utterance in (1), *article* and *finish* are the EL content morphemes, but *nci* ("that," a demonstrative) and *pian* (a Chinese noun classifier) function together as a determiner, i.e. a system morpheme.[1]

(1)   ni nei-pian ***article*** hai mei ***finish*** a?
        you that-CL article yet not finish PART/AFFIRM-Q
        "You haven't finished that article yet?"

A Chinese classifier is a morpheme that indicates a semantic class of nouns and regularly accompanies any noun of that class in certain syntactic constructions. It must always be used together with a singular demonstrative like "this" or "that" or a specific number like "one," "two," and so on. When this combination occurs with a content morpheme head, it syntactically functions as a system morpheme. It should also be noticed that there is no perfect aspect marking on the English verb *finish*, since Chinese does not have verb morphology of any sort for this and other grammatical purposes. Chinese does have a morpheme that realizes the grammatical concept of perfect aspect, but the verb itself is not inflected.

In (2) *paper* and *finish* are the EL content morphemes, but the EL system morphemes "-s" for plural marking and "-ed" for perfect aspect marking do not appear. In (3) the noun phrase *new library* is from the EL, but again the determiner *nei-ge* ("that"), a system morpheme, is from the ML.

(2) *wo you liang-fen* **paper** *mingtian bixu jiaoshangqu, ke wo xianzai yi-fen hai mei* **finish** *ne.*
I have two-CL paper tomorrow must turn in but I at the moment one-CL yet not finish PART/AFFIRM
"I must turn in two papers tomorrow, but at the moment I haven't finished one yet."

(3) shi-bu-shi qu nei-ge **new library**?
yes-not-yes go that-CL new library
"Are we going to that new library?"

In (4) both *in* and *May* are the EL content morphemes. The prepositional phrase *in May* expresses content because it is an adverbial of time. Also, the verb *graduate* is an EL content morpheme. As predicted, the EL system morphemes like "will" for tense marking are not switched.

(4) *tingshuo ni* **in May graduate**, *shi ma?*
hear you right in May graduate, PART/INTERROG
"I heard you will graduate in May, won't you?"

In (5) *summer* and *take course* are the EL content morphemes. It should be noticed that the Chinese preposition "zai" ("in") is optional in realizing an adverbial of time. In (6)–(8), English content morphemes co-occur with Chinese system morphemes. Also, while English requires the negative morpheme to cliticize onto an auxiliary verb, Chinese *bu* ("not"), a system morpheme from the ML, can stand alone.

(5) wo **summer** bu **take course** le.
I summer not take course PART/AFFIRM
"I won't take any course in summer."

(6) you xuduo **homework** yao zhuo; hai you hao ji-pian **article** xiang qu **library**-de **computer** shang **check** yixia.

have a lot of homework must do in addition have quite a few-CL article
want go library-POSS computer PREP/on check once
"I've a lot of homework to do. In addition, I've quite a few articles
I want to go to check on the library's computer."

(7) naxie **visiting scholar** bu shi hen youqian ma, bi women **student** you
qian duo le.
those visiting scholar not/EMPH COP very rich PART/AFFIRM PREP/
than us student have money more PART/AFFIRM
"Aren't those visiting scholars very rich? They have a lot more money
than us students."

(8) mei you zijide jiqi feichang b fanblan feichang **inconvenient**.
not have own machine very not convenient very inconvenient
"It's very inconvenient if I don't have my own machine, very
inconvenient."

Unlike Chinese, Japanese possesses inflectional morphology for number
and tense/aspect marking. Nevertheless, the same patterns emerge with
respect to the ML vs. EL distinction in CS, as shown in examples (9) through
(13). In (9) *stay* is an EL content morpheme used in conjunction with the
ML *suru* ("do"). In (10) *summer course* is an EL content morpheme phrase, but
o is an ML system morpheme marking the accusative case. In (11) *tuition*
and *expensive* are the EL content morphemes, but the EL definite article "the"
does not appear before *tuition*, and *totemo* ("very"), a system morpheme,
comes from the ML. In (12) *drug* is an EL content morpheme, but the
EL plural "-s," a system morpheme, does not appear. In (13) *essay* is an
EL content morpheme, but *sore* ("that"), a system morpheme, comes from
the ML.

(9) dore gurai koko ni **stay** suru no?
how long about here PREP/LOC stay do PART/Q
"About how long will you stay here?"

(10) ima wa **summer course** o totte iru n desu.
now PART/TOP summer courrse PART/OBJ take-PROG AUX/be PART
COP/be
"I'm taking summer courses now."

(11) ii desu keredomo **tuition** ga totemo **expensive** desu.
good COP/be but tuition PART/NOM very expensive COP/be
"It's good, but the tuition is very expensive."

(12) Nihon demo saikin kekkoo **drug** o yatte iru hito ga ooi yo.
Japan also recently rather drug PART/OBJ do-PROG AUX/be people
PART/NOM many PART/INTERJ
"Recently in Japan people who are doing drugs are also many."

(13) muzukashikatta to iu ka, aa sore wa **essay** datta kara wakara-nai, um.

difficult-PAST PART PART say PART PART that PART/TOP essay PART-PAST because understand-not PART
"It could be said to be difficult, mm because I didn't understand that essay, mm."

The above Chinese–English and Japanese–English CS examples provide empirical evidence that EL content and system morphemes are not equally activated in CS. Although EL content morphemes can be activated for CS if they are selected by speakers to meet their communicative intentions, EL system morphemes cannot. Also, it should be noted that although Chinese and Japanese have different basic word orders and Japanese alone possesses morphology for case and tense/aspect marking, the Morpheme Order Principle and the System Morpheme Principle apply to both language pairs involved in CS.

16.4.2   Lemma activation for morpho-syntactic procedures in CS

As shown in Figure 16.3, the activated language-specific lemmas in the bilingual mental lexicon include information about lexical–conceptual structure, predicate–argument structure, and morphological realization patterns of particular lexemes. Activated language-specific lemmas then send directions to the Formulator at the functional level for morpho-syntactic encoding. Such a bilingual production process is sequential: at the conceptual level the discourse mode is chosen with one language as the ML and then corresponding language-specific lemmas are activated at the lemma level to realize the speaker's preverbal message, resulting in language-specific morpho-syntax at the functional level. At the positional level, the Articulator produces surface morpho-phonological forms.

What should be noticed is that bilinguals may choose any of the languages they know as the ML for CS based on several factors, such as the languages known to the interlocutors, the topics for the current conversation, their motivations for CS, and the speech settings. The study of the factors implicated in choosing one language rather than the other as the ML is beyond the scope of this chapter. What should be emphasized is that whichever language is the ML, it will play a dominant role in CS by controlling the morpho-syntactic procedures.

All of the preceding examples show that in every utterance containing CS, whether Chinese–English or Japanese–English, the word order always follows that of the ML, rather than the EL. Although Chinese and English share the same basic V-O order, Chinese is very flexible in the arrangement of sentential elements. Once Chinese is chosen as the ML, it builds the sentential frame (i.e. predicate–argument structure and word order). For instance, in (5), the adverbial of time *(in) summer* follows the subject rather than being placed in the sentence initial or final position as in English. Further evidence is shown in Japanese–English CS instances. Unlike

Conceptual Level:

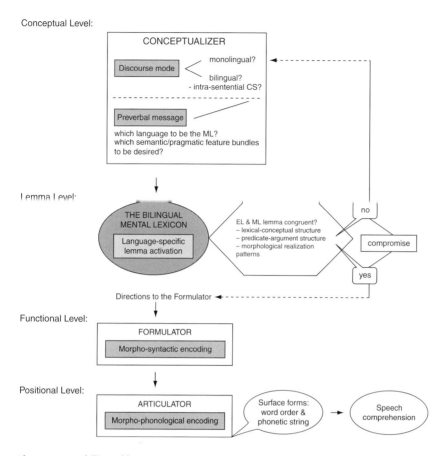

Figure 16.3 A bilingual lemma activation model (adapted from Levelt 1989)

English, Japanese has O-V order. Once Japanese is chosen as the ML, the verb final order is always maintained. For example, in (10) the object *summer course* goes before the verb. In sum, Chinese–English and Japanese–English CS instances provide further evidence that ML + EL constituents regularly consist of an ML morpho-syntactic frame (i.e. ML system morphemes and morpheme order) into which EL content morphemes are inserted.

Examples (14)–(16) illustrate Chinese–English CS with English as the ML. In (14) the infinitival clause with the dummy subject pronoun "it" is a typical English construction, but Chinese does not possess a parallel construction. In (15) both the main clause and the embedded clause are from the ML. In (16) the predicate *fabiao wenzhang* ("present papers") goes before the adverbial of place *at conferences*, which is an unacceptable word order in Chinese.

(14) It's not easy for students to get ***jiangxuejin***. Only ***youxiude*** students can get it.
     it's not easy for students to get scholarship. only excellent students can get it

"It's not easy for students to get a scholarship. Only excellent students can get one."

(15)   If I buy a used car, I'll buy a used **Riben che ershou Riben che** are **laokaode** *duo* and much cheaper.
       if I buy a used car, I'll buy a Japanese car second-hand Japanese car reliable a lot more and much cheaper
       "If I buy a used car, I'll buy a used Japanese car. Second-hand Japanese cars are a lot more reliable and much cheaper."

(16)   Some graduate students **fabiao wenzhang** at conferences, but it's difficult to get papers published.
       some graduate students present paper at conferences, but it's difficult to get papers published
       "Some graduate students present papers at conferences, but it's difficult to get papers published."

In (17)–(18) the Japanese speakers choose English as the ML. (17) again shows an infinitival clause with the dummy subject pronoun *it*. In (18) the English verb initial construction is used, rather than the verb final construction typical of Japanese.

(17)   It's **totemo muzukashi** to find a convenient and **yasui** apartment here.
       it's very difficult to find a convenient and cheap apartment here
       "It's very difficult to find a convenient and cheap apartment here."

(18)   **suupaa** is close from here, but I have to walk **juugo fun gurai** to the bus stop.
       supermarket is close from here, but I have to walk fifteen minutes about to the bus stop
       "The supermarket is close to here, but I have to walk about fifteen minutes to the bus stop."

16.5   Lemma congruence checking as an organizing principle

Lemma congruence between the participating languages in CS is defined as "a match between the ML and the EL at the lemma level with respect to linguistically relevant features" (Myers-Scotton and Jake 1995:985). The present chapter regards lemma congruence checking as an organizing principle for CS, and lemma congruence checking must take place at each of the three levels of abstract lexical structure: at the level of lexical–conceptual structure, predicate–argument structure, and morphological realization patterns. Relevant to the present discussion are the first two levels of abstract lexical structure.

16.5.1   Lemma congruence at the level of lexical–conceptual structure

As generally assumed, there is a universal set of semantic and pragmatic features available for the lexical–conceptual structure of lemmas. Also, as generally observed, there is cross-linguistic variation in the presence and conflation of these features. As shown in Figure 16.3, at the conceptual level speakers do not produce surface morphemes but rather make appropriate choices about the semantic and pragmatic information that they intend to convey. The semantic/pragmatic feature bundles chosen at the conceptual level activate the relevant lemmas in the mental lexicon that will support surface morphemes. But in CS the activated EL lemmas must be sufficiently congruent with those of the ML counterparts in terms of their lexical–conceptual structures (see Sebba, this volume, on the notion of congruence).

The CS instances discussed above show that the EL content morphemes can be inserted into the ML frames because these morphemes are projected from the EL lemmas whose semantic/pragmatic feature bundles are sufficiently congruent with those of the ML counterparts. However, the participating languages may differ in lexical–conceptual structure. If such a difference is only partial, there is still sufficient congruence as required for CS. In other words, even if there is not full congruence between the language pairs at the level of lexical–conceptual structure, CS is still possible. A partial difference between certain ML and EL lemmas' semantic/pragmatic feature bundles can be one of the major reasons why speakers switch to EL content morphemes at a certain point during a discourse involving CS. Below are some commonly observed instances of such a switch.

In (19), *paper* in English, in addition to "substance" or fibrous material in thin sheets, may mean any written or printed document, such as an article, an essay, a composition, or the like, but the Chinese equivalent morpheme "zhi" ("paper") itself only means a piece of paper used for writing or printing on, for wrapping or decorating walls, etc. Thus, "zhi" in Chinese does not share all the semantic feature bundles contained in *paper* in English. The speaker may switch to *paper* for his intended meaning.

(19)   wo you liang-fen ***paper*** mingtian bixu jiaoshangqu.
       I have two-CL paper tomorrow must turn in
       "I must turn in two papers tomorrow."

In (20), an *advisor* in English means a professor or instructor who offers advice or counsel to students regarding their academic progress, improvement, course requirements and sequential arrangements, thesis or dissertation writing, research in progress, and so on. Most *advisors* are also those who will recommend their students to professional agencies. However, a Chinese "daoshi" ("advisor") does not assume the same responsibilities. His/her only responsibility is to guide students in writing research papers, theses, or dissertations. The speaker switches to *advisor* to mean the individual similar to but not the same as "daoshi."

(20)   wo xiawu qu jian wode ***advisor***.
       I afternoon go see my advisor
       "I'm going to see my advisor this afternoon."

In (21), a *school bus* in English refers to a bus that mainly transports students to and from a school, in addition to other jobs it can do for a school. Although Chinese has the equivalent morpheme "xiaoche" ("school bus"), it usually, if not only, refers to a bus that transports a school's sports or performance team or equipment. In mainland China, very few schools possess such buses, and almost no *school bus* transports students to and from a school. The speaker switches to *school bus* to indicate its function in the English language context.

(21)   zhu zai zheli hen fanbian, meitian you ***school bus***.
       live PREP/LOC here very convenient everyday have school bus
       "It's very convenient to live here since there is a school bus everyday."

The same phenomenon has also been observed in Japanese–English CS instances. In (22), the concept of a *community force* may not only be American, but the general expression "community force" in the American context may include "neighborhood crime watch," "drug free zone," and so on. The Japanese expression similar to *community force* is "choukai" ("neighborhood association"), but such an association is mainly for organizing local social and cultural activities, overseeing environmental sanitation, taking care of the old, mediating a dispute, and so on. The speaker switches to *community force* probably to mean something beyond Japanese "choukai."

(22)   moshi Nihon ga soo iu ***community force*** mitaina no ga naku nattara
       Nihon mo ***America*** mitai ni nacchau no ja nai ka?
       if Japan PART/NOM so say community force like PART/NOM PART/NOM
       no become-PERF-if Japan also America same PREP/COND become PART/
       NOM COP/be not PART/Q
       "If Japan had no such thing as a community force, would Japan become America?"

In (23), the possible reason for the speaker to switch to *bedroom* lies in the fact that in many, if not most, Japanese families, the concept of "bedroom" is actually part of the general concept of "room." A traditional Japanese room is used not only for sleeping but also for eating, studying, meeting guests, or other daily family activities. The speaker switches to *bedroom* probably to make the type of room specific in the context.

(23)   futatsu no ***bedroom*** ga atte, hitori, Maria to iu ko wa hitori de ***one
       bedroom*** o motte imasu yo.

two PART/POSS bedroom PART/NOM COP one person Maria and call person PART/TOP one person PREP/by one bedroom PART/OBJ have-PROG AUX PART/AFFIRM

"We have two bedrooms. One person, called Maria, has one bedroom."

In (24), the speaker switches to *registration* for the possible reason that in Japanese colleges/universities, although students must register for their courses. They are not free to select the courses which they are interested in and want to take. The English morpheme may carry a special meaning not available in the Japanese equivalent and lets the speaker express his intended meaning more accurately.

(24)   anata wa **registration** o shimashita ka?
        you PART/TOP registration PART/OBJ do-PERF PART/INTERROG
        "Have you done your registration?"

Although every language allows its speakers to express their semantic and pragmatic intentions, actual semantic/pragmatic feature bundles contained in lemmas underlying actual lexical items may differ cross-linguistically. As observed, bilingual speakers may switch to particular lexical items from another language at a certain point during a discourse on condition that there is sufficient lemma congruence between the language pairs at the level of lexical–conceptual structure. If a difference in semantic/pragmatic feature bundles contained in language-specific lemmas is only partial, the condition of sufficient lemma congruence is still satisfied. Being aware of such a partial difference, bilingual speakers may switch to a relevant EL item to make their intended meaning clearer. This is because language cues may have different values (de Bot and Schreuder 1993). In CS, speakers may ignore the cue of the ML item and switch to that of an EL item to convey their intended meaning. In other words, when the language cue specifies a particular language at a certain point during a discourse involving CS, the lexical item from that language becomes activated. This means that it is necessary for conceptual information and language cues to work together in activating language-specific lemmas in the bilingual mental lexicon for speakers to realize their intended meanings.

16.5.2 Lemma congruence at the level of predicate–argument structure

In CS it is the ML that controls the predicate–argument structure because it supplies system morphemes, subcategorization frames for verbs, and morpheme order. Although morpho-syntactic procedures are realized by the Formulator, before lemmas send morpho-syntactic directions to the Formulator, lemmas from both languages can be activated at a certain point during a discourse. Thus, lemma congruence checking at the level of lexical–conceptual structure alone is not sufficient for CS to occur. Lemma congruence checking at the level of predicate–argument structure must also come into play.

As previously observed, in Chinese–English CS, speakers tend to use many EL verbs and verb phrases as well as EL nouns and noun phrases. One of the reasons for this is that Chinese and English share the basic V-O order. This allows the speakers to switch the EL verbs/verb phrases and nouns/noun phrases easily into the syntactic slots provided by the ML. In (25) *give me trouble* follows the V-O-O double object order in both languages; in (26) *make money* follows the V-O order in both languages; in (27) *drive* in its infinitive form is used as the object of the main verb *xue* ("learn") in the same word order as in English.

(25) wode che you **give me trouble** le.
      my car again give me trouble PART/PERF
      "My car has given me trouble again."

(26) ni dei xiang bangfa **make money**.
      you must think way make money
      "You must think of ways to make money."

(27) ta gang dao, ta dei xue **drive**.
      he just arrive he must learn drive
      "He's just arrived, and he must learn how to drive."

However, in Japanese–English CS there are very few English verbs or verb phrases switched into the Japanese morpho-syntactic frame. Instead, when speakers switch between Japanese and English, they switch nouns/ noun phrases and adjectives/adjective phrases. The possible reason for this is that if Japanese is chosen as the ML, its predicate–argument structure must be maintained or protected (see Chan, this volume).

16.5.3 Lemma incongruence and compromise strategies

One of the major reasons why languages differ is that different languages may lexicalize concepts differently. If the bilingual mode is chosen at the conceptual level, but the lemmas activated from the EL do not sufficiently match the ML counterparts, some compromise strategies must be taken in order for CS to occur. One of the compromise strategies is the production of EL islands. An EL island is a constituent consisting of an EL content morpheme with only other EL system morphemes. Such a compromise strategy can arise at the level of lexical–conceptual structure or at the level of predicate–argument structure.

In (28), the lexical–conceptual structure of the means of transportation is conflated in the EL noun *ride* as the direct object of the verb, while in the ML it is conflated in the verb *song* ("send"/"deliver"), but the verb itself may not contain any means of transportation. If the speaker says "ni neng-bu-neng song wo yixia?" (literally, "Can you send me once?"), it may simply mean "Can you see me off?" Whether "song"/"deliver" involves an automobile entirely depends on the context. If the same speaker wants to be specific, he would say "ni neng-bu-neng yong che song we yixia?" (literally, "Can you send/deliver me in your car once?"). The speaker chooses the EL expression probably because he wants to be more specific than he can be with the Chinese verb. Thus, when the EL lemma is activated, the whole VP is produced as an EL island.

(28) ni neng-bu-neng **give me a ride**?
    you can-not-can give me a ride
    "Can you give me a ride?"

In (29), since the speaker chooses the EL lemma underlying *call me*, the EL lexical–conceptual structure is activated and the whole VP is accessed as an EL island. While in the EL the semantic features of "communicate with by telephone" are conflated in the verb *call*, in the ML equivalent "da dianhua gei wo" ("make phone to me"), the same meaning is realized by both the verb and its direct object as well as its indirect object.

(29) name ni mingtian **call me**.
    then you tomorrow call me
    "Then you call me tomorrow."

In (30), the speaker chooses the EL lemma underlying *come to pick you up*, and thus the VP with a pronominal object before the particle satellite *up* is accessed. The infinitive *to*, an EL system morpheme, also appears in the island. The speaker prefers *pick up* because this phrasal verb means "to take on as a passenger," but the Chinese equivalent verb "jei" usually does not.

(30) na wo yidian **come to pick you up**.
    so I one o'clock come to pick you up
    "So, I'll come to pick you up at one o'clock."

Such cross-linguistic differences in lexical–conceptual structure are also shown in the Japanese–English CS instances. In (31), the speaker is talking about sex before marriage. He switches to the EL *before marriage sex*, where the EL word order is observed.

(31) nan to iu n desu ka, Amerika de **Christian** toka iu hito ga ooi deshoo dakara nanka **before marriage sex** ga dame mitai da.
    what PART say PART/NOM COP/be PART/QUE America PREP/LOC Christian so on say people PART/NOM many COP/be-AFFIRM so something before marriage sex PART/NOM prohibited like COP/be
    "Whatever you say, in America there're many Christians and other such people, so something like sex before marriage is prohibited."

In other cases, although there is sufficient congruence between the lexical–conceptual structures across the languages involved in CS, the predicate–argument structures may differ. If such incongruence occurs, a radical compromise strategy must be taken in order for the EL material to be accessed. In other words, the activated EL lemma must send special directions to the Formulator for the EL material to be realized in an EL island. In (32), the Theme *my computer work* is introduced by the preposition *with* in the EL, but in the ML any Theme must be introduced by the verb itself. The incongruence between the EL and the ML in predicate–argument structure motivates the EL island.

(32)   ta jingchang bangzhu wo **with my computer work**.
       he often help me with my computer work
       "He often helps me with my computer work."

In (32), the VP headed by *fail* is an EL island, with all the system mor-phemes from the EL. In the EL, *fail* is a causative verb, taking an Agent as grammatical subject. But in Chinese the lexical equivalent to "fail" is "shibai," which takes an Experiencer as grammatical subject (e.g. *She fails the exam*). Because there is incongruence between the EL and the ML in predicate–argument structure, the result is the production of an EL island.

(33)   ta jingchang **fails students in exams**.
       she often fails students in exams
       "She often fails students in exams."

In (34a), in the EL the Recipient in the VP can be introduced by a preposition like *to* in the indirect object dative construction. But the Chinese equivalent VP headed by "jiao" ("teach") only permits the double object construction: V NP NP, rather than the indirect object dative construction: V NP PP. For example, (34b) is a normal sentence, but (34c) is not.

(34)   (a.) ni biye hou keyi **teach English to non-native speakers**.
            you graduate after can teach English to non-native speakers
            "After you graduate, you can teach English to non-native speakers."
       (b.) ta jiao xiaohai yingyu.
            she teaches children English
       (c.) *ta jiao yingyu gei xiaohao.
            she teaches English to children

Again, since the speaker prefers the EL material, but the ML does not accept the mapping which the EL PP would project at the level of predicate–argument structure, the result is the production of an EL island.

In the Japanese–English CS utterance in (35) the speaker switches to an EL island that contains the NP *only two weeks* and the infinitival clause *to take a break*. The ML word order for the same NP would place *only* immediately after *two weeks* ("ni shuukan dake," "two weeks only"), and, in addition to the absence of infinitive clauses, the ML would keep the O-V order. Since the speaker chooses the EL expression, everything in this EL island must come from the EL, including the system morphemes -*s* for plural marking, an indefinite article *a*, and the infinitive marker *to*.

(35) EPI no student no vacation wa nakute, only two weeks to take a break
     EPI POSS student POSS vacation PART/TOP haven't , only two weeks to take a break
     "EPI students don't have vacation, only two weeks to take a break."

The above examples of CS reflect the notion that incongruence between the languages involved may occur at the level of lexical–conceptual structure and/or at the level of predicate–argument structure. The former is caused by an incomplete match between the ML and the EL lexemes, and the latter is caused by a mismatch between the language pairs in their grammatical argument structures. If such incongruence occurs at any of these levels, a compromise strategy must be taken in order to facilitate CS.

16.6   Conclusion

The naturally occurring CS data discussed in this chapter offer several implications for exploring the nature of the bilingual mental lexicon and the bilingual speech production process. First, the bilingual mental lexicon contains lemmas rather than lexemes from the component languages, and these lemmas are tagged for a specific language. Language-specific lemmas contain information about a word's meaning, semantics, pragmatics, syntax, and morphology, and such information is necessary for using the word appropriately and for constructing its syntactic environment. Second, the bilingual speech production process contains the same levels as those contained in the monolingual speech production process. However, at the conceptual level, the bilingual speaker makes several choices about the language mode, monolingual or bilingual, to be used, and about the semantic/pragmatic feature bundles to convey his/her communicative intention. Third, the bilingual's languages are turned "on" all the time during a bilingual CS discourse, but these languages are never equally activated at the same time. One language is more activated as the ML than the other as the EL. It is the speaker who chooses whichever language as the ML, and only the ML controls morpho-syntactic procedures and provides both content and system morphemes at a much higher frequency. In contrast, the EL normally supplies content morphemes inserted into the ML sentential frame. Fourth, the bilingual can activate lemmas from the EL during CS, but these activated EL lemmas must be sufficiently congruent with their ML counterparts at the three levels of abstract lexical structure: lexical–conceptual structure, predi-cate–argument structure, and morphological realization patterns. If lemma incongruence occurs between the languages involved in CS at any of these levels, radical compromise strategies must be taken in order for the EL material to be realized in CS configurations.

Note

1. The code-switching data discussed in this chapter were collected by Longxing Wei over several years in the service of a research project on Chinese–English and Japanese–English code-switching.

17

Code-switching and the brain

Marta Kutas
Eva Moreno
and
Nicole Wicha[1]

17.1 Introduction

This chapter examines the brain bases of bilingualism, with special emphasis on language switching. Bilingual speakers differ from monolinguals in that they frequently switch between their languages, sometimes but not always intentionally. Understanding the anatomical and functional organization of the bilingual or polyglot brain may lead to better understanding of the circumstances, mechanisms, and consequences of code-switching (hereafter CS). First it is necessary to examine whether the two languages of a bilingual are represented in distinct versus overlapping areas of the brain, and what brain areas are involved in orchestrating multiple languages, including switching among them. The chapter then focuses on event-related brain potential (ERP) studies of bilingualism and CS, as these brain measures afford inferences about the neurocognitive mechanisms of language processing. The chapter concludes with suggestions for some open questions that electrophysiological research could fruitfully address in the growing area of CS.

17.2 Bilingual brains are different

Learning more than one language alters both the anatomical and functional organization of the brain, and apparently not just for language. Mechelli et al. (2004), for example, point to a significant increase in grey matter density in the left inferior parietal cortex of bilinguals relative to monolinguals – greater with earlier L2 exposure and greater L2 fluency – as a specific instance of experience-dependent brain plasticity. Coggins et al. (2004) explain volumetric increases in the anterior midbody of the corpus callosum (involved in primary motor and somatosensory function) in highly proficient bilinguals as an accommodation to the increased phonemic capacity requirements of bilinguals. Whatever the explanations, certain regions of the bilingual brain reliably differ from the monolingual brain in size and/or in the pattern of neural activity (e.g. Reiterer et al. 2005a, 2005b).

Relative to monolinguals, bilinguals are, on average, slower at naming pictures of objects, produce fewer exemplars in fluency tasks, and experience more tip-of-the-tongue moments in both their languages than do their monolingual peers (e.g. Gollan and Acenas 2004; Gollan et al. 2002, 2005). Whether these particular differences and others similar in kind are a consequence of the larger search space of vocabulary knowledge, of greater interference and inhibition demands, or of simply less frequent use of (and thus weaker links to) each word within a given language, are topics of intense investigation in the bilingual literature (e.g., Bijeljac-Babic et al. 1997).

Perhaps, most surprisingly, there is some evidence for an advantage, beyond the obvious (communicating in another language), to being bilingual, even in the non-linguistic domain (e.g. Bialystok et al. 2006). Bilingual children, for example, outperform monolingual peers in identifying the alternate image in reversible figures (Bialystok and Shapero 2005) and in ignoring irrelevant perceptual information during card-sorting (Bialystok and Martin 2004). This bilingual advantage in tasks involving executive or attentional control holds across the lifespan (Bialystok 2006; Bialystok et al. 2004, 2006; Craik and Bialystok 2006). Bialystok and colleagues hypothesize that bilinguals are of necessity continually exercising and thus honing their executive skills, such as "selective attention to relevant aspects of a problem, inhibition of attention to misleading information and switching between competing alternatives" (Bialystok et al. 2004:291; see also Hernández et al. 2000, 2001). Clearly, these are the very component processes that are taxed by bilingualism in general and CS in particular – selecting words and structures from the active language, exerting inhibitory control over the currently inactive language, and switching between languages, together with maintaining the relevant word and message level representations needed, and all at the phenomenal speed with which human communication takes place.

17.3 L1–L2 brain overlap

The question of whether the two languages in a bilingual are represented and/or processed by the same brain region(s) or by different ones became a focus of debate following reports of bilingual aphasics displaying differential or selective patterns of language loss and/or recovery (see reviews by Fabbro 2001a; Ojemann and Whitaker 1978; Paradis 1985).

Intracranial Electrical Cortical Stimulation (IECS) procedures afforded inferences about language processing in bilingual patients with epilepsy or brain tumors undergoing neurosurgery (Lucas et al. 2004; Ojemann and Whitaker 1978; Rapport et al. 1983; Roux et al. 2004; Roux and Tremoulet 2002). Individual cases of bilinguals with diverse language histories and diverse language combinations were examined while brief electrical pulses were applied at different electrode sites (one at a time) as they named line-drawings, pointed to pictures of named objects, or read aloud. The stimulated brain sites most likely to disrupt L1 were more concentrated around typical language areas (e.g. posterior Sylvian fissure) than were the sites more likely to disrupt L2. Despite substantial variability within patients and within a particular location, stimulation disrupted L1 sites more consistently than L2 sites. IECS studies generally offered little if any support for the hypothesis that language representation in bilinguals has a greater than normal contribution from the right hemisphere (see also review by Paradis 2000a; Rapport et al. 1983), with the proviso that most stimulations occur in the left hemisphere. Like the patient data, the IECS findings also support only partial overlap in neural representations of the languages in bilinguals, with a mosaic pattern of L1–L2 representation where two adjacent cells could be language-specific.

Initial results of the scanning of intact bilingual brains with Positron Emission Tomography (PET) and functional Magnetic Resonance Imaging (fMRI), two techniques used to infer neural activity from changes in metabolic activity or blood flow, were similarly variable, with some researchers claiming identical brain areas for L1 and L2 (Klein et al. 1994, 1995) and others highlighting activation differences (Dehaene et al. 1997; Perani et al. 1996; Yetkin et al. 1996). Likewise, while some researchers report greater brain extent (number of activated pixels) for the less fluent language (Yetkin et al. 1996), others found the opposite pattern (Perani et al. 1996). Across these studies, however, participants varied considerably in their relative language proficiencies and performed different tasks ranging from word generation to story listening. Nonetheless, there tends to be greater intersubject variability in the cortical representation of L2 than of L1 (Dehaene et al. 1997).

Given these inconsistencies, researchers began to assess the influence of individual, language, and task characteristics that could reasonably be expected to account for the variability. This research tack is based on the assumption that the brain areas serving L1 and L2 can be identical in principle but may not be in practice because of differences in when or how each is acquired, and/or how well each is known, and/or the distance between the languages, the difficulty or level of language analysis, etc.

Some researchers, for example, argue that earlier L2 exposure leads to greater sharing of neural space with L1 (Kim et al. 1997). Other investigators, however, find that age of acquisition *per se* has little effect on either the precise location or neural extent of L2 representation if L2 proficiency is high (Illes et al. 1999; Perani et al. 1998; Pu et al. 2001). Language proficiency, by contrast, is found to have a significant, albeit differential, impact on the neural extent (number of activated pixels) of comprehension and production processes (Briellmann et al. 2004; Chee et al. 2001; Perani et al. 1996; Yetkin et al. 1996). This inverse correlation between activation and production proficiency may be a specific instance of a more general finding that increasing expertise is accompanied by a decrease in cortical activation (Briellmann et al. 2004).

Although the typological distance between the structures of two languages also might seem to be a reasonable factor influencing how the languages are represented, there is apparently no reliable evidence that it is. The degree of L1–L2 activation overlap is about the same for Italian and English as it is for typologically similar languages (e.g. Catalan and Spanish) (Perani et al. 1998) or two typologically diverse languages (e.g. English and Chinese) in both early and late bilinguals (Chee et al. 1999a, 1999b).

Some researchers have examined the possibility that the answer to the question of L1–L2 brain overlap varies with the specific language processes under investigation (e.g. phonological, morphological, syntactic, and semantic), which at times are modulated by proficiency in and/or age of exposure to L2. With respect to the issue of language processing, greater convergence was seen for semantic and phonological tasks in L1 than in L2 (Pillai et al. 2003), greater activation for negative compared to affirmative spoken sentences was seen only in L2 (Hasegawa et al. 2002), and more brain areas distinguished active from passive sentences in L1 than in L2, at least in late bilinguals (Yokoyama et al. 2006). With respect to proficiency and age, it has been claimed that proficiency has a major impact on neural processing for semantic judgments, and age of acquisition is more critical for grammatical processing (Wartenburger et al. 2003). Furthermore, while L2 proficiency is an important determinant for semantic processing, its effects are primarily beyond the word level (Xue et al. 2004). Finally, age of exposure influences linguistic tasks with isolated words, but not with more complex stimuli such as whole sentences (Frenck-Mestre et al. 2005).

17.3.1 General considerations of L1–L2 overlap

While the initial research focus on the degree or extent of overlap of the two (plus) languages of a multilingual has been refined to include the modulatory effects of individual factors (e.g. age of exposure, proficiency, daily usage), as well as linguistic and task factors (e.g. linguistic difficulty/complexity, language level/process), there exist, nonetheless, different accounts of which factors are most important for particular processes (for reviews see Abutalebi et al. 2001; Fabbro 2001a, 2001b; Perani and Abutalebi 2005; Vaid and Hull 2002).

Age and mode of acquisition, for example, play key roles in Ullman's model of bilingual processing (Ullman 2001), underscoring his view that it is how the two languages are acquired rather than differences in relative proficiencies that determine the brain areas engaged. All lexico-semantic knowledge in L1 and L2, as well as L2 grammar when learned later in life, is presumed to rely on a declarative memory system. By contrast, the grammatical knowledge of L1 is implicitly acquired, thus leading to differential L1–L2 activation in grammatical tasks. This model, however, fails to account for brain-based L1–L2 differences as a function of L2 proficiency. Alternatively, Perani and Abutalebi (2005) maintain that the brain areas involved in language learning change throughout the course of learning much as they do for non-language learning (Briellmann et al. 2004), such that the neural processing of L2 "converges" to that of L1 with increasing proficiency. They argue that the same brain mechanism supports grammatical processing in L1 and L2, with differences attributable to the different cognitive strategies adopted to compensate for lower L2 proficiency. Paradis (2000b, 2003) similarly argues that the apparent differential lateralization of brain function for L2 is strategic, with greater reliance on metalinguistic knowledge and pragmatics under right hemisphere control. On Indefrey's account (2006), late L2 acquisition onset, low L2 proficiency, and low exposure to L2 are all important in determining brain organization for L2, albeit with different weightings for different language processes. Specifically, word comprehension processes are influenced primarily by L2 proficiency, sentence comprehension processes primarily by L2 onset, and word production processes by all three factors.

In summary, there is no simple answer to the question of whether the neural representations of the two languages in a bilingual are or are not the same. Neuropsychological data and intraoperative electrocortical stimulation mapping data in bilinguals suggest that the brain regions serving L1 and L2 are not identical, although there may be substantial overlap. Neuroimaging data would seem to indicate that although L1 and L2 largely engage similar brain areas, there are individuals in whom there are circumstances when the activated brain areas differ. Some researchers interpret activation differences in the same general region as support for one language system, albeit with different degrees of activation, whereas for others it is evidence for the different neural representations of L1 and L2. When differences in brain regions for L1 and L2 are observed, it is more common to see greater activation during L2 processing than during L1 processing, presumably due to differences in age of exposure to L2, amount of L2 exposure, L2 proficiency, or some combination thereof. Moreover, these factors seem to make different contributions to different language tasks, presumably because different tasks tap into different linguistic and/or cognitive processes, although there is not yet a consensus as to which are the most relevant (e.g. comprehension vs. production, lexical vs. sentential, grammatical vs. semantic). At a minimum, researchers of bilingualism know that it is essential to determine age of acquisition as well as L1 and L2 proficiency, and to exercise caution when generalizing from any particular language task to language more generally.

Whatever the degree of neural overlap between L1 and L2, many questions remain. How do the different languages in bilinguals stay functionally segregated, if they do? What sorts of relationships exist between the languages at each level (lexical, phonological, morphological, syntactic)? How do bilingual speakers choose the right word in the right order in the intended language? How is access to the different languages controlled and how is interference prevented, if it is? Are both languages in a bilingual always "on" or can one be shut off when it is not in use? If so, then, is there a cost of switching to the unused language, always or only sometimes? To what extent do the answers to these questions differ as a function of bilingual characteristics, the stimuli, the language environment, language in use, and/or the task, among other factors?

These are the sorts of questions that electrophysiological researchers address by recording electrical brain activity from the scalps of bilinguals as they comprehend or produce language. For the most part, the electrical activity at the scalp reflects summed post-synaptic potentials (excitatory and inhibitory) generated primarily by pyramidal cells in the neocortex. The magnetic counterpart – the magnetoencephalograph (MEG) – reflects a subset of this activity generated by pyramidal cells that are oriented tangentially to the scalp surface. Researchers look to this electrical activity, locked in time to stimulus presentation or response onset and averaged across multiple occurrences of the relevant stimulus or response class – the event-related brain potential (ERP) – to track stimulus or response-related processing. By comparing two or more patterns of such voltage waveforms in time and space elicited under different experimental conditions, investigators make inferences about when (and where at the scalp) certain differences between the conditions first appear and what these differences might mean in terms of sensory-perceptional, motor, and cognitive constructs.

17.4　Electrophysiological patterns in bilingual readers and speakers

The ERP is a waveform of voltage in time, reflecting the difference in electrical potential between two recording electrodes, elicited by and synchronized in time to an event of interest, as a signal travels from a receptor to a percept, a concept, and on occasion to a memory representation or an overt response. The waveform consists of negative and positive peaks (with respect to a pre-event baseline), typically labeled with their polarity and latency (N100, a relative negativity peaking at 100ms after stimulus onset, or P200, a relative positivity peaking at 200ms after stimulus onset, both of which are obligatory sensory components that vary with parameters of the physical stimulus and attentional manipulations). Each peak (or temporal region of a waveform) can be characterized in terms of its amplitude, latency with respect to an event, and amplitude distribution across the scalp. Each of these characteristics of the ERP for different conditions and for each participant can be subjected to an analysis of variance or regression analysis in order to determine which differences between conditions are statistically reliable.

Although not identical to components, peaks are often taken as overt markers of latent components that index specific neural computations implementing certain psychological processes. Many such components have been described in the cognitive ERP literature. Two relatively late so-called endogenous components in particular have played important roles in psycholinguistic studies: the N400, a negative peak around 400ms sensitive to lexico-semantic processes, and the P600, a positive peak around 600ms sensitive to grammatical processes. By contrast to the early so-called exogenous components, such as the P1, N1, and P2, these components are much less sensitive to physical stimulus features, and much more sensitive to how an individual processes the eliciting stimulus or, in some cases, the absence of the "expected" stimulus. Two other endogenous components used in electrophysiological studies of language production are the lateralized readiness potential (LRP) and the nogo N200. The LRP is a derived measure that can be used under the appropriate experimental conditions to indicate preferential response activation, whereas the nogo N200 can be used in a go/nogo paradigm as an index of response inhibition. In response conflict and go/nogo paradigms, both of these ERP components can be used to track the time course of the encoding of features and response activation, thereby supporting inferences about the relative ordering of information availability during language production.

It is not at all uncommon to see differential patterns of electrical brain activity in monolinguals relative to bilinguals or within bilinguals for L1 versus L2. The difficulty is determining which differences are reliable and what functions they index. To date, the majority of electrophysiological investigations in bilinguals have looked at some aspect of language comprehension, focusing on the N400 (Kutas and Hillyard 1980b). Negativity in the N400 range (200–500ms post-stimulus onset) is a default response to all potentially meaningful items, not just language (words, pseudowords, sign language, gestures, line drawings, e.g. Ganis et al. 1996; Kutas et al. 1987; Wu and Coulson 2005). N400 amplitude is modulated by a number of factors that influence the ease with which information is accessed from semantic memory, such as word frequency (smaller for high frequency), word repetition (smaller with repetition), and semantic context (smaller with relatedness). The N400 is used in semantic priming paradigms as an index of associative/semantic priming, although the potential in the same window is also sensitive to phonological and orthographic relationships.

Within sentences, N400 amplitudes to given words are reduced by contextual constraints that seem to pre-activate aspects of upcoming items prior to their occurrence and/or ease their integration into the ongoing message-level representation upon their occurrence (e.g. Federmeier and Kutas 1999; Wicha et al. 2003, 2004). The effect of context is especially evident in the N400 semantic congruity effect: the difference in the ERP to a word that is a good semantic fit with a prior sentence context (congruent) and to one that is a bad semantic fit (semantically incongruent, although the N400 *per se* is not unique to semantic anomalies; e.g. "He shaved off his mustache and *eyebrows*"). Over frontal sites, N400 amplitudes vary with concreteness and with word class (Brown et al. 1999; Holcomb et al. 1999; Kounios and Holcomb 1994; Weber-Fox et al. 2003). N400 amplitude is also affected by language proficiency even in monolinguals (King and Kutas 1995; Weber-Fox et al. 2003). It develops rapidly in young adults learning a second language, with as little as fourteen hours of training sufficing to distinguish real words from nonsense words (McLaughlin et al. 2004).

The N400 has been used to examine lexico-semantic information processing in one or the other, or both, of a bilingual's two languages. Bilinguals typically show an N400 relatedness effect (smaller N400s to the second of a pair of semantically related than unrelated words) in both of their languages, much like monolinguals (see Kotz and Elston-Guttler 2004 for an exception). However, the timing and degree of access to information in semantic memory in each of a bilingual's languages seem to be modulated by both proficiency and age of acquisition. Bilinguals who are fluent in both their languages from birth tend to show equal amplitude N400 semantic priming effects in both (Kotz 2001). Bilinguals who are imbalanced either in proficiency or age of acquisition do not: larger N400 relatedness effects are seen during the processing of the more proficient language and for the earlier learned language (Kotz and Elston-Güttler 2004; Phillips et al. 2004).

In sentence processing studies, the focus is usually on the N400 congruity effect, which is linked to semantic expectancy and/or semantic integration. In a few cases, the N400 semantic congruity effect has been found to be about the same size in bilinguals (especially in L1) as in monolinguals (Ardal et al. 1990; Hahne and Friederici 2001; Proverbio et al. 2002; Sanders and Neville 2003; Weber-Fox and Neville 2001). In other cases, however, there are some noteworthy differences in the N400 congruity effects between monolinguals and bilinguals, and between the two languages of a bilingual in overall amplitude, onset and peak latencies, and/or relative amplitude distributions across the scalp. Importantly, these differences are modulated by proficiency (Proverbio et al. 2002) as well as age of acquisition (Weber-Fox and Neville 2001), although these two factors are often difficult to dissociate (Moreno and Kutas 2005).

Whether the N400 is taken to reflect semantic expectancy or integration, systematic variations in N400 onset and peak latency afford inferences about when semantic information becomes available for use. Some studies have reported longer latency onsets or peaks for the N400 congruity effect in bilinguals compared to monolinguals (Ardal et al. 1990; Hahne and Friederici 2001), within bilinguals for their less-dominant language compared to the more-dominant one (Ardal et al. 1990; Moreno and Kutas 2005) and for those who acquired the language later in life, though note that even for monolinguals, N400s are delayed in less proficient language users (Weber-Fox et al. 2003; Weber-Fox and Neville 2001). More specifically, the latency of the N400 congruity effect in L2 is positively correlated with age of exposure and inversely correlated with fluency (Moreno and Kutas 2005). The duration of the N400 congruity effect also may be longer for bilinguals in their less proficient language relative to monolingual readers (Hahne 2001; Hahne and Friederici 2001). The observation of slowed N400 congruity effects in both languages of a bilingual (relative to monolinguals) suggests that simply being bilingual may have processing consequences for certain semantic analyses. This is consistent with observations of slower reaction times even in L1 for bilinguals compared to monolinguals, although the N400 congruity effect does not always distinguish between monolinguals and bilinguals in the L1 (e.g. Proverbio et al. 2002). Similarly, the difference in timing between L1 and L2 clearly reflects differences in speed of access to lexical-semantic information in each language.

In summary then, bilinguals have access to word-level meanings in both their L1 and L2, although the speed and perhaps extent of effective access to that information is a function of language proficiency. Higher proficiency is associated with larger semantic priming effects and sometimes larger sentence level effects, although even the most highly proficient L2 users can be distinguished from strictly monolingual language users on N400 latency, amplitude, and/or distribution.

17.5   Bilingual (non-)selectivity

Fluent speakers of two or more languages are remarkably adept at accessing information from one language or the other selectively, although not always without cost. Nonetheless, given the apparently substantial overlap in the neural networks of a bilingual's two languages, it is noteworthy that many bilinguals do not seem to suffer much interference between their languages. Perhaps there is in fact no interference because the bilingual brain completely "shuts off" one language while the other is "on." Alternatively, the bilingual brain may regulate the use of two languages, both of which are always "on," so as to minimize interference. Or, perhaps interference is more pervasive than obvious in overt behavior. Whether only one language of a bilingual is "on" (selective) or both languages are "on" (non-selective) at any given moment is a particularly controversial question (e.g. Dijkstra and Heuven 2002). There are data consistent with both of these positions.

ERP researchers typically take cross-language priming/interference as evidence for activation of both languages as opposed to selective activation of just one. When a word in one language influences the ERP to the translation equivalent or to a semantically related word in the other language, it is assumed that both must be "active," at least to some degree. Similarly, if features of one language somehow modulate processing of the other, then it is assumed that both are effectively "active" to some extent at that time. Interaction/interference can be inferred from amplitude and/or latency alterations in many different ERP responses, depending on the brain process affected.

To date, a number of ERP investigations have suggested that fluent bilinguals can at least sometimes selectively activate one language, particularly when the processing task is monolingual (Rodriguez-Fornells et al. 2002). However, when the task performance requires that both languages be quickly available (Rodriguez-Fornells et al. 2005) or includes word stimuli such as interlingual homographs (words that share their form but not their meaning across two languages) that are an integral part of the lexicon in both languages, then interference/interaction is more likely (de Bruijn et al. 2001; Elston-Güttler et al. 2005b; Kerkhofs et al. 2006; Paulmann et al. 2006). Such interference is reflected in different ERP components indexing different cognitive processes including the N400, but is subject to modulation by context (Elston-Güttler et al. 2005a). Research with translational homonyms (two words in one language which translate to the same word in another, e.g. 'pine' and 'jaw' both translate to *Keifer* in German) also offers evidence for cross-language interference even when the processing task is monolingual (de Bruijn et al. 2001).

Unlike in the semantic domain where even late learners show N400 congruity effects similar to those of native speakers, bilinguals do not always show the typical monolingual ERP effects (P600 and left anterior negativity or LAN) to syntactic violations and grammatical analyses (Hahne 2001; Hahne and Friederici 2001; Hahne et al. 2006; Mueller et al. 2005; Sanders and Neville 2003). The P600 (Holcomb et al. 1999; Osterhout and Holcomb 1992) is elicited by both local and global grammatical processes, including violations of subject–verb agreement, pronoun agreement, phrase structure violations, subjacency violations, subcategorization violations, among others, but is also observed with no overt syntactic violation and even in non-linguistic contexts such as certain musical violations (e.g. Coulson et al. 1998; Patel et al. 1998). The LAN is a relatively early negativity often seen in association with violations of syntactic well-formedness as well as to manipulations of syntactic working memory (e.g. Kluender and Kutas 1993; Münte et al. 1993). For example, Mueller and colleagues (Mueller et al. 2005) found that although non-native speakers of Japanese were able to learn a mini-version of the language with 75% accuracy in grammatical sentence production and comprehension with only 4–10 hours of training, not all their ERP effects appeared native-like. In particular, whereas the bilingual and monolingual ERPs resembled each other for the P600 to word category and case violations, they were qualitatively different in response to more complex grammatical processes (e.g. thematic role assignment); moreover learners were characterized by a complete absence of the negativities (ELAN and N400) observed in monolinguals.

In sum, several different factors can influence the apparent selectivity of access to one language or another during language processing in bilinguals. The effects of these factors – especially relative language proficiencies, language environment, language of local context, and task demands – are all worth considering, as they are just as likely to be important when bilinguals actively use two languages, as in CS. Likewise, it is important to note that semantic and certain grammatical/syntactic processes are differentially impacted by bilingualism.

17.6   Switching: structure and function

The remaining sections focus on CS, first examining the neuroanatomy of CS then reviewing the handful of electrophysiological studies devoted to CS.

17.6.1   The subcortical–cortical network for language switching

Case studies of bilingual patients with cerebral lesions have been a major source of theorizing about the brain areas involved in translation, language mixing (clinically defined as mixing words between two or more languages within a single utterance), and language switching (clinically defined as switching between languages in complete sentences). Although translation, language mixing, and language switching are typically tied to separate brain mechanisms, the network specifics vary across proposals (e.g. Fabbro et al. 1997, 2000; Obler et al. 1978; Perecman 1984; Price et al. 1999). Herein, we use code-switching and language switching synonymously, encompassing switching within or between single utterances, as is common in the experimental literature.

Language switching hypothetically relies on inhibition of the non-target language via the left basal ganglia (Abutalebi et al. 2000; Fabbro et al., 1997; Mariën et al. 2005), and/or attentional/executive control mechanisms involving the anterior cingulate, prefrontal and frontal cortices (Fabbro et al. 2000; Hernandez et al. 2000, 2001), or bilateral supramarginal gyri and Broca's area (Price et al. 1999). Pathological or uncontrollable language switching is presumed to reflect deficits in selection processes and has been reported for all levels of linguistic processing, including phonological and morphological blends, intonation patterns, and syntax. The most common form, however, is lexical insertion of words from one language into sentences in another language (Perecman 1984), which sometimes occurs equally in both directions (e.g. Abutalebi et al. 2000; Fabbro et al. 2000), but is more often asymmetric (e.g. Aglioti and Fabbro 1993; Fabbro et al. 1997).

Patient data as well as neuroimaging data from healthy adults generally implicate a cortical–subcortical network (including the thalamus, basal ganglia, and frontal cortex) in language switching (Fabbro et al. 1997; Mariën et al. 2005). Some researchers consider the dorsolateral prefrontal cortex (DLPFC) key for controlling language switching and inhibiting the currently unused language, as damage to the DLPFC sometimes leads to uncontrollable language switching. Repetitive transcranial magnetic stimulation of the DLPFC in severely depressed bilinguals elicited the experience of thinking in and having an urge to speak in their less frequently used language (Holtzheimer et al. 2005). Similarly, neuroimaging studies show increased activation in the DLPFC during language switching (Hernandez et al. 2001; Hernandez et al. 2000), although not always (Crinion et al. 2006; Price et al. 1999). Likewise, damage to the basal ganglia and/or to their frontal projections leads to pathological and/or spontaneous CS. The left basal ganglia and thalamus are presumably important for *inhibitory* control of an unintended language, especially the more automatic language (e.g. Aglioti et al. 1996; Aglioti and Fabbro 1993). The left caudate also has been variously linked to the *selection* of desired lexical items, control of the language use in bilinguals, and the inhibition of the unintended language (e.g. Crinion et al. 2006).

Although presumed essential for multilingual language processing, this cortical–subcortical loop does not appear to be unique to multilinguals, or even to language (e.g. Aglioti 1997; Crosson 1999; Paradis and Goldblum 1989; Zatorre 1989). It has been linked to lexical selection in monolinguals (Crosson et al. 2003), as well as to lexical selection across languages in polyglots (e.g. Abutalebi et al. 2000), consistent with the possibility that bilinguals have co-opted existing mechanisms for lexical selection and inhibitory control within a language for multilingual control. In fact, a basal ganglia–frontal cortex pathway is more generally thought to be involved in cognitive control processes in multiple domains (memory and attention), not just language (Aglioti 1997; Alexander and Crutcher 1990).

In sum, data from patients as well as from neuroimaging studies in healthy adults have implicated both subcortical and (prefrontal) cortical structures in voluntary and involuntary language switching. Subcortical structures, especially in the basal ganglia, are presumably involved in language selection and/or inhibition mechanisms that are not necessarily specific to bilinguals, but important for their CS.

The bilingual psycholinguistic literature is rife with examples of the "cost of code switching" as inferred from longer reading times for bilingual versus monolingual texts (Macnamar and Kushnir 1971) or from longer lexical decision times for words that are immediately preceded by a different language than by the same one (Grainger and Beauvillain 1988; Grainger and O'Regan 1992). So, clearly CS can incur a cost. The question, however, is whether it always does so, or whether there are circumstances under which CS is not costly, and perhaps even beneficial (see Li 1996). Additionally, the predictability of a switch (as in a blocked stimulation design) has sometimes (although not always) been found to reduce (Altarriba et al. 1996; Meuter and Allport 1999) or eliminate costs (Chan et al. 1983). ERPs can provide us with a direct measure of the electrical (neocortical) brain activity associated with producing and processing switches of language. The handful of ERP studies of CS in bilinguals is reviewed next.

17.6.2 Brain response to the production of language switches

Jackson et al. (2001) recorded ERPs from native English speakers as they randomly named digits in L1 (English) or in L2 (French, German, Spanish, Mandarin, or Urdu); language was cued by the ink color. Participants were slower to name digits after a language switch, to the same extent regardless of switch direction, and also were slower to name digits in L2 than L1 on non-switched trials. Language switches were associated with a larger fronto-central N320 component and a later posterior positivity (late positive component or LPC) relative to non switch trials. The N320 was taken to index inhibition of the unwanted lexicon. Unlike the reaction time effect, this N320 effect was evident only for switches from L1 to L2, perhaps reflecting a greater need for resources to suppress an active L1 in order to produce an L2 word than vice versa. The enhanced LPC (385–700ms) was hypothesized to index the reconfiguration of stimulus–response linkages necessary to regain access to the previously inhibited lexicon.

Overall, these results support models in which effective production of one language requires inhibition of the other, though the inhibition mechanism need not be language specific. Inhibition, of course, need not be all or none, and may be influenced by age of exposure to L2 and/or language dominance.

17.6.3 Brain responses to the comprehension of language switches

Whereas naming a digit in one language may require deliberate suppression of its name in the other language, one can imagine that suppression might be less important during comprehension. To examine this issue, Jackson et al. (2004) presented bilinguals with a sequence of number names that alternated predictably between languages (e.g. *two-one-cinq-sept-four-eight*) and asked them to judge whether the number was even or odd, regardless of its language. Code-switches did not elicit an enhanced N320 (considered equivalent to a nogo N200), suggesting no suppression of the alternate lexicon. These results point to an overall difference between the effects of language switching at the word level on production and comprehension, particularly when the task requires both languages to be active (see also Rodríguez-Fornells et al. 2005). They suggest that the absence of the N320 effect might mean that switching costs during comprehension may occur outside the lexico-semantic system.

Moreno et al. (2002) were interested in determining whether the bilingual brain responds to a language switch as an orthographic/physical deviation (larger late positivity, e.g. Kutas and Hillyard 1980a), a semantic deviation (larger negativity, or N400, e.g. Kutas and Hillyard 1980b), or as both. To that end, ERPs were recorded in English–Spanish bilinguals reading highly constraining English sentences such as "He put a clean sheet on the ..." which could end with (1.) the most expected word ending in that sentential context ("bed"); (2.) a so-called lexical switch, or synonym of the expected word in English ("mattress"); or (3.) a code-switch, i.e. a translation equivalent of the expected word in Spanish ("cama"). Relative to expected endings (*bed*), within language switches (*mattress*) elicited a larger N400 while code-switches into Spanish (*cama*) elicited a large posterior late positive component (450–850 ms), consistent with the proposal that code-switches were treated more like unexpected events at the physical level than at the lexico-semantic level. The more proficient the bilingual in L2, the earlier in latency and the smaller in amplitude was this positivity to the code-switch.

Proverbio et al. (2004) also examined the nature of ERPs to CS, but within a group of professional simultaneous translators, presumably proficient in at least four different languages. These polyglots were examined in L1 (Italian) and L2 (English) as they read a sentence context followed ~1.5s later by a final word and made sense/nonsense judgments in two unmixed conditions with sentences and two mixed (but predictable code-switch) conditions. As expected, reaction times revealed switching costs: interpreters were slower to respond to mixed than unmixed sentence conditions even though there was no uncertainty about when the code-switches would occur. Several CS ERP results were reported, including larger N400s (300–500 ms) for language mixed final words compared to unmixed sentence endings, collapsed across congruity. Also, collapsed across congruity, N400s were reportedly larger when switching from the more-dominant to the less-dominant language than vice-versa.

Finally, although Alvarez et al. (2003) were more generally interested in characterizing the functional organization of L1 and L2 word processing in individuals early in the L2 acquisition process, their design offers data relevant to CS. Their primary focus was on ERP word repetition effects, as numerous studies have documented reductions in N400 amplitude upon word repetition (e.g. Bentin and Peled 1990; Besson et al. 1992). ERPs were recorded to a series of English and Spanish words (one every 2.7s) from English L1 speakers as they pressed a button for words from a particular semantic domain (i.e. body parts) in either language (approximately 10% of words). Alvarez et al. aimed to determine how much of the within–language effect on N400 reduction is semantically driven. Whereas within–language repetitions overlap in form and meaning, between-language repetitions of a word and its non-cognate translation share meaning but have minimal orthographic and phonological overlap. Critically, for present purposes, the main comparison of within-language repetitions versus between-language repetitions included CS in both directions. Even though participants could not be sure when a code-switch would occur, they could predict with great certainty what the code-switch would be when it did occur. As expected, immediate repetitions reduced N400 amplitudes, and these reductions were greater for within- compared to between-language repetitions, just as they are for exact repetitions versus semantic level repetitions. Moreover, although between-language ERP repetition effects were about the same size overall regardless of the direction of the switch, the time course of the repetition effect varied with switch direction, being earlier for switches into L1 than into L2. These findings are generally consistent with some asymmetry in the strength of lexical connections between L1 and L2, which Kroll and Stewart (1994) have hypothesized as a lifelong asymmetry, albeit modified by L2 fluency. If true, then with increasing L2 proficiency, there should be less of a difference in the size of the N400 repetition effect across a bilingual's two languages, as a function of switch direction.

In sum, only a handful of studies have examined the electrical brain activity accompanying language code-switches in production or comprehension. Code-switch-related effects have been observed on the N1, N320, N400, late positivity, and/or on a late (post N400) negativity, although never in the same study. It is difficult at present to compare results across experiments given the differences in experimental design and populations. It will be important to determine how certain factors contribute to the pattern of ERP effects observed, including: (1.) predictability in timing or content of the CS, (2.) frequency of the CS; (3.) the direction of the CS; (4.) language proficiency and/or dominance; (5.) age of acquisition; (6.) language process under investigation; and (7.) task demands. Although no unified picture of ERP effects of CS has yet emerged, it is unlikely that there will be a single ERP marker of language switching. More likely, different switch-related ERP effects will be elicited depending on which perceptual/cognitive/motor process is affected by switches.

17.7   Conclusions

Psychological and brain research are difficult for reasons that need no enumeration here. Research with bilinguals or polyglots is much harder still. If only researchers could "raise" multi-language individuals in controlled environments, conducting parametric studies and manipulating all the linguistic factors now known to be important for language learning and use. They can't. They make do by choosing more homogeneous populations, collecting information about language history, and assessing the language capabilities of the multilingual participants. Nonetheless there is more variance in the data than we can handle, and the literature remains somewhat inconsistent and incoherent. This, then, may be a good time to step back and be clear about what questions to ask. Simply recording some measure (brain or otherwise) in response to a CS without a clear theoretical motivation will just add to an already confusing mix of data patterns.

Although there is still some measure of uncertainty and disagreement as to the exact functional significance of various ERP components, there is some predictability to the pattern of effects obtained in particular paradigms and a limited range of hypotheses as to what manipulations and/or processes modulate them. It is thus possible to use known components to examine hypotheses about group or language differences at the level of sensory and attentional processes, consolidation into working memory, inhibition, relative response preparation, short term auditory memory or more generally attention independent change detection, semantic/conceptual level of analysis, error or conflict processing, prosodic boundaries, among others. None of these components, however, is a marker in the sense that we can look for it in an ERP waveform and from it alone (without knowledge of the stimuli, experimental design, and task demands) infer the engagement of an underlying cognitive/neural operation. These ERP components can, however, serve as markers under the appropriate set of experimental conditions chosen with specific alternative hypotheses in mind. An important point to note in this regard is that various components should not be dismissed as useless simply because they have not routinely or not yet been employed in language studies. Given the right question, every ERP component can be fruitfully harnessed to analyze both linguistic and non-linguistic processing in monolinguals and bilinguals. One can imagine ERP studies specifically aimed, for example, at assessing whether or not switching (during reading or listening) captures attention (focusing on attention-related components), or whether switching is sometimes expected but at other times considered an error (focusing on ERN, error related negativity).

Laboratory work is usually limited and limiting by its nature. It is certainly so in the study of CS: CS in the neuroimaging lab is a far cry from switching "in the wild" (see Gullberg et al., this volume). To the best of our knowledge, neuroimaging studies have not systematically taken into account why or when CS occurs in natural speech, and designed the stimuli accordingly. For example, in naturally spoken sentences, CS does not occur randomly. Yet, no neuroimaging designs have directly compared a code-switch at a natural juncture versus one that would never occur. ERP components such as the CPS (closure positive shift) and ERN, in particular, could be used to examine the processing consequences of CS at various positions between and across constituents, phrases, clauses, and other boundaries in written and spoken texts.

Investigations of inhibition in language switching would do well to include a condition requiring switching in a task that has nothing to do with language. Such data would help us to determine whether the neural circuitry involved in language switching is unique to bilinguals and language switching or shares some if not all of its features with other switching mechanisms in bilinguals and monolinguals alike. Moreover, to the extent possible, investigations of language switching would do well to compare switching in both directions, to examine the claim that it is easier to switch from L2 to L1 than vice versa. Related to this issue, some researchers report that bilingual children become exceptionally good at ignoring distractive information and at switching between different cognitive tasks compared to monolingual children (e.g. Bialystok 1999; Bialystok and Martin 2004; Bialystok and Shapero 2005). They hypothesize that the reason behind this is the development of enhanced cognitive control mechanisms in bilingual children, to be able to handle switching and attentional control demands from an early age. According to this suggestion, training in switching languages seems to generalize to other cognitive domains. Brain imaging techniques could become a useful tool to test this hypothesis.

An interesting population of study in the field of CS is that of professional interpreters (Petsche et al. 1993; Proverbio et al. 2004; Rinne et al. 2000). Some professional interpreters have commented on the fact that they can no longer read a novel and enjoy it just as it is written. By their own account, they feel compelled to think of how that sentence/word/expression would have been conveyed in another language. The systematic study of their brain functioning compared to bilingual controls might inform us about possible differences between trained and untrained "switchers." Such data in turn might aid in the development of criteria for determining what cognitive skills are needed to become a professional interpreter (switcher).

Further exploration of CS brain reaction could be especially informative with respect to the functional organization of lexical and semantic knowledge in bilinguals. Not every concept that is lexically coded in one language is coded in the other (in fact, this is an important reason for borrowing a word from an alternative lexicon – see Wei, this volume). Translations are often not exact equivalents. The encyclopaedic knowledge that a speaker possesses about a certain word will seldom exactly match the connotations s/he has with the translation equivalent, especially with regard to their shades of meaning (see Backus 1996; Dorleijn and Backus, this volume). Languages may express a particular concept in more than one way. One can imagine investigations of these issues using the N400 component. How does the degree of overlap in meaning between a word or phrase in L1 and L2 influence its integration into a sentence context? Can, and if so, how quickly do words in a language acquire new shades of meaning under the influence of the connotations of its equivalent in the alternative language ("loan semantics"). Systematically manipulating two or more languages with brain imaging measures will definitely enrich our knowledge of how bilingual brains store, use, interchange, and convey meaning using alternative codes or alternate the code at use. After all, languages often evolve due to influences from other languages during language-contact phenomena such as CS.

Note

1. M. Kutas and some of her laboratory's research described herein were supported by grants NICHD 22614 and NIA 08313. N. Wicha was supported by NIDCD DC000351 for some of the work cited, and by a San Antonio Life Sciences Institute grant and a College of Science faculty research award from the University of Texas at San Antonio while writing this chapter. Special thanks to Tom Urbach and the two editors for their invaluable comments on a previous draft of this chapter.

Part V

Formal models of code-switching

18

Generative approaches to code-switching
Jeff MacSwan

18.1 Introduction

Code-switching (hereafter CS) is a specific kind of language mixing. Unlike *borrowing*, which involves the full phonological and morphological integration of a word from one language (say, English *type*) into another (as Spanish *taipiar*), CS involves the mixing of phonologically distinctive elements into a single utterance, as illustrated in (1a), where the Spanish phrase *mi hermano* is mixed into an otherwise English sentence.

(1) (a.) **Mi hermano** bought some ice cream.
          "My brother …"
     (b.) *__*Él__ bought some ice cream.
          "He …"

While (1a) is a perfectly natural expression among Spanish–English bilingual code-switchers, (1b) is not. The contrast between (1a) and (1b) shows us that CS is patterned, rule-governed behavior, just like monolingual language. Linguists interested in the grammatical study of CS seek to discover the underlying mechanisms which define patterns of grammaticality for all constructions in any language pair.

At the Thirteenth Annual Round Table Meeting on Linguistics and Languages at Georgetown University, held in 1962, Haugen claimed to have originated the term code-switching. The word first appeared in print in Vogt's (1954) review of Weinreich's (1953) *Languages in Contact* and two years later in Haugen (1956). Benson (2001) identifies the work of Espinosa (1911) as the first scholarly engagement of bilingual language mixing. Although Espinosa noted some tendencies in the frequencies of word classes to be switched, he nonetheless saw CS patterns as essentially random in nature. Despite these early interests, an actual CS research literature did not emerge until the late 1960s and early 1970s, when work focusing on both social and grammatical aspects of language mixing began steadily appearing.

In research on grammatical aspects of CS, Gumperz and his colleagues (Gumperz 1967, 1970; Gumperz and Hernández-Chávez 1971), Hasselmo (1972), Timm (1975), and Wentz (1977) were among the earliest to observe that there are grammatical restrictions on language mixing: while some switches naturally occur among bilinguals, others are non-occurring or judged to be ill-formed. For example, Timm's list of restrictions noted that Spanish–English switching between a subject pronoun and a main verb, as in (1b) is ill-formed but not so when the subject pronoun is replaced with a lexical subject, as in (1a). Construction-specific constraints were typical of this early work; however, a literature would soon emerge in which the grammatical mechanisms underlying these descriptive observations were explored.

This chapter presents an overview of *generativist approaches to CS*, defined as theories of CS which posit explicit grammatical analyses of language mixing phenomena below sentential boundaries, and which rely upon research in mainstream generative grammar to inform their analysis. First we examine early generativist approaches to CS of the 1970s and early 1980s, developed in keeping with the basic framework of Chomsky's (1965) *Aspects* model. We then turn to proposals advanced in the era of Government–Binding Theory, the 1980s and early 1990s, before examining more recent work put forward in the spirit of the Minimalist Program. We conclude with thoughts on the direction of future theoretical research in CS.

18.2 *Aspects* era approaches

Chomsky's (1965) *Aspects of the Theory of Syntax* further developed the theory of transformational–generative grammar introduced in *Syntactic Structures* (Chomsky 1957). The basic architecture of the grammar still consisted of a base component, comprised of a set of phrase structure rules that defined the deep structure or initial phrase marker (tree) representation, and a set of transformational rules which mapped phrase marker into phrase marker to generate a surface structure. In the *Aspects* model, lexical items could be inserted in the tree if their syntactic features matched those generated by the base rules.

18.2.1 Constraints in linguistic theory

As early as 1955, Chomsky had noted that the transformational component in a hybrid generative–transformational system had the disadvantage of vastly increasing the expressive power of the grammar, permitting the formulation of grammatical processes that did not seem to occur in any language. In response to the problem, Chomsky (1964, 1965) and other researchers such as Ross (1967) posited *constraints* on transformational rules. Ross noticed, for instance, that a Noun Phrase (NP) could not be extracted out of a conjoined phrase, as in (2a), accounting for the ill-formedness in (2b), but could be extracted in the semantically equivalent (but syntactically divergent) example in (2c), where t denotes trace, the point of extraction of the NP, questioned as *what*.

(2)   (a.) John was having milk and cookies.
      (b.) *What$_i$ was John having milk and t_i?
      (c.) What$_i$ was John having milk with t_i?

While the focus of efforts to constrain the grammar was placed primarily on the transformational component, these extended to the phrase structure component as well, culminating in the formulation of X' Theory in Chomsky (1970) (see Newmeyer 1986). Nonetheless, constraints were typically viewed as psychologically real restrictions on the application of transformations to phrase markers, and were therefore understood to be imposed at the level of surface structure.

The idea of a constraint in syntactic theory appealed to a number of researchers in CS, and was used to articulate the grammatical restrictions observed in CS data. While some thought of these constraints in the technical sense, as actual grammatical constructs, others used the term informally, intending to refer only to descriptive restrictions on language mixing.

18.2.2   Equivalence-based analyses

Several researchers converged simultaneously on the notion that language switching is controlled by some kind of syntactic equivalence requirement. Lipski was among the first to express the idea, hypothesizing that elements appearing in an utterance after a switch must be "syntactically equivalent" (Lipski 1978:258). As Pfaff similarly suggested, "Surface structures common to both languages are favored for switches" (1979:314). Poplack (1978, 1981) articulated this perspective in terms of her well-known Equivalence Constraint, augmented by The Free Morpheme Constraint, given in (3) and (4).

(3)   *The Equivalence Constraint*
      Codes will tend to be switched at points where the surface structures of the languages map onto each other.

(4)   *The Free Morpheme Constraint*
      A switch may occur at any point in the discourse at which it is possible to make a surface constituent cut and still retain a free morpheme.

As a variationist (see Labov 1963), Poplack argues that linguistic rules correlate with social structure and should be stated in terms of statistical frequencies, hence (3) is expressed as a tendency. The general idea is nonetheless clear: CS is allowed within constituents so long as the word order requirements of both languages are met at surface structure. Surface structures derive from the (cyclical) application of transformations to phrase markers, which originate as the output of a phrase structure grammar. The constraint in (4) defines a restriction on morphology in CS contexts, also noted in Wentz and McClure (1977) and Pfaff (1979). To illustrate, (3) correctly predicts that the switch in (5) is disallowed, because the surface word order of English and Spanish differ with respect to object pronoun (clitic) placement; (4) correctly disallows (6), where an English stem is used with a Spanish bound morpheme without the phonological integration of the stem.

(5)   *told **le**, **le** told, him **dije**, **dije** him
       told to-him, to-him I-told, him I-told, I-told him
       "(I) told him."

$\hfill$ (Poplack 1981:176)

(6)   *__estoy__ eat-__iendo__
       I-am eat-ing

$\hfill$ (Poplack 1980:586)

Research since Poplack's initial proposals has found persuasive documentation that her Equivalence Constraint is empirically inadequate, that is, it does not account for the full range of relevant data (Stenson 1990; Lee 1991; Myers-Scotton 1993a; Mahootian 1993; MacSwan 1999b; Chan 1999; Muysken 2000). Note, for example, the contrast in (7) from Spanish–English CS, noted by Belaz et al. (1994).

(7)   (a.) The students **habían visto la película italiana**
       (b.) *The student had **visto la película italiana**
              "The student had seen the Italian movie."

The surface structure of Spanish and English are alike with regard to the construction in (7), yet a switch between the auxiliary and the verb renders the sentence ill-formed, but not so in the case of a switch between the subject and the verb. However, (3) predicts that both examples should be well-formed.

Also consider the examples in (8), from MacSwan (1999b), where code switches occur between a subject pronoun and a verb, both in their correct surface structure position for both Spanish and Nahuatl, yet one example is ill-formed and the other well-formed.

(8)   (a.) *__Tú__ tikoas tlakemetl
              tú ti-k-koa-s tlake-me-tl
              you/SING 2S-3Os-buy-FUT garment-PL-NSF
              "You will buy clothes."

(b.) *Él* kikoas tlakemetl
él 0-ki-koa-s tlak-eme-tl
he 3S-3Os-buy-FUT garment-PL-NSF
"He will buy clothes."

The descriptive adequacy of Poplack's Free Morpheme Constraint, on the other hand, remains controversial. While it is attested in numerous corpora (Bentahila and Davies 1983; Berk-Seligson 1986; Clyne 1987; MacSwan 1999b), others claim to have identified some counter-examples (Eliasson 1989; Bokamba 1989; Myers-Scotton 1993a; Nartey 1982; Halmari 1997; Chan 1999; Hlavac 2003). However, in presenting counter-examples to The Free Morpheme Constraint, researchers have often given too little attention to the specific phonological, morphological, and syntactic characteristics of the examples cited, making it difficult to determine whether they are in fact violations. For Poplack, items that are phonologically integrated into the language of the bound morpheme are regarded as *borrowings* rather than code-switches. This is made explicit in subsequent formulations of the constraint, as in Sankoff and Poplack (1981:5): "A switch may not occur between a bound morpheme and a lexical item unless the latter has been phonologically integrated into the language of the bound morpheme." Thus, examples in which an other-language stem has been phonologically integrated into the language of an inflectional affix do not constitute counter-examples to The Free Morpheme Constraint.

Poplack's constraints have been criticized as a *third grammar*, a term originally coined by Pfaff (1979) to designate a system designed to mediate between the two languages present in a mixed utterance, and applied specifically to Poplack's constraints by Lederberg and Morales (1985), Mahootian (1993), and MacSwan (2000), among others. As Lipski (1985:83–84) noted, such mechanisms should be admitted only as a last resort:

Strict application of Occam's Razor requires that gratuitous meta-structures be avoided whenever possible, and that bilingual language behavior be described as much as possible in terms of already existing monolingual grammars. As a result, preference must initially be given to modifications of existing grammars of Spanish and English, rather than to the formulation of a special bilingual generative mechanism, unless experimental evidence inexorably militates in favor of the latter alternative. Among the proposed integrative models which have been examined, the bilingual tagging mechanism of Sankoff and Poplack (1981) has the greatest degree of promise, since it deals directly with bilingual surface structure and adds no special meta-system to control bilingual language shifting.

However, although Sankoff and Poplack (1981) similarly expressed a strong preference for avoiding CS-specific mechanisms to mediate

between the two languages in contact, they nonetheless concluded that
something of the sort appeared to be necessary on empirical grounds.
Otherwise, the authors argued, the free union of Spanish and English
phrase structure grammars would yield ill-formed results. For instance,
whereas English requires pre-nominal adjectives (NP → Det Adj N),
Spanish requires post-nominal adjective placement (NP → Det N Adj). A
speaker is free to select the Spanish rule and lexically insert an English
determiner, Spanish noun and English adjective (*the **casa** white) or even
insert English lexical items for all categories (*the house white*). Therefore,
in order to constrain the grammars so that they do not generate violations of (3), Sankoff and Poplack introduced a superscripting ("bilingual
tagging") mechanism that restricted lexical insertion rules so that the
grammar contributing the phrase structure rule would also be the
grammar from which lexical insertion rules would be drawn. Hence,
under conditions of CS, the Spanish phrase structure rule would be
annotated as in (9a), generating (9b). The superscripting conventions
followed from *heritability conditions*, which essentially allowed phrase
structure rules to look ahead and restrict the application of lexical
insertion rules.

(9)   (a.) NP → Det $N^{sp:n}$ $Adj^{sp:adj}$
      (b.) the **casa blanca**
            "the white house"

Sankoff and Poplack do not make explicit the mechanisms for superscript insertion; rather, they indicate that phrase structure rules are so
superscripted when they are selected in the generation of a code-switched
utterance, and are subsequently used to trigger language-specific lexical
insertion rules (N → casa, for instance, in the case of $N^{sp:n}$). No account is
presented as to how the superscript insertion mechanism is able to anno-
tate the appropriate categories correctly – for instance, N and Adj in (9a),
but not Det, where either language may be inserted without negative
consequences. For these reasons, the superscripting mechanism, like The
Equivalence Constraint and The Free Morpheme Constraint, appears to
constitute a CS-specific mechanism, a marked disadvantage.[1]

Woolford (1983) similarly attempted to derive The Equivalence
Constraint working within the basic assumptions of the *Aspects* model.
Like Pfaff (1979) and others before her, Woolford emphasized that our
best account of CS would avoid reference to any kind of CS-specific grammar. And like Sankoff and Poplack, Woolford recognized the basic
dilemma of providing lexical items with access to the structure of the
sentence in which they were inserted:

Phrase structure rules are drawn freely from both grammars during the
construction of constituent structure trees, but the lexicon of each grammar is limited to filling only those terminal nodes created by phrase

structure rules drawn from the same language. Nevertheless, in the event that there are phrase structure rules common to both languages, such rules belong simultaneously to both languages. Lexical items can be freely drawn from either language to fill terminal nodes created by phrase structure rules common to both languages. (Woolford 1983:535)

In other words, Woolford believed that lexical insertion was unconstrained in the case of phrase structure rules common to both languages; but in the case of phrase structure rules that were not shared, lexical insertion was limited to the terminal nodes associated with the phrase structure rule of the grammar to which it belonged. Woolford's system does not seem to achieve its intended results as it predicts that Spanish–English CS would require that a language-unique phrase structure rule (for instance, NP → Det N Adj for Spanish) could only be lexically filled by Spanish items (predicting *the **casa blanca*** to be ill-formed, contrary to the facts). In addition, while Woolford's work is an excellent example of the articulation of the goals of CS research, she does not herself present the formal mechanism that might be responsible for achieving the results expected within her framework. No explanation as to how the unique phrase structure rules get linked to language-specific rules of lexical insertion is offered.

Woolford accounts for Poplack's Free Morpheme Constraint by postulating that "the lexicons and word formation components of the two grammars remain separate" (1983:526). While this approach seems preferable to Poplack's, where the prohibition against word-internal switching is simply stated in descriptive terms, no rationale for the separation of the lexicons in terms of principles independent of CS itself is offered, leaving the basis for asserting that the model is free of any CS-specific mechanisms inexplicit.

18.3 Government–Binding Theory

Government–Binding (GB) Theory (Chomsky 1981) introduced a number of dramatic shifts in generative grammar. The transformational component was reduced to a single operation, Move α, responsible for moving elements within base-generated phrase markers, and the phrase structure grammar itself was replaced with X' Theory, a generalized convention for category expansion introduced in Chomsky (1970) and further developed in Chomsky (1981). In GB Theory, the grammar was conceived as a system of interactive modules such as Case Theory, θ-Theory, and Binding Theory. Researchers focused on the discovery of grammatical relations such as *c-command* and *government*, and posited abstract principles designed to capture the more general nature of constraints on transformations (see van Riemsdijk and Williams 1986).

18.3.1 The Government Constraint

Working within the GB framework, Di Sciullo et al. (1986) proposed The Government Constraint, which posited that there is an anti-government requirement on CS boundaries. Using the standard definition of government in (10), the authors posed (11) as a condition on lexical insertion (where q indexes a category to the language-particular lexicon).

(10)   X governs Y if the first node dominating X also dominates Y, where X is a major category N, V, A, P and no maximal boundary intervenes between X and Y.

(11)   If X governs Y, … X_q … Y_q …

Di Sciullo et al.'s intuition was that (11) is a narrower and empirically more accurate version of (12), which they viewed as a common assumption in syntactic theory that is never made explicit.

(12)   All elements inserted into the phase structure tree of a sentence must be drawn from the same lexicon.

On these provisions, the authors maintained that CS "can be seen as a rather ordinary case of language use, requiring no specific stipulation" (Di Sciullo et al. 1986:7). In order to permit the head carrying the language index q to percolate up to its maximal projection, they formalized the condition on CS as The Government Constraint, given in (13).

(13)   *The Government Constraint*
  (a.) If L_q carrier has index q, then $Y^{max}{}_q$.
  (b.) In a maximal projection Y^{max}, the L_q carrier is the lexical element that asymmetrically c-commands the other lexical elements or terminal phrase nodes dominated by Y^{max}.

This formalism allows the language of a head to determine the syntax of its maximal projection and imposes the condition that two categories must be in the same language if the government relation holds between them.

  Much like Sankoff and Poplack's (1981) formalism, (13) (like (11)) attempts to trigger language-specific lexical insertion by identifying nodes within a phrase marker with a specific language label (termed a *language index*). Although the authors maintain that the mechanism underlying the language index is vacuously available to monolinguals as well, it nonetheless appears to add few advantages over Sankoff and Poplack's version. Indeed, the constraint in (13) must be seen as a primitive in the system of grammar or it would not have the desired effect, and the very motivation for proposing it is to account for the data of CS; hence, (13) also appears to be a CS-specific constraint.

  In addition, there are important counter-examples to (13), some of which were noted by Di Sciullo, et al. For instance, because government holds between a verb and its object and between a preposition and its object, (13) predicts that a verb or preposition must be in the language of its complement. This is shown to be incorrect by examples in (14), where switches occur in case-marked positions.

(14) (a.) *English–Spanish*
        This morning **mi hermano y yo fuimos a comprar** some milk
        "This morning my brother and I went to buy some milk."
      (b.) *French–Arabic*
        J'ai joué avec il-ku:ra
        I'have played with the-ball
        "I played with the ball."
      (c.) *Spanish–Nahuatl*
        Mi hermana kitlasojtla in Juan
        mi hermana 0-ki-tlasojtla in Juan
        my sister 3S-3Os-love IN Juan
        "My sister loves Juan."

18.3.2   The Functional Head Constraint

Belazi et al. (1994) proposed The Functional Head Constraint (FHC), which took advantage of a recent development in syntactic theory that distinguished between lexical and functional categories (Abney 1987). Functional categories, or functional heads, were responsible for selecting complements with specific feature matrices. For example, *for* is a head (C^0) and has a feature specifying that its complement must have the feature [-Tense]. Belazi, Rubin, and Toribio argued that the data of CS can be correctly described in terms of the generalization in (15).

(15) A code-switch may not occur between a functional head and its complement.

The authors developed the FHC, given in (16), intended as a refinement of Abney's (1987) proposal.

(16) *The Functional Head Constraint*
      The language feature of the complement f-selected by a functional head, like all other relevant features, must match the corresponding feature of that functional head.

By *language feature*, the authors mean a label identifying the language from which an item was contributed, such as [+Spanish] or [+English]. If the features do not agree (e.g. a Spanish functional head with an English complement), then the code-switch is blocked. Since (16) applies only to f-selected configurations (a complement selected by a functional head), switches between lexical heads and their complements are not constrained.

  Mahootian (1993) and Muysken (2000) see the FHC as a further elaboration of The Government Constraint, in that it identifies an independently

motivated principle of grammar but incorporates language-specific identifiers (for The Government Constraint, a language index; for the FHC, a
language feature). Belazi et al., like Di Sciullo et al. (1986) with respect to
The Government Constraint, maintained that the FHC does not constitute a
CS-specific constraint. However, although the constraints were formulated
in terms of independently motivated operations, the particular language
identifiers were not. Linguists take particular grammars to be derivative in
nature, not primitive constructs, and hence positing a label for a particular
language as a primitive in syntactic theory leads us to an ordering paradox,
as MacSwan (1999b) has pointed out. In addition, (15) remains controversial
as a descriptive generalization (Mahootian 1993; MacSwan 1999b; Muysken
2000).

However, MacSwan (1999b) noted that the content of Belaz et al.'s
theory is greatly improved if we regard [+English] as an informal reference
to a collection of formal features that define English. On this view, names
for particular languages act as proxies for bundles of features which
formally characterize them. The ordering paradox disappears, because
language features like [+English] or [+Spanish] are no longer taken to be
primitives in the theory of grammar. To evaluate the FHC, then, particular
hypotheses would be needed regarding which features of a language,
being distinct from features of another, result in a conflict. Such conflicts might arise in numerous configurations besides those where head-
complement relations hold, leading us to move beyond the FHC to
propose a wider diversity of grammatical configurations where CS might
be illicit.

18.3.3 The Null Theory

Mahootian (1993) proposed the Null Theory of CS, formulated within the
framework of Tree Adjoining Grammars (TAG) originally introduced by
Joshi (1985b) for applications in computational linguistics and natural
language processing. TAG differs from mainstream generative grammar
in that the lexical items encode partial tree structures, and use operations
of substitution and adjunction to assemble larger trees composed of multiple lexical items. For example, the verb *build* is represented in the lexicon
along with its projection, and therefore the branching direction of its
complement is lexically specified. A substitution operation allows a DP
(e.g. *a house*) to integrate with *build* by substituting the DP (along with its
category label) with the object category label of *build*.

Mahootian focused on the complement relation in phrase structure (see
Pandit 1990; Nishimura 1997), and claimed that (17) was adequate to
account for the facts of CS.

(17)   The language of a head determines the phrase structure position of
       its complements in code-switching just as in monolingual contexts.

Mahootian (1993) used a corpus of Farsi–English CS data that she collected in naturalistic observations. In Farsi, objects occur before the verb, contrasting with basic word order in English. She observed that in CS contexts the language of the verb determines the placement of the object, as (18) illustrates. These facts are consistent with (17).

(18) **You'll buy** xune-ye jaedid
you'll buy house-POSS new
"You'll buy a new house."

Mahootian noticed that the TAG formalism provides an advantage for the analysis of CS data. Because structures are encoded in the lexicon, no intervening control mechanism is needed to pair up lexical insertion rules with terminal nodes in a phrase marker, as seen in previous proposals. However, like Belazi et al. (1994), Mahootian's analysis was restricted to head-complement configurations (MacSwan 1999b; Muysken 2000). Not only was (17) too narrow in this regard, failing to comment on CS in other dimensions of syntax, but it also proved to be insufficiently restrictive. Note, for instance, the examples in (19), a phenomenon observed by Timm (1975). Although all complements are in the correct positions assigned by heads, (19a) is ill-formed but (19b) well-formed. The contrast in grammaticality appears to relate to the nature of the subject, a specifier (XP) rather than a pronominal head (van Gelderen and MacSwan 2008).

(19) (a.) *__*Él*__ bought some ice cream.
"He bought some ice cream."
(b.) **Mi hermano** bought some ice cream.
"My brother bought some ice cream."

Furthermore, recall also that in (7), *visto* "seen," the complement of *habían/ had*, is in the position assigned by its head, and therefore adheres to (17), yet (7a) is well-formed and (7b) is not. In (20), Spanish and Nahuatl word order is respected with regard to the placement of the verbal complement of negation, yet (20a) is ill-formed but (20b) is not.

(20) (a.) *__*No*__ nitekititoc
no ni-tekiti-toc
not 1S-work-DUR
"I'm not working."
(b.) Amo **estoy trabajando**
amo estoy trabaja-ndo
not be/3Ss work-DUR
"I'm not working."

These examples indicate that restrictions on CS are far more pervasive than the head-complement relation alone, and appear to move well beyond issues of phrase structure alone.

18.4   Minimalism

18.4.1   The lexicalist advantage

The importance of constructing a theory of CS that does not appeal to CS-specific mechanisms has been emphasized throughout the history of the field. However, in essential respects, the theoretical contexts in which many influential theories were formulated did not provide the tools needed to permit the implementation of a constraint-free theory of CS. An approach to syntax which built structure from the top down, as in the *Aspects* and later GB models, postponed lexical insertion until well after the word order had been laid out, posing a significant problem. The structure could not be sensitive to which language contributed a specific lexical item until the end, when lexical insertion occurred, but the language contributing the lexical item appeared to have strong consequences for the syntactic structure at the onset.

The desire to avoid CS-specific mechanisms in accounts of CS goes beyond issues of elegance and economy. The more serious problem is that such mechanisms threaten to trivialize the enterprise. Rather than explaining descriptive restrictions observed in CS data, CS-specific mechanisms simply note these restrictions within the grammar itself so that no explanation is needed, and so one is left still wondering what general principles of grammar might be at work in posing the observed restrictions. Within the Minimalist Program, structures are built from a stock of lexical items, essentially beginning with lexical insertion (formalized as *Select*). This important development permits CS researchers to probe the structural consequences of particular lexical items from specific languages, with no need to keep track of which languages may contribute which specific lexical elements during a final stage of lexical insertion.

18.4.2   The Minimalist Program

X' Theory effectively eliminated phrase structure grammar in favor of the view that structures are projected from lexical items; however, remnants remained, with reference to lexical insertion rules reasonably common among GB era syntacticians (Chomsky 1981; Stowell 1981; Lasnik and Uriagereka 1988). Apparent redundancies among various modules of grammar within the GB framework were troubling. Subcategorization, θ-Theory, and X' Theory all appeared to approach the same basic problems from a different angle, with none sufficient to manage the full array of issues associated with the base generation of an initial phrase marker. According to Chametzky (2003), the "lexical entry driven" approach to syntax was part of the general effort underlying X' reduction, with significant contributions from Stowell (1981) and Speas (1990), among others. With a return to its derivational roots, Minimalist syntax reduced generation to the simplest possible form – free *Merge* (Chomsky 1991, 1994), building structures from the ground (the lexical string) up (the hierarchical phrase structure), based on the specification of lexically encoded features. Independently, Borer (1984) had suggested an account of language variation in which parameters were also associated with the lexicon, rather than with the system of syntactic rules. Hence, the system of rules could be seen as invariant, with all variation associated with the lexicon, the traditional repository of arbitrariness.

In the Minimalist Program there are two components of grammar: C_{HL}, a computational system for human language, believed to be invariant across languages; and a lexicon, to which the idiosyncratic differences observed across languages are attributed. An operation called Select picks lexical items from the lexicon and introduces them into a *Numeration* or *Lexical Array* (LA), a finite subset of the lexicon used to construct a derivation. Merge takes items from the LA and forms new, hierarchically arranged syntactic objects. Movement operations (*Internal Merge*) apply to syntactic objects formed by Merge to re-arrange elements within a tree (Chomsky 1995, 2000). Phrase structure trees are thus built derivationally by the application of the operations Select and Merge, constrained by the condition that lexically encoded features match in the course of a derivation.

Movements are driven by feature valuation, and may be of two types. A head may undergo head movement and adjoin to another head, or a maximal projection may move to the specifier position of a head. In either case, the element moves for the purpose of valuing morphological features of case and φ (number, person, and gender). In addition, its movement may be overt or covert. Overt movements are driven by strong features and are visible at PF (Phonetic Form, where they are pronounced) and LF (Logical Form, where they are interpreted). Covert movements, driven by weak features, are visible only at LF.

Principles of Economy select among convergent derivations. One such principle, Full Interpretation (FI), requires that no symbol lacking a sensorimotor interpretation be admitted at PF. Applied at LF, FI entails that "every element of the representation have a (language-independent) interpretation" (Chomsky 1995:27). Thus, uninterpretable features (denoted -Interpretable) must be checked and deleted by LF. The +Interpretable features are categorial features plus φ-features of nominals; the +Interpretable features do not require valuation (checking). A derivation is said to converge at an interface level (PF or LF) if it satisfies FI at that level; it converges if FI is satisfied at both levels. A derivation that does not converge is also referred to as one that crashes. If features are not valued, the derivation crashes; if they mismatch, the derivation is canceled (that is, a different convergent derivation may not be constructed).

At some point in the derivation, an operation, Spell-Out, applies to strip away from the derivation those elements relevant only to PF; what

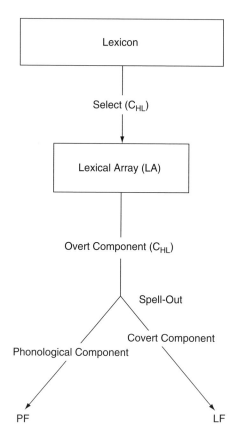

Figure 18.1 Model of the minimalist framework

remains is mapped to LF by a subsystem of C_{HL} called the *covert component*. The subsystem of C_{HL} that maps the lexicon to Spell-Out is the *overt component*. The phonological component is also regarded as a subsystem of C_{HL}. Note that the various components (overt, covert, phonological) are all part of C_{HL}, the computational system for human language. The model could be represented graphically as in Figure 18.1 (MacSwan 1999a).

It may be helpful to consider some illustrations of how feature checking drives movement in the Minimalist Program. As mentioned, movement may be of two types: (1.) a head (or X^0) moves by adjunction to another head, forming a complex X^0; or (2.) an XP moves to the Specifier position of another XP. Movement is driven by a need to value features, and the configuration into which the element moves for feature valuation constitutes its Checking Domain. XP movement is illustrated in (21). The tree in (21a) is formed by successive application of Merge, which uses lexically encoded categorial features (e.g. V, N, D, T) to build a classical phrase structure representation. The subject bears a case feature. T is a nominative case assigner that attracts the case feature of the subject to its Specifier position, bringing the full DP along. Because case is an uninterpretable feature, it must be valued and deleted before LF, or the derivation will crash. Hence, the DP is attracted to T, and moves to its Checking Domain, the Spec[ifier] of TP, as shown in (21b).

(21)   (a.)

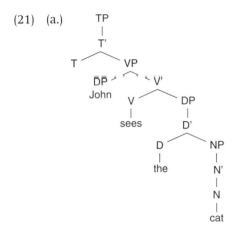

     (b.)

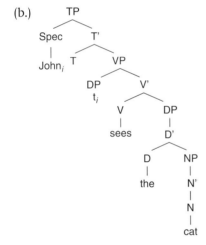

There are some terminological departures from earlier generative models. TP, or Tense Phrase, replaces IP, Inflection Phrase; DP, or Determiner Phrase, is headed by a determiner and dominates NP, as illustrated. The subject originates in a VP-internal position, following Koopman and Sportiche (1991), raising to the Spec of T to check its case feature. t is the trace of movement, co-indexed by i, as in classical approaches. Chomsky (1994, 2000) adopts a bare phrase structure approach, dispensing with intermediate bar levels when they are not relevant to output conditions. As is traditionally done, we have simplified aspects of the structure in (21) (and elsewhere) that are not relevant in the present context.

Now consider an example of head movement, illustrated in (22). The successive application of Merge results in the formation of a base structure. As in (21), the subject DP moves out of the VP shell to check its case feature. The resulting structure is shown in (22a). V, a head, moves to T by head adjunction in order to value and delete its φ-features, as shown in (22b).

(22) (a.)

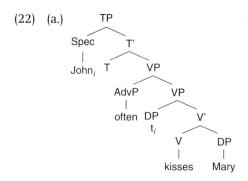

(b.)

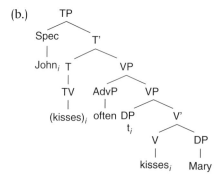

Feature strength (weak, strong) is the primary mechanism in the MP used to account for cross-linguistic variations in word order. Notice, for instance, the contrast in (23).

(23) (a.) John often kisses Mary
      (b.) John completely lost his mind
      (c.) Jean embrasse souvent Marie
      (d.) Jean perdit complètement la tête

In English, VP-adverbs precede verbs, but in French they follow them. We might assume, then, that in English V moves to T covertly, attracted by T's weak φ-features. This is represented in (22b) with the use of parentheses around the verb, illustrating that the phonetic features of the V have been left behind. By contrast, in French, T has strong φ-features, resulting in overt movement. In this case, all of V's features raise, with the result that it appears before its adverbial modifier in (23).

Feature strength can similarly be used to account for word order differences in the case of XP movement. For instance, if the case feature of T is strong, then the subject DP must move overtly out of its VP shell, bringing along its phonetic content. Overt movement of the subject DP results in preverbal subject word order (as in English, French, or Spanish). However, if the case feature is weak, then the subject DP will move covertly, resulting in postverbal word order (e.g. in Irish, Breton, or Zapotec). Let us now turn to an analysis of CS data within the Minimalist Program.

18.4.3 The analysis of code-switching in the Minimalist Program

The leading aim of the Minimalist Program is the elimination of all mechanisms that are not necessary and essential on conceptual grounds alone. Thus, only the minimal theoretical assumptions may be made to account for linguistic data, privileging more simplistic and elegant accounts over complex and cumbersome ones. These assumptions would naturally favor accounts of CS that make use of independently motivated principles of grammar over those that posit rules, principles, or other constructs specific to it. MacSwan (1999b, 2004) presents this research program in the context of the Minimalist Program as in (24), where the minimal CS-specific apparatus is assumed.

(24) Nothing constrains code-switching apart from the requirements of the mixed grammars.

Notice that (24) does not use "constrain" in a descriptive sense, to imply that there are no unacceptable code-switched sentences. Rather, constrain is used in its technical sense here, to mean that there are no statements, rules, or principles of grammar which refer to CS. In other words, (24) posits that all of the facts of CS may be explained just in terms of principles and requirements of the specific grammars used in each case. More formally, the claim is that for G_x a grammar of Lx and Gy a grammar of Ly, CS falls out of the union of the two grammars ($\{Gx \cup Gy\}$) and nothing more (MacSwan 1999a). In this respect ungrammaticality in CS is understood to relate to mechanisms motivated for the analysis of monolingual language, or which are conceptually necessary for reasons of optimal design.

Note that our conception of these conflicts is very much determined by our conception of the organization of the grammar. In classical GB theory, parametric differences were generally assumed to be properties of the computational system. For instance, noting that some subjacency violations of the English variety are acceptable in Italian, Rizzi (1982) proposed that the bounding nodes for the Subjacency Principle were parameterized (NP and IP in English, NP and CP in Italian). On this conception of parametric variation, in which the computational system itself differs across languages, it is very difficult to know how a conflict in language-specific requirements should be precisely defined. In an Italian–English mixed construction, for instance, what determines whether the sentence will be sensitive to IP or CP as a bounding node for the purposes of the Subjacency Principle? The answer depends upon which computational system is in use (Italian or English), and it is very unclear what factors might determine this in the absence of a system permitting CS-specific constraints to mediate conflicts.

In a Minimalist approach to CS which adheres to the research agenda stated in (24), lexical items may be drawn from the lexicon of either language to introduce features into the lexical array, which must then be valued (and deleted by LF, in the case of uninterpretable features) in just the same way as monolingual features must be valued, with no special mechanisms permitted. In this lexicalist approach, no CS-specific mechanism is required to mediate contradictory requirements of the systems in contact. The requirements are simply carried along with the lexical items of the respective languages.

18.4.3.1   Code-switching in head movement contexts

The contrast in (25), a repetition of (20), illustrates the inadequacy of analyses of CS focused exclusively on lexical categories labels (e.g. N, V, D, Adj, Neg).

(25)   (a.) ***No** nitekititoc
            no ni-tekiti-toc
            not 1S-work-DUR
            "I'm not working."
       (b.) Amo **estoy trabajando**
            amo estoy trabaja-ndo
            not be/PRES/1Ss work-DUR
            "I'm not working."

Although Spanish and Nahuatl have the same basic word order requirements with respect to negation, and the same basic functional and semantic properties are common to both examples, Spanish negation does not permit a Nahautl verb in its complement position in (25a), but Nahuatl negation followed by a Spanish verb is well-formed in (25b). The question of interest for (25) becomes, what lexically encoded properties distinguishing Nahautl and Spanish negation can reasonably be identified as the cause of the ill-formedness in one case but not in the other?

Zagona (1988) argues that Spanish *no* is a syntactic clitic and forms part of the Spanish verbal complex as a result of head movement. To make a case for this analysis, Zagona points out that Spanish *no* must be fronted with the verb in (26), unlike the adverbs in (27).

(26) ¿Qué no dijo Juan?
      what not say/1Ss/PAST Juan
      "What didn't Juan say?"

(27) (a.) *¿Qué sólo leyó Juan?
           what only read/1Ss/PAST Juan
           "What did Juan only read?"
      (b.) *¿Qué meramente leyó Juan?
           what merely read/1Ss/PAST Juan
           "What did Juan merely read?"

Zagona (1988) also points out that Spanish *no* cannot be contrastively stressed in (28a) as its English counterpart in (28b) can be, owing to the fact that clitics are inherently unstressable. The example in (28b) shows that in English, in contrast to Spanish, the negative element is not a syntactic clitic.

(28) (a.) *Juan no ha *no* hecho la tarea
           Juan not has not done the task
           "Juan hasn't not done the task."
      (b.) Juan hasn't *not* done the task

These facts suggest that in Spanish, the verb is a host for negation. Nahuatl, on the other hand, behaves differently from Spanish with regard to negation. A test similar to the one Zagona uses in (28) shows that Nahuatl patterns with English. Since clitics are inherently unstressable, we may conclude from (29) that *amo* is not a clitic in Nahuatl.

(29) Amo nio *amo* niktati nowelti
      amo ni-o amo ni-k-tati no-welti
      not 1S-go amo 1S-3Os-see my-sister
      "I'm not going to not see my sister."

The facts suggest the possibility of a ban on CS in head movement contexts. Such a ban, were it to be attested in a wide range of cases, would only serve as a descriptive generalization, not itself an explanation. An explanation would seek to derive the generalization from independent properties of grammar that prohibit cross-linguistic mixing in these contexts.

Restructuring is a well-studied and classic example of head movement. According to Rizzi (1982), Italian modals, aspectuals, and motion verbs comprise the class of restructuring verbs, which behave differently from other verbs, as illustrated in the Italian examples in (30) and (31).

(30) (a.) Finalmente si comincerà a costruire le nuove case popolari
           finally *si* begin/FUT to build the new houses people/GEN
      (b.) Finalmente le nuove case popolari si cominceranno a costruire
           "Finally we'll begin to build the new houses for the poor."

(31) (a.) Finalmente si otterrà di costruire le nuove case popolari
           finally *si* get.permission/FUT to build the new houses people/GEN

(b.) *Finalmente le nuove case popolari si otterranno di costruire
"Finally we'll get permission to build the new houses for the poor."

In Rizzi's analysis, *comincerà* "will begin," but not *otterrà* "will get per-mission," triggers an optional reanalysis of the form Vx (P) V$_2$ ⇒ V, where Vx is a verb of the restructuring class, (P) an optional intervening preposition, and V$_2$ is the verb of the embedded sentence. This restruc-turing process may be seen as a type of compounding by way of head movement, resulting in [$_V$ Vx V$_2$]. In (30) a reanalysis of the constituents allows the object of the embedded clause in an impersonal *si* construction to move to the subject position of the matrix clause; in (31) this promo-tion is barred because reanalysis cannot apply for *otterrà*. Importantly, reanalysis is optional in Italian; it has applied in (30b), allowing the pro-motion of the embedded object to subject position, but it has not applied in (31a) where the object of the embedded clause remains *in situ*.

Aspectual *essere* is used with a past participle in Italian passive imperso-nal *si* constructions. In constructions such as (32a), *essere* too may be viewed as a restructuring verb, allowing promotion of the embedded object to subject position, shown in (32b).

(32) (a.) Si è dato un regalo
           si essere given a gift
           "A gift is given."
      (b.) Un regalo si è dato
           a gift *si* essere given
           "A gift is given."

Within Rizzi's system, restructuring has applied to (32b) but not to (32a), forcing the promotion of [$_{NP}$ *un regalo*] in the former case (see Wurmbrand 1997; Roberts, 1997 for more recent studies of restructuring).

Examples involving the promotion of an embedded subject to the matrix clause correspond with restructuring of the verb complex by means of head movement. To test further whether CS is prohibited in head move-ment contexts, we may examine cases of CS in this context. Consider the French–Italian CS in (33).

(33) (a.) Si è **donné un cadeau**
           si essere given a gift
      (b.) ***Un cadeau** si è **donné**
           a gift si essere given

The movement of [$_{NP}$ *un cadeau*] indicates that reanalysis has occurred in (33b), just as it did in (32b). The verbal complexes are identical in (33a) and (33b): a mixture of the Italian aspectual auxiliary *è*, immediately adjacent to the French past participle *donné*.

Once again, the facts appear to indicate that CS in restructuring config-urations, an instance of head movement, is prohibited, leading us to conclude that a general ban on CS in head movement contexts is at play. As emphasized, the ban so stated is a descriptive generalization. In considering how such a prohibition might arise, we may develop a better understanding of how language mixing in bilinguals is constrained as an independent property of the language faculty, perhaps owing to conditions on interface levels within the organization of the grammar itself.

18.4.3.2 Code-switching and conditions on interface levels

Chomsky (2000, 2001a) and Boeckx and Stjepanovic (2001) have recently suggested that head movement is a phonological operation. The motivation for the idea derives from a need to address a range of issues in syntactic theory. In the context of CS research, associating head movement with the phonological component suggests some common ground between the ban on CS in head movement contexts and the prohibition against word-internal CS noted by Poplack (1981). In both instances, switching from one phonological representation to another within a word-like unit is disallowed. Recall Poplack's (1980) classic examples of the ban on word-internal mixing of the sort illustrated in (34).

(34) a. *Juan está **eat**-iendo
          Juan be/1Ss eat-DUR
          "Juan is eating."

      b. *Juan **eat**-ó
          Juan eat-PAST/3Ss
          "Juan ate."

      c. *Juan com-**ed**
          Juan eat-PAST
          "Juan ate."

      d. *Juan **eat**-ará
          Juan be/1Ss eat-FUT/3Ss
          "Juan will eat."

In cases such as (34), CS occurs within a single syntactic head, a structure represented in (35a). In the head movement cases, CS occurs in the context of a complex head, as in (35b).

(35) (a.)

      (b.)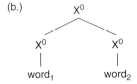

In order to remain true to our goal of positing no CS-specific constraints, the ban on switching in word-internal and head movement contexts may not be declaratively stated as a constraint on syntax, but must be derived from independent principles. As indicated in Figure 18.1, at Spell Out a derivation is split, with features relevant only to Phonetic Form (PF) sent to the phonological component where the phonological system maps them to PF, and interpretable material is treated by further application of the syntactic component in the mapping to Logical Form (LF) in anticipation of semantic interpretation.

A common assumption in CS research is that the linguistic identity of a word (as "Spanish" or "English" or "Arabic") is established by its morphological and phonological characteristics (Lipski 1978; Pfaff 1979; Woolford 1983; Di Sciullo et al.1986; Mahootian 1993; MacSwan 1999a, 1999b). For instance, the word *taipiar* may derive from English *type*, but *taipiar* is regarded as a "Spanish word" because it has phonological and morphological properties that are generally compatible with the grammar of the community of speakers known as "Spanish speakers." The same is true of nonce or novel borrowings. In an important respect, then, CS research is concerned with interface conditions on morphophonology and syntax across discretely represented linguistic systems.

The Minimalist framework assumes that processes of word formation apply before an item is introduced into the Lexical Array when syntactic operations begin (see Figure 18.1) (Chomsky 1995:20). Chomsky (1995, 1998) stresses that the phonological system has a dramatically different character from the syntactic system. Specifically – with π indicating the PF representation, λ the LF representation, and N the initial collection of lexical items – Chomsky (1995:229) posits that:

> ... at the point of Spell-Out, the computation splits into two parts, one forming π and the other forming λ. The simplest assumptions are (1) that there is no further interaction between computations and (2) that computational procedures are uniform throughout: any operation can apply at any point. We adopt (1), and assume (2) for the computation from N to λ, though not for the computation from N to π; the latter modifies structures (including the internal structure of lexical entries) by processes very different from those that take place in the N $\rightarrow$ λ computation.

We assume that affixation interacts with phonology (at least) pre-lexically (before items are selected into the Lexical Array), and that phonology is sensitive to word boundaries or discrete syntactic heads.

What properties of the grammar might explain the prohibition against switching head-internally, banning language mixing in structures such as (34)? Current approaches in phonology posit that lexical form (input) is mapped to the surface form (output) in one step, with no intermediate representations, and hypothesize that phonological constraints are prioritized with respect to each other on a language-specific basis. Each set of internally ranked constraints is a constraint dominance hierarchy, and a language-particular phonology is a set of constraint dominance hierarchies (see McCarthy 2002). Since language-particular phonologies differ with respect to their internal rankings, we might reasonably posit that bilinguals have a separately encapsulated phonological system for each language in their repertoire in order to avoid ranking paradoxes resulting from the availability of distinct constraint dominance hierarchies with conflicting priorities. This property of the bilingual language faculty emerges as a result of the design constraints imposed by the phonological system; without it, bilingualism would not be possible. It further leads us to anticipate that phonological systems may be switched between syntactic heads but not within them, since every syntactic head must be phonologically parsed at Spell Out, and the mapping of phonological structure occurs in a single step, with no intermediate representations and therefore no opportunities for switching from one phonological system to another. We state the condition as in (36) as the PF Interface Condition.

(36)   *The PF Interface Condition*

    (i.) Phonological input is mapped to the output in one step with no intermediate representations.

    (ii.) Each set of internally ranked constraints is a constraint dominance hierarchy, and a language-particular phonology is a set of constraint dominance hierarchies.

    (iii.) Bilinguals have a separately encapsulated phonological system for each language in their repertoire in order to avoid ranking paradoxes, which result from the availability of distinct constraint dominance hierarchies with conflicting priorities.

    (iv.) Every syntactic head must be phonologically parsed at Spell Out. Therefore, the boundary between heads (words) represents the minimal opportunity for CS.

By stipulating that syntactic heads subject to phonological parsing include both simple and complex heads, as illustrated in (35), we extend (36) to both word-internal CS and CS in head movement contexts. We might alternatively posit that head movement is itself a phonological operation that first builds a complex sequence of phonological features deriving from both adjoined heads, then attempts to subject them to phonological processing as a single word-like unit.

We may now appeal to the PF Interface Condition to account for the ban on CS in head movement contexts. Because the condition follows from independently motivated properties of the grammatical system, it complies with the research agenda articulated in (24), namely, the supposition that there are no rules or principles of grammar that refer to CS. We turn to a final example, CS among languages that differ with respect to their basic word order requirements, calling upon the PF Interface Condition to help identify syntactic properties of lexically null functional categories.

18.4.3.3   Explaining basic word order differences

Within the Minimalist Program, we assume a universal SVO base structure with a VP-internal subject. If the subject overtly raised to the specifier position of T^0 within this structure, an SVO order would result, with the subject pronounced above the verb. However, if the subject raises covertly, the resulting word order is VSO. The distinction between overt and covert movement is implemented in terms of feature strength. Weak features may be valued without pied-piping the phonetic content of a lexical item, while strong features require that the phonetic content comes along as well. Thus, the typological distinction between SVO and VSO languages may be captured in terms of the strength of the case feature in T^0 that triggers movement of the VP-internal subject.

Now consider the following CS facts involving mixing between SVO and VSO languages (see Chan, this volume):

(37)   (a.)   VS verb (Irish), SV subject (English)
> Beidh ***jet lag*** an tógáil a pháirt ann
> be-FUT . . . taking . . . its part in-it
> "Jet lag will be playing its part in it."

(Stenson 1990:180)

(b.)   VS verb (Irish), SV subject (English)
> Fuair sé ***thousand pounds***
> get-PAST he ..
> "He got a thousand pounds."

(Stenson 1990:180)

(c.)   VS verb (Breton), SV subject (French)
> Oa ket ***des armes***
> be-3S IMP NEG of-the . . .
> "There were no arms."

(Pensel 1979:68)

(d.)   VS verb (SLQ Zapotec), SV subject (Spanish)
> S-to'oh **mi esposa el coche**
> DEF-sell my wife the car
> "My wife will definitely sell the car."

(MacSwan 2004:305)

Descriptively, the pattern appears to be that the language of the verb determines the placement of the subject. A verb from a VS language places a subject after the verb, regardless of the language of the subject.

As in the analysis of monolingual examples, we assume that V^0 raises to T^0 to value its φ-features, forming a complex head via head adjunction, as illustrated in (22b). In the previous section, we noted a general prohibition against CS in head movement contexts, deriving from a condition at PF imposed by the architecture of the phonological system. In the present context, the condition guarantees that in any convergent derivation, T^0 is in the same language as V^0 if V^0-to-T^0 raising has occurred. As a result, the language of the verb restricts which language may contribute T^0, and the strength of the value of the case feature of T^0 is guaranteed to be consistent with the language of the verb. The analysis proceeds as follows. In the examples involving CS between a VS verb and an SV subject, the VP-internal subject raises to the specifier position of T^0 to value its case feature, as previously illustrated by (21b). Because the case feature of T^0 is weak in VS languages, the subject raises covertly, resulting in the attested VS word order. More concretely, consider (25d). The Spanish subject *mi esposa* raises to the specifier of Zapotec T^0 to value its case feature, weak for Zapotec, resulting in covert movement and VS word order.

Now consider the placement of objects in CS contexts. If an object moves covertly out of the VP-shell to the specifier position of v (a preverbal position), then the elements remain in the order SVO at PF. If the object moves overtly, however, an SOV word order is derived. The parameter responsible for this difference is associated with v. If the case feature of v is weak, SVO is formed; if it is strong, SOV results. The verb undergoes a checking relation with v by head movement as it moves up to T, guaranteeing once again that the language of the verb will determine the position of the object, just as in the case of subjects. The expected results are attested:

(38) (a.) VO (English) verb, OV object (Farsi)
           Tell them you'll buy ***xune-ye jaedid*** when you sell your own house
           tell them you'll buy house-POSS new when you sell your own house
           "Tell them you'll buy a new house when you sell your own house."
           (Mahootian 1993:152)

      (b.) OV verb (Farsi), VO object (English)
           Ten dollars ***dad-e***
           Ten dollars give-PERF
           "She gave ten dollars."
           (Mahootian 1993:150)

      (c.) VO verb (English), OV object (Japanese)
           … we never knew ***anna koto nanka***
           … we never knew such thing sarcasm
           " … we never knew such a thing as sarcasm."
           (Nishimura 1985a:76)

      (d.) OV verb (Japanese), VO object (English)
           In addition, his wife ***ni yattara***

in addition, his wife DAT give-COND
"In addition, if we give it to his wife ..."

(Nishimura 1985a:129)

(e.) VO verb (English), OV object (Korean)
I ate ***ceonyek*** quickly
I ate dinner quickly
"I ate dinner quickly."

(Lee 1991:130)

(f.) OV verb (Korean), VO object (English)
Na-nun ***dinner***-lul pali meokeotta
I-s dinner-o quickly ate
"I ate dinner quickly."

(Lee 1991:129)

18.5   Future directions of the field

A strong consensus in the field of CS, nearly since its inception, has been that a good theory of CS, minimally, is one that appeals to no "third grammar" (Pfaff 1979) or CS-specific device to regulate the interaction of the two systems. However, early non-lexicalist models of syntax posed a significant problem for this goal. In traditional non-lexicalist frameworks, words are only inserted into grammatical structures after they have been built, making it difficult to design a system of grammar that would be sensitive to the language-specific identity of words inserted into a phrase marker. Within the lexicalist proposals of more recent models within generative syntax, the lexicon itself projects the phrase structure, defines movements of elements within the tree, and encodes features responsible for essentially all aspects of language variation. This system thus permits us to identify in a concrete manner which specific features and array of values we should expect to see in any CS construction.

Minimalism, then, provides a framework that permits us to abandon the quest for constraints on CS, and engage in the linguistic analysis of mixed-language utterances in very much the same way we engage in the analysis of monolingual language. Over time, this research project promises to enhance our understanding of the nature of bilingualism, CS, and the architecture of the bilingual language faculty. Very much the same process is at work in contemporary linguistic theory quite generally, as Chomsky (1957:5) noted at the onset of the generative enterprise:

The search for rigorous formulation in linguistics has a much more serious motivation than mere concern for logical niceties or the desire to purify well-established methods of linguistic analysis. Precisely constructed models for linguistic structure can play an important role, both negative and positive, in the process of discovery itself. By pushing a precise but inadequate formulation to an unacceptable conclusion, we can often expose the exact source of this inadequacy and, consequently, gain a deeper understanding of the linguistic data.

Although the field of CS has its origins in sociolinguistics, where it has been fruitfully studied by scholars interested in discourse and conversational analysis, it also shares important characteristics with psycholinguistics – more specifically, with the study of language acquisition. In both enterprises, one makes specific assumptions about the special circumstances of language use, and engages in extensive and detailed linguistic analysis in the interest of verifying, rejecting, or refining them. Recent developments in the field of CS have permitted us to move beyond traditional battles over which proposed CS-specific constraint is accurate and which is not, calling upon us to examine CS in the context of specific constructions, operations, and grammatical features across a wide range of language pairs (see Chan, this volume). The goal, as the field continues on its present course, is to propose increasingly better theories about the nature of the bilingual language faculty as a reflection of the facts of CS, informing the field of bilingualism as well as general linguistic theory.

Note

1. Sankoff (1998) provides a speech production model of CS which he believes is consistent with The Equivalence Constraint, but with similar limitations.

19

A universal model of code-switching and bilingual language processing and production

Carol Myers-Scotton
and
Janice Jake

19.1 Introduction

The Matrix Language Frame (MLF) model (Myers-Scotton 1993a, 1997), augmented by the 4-M model of morpheme classification (Myers-Scotton and Jake 2000; Myers-Scotton 2002a), provides a major linguistic theory of language contact dedicated to bilingual processing and production. This model has inspired many studies of bilingual speech within diverse language pairings and accounts for a variety of bilingual behaviors, principally code-switching (hereafter CS). Unlike most other approaches to CS, the MLF model enjoys widespread appeal among linguists and psycholinguists alike.

19.1.1 No chaos allowed: the Uniform Structure Principle

This chapter elaborates and illustrates the research program framed by the MLF model. What is new is that it emphasizes how a principle of uniform structure drives the explanation of what does and does not occur in CS. The first goal of this chapter is to show how the Uniform Structure Principle (USP) implies a particular view of processing and production in bilingual speech, especially in CS. *Bilingual speech* is defined as surface level morphemes from two or more language varieties in the same clause. With the 4-M model, the USP clarifies and strengthens the Matrix Language Frame (MLF) model, as a model of CS. A succinct way of viewing the USP is the phrase, "no chaos allowed." This may be obvious for monolingual speech; that it applies to bilingual speech is not so obvious. *A priori*, the ways in which languages participate in bilingual speech are unconstrained. In particular, the source of grammatical structure within a bilingual clause could be shared in any number of ways. But this does not happen.

For bilingual speech, "no chaos allowed" means a particular asymmetry between the participating languages. This is formalized in the USP, as follows:

A given constituent type in any language has a uniform abstract structure and the requirements of well-formedness for this constituent type must be observed whenever the constituent appears. In bilingual speech, the structures of the Matrix Language (ML) are always preferred. Embedded Language (EL) islands (phrases from other varieties participating in the clause) are allowed if they meet EL well-formedness conditions, as well as those ML conditions applying to the clause as a whole (e.g. phrase placement).   (cf. Myers-Scotton 2002a)

The second goal here is to make more explicit how specific morphemes are classified under the 4-M model and to show how differences in morpheme type explain their distribution in CS. These distributions will be shown to reflect the USP. In doing this, the chapter focuses on CS in general, but gives special attention to prepositions, complementizers, and pronouns.

First, the MLF model of CS and its relation to the USP is summarized. Next, the view of language production motivated by empirical CS data and the MLF model is outlined, as is the 4-M model and how it relates to the USP and the MLF model. Finally, the descriptive sections of the chapter are shown to support the theoretical goal of explaining the asymmetries that pattern CS data. With the USP as an overarching framework in which the MLF and 4-M models add specific hypotheses, a set of principled predictions emerges about what does and does not occur in CS. These predictions should have relevance to other types of contact phenomena as well.

19.2   Summary of the MLF model

The key feature of the MLF model is that it differentiates both the participating languages and morpheme types at a number of abstract levels. It emphasizes asymmetry, claiming crucially a dominant role in the bilingual clause for only one of the participating languages, the ML. That is, reflecting the USP, the MLF model limits the EL's main role to providing either content morphemes in mixed constituents or EL phrase-level constituents (EL islands), or both. Asymmetry under the model also differentiates content and system morphemes and their participation in CS. The model assumes that these two asymmetries apply universally in Classic CS and empirical evidence largely supports this. *Classic CS* is defined here as CS in which empirical evidence shows that abstract grammatical structure within a clause comes from only one of the participating languages. Which of the participating languages is the ML is determined for each corpus. Within a corpus, the ML may vary from clause to clause, although this is unusual.

The MLF model has always defined content and system morphemes differently from those classifications based on the lexical vs. functional distinction, or the open vs. closed class distinction. Specifically, system morphemes are not the same as the functional elements or closed-class items in other linguistic models. They are defined in opposition to content morphemes. Content morphemes are defined as assigning or receiving thematic roles; system morphemes do not. Prototypical system morphemes are affixes and some function words that are free forms but do not occur alone, such as determiners and clitics.

The MLF model contains two principles that can be interpreted as hypotheses about the differing roles of the participating languages. These were first presented in Myers-Scotton (1993a, 1997:82) as the Morpheme Order Principle (MOP) and the System Morpheme Principle (SMP). They specify the elements in a bilingual constituent that must come from only one participating language; in effect, support of these principles identifies this language as the ML.

19.2.1 Exemplifying the MLF model

Example (1) comes from a corpus of Turkish–Dutch CS, where elements from the EL appear in italics. Turkish is verb-final, and in this example the inflected (main) verb *yap* "do" occurs after its predicate (the Dutch infinitive), not before it as it would in Dutch. This configuration supports the MOP, which states that only one of the participating languages supplies morpheme order in such constituents. Note as well that all instances of subject–verb agreement come from Turkish. This supports the SMP, which states that only one of the participating languages supplies a certain type of system morpheme (SM), now called an outsider late SM under the 4-M model. Subject–verb agreement is such a morpheme. Based on the example's support of the MOP and the SMP, Turkish is identified as the ML.

(1) *Turkish–Dutch*
     O diyor ben **uitmak-en**   yap-tı-m diyordu kız-ınam
     he say.PROG.3SG 1SG finish-INF do-PRET - 1SG say.IMP.3SG girl-with
     "He says 'I broke up with a girl'."

                                                              (Backus 1992:107)

Example (2) supports both principles as well. Note the order of *certificate* and its modifiers; they follow Swahili word order, not that of English. In addition, although the main verb is from English (*depend*), subject-agreement, an outsider morpheme, (*i-*, class 9) comes from Swahili, agreeing with a subject mentioned before (*saa hiyo* is an introductory phrase, not the subject). These data support Swahili as the ML in this example.

(2)   *Swahili–English*
Ø-saa hi-yo i-na-***depend***   na Ø -***certificate*** z-ako
c.9-time DEM-c.9 c.9-non-PAST-depend with c.10-certificate c.10-your
z-a Ø-shule
c.10-ASSOC c.10-school
"At this time, it depends on your school certificates."

(Myers-Scotton 2004:108)

19.2.2   Three premises summarizing the MLF model

Three basic premises have always structured the MLF model (Myers-Scotton 1993a, 1997):

(1.) Participating languages do not play equal roles in the bilingual clause.
(2.) In bilingual constituents within this clause, not all morpheme types can come equally from the ML and EL.
(3.) The SMP limits the occurrence of system morphemes that build clausal structure of the ML.

19.2.3   Relating the MLF model to other data

The implicit domain of the MLF model always has been participating varieties that are not mutually intelligible. It may well apply to other varieties, but that would be an unintended bonus. As already noted, the model applies only to what is defined above as Classic CS. This type of CS contrasts with Composite CS in which the abstract grammatical structure underlying surface configurations still comes largely from one language, but also partially from another. The Abstract Level model (see Myers-Scotton and Jake 2001; Myers-Scotton 2002a) is especially relevant to Composite CS. More research may show Composite CS to be more common than Classic CS. The USP applies to both types of CS, of course, to the extent there is an ML, and so does the 4-M model; both are universal.

19.3   The language production model

A general language production model of four levels, the conceptual level, the mental lexicon, the formulator, and the surface level (see Levelt 1989) accommodates CS and other contact phenomena. The conceptual level is pre-linguistic, and includes speaker intentions, as well as other cognitive components, such as memory. The critical factor in resolving competition at the conceptual level is which lemma entry (either from the ML or the EL) best conveys the speaker's semantic and pragmatic intentions (La Heij 2005). Intentions activate semantic and pragmatic features that are bundled together, pointing to language-specific lemmas in the mental lexicon.

If CS becomes part of the cognitive plan, the ML is selected at the conceptual level. Speakers must be able to produce well-formed utterances for the language selected as the ML because it provides the grammatical frame of the bilingual clause; they may be less proficient in the EL, but are not necessarily so. Often the ML is the speakers' L1, although not necessarily. Selecting a language as the ML is largely unconscious, although the process draws on various resources, especially the participant's cognitive system (i.e. memory about social aspects of contexts compared with the nature of current contexts).

But satisfying semantic and pragmatic intentions at the conceptual level is not the only issue. CS data imply a matching process – checking – between the abstract requirements regarding the structural well-formedness of the ML and a potential EL element in a bilingual clause (Myers-Scotton and Jake 1995). This is referred to as *congruence checking*. There must be some degree of semantic match, but more critical is a grammatical match.

Lemmas in the mental lexicon include directions that map semantic information to grammatical structure, directions needed at the next level, the formulator. Thus, lemmas contain information beyond word meaning about thematic roles and selectional restrictions that have syntactic consequences, such as argument structure. For example, the verb *hit* assigns the thematic roles of Agent and Patient to a subject and object, respectively. Other lemmas in the mental lexicon underlie late SMs that become salient at the level of the formulator and will build syntactic structure (see §19.4.1).

Lemmas point to language-specific morpho-syntactic constraints located in the formulator. The formulator assembles larger constituents. The mental lexicon also contains language-specific Generalized Lexical Knowledge (GLK) that reflects the grammatical competence of speakers in their languages (Myers-Scotton and Jake 1995; Myers-Scotton 2002a). GLK plays an important role in congruence checking between languages and explains how EL lemmas without close ML counterparts occur in CS because their features can be checked against ML Generalized Lexical Knowledge.

Incomplete congruence can have repercussions for CS. Significant incongruence may mean that optimal CS mixed constituents with EL elements entirely framed by the ML do not occur. Instead, compromise strategies such as entire, well-formed phrases in the EL (EL islands), may occur. Sometimes EL content morphemes occur in ML frames as bare forms, without the SMs that would make the phrase well-formed in the ML. Note that the occurrence of bare forms implies that the ML is an abstract construct and not necessarily identical with the morpho-syntax of the language that is its source.

19.4 The 4-M model

The 4-M model does not replace the MLF model; rather, it offers a more precise description of morpheme types by viewing them in terms of their syntactic roles and how they are activated in language production. For convenience, the model employs the term "morpheme" to refer both to the abstract entries in the mental lexicon that underlie surface realizations and to the surface realizations themselves. The model separates out three types of system morpheme: early SMs, and two types of late SMs, bridges and outsiders. The MLF model's SMP is often misunderstood as applying to *all* SMs. However, it was always intended to constrain only one type of SM, now called outsiders (Myers-Scotton 1993a, 1997:82). The 4-M model keeps the division between content and system morphemes, but explicitly recognizes significant divisions between morpheme types.

The primary division is between morphemes that are conceptually-activated (e.g. nouns and verbs) and those that are structurally-assigned (e.g. AGR elements). Content morphemes are conceptually-activated. They are based on the speaker's pre-linguistic intentions; recall the semantic/pragmatic feature bundles that speakers' intentions activate. But early SMs (e.g. plural affixes) are also conceptually-activated; they flesh out the meaning of their content morpheme heads that "indirectly elect" them (see Bock and Levelt 1994). Because they are structurally-assigned, late SMs contrast with both content morphemes and early SMs in an important way with many ramifications for both monolingual and language contact data.

19.4.1 The Differential Access Hypothesis

In CS, and in line with what the USP would predict, the distribution of morpheme types across the ML and EL is quite different. Not only are there distribution differences between content and system morphemes, but also within the category of SMs itself. Recognizing this motivates new ways of classifying morphemes and leads to the 4-M model. In turn, how the 4-M model classifies morpheme types leads to a hypothesis that abstract differences at the production level account for surface level differences in morpheme types. The Differential Access Hypothesis (DAH) offers an explanation for the observed differences. The DAH is the following:

The different types of morpheme under the 4-M model are differentially accessed in the abstract levels of the production process. Specifically, content morphemes and early SMs are accessed at the level of the mental lexicon, but late SMs do not become salient until the level of the formulator.

(cf. Myers-Scotton 2002a:78, 2005a)

The hypothesis suggests the following scenario. As already noted, lemmas underlying content and early SMs send language-specific directions to the formulator to build larger linguistic units. To build these units, these directions contain information about assigning late SMs. These late SMs become salient only when they are structurally-assigned at the formulator. Separating the activation of abstract elements underlying surface

morpheme types echoes Garrett's view that "major and minor grammatical category words behave quite differently" (1993:81). However, he and
others, such as Ullman (2001), who posits that the grammar and lexicon
are two separate systems, do not differentiate the distribution of different
types of SMs.

This theory differs from contemporary linguistic theories that project
"functional" elements as the heads of maximal projections. The following
sections exemplify EL morphemes in CS in terms of SM types, showing
how their distribution follows the USP and implies the DAH.

19.4.2 Early SMs

Early SMs are so-designated because they, along with their content morpheme heads, become salient in the mental lexicon as the basic building
blocks of constituent structure, such as NP, VP, AP. Yet, they are still SMs
because only content morphemes receive and assign thematic roles. Early
SMs typically occur with the content morpheme heads that select them.
Early SMs may be free or bound. For example, definite articles are early
SMs but always occur with nouns in English.

Plural and derivational affixes are examples of early SMs. Unfortunately,
to date, few studies include quantitative evidence on the distribution of
either type of early SM. However, in one quantitative study considering
determiners in bilingual NPs in a Spanish–English corpus, 151/161 (94%)
of English nouns in well-formed mixed NPs occur with Spanish determiners, such as *el **garage*** (Jake et al. 2002). Because Spanish can be
identified as the ML, the overwhelming number of these mixed NPs
supports the USP because ML structure is maintained in these NPs even
though the noun is from English. However, as early SMs, definite articles
can come from the EL without violating the SMP, and occasionally do, as
in Palestinian Arabic–English CS *el pharmacy is very boring [. . .]* (Okasha
1999:110).

Verb satellites (also called particles) that occur with what are often
called phrasal verbs are also early SMs because they depend on their
heads for their appearance and they add meaning to their heads. Under
the MLF model, these and other derivational morphemes may come from
the EL because they are not the type of morpheme that the SMP restricts.
EL phrasal verbs often appear with their EL verb satellites. An example
from Swahili–English CS shows this, *u-na-**chase after*** ("you are chasing
after"), as does another example from Arabic–English: [an engine is]
locked up. In an Ewe–English example, an Ewe object suffix -*e* "him" can
attach to the verb, as required in Ewe, but the particle remains in the EL,
English: ***keep**-e **away from*** *Eun* ("keep him away from Eun") (Amuzu
1998:53). That Ewe supplies the third person singular object suffix
shows how the USP is supported as grammatical structure from the ML
is maintained.

19.4.2.1 Plural markers as early SMs

Perhaps the most common early SM studied in Classic CS corpora is the plural marker. The language of origin of the plural marker in CS varies in four ways: the possible combinations are these: (1.) EL plural marking only, (2.) no plural marking at all, (3.) ML plural marking only, (4.) plural marked from both the EL and ML.

(1.) Most often, plural is marked on an EL noun by its EL plural affix, but no overt ML affix, as in Welsh–English CS in the phrase: *y* **motorway-s** *na'r* **dual carriageway-s** ("on the motorways nor the dual carriageways") (Deuchar 2006). In a Moroccan Arabic–Dutch example, *duk* **artikel-en** ("those articles"), the Dutch (EL) noun occurs with a Dutch plural suffix, but its plural determiner from Arabic (ML) shows agreement, thereby maintaining ML structure and the USP's dictates (Boumans 1998:37). In example (3) *workers* has no ML plural marking, but its agreements indicate that the EL noun is operating as a class 2 Swahili noun. The demonstrative *hawa* ("these") and the associative *wa* ("of") show plural agreement (class 2).

(3) *Swahili–English*
Mbona ha-wa **worker-s** wa **East Africa Power and Lighting** wa-ka-end-a **strike** [. . .]
Why dem-c.2 worker-PL c.2-ASSOC East Africa Power and Lighting c.2-CONSEC-go strike
"Why did workers of East Africa Power and Lighting go [on] strike [. . .]?"

(Myers-Scotton 1993a, 1997:96)

In some language pairs with morphologically rich MLs, this is a frequent pattern. Even though an EL noun occurs without the ML plural marker, there is evidence that the ML assigns plurality features to the EL noun (see Myers-Scotton 2002a:127–31).

(2.) In some language pairs, an EL noun appears with no plural markings. In *na* **date** *zingine* ("with other dates") from Swahili–English, even though *date* has no plural at all, its modifier (*zi-ngine*) has a prefix from noun class 10 (*zi-*), indicating **date** is intended as a class 10 plural.

(3.) Perhaps less frequently, but still often, an ML affix marks plurality and there is no EL plural affix. For example, a Turkish (ML) plural suffix (*-lar*) occurs in the otherwise Dutch (EL) phrase **klant**-*lar* **wegjag-en** (customer-pl away-chase-INF "chase away customers") (Boeschoten 1991:90).

(4.) Finally, sometimes both EL and ML early SMs occur with an EL content morpheme head; they are usually affixes. Both convey plurality, although they may contain other information as well. This "double morphology" can occur with other early SMs, but occurs most often with plural affixes. For example, in the Acholi–English example *lu-civilian-s* ("the civilians"), Acholi *lu* encodes both definiteness and plural (Myers-Scotton 2005d) and English *-s* also encodes plural.

19.4.2.2 Early SMs and internal EL islands

When an EL early SM, particularly a plural marker, occurs with its EL content morpheme head, it often occurs in a construction of EL elements framed by the ML, as in Spanish–English *tant-a-s* **thing-s** ("so.many-FEM-PL thing-s"). In such instances, early SMs together with their content morpheme heads are small EL islands (internal EL islands). These islands are well-formed in the EL, but are part of a larger mixed constituent framed by the ML. They are like other EL islands, but are smaller than phrasal level constituents, full EL islands (e.g. the PP, **on the weekend**). Many internal EL islands contain the crucial "chunks" of collocations that are then framed by the ML (see Backus 2003, on multi-morphemic "chunks"). For example, French–English *la* **real thing** (King 2000:100), Cajun–French *le* **highest class** (Brown 1986:404), and *sa* **little salary** (see (4) below) do not occur as maximal EL constituents. Instead, they occur framed by an ML element. This is evidence that the USP is observed in bilingual speech whenever possible.

(4) *Wolof–English*
     Sa **little salary** rek la [. . .]
     2SG.POSS little salary only 3SG.COP [. . .]
     "It is only your little salary, [. . .]"

(Haust 1995:52)

19.4.3 Late system morphemes

In contrast to early SMs, two types of late SMs are structurally-assigned. The term "late" suggests that they are not activated until a later production level. While early SMs largely build semantic structure, late SMs build syntactic structure. These late SMs are labeled "bridges" and "outsiders." The DAH, discussed in §19.4.1, explains observable differences in data distribution by postulating a fundamental difference in how late SMs are accessed. It states that not all morphemes become salient at the same level of language production. Information about content morphemes and early SMs is available at the level of the mental lexicon; late SMs do not become salient until the level of the formulator. The role of late SMs is to construct larger constituents out of conceptually-activated morphemes; they assemble phrases and connect phrases to realize full clauses. Put simply, late SMs satisfy the requirements of the USP that constituents maintain a consistent structure. "The late system morphemes [. . .] indicate relationships within the clauses; they are the cement that holds the clause together" (Myers-Scotton 2006a:269).

19.4.3.1 Bridge late SMs

Bridge late SMs provide "bridges" between elements that make up larger constituents. There is an important difference between bridge SMs and outsider SMs. For information about their form (and, indeed, their presence), bridges depend on information *within* their maximal projection, while outsider SMs depend on information *outside* the maximal projection in which they appear. Also, bridges seem to have an invariant form (they constitute a single allomorph); in contrast, outsiders seem to be part of a paradigm or conjugation (with more than one allomorph). English *of* is an example of a bridge SM, as in *requirements of the college*; so is *'s* in *Lena's shoe*. In French, *de* is an equivalent bridge, as in *le français de Bruxelles* ("the French of Brussels"). Example (5) shows a similar bridge from Hindi (*kii*) with a partitive meaning.

(5) *Hindi–English*
    merii paatnii saaRii kii **choice** kar-egii
    my wife saree of choice do-FUT.3SG.FEM
    "My wife will choose a saree."

    (Ritchie and Bhatia 1999:273)

Because language-specific requirements for phrasal well-formedness vary, bridges are required in some languages, but not in others. For example, in many languages, weather expressions require a bridge. In these expressions, the subject pronoun does not receive a thematic role, e.g. French **il** *pleut* or English **it** *is raining*. In such expressions, the pronoun *it* is different from referring indefinite/antecedent third person singular *it*, a content morpheme in English (as in *Where is the book? It is on the table.*). Similarly, in American English, in certain expressions, determiners are bridges, not early SMs, as in this exchange: *Where's John? He had to go to* **the** *hospital.* No definite hospital is indicated.

In CS corpora, most bridges come from the ML. Example (6) from an Acholi–English corpus shows a bridge *me* coming from the ML, Acholi. In the entire corpus, an English bridge occurs in only one formulaic EL island (*cost* **of** *living*). Altogether, 42 Acholi associative constructions have at least one NP from English.

(6) *Acholi–English*
    Chances me **accident** pol ka i-**boarding taxi**
    chances ASSOC accident many if 2SG-board taxi
    "[The] chances of [an] accident [are] many if you board [a] taxi."

    (Myers-Scotton 2005d:12)

EL bridges occur very rarely in mixed constituents, although there is an exception noted in the literature. When Arabic is the EL, sometimes it supplies the bridge *djal* in a clause framed by French as in French–Moroccan Arabic *connaissance* **dyal** *la personne* "knowledge of the person" (Bentahila and Davies 1998:38). The presence of *dyal* in such cases does not violate the SMP. It is clearly a bridge SM, not an outsider.

19.4.3.2   Outsider late SMs

The second type of late SM is the outsider. As noted above, this morpheme type differs from bridges in that the presence and form of an outsider depends on information that is outside of the element with which it occurs. This information can come from another element in another constituent, or from the discourse as a whole. For example, subject–verb agreement is realized by outsider late SMs. However, in pro-drop languages, a late SM may be co-indexed with a null pronoun, whose relevant grammatical features come from the larger discourse. For example, in Spanish, the *-en* on the verb *corr-en* (run-3PL) is a late SM when it occurs as *los estudiantes corren* ("the students run") or simply *corren* ("[they] run").

There is good evidence from various sources that outsiders behave differently from other morphemes in many linguistic phenomena – see Myers-Scotton and Jake (2000) on Broca's aphasia and second language acquisition; Myers-Scotton (2002a) on speech errors and attrition; Myers-Scotton (2003) on split or mixed languages; and Wei (2000a) on second language acquisition. There is also scattered evidence in the literature about the distinctive distribution of outsiders in various contact phenomena. For example, Johanson (1998:251–3) notes that Turkic languages frequently borrowed conjunctions from other languages, but they "practically never" borrowed what he calls "relators." These relators include case markers, which are outsider SMs.

Certainly, outsiders are the most crucial and unambiguous purveyors of grammatical structures. They provide a more precise indexing of relations that extends beyond word order and basic constituent structure. Outsiders "knit together elements at another level" (Myers-Scotton 2005c:25). The grammatical relations indexed by outsiders reinforce semantic coherence within the clause and within the larger discourse. Furthermore, "[t]hese characteristics are the basis for an argument that outsider morphemes are the main bastion for maintaining uniform structure [the USP] in a clause" (2005c:25). Given that these characteristics define outsiders, it follows that the distribution of outsider late SMs should be the most defining feature of Classic CS – and it is. With few exceptions, outsiders always come from the ML in mixed constituents.

In some CS data sets, ML outsiders as AGR features occur with EL verbs, as in example (7): the third person singular prefix *i-* on *appartenir* shows subject–verb agreement, referring to *richesse*, the subject of the clause. The object prefix *-tu-* ("us") refers to the speaker and previously mentioned others. In addition, the class 9 prefix *y-* on *y-ote* ("of all") is also an outsider, as is the prefix on *y-ake* ("his").

(7) *Shaba Swahili–French*
    Donc, (h)ii **richesse** y-ote (h)ii i-na-tu-***appartenir*** shi
    So, c.9.DEM riches c.9-all c.9.DEM c.9-NON-PAST.OBJ.1PL-belong us
    ba-toto y-ake
    c.2-child c.9-his
    "So, all these riches, it belongs to us, his children."
                                                        (De Rooij 1996:186)

When the ML is a language with case assigning verbs (and/or preposi-tions), case markers are also outsiders. Almost without exception, EL elements receive the expected ML case marker as in (8), in which Dutch *terras* receives locative case from Turkish. Similarly, in (9), English *grass* is inflected with prepositional case from Russian.

(8) *Turkish–Dutch*
    evet, **terras**-ta oturuyorlar
    yes cafe-LOC sit-PROG.3PL
    "Yes, they are sitting at the outdoor cafe."
                                                        (Backus 1996:140)

(9) *Russian–English*
    Zachem ty na **grass**-e valjajesih'sja
    what-for you.SG on grass-PREP.SG roll-around
    "Why are you rolling around on the grass?"
                                                        (Schmitt 2006)

19.5 An overview of morpheme types

An important advantage of the 4-M model over other approaches to clas-sifying morphemes is that it eliminates the problem that lexical category membership does not predict morpheme type. That is, members of a category need not be members of the same 4-M morpheme type. In fact, in terms of the 4-M model's defining features for morpheme types, some morphemes in the lexical types we consider here (prepositions, pronouns, and complementizers) are content morphemes, but others are early SMs, and still others are either bridge or outsider late SMs. The Chomskyan lexical–functional element dichotomy does not account for these differ-ences. The premises of the 4-M model that allow for such a flexible classi-fication are supported by findings in CS data, other contact phenomena, and evidence from various types of language acquisition and loss. Simply put, not all prepositions, pronouns, or complementizers have the same distribution.

19.5.1 Prepositions
Linguistic theory has long recognized that prepositions do not behave as a uniform class (see e.g. Abney 1987). Under the 4-M model, prepositions

can be content morphemes or any of the three types of SMs. Sometimes the same phonological form fits into more than one category. For example, in *He walked across the street*, *across* assigns a thematic role and is a content morpheme. In CS, content morpheme prepositions can come from the EL, as in (10). There are not many examples of such EL prepositions in mixed constituents; more frequently, they occur in PPs that are EL islands (e.g. *before tomorrow evening*).

(10)   *Swahili–English*
       Labda, [. . .] ***bring it at my home***. U-let-e ***before*** kesho jioni.
       perhaps, bring it to my home. 2SG-bring-SUBJUNCT before tomorrow
       evening
       "Perhaps you should bring it to my house. You should bring it before
       tomorrow evening."
                                                          (Myers-Scotton 1993a, 1997:124)

Some prepositions can also be indirectly elected at the conceptual level, and are then early system morphemes: in *he comes across as ill-prepared*, *across* occurs with *come*, its content morpheme head. The discussion in §19.4.2 above includes examples in which prepositions are satellites of phrasal verbs, and suggests that the satellite comes from the same language as the verb, either EL or ML verb. However, sometimes such early SMs occur in the EL even when the verb is in the ML. In (11), the expression "change [something] around" is realized in both Spanish and English, with English supplying the preposition *around*.

(11)   *Spanish–English*
       Sabes   los cambian ***around***
       know.PRES.2SG them change.PRES.3PL around
       "You know they change them around."
                                                          (Pfaff 1979:303)

Sometimes prepositions are late SMs that are not activated until the level of the formulator; these primarily contribute structure, and not content. For example, prepositions that are bridge SMs make a phrasal constituent well-formed. Although EL bridge prepositions can occur in mixed constituents, very few actually do. As noted above in some French–Arabic CS, Arabic *djal* (equivalent to "of") occurs in associative constituents in French-framed CPs. Below are discussed some instances of EL bridges that occur with more frequency, namely, Comp bridges.

Some locative prepositions are bridges; they do not encode directionality or motion, but locate a figure with respect to a ground (see Talmy 2000). For example, in *Joe's in school*, *in* adds little conceptual information to the mapping of the theme (*Joe*) to the ground (*school*). Such bridge prepositions show variation (e.g. *Joe's at school*). However, *in* can also be a content morpheme or an early SM. In *He's all done in*, *in* is an early SM. Further, *in* is a content morpheme in *In this example, they illustrate the distinction*; like other content morphemes, the thematic role assigned by *in* can be questioned, as in *Where do they illustrate the distinction?*

In some languages, prepositions are also outsiders. Consider Spanish *a*. It can be a content morpheme assigning directionality, as in *va **a** Hamburg* "he/she goes to Hamburg," or an early SM, as in *miremos **al** año que viene*, ("we are looking forward to the coming year") (*al* = *a* + *el* "to+the.m.def"). As a bridge, it connects purpose infinitives with matrix CPs, as in *prepare **a** venir* ("prepare to come"). Finally, *a* occurs as an outsider when it assigns case to animate direct objects, as in *veo **a** Eva* "I see Eva." The prediction is that as ML, Spanish will supply personal *a* to objects in mixed constituents, as in *refieres a tus coworkers* ("you are talking about your coworkers") (Jake et al. 2002), but that as EL, Spanish NP animate objects do not have to occur with personal *a*, as in *the police officers have seen **un ladrón*** ("The police officers have seen a thief") (Belazi et al. 1994:230).

The 4-M model articulates how morphemes are classified. Even so, the fact that one prepositional form can be activated at more than one level and is thus subject to different conditions in CS demands careful analysis. The SMP requires that all outsider prepositions come from the ML in mixed constituents. The distribution of bridges in most CS also supports the USP; one language, the ML, provides most of the grammatical frame.

19.5.2   Pronouns

Pronouns are another lexical category that is not uniform because they can be members of any of the four morpheme types (see Jake 1994). Some are content morphemes; i.e. they occur in argument position and receive thematic roles. As content morphemes, EL pronouns can occur in clauses framed by the ML. For example Klintborg (1995) reports English pronouns in Swedish-framed clauses in Swedish–American English CS, as in *När vi var hemma sista gånge **me and** min hustru* ("When we were home last time me and my wife") and *[. . .] **he** var smed för tyket* ("[. . .] he was a blacksmith by trade").

But even when pronouns are content morphemes, EL pronouns occur very infrequently except in EL islands. Why? First, preference is for ML elements. Also, ML counterparts play a role. When pronouns in the ML are clitics or affixes licensing null pronouns in argument position, they are outsider SMs and must come from the ML (see the Blocking Hypothesis (Myers-Scotton 1993a, 1997:120) which requires congruence with the ML).

However, EL content morpheme pronouns that establish topics or contrast occur widely in bilingual clauses. They convey both conceptual and procedural information, as noted by Wilson and Sperber (1993:21). Example (12) shows an English pronoun within a Malay grammatical frame, expressing a "dual notion of fusion and contrast" (Jacobson 2000;68).

(12)   *Malay–English*
       Oh! About the recent controversy? I tak bersetujulah kalau **women stay at home**.
       Oh! About the recent controversy? I not agree-emph if . . .
       "Oh! About the recent controversy? I don't agree that women should stay at home."

Other examples from diverse language pairs abound. Haust (1995) includes examples of Mandinka emphatic pronouns occurring in English-framed CPs and Wolof-framed CPs. English contrastive topic pronouns occur in Spanish-framed CPs, as in **You** *estás diciéndole* [sic] *la pregunta* **in the wrong person** ("You are asking the question in the wrong person") (Sankoff and Poplack 1981:13).

   Some researchers have commented on "pronoun doubling," as in (13), but this is not the true doubling that occurs with early SMs. Each pronoun is activated independently and occurs in a separate position in the bilingual CP. In (13), for example, the Arabic discourse emphatic pronoun *nta* ("you") is adjoined under Comp and the French *tu* ("you") is an agreement clitic not in argument position. A null pronoun is assumed to occur in subject position. In (14), Arabic *?ihna* ("we") is adjoined under Comp and English *we* occurs in subject position.

(13)   *Morrocan Arabic–French*
       nta **tu va travailler**
       2SG.EMPH 2SG go work-INF
       "You, you are going to work."
                                                  (Bentahila and Davies 1983:313)

(14)   *Palestinian Arabic–English*
       ?iħna **we are supposed to be** nudris-**ing**
       1PL.TOP . . . study-PROG
       "We, we are supposed to be studying."
                                                  (Myers-Scotton et al. 1996:27)

And in the Spanish–English example cited above, the English emphatic pronoun *you* is a topic, and a Spanish null pronoun occurs as the subject.

   In sum, the distribution of pronouns in CS reflects their classification under the 4-M model. The requirements of the MLF model foreshadow the import of this classification. Both the SMP, which requires ML outsider pronouns in mixed constituents, and the Blocking Hypothesis, which requires cross-linguistic congruence, imply how critical it is to recognize morpheme type at the abstract level of clause construction. Taken together, they maintain the integrity of the frame in line with the USP.

19.5.3 Complementizers and other clause connectors

Complementizers and complementizer-like elements are similar to prepositions and pronouns in not showing a uniform distribution in CS. In current syntactic theory, COMP is the head of any clause identified as CP, projection of Complementizer. Variation among COMP elements themselves and cross-linguistic variation in their patterning in CS complicate their discussion. Also, there is no uniform agreement regarding what elements are rightly classified under COMP. Complementizers include not just elements such as *that*, but also subordinating conjunctions, relative clause markers, other elements that indicate clause boundaries, and even coordinating conjunctions. These elements are discussed according to how they are elected and how they participate in the construction of a CP.

Like pronouns, most complementizers convey procedural knowledge. Many constrain the truth-conditions of propositions and participate in the discourse-thematic structure of propositions. For example, *porque* "because" in (15) assigns a discourse-level thematic role of Cause or Reason.

(15) *Spanish–English*
   trabajé menos porque ***then I didn't know some of his business***
   work.PRET.1SG less because . . .
   "I worked less because then [i.e. at that time] I didn't know some of his business."

(Pfaff 1979:312)

Most complementizers straddle two CPs. In this way, they are at the intersection between inter-sentential CS and intra-sentential CS. In example (15), *porque* is the head of the subordinate CP (hereafter CP2), yet it is within the domain of a matrix clause (hereafter CP1), and is in the language of CP1.

19.5.3.1 Overview of complementizer types

Several factors play a role in determining the source of complementizers. These include the type of morpheme, the grammatical requirements of the participating languages, and the overall pattern in the discourse. Complementizers from one of the participating languages are preferred if that language is typically the ML in mixed constituents throughout the corpus.

Under the 4-M model, some complementizers and complementizer-like elements are bridge SMs, especially complementizers such as "*that*." Similar complementizers are multi-morphemic elements that include a bridge and an outsider SM. For example, in Arabic, *?inn-* ("that-") occurs with a suffix agreeing with the subject of CP2. Finally, many subordinators and coordinators are content morphemes (e.g. French *alors* "then" or German *aber* "but"). In many corpora, content morpheme subordinators and coordinators tend to come from the ML of either CP. In (15) above, *porque* comes from the ML of CP1.

19.5.3.2   The language of the complementizer

If CS occurs at the clause boundary, is the complementizer in the language framing CP1 or CP2? It appears that in some language pairs, the complementizer can come from either language. In Spanish–English CS, for example, *que* can introduce an English CP (see 16), and *that* can introduce a Spanish CP (see 17). However, the complementizer can also be in the ML of CP2, as in (18) and (19).

(16)   Tonces salió eso que she wanted to take mechanics
        "Then it turned out that she wanted to take mechanics."
                                                        (Lipski 1978:258)

(17)   They sell so much of it that   *lo están sacando* y many people [. . .]
        . . . it be.3PL take-PART and . . .
        "They sell so much of it that   they're taking it out and many people
        [. . .]"
                                                        (Pfaff 1979:312)

(18)   **Sí**, but the thing is *que empiezan bien recio* and [. . .]
        "Yes, but the thing is that [(they)] start[3PL] pretty fast and [. . .]"
                                                        (Pfaff 1979:315)

(19)   El profesor dijo *that the student had received an A*
        "The professor said that the student had received an A."
                                                        (Belazi et al. 1994:234)

19.5.3.3   *That*-type complementizers as bridges

The distribution of complementizers such as *that* and *que* supports their analysis as bridge SMs. *That*-like complementizers allow a larger constituent, a multi-clause structure, to be constructed out of an embedded CP and a matrix CP. And unlike content morphemes and early SMs, bridges convey little representational meaning. In this way, *that*-like complementizers are different from other complementizers such as *when* and *before*, and their equivalents across languages.

It is not surprising that bridge complementizers can come from either language with CS at clause boundaries. This is because, although bridges join two constituents together, they are invariant placeholders satisfying well-formedness conditions for the larger unit. In some language pairs, *that*-like complementizers come from one specific participating language, regardless of the ML of CP1 or CP2. For example, in Chicheŵa–English CS, the bridge complementizer always comes from Chicheŵa, as in (20). In Simango's (1996) corpus, *kuti* introduces over 20 English-framed clauses, but *that* never introduces any English clauses.

(20) *Chicheŵa–English*

[. . .] a-ka-tsimikiz-e kuti **this was the end**
[. . .] 3SG-CONSEC-confim-SUBJUNCT that . . .
"[. . .] he confirms that this was the end."

(Simango 1996)

This suggests that language-specific factors are involved. For example Chicheŵa requires a complementizer, whereas English does not.

19.5.3.4 Outsider complementizers

As noted above, Arabic *?inn-* agrees with the subject of CP2. In Arabic–English CS, these multi-morphemic complementizers always come from Arabic. For example, Okasha (1999) reports that *?inn-* introduces 10 clauses entirely in English, as in (21), and 15 bilingual clauses framed in English. No English complementizers occur with Arabic clauses.

(21) *Palestinian Arabic–English*

kaan el-**doctor** yišuk ?innu **it is not reliable**
PERF.3MASC.be the-doctor imperf.3MASC.doubt that.3MASC it is not reliable
'[he] was, the doctor, doubting that it was not reliable'

(Okasha 1999:71)

In the case of Arabic–English CS, the USP is better satisfied when the complementizer comes from the ML of CP1. This configuration means that the following IP (clause) is in the EL of CP2. That is, *?inn-* does not just bridge two CPs; it coindexes an embedded CP with the ML of CP1, and frames the entire multi-clausal constituent in one language, Arabic. Thus the English clause in (21) is an embedded IP island (and English is not the ML of CP2).

Not only are Arabic bridge complementizers inflected with outsider SMs, but so are subordinators, which are content morphemes in many languages. In (22) *li?anhum* "because" agrees with the third person plural subject *they* of the English IP.

(22) *Palestinian Arabic–English*

[. . .] huma biyidfa9ooli kul haga li?anuhum **they can afford it**
[. . .] they HAB.IMP.3PL.pay.1SG every thing because.3PL . . .
"[. . .] they pay for everything [for me] because they can afford it."

(Okasha 1999:123)

19.5.3.5 Content morpheme complementizers

Adverbial-like subordinators are conceptually-activated content morphemes. They introduce discourse-thematic roles. When they are uninflected, the language of the complementizer can be different from the language of the CP it introduces. Thus, *porque* "because" can introduce an English CP, as in (15) above. And in many other language pairs, the language of such subordinators appears free. For example, in Wolof–French

CS, French subordinators introduce clauses that are bilingual or mixed (Swigart 1992a, 1992b, 1992c).

Under the 4-M model, most coordinating conjunctions are also content morphemes. They reflect procedural knowledge and are truth conditional, although some have more procedural content than others. In (23), English conjoins two Xhosa clauses.

(23)   *Xhosa–English*
       [...] ba-se-msebenzi-ni **and** umalume be-ka-khal-a kude ku-na-thi [...]
       [...] 2.PL-LOC-work-LOC and my.uncle PST of-stay-FV far LOC-have-us
       [...]
       "[...] they were at work and my uncle lived far from us [...]"
                                                        (Myers-Scotton 2005b)

19.5.3.6   Summary: The language of the complementizer

In summary, although EL complementizers do not appear in CS as freely as some categories, participation largely depends on their morpheme type. EL subordinators and coordinators, usually content morphemes, are quite robust. However, subordinators or *that*-like complementizers that include an outsider seem to always come from the ML, even when the outsider depends on a CP2 whose clause is otherwise framed by the EL. *That*-like complementizers which are bridges are a mixed bag. With some languages, these complementizers must come from the ML, with others they do not.

When the complementizer of CP2 is in the ML of CP1, it reinforces uniformity across clauses. This suggests that only when the complementizers of the participating languages are congruent enough not to violate language specific requirements do complementizers come from the ML of CP2 (e.g. Spanish–English CS). However, no matter what the morpheme type, whatever ML dominates in the discourse seems to preference complementizers from that language, reflecting a more general organizing principle, the USP.

19.6   Conclusion

One goal of this chapter has been to offer implications for the nature of bilingual production and processing that arise from considering naturally occurring CS corpora in terms of the MLF model and the 4-M model. In turn, this leads us to a more universally applicable characterization of linguistic structure, the Uniform Structure Principle (USP). In bilingual utterances, there is no *a priori* reason to expect uniformity in clause structure; the significance of the principle for contact linguistics is that the USP predicts uniformity. It preferences the structures of only one of the participating languages. The extent to which this principle is supported implies certain preferences for how the cognitive component supporting bilingual speech is structured.

Early researchers in contact linguistics avoided CS, focusing instead on possible contact-induced change or dialectal variation. For example, the father of modern contact linguistics, Weinreich (1954, 1967) famously dismissed bilingual CS clauses in a way that implied that looking for organizing principles in CS was a theoretical dead end. In contrast, the USP, along with the MLF and 4-M models, predict that a principled account of CS is possible. Thus, the mantra of the USP is "no chaos allowed." Such an account depends on premises about predictable divisions between the roles of participating languages and morpheme types. In turn, these divisions motivate a model of language production and present implications about organization within the cognitive components supporting language.

19.6.1   Predictable patterns

The bulk of this chapter is descriptive, but with the theoretical goal of demonstrating how the asymmetries that one finds in CS show a predictable pattern. The goal here has been to demonstrate that the contributions of morphemes of participating languages depend on the four morpheme types and to relate this observation to production. When one views morphemes in terms of these types and in terms of the Differential Access Hypothesis, a principled explanation for differences in their cross-linguistic distributions in CS is forthcoming. Three examples illustrate insights of this chapter.

First, it is predicted that double plural marking on EL nouns is possible, but that double subject–verb agreement or double case marking is not. This disparity is owed to the difference in how these morphemes are accessed in language production. Plural affixes are early SMs while subject–verb agreement and case markers are outsider SMs. EL early SMs can be accessed with their content heads because they are conceptually activated and available in the mental lexicon, but outsiders become salient only later, at the level of the formulator.

Second, a strong preference for the ML to supply "*that*-type" complementizers at clause boundaries is predicted. However, subordinating complementizers are less constrained and they come from either language. The reason again is differences in morpheme type and hypotheses about their production history. *That*-type complementizers are bridge SMs and, although not as critical in building clauses as outsiders, are still part of constituent structure and are salient at the level of the formulator. When they come from the ML, the USP is satisfied. In contrast, many subordinators are content morphemes; they are activated by speakers' intentions (conceptually activated), and are available in the mental lexicon.

Third, prepositions fall into all four types under the 4-M model, but not all types are predicted to come from the EL, or with the same frequency. In fact, EL prepositions do not occur frequently, and this may be because of their role in structuring constituents and the requirement of uniform structure, i.e. the USP. Among prepositions, early SMs are more frequent, perhaps because they allow for an elaboration of pragmatic and semantic structure without creating syntactic structure. Prepositions that are content morphemes (i.e. that assign thematic roles) are the most unconstrained; even so, they are not frequent.

Of the three types of SMs, early SMs are the least constrained because they are conceptually activated, whereas bridges and outsiders are structurally assigned. Even so, the most frequent early SMs seem to be the most contentful ones, plural affixes and definite articles. Only a few types of EL bridge SMs occur, and no EL outsider SMs occur in mixed constituents (except for fairly rare types of EL islands). More research needs to be done on EL islands, but the overall point about prepositions holds for all lexical categories: morpheme type, as discussed at many points above, makes the difference in their distribution.

19.6.2 Cognitive support systems

Such differences in morpheme distribution across languages are systematic and follow from the MLF and 4-M models, as well as the USP; they are also empirically verifiable. However, these differences also imply some speculations about language production and the cognitive systems supporting language. First, the division of labor between languages in CS, with only one language providing the morpho-syntactic frame of the bilingual clause, seems to imply some sort of divisions within the cognitive component supporting this surface asymmetry. Certainly, any intra-clause CS implies that both languages are active during bilingual production, but that the ML has a higher level of activation.

Second, the USP implies that cognitive energy is conserved by allowing only minor-level switches to EL islands. If we look at the frequency with which EL content morphemes are integrated into an ML-framed structure and juxtapose this frequency with the USP's injunction against changing languages, one conclusion is that accessing words from the EL requires a different type or level of activation than creating morpho-syntactic structure.

Third, the role of the EL is explicitly limited. Most obviously, the EL never structures any constituents that include ML morphemes. This means that the EL has little opportunity to supply any outsider SMs to the bilingual clause except in EL islands, but typical EL islands have few structures that would require outsiders. Further, except for occasional early SMs or even less frequent bridge SMs, the EL supplies only content morphemes within constituents structured by the ML. The dearth of outsider SMs from the EL motivates the conclusion that the cognitive component supporting this morpheme type may be independent from that which coordinates simpler syntactic constructions. Keep in mind the complex tasks that this mental architecture must accomplish: outsiders are critical in signaling thematic roles and other relationships of the semantic–syntactic interface; without them, there can be no clause.

19.6.3   Testing hypotheses

Finally, as already noted at many points above, CS data support the DAH that is derived from the 4-M model. This hypothesis suggests a language production model in which some of the elements underlying surface level morphemes are salient at one level and others are not salient until another level. Specifically, late SMs are not salient until they are called by the lemmas underlying content morphemes to construct larger constituents in the formulator. Obviously, the extent to which this hypothesis is supported has relevance beyond CS and other types of contact phenomena to both child and second language acquisition, among other topics. The results of psycholinguistic experiments testing this hypothesis will add crucial support to a language processing model that accommodates the notion of saliencies at different levels (Myers-Scotton 2006b). Not only does this matter for production models, but also for comprehension models.

19.6.4   Supporting the Uniform Structure Principle (USP)

In sum, this chapter has shown how the distribution of morpheme types in Classic CS, at least, is compatible with predictions of the MLF and 4-M models, and the USP. As an empirical window on divisions of labor between participating languages, CS implies intriguing hypotheses about some ways in which language is supported in our cognitive systems.

References

Aarons, Debra and Morgan, Ruth (2003). Classifier predicates and the creation of multiple perspectives in South African Sign Language. *Sign Language Studies*, **3** (2), 125–156.

Abney, Steven (1987). The English noun phrase in its sentential aspect. Ph.D. dissertation, Massachusetts Institute of Technology.

Aboud, Frances E. (1976). Social developmental aspects of language. *Papers in Linguistics*, **9** (3–4), 15–37.

Abutalebi, Jubin; Cappa, Stefano F. and Perani, Daniela (2001). The bilingual brain as revealed by functional neuroimaging. *Bilingualism: Language and Cognition*, **4** (2), 179–190.

Abutalebi, Jubin; Miozzo, Antonio and Cappa, Stefano F. (2000). Do subcortical structures control "language selection" in polyglots? Evidence from pathological language mixing. *Neurocase*, **6** (1), 51–56.

Adams, James N. (2003). *Bilingualism and the Latin language*. Cambridge, UK and New York: Cambridge University Press.

Adams, Margarita G. (2003). *Historia de la educación de los sordos en México y Lenguaje por Señas Mexicano [History of the education of the deaf in Mexico and Mexican Sign Language]*. San Diego, CA: Dawn Sign Press.

Aglioti, Salvatore (1997). The role of the thalamus and basal ganglia in human cognition. *Journal of Neurolinguistics*, **10** (4), 255–265.

Aglioti, Salvatore; Beltramello, Alberto; Girardi, Flavia and Fabbro, Franco (1996). Neurolinguistic and follow-up study of an unusual pattern of recovery from bilingual subcortical aphasia. *Brain*, **119** (5), 1551–1564.

Aglioti, Salvatore and Fabbro, Franco (1993). Paradoxical selective recovery in a bilingual aphasic following subcortical lesions. *Neuroreport*, **4** (12), 1359–1362.

Agnihotri, Rama Kant (1979). Processes of assimilation: A sociolinguistic study of Sikh children in Leeds. Ph.D. dissertation, University of York.

Aguirre, Adalberto, Jr. (1985). An experimental study of code alternation. *International Journal of the Sociology of Language*, **53**, 59–81.

Aikhenvald, Alexandra Y. (2003). Multilingualism and ethnic stereotypes: The Tariana of Northwest Amazonia. *Language in Society*, **32** (1), 1–21.

Aitchison, Jean (1996). *The seeds of speech: Language origin and evolution.* Cambridge, UK and New York: Cambridge University Press.

Alexander, Garrett E. and Crutcher, Michael D. (1990). Functional architecture of basal ganglia circuits: Neural substrates of parallel processing. *Trends in Neurosciences*, **13** (7), 266–271.

Alfonzetti, Giovanna (1998). The conversational dimension in code-switching between Italian and dialect in Sicily. In P. Auer (ed.), *Code-Switching in Conversation: Language, Interaction and Identity*, pp. 180–211. London and New York: Routledge.

Al-Khatib, Hayat (2003). Language alternation among Arabic and English youth bilinguals: Reflecting or constructing social realities? *International Journal of Bilingual Education and Bilingualism*, **6** (6), 409–422.

Allen, Shanley; Genesee, Fred; Fish, Sarah and Crago, Martha (2001). Patterns of code-mixing in English-Inuktitut bilinguals. In M. Andronis, C. Ball, H. Elston and S. Neuvel (eds.), *CLS 37: The Panels. 2001. Proceedings from the Parasessions of the Thirty-seventh Meeting of the Chicago Linguistics Society: 37th Annual Meeting of the Chicago Linguistics Society*, pp. 171–188. Chicago: Chicago Linguistics Society.

Altarriba, Jeanette; Kroll, Judith F.; Sholl, Alexandra and Rayner, Keith (1996). The influence of lexical and conceptual constraints on reading mixed-language sentences: Evidence from eye fixations and naming times. *Memory & Cognition*, **24** (4), 477–492.

Altarriba, Jeanette and Mathis, Katherine M. (1997). Conceptual and lexical development in second language acquisition. *Journal of Memory and Language*, **36** (4), 550–568.

Alvarez, Ruben P.; Holcomb, Phillip J. and Grainger, Jonathan (2003). Accessing word meaning in two languages: An event-related brain potential study of beginning bilinguals. *Brain and Language*, **87** (2), 290–304.

Alvarez-Caccamo, Celso (1998). From "switching code" to "code-switching": Towards a reconceptualisation of communicative codes. In P. Auer (ed.), *Code-switching in conversation: Language, interaction and identity*, pp. 29–50. London and New York: Routledge.

Amuzu, Evershed (1998). Aspects of grammatical structure in Ewe–English codeswitching. M. A. dissertation, University of Oslo.

Andersen, Elaine and Johnson, Carolyn (1973). Modifications in the speech of an eight-year-old to younger children. *Stanford Occasional Papers in Linguistics*, **3**, 149–160.

Andersen, Elaine S. (1990). *Speaking with style: The sociolinguistic skills of children.* London and New York: Routledge.

Andersen, Roger W. (1982). Determining the linguistic attributes of language attrition. In R. D. Lambert and B. F. Freed (eds.), *The Loss of language skills*, pp. 83–118. Rowley, MA: Newbury House.

Androutsopoulos, Jannis (2006). Mehrsprachigkeit im deutschen Internet: Sprachwahl und sprachwechsel in Ethno-Portalen. In P. Schlobinski (ed.), *Duden thema Deutsch, Band 7. Von "hdl" bis "cul8r": Sprache und kommunikation in den Neuen Medien*, pp. 172–196. Mannheim: Dudenverlag.

Appel, René and Muysken, Pieter (1987). *Language contact and bilingualism*. London: Edward Arnold.

Ardal, Sten; Donald, Merlin W.; Meuter, Renata; Muldrew, Shannon and Luce, Moira (1990). Brain responses to semantic incongruity in bilinguals. *Brain and Language*, **39** (2), 187–205.

Auer, Peter (1984). *Bilingual conversation*. Amsterdam and Philadelphia: John Benjamins.

Auer, Peter (1988). A conversation analytic approach to code-switching and transfer. In M. Heller (ed.), *Codeswitching: Anthropological and sociolinguistic perspectives*, pp. 187–214. Berlin and New York: Mouton de Gruyter.

Auer, Peter (1995). The pragmatics of code-switching: A sequential approach. In L. Milroy and P. Muysken (eds.), *One speaker, two languages: Cross-disciplinary perspectives on code-switching*, pp. 115–135. Cambridge, UK and New York: Cambridge University Press.

Auer, Peter (ed.) (1998). *Code-switching in conversation: Language, interaction and identity*. London and New York: Routledge.

Auer, Peter (1999). From codeswitching via language mixing to fused lects: Toward a dynamic typology of bilingual speech. *International Journal of Bilingualism*, **3** (4), 309–332.

Auer, Peter (2000). Why should we and how can we determine the "base language" of a bilingual conversation? *Estudios de Sociolingüística*, **1** (1), 129–144.

Auer, Peter (2005). A postscript: Code-switching and social identity. *Journal of Pragmatics. Special Issue: Conversational Code-Switching*, **37** (3), 403–410.

Austin, John L. (1965). *How to do things with words: The William James lectures delivered at Harvard University in 1955*. Oxford and New York: Oxford University Press.

Axelsson, Ann-Sofie; Abelin, Åsa and Schroeder, Ralph (2003). Anyone speak Spanish? Language encounters in multi-user virtual environments and the influence of technology. *New Media and Society*, **5** (4), 475–498.

Azuma, Shoji (1996). Speech production units among bilinguals. *Journal of Psycholinguistic Research*, **25** (3), 397–416.

Azuma, Shoji and Meier, Richard P. (1997). Open class and closed class: Sentence-imitation experiments on intrasentential code-switching. *Applied Psycholinguistics*, **18** (3), 257–276.

Backus, Ad (1992). *Patterns of language mixing: A study in Turkish–Dutch bilingualism*. Wiesbaden: Harrassowitz.

Backus, Ad (1996). *Two in one: Bilingual speech of Turkish immigrants in the Netherlands*. Tilburg, The Netherlands: Tilburg University Press.

Backus, Ad (2000). The role of semantic specificity in insertional codeswitching: Evidence from Dutch–Turkish. In R. Jacobson (ed.), *Codeswitching worldwide II*, pp. 125–154. Berlin and New York: Mouton de Gruyter.

Backus, Ad (2003). Units in code switching: Evidence for multimorphemic elements in the lexicon. *Linguistics*, **41** (1), 83–132.

Backus, Ad (2004). Turkish as an immigrant language in Europe. In T. K. Bhatia and W. C. Ritchie (eds.), *The handbook of bilingualism*, pp. 689–724. Oxford and Malden, MA: Blackwell.

Backus, Ad (2005). Codeswitching and language change: One thing leads to another? *International Journal of Bilingualism*, **9** (3–4), 307–340.

Bahr, Ruth and Frisch, Stefan (2002). The problem of codeswitching in voice identification. In A. Braun and H. R. Masthoff (eds.), *Phonetics and its applications: Festschrift for Jens-Peter Köster on the occasion of his 60th birthday*, pp. 86–96. Stuttgart: Steiner.

Bankston, Carl L., III and Henry, Jacques M. (1998). The silence of the gators: Cajun ethnicity and intergenerational transmission of Louisiana French. *Journal of Multilingual and Multicultural Development*, **19** (1), 1–23.

Barnett, Ruthanna; Codó, Eva; Eppler, Eva; Forcadell, Montse; Gardner-Chloros, Penelope; van Hout, Roeland; Moyer, Melissa; Torras, Maria Carme; Turell, Maria Teresa; Sebba, Mark; Starren, Marianne and Wensing, Sietse (2000). The LIDES coding manual: A document for preparing and analysing language interaction data. *International Journal of Bilingualism*, **4** (2), 131–270.

Barrett, Rusty (1998). Markedness and styleswitching in performances by African American drag queens. In C. Myers-Scotton (ed.), *Codes and consequences: Choosing linguistic varieties*, pp. 139–161. Oxford and New York: Oxford University Press.

Bates, Elizabeth and Liu, Hua (1996). Cued shadowing. *Language and Cognitive Processes*, **11** (6), 577–581.

Bautista, Maria Lourdes S. (2004). Tagalog–English code switching as a mode of discourse. *Asia Pacific Education Review*, **5** (2), 226–233.

Beauvillain, Cécile and Grainger, Jonathan (1987). Accessing interlexical homographs: Some limitations of a language-selective access. *Journal of Memory and Language*, **26** (6), 658–672.

Beebe, Leslie M. (1981). Social and situational factors affecting the communicative strategy of dialect code-switching. *International Journal of the Sociology of Language*, **32**, 139–149.

Belazi, Heidi M.; Rubin, Edward J. and Toribio, Almeida Jacqueline (1994). Code switching and X-bar theory: The functional head constraint. *Linguistic Inquiry*, **25** (2), 221–237.

Bell, Allan (1984). Language style as audience design. *Language in Society*, **13** (2), 145–204.

Bell, Allan (1997). Language style as audience design. In Nikolas Coupland and Adam Jaworski (eds.), *Sociolinguistics: A reader*, pp. 240–250. New York: St. Martin's Press.

Bell, Allan (2001). Back in style: Reworking audience design. In P. Eckert and J. R. Rickford (eds.), *Style and sociolinguistic variation*, pp. 139–169. Cambridge, UK and New York: Cambridge University Press.

Benson, Erica J. (2001). The neglected early history of codeswitching research in the United States. *Language and Communication*, **21** (1), 23–36.

Bentahila, Abdelâli and Davies, Eirlys E. (1983). The syntax of Arabic–French code-switching. *Lingua*, **59** (4), 301–330.

Bentahila, Abdelâli and Davies, Eirlys E. (1992). Code-switching and language dominance. In R. J. Harris (ed.), *Cognitive processing in bilinguals*, pp. 443–458. Amsterdam: Elsevier.

Bentahila, Abdelâli and Davies, Eirlys E. (1995). Patterns of code-switching and patterns of language contact. *Lingua*, **96** (2), 75–93.

Bentahila, Abdelâli and Davies, Eirlys E. (1998). Codeswitching: An unequal partnership? In R. Jacobson (ed.), *Codeswitching worldwide*, pp. 25–49. Berlin and New York: Mouton de Gruyter.

Bentahila, Abdelâli and Davies, Eirlys E. (2002). Language mixing in Rai music: Localisation or globalisation? *Language and Communication*, **22** (2), 187–207.

Bentin, Shlomo and Peled, Bat-Shahar (1990). The contribution of task-related factors to ERP repetition effects at short and long lags. *Memory & Cognition*, **18** (4), 359–366.

Bergman, Coral R. (1976). Interference vs. independent development in infant bilingualism. In G. D. Keller, R. V. Teschner and S. Viera (eds.), *Bilingualism in the bicentennial and beyond*, pp. 86–95. Jamaica, NY: Bilingual Press/Editorial Bilingüe.

Berk-Seligson, Susan (1986). Linguistic constraints on intrasentential code-switching: A study of Spanish/Hebrew bilingualism. *Language in Society*, **15** (3), 313–348.

Bernardini, Petra and Schlyter, Suzanne (2004). Growing syntactic structure and code-mixing in the weaker language: The ivy hypothesis. *Bilingualism: Language and Cognition*, **7** (1), 49–69.

Besson, Mireille; Kutas, Marta and Van Petten, Cyma (1992). An event-related potential (ERP) analysis of semantic congruity and repetition effects in sentences. *Journal of Cognitive Neuroscience*, **4** (2), 132–149.

Bhatia, Tej K. and Ritchie, William C. (1996). Bilingual language mixing, universal grammar, and second language acquisition. In W. C. Ritchie and T. K. Bhatia (eds.), *Handbook of second language acquisition*, pp. 627–688. New York: Academic Press.

Bhatt, Rakesh Mohan (1995). Code-switching and the functional head constraint. In J. M. Fuller, H. Han and D. Parkinson (eds.), *ESCOL '94: Proceedings of the Eleventh Eastern States Conference on Linguistics*, pp. 1–12.

Ithaca, NY: Cornell University, Department of Modern Languages and Linguistics.

Bhatt, Rakesh Mohan (1997). Code-switching, constraints, and optimal grammars. *Lingua*, **102** (4), 223–251.

Bialystok, Ellen (1999). Cognitive complexity and attentional control in the bilingual mind. *Child Development*, **70** (3), 636–644.

Bialystok, Ellen (2006). Effect of bilingualism and computer video game experience on the Simon task. *Canadian Journal of Experimental Psychology*, **60** (1), 68–79.

Bialystok, Ellen; Craik, Fergus I. M.; Klein, Raymond and Viswanathan, Mythili (2004). Bilingualism, aging, and cognitive control: Evidence from the Simon task. *Psychology and Aging*, **19** (2), 290–303.

Bialystok, Ellen; Craik, Fergus I. M. and Ruocco, Anthony C. (2006). Dual-modality monitoring in a classification task: The effects of bilingualism and ageing. *Quarterly Journal of Experimental Psychology*, **59** (11), 1968–1983.

Bialystok, Ellen and Martin, Michelle M. (2004). Attention and inhibition in bilingual children: Evidence from the dimensional change card sort task. *Developmental Science*, **7** (3), 325–339.

Bialystok, Ellen and Shapero, Dana (2005). Ambiguous benefits: The effect of bilingualism on reversing ambiguous figures. *Developmental Science*, **8** (6), 595–604.

Biber, Douglas (1988). *Variation across speech and writing*. Cambridge, UK and New York: Cambridge University Press.

Bijeljac-Babic, Ranka; Biardeau, Agnès and Grainger, Jonathan (1997). Masked orthographic priming in bilingual word recognition. *Memory & Cognition*, **25** (4), 447–457.

Blom, Jan-Petter and Gumperz, John J. (1972). Social meaning in linguistic structure: Code-switching in Norway. In J. J. Gumperz and D. H. Hymes (eds.), *Directions in sociolinguistics: The ethnography of communication*, pp. 407–434. New York: Holt, Rinehart and Winston. Reprinted in Li Wei (ed.) (2000) (q.v.).

Bloomfield, Leonard (1933). *Language*. New York: Henry Holt and Company.

Blot, Kevin J.; Zárate, Michael A. and Paulus, Paul B. (2003). Code-switching across brainstorming sessions: Implications for the revised hierarchical model of bilingual language processing. *Experimental Psychology*, **50** (3), 171–183.

Bock, Kathryn (1996). Language production: Methods and methodologies. *Psychonomic Bulletin and Review*, **3** (4), 395–421.

Bock, Kathryn and Levelt, Willem (1994). Language production: Grammatical encoding. In M. Gernsbacher (ed.), *Handbook of psycholinguistics*, pp. 945–984. New York: Academic Press.

Boeckx, Cedric and Stjepanovic, Sandra (2001). Head-ing toward PF. *Linguistic Inquiry*, **32** (2), 345–355.

Boeschoten, Hendrik (1991). Asymmetrical code-switching in immigrant communities. *Proceedings of the Workshop on Constraints, Methodology and Models of the ESF-Network on Code-switching and Language Contact*, pp. 85–104. Strasbourg: European Science Foundation.

Boeschoten, Hendrik (1998). Codeswitching, codemixing, and code alternation: What a difference. In R. Jacobson (ed.), *Codeswitching worldwide*, pp. 15–24. Berlin and New York: Mouton de Gruyter.

Bokamba, Eyamba G (1989). Are there syntactic constraints on code-mixing? *World Englishes*, **8** (3), 277–292.

Bolle, Jette (1994). Sranan Tongo–Nederlands: Code-wisseling in ontlenig. M. A. dissertation, University of Amsterdam.

Bolonyai, Agnes (1998). In-between languages: Language shift/maintenance in childhood bilingualism. *International Journal of Bilingualism*, **2** (1), 21–43.

Bolonyai, Agnes (2000). "Elective affinities": Language contact in the abstract lexicon and its structural consequences. *International Journal of Bilingualism*, **4** (1), 81–106.

Bolonyai, Agnes (2002). Case systems in contact: Syntactic and lexical case in bilingual child language. *Southwest Journal of Linguistics*, **21** (2), 1–35.

Bolonyai, Agnes (2005). "Who was the best?": Power, knowledge and rationality in bilingual girls' code choices. *Journal of Sociolinguistics*, **9** (1), 3–27.

Bolonyai, Agnes (2007). (In)vulnerable agreement in incomplete bilingual L1 learners. *International Journal of Bilingualism*, **11** (1), 3–23.

Borer, Hagit (1984). *Parametric syntax: Case studies in Semitic and Romance languages*. Dordrecht: Foris.

Boumans, Louis (1998). *The syntax of codeswitching: Analysing Moroccan Arabic/Dutch conversations*. Tilburg, The Netherlands: Tilburg University Press.

Boumans, Louis (2002). Meertaligheid op Marokkaanse elektronische prikborden. *Levende Talen Tijdschrift*, **3** (1), 11–22.

Bourdieu, Pierre (1991). *Language and symbolic power (edited by John B. Thompson, translated by Gino Raymond and Matthew Adamson)*. Cambridge, UK and New York: Cambridge University Press; Oxford: Polity Press.

Boysson-Bardies, Benedicte de and Vihman, Marilyn May (1991). Adaptation to language: Evidence from babbling and first words in four languages. *Language*, **67** (2), 297–319.

Branigan, Holly P.; Pickering, Martin J. and Cleland, Alexandra A. (2000). Syntactic co-ordination in dialogue. *Cognition*, **75** (2), B13–B25.

Breitborde, Lawrence B. (1983). Levels of analysis in sociolinguistic explanation: Bilingual code switching, social relations, and domain theory. *International Journal of the Sociology of Language*, **39**, 5–43.

Briellmann, Regula S.; Saling, Michael M.; Connell, Ailie B.; Waites, Anthony B.; Abbott, David F. and Jackson, Graeme D. (2004).

A high-field functional MRI study of quadri-lingual subjects. *Brain and Language*, **89** (3), 531–542.

Broeder, Peter and Extra, Guus (1999). *Language, ethnicity, and education: Case studies on immigrant minority groups and immigrant minority languages.* Clevedon: Multilingual Matters.

Broersma, Mirjam and de Bot, Kees (2006). Triggered codeswitching: A corpus-based evaluation of the original triggering hypothesis and a new alternative. *Bilingualism: Language and Cognition*, **9** (1), 1–13.

Brown, Becky (1986). Cajun/English code-switching: A test of formal models In D. Sankoff (ed.), *Diversity and diachrony*, pp. 399–406. Amsterdam and Philadelphia: John Benjamins.

Brown, Colin M.; Hagoort, Peter and ter Keurs, Mariken (1999). Electrophysiological signatures of visual lexical processing: Open- and closed-class words. *Journal of Cognitive Neuroscience*, **11** (3), 261–281.

Brown, Penelope (1993). Gender, politeness, and confrontation in Tenejapa. In D. Tannen (ed.), *Gender and conversational interaction*, pp. 144–162. Oxford and New York: Oxford University Press.

Brown, Penelope and Levinson, Stephen C. (1999). *Politeness: Some universals in language usage.* Cambridge, UK and New York: Cambridge University Press.

Bullock, Barbara E. and Toribio, Almeida Jacqueline (2004). Introduction: Convergence as an emergent property in bilingual speech. *Bilingualism: Language and Cognition. Special Issue: Bilingualism and linguistic convergence*, **7** (2), 91–93.

Bullock, Barbara E.; Toribio, Almeida Jacqueline; Davis, Kristopher Allen and Botero, Christopher G. (2005). Phonetic convergence in bilingual Puerto Rican Spanish. In V. Chand, A. Kelleher, A. J. Rodríguez and B. Schmeiser (eds.), *WCCFL 23: Proceedings of the 23rd West Coast Conference on Formal Linguistics*, pp. 113–125. Somerville, MA: Cascadilla Press.

Bullock, Barbara E.; Toribio, Almeida Jacqueline; González, Verónica and Dalola, Amanda (2006). Language dominance and performance outcomes in bilingual pronunciation. In M. G. O'Brien, C. Shea and J. Archibald (eds.), *Proceedings of the 8th Generative Approaches to Second Language Acquisition Conference (GASLA 2006): The Banff Conference*, pp. 9–16. Somerville, MA: Cascadilla Press.

Bullock, Barbara E. and Toribio, Almeida Jacqueline (eds.) (2004). Bilingualism and linguistic convergence. Special issue of *Bilingualism: Language and Cognition*, **7** (2).

Bürki-Cohen, Judith; Grosjean, François and Miller, Joanne (1989). Base language effects on word identification in bilingual speech: Evidence from categorical perception experiments. *Language and Speech*, **32** (4), 355–371.

Cameron, Deborah (1990). Demythologizing sociolinguistics: Why language does not reflect society. In J. E. Joseph and T. J. Taylor (eds.),

Ideologies of language, pp. 79–93. London: Routledge. Reprinted in N. Coupland and A. Jaworski (eds.) (1997) *Sociolinguistics: A reader and coursebook*, pp. 55–67. New York: St. Martin's Press.

Cameron, Deborah (1992). *Feminism and linguistic theory*. New York: Palgrave.

Campbell, Jamie I. D. (2005). Asymmetrical language switching costs in Chinese–English bilinguals' number naming and simple arithmetic. *Bilingualism: Language and Cognition*, **8** (1), 85–91.

Cantone, Katja Francesca (2007). *Code-switching in bilingual children*. Dordrecht: Springer.

Cantone, Katja Francesca and Müller, Natascha (2005). Codeswitching at the interface of language-specific lexicons and the computational system. *International Journal of Bilingualism*, **9** (2), 205–225.

Cantone, Katja Francesca and Müller, Natascha (2008). Un nase or una nase? What gender marking within switched DPs reveals about the architecture of the bilingual language faculty. *Lingua*, **118** (6), 810–826.

Caramazza, Alfonso; Yeni-Komshian, Grace; Zurif, Edgar and Carbone, Ettore (1973). The acquisition of a new phonological contrast: The case of stop consonants in French–English bilinguals. *The Journal of the Acoustical Society of America*, **54** (2), 421–428.

Chambers, J. K. (2002). Dynamics of dialect convergence. *Journal of Sociolinguistics*, **6** (1), 117–130.

Chambers, J. K. (2003). *Sociolinguistic theory: Linguistic variation and its social significance*. (2nd edn.). Oxford and Malden, MA: Blackwell.

Chametzky, Robert A. (2003). Phrase structure. In R. Hendrick (ed.), *Minimalist syntax*, pp. 192–225. Oxford and Malden, MA: Blackwell.

Chan, Brian Hok-Shing (1998a). Functional heads, Cantonese phrase structure and Cantonese–English code-switching. *UCL Working Papers in Linguistics* **10**, 253–284.

Chan, Brian Hok-Shing (1998b). How does Cantonese–English code-mixing work? In M. C. Pennington (ed.), *Language use in Hong Kong at century's end*, pp. 191–216. Hong Kong: Hong Kong University Press.

Chan, Brian Hok-Shing (1999). Aspects of the syntax, production and pragmatics of code-switching, with special reference to Cantonese–English. Ph.D. dissertation, University College London.

Chan, Brian Hok-Shing (2003). *Aspects of the syntax, the pragmatics, and the production of code-switching: Cantonese and English*. New York: Peter Lang.

Chan, Brian Hok-Shing (2008). Code-switching, word order and the lexical/functional category distinction. *Lingua*, **118** (6), 777–809.

Chan, Mun-chee; Chau, Helen L. and Hoosain, Rumjahn (1983). Input/output switch in bilingual code switching. *Journal of Psycholinguistic Research*, **12** (4), 407–416.

Chee, Michael W. L.; Caplan, David; Soon, Chun Siong; Sriram, N.; Tan, Edsel W. L.; Thiel, Thorsten and Weekes, Brendan (1999a).

Processing of visually presented sentences in Mandarin and English studied with fMRI. *Neuron*, **23** (1), 127–137.

Chee, Michael W. L.; Tan, Edsel W. L. and Thiel, Thorsten (1999b). Mandarin and English single word processing studied with functional magnetic resonance imaging. *Journal of Neuroscience*, **19** (8), 3050–3056.

Chee, Michael W. L.; Hon, Nicholas; Lee, Hwee Ling and Soon, Chun Siong (2001). Relative language proficiency modulates BOLD signal change when bilinguals perform semantic judgments. *NeuroImage*, **13**, 1155–1163.

Cheng, Lisa Lai-Shen and Sybesma, Rint (1999). Bare and not-so-bare nouns and the structure of NP. *Linguistic Inquiry*, **30** (4), 509–542.

Cheshire, Jenny (1982). *Variation in an English dialect: A sociolinguistic study*. Cambridge, UK and New York: Cambridge University Press.

Cheshire, Jenny and Gardner-Chloros, Penelope (1998). Code-switching and the sociolinguistic gender pattern. *International Journal of the Sociology of Language*, **129**, 5–34.

Choi, Jae Oh (1991). Korean–English code switching: Switch-alpha and linguistic constraints. *Linguistics*, **29** (5), 877–902.

Chomsky, Noam (1955). The logical structure of linguistic theory. Ph.D. dissertation, University of Pennsylvania.

Chomsky, Noam (1957). *Syntactic structures*. The Hague: Mouton.

Chomsky, Noam (1964). *Current issues in linguistic theory*. The Hague: Mouton.

Chomsky, Noam (1965). *Aspects of the theory of syntax*. Cambridge, MA: MIT Press.

Chomsky, Noam (1970). Remarks on nominalization. In R. A. Jacobs and P. S. Rosenbaum (eds.), *Readings in English transformational grammar*, pp. 184–221. Waltham, MA: Ginn.

Chomsky, Noam (1981). *Lectures on government and binding*. Dordrecht: Foris.

Chomsky, Noam (1991). Linguistics and cognitive science: Problems and mysteries. In A. Kasher (ed.), *The chomskyan turn*, pp. 26–53. Oxford and Cambridge, MA: Basil Blackwell.

Chomsky, Noam (1994). Bare phrase structure. *MIT Occasional Papers in Linguistics*, **5**, 1–48.

Chomsky, Noam (1995). *The minimalist program*. Cambridge, MA: MIT Press.

Chomsky, Noam (1998). Some observations on economy in generative grammar. In P. Barbosa, D. Fox, P. Hagstrom, M. McGinnis and D. Pesetsky (eds.), *Is the best good enough? Optimality and competition in syntax*, pp. 115–127. Cambridge, MA: MIT Press.

Chomsky, Noam (2000). Minimalist inquiries: The framework. In R. Martin, D. Michaels and J. Uriagereka (eds.), *Step by step: Essays on minimalist syntax in honor of Howard Lasnik*, pp. 89–155. Cambridge, MA: MIT Press.

Chomsky, Noam (2001a). Beyond explanatory adequacy. *MIT Occasional Papers in Linguistics*, **20**, 1–28.

Chomsky, Noam (2001b). Derivation by phase. In M. Kenstowicz (ed.), *Ken Hale: A life in language*, pp. 1–52. Cambridge, MA: MIT Press.

Clark, Herbert H. and Gerrig, Richard J. (1990). Quotations as demonstrations. *Language*, **66** (4), 764–805.

Clyne, Michael (1972). Perception of code-switching by bilinguals: An experiment. *International Review of Applied Linguistics*, **16**, 45–48.

Clyne, Michael (1986). Towards a systematization of language contact dynamics. In J. A. Fishman, A. Tabouret-Keller, M. Clyne, B. Krishnamurti and M. Abdulaziz (eds.), *The Fergusonian Impact: In honor of Charles A. Ferguson on the occasion of his 65th birthday. Vol. 2*, pp. 483–492. Berlin and New York: Mouton de Gruyter.

Clyne, Michael (1987). Constraints on code switching: How universal are they? *Linguistics*, **25** (4), 739–764.

Clyne, Michael G. (1967). *Transference and triggering: Observations on the language assimilation of postwar German-speaking migrants in Australia*. The Hague: Martinus Nijhoff.

Clyne, Michael G (2003). *Dynamics of language contact: English and immigrant languages*. Cambridge, UK and New York: Cambridge University Press.

Codó, Eva (1998). Analysis of language choice in intercultural service encounters. M. A. dissertation, Universitat Autònoma de Barcelona.

Coetsem, Frans van (1988). *Loan phonology and the two transfer types in language contact*. Dordrecht: Foris.

Coggins, Porter E., III; Kennedy, Teresa J. and Armstrong, Terry A. (2004). Bilingual corpus callosum variability. *Brain and Language*, **89** (1), 69–75.

Collot, Milena and Belmore, Nancy (1996). Electronic language: A new variety of English. In S. C. Herring (ed.), *Computer-mediated communication: Linguistic, social, and cross-cultural perspectives*, pp. 13–29. Amsterdam and Philadelphia: John Benjamins.

Comeau, Liane; Genesee, Fred and Lapaquette, Lindsay (2003). The modeling hypothesis and child bilingual codemixing. *International Journal of Bilingualism*, **7** (2), 113–126.

Comrie, Bernard (1989). *Language universals and linguistic typology: Syntax and morphology* (2nd edn.). Chicago: University of Chicago Press.

Cook, Vivian (ed.) (2003). *Effects of the second language on the first*. Clevedon: Multilingual Matters.

Cook-Gumperz, Jenny and Gumperz, John J. (1976). Context in children's speech. In J. Cook-Gumperz and J. J. Gumperz (eds.), *Papers on language and context: Working papers of the Language Behavior Research Laboratory, No. 46*, Berkeley, CA: Language Behavior Research Laboratory, University of California.

Costa, Albert (2005). Lexical access in bilingual production. In J. F. Kroll and A. M. B. de Groot (eds.), *Handbook of bilingualism: Psycholinguistic* *approaches*, pp. 308–325. Oxford and New York: Oxford University Press.

Costa, Albert; La Heij, Wido and Navarrete, Eduardo (2006). The dynamics of bilingual lexical access. *Bilingualism: Language and Cognition. Special Issue: Lexical Access in Bilingual Speech Production*, **9** (2), 137–151.

Costa, Albert and Santesteban, Mikel (2004). Lexical access in bilingual speech production: Evidence from language switching in highly proficient bilinguals and L2 learners. *Journal of Memory and Language*, **50** (4), 491–511.

Costa, Albert and Santesteban, Mikel (2006). The control of speech production by bilingual speakers: Introductory remarks. *Bilingualism: Language and Cognition. Special Issue: Lexical Access in Bilingual Speech Production*, **9** (2), 115–117.

Coulson, Seana; King, Jonathan W. and Kutas, Marta (1998). Expect the unexpected: Event-related brain response to morphosyntactic violations. *Language and Cognitive Processes*, **13** (1), 21–58.

Coupland, Nikolas (1985). "Hark, hark, the lark": Social motivations for phonological style-shifting. *Language and Communication*, **5** (3), 153–171.

Coupland, Nikolas and Giles, Howard (eds.) (1988). Communicative accommodation: Recent developments. *Language & Communication*, **8** (3–4), 175–327.

Crago, Martha B. (1992). Ethnography and language socialization: A cross-cultural perspective. *Topics in Language Disorders*, **12** (3), 28–39.

Crago, Martha B. and Cole, Elizabeth (1991). Using ethnography to bring children's communicative and cultural worlds into focus. In T. M. Gallagher (ed.), *Pragmatics of language: Clinical practice issues*, pp. 99–131. San Diego, CA: Singular Publishing Group.

Craik, Fergus I. M. and Bialystok, Ellen (2006). Cognition through the lifespan: Mechanisms of change. *Trends in Cognitive Sciences*, **10** (3), 131–138.

Crinion, J.; Turner, R.; Grogan, A.; Hanakawa, T.; Noppeney, U.; Devlin, J. T.; Aso, T.; Urayama, S.; Fukuyama, H.; Stockton, K.; Usui, K.; Green, D. W. and Price, C. J. (2006). Language control in the bilingual brain. *Science*, **312** (5779), 1537–1540.

Croft, William (2000). *Explaining language change: An evolutionary approach*. Harlow, UK and New York: Longman.

Croft, William (2003). *Typology and universals* (2nd edn.). Cambridge, UK and New York: Cambridge University Press.

Cromdal, Jakob and Aronsson, Karin (2000). Footing in bilingual play. *Journal of Sociolinguistics*, **4** (3), 435–457.

Crosson, Bruce (1999). Subcortical mechanisms in language: Lexical-semantic mechanisms and the thalamus. *Brain and Cognition*, **40** (2), 414–438.

Crosson, Bruce; Benefield, Hope; Cato, M. Allison; Sadek, Joseph R.; Moore, Anna Bacon; Wierenga, Christina E.; Gopinath,

Kaundinya; Soltysik, David; Bauer, Russell M.; Auerbach, Edward J.; Gökçay, Didem; Leonard, Christiana M. and Briggs, Richard W. (2003). Left and right basal ganglia and frontal activity during language generation: Contributions to lexical, semantic, and phonological processes. *Journal of the International Neuropsychological Society*, **9** (7), 1061–1077.

Crystal, David (2001). *Language and the internet*. Cambridge, UK and New York: Cambridge University Press.

Cummins, James (1979). Linguistic interdependence and the educational development of bilingual children. *Review of Educational Research*, **49** (2), 222–251.

Dalrymple-Alford, E. C. (1985). Language switching during bilingual reading. *British Journal of Psychology*, **76** (1), 111–122.

Davidson, Judy A. (1984). Subsequent versions of invitations, offers, requests and proposals dealing with potential or actual rejection. In J. M. Atkinson and J. Heritage (eds.), *Structures of social action: Studies in Conversation Analysis*, pp. 102–128. Cambridge, UK and New York: Cambridge University Press.

Davidson, Judy A. (1990). Modifications of invitations, offers and rejections. In G. Psathas (ed.), *Interaction competence*, pp. 149–180. Washington D.C.: International Institute for Ethnomethodology and Conversation Analysis/University Press of America.

Davies, Eirlys E. and Bentahila, Abdelâi (in press). Code switching as a poetic device: Examples from Rai lyrics. *Language and Communication*.

Davis, Jeffrey (1989). Distinguishing language contact phenomena in ASL interpretation. In C. Lucas (ed.), *The sociolinguistics of the deaf community*, pp. 85–102. San Diego, CA: Academic Press.

Davis, Jeffrey E. (1990). Interpreting in a language contact situation: The case of English-to-ASL Interpretation. Ph.D. dissertation, University of New Mexico.

de Bot, Kees (1992). A bilingual production model: Levelt's "speaking" model adapted. *Applied Linguistics*, **13** (1), 1–24.

de Bot, Kees (2002). Cognitive processing in bilinguals: Language choice and code-switching. In R. B. Kaplan (ed.), *The Oxford handbook of applied linguistics*, pp. 287–300. Oxford and New York: Oxford University Press.

de Bot, Kees and Clyne, Michael (1989). Language reversion revisited. *Studies in Second Language Acquisition*, **11** (2), 167–177.

de Bot, Kees and Schreuder, Robert (1993). Word production and the bilingual lexicon. In R. Schreuder and B. Weltens (eds.), *The bilingual lexicon*, pp. 191–214. Amsterdam and Philadelphia: John Benjamins.

de Bot, Kees and Weltens, Bert (1985). Taalverlies: Beschrijven versus verklaren. *Handelingen van het 38e Nederlands Filologencongres*, pp. 51–61.

de Bruijn, Ellen R. A.; Dijkstra, Ton; Chwilla, Dorothee J. and Schriefers, Herbert J. (2001). Language context effects on interlingual homograph recognition: Evidence from event-related potentials and response times in semantic priming. *Bilingualism: Language and Cognition*, **4** (2), 155–168.

de Rooij, Vincent A. (1996). *Cohesion through contrast: Discourse structure in Shaba Swahili/French conversations*. Amsterdam: IFOTT.

Dechert, Hans W. and Raupach, Manfred (1989). *Transfer in language production*. Norwood, NJ: Ablex Publishing Corporation.

Dehaene, Stanislas; Dupoux, Emmanuel; Mehler, Jacques; Cohen, Laurent; Paulesu, Eraldo; Perani, Daniela; van de Moortele, Pierre-Francois; Lehéricy, Stéphane and Le Bihan, Denis (1997). Anatomical variability in the cortical representation of first and second language. *Neuroreport: An International Journal for the Rapid Communication of Research in Neuroscience*, **8** (17), 3809–3815.

Deuchar, Margaret (1999). Are function words non-language-specific in early bilingual two-word utterances? *Bilingualism: Language and Cognition*, **2** (1), 23–34.

Deuchar, Margaret (2005). Congruence and Welsh–English code-switching. *Bilingualism: Language and Cognition*, **8** (3), 255–269.

Deuchar, Margaret (2006). Welsh–English codeswitching and the Matrix Language Frame model. *Lingua*, **116** (11), 1986–2011.

Deuchar, Margaret and Quay, Suzanne (1998). One vs. two systems in early bilingual syntax: Two versions of the question. *Bilingualism: Language and Cognition*, **1** (3), 231–243.

Deuchar, Margaret and Quay, Suzanne (2000). *Bilingual acquisition: Theoretical implications of a case study*. Oxford and New York: Oxford University Press.

Di Luzio, Aldo (1984). On the meaning of language choice for sociocultural indentity of bilingual migrant children. In P. Auer and A. Di Luzio (eds.), *Interpretive sociolinguistics: Migrants – children – migrant children*, pp. 55–86. Tübingen: Gunter Narr Verlag.

Di Sciullo, Anne-Marie; Muysken, Pieter and Singh, Rajendra (1986). Government and code-mixing. *Journal of Linguistics*, **22** (1), 1–24.

Dijkstra, Ton (2005). Bilingual visual word recognition and lexical access. In J. F. Kroll and A. M. de Groot (eds.), *Handbook of bilingualism: Psycholinguistic approaches*, pp. 179–201. Oxford and New York: Oxford University Press

Dijkstra, Ton and van Heuven, Walter J. B. (1998). The BIA model and bilingual word recognition. In J. Grainger and A. M. Jacobs (eds.), *Localist connectionist approaches to human cognition*, pp. 189–225. Mahwah, NJ: Lawrence Erlbaum Associates.

Dijkstra, Ton and Van Heuven, Walter J. B. (2002). The architecture of the bilingual word recognition system: From identification to decision. *Bilingualism: Language and Cognition*, **5** (3), 175–197.

Docherty, Gerry J.; Foulkes, Paul; Tillotson, Jennifer and Watt, Dominic J. L. (2006). On the scope of phonological learning: Issues arising from socially structured variation. In L. M. Goldstein,

D. H. Whalen and C. T. Best (eds.), *Laboratory phonology 8*, pp. 393–421. Berlin and New York: Mouton de Gruyter.

Döpke, Susanne (1992). *One parent, one language: An interactional approach.* Amsterdam and Philadelphia: John Benjamins.

Dorian, Nancy C. (1981). *Language death: The life cycle of a Scottish Gaelic dialect.* Philadelphia: University of Pennsylvania Press.

Dorleijn, Margreet (2002). "Ik leg mijn schoen met Sinterklaas" Leenvertalingen in het Turks en het Nederlands. ["I lay my shoe with Santa Claus" Loan translations in Turkish and Dutch]. In H. Bennis, G. Extra, P. Muysken and J. Nortier (eds.), *Een buurt in beweging: Talen en culturen in het Utrechtse Lombok en Transvaal*, pp. 217–234. Amsterdam: Aksant.

Dorleijn, Margreet and van der Heijden, Hanneke (2000). Verbs and their objects in Turkish spoken in the Netherlands. Paper presented at *The 10th International Conference on Turkish Linguistics, August 16–18, Bogazici Üniversitesi, Istanbul.*

Dulay, Heidi C. and Burt, Marina K. (1974). Natural sequences in child second language acquisition. *Language Learning*, **24** (1), 37–53.

Dussias, Paola E. (2001). Psycholinguistic complexity in codeswitching. *International Journal of Bilingualism*, **5** (1), 87–100.

Dussias, Paola E. (2002). On the relationship between comprehension and production data in codeswitching. In C. R. Wiltshire and J. Camps (eds.), *Romance phonology and variation: Selected papers from the 30th Linguistic Symposium on Romance Languages, Gainesville, Florida, February 2000*, pp. 27–38. Amsterdam and Philadelphia: John Benjamins.

Dussias, Paola E. (2003). Spanish–English code mixing at the auxiliary phrase: Evidence from eye-movement data. *Revista Internacional de Lingüística Iberoamericana*, **1** (2), 7–34.

Dyer, Judy (2004). "What kind of English is that?" Using metalinguistic comments to investigate a bilingual 6-year-old's acquisition of a second English dialect. Paper presented at *The 33rd New Ways of Analysing Variation*, Ann Arbor, Michigan.

Eckert, Penelope (2000). *Linguistic variation as social practice: The linguistic construction of identity in Belten High.* Oxford and Malden, MA: Blackwell.

Eckert, Penelope and Rickford, John R. (2001). *Style and sociolinguistic variation.* Cambridge, UK and New York: Cambridge University Press.

El Aissati, Abderrahman (1996). Language loss among native speakers of Moroccan Arabic in the Netherlands. Ph.D. dissertation, University of Nijmegen.

El Aissati, Abderrahman (2002). Verandering en verankering. In H. Bennis, G. Extra, P. Muysken and J. Nortier (eds.), *Een buurt in beweging: Talen en culturen in het Utrechtse Lombok en Transvaal*, pp. 251–262. Amsterdam: Aksant.

Eldridge, John (1996). Code-switching in a Turkish secondary school. *English Language Teaching Journal*, **50** (4), 303–311.

Eliasson, Stig (1989). English–Maori language contact: Code-switching and the free-morpheme constraint. *Reports from Uppsala University Department of Linguistics*, **18**, 1–28.

Elman, Jeffrey L.; Diehl, Randy L. and Buchwald, Susan E. (1977). Perceptual switching in bilinguals. *Journal of the Acoustical Society of America*, **62**, 971–974.

Els, Theo van (1986). An overview of European research on language attrition. In B. Weltens, K. de Bot and T. v. Els (eds.), *Language attrition in progress*, pp. 3–18. Dordrecht: Foris.

Elston-Güttler, Kerrie E.; Gunter, Thomas C. and Kotz, Sonja A. (2005a). Zooming into L2: Global language context and adjustment affect processing of interlingual homographs in sentences. *Cognitive Brain Research*, **25** (1), 57–70.

Elston-Güttler, Kerrie E.; Paulmann, Silke and Kotz, Sonja A. (2005b). Who's in control? Proficiency and L1 influence on L2 processing. *Journal of Cognitive Neuroscience*, **17** (10), 1593–1610.

Emmorey, Karen (2002). *Language, cognition, and the brain: Insights from sign language research*. Mahwah, NJ: Lawrence Erlbaum Associates.

Emmorey, Karen; Borinstein, Helsa B. and Thompson, Robin (2005). Bimodal bilingualism: Code-blending between spoken English and American Sign Language. In J. Cohen, K. T. McAlister, K. Rolstad and J. MacSwan (eds.), *ISB4: Proceedings of the 4th International Symposium on Bilingualism*, pp. 663–673. Somerville, MA: Cascadilla Press.

Ervin-Tripp, Susan M. (1964). An analysis of the interaction of language, topic, and listener. *American Anthropologist*, **66** (6, pt. 2), 86–102.

Ervin-Tripp, Susan M. (1973). Children's sociolinguistic competence and dialect diversity. In A. S. Dil (ed.), *Language acquisition and communicative choice: Essays by Susan M. Ervin-Tripp*, pp. 262–301. Stanford: Stanford University Press.

Ervin-Tripp, Susan and Reyes, Iliana (2005). Child codeswitching and adult content contrasts. *International Journal of Bilingualism*, **9** (1), 85–102.

Espinosa, Aurelio M. (1911). Studies in New Mexican Spanish, Part II: Morphology. *Revue de Dialectologie Romane*, **3**, 251–286.

Eversteijn, Nadia (2002). "We praten Turks over de zaktelefoon" Processen van in- en uitsluiting door taalkeuze en codewisseling onder Turkse jongeren. In H. Bennis, G. Extra, P. Muysken and J. Nortier (eds.), *Een buurt in beweging: Talen en culturen in het Utrechtse Lombok en Transvaal*, pp. 169–181. Amsterdam: Aksant.

Extra, Guus; Aarts, Rian; Avoird, Tim van der; Broeder, Peter and Yagmur, Kutlay (2001). *Meertaligheid in Den Haag: De status van allochtone talen thuis en op school*. Amsterdam: European Cultural Foundation.

Extra, Guus and Verhoeven, Ludo (eds.) (1998). *Bilingualism and migration*. Berlin and New York: Mouton de Gruyter.

Fabbro, Franco (2001a). The bilingual brain: Bilingual aphasia. *Brain and Language*, **79** (2), 201–210.

Fabbro, Franco (2001b). The bilingual brain: Cerebral representation of languages. *Brain and Language,* **79** (2), 211–222.

Fabbro, Franco; Peru, Andrea and Skrap, Miran (1997). Language disorders in bilingual patients after thalamic lesions. *Journal of Neurolinguistics,* **10** (4), 347–367.

Fabbro, Franco; Skrap, Miran and Aglioti, Salvatore (2000). Pathological switching between languages after frontal lesions in a bilingual patient. *Journal of Neurology, Neurosurgery & Psychiatry,* **68** (5), 650–652.

Fantini, Alvino E. (1985). *Language acquisition of a bilingual child: A sociolinguistic perspective (to age ten).* San Diego, CA: College Hill Press.

Farrar, Kimberley and Jones, Mari C. (2002). Introduction. In M. C. Jones and E. Esch (eds.), *Language change: The interplay of internal, external, and extra-linguistic factors,* pp. 1–16. Berlin and New York: Mouton de Gruyter.

Faurot, Karla; Dellinger, Dianne; Eatough, Andy and Parkhurst, Steve (1999). The identity of Mexican Sign as a language. Retrieved on July 31, 2007 from http://www.sil.org/mexico/lenguajes-de-signos/G009i-Identity-MFS.pdf.

Federmeier, Kara D. and Kutas, Marta (1999). A rose by any other name: Long-term memory structure and sentence processing. *Journal of Memory and Language,* **41** (4), 469–495.

Ferguson, Charles A. (1959). Diglossia. *Word* **15**, 325–344.

Ferreira, Fernanda; Henderson, John M.; Anes, Michael D.; Weeks, Phillip A., Jr. and McFarlane, David K. (1996). Effects of lexical frequency and syntactic complexity in spoken-language comprehension: Evidence from the auditory moving-window technique. *Journal of Experimental Psychology: Learning, Memory, and Cognition,* **22** (2), 324–335.

Field, Fredric (2005). Long-term effects of CS: Clues to structural borrowing. *International Journal of Bilingualism,* **9** (3–4), 341–360.

Finkbeiner, Matthew; Gollan, Tamar H. and Caramazza, Alfonso (2006). Lexical access in bilingual speakers: What's the (hard) problem? *Bilingualism: Language and Cognition. Special Issue: Lexical Access in Bilingual Speech Production,* **9** (2), 153–166.

Finnis, Katerina (2008). Language use and socio-pragmatic meaning: Code-switching amongst British-born Greek-Cypriots. Ph.D. dissertation, Birkbeck College, University of London.

Firth, Alan (1995). Talking for a change: Negotiating by telephone in commodity trading. In A. Firth (ed.), *The discourse of negotiation: Studies of language in the workplace,* pp. 183–222. Oxford, UK and Tarrytown, NY: Pergamon.

Fischer, Susan D. (1974). Sign language and linguistic universals. In C. Rohrer and N. Ruwet (eds.), *Actes du colloque Franco-Allemand de Grammaire Transformationelle, band II: Études de sémantique et autres,* pp. 187–204. Tübingen: Max Niemeyer Verlag.

Fishman, Joshua A. (1965/2000a). Who speaks what language to whom and when? *La Linguistique*, **2**, 67–68. Reprinted in Li Wei (ed.), *The bilingualism reader*, pp. 89–108. London and New York: Routledge.

Fishman, Joshua A. (1967/2006). Bilingualism with and without diglossia; diglossia with and without bilingualism. *Journal of Social Issues*, **23** (2), 29–38. Reprinted in Li Wei (ed.), *The bilingualism reader* (2nd edn.), pp. 47–55. London and New York: Routledge.

Fishman, Joshua A. (1972). Domains and the relationship between micro- and macrosociolinguistics. In J. J. Gumperz and D. H. Hymes (eds.), *Directions in sociolinguistics: The ethnography of communication*, pp. 435–453. New York: Holt, Rinehart and Winston.

Fishman, Joshua A. (2000b). Reversing language shift: RLS theory and practice revisited. In G. Kindell and M. P. Lewis (eds.), *Assessing ethnolinguistic vitality: Theory and practice. Selected papers from the Third International Language Assessment Conference*, pp. 1–25. Dallas, TX: SIL International.

Flege, James Emil and Eefting, Wieke (1987). Production and perception of English stops by native Spanish speakers. *Journal of Phonetics*, **15** (1), 67–83.

Franceschini, R. (1998). Code-switching and the notion of code in linguistics: Proposals for a dual focus model. In P. Auer (ed.), *Code-switching in Conversation: Language, Interaction and Identity*, pp. 51–74. London and New York: Routledge.

Freedman, Sandra E. and Forster, Kenneth I. (1985). The psychological status of overgenerated sentences. *Cognition*, **19** (2), 101–131.

Frenck-Mestre, Cheryl; Anton, Jean Luc; Roth, Muriel; Vaid, Jyotsna and Viallet, François (2005). Articulation in early and late bilinguals' two languages: Evidence from functional magnetic resonance imaging. *Neuroreport: For Rapid Communication of Neuroscience Research*, **16** (7), 761–765.

Fuller, Janet M. (1999). The role of English in Pennsylvania German development: Best supporting actress? *American Speech*, **74** (1), 38–55.

Gafaranga, Joseph (1999). Language choice as a significant aspect of talk organization: The orderliness of language alternation. *Text*, **19** (2), 201–225.

Gafaranga, Joseph (2000). Medium repair vs. other-language repair: Telling the medium of a bilingual conversation. *International Journal of Bilingualism*, **4** (3), 327–350.

Gafaranga, Joseph (2005). Demythologising language alternation studies: Conversational structure vs. social structure in bilingual interaction. *Journal of Pragmatics*, **37** (3), 281–300.

Gafaranga, Joseph and Britten, Nicky (2003). "Fire away": The opening sequence in general practice consultations. *Family Practice*, **20** (3), 242–247.

Gafaranga, Joseph and Britten, Nicky (2005). Talking an institution into being: The opening sequence in general practice consultations. In

K. Richards and P. Seedhouse (eds.), *Applying conversation analysis*, pp. 75–90. Basingstoke and New York: Palgrave Macmillan.

Gafaranga, Joseph and Torras i Calvo, Maria Carme (2001). Language versus medium in the study of bilingual conversation. *International Journal of Bilingualism*, **5** (2), 195–219.

Gafaranga, Joseph and Torras, Maria-Carme (2002). Interactional otherness: Towards a redefinition of codeswitching. *International Journal of Bilingualism*, **6** (1), 1–22.

Gal, Susan (1979). *Language shift: Social determinants of linguistic change in bilingual Austria*. New York: Academic Press.

Gal, Susan (1988). The political economy of code choice. In M. Heller (ed.), *Codeswitching: Anthropological and sociolinguistic perspectives*, pp. 245–264. Berlin and New York: Mouton de Gruyter.

Gal, Susan (1989). Lexical innovation and loss: The use and value of restricted Hungarian. In N. C. Dorian (ed.), *Investigating obsolescence: Studies in language contraction and death*, pp. 313–331. Cambridge, UK and New York: Cambridge University Press.

Ganis, Giorgio; Kutas, Marta and Sereno, Martin I (1996). The search for "common sense": An electrophysiological study of the comprehension of words and pictures in reading. *Journal of Cognitive Neuroscience*, **8** (2), 89–106.

Gardner-Chloros, Penelope (1991). *Language selection and switching in Strasbourg*. Oxford and New York: Oxford University Press.

Gardner-Chloros, Penelope (1992). The sociolinguistics of the Greek-Cypriot community in London. In M. Karyolemou (ed.), *Plurilinguismes: Sociolinguistique du Grec et de la Grèce, 4*, pp. 112–136. Paris: Centre d'études et de recherches en planification linguistique (CERPL).

Gardner-Chloros, Penelope; Charles, Reeva and Cheshire, Jenny (2000). Parallel patterns? A comparison of monolingual speech and bilingual codeswitching discourse. *Journal of Pragmatics. Special Issue: Codeswitching*, **32** (9), 1305–1341.

Gardner-Chloros, Penelope and Edwards, Malcolm (2004). Assumptions behind grammatical approaches to code-switching: When the blueprint is a red herring. *Transactions of the Philological Society*, **102** (1), 103–129.

Gardner-Chloros, Penelope and Finnis, Katerina (2004). How code-switching mediates politeness: Gender-related speech among London Greek-Cypriots. *Estudios de sociolingüística: Linguas, sociedades e culturas*, **4** (2), 505–532.

Garfinkel, Harold (1967). *Studies in ethnomethodology*. Englewood Cliffs, NJ: Prentice Hall.

Garfinkel, Harold and Sacks, Harvey (1970). On formal structures of practical social action. In J. C. McKinney and E. A. Tiryakian (eds.), *Theoretical sociology: Perspectives and developments*, pp. 338–366. New York: Appleton-Century-Crofts.

Garrett, Merrill F. (1993). Errors and their relevance for models of language production. In G. Blanken, J. Dittmann, H. Grimm, J. C. Marshall and C.-W. Wallesch (eds.), *Linguistic disorders and pathologies: An international handbook*, pp. 72–92. Berlin: Walter de Gruyter.

Gass, Susan (1996). Second language acquisition and linguistic theory: The role of language transfer. In W. C. Ritchie and T. K. Bhatia (eds.), *Handbook of second language acquisition*, pp. 317–345. San Diego, CA: Academic Press.

Gass, Susan M. (2001). Sentence matching: A re-examination. *Second Language Research*, **17** (4), 421–441.

Gass, Susan M. and Selinker, Larry (1983). *Language transfer in language learning*. Rowley, MA: Newbury House

Gawlitzek-Maiwald, Ira and Tracy, Rosemarie (1996). Bilingual bootstrapping. *Linguistics*, **34** (5), 901–926.

Genesee, Fred (1989). Early bilingual development: One language or two? *Journal of Child Language*, **16** (1), 161–179.

Genesee, Fred; Boivin, Isabelle and Nicoladis, Elena (1996). Talking with strangers: A study of bilingual children's communicative competence. *Applied Psycholinguistics*, **17** (4), 427–442.

Genesee, Fred; Nicoladis, Elena and Paradis, Johanne (1995). Language differentiation in early bilingual development. *Journal of Child Language*, **22** (3), 611–631.

Genesee, Fred; Paradis, Johanne and Crago, Martha B. (2004). *Dual language development and disorders: A handbook on bilingualism and second language learning*. Baltimore: Paul H. Brookes Publishing.

Genesee, Fred and Sauve, D. (2000). Grammatical constraints on child bilingual codemixing. Paper presented at *The Annual Conference of the American Association for Applied Linguistics, 12 March, Vancouver, Canada*.

Giles, Howard (1973). Accent mobility: A model and some data. *Anthropological Linguistics*, **15** (2), 87–105.

Giles, Howard (1977). *Language, ethnicity, and intergroup relations*. New York: Academic Press.

Giles, Howard; Coupland, Justine and Coupland, Nikolas (1991). *Contexts of accommodation: Developments in applied sociolinguistics*. Cambridge, UK and New York: Cambridge University Press.

Giles, Howard and Powesland, Peter F. (1975). A social psychological model of speech diversity. In H. Giles and P. F. Powesland (eds.), *Speech style and social evaluation*, pp. 154–170. New York: Harcourt Brace.

Giusti, Giuliana (1997). The categorial status of determiners. In L. Haegeman (ed.), *The new comparative syntax*, pp. 95–123. Harlow, UK: Addison Wesley Longman.

Gleason, Jean Berko (1987). Sex-differences in parent-child interactions. In S. U. Philips, S. Steele and C. Tanz (eds.), *Language, gender, and sex in comparative perspective*, pp. 189–199. Cambridge, UK and New York: Cambridge University Press.

Goffman, Erving (1967). *Interaction ritual: Essays on face-to-face behavior.* New York: Doubleday.

Goglia, Francesco (2006). Communicative strategies in the Italian of Igbo-Nigerian immigrants in Padova, Italy: A contact-linguistic approach. Ph.D. dissertation, University of Manchester.

Gollan, Tamar H. and Acenas, Lori-Ann R. (2004). What is a TOT? Cognate and translation effects on tip-of-the-tongue states in Spanish–English and Tagalog–English bilinguals. *Journal of Experimental Psychology: Learning, Memory, and Cognition*, **30** (1), 246–269.

Gollan, Tamar H.; Montoya, Rosa I.; Fennema-Notestine, Christine and Morris, Shaunna K. (2005). Bilingualism affects picture naming but not picture classification. *Memory and Cognition*, **33** (7), 1220–1234.

Gollan, Tamar H.; Montoya, Rosa I. and Werner, Grace A. (2002). Semantic and letter fluency in Spanish–English bilinguals. *Neuropsychology*, **16** (4), 562–576.

Goodz, Naomi S. (1994). Interactions between parents and children in bilingual families. In F. Genesee (ed.), *Educating second language children: The whole child, the whole curriculum, the whole community*, pp. 61–81. Cambridge, UK and New York: Cambridge University Press.

Gordon, Raymond G., Jr. (ed.) (2005). *Ethnologue: Languages of the world, Fifteenth edition.* Dallas, TX: SIL International. (Online version: http://www.ethnologue.com/)

Grainger, Jonathan and Beauvillain, Cécile (1988). Associative priming in bilinguals: Some limits of interlingual facilitation effects. *Canadian Journal of Psychology/Revue Canadienne de Psychologie*, **42** (3), 261–273.

Grainger, Jonathan and O'Regan, J. Kevin (1992). A psychophysical investigation of language priming effects in two English–French bilinguals. *European Journal of Cognitive Psychology. Special Issue: Multilingual community*, **4** (4), 323–339.

Green, David W. (1998). Mental control of the bilingual lexico-semantic system. *Bilingualism: Language and Cognition*, **1** (2), 67–81.

Gregory, Stanford W. (1990). Analysis of fundamental frequency reveals covariation in interview partners' speech. *Journal of Nonverbal Behavior*, **14** (4), 237–251.

Grosjean, François (1980). Spoken word recognition processes and the gating paradigm. *Perception & Psychophysics*, **28** (4), 267–283.

Grosjean, François (1985). The bilingual as a competent but specific speaker-hearer. *Journal of Multilingual and Multicultural Development*, **6** (6), 467–477.

Grosjean, François (1988). Exploring the recognition of guest words in bilingual speech. *Language and Cognitive Processes*, **3** (3), 233–274.

Grosjean, François (1995). A psycholinguistic approach to code-switching: The recognition of guest words by bilinguals. In L. Milroy and P. Muysken (eds.), *One speaker, two languages: Cross-disciplinary* *perspectives on code-switching*, pp. 259–275. Cambridge, UK and New York: Cambridge University Press.

Grosjean, François (1998). Studying bilinguals: Methodological and conceptual issues. *Bilingualism: Language and Cognition*, **1** (2), 131–149.

Grosjean, François (2001). The bilingual's language modes. In J. L. Nicol (ed.), *One mind, two languages: Bilingual language processing*, pp. 1–22. Oxford and Malden, MA: Blackwell.

Grosjean, François and Miller, Joanne L. (1994). Going in and out of languages: An example of bilingual flexibility. *Psychological Science*, **5** (4), 201–206.

Grosjean, François and Soares, Carlos (1986). Processing mixed language: Some preliminary findings. In J. Vaid (ed.), *Language processing in bilinguals: Psycholinguistic and neuropsychological perspectives*, pp. 145–179. Hillsdale, NJ: Lawrence Erlbaum Associates.

Grzega, Joachim (2003). Borrowing as a word-finding process in cognitive historical onomasiology. *Onomasiology Online*, **4**, 22–42.

Guerra Currie, Anne-Marie P. (1999). A Mexican sign language lexicon: Internal and cross-linguistic similarities and variations. Ph.D. dissertation, University of Texas at Austin.

Guerra Currie, Anne-Marie P.; Meier, Richard P. and Walters, Keith (2002). A crosslinguistic examination of the lexicons of four signed languages. In R. P. Meier, K. Cormier and D. Quinto-Pozos (eds.), *Modality and structure in signed and spoken languages*, pp. 224–236. Cambridge, UK and New York: Cambridge University Press.

Gullberg, Marianne and Indefrey, Peter (eds.) (2006). *The cognitive neuroscience of second language acquisition*. Oxford and Malden, MA: Blackwell.

Gullberg, Marianne; Indefrey, Peter and Muysken, Pieter (in prep.). Band'i dje e vlaggetje colo cora: The experimental study of code-switched sentence production in Papiamento–Dutch bilinguals.

Gumperz, John (1967). On the linguistic markers of bilingual communication. *Journal of Social Issues*, **28** (2), 48–57.

Gumperz, John (1970). Verbal strategies and multilingual communication. In J. E. Alatis (ed.), *Report of the Twenty-first Annual Round-Table Meeting on Linguistics and Language Studies*, pp. 129–147. Washington, DC: Georgetown University Press.

Gumperz, John J. (1976). The sociolinguistic significance of conversational code-switching. In J. Cook-Gumperz and J.J. Gumperz (eds.), *Papers on language and context: Working Papers No. 46*, pp. 1–46. Berkeley, CA: University of California Language Behavior Research Laboratory.

Gumperz, John J. (1982a). *Discourse strategies*. Cambridge, UK and New York: Cambridge University Press.

Gumperz, John J. (1982b). *Language and social identity*. Cambridge, UK and New York: Cambridge University Press.

Gumperz, John J. and Hernández-Chávez, Eduardo (1971). Cognitive aspects of bilingual communication. In W. H. Whiteley (ed.), *Language use* *and social change: Problems of multilingualism with special reference to Eastern Africa*, pp. 111–125. Oxford and New York: Oxford University Press.

Gürel, Ayse (2004). Selectivity in L2-induced L1 attrition: A psycholinguistic account. *Journal of Neurolinguistics. Special Issue: Attrition*, **17** (1), 53–78.

Gutiérrez-Clellen, Vera and Kreiter, Jacqueline (2003). Understanding child bilingual acquisition using parent and teacher reports. *Applied Psycholinguistics*, **24** (2), 267–288.

Gutiérrez-Clellen, Vera and Peña, Elizabeth (2001). Dynamic assessment of diverse children: A tutorial. *Language, Speech, and Hearing Services in Schools*, **32** (4), 212–224.

Gutiérrez-Clellen, Vera F. (1996). Language diversity: Implications for assessment. In K. N. Cole, P. S. Dale and D. J. Thal (eds.), *Assessment of communication and language*, pp. 29–56. Baltimore: Paul H. Brookes.

Hagoort, Peter; Brown, Colin and Groothusen, Jolanda (1993). The syntactic positive shift (SPS) as an ERP measure of syntactic processing. *Language and Cognitive Processes. Special Issue: Event-related brain potentials in the study of language*, **8** (4), 439–483.

Hahne, Anja (2001). What's different in second-language processing? Evidence from event-related brain potentials. *Journal of Psycholinguistic Research. Special Issue: Brain imaging and language processing*, **30** (3), 251–266.

Hahne, Anja and Friederici, Angela D. (2001). Processing a second language: Late learners' comprehension mechanisms as revealed by event-related brain potentials. *Bilingualism: Language and Cognition. Special Issue: The cognitive neuroscience of bilingualism*, **4** (2), 123–141.

Hahne, Anja; Mueller, Jutta L. and Clahsen, Harald (2006). Morphological processing in a second language: Behavioral and event-related brain potential evidence for storage and decomposition. *Journal of Cognitive Neuroscience*, **18** (1), 121–134.

Haiman, John (1980). The iconicity of grammar: Isomorphism and motivation. *Language*, **56** (3), 515–540.

Haiman, John (1983). Iconic and economic motivation. *Language*, **59** (4), 781–819.

Hakuta, Kenji and D'Andrea, Daniel (1992). Some properties of bilingual maintenance and loss in Mexican background high-school students. *Applied Linguistics*, **13** (1), 72–99.

Halmari, Helena (1992). Codeswitching strategies as a mirror of language loss: A case study of two child bilinguals. In D. Staub and C. Delk (eds.), *The proceedings of the Twelfth Second Language Research Forum*, pp. 200–215. Michigan State University, East Lansing, MI: Papers in Applied Linguistics – Michigan.

Halmari, Helena (1997). *Government and codeswitching: Explaining American Finnish*. Amsterdam and Philadelphia: John Benjamins.

Halmari, Helena (2005). "I'm forgetting both": L1 maintenance and codeswitching in Finnish–English language contact. *International Journal of Bilingualism*, **9** (3-4), 397–433.

Hamers, Josiane F. and Blanc, Michel H. A. (2000). *Bilinguality and bilingualism* (2nd edn.). Cambridge, UK and New York: Cambridge University Press.

Hamers, Josiane F. and Lambert, Wallace E. (1972). Bilingual interdependencies in auditory perception. *Journal of Verbal Learning and Verbal Behavior*, **11** (3), 303–310.

Hammer, Carol Scheffner (1998). Toward a "thick description" of families: Using ethnography to overcome the obstacles to providing family-centered early intervention services. *American Journal of Speech Language Pathology*, **7** (1), 5–22.

Hammer, Carol Scheffner (2000). Language acquisition and intervention in context. Paper presented at *The Georgetown University Roundtable on Languages and Linguistics*, Washington, D.C.

Hartsuiker, Robert J.; Pickering, Martin J. and Weltkamp, Eline (2004). Is syntax separate or shared between languages? Cross-linguistic syntactic priming in Spanish–English bilinguals. *Psychological Science*, **15** (6), 409–414.

Hasegawa, Mihoko; Carpenter, Patricia A. and Just, Marcel Adam (2002). An fMRI study of bilingual sentence comprehension and workload. *NeuroImage*, **15** (3), 647–660.

Hasselmo, Nils (1972). Code-switching as ordered selection. In E. S. Firchow, K. Grimstad, N. Hasselmo and W. A. O'Neil (eds.), *Studies for Einar Haugen presented by friends and colleagues*, pp. 261–280. The Hague: Mouton.

Haugen, Einar I. (1956). *Bilingualism in the Americas: A bibliography and research guide*. University of Alabama Press.

Haugen, Einar I. (1972a). The analysis of linguistic borrowing. In A. S. Dil (ed.), *The ecology of language: Essays by Einar Haugen*, pp. 79–109. Stanford: Stanford University Press.

Haugen, Einar I. (1972b). The stigmata of bilingualism. In A. S. Dil (ed.), *The ecology of language: Essays by Einar Haugen*, pp. 307–324. Stanford: Stanford University Press.

Hauser, Peter C. (2000). An analysis of codeswitching: American Sign Language and Cued English. In M. Metzger (ed.), *Bilingualism and identity in deaf communities*, pp. 43–78. Washington, D.C.: Gallaudet University Press.

Haust, Delia (1995). *Codeswitching in Gambia: Eine soziolinguistische Untersuchung von Mandinka, Wolof und Englisch in Kontakt*. Köln: Rüdiger Köppe Verlag.

Haust, Delia and Dittmar, Norbert (1998). Taxonomic or functional models in the description of codeswitching? Evidence from Mandinka and Wolof in African contact situations. In R. Jacobson (ed.), *Codeswitching worldwide*, pp. 79–90. Berlin and New York: Mouton de Gruyter.

Have, Paul ten (1999). *Doing conversation analysis: A practical guide*. London: Sage.

Hazan, Valerie L. and Boulakia, Georges (1993). Perception and production of a voicing contrast by French–English bilinguals. *Language and Speech*, **36** (1), 17–38.

Heine, Bernd and Kuteva, Tania (2003). On contact-induced grammaticalization. *Studies in Language*, **27** (3), 529–572.

Heller, Monica (ed.) (1988a). *Codeswitching: Anthropological and sociolinguistic perspectives*. Berlin and New York: Mouton de Gruyter.

Heller, Monica (1988b). Strategic ambiguity: Codeswitching in the management of conflict. In M. Heller (ed.), *Codeswitching: Anthropological and sociolinguistic perspectives*, pp. 79–98. Berlin and New York: Mouton de Gruyter.

Heller, Monica (1995). Language choice, social institutions, and symbolic domination. *Language in Society*, **24** (3), 373–405.

Heredia, Roberto R. and Stewart, Mark T. (2002). On-line methods in bilingual spoken language research. In R. R. Heredia and J. Altarriba (eds.), *Bilingual sentence processing*, pp. 7–28. Amsterdam: Elsevier.

Heritage, John (1984). *Garfinkel and ethnomethodology*. Cambridge: Polity Press.

Heritage, John C. and Watson, D. Rodney (1979). Formulations as conversational objects. In G. Psathas (ed.), *Everyday language: Studies in ethnomethodology*, pp. 123–162. New York: Irvington.

Hernandez, Arturo E.; Dapretto, Mirella; Mazziotta, John and Bookheimer, Susan (2001). Language switching and language representation in Spanish–English bilinguals: An fMRI study. *NeuroImage*, **14** (2), 510–520.

Hernandez, Arturo E.; Martinez, Antigona and Kohnert, Kathryn (2000). In search of the language switch: An fMRI study of picture naming in Spanish–English bilinguals. *Brain and Language*, **73** (3), 421–431.

Heselwood, Barry and McChrystal, Louise (2000). Gender, accent features and voicing in Panjabi–English bilingual children. *Leeds Working Papers in Linguistics and Phonetics*, **8**, 45–70.

Hewitt, Roger (1986). *White Talk Black Talk*. Cambridge, UK and New York: Cambridge University Press.

Hinrichs, Lars (2006). *Codeswitching on the web: English and Jamaican Creole in e-mail communication*. Amsterdam and Philadelphia: John Benjamins.

Hlavac, Jim (2000). Croatian in Melbourne: Lexicon, switching and morphosyntactic features in the speech of second-generation bilinguals. Ph.D. dissertation, Monash University.

Hlavac, Jim (2003). *Second-generation speech: Lexicon, code-switching and morpho-syntax of Croatian–English bilinguals*. New York: Peter Lang.

Hock, Hans H. (1991). *Principles of historical linguistics: Second edition, revised and updated*. Berlin and New York: Mouton de Gruyter.

Hoffmeister, Robert and Moores, Donald F. (1987). Code switching in deaf adults. *American Annals of the Deaf*, **132** (1), 31–34.

Højrup, Thomas (1983). The concept of life-mode: A form-specifying mode of analysis applied to contemporary Western Europe. *Ethnologia Scandinavica*, **13**, 15–50.

Holcomb, Phillip J.; Kounios, John; Anderson, Jane E. and West, W. Caroline (1999). Dual-coding, context-availability, and concreteness effects in sentence comprehension: An electrophysiological investigation. *Journal of Experimental Psychology: Learning, Memory, and Cognition*, **25** (3), 721–742.

Holtzheimer, Paul; Fawaz, Walid; Wilson, Christopher and Avery, David (2005). Repetitive transcranial magnetic stimulation may induce language switching in bilingual patients. *Brain and Language*, **94** (3), 274–277.

Hulk, Aafke and Müller, Natascha (2000). Bilingual first language acquisition at the interface between syntax and pragmatics. *Bilingualism: Language and Cognition. Special Issue: Syntactic aspects of bilingual acquisition*, **3** (3), 227–244.

Hulk, Aafke and van der Linden, Elisabeth (2005). The role of illocutionary operators in the emerging grammars of bilingual children. *International Journal of Bilingualism*, **9** (2), 179–203.

Hymes, Dell (1972). Models of the interaction of language and social life. In J. J. Gumperz and D. H. Hymes (eds.), *Directions in sociolinguistics: The ethnography of communication*, pp. 35–71. New York: Holt, Rinehart and Winston.

Hymes, Dell H. (1974). *Foundations in sociolinguistics: An ethnographic approach*. Philadelphia: University of Pennsylvania Press.

Illes, Judy; Francis, Wendy S.; Desmond, John E.; Gabrieli, John D. E.; Glover, Gary H.; Poldrack, Russell; Lee, Christine J. and Wagner, Anthony D. (1999). Convergent cortical representation of semantic processing in bilinguals. *Brain and Language*, **70** (3), 347–363.

Indefrey, Peter (2006). A meta-analysis of hemodynamic studies on first and second language processing: Which suggested differences can we trust and what do they mean? *Language Learning*, **56** (Suppl. 1), 279–304.

Isurin, Ludmila (2000). Deserted island or a child's first language forgetting. *Bilingualism: Language and Cognition*, **3** (2), 151–166.

Jackendoff, Ray (1977). *X syntax: A study of phrase structure*. Cambridge, MA: MIT Press.

Jackson, Georgina M.; Swainson, Rachel; Cunnington, Ross and Jackson, Stephen R. (2001). ERP correlates of executive control during repeated language switching. *Bilingualism: Language and Cognition. Special Issue: The cognitive neuroscience of bilingualism*, **4** (2), 169–178.

Jackson, Georgina M.; Swainson, Rachel; Mullin, A.; Cunnington, Ross and Jackson, Stephen R. (2004). ERP correlates of a receptive language-switching task. *The Quarterly Journal of Experimental Psychology. Section A: Human Experimental Psychology*, **57A** (2), 223–240.

Jacobs, Haike and Gussenhoven, Carlos (2000). Loan phonology: Perception, salience, the lexicon and OT. In J. Dekkers, F. van der Leeuw and J. van de Weijer (eds.), *Optimality theory: Phonology, syntax, and acquisition*, pp. 193–209. Oxford and New York: Oxford University Press.

Jacobson, Rodolfo (2000). Language alternation: The third kind of codeswitching mechanism. In R. Jacobson (ed.), *Codeswitching worldwide II*, pp. 59–74. Berlin and New York: Mouton de Gruyter.

Jake, Janice L. (1994). Intrasentential code switching and pronouns: On the categorial status of functional elements. *Linguistics*, **32** (2), 271–298.

Jake, Janice L. (1998). Constructing interlanguage: Building a composite matrix language. *Linguistics*, **36** (2), 333–382.

Jake, Janice L. and Myers-Scotton, Carol (1997). Codeswitching and compromise strategies: Implications for lexical structure. *International Journal of Bilingualism*, **1** (1), 25–39.

Jake, Janice L.; Myers-Scotton, Carol and Gross, Steven (2002). Making a minimalist approach to codeswitching work: Adding the matrix language. *Bilingualism: Language and Cognition*, **5** (1), 69–91.

Jarvis, Scott (2000). Methodological rigor in the study of transfer: Identifying L1 influence in the interlanguage lexicon. *Language Learning*, **50** (2), 245–309.

Jisa, Harriet (2000). Language mixing in the weak language: Evidence from two children. *Journal of Pragmatics*, **32** (9), 1363–1386.

Johanson, Lars (1993). Code-copying in immigrant Turkish. In G. Extra and L. Verhoeven (eds.), *Immigrant languages in Europe*, pp. 197–221. Clevedon: Multilingual Matters.

Johanson, Lars (1998). Frame-changing code-copying in immigrant varieties. In G. Extra and L. Verhoeven (eds.), *Bilingualism and migration*, pp. 247–260. Berlin and New York: Mouton de Gruyter.

Jørgensen, J. Normann (1998). Children's acquisition of code-switching for power wielding. In P. Auer (ed.), *Code-switching in conversation: Language, interaction and identity*, pp. 237–261. London and New York: Routledge.

Joshi, Aravind K. (1985a). How much context-sensitivity is necessary for assigning structural descriptions? Tree adjoining grammars. In D. R. Dowty, L. Karttunen and A. M. Zwicky (eds.), *Natural language parsing: Psychological, computational, and theoretical perspectives*, pp. 206–250. Cambridge, UK and New York: Cambridge University Press.

Joshi, Aravind K. (1985b). Processing of sentences with intrasentential code switching. In D. R. Dowty, L. Karttunen and A. M. Zwicky (eds.), *Natural language parsing: Psychological, computational, and theoretical perspectives*, pp. 190–205. Cambridge, UK and New York: Cambridge University Press.

Kachman, William Paul (1991). An investigation of code switching behavior of deaf children. Ph.D. dissertation, University of Maryland.

Kachru, Braj B (1978). Toward structuring code-mixing: An Indian perspective. *International Journal of the Sociology of Language*, **16**, 27–46.

Kamwangamalu, Nkonko Mudipanu (1989). The morphosyntactic aspects of French/English-Bantu code-mixing: Evidence for universal constraints. In B. Music, R. Graczyk and C. R. Wiltshire (eds.), *CLS 25: Papers from the 25th Annual Regional Meeting of the Chicago Linguistic Society: Part Two: Parasession on Language in Context*, pp. 157–170. Chicago: Chicago Linguistic Society.

Kan, Pui Fong and Kohnert, Kathryn (2005). Preschoolers learning Hmong and English: Lexical-semantic skills in L1 and L2. *Journal of Speech, Language, and Hearing Research*, **48** (2), 372–383.

Kaufman, Dorit (2001). Tales of L1 attrition: Evidence from pre-puberty children. In T. Ammerlaan, M. Hulsen, H. Strating and K. Yağmur (eds.), *Sociolinguistic and psycholinguistic perspectives on maintenance and loss of minority languages*, pp. 185–202. Münster: Waxmann.

Kaufman, Dorit and Aronoff, Mark (1991). Morphological disintegration and reconstruction in first language attrition. In H. W. Seliger and R. M. Vago (eds.), *First language attrition: Structural and theoretical perspectives*, pp. 175–188. Cambridge, UK and New York: Cambridge University Press.

Kayne, Richard S. (1994). *The antisymmetry of syntax*. Cambridge, MA: MIT Press.

Kellerman, Eric and Sharwood Smith, Michael (1986). *Crosslinguistic influence in second language acquisition*. New York: Pergamon Institute of English.

Kerkhofs, Roel; Dijkstra, Ton; Chwilla, Dorothee J. and de Bruijn, Ellen R. A. (2006). Testing a model for bilingual semantic priming with interlingual homographs: RT and N400 effects. *Brain Research*, **1068** (1), 170–183.

Kerswill, Paul (1996). Children, adolescents, and language change. *Language Variation and Change*, **8** (2), 177–202.

Khattab, Ghada (2002a). /l/ Production in English–Arabic bilingual speakers. *International Journal of Bilingualism*, **6** (3), 335–353.

Khattab, Ghada (2002b). /r/ Production in English and Arabic bilingual and monolingual speakers. *Leeds Working Papers in Linguistics and Phonetics*, **9**, 91–129.

Khattab, Ghada (2002c). VOT in English and Arabic bilingual and monolingual children. In D. B. Parkinson and E. Benmamoun (eds.), *Perspectives on Arabic linguistics XIII–XIV: Papers from the thirteenth and fourteenth annual Symposia on Arabic Linguistics*, pp. 1–38. Amsterdam and Philadelphia: John Benjamins.

Khattab, Ghada (2003). Sociolinguistic competence and the bilingual's choice of phonetic variants: Auditory and instrumental data from English–Arabic bilinguals. Ph.D. dissertation, University of Leeds.

Khattab, Ghada (2006). Phonological acquisition by Arabic–English bilingual children. In Z. Hua and B. Dodd (eds.), *Phonological development and disorders in children: A multilingual perspective*, pp. 383–412. Clevedon: Multilingual Matters.

Khattab, Ghada (2007). Variation in vowel production by English–Arabic bilinguals. In J. Cole and J. I. Hualde (eds.), *Papers in laboratory phonology IX*, pp. 383–410. Berlin and New York: Mouton de Gruyter.

Kibogoya, Ado (1995). Kiswahili/English code-switching: Some morphological and syntactic aspects. Ph.D. dissertation, Lancaster University.

Kim, Karl H. S.; Relkin, Norman R.; Lee, Kyoung-Min and Hirsch, Joy (1997). Distinct cortical areas associated with native and second languages. *Nature*, **388** (6638), 171–174.

King, Jonathan W. and Kutas, Marta (1995). Who did what and when? Using word- and clause-level ERPs to monitor working memory usage in reading. *Journal of Cognitive Neuroscience*, **7** (3), 376–395.

King, Ruth (2000). *The lexical basis of grammatical borrowing: A Prince Edward Island French case study*. Amsterdam and Philadelphia: John Benjamins.

Klein, Denise; Milner, Brenda; Zatorre, Robert J.; Meyer, Ernst and Evans, Alan C. (1995). The neural substrates underlying word generation: A bilingual functional-imaging study. *Proceedings of the National Academy of Sciences of the United States of America*, **92** (7), 2899–2903.

Klein, Denise; Zatorre, Robert J.; Milner, Brenda; Meyer, Ernst and Evans, Alan C. (1994). Left putaminal activation when speaking a second language: Evidence from PET. *Neuroreport*, **5** (17), 2295–2297.

Klein, Flora (1980). A quantitative study of syntactic and pragmatic indications of change in the Spanish of bilinguals in the US. In W. Labov (ed.), *Locating language in time and space*, pp. 69–82. New York: Academic Press.

Klima, Edward S. and Bellugi, Ursula (1979). *The signs of language*. Cambridge, MA: Harvard University Press.

Klintborg, Staffan (1995). Swanson's swan song. The dying of Swedish in America. *Moderna Sprak*, **89** (1), 15–29.

Kluender, Robert and Kutas, Marta (1993). Bridging the gap: Evidence from ERPs on the processing of unbounded dependencies. *Journal of Cognitive Neuroscience*, **5** (2), 196–214.

Kohnert, Kathryn; Yim, Dongsun; Nett, Kelly; Kan, Pui Fong and Duran, Lillian (2005). Intervention with linguistically diverse preschool children: A focus on developing home language(s). *Language, Speech, and Hearing Services in Schools*, **36** (3), 251–263.

Kohnert, Kathryn J. and Bates, Elizabeth (2002). Balancing bilinguals II: Lexical comprehension and cognitive processing in children learning Spanish and English. *Journal of Speech, Language, and Hearing Research*, **45** (2), 347–359.

Kolers, Paul A. (1966). Reading and talking bilingually. *American Journal of Psychology*, **79** (3), 357–376.

Koopman, Hilda and Sportiche, Dominique (1991). The position of subjects. *Lingua*, **85** (2–3), 211–258.

Kootstra, Gerrit Jan; Van Hell, Janet and Dijkstra, Ton (in preparation). Interactive alignment and syntactic choice in code-switching in bilinguals.

Köppe, Regina and Meisel, Jürgen M. (1995). Code-switching in bilingual first language acquisition. In L. Milroy and P. Muysken (eds.), *One speaker, two languages: Cross-disciplinary perspectives on code-switching*, pp. 276–301. Cambridge, UK and New York: Cambridge University Press.

Kotz, Sonja A. (2001). Neurolinguistic evidence for bilingual language representation: A comparison of reaction times and event-related brain potentials. *Bilingualism: Language and Cognition. Special Issue: The cognitive neuroscience of bilingualism*, **4** (2), 143–154.

Kotz, Sonja A. and Elston-Güttler, Kerrie (2004). The role of proficiency on processing categorical and associative information in the L2 as revealed by reaction times and event-related brain potentials. *Journal of Neurolinguistics. Special Issue: Automatic and Controlled Language Processes*, **17** (2–3), 215–235.

Kounios, John and Holcomb, Phillip J. (1994). Concreteness effects in semantic processing: ERP evidence supporting dual-coding theory. *Journal of Experimental Psychology: Learning, Memory, and Cognition*, **20** (4), 804–823.

Kouritzin, Sandra G. (1999). *Face[t]s of first language loss.* Mahwah, NJ: Lawrence Erlbaum Associates.

Kouwenberg, Silvia and Muysken, Pieter (1995). Papiamento. In J. Arends, P. Muysken and N. Smith (eds.), *Pidgins and Creoles: An introduction*, pp. 205–218. Amsterdam and Philadelphia: John Benjamins.

Kovács, Magdolna (2001). *Code-switching and language shift in Australian Finnish in comparison with Australian Hungarian.* Åbo: Åbo Akademi University Press.

Kroll, Judith F.; Bobb, Susan C. and Wodniecka, Zofia (2006). Language selectivity is the exception, not the rule: Arguments against a fixed locus of language selection in bilingual speech. *Bilingualism: Language and Cognition. Special Issue: Lexical Access in Bilingual Speech Production*, **9** (2), 119–135.

Kroll, Judith F. and de Groot, Annette M. B. (1997). Lexical and conceptual memory in the bilingual: Mapping form to meaning in two languages. In A. M. de Groot and J. F. Kroll (eds.), *Tutorials in bilingualism: Psycholinguistic perspectives*, pp. 169–199. Mahwah, NJ: Lawrence Erlbaum Associates.

Kroll, Judith F. and Stewart, Erika (1994). Category interference in translation and picture naming: Evidence for asymmetric connection between bilingual memory representations. *Journal of Memory and Language*, **33** (2), 149–174.

Kuhberg, Heinz (1992). Longitudinal L2-attrition versus L2-acquisition in three Turkish children – empirical findings. *Second Language Research*, **8** (2), 138–154.

Kuhl, Patricia K. and Meltzoff, Andrew N. (1996). Infant vocalizations in response to speech: Vocal imitation and developmental change. *Journal of the Acoustical Society of America*, **100** (4, Pt. 1), 2425–2438.

Kuntze, Marlon (2000). Codeswitching in ASL and written English language contact. In K. Emmorey and H. Lane (eds.), *The signs of language revisited: An anthology to honor Ursula Bellugi and Edward Klima*, pp. 287–302. Mahwah, NJ: Lawrence Erlbaum Associates.

Kutas, Marta and Hillyard, Steven A. (1980a). Event-related brain potentials to semantically inappropriate and surprisingly large words. *Biological Psychology*, **11** (2), 99–116.

Kutas, Marta and Hillyard, Steven A. (1980b). Reading senseless sentences: Brain potentials reflect semantic incongruity. *Science*, **207** (4427), 203–205.

Kutas, Marta and Hillyard, Steven A. (1984). Brain potentials during reading reflect word expectancy and semantic association. *Nature*, **307** (5947), 161–163.

Kutas, Marta; Neville, Helen J. and Holcomb, Phillip J. (1987). A preliminary comparison of the N400 response to semantic anomalies during reading, listening and signing. In R. J. Ellingson, N. M. F. Murray and A. M. Halliday (eds.), *The London Symposia: Electroencephalography and clinical neurophysiology, supplement 39*, pp. 325–330. Amsterdam: Elsevier.

Kyuchukov, Hristo (2006). Code-switching among Muslim Roms in Bulgaria. *International Journal of the Sociology of Language*, **179**, 41–51.

La Heij, Wido (2005). Selection processes in monolingual and bilingual lexical access. In J. F. Kroll and A. M. B. de Groot (eds.), *Handbook of bilingualism: Psycholinguistic approaches*, pp. 289–307. Oxford and New York: Oxford University Press.

Labov, William (1963). The social motivation of a sound change. *Word*, **19**, 273–309.

Labov, William (1972). *Sociolinguistic patterns*. Philadelphia: University of Pennsylvania Press.

Ladegaard, Hans J. and Bleses, Dorthe (2003). Gender differences in young children's speech: The acquisition of sociolinguistic competence. *International Journal of Applied Linguistics*, **13** (2), 222–233.

Lado, Robert (1957). *Linguistics across cultures: Applied linguistics for language teachers*. Ann Arbor: University of Michigan Press.

Lanza, Elizabeth (1992). Can bilingual two-year-olds code-switch? *Journal of Child Language*, **19** (3), 633–658.

Lanza, Elizabeth (1997). Language contact in bilingual two-year-olds and code-switching: Language encounters of a different kind? *International Journal of Bilingualism*, **1** (2), 135–162.

Lasnik, Howard and Uriagereka, Juan (1988). *A course in GB syntax: Lectures on binding and empty categories*. Cambridge, MA: MIT Press.

Lauttamus, Timo (1990). *Code-switching and borrowing in the English of Finnish Americans in an interview setting*. Joensuu: University of Joensuu.

Le Page, Robert Brock and Tabouret-Keller, Andrée (1985). *Acts of identity: Creole-based approaches to language and ethnicity*. Cambridge, UK and New York: Cambridge University Press.

Lederberg, Amy R. and Morales, Cesáreo (1985). Code switching by bilinguals: Evidence against a third grammar. *Journal of Psycholinguistic Research*, **14** (2), 113–136.

Lee, Alison; **Hewlett, Nigel and Nairn, Moray** (1995). Voice and gender in children. In S. Mills (ed.), *Language and gender: Interdisciplinary perspectives*, pp. 194–204. Harlow, UK: Longman.

Lee, Dorothy (1983). Sources and aspects of code-switching in the signing of a deaf adult and her interlocutors. Ph.D. dissertation, University of Texas at Austin.

Lee, Mee Hwa (1991). A parametric approach to code-mixing. Ph.D. dissertation, State University of New York.

Lehtinen, Meri (1966). An analysis of a Finnish–English bilingual corpus. Ph.D. dissertation, Indiana University.

Leonard, Laurence B. (2001). Specific language impairment across languages. In D.V. M. Bishop and L. B. Leonard (eds.), *Speech and language impairments in children: Causes, characteristics, intervention, and outcome*, pp. 115–129. Hove, UK: Psychology Press.

Leseman, Paul P.M. (2000). Bilingual vocabulary development of Turkish preschoolers in The Netherlands. *Journal of Multilingual and Multicultural Development*, **21** (2), 93–112.

Levelt, Willem J.M. (1989). *Speaking: From intention to articulation*. Cambridge, MA: MIT Press.

Levinson, Stephen C. (1983). *Pragmatics*. Cambridge, UK and New York: Cambridge University Press.

Li, Ping (1996). Spoken word recognition of code-switched words by Chinese–English bilinguals. *Journal of Memory and Language*, **35** (6), 757–774.

Li Wei (1994). *Three generations, two languages, one family: Language choice and language shift in a Chinese community in Britain*. Clevedon: Multilingual Matters.

Li Wei (1998). The "why" and "how" questions in the analysis of conversational code-switching. In P. Auer (ed.), *Code-switching in conversation: Language, interaction and identity*, pp. 156–179. London and New York: Routledge.

Li Wei (ed.) (2000). *The bilingualism reader*. London and New York: Routledge.

Li Wei (2002). "What do you want me to say?" On the conversation analysis approach to bilingual interaction. *Language in Society*, **31** (2), 159–180.

Li Wei (2005). "How can you tell?" Towards a common sense explanation of conversational code-switching. *Journal of Pragmatics*, **37** (3), 375–389.

Li Wei; **Milroy, Lesley and Ching, Pong Sin** (2000). A two-step sociolinguistic analysis of code-switching and language choice: The example of a bilingual Chinese community in Britain. In Li Wei (ed.), *The bilingualism reader*, pp. 188–209. London and New York: Routledge.

Liceras, Juana M. (2002). Uninterpretable features and the issue of language dominance. Paper presented at *The European Research Conference on Theoretical and Experimental Linguistics, Corinth, Greece, June 1–2, 2002.*

Liceras, Juana M.; Spradlin, K. Todd and Fernández Fuertes, Raquel (2005). Bilingual early functional-lexical mixing and the activation of formal features. *International Journal of Bilingualism*, **9** (2), 227–252.

Lindholm, Kathryn J. and Padilla, Amado M. (1978). Language mixing in bilingual children. *Journal of Child Language*, **5** (2), 327–335.

Lipski, John M. (1978). Code-switching and the problem of bilingual competence. In M. Paradis (ed.), *Aspects of bilingualism*, pp. 250–264. Columbia, SC: Hornbeam Press.

Lipski, John M. (1985). *Linguistic aspects of Spanish–English language switching.* Tempe, AZ: Center for Latin American Studies, Arizona State University.

Lipski, John M. (2004). Is "Spanglish" the third language of the South? Truth and fantasy about U.S. Spanish. *Invited keynote lecture, LAVIS-III, Language Variation in the South, University of Alabama, Tuscaloosa, April 16, 2004.*

Loebell, Helga and Bock, Kathryn (2003). Structural priming across languages. *Linguistics*, **41** (5(387)), 791–824.

Lucas, Ceil and Valli, Clayton (1992). *Language contact in the American deaf community.* San Diego, CA: Academic Press.

Lucas, Timothy H. II; McKhann, Guy M. II and Ojemann, George A. (2004). Functional separation of languages in the bilingual brain: A comparison of electrical stimulation language mapping in 25 bilingual patients and 117 monolingual control patients. *Journal of Neurosurgery*, **101** (3), 449–457.

Luo, Shiow-Huey and Wiseman, Richard L. (2000). Ethnic language maintenance among Chinese immigrant children in the United States. *International Journal of Intercultural Relations*, **24** (3), 307–324.

Macaulay, Ronald K. S. (1977). *Language, social class, and education: A Glasgow study.* Edinburgh: Edinburgh University Press.

MacLeod, Colin M. (1991). Half a century of research on the Stroop effect: An integrative review. *Psychological Bulletin*, **109** (2), 163–203.

Macnamara, John (1967a). The bilingual's linguistic performance – A psychological overview. *Journal of Social Issues*, **23** (2), 58–77.

Macnamara, John (1967b). The linguistic independence of bilinguals. *Journal of Verbal Learning & Verbal Behavior*, **6** (5), 729–736.

Macnamara, John; Krauthammer, Marcel and Bolgar, Marianne (1968). Language switching in bilinguals as a function of stimulus and response uncertainty. *Journal of Experimental Psychology*, **78** (2, Pt.1), 208–215.

Macnamara, John and Kushnir, Seymour L. (1971). Linguistic independence of bilinguals: The input switch. *Journal of Verbal Learning & Verbal Behavior*, **10** (5), 480–487.

MacSwan, Jeff (1999a). *A minimalist approach to intrasentential code switching.* New York: Garland.

MacSwan, Jeff (1999b). *A minimalist approach to intrasentential code switching: Spanish–Nahuatl bilingualism in Central Mexico*. London and New York: Routledge.

MacSwan, Jeff (2000). The architecture of the bilingual language faculty: Evidence from intrasentential code switching. *Bilingualism: Language and Cognition*, **3** (1), 37–54.

MacSwan, Jeff (2004). Code Switching and grammatical theory. In T. K. Bhatia and W. C. Ritchie (eds.), *The handbook of bilingualism*, pp. 283–311. Oxford and Malden, MA: Blackwell.

Mæhlum, Brit (1990). Codeswitching in Hemnesberget – myth or reality? In E. H. Jahr and O. Lorentz (eds.), *Tromsø linguistics in the Eighties*, pp. 338–355. Oslo: Novus Press. Reprinted in *Journal of Pragmatics*, 1996, **25** (6), 749–761.

Mahootian, Shahrzad (1993). A null theory of code switching. Ph.D. dissertation, Northwestern University.

Mahootian, Shahrzad and Santorini, Beatrice (1996). Code switching and the complement/adjunct distinction. *Linguistic Inquiry*, **27** (3), 464–479.

Mariën, Peter; Abutalebi, Jubin; Engelborghs, Sebastiaan and De Deyn, Peter P. (2005). Pathophysiology of language switching and mixing in an early bilingual child with subcortical aphasia. *Neurocase*, **11** (6), 385–398.

Marslen-Wilson, William (1973). Linguistic structure and speech shadowing at very short latencies. *Nature*, **244**, 522–523.

McCardle, Peggy; Kim, Julia; Grube, Carl and Randall, Virginia (1995). An approach to bilingualism in early intervention. *Infants and Young Children*, **7** (3), 63–73.

McCarthy, John J. (2002). *A thematic guide to optimality theory*. Cambridge, UK and New York: Cambridge University Press.

McClure, Erica (1977). Aspects of code-switching in the discourse of bilingual Mexican-American children. In M. Saville-Troike (ed.), *Linguistics and anthropology*, pp. 93–115. Washington, D.C.: Georgetown University Press.

McClure, Erica (1981). Formal and functional aspects of the codeswitched discourse of bilingual children. In R. P. Durán (ed.), *Latino language and communicative behavior*, pp. 69–94. Norwood, NJ: Ablex.

McClure, Erica (1998). The relationship between form and function in written national language – English codeswitching: Evidence from Mexico, Spain and Bulgaria. In R. Jacobson (ed.), *Codeswitching worldwide*, pp. 125–152. Berlin and New York: Mouton de Gruyter.

McClure, Erica and McClure, Malcom (1988). Macro- and micro-sociolinguistic dimensions of code-switching in Vingard (Romania). In M. Heller (ed.), *Codeswitching: Anthropological and sociolinguistic perspectives*, pp. 25–52. Berlin and New York: Mouton de Gruyter.

McConvell, Patrick (1988). Mix-im-up: Aboriginal code-switching, old and new. In M. Heller (ed.), *Codeswitching: Anthropological and* *sociolinguistic perspectives*, pp. 97–149. Berlin and New York: Mouton de Gruyter.

McConvell, Patrick and Meakins, Felicity (2005). Gurindji Kriol: A mixed language emerges from code-switching. *Australian Journal of Linguistics*, **25** (1), 9–30.

McLaughlin, Judith; Osterhout, Lee and Kim, Albert (2004). Neural correlates of second-language word learning: Minimal instruction produces rapid change. *Nature Neuroscience*, **7** (7), 703–704.

McLellan, James A. H. (2005). Malay–English language alternation in two Brunei Darussalam on-line discussion forums. Ph.D. dissertation, Curtin University of Technology.

McNeill, David (1992). *Hand and mind: What gestures reveal about thought.* Chicago: University of Chicago Press.

Mechelli, Andrea; Crinion, Jenny T.; Noppeney, Uta; O'Doherty, John; Ashburner, John; Frackowiak, Richard S. and Price, Cathy J. (2004). Structural plasticity in the bilingual brain: Proficiency in a second language and age at acquisition affect grey-matter density. *Nature*, **431**, 757.

Mees, Inger M. (1990). Patterns of sociophonetic variation in the speech of Cardiff school children. In N. Coupland (ed.), *English in Wales. Diversity, conflict, and change*, pp. 167–194. Clevedon: Multilingual Matters.

Meeuwis, Michael and Blommaert, Jan (1998). A monolectal view of code-switching: Layered code-switching among Zairians in Belgium. In P. Auer (ed.), *Code-switching in conversation: Language, interaction and identity*, pp. 76–100. London and New York: Routledge.

Meier, Richard P. (2002). Why different, why the same? Explaining effects and non-effects of modality upon linguistic structure in sign and speech. In R. P. Meier, K. Cormier and D. Quinto-Pozos (eds.), *Modality and structure in signed and spoken languages*, pp. 1–25. Cambridge, UK and New York: Cambridge University Press.

Meijer, Paul J. A. and Fox Tree, Jean E. (2003). Building syntactic structures in speaking: A bilingual exploration. *Experimental Psychology*, **50** (3), 184–195.

Meisel, Jürgen M. (1994). Code-switching in young bilingual children: The acquisition of grammatical constraints. *Studies in Second Language Acquisition*, **16** (4), 413–439.

Merino, Barbara J. (1992). Acquisition of syntactic and phonological features in Spanish. In H. W. Langdon and L.-R. L. Cheng (eds.), *Hispanic children and adults with communication disorders: Assessment and intervention*, pp. 57–98. Gaithersburg, MD: Aspen Publishers.

Metzger, Melanie (1995). Constructed dialogue and constructed action in American Sign Language. In C. Lucas (ed.), *Sociolinguistics in deaf communities*, pp. 255–271. Washington, D.C.: Gallaudet University Press.

Meuter, Renata F. I. (2005). Language selection in bilinguals: Mechanisms and processes. In J. F. Kroll and A. M. de Groot (eds.),

Handbook of bilingualism: Psycholinguistic approaches, pp. 349–370. Oxford and New York: Oxford University Press.

Meuter, Renata F. I. and Allport, Alan (1999). Bilingual language switching in naming: Asymmetrical costs of language selection. *Journal of Memory and Language*, **40** (1), 25–40.

Miccio, Adele W. and Hammer, Carol Scheffner (2006). Bilingual Spanish–English phonological acquisition: The longitudinal course of change. Paper presented at *The Annual Meeting of the American Speech-Language-Hearing Association, Miami, FL, November 16–18, 2006.*

Milroy, Lesley (1980). *Language and social networks.* Baltimore: University Park Press.

Milroy, Lesley and Gordon, Matthew J. (2003). *Sociolinguistics: Method and interpretation.* Oxford and Malden, MA: Blackwell.

Milroy, Lesley and Li Wei (1995). A social network approach to code-switching: The example of a bilingual community in Britain. In L. Milroy and P. Muysken (eds.), *One speaker, two languages: Cross-disciplinary perspectives on code-switching*, pp. 136–157. Cambridge, UK and New York: Cambridge University Press.

Milroy, Lesley and Muysken, Pieter (1995). *One speaker, two languages: Cross-disciplinary perspectives on code-switching.* Cambridge, UK and New York: Cambridge University Press.

Mitchell, Rosamond and Myles, Florence (2004). *Second language learning theories* (2nd edn.). London: Edward Arnold.

Montrul, Silvina (2002). Incomplete acquisition and attrition of Spanish tense/aspect distinctions in adult bilinguals. *Bilingualism: Language and Cognition*, **5** (1), 39–68.

Montrul, Silvina (2004). Convergent outcomes in L2 acquisition and L1 loss. In M. S. Schmid, B. Kopke, M. Keijzer and L. Weilemar (eds.), *First language attrition: Interdisciplinary perspectives on methodological issues*, pp. 259–279. Amsterdam and Philadelphia: John Benjamins.

Moravcsik, Edit (1975). Verb borrowing. *Wiener Linguistische Gazette*, **8**, 3–31.

Moreno, Eva M.; Federmeier, Kara D. and Kutas, Marta (2002). Switching languages, switching *palabras* (words): An electrophysiological study of code switching. *Brain and Language*, **80** (2), 188–207.

Moreno, Eva M. and Kutas, Marta (2005). Processing semantic anomalies in two languages: An electrophysiological exploration in both languages of Spanish–English bilinguals. *Cognitive Brain Research*, **22** (2), 205–220.

Mougeon, Raymond and Beniak, Edouard (1991). *Linguistic consequences of language contact and restriction: The case of French in Ontario, Canada.* Oxford and New York: Oxford University Press.

Mougeon, Raymond; Nadasdi, Terry and Rehner, Katherine (2005). Contact-induced linguistic innovations on the continuum of language use: The case of French in Ontario. *Bilingualism: Language and Cognition.*

Special Issue: The role of transfer in language variation and change: Evidence from contact varieties of French, **8** (2), 99–115.

Moyer, Melissa G. (1998). Bilingual conversation strategies in Gibraltar. In P. Auer (ed.), *Code-switching in conversation: Language, interaction and identity*, pp. 215–236. London and New York: Routledge.

Mueller, Jutta L.; Hahne, Anja; Fujii, Yugo and Friederici, Angela D. (2005). Native and nonnative speakers' processing of a miniature version of Japanese as revealed by ERPs. *Journal of Cognitive Neuroscience*, **17** (8), 1229–1244.

Müller, Natascha and Hulk, Aafke (2001). Crosslinguistic influence in bilingual language acquisition: Italian and French as recipient languages. *Bilingualism: Language and Cognition*, **4** (1), 1–21.

Müller, Natascha; Kupisch, Tanja; Schmitz, Katrin and Cantone, Katja (2006). *Einführung in die Mehrsprachigkeitsforschung: Deutsch, Französisch, Italienisch*. Tübingen: Gunter Narr Verlag.

Münte, Thomas F.; Heinze, Hans-Jochen and Mangun, George R. (1993). Dissociation of brain activity related to syntactic and semantic aspects of language. *Journal of Cognitive Neuroscience*, **5** (3), 335–344.

Muysken, Pieter (1981). Halfway between Quechua and Spanish: The case for relexification. In A. R. Highfield and A. Valdman (eds.), *Historicity and variation in creole studies*, pp. 52–78. Ann Arbor: Karoma.

Muysken, Pieter (1988). Media Lengua and linguistic theory. *The Canadian Journal of Linguistics/La Revue canadienne de Linguistique*, **33** (4), 409–422.

Muysken, Pieter (1995). Code-switching and grammatical theory. In L. Milroy and P. Muysken (eds.), *One speaker, two languages: Cross-disciplinary perspectives on code-switching*, pp. 177–198. Cambridge, UK and New York: Cambridge University Press.

Muysken, Pieter (1996). Media Lengua. In S. G. Thomason (ed.), *Contact languages: A wider perspective*, pp. 365–426. Amsterdam and Philadelphia: John Benjamins.

Muysken, Pieter (2000). *Bilingual speech: A typology of code-mixing*. Cambridge, UK and New York: Cambridge University Press.

Muysken, Pieter (2005). Two languages in two countries: The use of Spanish and Quechua in songs and poems from Peru and Ecuador. In G. Delgado and J. M. Schechter (eds.), *Quechua verbal artistry: The inscription of Andean voices [Arte expresivo Quechua: la inscripción de voces andinas]*, pp. 35–60. Bonn: Bonner Amerikanistische Studien.

Muysken, Pieter; Kook, Hetty and Vedder, Paul (1996). Papiamento/ Dutch code-switching in bilingual parent-child reading. *Applied Psycholinguistics*, **17** (4), 485–505.

Myers-Scotton, Carol (1983). The negotiation of identities in conversation: A theory of markedness and code choice. *International Journal of the Sociology of Language*, **44**, 115–136.

Myers-Scotton, Carol (1986). Diglossia and code-switching. In J. A. Fishman, A. Tabouret-Keller, M. Clyne, B. Krishnamurti and M. Abdulaziz (eds.),

The Fergusonian Impact: In honor of Charles A. Ferguson on the occasion of his 65th birthday. Vol. 2, pp. 403–415. Berlin and New York: Mouton de Gruyter.

Myers-Scotton, Carol (1991). Intersections between social motivations and structural processing in code-switching. *Papers for the workshop on constraints, conditions and models*, pp. 57–82. Strasbourg: European Science Foundation.

Myers-Scotton, Carol (1993a). *Duelling languages: Grammatical structure in codeswitching*. Oxford and New York: Oxford University Press.

Myers-Scotton, Carol (1993b). *Social motivations for codeswitching: Evidence from Africa*. Oxford and New York: Oxford University Press.

Myers-Scotton, Carol (1995). A lexically based model of code-switching. In L. Milroy and P. Muysken (eds.), *One speaker, two languages: Cross-disciplinary perspectives on code-switching*, pp. 233–256. Cambridge, UK and New York: Cambridge University Press.

Myers-Scotton, Carol (1997). *Duelling languages: Grammatical structure in codeswitching* (2nd edn. with added afterword). Oxford and New York: Oxford University Press.

Myers-Scotton, Carol (1998). A way to dusty death: The matrix language turnover hypothesis. In L. A. Grenoble and L. J. Whaley (eds.), *Endangered languages: Current issues and future prospects*, pp. 289–316. Cambridge, UK and New York: Cambridge University Press.

Myers-Scotton, Carol (2002a). *Contact linguistics: Bilingual encounters and grammatical outcomes*. Oxford and New York: Oxford University Press.

Myers-Scotton, Carol (2002b). Frequency and intentionality in (un-) marked choices in codeswitching: "This is a 24-hour country". *International Journal of Bilingualism*, **6** (2), 205–219.

Myers-Scotton, Carol (2003). What lies beneath: Split (mixed) languages as contact phenomena. In Y. Matras and P. Bakker (eds.), *The mixed language debate: Theoretical and empirical advances*, pp. 73–106. Berlin and New York: Mouton de Gruyter.

Myers-Scotton, Carol (2004). Precision tuning of the Matrix Language Frame (MLF) Model of codeswitching. *Sociolinguistica*, **18**, 106–117.

Myers-Scotton, Carol (2005a). Embedded language elements in Acholi/English codeswitching: What's going on? *Language Matters*, **36** (1), 3–18.

Myers-Scotton, Carol (2005b). Supporting a differential access hypothesis: Code switching and other contact data. In J. F. Kroll and A. M. de Groot (eds.), *Handbook of bilingualism: Psycholinguistic approaches*, pp. 326–348. Oxford and New York: Oxford University Press.

Myers-Scotton, Carol (2005c). Uniform structure: Looking beyond the surface in explaining codeswitching. *Special Issue on Codeswitching, Rivista di Linguistica*, **17**, 15–34.

Myers-Scotton, Carol (2005d). Xhosa–English bilingual corpus. Unpublished.

Myers-Scotton, Carol (2006a). *Multiple voices: An introduction to bilingualism*. Oxford and Malden, MA: Blackwell.

Myers-Scotton, Carol (2006b). Natural codeswitching knocks on the laboratory door. *Bilingualism: Language and Cognition. Special Issue: Lexical Access in Bilingual Speech Production*, **9** (2), 203–212.

Myers-Scotton, Carol and Jake, Janice L. (1995). Matching lemmas in a bilingual language competence and production model: Evidence from intrasentential code switching. *Linguistics*, **33** (5), 981–1024.

Myers-Scotton, Carol and Jake, Janice L. (2000). Four types of morpheme: Evidence from aphasia, code switching, and second-language acquisition. *Linguistics*, **38** (6), 1053–1100.

Myers-Scotton, Carol and Jake, Janice L. (2001). Explaining aspects of code-switching and their implications. In J. L. Nicol (ed.), *One mind, two languages: Bilingual language processing*, pp. 84–116. Oxford and Malden, MA: Blackwell.

Myers-Scotton, Carol; Jake, Janice L. and Okasha, Maha (1996). Arabic and constraints on codeswitching. In M. Eid and D. B. Parkinson (eds.), *Perspectives on Arabic linguistics IX: Papers from the Ninth Annual Symposium on Arabic Linguistics*, pp. 9–43. Amsterdam and Philadelphia: John Benjamins.

Myers-Scotton, Carol and Ury, William (1977). Bilingual strategies: The social functions of code-switching. *International Journal of the Sociology of Language*, **13**, 5–20.

NAEYC (1995). *Responding to linguistic and cultural diversity recommendations for effective early childhood education: A position statement of the National Association for the Education of Young Children*. Washington, D.C.: NAEYC.

Nartey, Jonas (1982). Code-switching, interference or faddism? Language use among educated Ghanians. *Anthropological Linguistics*, **24** (2), 183–192.

Naseh Lotfabbadi, Leyla (2002). Disagreement in agreement: A study of grammatical aspects of codeswitching in Swedish/Persian bilingual speech. Ph.D. dissertation, Stockholm University.

Neeleman, Ad and Weerman, Fred (1999). *Flexible syntax: A theory of case and arguments*. Dordrecht: Kluwer Academic.

Neisser, Ulric (1984). Interpreting Harry Bahrick's discovery: What confers immunity against forgetting? *Journal of Experimental Psychology: General*, **113** (1), 32–35.

Newmeyer, Frederick J. (1986). *Linguistic theory in America* (2nd edn.). New York: Academic Press.

Newport, Elissa L. and Supalla, Ted (2000). Sign language research at the millenium. In K. Emmorey and H. Lane (eds.), *The signs of language revisited: An anthology to honor Ursula Bellugi and Edward Klima*, pp. 103–114. Mahwah, NJ: Lawrence Erlbaum Associates.

Nicoladis, Elena (2006). Cross-linguistic transfer in adjective-noun strings by preschool bilingual children. *Bilingualism: Language and Cognition*, **9** (1), 15–32.

Nicoladis, Elena and Genesee, Fred (1997). Language development in preschool bilingual children. *Journal of Speech-Language Pathology and Audiology*, **21** (4), 258–270.

Nicoladis, Elena and Genesee, Fred (1998). Parental discourse and codemixing in bilingual children. *International Journal of Bilingualism*, **2** (1), 85–99.

Nishimura, Miwa (1985a). Intrasentential codeswitching in Japanese and English. Ph.D. dissertation, University of Pennsylvania.

Nishimura, Miwa (1985b). Intrasentential code-switching: The case of language assignment. In J. Vaid (ed.), *Language processing in bilinguals: psycholinguistic and neuropsychological perspectives*, pp. 123–144. Hillsdale, NJ: Laurence Erlbaum Associates.

Nishimura, Miwa (1995). Varietal conditioning in Japanese/English code-switching. *Language Sciences*, **17** (2), 123–145.

Nishimura, Miwa (1997). *Japanese/English code-switching: Syntax and pragmatics*. New York: Peter Lang.

Nishimura, Miwa and Yoon, Keumsil Kim (1998). Head directionality and intrasentential code-switching: A study of Japanese Canadian and Korean Americans' bilingual speech. In D. J. Silva (ed.), *Japanese/Korean linguistics, vol. 8*, pp. 121–131. Stanford: CSLI Publications.

Nortier, Jacomine (1990). *Dutch–Moroccan Arabic code switching among Moroccans in the Netherlands*. Dordrecht: Foris.

Nortier, Jacomine (1995). Codeswitching in Moroccan Arabic/Dutch vs. Moroccan Arabic/French language contact. *International Journal of the Sociology of Language*, **12**, 81–96.

Obler, Loraine K.; Albert, Martin L.; Goodglass, Harold and Benson, D. Frank (1978). Aphasia type and aging. *Brain and Language*, **6** (3), 318–322.

Odlin, Terrence (2003). Cross-linguistic influence. In C. J. Doughty and M. H. Long (eds.), *The handbook of second language acquisition*, pp. 436–486. Oxford and Malden, MA: Blackwell.

Ojemann, George A. and Whitaker, Harry A. (1978). The bilingual brain. *Archives of Neurology*, **35** (7), 409–412.

Okasha, Maha (1999). Structural constraints on Arabic/English code-switching: Two generations. Ph.D. dissertation, University of South Carolina.

Olshtain, Elite and Barzilay, Margaret (1991). Lexical retrieval difficulties in adult language attrition. In H. W. Seliger and R. M. Vago (eds.), *First language attrition: Structural and theoretical perspectives*, pp. 139–150. Cambridge, UK and New York: Cambridge University Press.

Osgood, Charles E. (1953). *Method and theory in experimental psychology*. Oxford and New York: Oxford University Press.

Osterhout, Lee and Holcomb, Phillip J. (1992). Event-related brain potentials elicited by syntactic anomaly. *Journal of Memory and Language*, **31** (6), 785–806.

Otheguy, Ricardo (1993). A reconsideration of the notion of loan translation in the analysis of U.S. Spanish. In A. Roca and J. M. Lipski (eds.), *Spanish in the United States: Linguistic contact and diversity*, pp. 21–45. Berlin and New York: Mouton de Gruyter.

Ouhalla, Jamal (1993). Functional categories, agrammatism and language acquisition. *Linguistische Berichte*, **143**, 3–36.

Owens, Jonathan (1996). Idiomatic structure and the theory of genetic relationship. *Diachronica*, **13** (2), 283–318.

Pakir, Anne (1989). Linguistic alternants and code selection in Baba Malay. *World Englishes*, **8** (3), 379–388.

Palfreyman, David and al Khalil, Muhamed (2003). "A funky language for teenzz to Use": Representing Gulf Arabic in instant messaging. *Journal of Computer-Mediated Communication*, **9** (1), 18–48.

Pandit, Ira (1986). *Hindi–English code-switching: Mixed Hindi–English*. Delhi: Datta Book Centre.

Pandit, Ira (1990). Grammaticality in code switching. In R. Jacobson (ed.), *Codeswitching as a worldwide phenomenon*, pp. 33–69. New York: Peter Lang.

Paradis, Johanne; Crago, Martha; Genesee, Fred and Rice, Mabel (2003). French–English bilingual children with SLI: How do they compare with their monolingual peers? *Journal of Speech, Language, and Hearing Research*, **46** (1), 113–127.

Paradis, Johanne; Nicoladis, Elena and Genesee, Fred (2000). Early emergence of structural constraints on code-mixing: Evidence from French–English bilingual children. *Bilingualism: Language and Cognition*, **3** (3), 245–261.

Paradis, Michel (1981). Neurolinguistic organization of a bilingual's two languages. In J. E. Copeland and P. W. Davis (eds.), *The seventh LACUS Forum, 1980*, pp. 486–494. Columbia, SC: Hornbeam Press.

Paradis, Michel (1985). On the representation of two languages in one brain. *Language Sciences*, **7** (1), 1–39.

Paradis, Michel (1987). Neurolinguistic perspectives on bilingualism. In M. Paradis and G. Libben (eds.), *The assessment of bilingual aphasia*, pp. 1–17. Hillsdale, NJ: Lawrence Erlbaum Associates.

Paradis, Michel (1993). Linguistic, psycholinguistic, and neurolinguistic aspects of "interference" in bilingual speakers: The activation threshold hypothesis. *International Journal of Psycholinguistics*, **2** (26), 133–145.

Paradis, Michel (1998). Aphasia in bilinguals: How atypical is it? In P. Coppens, Y. Lebrun and A. Basso (eds.), *Aphasia in atypical populations*, pp. 35–66. Mahwah, NJ: Lawrence Erlbaum Associates.

Paradis, Michel (2000a). Generalizable outcomes of bilingual aphasia research. *Folia Phoniatrica et Logopaedica*, **52** (1–3), 54–64.

Paradis, Michel (2000b). The neurolinguistics of bilingualism in the next decades. *Brain and Language*, **71** (1), 178–180.

Paradis, Michel (2001). An integrated neurolinguistic theory of bilingualism (1976-2000). In R. M. Brend, A. K. Melby and A. R. Lommel (eds.),

LACUS Forum XXVII: Speaking and comprehending, pp. 5–15. Fullerton, CA: LACUS.

Paradis, Michel (2003). The bilingual Loch Ness monster raises its non-asymmetric head again – or, Why bother with such cumbersome notions as validity and reliability? Comments on Evans et al. (2002). *Brain and Language*, **87** (3), 441–448.

Paradis, Michel (2004). *A neurolinguistic theory of bilingualism*. Amsterdam and Philadelphia: John Benjamins.

Paradis, Michel and Goldblum, Marie-Claire (1989). Selective crossed aphasia in a trilingual aphasic patient followed by reciprocal antago-nism. *Brain and Language. Special Issue: Bilingualism and neurolinguistics*, **36** (1), 62–75.

Pardo, Jennifer S. (2006). On phonetic convergence during conversa-tional interaction. *The Journal of the Acoustical Society of America*, **119** (4), 2382–2393.

Park, Jun-Eon (1990). Korean/English intrasentential code-switching: Matrix language assignment and linguistic constraints. Ph.D. disserta-tion, University of Illinois at Urbana Champaign.

Patel, Aniruddh D.; Gibson, Edward; Ratner, Jennifer; Besson, Mireille and Holcomb, Phillip J. (1998). Processing syntactic relations in language and music: An event-related potential study. *Journal of Cognitive Neuroscience*, **10** (6), 717–733.

Patterson, Janet L. and Pearson, Barbara Zurer (2004). Bilingual lex-ical development: Influences, contexts, and processes. In B. A. Goldstein (ed.), *Bilingual language development and disorders in Spanish–English speakers*, pp. 77–104. Baltimore, MD: Paul H. Brookes.

Paul, Rhea (2001). *Language disorders from infancy through adolescence: Assessment and intervention* (2nd edn.). St. Louis, MO: Mosby.

Paulmann, Silke; Elston-Guttler, Kerrie E.; Gunter, Thomas C. and Kotz, Sonja A. (2006). Is bilingual lexical access influenced by language context? *Neuroreport*, **17** (7), 727–731.

Pavlenko, Aneta (2000). L2 influence on L1 in late bilingualism. *Issues in Applied Linguistics*, **11** (2), 175–205.

Pearson, Barbara Zurer (2007). Social factors in childhood bilingualism in the United States. *Applied Psycholinguistics*, **28** (3), 399–410.

Pensel, Itron (1979). Testeni. *Hor Yezh*, **126**, 47–73.

Perani, Daniela and Abutalebi, Jubin (2005). The neural basis of first and second language processing. *Current Opinion in Neurobiology*, **15** (2), 202–206.

Perani, Daniela; Dehaene, Stanislas; Grassi, Franco; Cohen, Laurent; Cappa, Stefano F.; Dupoux, Emmanuel; Fazio, Ferrucio and Mehler, Jacques (1996). Brain processing of native and foreign languages. *Neuroreport*, **7** (15–17), 2439–2444.

Perani, Daniela; Paulesu, Eraldo; Galles, Nuria Sebastian; Dupoux, Emmanuel; Dehaene, Stanislas; Bettinardi, Valentino; Cappa,

Stefano F.; Fazio, Ferruccio and Mehler, Jacques (1998). The bilingual brain: Proficiency and age of acquisition of the second language. *Brain: A Journal of Neurology*, **121** (10), 1841–1852.

Perecman, Ellen (1984). Spontaneous translation and language mixing in a polyglot aphasic. *Brain and Language*, **23** (1), 43–63.

Pérez Firmat, Gustavo (1987). Bilingual blues. In R. Durán, J. Ortiz Cofer and G. Pérez Firmat (eds.), *Triple crown: Chicano, Puerto Rican, and Cuban-American Poetry*, p. 164. Tempe, AZ: Bilingual Press.

Perozzi, Joseph A. and Chávez Sánchez, María Lourdes (1992). The effect of instruction in L1 on receptive acquisition of L2 for bilingual children with language delay. *Language, Speech, and Hearing Services in Schools*, **23** (4), 348–352.

Petersen, Jennifer (1988). Word-internal code-switching constraints in a bilingual child's grammar. *Linguistics*, **26** (3(295)), 479–493.

Petitto, Laura Ann; Katerelos, Marina; Levy, Bronna G.; Gauna, Kristine; Tétreault, Karine and Ferraro, Vittoria (2001). Bilingual signed and spoken language acquisition from birth: Implications for the mechanisms underlying early bilingual language acquisition. *Journal of Child Language*, **28** (2), 453–496.

Petsche, Hellmuth; Etlinger, Susan C. and Filz, Oliver (1993). Brain electrical mechanisms of bilingual speech management: An initial investigation. *Electroencephalography & Clinical Neurophysiology*, **86** (6), 385–394.

Pfaff, Carol W. (1979). Constraints on language mixing: Intrasentential code-switching and borrowing in Spanish/English. *Language*, **55** (2), 291–318.

Pfau, Roland (2002). Applying morphosyntactic and phonological readjustment rules in natural language negation. In R. P. Meier, K. Cormier and D. Quinto-Pozos (eds.), *Modality and structure in signed and spoken languages*, pp. 263–295. Cambridge, UK and New York: Cambridge University Press.

Phillips, Natalie A.; Segalowitz, Norman; O'Brien, Irena and Yamasaki, Naomi (2004). Semantic priming in a first and second language: Evidence from reaction time variability and event-related brain potentials. *Journal of Neurolinguistics. Special Issue: Automatic and Controlled Language Processes*, **17** (2–3), 237–262.

Pienemann, Manfred (1999). *Language processing and second language development: Processability theory*. Amsterdam and Philadelphia: John Benjamins.

Pike, Kenneth L. (1967). *Language in relation to a unified theory of the structure of human behavior*. The Hague: Mouton.

Pillai, Jay J.; Araque, Julio M.; Allison, Jerry D.; Sethuraman, Sankar; Loring, David W.; Thiruvaiyaru, Dharma; Ison, Claro B.; Balan, Aparna and Lavin, Tom (2003). Functional MRI study of semantic and phonological language processing in bilingual subjects: Preliminary findings. *Neuroimage*, **19** (3), 565–576.

Polinsky, Maria (1995). Cross-linguistic parallels in language loss. *Southwest Journal of Linguistics*, **14** (1–2), 87–123.

Pomerantz, Anita (1984). Agreeing and disagreeing with assessments: Some features of preferred/dispreferred turn shapes. In J. M. Atkinson and J. Heritage (eds.), *Structures of social action: Studies in conversation analysis*, pp. 57–101. Cambridge, UK and New York: Cambridge University Press.

Poplack, Shana (1978). *Quantitative analysis of constraints on code-switching.* New York: City University of New York, Centro de Estudios Puertorriqueños.

Poplack, Shana (1980). Sometimes I'll start a sentence in Spanish Y TERMINO EN ESPAÑOL: Toward a typology of code-switching. *Linguistics*, **18** (7–8), 581–618.

Poplack, Shana (1981). The syntactic structure and social function of code-switching. In R. P. Durán (ed.), *Latino language and communicative behavior*, pp. 169–184. Norwood, NJ: Ablex.

Poplack, Shana (1987). Contrasting patterns of code-switching in two communities. In E. Wande, J. Anward, B. Nordberg, L. Steensland and M. Thelander (eds.), *Aspects of multilingualism: Proceedings from the Fourth Nordic Symposium on Bilingualism, 1984*, pp. 51–77. Uppsala: Borgströms.

Poplack, Shana (1988). Contrasting patterns of code-switching in two communities. In M. Heller (ed.), *Codeswitching: Anthropological and sociolinguistic perspectives*, pp. 215–244. Berlin and New York: Mouton de Gruyter.

Poplack, Shana (1990). Variation theory and language contact: Concepts, methods and data. *Papers for the workshop on concepts, methodology and data: ESF Network on Code Switching and Language Contact, Basel, January 12–13, 1990*, pp. 33–66. Strasbourg: European Science Foundation.

Poplack, Shana and Meechan, Marjory (1995). Patterns of language mixture: Nominal structure in Wolof–French and Fongbe–French bilingual discourse. In L. Milroy and P. Muysken (eds.), *One speaker, two languages: Cross-disciplinary perspectives on code-switching*, pp. 199–232. Cambridge, UK and New York: Cambridge University Press.

Poplack, Shana and Meechan, Marjory (1998). Introduction: How languages fit together in codemixing. *International Journal of Bilingualism*, **2** (2), 127–138.

Poplack, Shana and Sankoff, David (1984). Borrowing: The synchrony of integration. *Linguistics*, **22** (1), 99–135.

Poplack, Shana; Sankoff, David and Miller, Christopher (1988). The social correlates and linguistic processes of lexical borrowing and assimilation. *Linguistics*, **26** (1(293)), 47–104.

Poplack, Shana; Wheeler, Susan and Westwood, Anneli (1987). Distinguishing language contact phenomena: Evidence from Finnish–English bilingualism. In P. Lilius and M. Saari (eds.), *The Nordic Languages and Modern Linguistics 6: Proceedings of the Sixth International*

Conference of Nordic and General Linguistics in Helsinki, August 18–22, 1986, pp. 33–56. Helsinki: University of Helsinki Press.

Poplack, Shana; Wheeler, Susan and Westwood, Anneli (1989). Distinguishing language contact phenomena: Evidence from Finnish–English bilingualism. *World Englishes*, **8** (3), 389–406.

Poulisse, Nanda (1999). *Slips of the tongue: Speech errors in first and second language production*. Amsterdam and Philadelphia: John Benjamins.

Poulisse, Nanda and Bongaerts, Theo (1994). First language use in second language production. *Applied Linguistics*, **15** (1), 36–57.

Price, Cathy J.; Green, David W. and von Studnitz, Roswitha (1999). A functional imaging study of translation and language switching. *Brain*, **122** (12), 2221–2235.

Proverbio, Alice Mado; Cok, Barbara and Zani, Alberto (2002). Electrophysiological measures of language processing in bilinguals. *Journal of Cognitive Neuroscience*, **14** (7), 994–1017.

Proverbio, Alice Mado; Leoni, Giuliana and Zani, Alberto (2004). Language switching mechanisms in simultaneous interpreters: An ERP study. *Neuropsychologia*, **42** (12), 1636–1656.

Psathas, George (1995). *Conversation analysis: The study of talk-in-interaction*. London: Sage.

Pu, Yonglin; Liu, Ho-Ling; Spinks, John A.; Mahankali, Srikanth; Xiong, Jinhu; Feng, Ching-Mei; Tan, Li Hai; Fox, Peter T. and Gao, Jia-Hong (2001). Cerebral hemodynamic response in Chinese (first) and English (second) language processing revealed by event-related functional MRI. *Magnetic Resonance Imaging*, **19** (5), 643–647.

Pujolar, Joan (2001). *Gender, heteroglossia, and power: A sociolinguistic study of youth culture*. Berlin and New York: Mouton de Gruyter.

Purcell, April K. (1984). Code shifting Hawaiian style: Children's accommodation along a decreolizing continuum. *International Journal of the Sociology of Language*, **46**, 71–86.

Quadros, Ronice Müller de (1999). Phrase structure of Brazilian sign language. Ph.D. dissertation, Pontifícia Universidade Católica do Rio Grande do Sul.

Quinto-Pozos, David (2002). Contact between Mexican sign language and American sign language in two Texas border areas. Ph.D. dissertation, University of Texas at Austin.

Rakowsky, Amy B. (1989). A study of intra-sentential code-switching in Spanish–English bilinguals and second language learners. Ph.D. dissertation, Brown University.

Rampton, Ben (1995). *Crossing: Language and ethnicity among adolescents*. Harlow, UK and New York: Longman.

Rampton, Ben (1999). Styling the other: Introduction. *Journal of Sociolinguistics*, **3** (4), 421–427.

Rampton, Ben (2005). *Crossing: Language and ethnicity among adolescents* (2nd edn.). Manchester NH: St. Jerome Publishing.

Rapport, Richard L.; Tan, C. T. and Whitaker, Harry A. (1983). Language function and dysfunction among Chinese- and English-speaking polyglots: Cortical stimulation, Wada testing, and clinical studies. *Brain and Language*, **18** (2), 342–366.

Rathmann, Christian (2000). Does the presence of a person agreement marker predict word order in SLs? Paper presented at *The 7th International Conference on Theoretical Issues in Sign Language Research*, July, 23–27. Amsterdam, The Netherlands.

Redlinger, Wendy E. and Park, Tschang-zin (1980). Language mixing in young bilinguals. *Journal of Child Language*, **7** (2), 337–352.

Reid, Euan (1978). Social and stylistic variation in the speech of children. Some evidence from Edinburgh. In P. Trudgill (ed.), *Sociolinguistic patterns in British English*, pp. 158–173. London: Edward Arnold.

Reiterer, Susanne; Berger, Michael L.; Hemmelmann, Claudia and Rappelsberger, Peter (2005a). Decreased EEG coherence between prefrontal electrodes: A correlate of high language proficiency? *Experimental Brain Research*, **163** (1), 109–113.

Reiterer, Susanne; Hemmelmann, Claudia; Rappelsberger, Peter and Berger, Michael L (2005b). Characteristic functional networks in high- versus low-proficiency second language speakers detected also during native language processing: An explorative EEG coherence study in 6 frequency bands. *Cognitive Brain Research*, **25** (2), 566–578.

Restrepo, María Adelaida (2003). Spanish language skills in bilingual children with specific language impairment. In S. Montrul and F. Ordóñez (eds.), *Linguistic theory and language development in Hispanic languages: Papers from the 5th Hispanic Linguistics Symposium and the 4th Conference on the Acquisition of Spanish and Portuguese*, pp. 365–374. Somerville, MA: Cascadilla Press.

Restrepo, María Adelaida and Gutiérrez-Clellen, Vera F. (2004). Grammatical impairments in Spanish–English bilingual children. In B. A. Goldstein (ed.), *Bilingual language development and disorders in Spanish–English speakers*, pp. 213–234. Baltimore, MD: Paul H. Brookes.

Richards, Keith (2005). Introduction. In K. Richards and P. Seedhouse (eds.), *Applying conversation analysis*, pp. 1–18. Basingstoke: Palgrave Macmillan.

Rindler Schjerve, Rosita (1998). Codeswitching as an indicator for language shift? Evidence from Sardinian–Italian bilingualism. In R. Jacobson (ed.), *Codeswitching worldwide*, pp. 221–248. Berlin and New York: Mouton de Gruyter.

Rinne, Juha O.; Tommola, Jorma; Laine, Matti J.; Krause, Bernd J.; Schmidt, Daniela; Kaasinen, Valtteri; Teräs, Mika; Sipilä, Hannu and Sunnari, Marianna (2000). The translating brain: Cerebral activation patterns during simultaneous interpreting. *Neuroscience Letters*, **294** (2), 85–88.

Ritchie, William and Bhatia, Tej K. (1999). Codeswitching, grammar, and sentence production: The problem of light verbs. In E. C. Klein and

G. Martohardjono (eds.), *The development of second language grammars: A generative approach*, pp. 269–287. Amsterdam: John Benjamins.

Ritter, Elizabeth (1995). On the syntactic category of pronouns and agreement. *Natural Language and Linguistic Theory*, **13** (3), 405–443.

Rizzi, Luigi (1982). *Issues in Italian syntax*. Dordrecht: Foris.

Roberts, Ian (1997). Restructuring, head movement, and locality. *Linguistic Inquiry*, **28** (3), 423–460.

Roberts, Julie and Labov, William (1995). Learning to talk Philadelphian: Acquisition of short "a" by preschool children. *Language Variation and Change*, **7** (1), 101–112.

Roberts, Leah and Verhagen, Josje (forthcoming). Auditory sentence matching.

Rodríguez-Fornells, Antoni; De Diego Balaguer, Ruth and Münte, Thomas F. (2006). Executive control in bilingual language processing. *Language Learning*, **56** (Suppl. 1), 133–190.

Rodríguez-Fornells, Antoni; Rotte, Michael; Heinze, Hans-Jochen; Nösselt, Tömme and Münte, Thomas F. (2002). Brain potential and functional MRI evidence for how to handle two languages with one brain. *Nature*, **415** (6875), 1026–1029.

Rodríguez-Fornells, Antoni; van der Lugt, Arie; Rotte, Michael; Britti, Belinda; Heinze, Hans-Jochen and Münte, Thomas F. (2005). Second language interferes with word production in fluent bilinguals: Brain potential and functional imaging evidence. *Journal of Cognitive Neuroscience*, **17** (3), 422–433.

Roelofs, Ardi and Verhoef, Kim (2006). Modeling the control of phonological encoding in bilingual speakers. *Bilingualism: Language and Cognition*, **9** (2), 167–176.

Romaine, Suzanne (1984). *The language of children and adolescents: The acquisition of communicative competence*. Oxford and Malden, MA: Blackwell.

Romaine, Suzanne (1995). *Bilingualism* (2nd edn.). Oxford and Malden, MA: Blackwell.

Ross, John Robert (1967). Constraints on variables in syntax. Ph.D. dissertation, MIT.

Ross, Malcolm (2001). Contact-induced change in Oceanic languages in north-west Melanesia. In A. Y. Aikhenvald and R. M. W. Dixon (eds.), *Areal diffusion and genetic inheritance: problems in comparative linguistics*, pp. 134–166. Oxford and New York: Oxford University Press.

Roux, Franck-Emmanuel; Lubrano, Vincent; Lauwers-Cances, Valérie; Trémoulet, Michel; Mascott, Christopher R. and Démonet, Jean-François (2004). Intra-operative mapping of cortical areas involved in reading in mono- and bilingual patients. *Brain: A Journal of Neurology*, **127** (8), 1796–1810.

Roux, Franck-Emmanuel and Trémoulet, Michel (2002). Organization of language areas in bilingual patients: A cortical stimulation study. *Journal of Neurosurgery*, **97** (4), 857–864.

Sachdev, Itesh and Giles, Howard (2006). Bilingual accommodation. In T. K. Bhatia and W. C. Ritchie (eds.), *The handbook of bilingualism*, pp. 353–378. Oxford and Malden, MA: Blackwell.

Sachs, Jacqueline; Lieberman, Philip and Erickson, Donna (1973). Anatomical and cultural determinants of male and female speech. In R. W. Shuy and R. W. Fasold (eds.), *Language attitudes: Current trends and prospects*, pp. 74–84. Washington, D.C.: Georgetown University Press.

Sacks, Harvey (1984). Notes on methodology. In J. M. Atkinson and J. Heritage (eds.), *Structures of social action: Studies in conversation analysis*, pp. 21–27. Cambridge, UK and New York: Cambridge University Press.

Sacks, Harvey; Schegloff, Emanuel A. and Jefferson, Gail (1970). A simplest systematics for the organization of turn-taking in conversation. In J. Schenkein (ed.), *Studies in the organization of conversational interaction*, pp. 7–55. New York: Academic Press.

Saito, Mamoru and Fukui, Naoki (1998). Order in phrase structure and movement. *Linguistic Inquiry*, **29** (3), 439–474.

Salmons, Joe (1990). Bilingual discourse marking: Code switching, borrowing, and convergence in some German-American dialects. *Linguistics*, **28** (3), 453–480.

Sanders, Lisa D. and Neville, Helen J. (2003). An ERP study of continuous speech processing. II. Segmentation, semantics, and syntax in nonnative speakers. *Cognitive Brain Research*, **15** (3), 214–227.

Sankoff, David (1998). A formal production-based explanation of the facts of code-switching. *Bilingualism: Language and Cognition*, **1** (1), 39–50.

Sankoff, David and Poplack, Shana (1981). A formal grammar for codeswitching. *Papers in Linguistics*, **14**, 3–45.

Sankoff, David; Poplack, Shana and Vanniarajan, Swathi (1990). The case of the nonce loan in Tamil. *Language Variation and Change*, **2** (1), 71–101.

Sankoff, Gillian (1980). *The social life of language*. Philadelphia: University of Pennsylvania Press.

Sarkar, Mela and Winer, Lise (2006). Multilingual codeswitching in Quebec rap: Poetry, pragmatics and performativity. *International Journal of Multilingualism*, **3** (3), 173–192.

Saunders, George (1982). *Bilingual children: Guidance for the family*. Clevedon: Multilingual Matters.

Schachter, Jacquelyn (1993). A new account of language transfer. In S. M. Gass and L. Selinker (eds.), *Language transfer in language learning*, pp. 32–46. Amsterdam and Philadelphia: John Benjamins.

Schaerlaekens, Anne-Marie; Zink, Inge and Verheyden, L (1995). Comparative vocabulary development in kindergarten classes with a mixed population of monolinguals, simultaneous and successive bilinguals. *Journal of Multilingual and Multicultural Development*, **16** (6), 477–495.

Schegloff, Emanuel A (1980). Preliminaries to preliminaries: "Can I ask you a question?" *Sociological Inquiry*, **50** (3–4), 104–152.

Schembri, Adam (2003). Rethinking "classifiers" in signed languages. In K. Emmorey (ed.), *Perspectives on classifier constructions in sign languages*, pp. 3–34. Mahwah, NJ: Lawrence Erlbaum Associates.

Schenkein, Jim (1978). Sketch of an analytic mentality for the study of conversational interaction. In J. Schenkein (ed.), *Studies in the organization of conversational interaction*, pp. 1–6. New York: Academic Press.

Schieffelin, Bambi B. and Ochs, Elinor (1986). Language socialization. *Annual Review of Anthropology*, **15**, 163–191.

Schlyter, Suzanne (1990). Introducing the DUFDE project. In J. M. Meisel (ed.), *Two first languages: Early grammatical development in bilingual children*, pp. 73–84. Dordrecht: Foris.

Schlyter, Suzanne (1993). The weaker language in bilingual Swedish–French children. In K. Hyltenstam and Å. Viberg (eds.), *Progression and regression in language: Sociocultural, neuropsychological, and linguistic perspectives*, pp. 289–308. Cambridge, UK and New York: Cambridge University Press.

Schmidt, Johannes (1872). *Die verwantschaftsverhältnisse der indogermanischen sprachen*. Weimar: Böhlau.

Schmitt, Elena (2000). Overt and covert codeswitching in immigrant children from Russia. *International Journal of Bilingualism*, **4** (1), 9–28.

Schmitt, Elena (2006). Russian–English corpus. Unpublished ms.

Schuchardt, Hugo (1890). Kreolische studien IX: Über das Malaioportugiesische von Batavia und Tugu. *Sitzungsberichte der kaiserlichen Akademie der Wissenschaften, Philosophisch-Historischen Classe, XII, Sitzung Vom 9 Juli, 1890*, **122** (9), 1–256.

Schwartz, Bonnie D. and Sprouse, Rex A. (1996). L2 cognitive states and the Full Transfer/Full Access Model. *Second Language Research*, **12** (1), 40–72.

Searle, John R. (1969). *Speech acts: An essay in the philosophy of language*. Cambridge, UK and New York: Cambridge University Press.

Sebba, Mark (1998). A congruence approach to the syntax of codeswitching. *International Journal of Bilingualism*, **2** (1), 1–19.

Sebba, Mark and Wootton, Tony (1998). We, they and identity: Sequential versus identity-related explanation in code-switching. In P. Auer (ed.), *Code-switching in conversation: Language, interaction and identity*, pp. 262–289. London and New York: Routledge.

Seliger, Herbert (1989). Deterioration and creativity in childhood bilingualism. In K. Hyltenstam and L. K. Obler (eds.), *Bilingualism across the lifespan: Aspects of acquisition, maturity, and loss*, pp. 173–184. Cambridge, UK and New York: Cambridge University Press.

Seliger, Herbert W. (1991). Language attrition, reduced redundancy, and creativity. In H. Seliger and R. Vago (eds.), *First language attrition: Structural and theoretical perspectives*, pp. 227–240. Cambridge, UK and New York: Cambridge University Press.

Seliger, Herbert W. (1996). Primary language attrition in the context of bilingualism. In W.C. Ritchie and T.K. Bhatia (eds.), *Handbook of second language acquisition*, pp. 605–626. San Diego, CA: Academic Press.

Seliger, Herbert W. and Vago, Robert M. (eds.) (1991). *First language attrition: Structural and theoretical perspectives*. Cambridge, UK and New York: Cambridge University Press.

Selinker, Larry (1972). Interlanguage. *International Review of Applied Linguistics in Language Teaching*, **10** (3), 209–231.

Sella-Mazi, Eleni (2001). *Bilingualism and society: Greek reality* [Διγλωσσία και κοινωνία: Η ελληνική πραγματικότητα]. Athens: Proskinio Publications [Προσκήνιο].

Sharwood Smith, Michael A. (1989). Crosslinguistic influence in language loss. In K. Hyltenstam and L. Obler (eds.), *Bilingualism across the lifespan: Aspects of acquisition, maturity, and loss*, pp. 185–201. Cambridge, UK and New York: Cambridge University Press.

Siebenhaar, Beat (2005). Varietätenwahl und code switching in Deutschschweizer Chatkanälen: Quantitative und qualitative analysen. NET.WORX, Nr. 43. Retrieved on September 20, 2007 from http://www.mediensprache.net/networx/networx-43.pdf.

Sifianou, Maria (1992). *Politeness phenomena in England and Greece: A cross-cultural perspective*. Oxford and New York: Oxford University Press.

Silva-Corvalán, Carmen (1991). Spanish language attrition in a language contact situation with English. In H.W. Seliger and R. Vago (eds.), *First language attrition: Structural and theoretical perspectives*, pp. 151–171. Cambridge, UK and New York: Cambridge University Press.

Silva-Corvalán, Carmen (1994). *Language contact and change: Spanish in Los Angeles*. Oxford and New York: Oxford University Press.

Silverman, David (1997). *Discourses of counselling: HIV counselling as social interaction*. London: Sage.

Silverman, David (1998). *Harvey Sacks: Social science and conversation analysis*. Cambridge: Polity Press.

Simango, S. Ron (1996). Chicheŵa–English codeswitching. Unpublished corpus.

Singh, Rajendra (1983). We, they, and us: A note on code-switching and stratification in North India. *Language in Society*, **12** (1), 71–73.

Skaaden, Hanne (2005). First language attrition and linguistic creativity. *International Journal of Bilingualism*, **9** (3–4), 435–452.

Slabbert, Sarah and Myers-Scotton, Carol (1997). The structure of Tsotsitaal and Iscamtho: Code switching and in-group identity in South African townships. *Linguistics*, **35** (2(348)), 317–342.

Slobin, Dan I. (1996). From "thought and language" to "thinking for speaking." In J.J. Gumperz and S.C. Levinson (eds.), *Rethinking linguistic relativity*, pp. 70–96. Cambridge, UK and New York: Cambridge University Press.

Slobin, Dan I.; Hoiting, Nini; Kuntze, Marlon; Lindert, Reyna; Weinberg, Amy; Pyers, Jennie; Anthony, Michelle; Biederman, Yael and Thumann, Helen (2003). A cognitive/functional perspective on the acquisition of "classifiers." In K. Emmorey (ed.), *Perspectives on classifier constructions in sign languages*, pp. 271–296. Mahwah, NJ: Lawrence Erlbaum Associates.

Smith, Jennifer; Durham, Mercedes and Fortune, Liane (2007). "Mam, my trousers is fa'in doon!": Community, caregiver, and child in the acquisition of variation in a Scottish dialect. *Language Variation and Change*, **19** (1), 63–99.

Soares, Carlos and Grosjean, François (1984). Bilinguals in a monolingual and a bilingual speech mode: The effect of lexical access. *Memory & Cognition*, **12** (4), 380–386.

Sobin, Nicholas J (1984). On code-switching inside NP. *Applied Psycholinguistics*, **5** (4), 293–303.

Sorace, Antonella (1996). The use of acceptability judgments in second language acquisition research. In W. C. Ritchie and T. K. Bhatia (eds.), *Handbook of second language acquisition*, pp. 375–409. San Diego, CA: Academic Press.

Sorace, Antonella (2000). Differential effects of attrition in the L1 syntax of near-native L2 speakers. In S. C. Howell, S. A. Fish and T. Keith-Lucas (eds.), *Proceedings of the 24th annual Boston University Conference on Language Development*, pp. 719–725. Somerville, MA: Cascadilla Press.

Sorace, Antonella (2004). Native language attrition and developmental instability at the syntax–discourse interface: Data, interpretations and methods. *Bilingualism: Language and Cognition*, **7** (2), 143–145.

Speas, Margaret (1990). *Phrase structure in natural language*. Dordrecht: Kluwer Academic Publishers.

Spradlin, Kenton; Liceras, Juana and Fernández-Fuertes, Raquel (2003). The "grammatical features spell-out hypothesis" as a diagnostic for bilingual competence. Paper presented at *The 4th International Symposium on Bilingualism (ISB4), Arizona State University, April 30-May 3, 2003*.

Sridhar, Shikaripur N. and Sridhar, Kamal K. (1980). The syntax and psycholinguistics of bilingual code mixing. *Canadian Journal of Psychology/ Revue Canadienne de Psychologie*, **34** (4), 407–416.

Stavans, Ilan (2003). *Spanglish: The making of a new American language*. New York: Harper Collins.

Stenson, Nancy (1990). Phrase structure congruence, government, and Irish–English code-switching. In R. Hendrick (ed.), *The syntax of the modern Celtic languages*, pp. 137–197. San Diego, CA: Academic Press.

Stolt, Birgit (1964). *Die sprachmischung in Luthers Tischreden: Studien zum problem der zweisprachigkeit*. Stockholm: Almqvist and Wiksell.

Stowell, Timothy (1981). Origins of phrase structure. Ph.D. dissertation, MIT.

Street, Richard L., Jr. and **Cappella, Joseph N.** (1989). Social and linguistic factors influencing adaptation in children's speech. *Journal of Psycholinguistic Research*, **18** (5), 497–519.

Supalla, Samuel J. and McKee, Cecile (2002). The role of manually coded English in language development of deaf children. In R. P. Meier, K. Cormier and D. Quinto-Pozos (eds.), *Modality and structure in signed and spoken languages*, pp. 143–165. Cambridge, UK and New York: Cambridge University Press.

Supalla, Ted (1986). The classifier system in American Sign Language. In C. G. Craig (ed.), *Noun classes and categorization: Proceedings of a symposium on categorization and noun classification, Eugene, Oregon, October 1983*, pp. 181–214. Amsterdam and Philadelphia: John Benjamins.

Supalla, Ted (1990). Serial verbs of motion in ASL. In S. D. Fischer and P. Siple (eds.), *Theoretical issues in sign language research*, pp. 127–152. Chicago: University of Chicago Press.

Swigart, Leigh (1992a). Practice and perception: Language use and attitudes in Dakar. Ph.D. dissertation, University of Washington.

Swigart, Leigh (1992b). Two codes or one? The insiders' view and the description of codeswitching in Dakar. *Journal of Multilingual and Multicultural Development*, **13** (1–2), 83–102.

Swigart, Leigh (1992c). Women and language choice in Dakar: A case of unconscious innovation. *Women and Language*, **15** (1), 11–20.

Tabors, Patton O. (1997). *One child, two languages: A guide for preschool educators of children learning English as a second language*. Baltimore: Paul H. Brookes.

Tabors, Patton O.; Páez, Mariela M. and López, Lisa M. (2003). Dual language abilities of bilingual four-year olds: Initial findings from the early childhood study of language and literacy development of Spanish-speaking children. *NABE Journal of Research and Practice*, Winter, 70–91.

Taeschner, Traute (1983). *The sun is feminine: A study on language acquisition in bilingual children*. Berlin: Springer.

Talmy, Leonard (1985). Lexicalization patterns: Semantic structures in lexical forms. In T. Shopen (ed.), *Language typology and syntactic description III: Grammatical categories and the lexicon*, pp. 57–149. Cambridge, UK and New York: Cambridge University Press.

Talmy, Leonard (2000). *Toward a cognitive semantics* (vols. 1–2). Cambridge, MA: MIT Press.

Tay, Mary W. J. (1989). Code switching and code mixing as a communicative strategy in multilingual discourse. *World Englishes*, **8** (3), 407–417.

Taylor, Insup (1971). How are words from two languages organized in bilinguals' memory? *Canadian Journal of Psychology/Revue Canadienne de Psychologie*, **25** (3), 228–240.

Terasaki, Alene K. (1976). Pre-announcement sequences in conversation. *Social Science Working Paper 99*. Irvine, CA: School of Social Sciences, University of California, Irvine.

Thomason, Sarah G. (2001). *Language contact: An introduction*. Washington, D.C.: Georgetown University Press.

Thomason, Sarah Grey and Kaufman, Terrence (1988). *Language contact, creolization, and genetic linguistics*. Berkeley, CA: University of California Press.

Thordardottir, Elin T.; Weismer, Susan Ellis and Smith, Mary E. (1997). Vocabulary learning in bilingual and monolingual clinical intervention. *Child Language Teaching and Therapy*, **13** (3), 215–227.

Timm, Leonora A. (1975). Spanish–English code-switching: El porqué y how-not-to. *Romance Philology*, **28** (4), 473–482.

Timm, Leonora A. (1978). Code switching in *War and Peace*. In M. Paradis (ed.), *The Fourth LACUS Forum 1977*, pp. 236–249. Columbia: Hornbeam Press.

Toribio, Almeida Jacqueline (2001a). Accessing bilingual code-switching competence. *International Journal of Bilingualism*, **5** (4), 403–436.

Toribio, Almeida Jacqueline (2001b). On the emergence of bilingual code-switching competence. *Bilingualism: Language and Cognition*, **4** (3), 203–231.

Toribio, Almeida Jacqueline (2004). Convergence as an optimization strategy in bilingual speech: Evidence from code-switching. *Bilingualism: Language and Cognition. Special Issue: Bilingualism and linguistic convergence*, **7** (2), 165–173.

Toribio, Almeida Jacqueline; Bullock, Barbara E.; Botero, Christopher G. and Davis, Kristopher Allen (2005). Perseverative phonetic effects in bilingual code-switching. In R. S. Gess and E. J. Rubin (eds.), *Theoretical and experimental approaches to Romance linguistics: Selected papers from the 34th Linguistic Symposium on Romance Languages (LSRL), Salt Lake City, March 2004*, pp. 291–306. Amsterdam and Philadelphia: John Benjamins.

Torras, Maria-Carme (1998). Code negotiation and code alternation in service encounters in Catalonia. MA dissertation, Lancaster University.

Torras, Maria-Carme and Gafaranga, Joseph (2002). Social identities and language alternation in non-formal institutional bilingual talk: Trilingual service encounters in Barcelona. *Language in Society*, **31** (4), 527–548.

Treffers-Daller, Jeanine (1991). Towards a uniform approach to code-switching and borrowing. In *Papers for the workshop on constraints, conditions and models*, pp. 259–279. Strasbourg: European Science Foundation.

Treffers-Daller, Jeanine (1992). Switching between French and Dutch: (dis)similarities in the switching patterns of men and women. Paper presented at the *International Conference on Code-Switching, Nijmegen, Holland, June 1992*.

Treffers-Daller, Jeanine (1994). *Mixing two languages: French-Dutch contact in a comparative perspective*. Berlin: Mouton de Gruyter.

Treffers-Daller, Jeanine (1998). Variability in code-switching styles: Turkish-German code-switching patterns. In R. Jacobson (ed.), *Codeswitching worldwide*, pp. 177–200. Berlin: Mouton de Gruyter.

Treffers-Daller, Jeanine (1999). Borrowing and shift-induced interference: Contrasting patterns in French-Germanic contact in Brussels and Strasbourg. *Bilingualism: Language and Cognition*, **2** (1), 1–22.

Treffers-Daller, Jeanine (2005a). Brussels French *une fois*: Transfer-induced innovation or system-internal development? *Bilingualism: Language and Cognition*, **8** (2), 145–157.

Treffers-Daller, Jeanine (2005b). Evidence for insertional codemixing: Mixed compounds and French nominal groups in Brussels Dutch. *International Journal of Bilingualism*, **9**, 3–4.

Treffers-Daller, Jeanine and Mougeon, Raymond (2005). The role of transfer in language variation and change: Evidence from contact varieties of French. *Bilingualism: Language and Cognition*, **8** (2), 93–98.

Trubetzkoy, Nikolai S. (1939/1969). *Principles of phonology*. Berkeley: University of California Press (1969). Translation by Christiane A. M. Baltaxe of *Grundzüge der Phonologie*. Göttingen: Vandenhoek and Ruprecht (1939).

Trudgill, Peter (1974). *The social differentiation of English in Norwich*. Cambridge, UK and New York: Cambridge University Press.

Trudgill, Peter (1975). *Accent, dialect and the school*. London: Edward Arnold.

Tsimpli, Ianthi; Sorace, Antonella; Heycock, Caroline and Filiaci, Francesca (2004). First language attrition and syntactic subjects: A study of Greek and Italian near-native speakers of English. *International Journal of Bilingualism*, **8** (3), 257–277.

Tuc, Ho-Dac (2003). *Vietnamese–English bilingualism: Patterns of code-switching*. London and New York: Routledge.

Turian, Donna and Altenberg, Evelyn P. (1991). Compensatory strategies of child first language attrition. In H. W. Seliger and R. M. Vago (eds.), *First language attrition*, pp. 207–226. Cambridge, UK and New York: Cambridge University Press.

Ullman, Michael T. (2001). The neural basis of lexicon and grammar in first and second language: The declarative/procedural model. *Bilingualism: Language and Cognition*, **4** (2), 105–122.

Vaid, Jyotsna and Hull, Rachel (2002). Re-envisioning the bilingual brain using functional neuroimaging: Methodological and interpretive issues. In F. Fabbro (ed.), *Advances in the neurolinguistics of bilingualism: essays in honor of Michel Paradis*, pp. 315–355. Udine, Italy: Udine University Press.

Vainikka, Anne and Young-Scholten, Martha (1996a). The early stages in adult L2 syntax: Additional evidence from Romance speakers. *Second Language Research*, **12** (2), 140–176.

Vainikka, Anne and Young-Scholten, Martha (1996b). Gradual development of L2 phrase structure. *Second Language Research*, **12** (1), 7–39.

Valdés Fallis, Guadalupe (1976). Social interaction and code-switching patterns: A case study of Spanish/English alternation. In G. D. Keller, R. V. Teschner and S. Viera (eds.), *Bilingualism in the bicentennial and beyond*, pp. 53–85. New York: Bilingual Press.

Valdés, Guadalupe (1988). The language situation of Mexican-Americans. In S.-L. C. Wong and S. McKay (eds.), *Language diversity: Problem or resource? A social and educational perspective on language minorities in the United States*, pp. 111–139. New York: Newbury House Publishers.

Valdés, Guadalupe (2001). *Learning and not learning English: Latino students in American schools*. New York: Teachers College Press.

van Gelderen, Elly and MacSwan, Jeff (in press). Interface conditions and codeswitching: An F-movement analysis of pronouns and lexical DPs. *Lingua*.

van Riemsdijk, Henk C. and Williams, Edwin (1986). *Introduction to the theory of grammar*. Cambridge, MA: MIT Press.

van Tuijl, Cathy; Leseman, Paul P. M. and Rispens, Jan (2001). Efficacy of an intensive home-based educational intervention programme for 4- to 6-year-old ethnic minority children in the Netherlands. *International Journal of Behavioral Development*, **25** (2), 148–159.

Vedder, Paul; Kook, Hetty and Muysken, Pieter (1996). Language choice and functional differentiation of languages in bilingual parent–child reading. *Applied Psycholinguistics*, **17** (4), 461–484.

Veh, Birgitta (1990). Syntaktische aspekte des code-switching bei bilingualen kindern (Französisch–Deutsch) im Vorschulalter. M. A. dissertation, University of Hamburg.

Verma, Mahendra K.; Corrigan, Karen P. and Firth, Sally (1992). The developing phonological system of Panjabi/Urdu speaking children learning English as a second language in Britain. In J. Leather and A. James (eds.), *New Sounds 92: Proceedings of the 1992 Amsterdam Symposium on the Acquisition of Second-Language Speech*, pp. 174–199. Amsterdam: University of Amsterdam.

Viberg, Åke (1993). Crosslinguistic perspectives on lexical organization and lexical progression. In K. Hyltenstam and Å. Viberg (eds.), *Progression and regression in language: Sociocultural, neuropsychological, and linguistic perspectives*, pp. 340–385. Cambridge, UK and New York: Cambridge University Press.

Vihman, Marilyn M. (1985). Language differentiation by the bilingual infant. *Journal of Child Language*, **12** (2), 297–324.

Vihman, Marilyn M. (1998). A developmental perspective on codeswitching: Conversations between a pair of bilingual siblings. *International Journal of Bilingualism*, **2** (1), 45–84.

Vihman, Marilyn M. and Boysson-Bardies, Benedicte de (1994). The nature and origins of ambient language influence on infant vocal production and early words. *Phonetica*, **51**, 159–169.

Vinther, Thora (2002). Elicited imitation: A brief overview. *International Journal of Applied Linguistics*, **12** (1), 54–73.

Vogt, Hans (1954). Review of *Languages in Contact*. *Word*, **10**, 79–82.

Volterra, Virginia and Taeschner, Traute (1978). The acquisition and development of language by bilingual children. *Journal of Child Language*, **5** (2), 311–326.

Wakefield, James A.; Bradley, Peggy E.; Yom, Byong-Hee Lee and Doughtie, Eugene B. (1975). Language switching and constituent structure. *Language and Speech*, **18** (1), 14–19.

Wartenburger, Isabell; Heekeren, Hauke R.; Abutalebi, Jubin; Cappa, Stefano F.; Villringer, Arno and Perani, Daniela (2003). Early setting of grammatical processing in the bilingual brain. *Neuron*, **37** (1), 159–170.

Weber-Fox, Christine; Davis, Laura J. and Cuadrado, Elizabeth (2003). Event-related brain potential markers of high-language proficiency in adults. *Brain and Language*, **85** (2), 231–244.

Weber-Fox, Christine and Neville, Helen J. (2001). Sensitive periods differentiate processing of open- and closed-class words: An ERP study of bilinguals. *Journal of Speech, Language, and Hearing Research*, **44** (6), 1338–1353.

Wei, Longxing (2000a). Types of morphemes and their implications for second language morpheme acquisition. *International Journal of Bilingualism*, **4** (1), 29–43.

Wei, Longxing (2000b). Unequal election of morphemes in adult second language acquisition. *Applied Linguistics*, **21** (1), 106–140.

Wei, Longxing (2001). Lemma congruence checking between languages as an organizing principle in intrasentential code-switching. *International Journal of Bilingualism*, **5** (2), 153–173.

Wei, Longxing (2002). The bilingual mental lexicon and speech production process. *Brain and Language. Special Issue: Mental lexicon II*, **81** (1–3), 691–707.

Weinreich, Uriel (1950). Di forshung fun "mishshprakhike" yidishe folkslider. *YIVO-Bleter*, **34**, 282–288.

Weinreich, Uriel (1953/1964/1967). *Languages in contact: Findings and problems*. New York: Linguistic Circle of New York and The Hague: Mouton.

Weinreich, Uriel (1954). Is a structural dialectology possible? *Word*, **10**, 388–400.

Wentz, James (1977). Some considerations in the development of a syntactic description of code-switching. Ph.D. dissertation, University of Illinois at Urbana-Champaign.

Wentz, James and McClure, Erica (1977). Aspects of the syntax of the code-switched discourse of bilingual children. In F. Ingemann (ed.), *1975 Mid-America Linguistics Conference papers*, Lawrence, KS: University of Kansas.

White, Lydia (2000). Second language acquisition: From initial to final state. In J. Archibald (ed.), *Second language acquisition and linguistic theory*, pp. 130–155. Oxford and Malden, MA: Blackwell.

Wicha, Nicole Y.Y.; Bates, Elizabeth A.; Moreno, Eva M. and Kutasa, Marta (2003). Potato not Pope: Human brain potentials to gender expectation and agreement in Spanish spoken sentences. *Neuroscience Letters*, **346**, 165–168.

Wicha, Nicole Y.Y.; Moreno, Eva M. and Kutas, Marta (2004). Anticipating words and their gender: An event-related brain potential study of semantic integration, gender expectancy, and gender agreement in Spanish sentence reading. *Journal of Cognitive Neuroscience*, **16** (7), 1272–1288.

Williams, Glyn (1992). *Sociolinguistics: A sociological critique*. London and New York: Routledge.

Williams, Lee (1977). The perception of stop consonant voicing by Spanish–English bilinguals. *Perception and Psychophysics*, **21** (4), 289–297.

Wilson, Deirdre and Sperber, Dan (1993). Linguistic form and relevance. *Lingua*, **90** (1–2), 1–25.

Winford, Donald (2003). *An introduction to contact linguistics*. Oxford and Malden, MA: Blackwell.

Winford, Donald (2005). Contact-induced changes: Classification and processes. *Diachronica*, **22** (2), 373–427.

Winter, Joanne and Pauwels, Anne (2000). Gender and language contact research in the Australian context. *Journal of Multilingual and Multicultural Development*, **21** (6), 508–522.

Wolfram, Walt (1969). *A sociolinguistic description of Detroit Negro speech*. Washington, D.C.: Center for Applied Linguistics.

Wong-Fillmore, Lily (1991). When learning a second language means losing the first. *Early Childhood Research Quarterly*, **6** (3), 323–347.

Wooffitt, Robin (2005). *Conversation analysis and discourse analysis: A comparative and critical introduction*. London: Sage.

Woolard, Kathryn A. (1988). Code-switching and comedy in Catalonia. In M. Heller (ed.), *Codeswitching: Anthropological and sociolinguistic perspectives*, pp. 53–76. Berlin and New York: Mouton de Gruyter.

Woolard, Kathryn A. (1998). Simultaneity and bivalency as strategies in bilingualism. *Journal of Linguistic Anthropology*, **8** (1), 3–29.

Woolford, Ellen (1983). Bilingual code-switching and syntactic theory. *Linguistic Inquiry*, **14** (3), 520–536.

Wray, Alison (2002). *Formulaic language and the lexicon*. Cambridge, UK and New York: Cambridge University Press.

Wu, Ying Choon and Coulson, Seana (2005). Meaningful gestures: Electrophysiological indices of iconic gesture comprehension. *Psychophysiology*, **42** (6), 654–667.

Wurmbrand, Susi (1997). Deconstructing restructuring. Paper presented at *The III Langues et Grammaire*, Paris, France.

Xue, Gui; Dong, Qi; Jin, Zhen; Zhang, Lei and Wang, Yue (2004). An fMRI study with semantic access in low proficiency second language learners. *Neuroreport*, **15** (5), 791–796.

Yates, Simeon J. (1996). Oral and written linguistic aspects of computer conferencing: A corpus based study. In S.C. Herring (ed.), *Computer-mediated communication: Linguistic, social, and cross-cultural perspectives*, pp. 29–46. Amsterdam and Philadelphia: John Benjamins.

Yetkin, Oguz; Yetkin, Fatma Zerrin; Haughton, Victor M. and Cox, Robert W. (1996). Use of functional MR to map language in multilingual volunteers. *American Journal of Neuroradiology*, **17** (3), 473–477.

Yokoyama, Satoru; Okamoto, Hideyuki; Miyamoto, Tadao; Yoshimoto, Kei; Kim, Jungho; Iwata, Kazuki; Jeong, Hyeonjeong; Uchida, Shinya; Ikuta, Naho; Sassa, Yuko; Nakamura, Wataru; Horie, Kaoru; Sato, Shigeru and Kawashima, Ryuta (2006). Cortical activation in the processing of passive sentences in L1 and L2: An fMRI study. *NeuroImage*, **30** (2), 570–579.

Young, Russell and Tran, Myluong (1999). Language maintenance and shift among Vietnamese in America. *International Journal of the Sociology of Language*, **140**, 77–82.

Yule, George (1997). *Referential communication tasks*. Hillsdale, NJ: Lawrence Erlbaum Associates.

Zagona, Karen T. (1988). *Verb phrase syntax: A parametric study of English and Spanish*. Boston: Kluwer Academic.

Zatorre, Robert J. (1989). On the representation of multiple languages in the brain: Old problems and new directions. *Brain and Language*, **36** (1), 127–147.

Zentella, Ana Celia (1997). *Growing up bilingual: Puerto Rican children in New York*. Oxford and Malden, MA: Blackwell.

Zhang, Wei (2005). Code-choice in bidialectal interaction: The choice between Putonghua and Cantonese in a radio phone-in program in Shenzhen. *Journal of Pragmatics. Special Issue: Conversational Code-Switching*, **37** (3), 355–374.

Zheng, Lin (1997). Tonal aspects of code-switching. *Monash University Linguistics Papers*, **1** (1), 53–63.

Zwartjes, Otto (1997). Love songs from al-Andalus: History, structure, and meaning of the Kharja. Leiden: Brill Academic.

Index of subjects

Abstract Level Model 339
accent 144, 146, 156, 158-159, 166
  filter 159
  shifting 148
acceptability judgment *see* grammaticality
  judgment
accommodation 74, 113, 143, 144, 145, 148,
  152, 157, 158, 159, 167, 177, 229, 231, 232,
  245, 259
anatomical/functional organization of the
  bilingual brain 289-290
  L1-L2 brain overlap 290-294
activation 30, 154, 172, 287
  cortical 292, 293-294, 295
Activation Threshold Hypothesis 64
adposition 87
adstrate 59
age of exposure/acquisition 291, 292, 296-297,
  301, 303
AGR, 209
agreement 44-45, 298, 338, 346
analogical change 74
anterior cingulate cortex 299
Arabic script 135
architecture of the bilingual language faculty
  214, 334
article (definite, indefinite) 49-50, 84, 139-140,
  194-196, 197, 211
Article Phrase (ArtP) 194-195
aspect *see* tense
aspiration *see* VOT
assessment of disordered language 248-251
attrition 8, 26, 75, 142, 148, 155, 158, 253-256,
  258, 259-269, 346
audience design 112-113
auxiliary 45-47, 201, 218

basal ganglia 299, 300
base language 66, 133, 156-157, 159, 164, 167,
  168-173, 175, 180, 262, 268
bilingual, types of
  balanced 7, 185, 186
  early 7, 256
  elite 9
  heritage 8-9

late/second language 9, 255, 292
  naturalistic/folk 9
  non-balanced 185, 213, 262, 264
  sequential 204
  simultaneous 7, 204, 210-213, 217, 256
  symmetrical 7
  true 7
Bilingual Bootstrapping Hypothesis 213
bilingual communities *see* speech communities
bilingual competence *see* competence
bilingual homophones 172, 173, 177-178
Bilingual Interactive Activation Model 63
Bilingual Model of Lexical Access 63
Bilingual Speech Model 188
bivalency 158
blog/weblog 130
borrowing
  lexical 4, 5, 41-42, 58, 62, 65-66, 70, 76, 77,
    78-79, 101, 103, 149, 163, 164-166, 170,
    173, 201, 214, 224-225, 243, 266, 267,
    309, 313
  nonce 5, 150, 166, 177, 184, 201, 330
  structural 78, 79, 80, 81, 87, 89,
    254, 263
bridge *see* morphemes

calque *see* loan translation
case (markers/marking/system) 24-26, 88-89,
  201, 225, 264-265, 268, 274, 275, 321,
  346, 347
Case Phrase (KP) 194-196, 197
category labels 326
chat/chatgroup 130, 132, 133, 134
classifers/classifier constructions, in sign
  language 221, 223, 225
  entity 224
  handle 224, 233
  polycomponential 223, 224, 225, 233,
    235, 236
  shape specifiers 224
  size specifier 224
classifier/Classifier Phrase (CLP), for nouns
  194-196, 197, 275-276
closed class items/words 202, 205,
  247, 338

CMC (Computer Mediated Communication) 127, 140
  types of 129–130
code-blend/code-blending 228
code-changing 66
code copying 80, 263
code-mixing 21, 66, 67–68, 101, 150, 260
  in children 200, 204–208, 242–243
  in sign 227, 228
code-shifting 147
code-switching, approaches to 14–16
code-switching, as a conversational resource 99, 118–119
code-switching, attitudes towards 11–13, 99, 104, 204, 258
code-switching, between sign and speech 226–228
code-switching, constraints on 200–204, 310–318
  phonological 177–179
  universal 182–188, 214–220, 325
code-switching, misperceptions of 4–5, 242, 244
code-switching, social context for 13–14, 249–250
code-switching, social functions of 9–13, 110–112, 138–139, 229–232, 243–244, 261
code-switching, sociolinguistic factors 98–99
code-switching, types of 65–68
  alternation/alternational 3, 67, 68, 76–77, 85, 133, 186, 262, 268
  Classic 3, 4, 67, 337, 343, 346, 357
  composite 67, 263, 264–265, 268, 339
  congruent lexicalization 3–4, 67, 68, 186
  conversational 104, 106–107
  covert *see* convergence
  flagged 25, 60, 103, 260
  functional 150
  insertion/insertional 3–4, 67, 68, 77, 78, 79, 133, 134, 137, 186, 267, 268, 300
  inter-sentential/inter-utterance 3, 134, 138, 157, 182, 199, 242, 246, 262, 263, 351
  internet 133–135
  intra-sentential/intra-utterance 3–4, 40, 67, 133, 134, 138, 155, 157, 173, 182, 199–200, 209, 242, 244, 262–263, 270, 351
  metaphorical 107
  motivated 60
  performance 60
  reiterative 229–232, 236
  sign 228–236
  situational 102, 104, 106–107
  smooth 24, 60
  tag 4, 262, 267
  variant switching 107
code-switching vs. other contact phenomena 5–6, 59–62
cognitive processes 15–16, 293, 356–357
collocations 78–79, 80, 83, 84, 85–86, 91, 344
community of practice 113, 140
competence, linguistic 148, 241, 248, 252, 254, 256, 260, 262
  grammatical 56, 99, 143, 145, 185, 198, 220, 242, 244, 257, 340
  pragmatic 147, 242
  socio-phonetic 148–154
  sociolinguistic 142–143, 145–148, 257

complementizers 201, 202, 218, 351–354
  language of 352, 354
  as content morphemes 353–354
  as bridge morphemes 352–353
  as outsider morphemes 353
Complementizer Phrase (CP) 351, 355
compounds/compounding 215–217
compromise strategies 49–51, 56, 284–287, 288, 340
conceptual level 272, 274, 275, 284, 287, 339–340
conceptualizer 63, 272
confederate scripting 27, 35–36
congruence 41–42, 55, 64–65, 74, 221, 263, 274
congruence checking 340
congruent lexicalization *see* code-switching; types of
Constraint on Closed-Class Items 202, 205
constructed action 224, 225, 233, 235, 237
content judgment 27, 32
control *see* inhibition
convergence 8, 51–55, 59, 67, 69–72, 101, 143, 147, 158, 159, 263, 264
  phonetic 143, 151–152, 154, 163, 167, 173, 175, 177, 268
Conversational Analysis Model 119–123
conversational order 117, 118, 119, 121, 125
correspondence 41–42
cortical-subcortical network 299–301
crossing 106, 158
cross-language priming 29, 298
cross-linguistic influence 59–60, 176, 210, 254, 265
crutching 9, 261
cued shadowing 27, 28–29, 38
cued speech 228

definiteness/indefiniteness 193
deixis/deictic 89, 224, 225, 230
determiners 44, 49–50, 53, 178, 194, 211–212, 275, 342
Determiner Phrase (DP) 24–26, 193–197, 211–212, 219–220
demonstratives *see* determiners
diachrony 76, 78–79, 81
Differential Access Hypothesis (DAH) 341, 344
  predictions of 355–356
  testing of 357
diglossia 6, 100, 107
discourse patterns, in loan translations 89–90
discursive strategies 10–11
dispreference markers 120
Director-Matcher task 37–39
divergence 143, 147, 151, 153, 154, 159, 257
dorsolateral prefrontal cortex (DLPFC) 300
double marking (of function words or bound morphemes) 187, 195, 197, 343, 355
Double Morphology Principle 184
Dynamic assessment 251

economy 186, 192, 193, 197
elicited imitation *see* sentence repetition
e-mail 130, 131–132, 133
Embedded Language (EL) 42, 77, 184, 186, 198, 275–278, 342–344, 348, 349–350
  activation of 356
  island 284–287, 337, 349
  role of 356–357
  vs. Matrix Language (ML) 262

Embedded Language Island Principle 184
emic 117–118, 119, 121–122, 123, 124, 126
equivalence 41–42, 51, 64, 90, 178, 263, 264, 266, 311
Equivalence Constraint 41, 183–184, 200–201, 206, 207, 311–313, 314–315
ERP (Event-Related Potentials) 27, 36, 289, 294–297, 298–299, 301–303
erosion *see* attrition
Ethno Portalen 134
etic 117, 122
eye-tracking 33

facilitation 30, 177
fMRI (functional Magnetic Resonance Imaging) 27, 291
first concern elicitors 116, 117
formulation 118
formulator 63, 272, 339, 344, 355–356
Forum (Internet forum) 128, 130, 131, 132, 133
4-M model 274, 337, 340–341, 347, 354, 355, 357
Free Morpheme Constraint 183–184, 200–201, 205, 207, 247, 311–312, 313, 314, 315
free speech 27, 34
Full Transfer/Full Access model 72
function words 140, 184, 193–197, 205, 207, 247
functional level 273
functional categories/heads 184, 209, 216–219, 220, 317–318, 338, 342
  vs. lexical categories/heads 338
Functional Head Constraint (FHC) 183, 203, 208, 317–318
functional Magnetic Resonance Imaging *see* fMRI

gating 27, 28
gender 112, 144, 243
  grammatical 44, 50–51, 53–54, 194, 211–212, 321
gesture 222, 224
Generalized Lexical Knowledge (GLK) 340
Government Constraint 24, 183, 202–203, 208, 209, 316–317
grammar
  descriptive 1
  prescriptive 1, 51
Grammatical Deficiency Hypothesis 209
grammatical features spell-out hypothesis 212
grammaticality judgment 27, 31–33, 38, 185, 204
grammaticalization, contact-induced 87
guest language 66, 157, 167, 169–173

harmonization 48, 50–51, 53, 55, 56
head movement 321, 324, 326–333
heritage speakers *see* bilingual, types of
hybrid syntactic structures 52

iconicity 225–226, 230, 236
identity 10, 97, 104, 105, 136, 137, 138, 143, 157, 159, 192, 243, 252, 259
  construction 106, 127, 128, 130, 131, 140, 158–159
idioms *see* collocations
in-group communication
inhibition 30, 290, 295, 299, 301, 305
  psycholinguistic approaches to 62–65

Inhibitory Control 290, 300
  Model 63
interface levels 329–332
interference 58, 59, 60, 62, 64, 65–66, 70, 72, 75, 78–79, 81, 89, 101, 107, 158, 177, 263, 267, 290, 297–298
  dynamic 61–62, 69
  effect in naming 30–31
  static 61–62, 69
  through shift 70
Internet 127, 129–130, 133–135
intersystem influence, *see* transfer
intervention/remediation 249–251
Intracranial Electrical Cortical Stimulation (IECS) 290–291, 293
isomorphism 192, 193, 197
Ivy Hypothesis 213

language acquisition
  imperfect/incomplete 253–255, 256–257, 263, 264, 269–266
language alternation 68, 122, 125, 145
language change 59, 69–72, 74, 260, 267–268, 269
language choice 100, 101, 119, 121, 123, 125, 134, 139, 145, 147, 157, 207, 244–246, 255, 259
  marked 100, 134, 147, 157
  unmarked 100, 106, 134, 147, 157, 158
language disorders 248–249, 250, 251
language dominance 212–213, 301, 303
language maintenance 254, 255, 257, 258, 267
language mixing 124, 145, 186, 254, 263, 299
  in children 208–213, 220, 253
language mode
  bilingual 64, 140, 159, 173, 174, 284
  code-switching mode 34, 48–49, 158
language negotiation 125
  implicit 121
language/speech production 242, 270–273, 287–288, 292, 295, 354, 355
language shift 255, 256, 267
language shifting 2
language status 257–258
language switching 15–16, 21–22, 27, 29–31, 37, 58, 167–173, 289, 299
Late Positive Component (LPC) 301, 302
Left Anterior Negativity (LAN) 298
left inferior parietal cortex 289
lemma/lemma level 63, 270, 274, 340
  activation 271, 272, 275–280
  congruence 280–284, 287
  incongruence 284–287
lexical categories/heads 183, 217, 220, 317
  vs. functional categories/heads 338
lexical change 77, 78, 79, 81, 87
lexical decision task 27, 29
lexical selection, in monolinguals 64, 300
lexical-conceptual level/lexical-conceptual structure 42, 270–271, 280–283, 284–287
linearization 193
loan phonology 165
loan translation 5, 8
  approaches to 80–82
  categories of 82
  definitions of 75–76

vs. code-switching 76–77
vs. interference/transference 78
vs. lexical borrowing 77
vs. structural borrowing 78, 79, 263

macrolinguistic 99–107
macro-level sociolinguistic 16–17, 131, 140, 157
Magnetoencephalography (MEG) 294
Marked/unmarked *see* language choice
Markedness Model/Markedness Theory 100, 106
Matrix Language (ML) 42, 77, 80, 171, 184, 186,
    189, 196, 197–198, 275–278, 337–339, 346,
    349–350, 351
  composite 3, 80, 264
  turnover hypothesis 267
  vs. Embedded Language (EL) 262
Matrix Language Frame (MLF) Model 42, 66, 80,
    184, 189, 197–198, 270, 273, 337–339, 354,
    355, 357
mental lexicon 270–273, 287, 339, 344
micro-level sociolinguistic 16–17, 131, 149,
    157, 159
Minimalist Program 189, 192, 214, 320–325, 334
mixed compound verbs 187, 190–191
mixed languages 4, 16, 346
Morpheme Order Principle (MOP) 184, 275, 338
morpheme
  bridge 274, 341, 344, 345–346, 348–349,
    352–353
  bound 183, 184, 193, 200–201, 312, 313
  conceptually-activated 341, 344, 356
  content 184, 189, 274, 275–278, 281, 337–338,
    341, 348, 353–354
  content, in loan translation 82–86
  directly elected 274–275
  early system 184, 274, 341, 342–344, 348
  free 183, 200
  functional, in loan translation 86–88
  grammatical, in loan translation 88–89
  indirectly elected 274–275, 341
  late system 274, 344–347
  outsider 274, 338, 341–342, 344, 345, 346,
    349, 353
  structurally-assigned 274, 341, 344, 356
  system 184, 274, 337, 341
morphological realization patterns 42, 270–271
mouthing 223, 226, 227, 228
moving window 27, 33
music 12
MUD (multi-user dungeon domain/
    dimension) 130

N400 295–297, 302
naming task 27, 29–31, 38
nativization *see* neutralization
naturalistic data/natural speech 22–26, 39, 58,
    64, 97–98, 172, 176–177, 201, 204, 305,
    319, 354
  phonetics of 176–177
neuroimaging 36, 63, 293, 300
neutralization 48–49, 50, 56
nogo N200 295, 302
nonce *see* borrowing
normative 118, 119, 123–124, 126
noun class 45
Null Theory 185, 186–187, 318–319
number 89, 194, 195, 212, 276, 321,
    343–344, 355

off-line techniques 26, 32
on-line techniques 26, 32
open class items/words 202, 205, 338
Optimality Theory 165, 186
orthography/orthographic systems 29, 131,
    137–140, 295, 302

P600 36, 295, 298
participle 45–47, 53, 201, 206, 218
pathological/uncontrolled switching 7, 299, 300
perception, phonetic 167, 168–171, 179, 180
performance 56, 188, 198, 220, 257
person 321
PET (Positron Emission Tomography) 27, 291,
    294–297
PF (Phonetic Form) Adjunction Theorem 184
PF Disjunction Theorem 214–216
PF Interface 192, 330
  Condition 331–332
phonetic categories/categorization 15, 27, 28,
    168, 176, 179
phonetic convergence *see* convergence
phonetic/phonological repertoire/register 143,
    145, 167, 177
phonology
  phonological constraints on CS 177–179
  phonological dissimilarity 170, 179
  phonological integration 163, 165–167, 170,
    183, 214, 224, 309, 312, 313
phrase structure categories, cross-linguistic
    equivalence of 41, 42–43
plural *see* number
plurilingual communities *see* speech
    communities
poetry 12, 23
politeness 108–112
polycomponential signs, *see* classifiers
portmanteau construction 187, 191–193
pre-announcement 116
predicate-argument structure 42, 270–271, 274,
    283, 284, 285–287
preliminary 116
prepositions 274, 316, 347–349, 355–356
  as bridge morphemes 348–349
  as content morphemes 348
  as early system morphemes 348
  as outsider morphemes 349
prestige
  covert 10, 98
  overt 10, 98
processing 63–65, 167, 172, 179, 193, 272, 273,
    289, 292, 298–299, 300, 354
  costs 167, 301, 302
  strategies 167, 188, 197–198
production 242, 270–273, 287–288, 292, 295,
    354, 355
  phonetic 167, 171–177, 179–180
proficiency 7–9, 145, 185, 267, 291–292, 293,
    296–297, 303
  code-switching as a measure of 1, 3, 242, 244,
    252, 254, 262
pronouns 225, 246, 310, 312, 349–350
prosody/prosodic systems 179, 180

reading tasks 27, 33
recipient language agentivity 70
restructuring 91, 254, 259–269, 327–329
Roman script 29, 135, 136, 137

second language acquirers/learners *see* bilinguals, types of; late
second language acquisition (SLA) 58, 65, 72–73, 249, 265, 346
selection/selective activation 62, 297–299
semantic congruity effect 296–297, 298
semantic extension 5, 8, 76, 83, 87, 91
semantic priming
    effect 296–299
    paradigm 295
semilingualism 11
sentence matching 27, 32–33
sentence recall 27, 35
sentence repetition 27, 34
sequentiality 117, 119, 120–121, 123, 126
sentence completion 27, 35, 38–39
sign language
    phonology 224–225, 236
    vs. speech 222–226
similarity, phonetic/phonological 156
simultaneity (in sign language) 223–224, 226–227, 235, 236
social networks 16, 99, 101, 146
source language agentivity 70
Specific Language Impairment (SLI) 248, 249, 251
Speech Act Theory 115–117
speech community 10, 22, 37, 51, 56–57, 82, 91, 98, 101–104, 108–112, 128, 145, 146–147, 185, 188, 248, 259
speech production model (Levelt) 63, 270, 272, 339–340
Spell Out 321, 330, 331
split languages 346
Sprachbund 55, 80
structural change 78, 79, 81, 87, 257
style shifting 2, 67, 113, 144, 241
stylistic use of CS/styling 127
subcategorization 43, 84, 85, 88, 183, 271, 298
    Constraint 202
subset hypothesis 63

substrate 59
superstrate 59
syntactic priming 35, 193
switching costs *see* processing; costs
synchrony 76, 77, 78–79, 81
System Morpheme Principle (SMP) 184, 185, 275, 338

tag-switching *see* code-switching; types of
talk organization 116, 119, 124, 126
talk-in-interaction 114
tense 45, 193, 209, 225, 276
Tense (T)/Tense Phrase (TP) 218–219
they-code 104–106, 134
three-stage model 210
tone 165, 178–179
transfer/transference 41, 58, 59, 60, 61, 62, 65, 66, 68, 69–74, 78–79, 81, 89, 211, 263
transversion 66
Tree Adjoining Grammar 189, 318
trigger/triggering *see* facilitation
turn constructional units 120, 123

Universal Grammar (UG) 51, 72, 185, 186–187, 203
Uniform Structure Principle (USP) 336–337, 354–355, 357
uninterpretable features 212, 321

voice onset time (VOT) 33, 168–172, 174–175

we-code 104–106, 134
word association task 27, 31
word order 188–193, 201, 206, 216–217, 218–220, 225, 264, 278, 278–280, 284, 286, 319, 326, 332–334, 338
written code-switching 22–23, 102
written speech vs. oral 127, 128–129, 131, 140

X-bar Theory 311, 315, 320
XP Movement 325

Index of languages

Acholi 344, 345
Adaŋme 183
Alsatian 46
American Sign Language (ASL) 223, 224–225, 227, 228, 229–235, 236
Arabic 23, 53–54, 134–135, 317, 342, 348
  Algerian 12
  Lebanese 147, 148–155, 156–157, 158, 176–177
  Moroccan 13, 42–43, 44, 49–51, 135, 136, 137–140, 183, 195, 202, 263, 343, 345, 350
  Nigerian 80, 91
  Palestinian 342, 350, 353
  Tunisian 202

Berber 135, 136, 137–138
Breton 332
Buang (Papua New Guinea) 10
Bulgarian 10
Byelorussian 4

Catalan 121, 158
Catalan Sign Language (LSC) 229
Chichewa 352–353
Chinese 99, 120, 145, 170, 194, 275–277, 278, 278–280, 281–282, 284, 285, 286
  Cantonese 105, 194, 195, 196
  Mandarin 178

Dutch 3, 35, 37–39, 49–50, 61, 67, 70, 76–78, 83–90, 92, 135, 136–140, 177–178, 191, 247, 338, 343, 347

English 2–3, 4, 10–11, 12, 22, 24–26, 33, 35, 36, 42, 46–47, 48, 52, 53, 54–55, 60–61, 69, 81, 102, 103–104, 105, 110–111, 120, 121–124, 134, 137, 145, 146–147, 148–155, 156–157, 158, 166, 169–172, 174–176, 176–178, 182–184, 188–189, 190–191, 192, 194–196, 200–201, 203, 205–206, 209, 212, 213, 215–216, 220, 227, 228, 242, 243, 244, 245, 246–247, 248, 258, 259, 260, 261, 262, 264, 266, 267–268, 275–278, 278–280, 281–283, 284, 302, 309, 312–314, 317, 319, 332, 333–334, 338–339, 342, 343, 344, 345, 347, 348, 349, 350, 351, 352–354

African American Vernacular English (AAVE) 147
  Hawaiian 147
  Middle 23
Estonian 207, 246, 247
Ewe 342

Farsi (Persian) 188, 319, 333
Finnglish 4
Finnish 24–26, 166, 184, 201, 267–268
Fongbe 184
Franglais 4
French 5–6, 7–8, 12, 13–14, 42–43, 44, 46, 49–51, 53–54, 61, 67, 70, 103, 105, 121–123, 124–125, 139–140, 169, 170, 171–172, 183, 184, 195, 200, 202, 203, 206, 208–209, 215–216, 220, 227, 244, 246, 247, 263, 317, 328, 332, 344, 345, 347, 348, 350
  Cajun 344
  Frenchville 4, 10

German 7–8, 46, 70, 134, 147, 199, 205–207, 208–209, 210, 211–212, 213, 214–216, 217–220, 246
  Pennsylvania 75
  Swiss 106, 134
Greek 29, 104, 109–111
Guaraní 6
Gurindji Kriol 6, 16–17

Haitian Creole 12
Hebrew 23, 183, 196, 258
Hindi 105, 183, 189, 191, 194, 345
Hungarian 261, 262, 263, 266, 268

Igbo 104
Ingleñol 4
Inuktitut 246
Irish 332
Italian 106, 147, 183, 199, 201, 203, 205–207, 208–209, 210, 211–212, 213, 214–216, 217–220, 327–328
Italian Sign Language (LIS) 225

Jamaican Creole 12, 106, 134
Japanese 5, 10–11, 184, 189, 191, 192, 194,
    277–278, 278–280, 282–283, 284, 285,
    286–287, 333–334

Kannada 184
Kinyarwanda 121–122, 124–125
Korean 184, 189, 190, 194, 196, 333–334

Latin 23
Lingala 105

Malay 13, 54–55, 349
Mandinka 190, 350
Marathi 42, 48, 184, 190
Media Lengua 6
Mexican Sign Language (LSM) 228,
    229–235, 236

Nahuatl 184, 312–313, 317, 319,
    326–327
Norwegian 246, 247

Old French Sign Language (OLSF) 229

Papiamentu 37–39
Persian (Farsi) 3, 134, 188,
    319, 333
Portinglês 4
Punjabi 105, 106, 191

Quebec Sign Language (LSQ) 227, 229
Quechua 6, 23, 68

Romani 10
Russian 4, 23, 260, 347

Shona 195
Spanglish 13

Spanish 2, 4, 5–6, 10, 12, 22, 23, 33, 36, 46, 53,
    60–61, 67, 71, 81, 102, 103–104, 121, 145,
    146–147, 158, 165, 169, 182–183, 196,
    200–201, 203, 205–206, 212, 215–216, 242,
    243, 244, 245, 247, 248, 259, 261, 302, 309,
    312–314, 317, 319, 326–327, 329, 332, 342,
    344, 348, 349, 350, 351, 352
Spanish Sign Language (LSE) 229
Sranan 3, 67
Swahili/Kiswahili 3, 45, 46–47, 52, 105, 123–125,
    184, 338–339, 342, 343, 347, 348
Swedish 3, 213, 349

Taglish 54
Tagolog 54
Tamil 184, 190, 191, 194, 196
Tariana (Brazil) 11
Thai 145
Tok Pisin 10
Tsotistaal (South Africa) 190
Tucano (Brazil) 11
Turkish 10, 49, 76–78, 83–90, 92, 104, 136–139,
    140, 191, 194, 338, 343, 347

Ukranian 4
Urdu 301

Vietnamese 178–179

Welsh 184, 343
Wolof (Senegal) 61, 105, 184, 344, 350

Xhosa (South Africa) 354

Yabem (Papua New Guinea) 10
Yiddish 23
Yoruba (West Africa) 104

Zapotec (Mexico) 332